THE INCREDIBLE LIFE & MYST

DOROTHY KILGALLEN

SARA JORDAN-HEINTZ

PAGE TURNER
BOOKS INTERNATIONAL

The Incredible Life & Mysterious Death of Dorothy Kilgallen

Library of Congress Control Number: 2023945256
ISBN 9798218177010

www.pageturnerbooks.biz

www.dorothykilgallen.net

Table of Contents

"Congress shall make no law respecting an establishment of religion, or prohibiting the free exercise thereof; or abridging the freedom of speech, or of the press; or the right of the people peaceably to assemble, and to petition the Government for a redress of grievances."

— First Amendment of the United States Constitution

"Cowards die many times before their deaths; the valiant never taste of death but once."—**William Shakespeare's *Julius Caesar***

AUTHOR BIO

Sara Jordan-Heintz is an award-winning newspaper reporter, historian and editor. Her human interest pieces, business profiles and news articles have been published nationwide through the Associated Press and *USA Today* Network. Her writing also appears in a variety of nationally distributed magazines.

Her cultural critique of the 1950-era Betty Crocker's *Picture Cook Book* was published in *Queen's Quarterly*, a Canadian peer-reviewed academic journal of cultural studies that was established in 1893. Those who have contributed to the *Quarterly* include Sinclair Ross, Margaret Laurence, W.O. Mitchell and Margaret Atwood.

She began writing for her family business *Midwest Today* magazine in her early teens. In 2006, at age 16, she started work on the Kilgallen article, which was published in 2007. The article attracted notice, and has since been cited and referenced in several books and on various websites and forums.

Jordan-Heintz is a recipient of the Genevieve Mauck Stoufer Outstanding Young Iowa Journalists Award. She has received additional honors from the Iowa Newspaper Association and Associated Press.

As a working journalist, she has interviewed presidential candidates, U.S. cabinet members, prisoners of war, activists, refugees, law enforcement, historians, authors, filmmakers, scientists, musicians, inventors, designers, art collectors, and others. She's covered natural disasters and the COVID-19 pandemic.

Her biography on classic stars from the Heartland entitled *Going Hollywood: Midwesterners in Movieland* was released in 2019.

She graduated with honors and holds a Bachelor of Arts degree in American Studies and history from the University of Iowa. She lives in Iowa with her husband Andy Heintz, also a writer, their young daughter Louisa, and tuxedo cat Madeline.

To Dolly Mae

And to the next generation of female journalists.
May your voices be heard.

(*Clockwise from top left*): Dorothy with her *What's My Line?* colleagues Arlene Francis, Bennett Cerf and John Daly. Kilgallen and Marilyn Monroe were spied on by the FBI. Dorothy was glamorous on her last show (clip). She worked hard but enjoyed the good life and had a fancy townhouse. She loved singer Johnnie Ray, but traveled the world with husband Richard. She got the only "private" interview with Jack Ruby.

Author's Note

When I wrote an article entitled "Who Killed Dorothy Kilgallen?" in 2007 for *Midwest Today*—a widely respected glossy regional magazine—I could not have foreseen my investigative piece would become the Rosetta Stone for fans of Ms. Kilgallen who had always questioned the suspicious circumstances surrounding her death.

She was not only a panelist on the popular game show, *What's My Line?*, but also a working journalist whose newspaper articles reached tens of millions of daily readers. In a series of articles spanning the final two years of her life, she publicly and very courageously challenged the government's cover-up of the truth about the assassination of John F. Kennedy by presenting new and disturbing facts about the case, poking giant holes in the Warren Commission Report. Dorothy is the only reporter to have scored exclusive interviews with Jack Ruby, and vowed to discover who really killed Kennedy. Sadly, she died trying, and her research papers were never found.

Although I am pleased I was able to kindle such public interest in this fascinating woman, by virtue of my "deep dive" research, I am dismayed to see Dorothy's story turn into a cottage industry for one author in particular whose books, in my opinion, contain reams of repetition, wild theories and self-aggrandizement. Much of his original information came from my article, after he contacted me several years ago requesting an interview. Not all of this is appropriately credited. But he also has relied in some cases on "anonymous sources" that make it impossible to assess their credibility.

Dorothy deserves better. Hence I decided to set the record straight with this new book, *The Incredible Life & Mysterious Death of Dorothy Kilgallen*.

You'll notice I divide the book into three parts: pre-JFK assassination, the assassination and its aftermath, and Dorothy's own demise.

Reviewing the voluminous collection of Dorothy's syndicated *Voice of Broadway* columns and bylined front page articles led me to conclusively believe she was one hell of a good journalist. She had an eagle-eye for detail, a highly-sensitive bullshit detector and a vast pipeline of sources. Her reporting illustrates she did possess information damaging to the Warren

Commission's official rulings which she planned to reveal in a book separate from the posthumously released *Murder One*.

She was a skilled writer whose word pictures were savored by her legion of followers, and—sadly—largely lost today to the annals of newspaper archives. I have worked to resurrect her "voice" throughout this book, allowing her prose to take center stage: the humorous story of her first time traveling on a jet plane in 1959; tips for tourists in New York City; takedowns of sexist critics; coverage of royal weddings and murder trials; prescient reportage of geopolitics; her whimsical journey to Ireland with her husband her last summer alive, to name just a few.

Dorothy had an interest in art and interior decorating, and was known for her lavish dinner parties. She repeatedly garnered accolades as one of the best-dressed women in the nation. This on top of being a television and radio personality and syndicated columnist.

But most importantly, Dorothy was a mother to three very different children, and while her marriage to Richard Kollmar was far from being a storybook romance, evidence exists of their loyalty and deep affection for one another, despite their infidelities.

I was the first writer to publicly print the name of the number one (unofficial) suspect in Kilgallen's murder, whom her first biographer Lee Israel called the Out-of-Towner; the first to obtain exclusive—and contradictory—quotes from him in which he unwittingly implicated himself; the first author to quote from a videotaped interview with the hairdresser who found Dorothy dead (but was never questioned by police); the first to quote a second hairdresser with personal knowledge that DK's life had been threatened; the first to quote an eyewitness who saw Dorothy just before she died with a man at the Regency hotel bar, following the Sunday night broadcast of *What's My Line?*, on which she appeared for the last time; the first to obtain information directly from a chemist who had worked in the Manhattan Medical Examiner's office and later used new technology to establish that Kilgallen died from three barbiturates, not just one—which pointed to murder; the first to lay out details of Dorothy's quest as an award winning newspaper reporter to discover the truth of John Kennedy's assassination.

Since my original article on Dorothy was published years ago, much new information has become available on the Kennedy assassination. For this book, I have made extensive use of recently declassified government documents that contain numerous important revelations about the case that the U.S. media for the most part have ignored. I am now able to show how these correlate directly with what DK wrote.

Some anonymous critics have posted *ad hominem* attacks on Dorothy Kilgallen on the internet, arguing she didn't have any knowledge about JFK's murder that could have gotten her killed. They point out authors like Mark Lane, who wrote a popular book decrying the Warren Report, survived. But there is a simple explanation for this: Unlike authors whose writing attracts a limited number of people over a period of months or years, as a reporter for the Hearst newspaper chain, Dorothy could reach tens of millions of Americans in less than twenty-four hours and influence their thinking. Plus her major "exclusives" were often republished by other papers as well.

As respected CBS producer/writer and close Dorothy friend Marlin Swing told us, when he called to praise my *Midwest Today* story on her, "She was a very powerful woman. People don't have any idea of the power and contacts she had."

The CIA certainly knew. It had fifty-three of its field offices monitoring Kilgallen when she traveled abroad. The FBI perceived her as a threat, and director J. Edgar Hoover personally wrote memos about her, even dispatching federal agents to her New York townhouse to confront her when she managed to acquire highly sensitive information before it even reached Lyndon Johnson's desk. (She refused to reveal sources).

Most importantly, I have been able to establish—through exclusive taped interviews my father and fellow journalist, Larry Jordan did (after my original article was published) with the man suspected of having a hand in Dorothy's demise—that he had previously participated in a covert operation staged by the Central Intelligence Agency. Juxtaposing his comments with newly declassified government documents, I am able to describe with specificity the contemptible mission in which he was engaged. It was launched by CIA director Allen Dulles, overseen by E. Howard Hunt and Frank Sturgis, and involved political assassinations for which he said he was "highly trained." This shocking truth contextualizes Dorothy Kilgallen's death as never before and is revealed here for the first time as the "smoking gun" of her mysterious case.

For the skeptics who dismiss any information—no matter how credible—that conflicts with the "official" account of Kennedy's death as "conspiracy theories," I would pose this question: *If Lee Harvey Oswald was the lone assassin of President Kennedy and there was no conspiracy, why is "national security" invoked for not releasing all the records?*

I arrived at researching this book, metaphorically, like an architect arrives at a dwelling left in ruins. Piece by piece, source by source, the structure, or in this case, a narrative, began to take shape.

I hope you agree it's a story worth telling.

—Sara Jordan-Heintz

Prologue

At 10:30 p.m. Eastern Standard Time on Sunday, Nov. 7, 1965, fourteen million viewers tuned their television sets to CBS to watch the latest installment of *What's My Line?*—by then a fifteen-year ritual, signaling the end of the weekend—that one final reprieve before the Monday rat race began.

On the panel that night were the show's mainstays, actress Arlene Francis, Random House co-founder Bennett Cerf, actor Tony Randall, and first out on the stage, syndicated columnist Dorothy Kilgallen. The panelists were tasked with discovering what three professionals did for a living, as well as uncovering the identity of the mystery celebrity guest, for which they were always blindfolded.

First guest Spoony Singh's physical appearance elicited insensitive guffaws from the audience (he was clad in a Sikh turban.) He stumped the panel as the founder of the Hollywood Wax Museum. Next, Kilgallen correctly guessed that demure southerner Katherine Stone sold dynamite. As was expected, the appearance of mystery guest Joey Heatherton brought woof whistles from the audience.

With minutes left remaining of the half hour show, host John Daly brought out one final challenger—football writer Elinor Kaine. Just moments after Daly announced the panel had run out of time, Kilgallen chimed in with the guess that the glamorous, youthful contestant was a writer. As the show neared its end, with Cerf and Daly engaged in their signature repartee, Cerf called Ms. Kaine a "pretty football writer" adding, "She better dig up a field goal kicker for the New York Giants, or it's going to be too bad." To which Kilgallen broke in, "Oh, I thought you were going to say something about a forward pass," alluding to Cerf's ubiquitous commentary on a guest's physical attractiveness. The audience laughed, but Randall—seated next to her—gave her a disapproving look.

It wasn't unusual for the cast and even its weekly guests to imbibe after the show, meeting up at a posh New York City watering hole. Kilgallen had a "late date" at the Regency Hotel with a "mystery man" not identified by any witnesses at the time. She found her way home in the wee hours of the morning, while her townhouse's inhabitants, which included husband Richard Kollmar, son Kerry, his tutor Ibne Hassan and

Evelyn and James Clement—her live-in maid and butler—slumbered.

The Clements, who lived on the main level, would claim Kilgallen returned home that evening accompanied by a man. Later, after detecting the sound of a back door shutting, the couple assumed the visitor had parted ways with their employer.

It was no secret Dorothy and her husband led separate personal lives. As a duo, they had entered the homes of millions of listeners with their radio program *Breakfast with Dorothy and Dick* broadcast from their residence each morning at 8:15 a.m. But DK hardly needed her husband's jovial radio voice and charms to eke out a living. It was her work ethic and tenacity that paid the bills and maintained the couple's lavish lifestyle.

By 1965, age fifty-two, Kilgallen had been a decades-long triple threat: radio show host, television personality appearing on *What's My Line?* since 1950, and an acclaimed journalist, known not only for her column *The Voice of Broadway* gobbled up daily by a legion of celebrity gossip hounds, but for having shattered the glass ceiling through working as a crime reporter, beginning in the early 1930s. Ernest Hemingway once dubbed her "the greatest female writer in the world."

On the morning of Nov. 8, 1965, Kilgallen was found dead in her home, the result of a drug and alcohol overdose. Her research file pertaining to her latest book project was missing, which colleagues said contained notes and documents on her investigation of the John F. Kennedy assassination, a case in which she had vowed to "blow the lid off."

Dorothy publicly discredited the Warren Commission's findings that stated that Lee Harvey Oswald acted alone; Oswald did not know Jack Ruby prior to being shot and killed by him on live television; and there was not a conspiracy to assassinate the president. Dorothy had scored not one, but two, exclusive, one-on-one interviews with the enigmatic Ruby—much to the envy of her journalistic colleagues. Kilgallen had even secured a copy of Ruby's Warren Commission testimony before it landed on President Lyndon B. Johnson's desk and published it nationwide, accompanied by her own commentary.

She was an ace reporter with an ace in the hole.

In the weeks before her death, she made a clandestine visit to New Orleans, with a planned second trip she called "cloak and daggerish" to meet with a source that would yield details on the assassination. She also visited anti-Castro hotspot Miami, Florida.

Charles Simpson, one of her trusted hairdressers, recalled decades later, "She never quit. She dug up something about the assassination of President Kennedy that somebody didn't want her to know. She even told us on her own volition: 'I used to share things with you guys [Simpson and fellow hairstylist Marc Sinclaire], but after I have found out now what I know, if the wrong people knew what I know, it would cost me my life.' And she was dead about nine months later."

PART I

1
Girl Around The World

She was born Dorothy Mae Kilgallen on July 3, 1913, in Chicago to James L. (Jim) and Mae Kilgallen, nee Ahern. Jim referred to her as having "black hair and big Irish blue eyes." (In a February 1952 column DK would tell a reader who asked that her eyes were "not very blue, except sometimes. Mostly just gray.)"

She idolized her father, who worked as a news reporter for more than seventy-five years before his death in 1982. Mae decided on her name because Dorothy means "a gift from Heaven." She had high hopes her daughter would pursue a career in teaching, but Dorothy had other ambitions.

Her younger lookalike sister Eleanor was born in 1919 in Indianapolis. She too would choose a profession connected to the entertainment business. A student of the Juilliard Institute of Musical Arts, Eleanor started her career as a casting director for NBC Radio, then CBS Radio and Young and Rubicam.

Dorothy as a budding reporter.

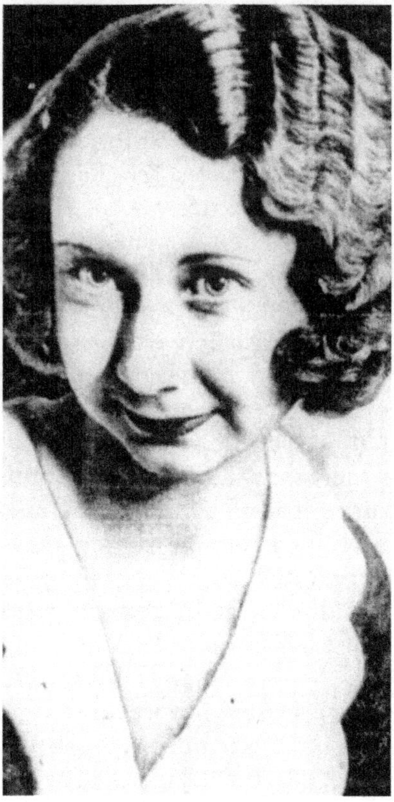

Eleanor teamed with longtime business partner Monique James and launched Casting Consultants, later purchased by MCA, where Eleanor represented clients including Alec Guinness, Laurence Olivier and Michael Redgrave. She and James helped launch the careers of Warren Beatty, Kim Cattrall, Jamie Lee Curtis, Jack Klugman, Katherine Ross, Susan St. James and long-term client George Peppard.

"Eleanor was beautiful, with alabaster skin, proper with her white gloves, surprising with her Broadway lingo, sharp and committed," actor Norman Lloyd would write in his autobiography *Stages: Of Life in Theatre,*

Film and Television.

Jim recalled Dorothy enjoying her visits to the newsroom during his time as managing editor of the *Indianapolis Daily Times*.

Dorothy idolized "Latin Lover" film star Ramon Novarro. She enjoyed writing, producing, directing and starring in plays she'd put on for neighborhood children. Young Kilgallen had a desire to grow up to be a "somebody."

James joined the International News Service in 1920, making a name for himself chronicling the Lindbergh baby kidnapping, was a correspondent during War War II stationed in the Pacific and in Europe—being one of the first reporters to examine the ruins of Hitler's bunker in Berlin—and was with General Eisenhower at the signing of the armistice with the Germans in the little red schoolhouse in Reims, France.

Dorothy wrote of her father, "When I was a very small girl, he fascinated me with tales of murder trials, Ku Klux Klan meetings, trapped coal miners and rioting strikers."

She attended Erasmus Hall High School in Brooklyn, graduating in 1930. (Other famous alums include Barbara Stanwyck, Susan Hayward, Mae West, Eli Wallach, Neil Diamond and Barbra Streisand).

Dorothy earned "excellent" marks in English and "poor" grades in math. She worked for the school's magazine and was known for her high IQ.

At age 17, she enrolled at New Rochelle College, a private Catholic school in existence from 1904 to 2019. She was there only a year before dropping out in 1931 to accept a twenty-dollar-a-week job with the Hearst Corporation's *New York Evening Journal* newspaper, which her father had helped her secure.

"When it came time for me to be a reporter, I was sent to the morgue to identify bodies, assigned to police stations to check on various unpleasant felonies, ordered by my editors alternately to write drama reviews and ask bereaved gentlemen whether they had recently killed their wives. Once, in the course of duty, I had a gun pulled on me on the steps of Sing Sing Prison. (I halted)," she would later recall.

Female journalists of the time were typically relegated to covering society news and writing columns on domesticity. Dorothy enjoyed the surge of adrenaline of sitting mere feet away from the accused in murder trials. As a young reporter, she obtained the first exclusive interview with Bruno Richard Hauptmann, the German-born carpenter who was convicted of the abduction and murder of the twenty-month-old baby of aviator Charles Lindbergh and his wife Anne Morrow Lindbergh.

The court case kicked off on Jan. 3, 1935, at Flemington, New Jersey, and lasted five weeks—largely circumstantial in nature. Found guilty of first degree murder, he died in the electric chair on April 3, 1936.

In the fall of 1936, at just 23 years old, Dorothy gained the experience of a lifetime when her newspaper agreed to send her on a race around the world. The gimmick was to show readers how modern transportation opened up parts of the globe that had been previously uncharted by most Americans, and of course, to sell newspapers by reporting on all the adventures and misadventures that ensued.

Dorothy had just two days to get sixteen visas and secure a passport. She promised her father she'd attend Mass en route whenever possible when she wasn't battling flight delays, inclement weather, political upheaval and social unrest. The cub reporter also had to find the time to transcribe her travel notes and turn them into copy for her paper's hungry readers.

As the only woman participant, she competed against Leo Kieran with *The New York Times* and Herbert R. Ekins of the *World-Telegram*. The race began on September 30 with a departure from the Naval air station in Lakehurst, New Jersey where they boarded the Hindenburg, the doomed dirigible that would explode a year later on May 6, 1937.

Upon arriving in Frankfurt, Germany, Ekins gained the upper hand when he boarded a KLM DC-2. Kilgallen and Kieran decided to stick close together during much of the race.

"For Kilgallen and Kieran, it was planes, trains, and automobiles

Dorothy with rival journalists Leo Kieran and Herbert Ekins as they get ready to depart from Lakehurst, NJ on their around the world race.

as they battled delays on their journey to Brindisi, on the heel of Italy," reported *Air & Space* magazine. "Kieran abandoned a slow train and hired a driver, who drove him down through Italy at breakneck speed. He and Kilgallen had cast their lot with the British flag carrier, Imperial Airways; they planned to take an airliner from Brindisi to Hong Kong. Imperial was to prove safe, cautious—and slow. They lost seven hours when their departure for Athens was delayed by winds, which was just as well for Kilgallen, who had arrived in Brindisi late because a locomotive had broken down. During the trip to Hong Kong, Kilgallen noted repeatedly that the airline's schedule seemed to be based on mealtimes."

For a young woman who up to that time had only resided in the American Midwest and New York City, Dorothy's feet must have floated inches off the ground as she explored Bangkok, Siam and French Indochina. She turned down a private interview with Adolf Hitler, then Führer of Germany.

On October 6, she arrived in Athens from Brindisi, Italy and got to see the Parthenon by moonlight en route to Alexandria. The paper's headline summed up the breakneck speed with which she traveled: "Girl Hopes For Breakfast in Europe, Lunch in Africa, Supper in Asia."

"Leo Kieran, my fellow globe-trotter, and I made the ascent of the Acropolis together and wandered around in awed silence among the fallen columns and crumbling ruins of what is still the most exquisitely formed of the world's buildings."

Her October 7 dispatch described her brief time in Gaza, Palestine.

"The wheels of time have turned with almost invisible slowness here for many centuries, but I zipped through Gaza, just another milk station on the way around the world, so fast today that it must have made Samson turn a whisker.

"I spent exactly an hour and a half in the Holy Land, swinging down from Alexandria onto the Asiatic continent at 8:20 a.m.—1:20 a.m. Akron time—and was off for Rutbah Wells (Iraq), which I hope the pilot can find, at 9:50.

"We made the stirring trip from Africa in four hours, 20 minutes—a two-continent hop with an amazing diversity of scenery.

"The blaring orb of the rising sun lifted the mists over the delta of the Nile, reputed to be the world's most fertile soil. Then from the rich deposit of Mother Nile, we sailed suddenly over the bleakest desert imaginable, endless miles of fawn-colored sand to the right and the dazzling Mediterranean on the left, until we sighted below us a narrow greenish-blue ribbon rolling away to the south..."

Dorothy's description of Palestine and specifically Gaza is in sharp contrast to what is happening there today. It had been a peaceful region but became a flashpoint for war in October 2023. The Gaza Strip, West

Bank, and parts of modern Israel are all part of Palestine. It is a state whose legal status is the subject of controversy although it is currently recognized by 138 of 193 United Nations member states.

When Kieran and Kilgallen arrived in Hong Kong to board a steamship for Manila and then Pan American's China Clipper on their way back to the States, they discovered Ekins was way ahead of them. He had taken a non-passenger Pan Am trial flight. He violated the contest's rules by presenting himself as a crewmember to get on board. Ekins won the race, traveling for a total of eighteen days, eleven hours and forty-five minutes.

Meanwhile Kieran and Kilgallen were stranded in Manila while a typhoon battered the island. The pair reached Honolulu on October 22. Dorothy arranged for a flight from San Francisco to New York on a Vultee plane. She completed the journey in twenty-four days, twelve hours and thirty-one minutes, making her the second place champion, with Kieran a mere two hours behind her.

Dorothy became the second woman in history to traverse the globe, following Nellie Bly's famed adventure of 1889, but DK was the first to do so while also using commercial airlines. First Lady Eleanor Roosevelt wrote to congratulate DK. Kilgallen published a memoir about the trip entitled *Girl Around the World*. Her father Jim wrote a touching foreword to the book, marveling that his daughter was growing up so quickly, already a seasoned traveler and budding journalist. Copies of the book today, sadly, are extremely hard to find.

Dorothy wrote of the people she met, exotic cuisine she sampled, and the turbulence of traveling by rail, plane and boat. She conversed with a French-speaking police commissioner in Hanoi, French Indochina (today Vietnam), and relayed their exchange in her book. "'Are you English?' he asked me, using that tongue brokenly. When I told him I was American, he answered flatteringly: 'Of course...what else could you be...with such courage?'"

Upon completing her around the globe assignment, she was sent to Hollywood to report on the film colony. She made her acting debut (a brief performance) in the December 1936 mystery *Sinner Take All*, playing "sob sister" Jane Mills. The following year, she wrote a concept screenplay for Warner Brothers, based on her book. It was turned into the crime-mystery *Fly Away Baby*, starring Glenda Farrell and Barton MacLane.

Dorothy was writing a column called *Hollywood Scene as Seen by Dorothy Kilgallen*. The name was later tweaked to *As Seen in Hollywood by Dorothy Kilgallen*.

The First of Many Feuds

In some columns, DK was critical of movie star Constance Bennett, whom she wrote was experiencing a decline in popularity. On Jan.

23, 1937, Bennett sued for libel. Dorothy was forced to print this apology:

"Miss Bennett's pictures have been successful and there was no intention on the part of Twentieth Century-Fox to induce cancellation of the contract at any time. The writer regrets her erroneous reference to the matter, and desires to withdraw the statements completely, with her apologies to Miss Bennett thereof."

Angering a Hollywood legend so early on in DK's career could be chalked up to her inexperience. Perhaps she thought it might boost circulation and help her catch the eye of her boss, William Randolph Hearst. Another theory was that the "scoop" had been given to her by rival columnist Louella Parsons, who felt threatened by the competition and wanted to get rid of the young reporter.

Hearst Not Without Controversy

William Randolph Hearst's long career was not without controversy. He bought the *New York Morning Journal* in 1895, followed by the *New York Evening Journal* the next year. The *Morning Journal* gained notoriety for its circulation war with Joseph Pulitzer's *New York World-Telegram* through yellow journalism. Readers were wooed with illustrations, color pages and salacious headlines, including coverage of the Spanish-American War. Hearst is reputed to have wired his illustrator in Cuba, "You furnish the pictures, I'll furnish the war."

"*The Journal* was among the earliest American newspapers to give published credit to its reporters, columnists, editorial writers, cartoonists, and photographers," Ransom Center Senior Research Curator of Photography Roy Flukinger wrote. "The newspaper was consistent in its pride for the individual achievements of its staff members and from this first decade onwards took up the professional practice of granting credit lines to much of its published imagery by its staff photographers and artists.

"It is important to note that, in addition to subscribing to various other news services, the Hearst Corporation would also establish a successful news and picture syndication service of its own. Growing out of his rivalry with competing publisher Joseph Pulitzer, the Hearst's *New York Morning Journal* was denied membership in 1897 to America's dominant news service, the Associated Press (AP). Although the magnate quickly gained backdoor access by simply buying up another newspaper with an earlier AP membership, his pique had been raised. In typical Hearst fashion he began to eschew both the AP and rival Edward Willis Scripps's United Press (UP) by establishing his own fledgling news syndication service around 1900. Nine years later Hearst entered the contract news syndication business with the formal establishment of his International News Service (INS) that distributed news stories by both mail and wire."

The *New York American* (originally called the *New York Journal*, then renamed American in 1901), a morning paper, and the *New York Evening*

The presses are ready to roll at one of New York City's daily newspapers.

Journal, an afternoon paper, merged on June 25, 1937 to become the *New York Journal-American*, Dorothy's flagship newspaper for her entire career as a journalist.

DK's First Royal Assignment

Hearst gave DK the coveted assignment of covering the coronation of King George VI, which took place on May 12, 1937. It was a tumultuous time in Great Britain. King George V had died in January of 1936 and his son Edward took the throne, only to abdicate that December to marry American divorcee Wallis Simpson.

DK called London a "fairy tale town" with its "beauty and splendor" on display for the historic occasion. She gushed over the jewels and gowns worn by the royal family.

"If there are poor people in this city, if there are those who are hungry and sick and unhappy, they are hidden for these days of magic," she wrote.

2
Balancing Act

In November 1938, DK was back in New York. She began writing a new column for the newspaper called *The Voice of Broadway*. Her articles were sharp, concise and dishy, encompassing every aspect of the entertainment world. Dorothy, by virtue of her syndication across the country, became as well-known as the celebrities about whom she wrote.

"It's essentially what I think about things and what appeals to the public," she said of the format.

By 1941, Dorothy Kilgallen's *VOB* column was running in twenty-four newspapers and growing, but it only made her one-hundred and fifty dollars a week. That August, she began hosting a fifteen-minute afternoon radio show of the same title, which aired on CBS. It promised listeners the "story behind the story" of New York City night life, peppered with celebrity interviews. Sponsored by Johnson & Johnson, her new manager Mark Hanna had helped secure the gig. The radio program earned DK four times as much as she made writing her newspaper column.

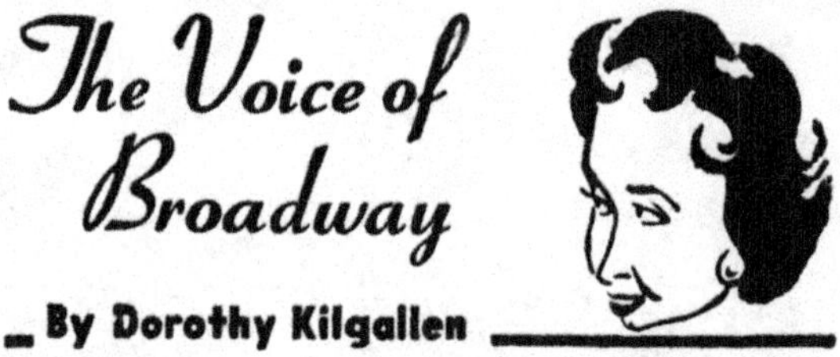

Dorothy Falls For Charismatic Thespian

Against the backdrop of a busy reporter's life, Dorothy still found time for romance. In 1938, she spotted an attractive young actor named Richard Kollmar, who was appearing in a Broadway play called *Knickerbocker Holiday*.

Born in Brooklyn, New York on Dec. 31, 1910, to John and Christine Kollmar, he was the great-great grandson of Daniel D. Tompkins, who served as the sixth Vice President of the United States. While he was still an infant, his family moved to Ridgewood, New Jersey, an area that was known as being white upper-class. His father was an architect.

Richard had a troubled adolescence, and by the time he was twelve years of age, he had run away from home at least a dozen times. Notably, he made it as far as St. Louis. His goal was to become a movie star.

Dorothy with her fiancé Dick Kollmar in 1940.

After being picked up in Missouri by his father, young Richard Kollmar was sent away to a work school for troubled boys, affiliated with the Episcopal Church. He then secured admission to Saint Stephens College, later known as Bard. In a year's time he flunked out, and transferred to Tusculum College in Greenville, Tennessee. While there, he enjoyed singing in the glee club and garnered appreciation for his deep, resonant baritone voice. He was also editor of the school newspaper. He befriended other thespians and had an active social life.

He went on to Yale Dramatic School, but dropped out after he won a role on a radio drama in New York City in 1934. He also was hired to do a series of radio commercials and even served as master of ceremonies for a fashion show.

One Sunday morning he sang on the radio for the first time, doing southern mountain songs. That gig helped him get an agent, Dorothy Bernon, who in turn secured the part in *Knickerbocker Holiday*. It opened at the Ethel Barrymore Theater on Oct. 19, 1938, and closed March 11, 1939, following one-hundred and sixty-eight performances. The director was Josh Logan and the cast included Walter Huston, who would later be known for his work in films.

Impressed by Kollmar's talent, DK mentioned him in one of her columns, after which his press agent formally introduced them. They lunched at the Algonquin.

According to Lee Israel, "He proposed on their sixth date, the courtship having been interrupted while he left town with the show.

Dorothy told him that she wanted very much to be his wife, but that the problem of religion had first to be solved. Richard was an Episcopalian, and she would not consider marrying outside the Catholic Church. He would have to convert."

While Dick's mother Christine, and Dorothy's mother Mae, were not in favor of the marriage, Jim Kilgallen gave his blessing and John Kollmar convinced his wife that she would have to consent, or risk losing her only son.

Before the couple exchanged nuptials, in 1939 Richard got a role in the musical *Too Many Girls* alongside Desi Arnaz.

As an indication of Dorothy's increasing stature as a columnist, several of the most important clubs in New York lined up to help the couple celebrate their engagement. Parties were held at the 21 Club, The Rainbow Room, Leon & Eddies, the Monte Carlo and the Stork Club.

Though Richard had made some money and had some extravagant ways—buying a pre-owned black Cadillac and hiring a man to chauffeur him on special occasions (including his first date with DK)—he was thunderstruck by Dorothy's extravagance. Prior to their marriage he had an eleventh hour panic attack at the prospect of her bankrupting him, especially after she ordered a $700 carpet and other lavish furnishings for their new apartment. But he decided he loved her enough to roll the dice.

Dorothy and Dick tied the knot at a noon Mass on April 6, 1940. Sister Eleanor was maid of honor alongside Mrs. Frederic A. Willis who was matron of honor. Mary Anita Loos, the niece of screenwriter Anita Loos, was a bridesmaid. The eight hundred guests included a mix of family, friends and celebrities such as actor Tyrone Power and his wife, French actress Annabella, Ethel Merman, Milton Berle, Louella Parsons and Gertrude Lawrence. It's still unclear who picked up the tab for this huge wedding and the reception that followed at the Viennese Room of the Saint Regis Hotel at which guests sipped champagne and enjoyed a sumptuous meal.

But it was no mystery as to how the newlyweds could afford a honeymoon in Varadero, Cuba. Their trip was paid for by the North American gambling syndicate.

The Kollmars' first child Richard, Jr. was born in 1941, followed by Jill in 1943. The prospect of DK becoming a mother concerned Hearst exec Richard Berlin, perhaps because most women of that era struggled to "have it all" with many quitting their jobs upon marrying and certainly by the time a child had entered the scene. With the aid of household staff, a nanny and a secretary, Dorothy balanced home and work life. She was a self-professed "terrible cook" and left those duties to the professionals.

Meanwhile, husband Richard's career was thriving. By 1943 he had become a Broadway producer, and hired Fats Waller to compose a musical that year called *Early To Bed*. That was a daring move at the time, because it was unheard of for a Black composer to be writing the musical score for a white show.

By then, Waller had established himself as a respected jazz pianist, organist, composer, violinist, singer and comedic entertainer. One night he was kidnapped in Chicago while leaving a performance and taken by four men to an establishment owned by mobster Al Capone. Waller was surprised to find a party going on inside, at which point—with a gun to his back—he was pushed toward a piano and told to play. Absolutely terrified, Fats soon realized he was the "surprise guest" for Capone's birthday party, but then was relieved to discover that the kidnappers had no intention of doing him any harm.

It is to Kollmar's credit that he did not let the prevailing prejudice of his day influence him; he signed Waller to compose music for his theatrical production. Fats was credited with writing at least four hundred songs during his career—but at times of financial distress, when he needed quick cash, he often would sell his compositions to other songwriters and they got the credit. Two examples were *I Can't Give You Anything But Love* and *On the Sunny Side Of the Street.*

Sadly, Waller died in mid-December 1943.

DK's column, in which she'd sometimes dub herself "Miss Midnight," writing her "Midnight Memo," grew in popularity with expanded reach through syndication.

She regaled readers with celebrity tidbits such as seeing Milton Berle grab a hot dog at a Broadway stand; Greta Garbo (notoriously reclusive) share an umbrella with a man on E. 49th Street; Morton Downey's brogue mingling with Gregory Ratoff's incredible dialect at the Stork Club. In one item, she revealed how at a particularly swank party the host hired a hairdresser "just to keep the ladies' coiffures in condition during the course of the evening."

War News Mixed In With Celebrity Gossip

While her father Jim traveled abroad to cover the war, Dorothy remained on the home front.

In early January 1942, DK included an item in her column that defended the controversial head of the FBI. She wrote, "J. Edgar Hoover is ready with a blistering answer to critics who have been seeking to lay a great part of the blame for the Pearl Harbor disaster in his lap. Hoover tried to warn the government of Jap fifth-columning in Hawaii but allegedly was blocked by Army and Navy officials who were sure the Japs couldn't get within miles of Honolulu. He will 'name names' if a showdown comes."

In June 1943, Dorothy wrote a piece entitled "They Who Fight" which revealed she chatted with soldiers and sailors while she attended Broadway shows and events. She wrote, in part, "It is stimulating to talk to them and listen to them, especially if you have any connection with show business, because they are quick to demonstrate what an important part show business plays in their lives whether they are on furlough in New York, or just dreaming about it in some South Pacific jungle.

"Perhaps, because they are young and 'hep,' they are the best audience in the world for a musical show, a swing band, a Broadway column, or a radio comic. They like fun the way it is dished out in America, and when they are here they enjoy it and when they are far away they talk about it under desert stars and on the decks of ships in strange seas, and they write home about it as if to say, 'Hold everything. Keep the overture playing. Keep the champagne and the beer on ice. Keep the girls smiling. We'll be back—and we want it to be like the dreams we're dreaming over here.'"

In a later column, she paid tribute to the entertainment industry's contribution to the war effort.

"Next to the actual taste of victory itself nothing is so palatable to the spirit of fighting men as a good movie, a personal appearance by a stage or screen star, a favorite radio program, or a zippy recording," she wrote. "...It seems that in wartime nothing is more of an artistic triumph than a sweater-girl; I don't know what the Mona Lisa meant to warriors in her times, but everyone's well aware of what Betty Grable and Lana Turner mean to ours. It's not art for art's sake, but it's art for GI Joe."

Dorothy and Dick Become a Power Couple

Dorothy was gaining new readers all the time with her witty and newsy columns as her hubby was embarking on a career in radio. He was signed to portray Dennis Pierce on the CBS radio series *Pretty Kitty Kelly*. But he became best known as the popular detective Boston Blackie on a radio show by the same name on the Mutual Broadcasting System, which aired from 1945 to 1950.

Although the couple pursued their separate careers, they did team up for a venture that was highly successful. Their radio show, *Breakfast With Dorothy and Dick*, launched on April 15, 1945.

Though the program had its homespun qualities—it was literally broadcast from their dining room table—they did not pretend to be the couple next door.

Chatty and personal, their show sparkled with name-dropping, giving listeners a forty-five-minute glimpse into how the other half lives. "Good morning, darling" (said by DK), good morning, sweetie" (Richard said in reply) was the signature opening line. With the microphone on the table amongst the breakfast dishes, the couple conversed about family incidents, parties and plays, in a quiet and intimate tone. Sometimes their topics were rather mundane, as when Dorothy groused good-humoredly about her inability to find truly black ink for her fountain pen but kept ending up with bottles of dark blue ink instead.

The show reached an estimated twenty million listeners, leading to companies vying for sponsorship opportunities. The show aired on powerhouse station WOR-AM from 1945 through 1963.

WOR was a prestigious, pioneering broadcaster, who launched in 1922, transmitting with less power than a modern microwave oven, using a wire strung between two poles on the top of the Bamberger's department store in New Jersey. This configuration was replaced within a few months by a two hundred-foot-wide antenna array, and eight months in, WOR became the first American station heard in Europe.

By the time the Kollmars joined the program roster, the station was transmitting with 50,000 watts—the most power allowable for AM outlets then and since—and attracted a massive listening audience.

John Crosby with the Publishers Newspaper Syndicate wrote an amusing dispatch from London (where he had relocated), comparing Dorothy and Dick to the British royal family. His article, which appeared after the show went off the air, fittingly paid it tribute.

He concluded the two famous Americans had a lot more fun than the Brits. He called the couple his "pseudo-family," writing, "Aaah, the vicarious adventures I went through with Dorothy and Dick—their problems with the children, the parties they went to, the places they went last night, whom they saw, what they wore, what the glamorous people they ran with wore and ate and said, their little quarrels. It was like having two lives, Dorothy and Dick's and my own, and I've missed them."

Crosby mused, "Well, I've got a new pseudo-family, at long last,

Richard, Dorothy and children Dick, Jr. and Jill promoting Colonial House candies on their radio show.

which I read about every day in the *Times of London* or the *Telegraph*...I thought it over a long time before adopting the Royal Family for my pseudo-family. For one thing the prose style of the court circulars are pretty tough sledding at breakfast. 'His Highness the Sultan of Zanzibar was entertained to luncheon by the Princess Margaret, Countess of Snowdon'...I didn't think the Royal Family would give me the same sense of belonging, of participating that Dorothy and Dick did. It was a step up socially but a step down emotionally.

"I used to get a tremendously vicarious sense of upset at hearing that Dick had used the wrong fork again at somebody's party (as he almost always did). Obviously the Royal Family never use the wrong fork. Even if they did they wouldn't put it in the court circular...

"I hate to say it, but the parties my new family go to are nowhere near as interesting as the ones Dorothy and Dick used to attend. The other day the Duke of Edinburgh went helling off to a Boy's Club reception at the Fishmongers Hall. The Princess-Royal went to a luncheon of the Worshipful Company of Skinners, whoever they are. The Queen Mother opened a factory in Dundee. Pretty grubby lot of social events next to the company Dorothy and Dick used to keep—authors, composers, actresses, socialites. No fishmongers and never any skinners. (Dorothy Kilgallen wouldn't be caught in the same room with a fishmonger)."

October 1947 brought Dorothy notice for her crime solving skills. She scored a private interview with suspected murderer Janet Graham and was able to obtain a confession from the woman that she and Charles Mason had killed her mother. For these efforts, Dorothy won cigarette company Pall Mall's *The Big Story* contest and received a $500 prize. The story was re-enacted on the radio by an all-star cast and broadcast on CBS. This radio—later television—series was based on real experiences of newspaper reporters from all over the United States.

As the decade was nearing its end, in April 1949, DK penned a column offering up predictions for what the world would be like in 1959. Here are some of the pithy comments she offered to readers, "If it takes you more than half an hour to get to Miami, you'll know you're on a slow jet...*Rhapsody in Blue* will be on one side of a dime record...Magazines containing more printed words than pictures will be purchased only by professors...Mamas will pray for girl twins to pose for Toni (home perm) ads.

"There'll be a strong wiretappers' union...Leo Durocher will hand over his year's salary to the commissioner and it will barely cover his fines...The new automobiles will be so low slung that the best way to drive them will be lying face down. You'll also have to take the price lying down...Tallulah Bankhead will sue eight towns because they have streets named Taullulah...There won't be a job for any show girl under six feet... Rogers and Hammerstein will make money with their own chain of banks, no outside investors permitted."

3
Cub Reporter Turned Journalistic Lion

By 1950, Dorothy's column was running in about one hundred fifty papers, garnering twenty million readers. The Kilgallen approach, according to *Time* magazine, was a mixture of catty gossip ("A world-famous movie idol, plastered, commanded a pretty girl to get into his limousine, take off all her clothes"); odd tidbits of inconsequential information ("The Duke of Windsor eats caviar with a spoon"); and dark warnings ("Anti-American factions are planning to blow up the Panama Canal"; "Venezuela is on the brink of a civil war. The strong men in the government are quarreling among themselves.")

Oftentimes, celebrity news was presented as vignettes, punchy and jaunty: "...Greta Garbo looked dazzling at the Colony the other day when she lunched with Countess Bernadotte and Jacques Sarlie. She was hatless, and her hair was perfectly straight, but enormously becoming...Linda Darnell's nightclub act needs a lot of work, Chicago experts report...Jean Martin Black, ex-wife of the Chock Full O'Nuts tycoon, is seriously ill, chums say. They're calling it a nervous breakdown."

Kilgallen's deal "bring me three detrimental stories concerning other stars and I will include a good piece about your client," became the way she ran her column. She cruised New York nightspots like the Stork Club, Copacabana, Eden Roc, Delmonico's and the Cotillion Room, picking up stories, writing them on matchbooks and tossing them in her purse. She frequented P.J. Clarke's for lunch, occupying the same big round table in the back corner of the room that is still there, and like the *éminence grise* that she'd become, she held court with all kinds of politicos, celebrities, wits and movie stars paying homage. Reuben's Restaurant in New York City even named a sandwich after her. The Dorothy Kilgallen sold for a dollar and ten cents.

As Dorothy's fame grew, she was profiled in newspapers and magazines. She did advertisements for Camel cigarettes, Douglas D-6 planes and Allen Rubber-Top carpet, to name a few.

Everybody's Favorite Guessing Game

On Thursday, Feb. 2, 1950, Dorothy became a regular panelist on a new game show, first called *Occupation Unknown*, but then renamed *What's My Line?*, in which she would appear weekly for the next fifteen years.

Dorothy Kilgallen, Bennett Cerf, Arlene Francis, Hal Block and host John Daly.

Contestants were brought on with unusual occupations and were interviewed by the panelists. Only questions that could be answered with a "yes" or "no" were allowed, with the contestant winning five dollars for every "no" answer. Ten "no's" and the contestant won the game (and fifty dollars). The viewers at home and in the theater knew the occupation of each guest from words that were flashed on the screen at the start of questioning.

Situated alongside her during the debut episode were former New Jersey governor Harold Hoffman, poet Louis Untermeyer and psychiatrist Richard Hoffman (no relation to the governor). John Daly served as moderator.

The initial format was rather cornball in nature and had the panelists, host and contestant all wedged together on one side of the stage (instead of utilizing the entire space as later episodes would). People openly smoked. After signing in on a board, the challenger would then be asked to walk the length of the panel to be examined close up. Panelists would then be allowed to take "a wild free guess" before the game began.

During the introduction of the debut show, DK alone was poised enough to speak directly into the camera and not fumble around with notes like the others, who were clearly ill at ease. When the first contestant, hat check girl Pat Finch, appeared on stage, she was asked to parade before the panel and had awkward questions posed to her, including what perfume she wore (no, it was not My Sin) and to balance a book on her head (she couldn't). Dorothy, likely trying to ascertain the woman's income level, asked to see the label in her suit jacket. The mystery guest, whom they did not guess, was baseball shortstop Phil Rizzuto.

Famed CBS producer Marlin Swing, who was not affiliated with *WML?*, was a close friend of Dorothy's. He told *Midwest Today* magazine, "In looking back at the early episodes, I thought 'how did this show last?' And for a Goodson-Todman show, it was so poorly thrown together."

After airing alternate Wednesdays, then alternate Thursdays, it landed in an established tine slot of Sundays at 10:30 p.m. EST on Oct. 1, 1950, anchored there until the end of its network run on Sept. 3, 1967.

In Dorothy, viewers saw a highly intelligent, competitive woman who strived to determine the professions of the contestants. She attributed the ability to flush out information from her years as a reporter, through covering court trials, for being a voracious reader and playing "think games" at private parties.

Random House co-founder Bennett Cerf joined the panel in 1951, replacing Untermeyer. Actress Arlene Francis and comedy writer Hal Block were also panel regulars. Comedian Steve Allen replaced Block in 1953, then left in 1954 to start *The Tonight Show*. His empty seat was then filled by Fred Allen (no relation). When Fred died in 1956, it was decided his empty seat would be filled by a guest star each week, instead of securing a permanent replacement. Steve Allen, Joey Bishop, Tony Randall, Johnny Carson, William Shatner, David Niven and Greer Garson all guest starred on the panel.

Arlene Francis, born Arline Francis Kazanjian, on Oct. 20, 1907, in Boston, was a pioneering woman of television. In addition to her work on *WML?*, she had hosted a highly-rated daily radio interview program called *The Arlene Francis Show* on WOR in New York from 1961 to 1990. She was host of NBC's *Home* newsmagazine (1954-57) and made several appearances on Broadway and in film.

Original show announcers were Lee Vines and Hal Simms. Johnny Olson took over the role in 1961 and remained with the show for its duration. He built a career as a game show announcer working up until his death in 1985. Modern audiences may remember his exuberant "Come on down!" on *The Price is Right*.

Often first out on the stage, Kilgallen was announced as "the popular columnist whose *Voice of Broadway* appears in papers coast to coast, Miss Dorothy Kilgallen."

WML? was broadcast live from New York City on Sunday nights at 10:30 p.m. EST, from a drab, seven-story theater on 54th Street that was later remodeled into the famed discotheque Studio 54. Men on the panel wore black ties and suit coats, while the ladies donned gloves, false eyelashes and glistening evening gowns. Jewels glittered under the bright studio lighting.

A who's who affair, stars vied for the opportunity to come on the show and promote their latest film or album, either by appearing as the mystery guest or seated on the panel. Mystery celebrity guests included, but are not limited to: Lucille Ball, Lauren Bacall, Jayne Mansfield, Jack Benny, Joan Crawford, Eleanor Roosevelt, Charles Boyer, Alfred Hitchcock, Gloria Swanson, Nat King Cole, Frank Lloyd Wright, Salvador Dali, Joe DiMaggio, Mickey Mantle, Paul Newman, Natalie Wood, Sean Connery, Liberace and hundreds more.

At Christmas 1950 Dorothy was asked to demonstrate an early color TV test by CBS.

The show's host, John Charles Daly Jr., was a polished sophisticate with many years experience working in journalism. He and Kilgallen may have swapped tales of their time reporting on major news stories of domestic and international significance. Born on Feb. 20, 1914, in Johannesburg, South Africa, his American father had worked there as a geologist. After his father died of tropical fever, Mrs. Daly moved him and his older brother to Boston. He was educated at Tilton School in Tilton, New Hampshire, followed by Boston College.

Daly had worked in a wool factory and for a transit company in Washington before landing a job as a reporter for NBC Radio, followed by CBS. He later served as a White House correspondent for CBS, gaining the opportunity to travel the world reporting for CBS Radio Network. During World War II, he was the first national correspondent to report the attack on Pearl Harbor, Sunday, Dec. 7, 1941. He was also the first journalist to announce wire service reports of the death of President Franklin D. Roosevelt on April 12, 1945. In 1948, Daly appeared as a panelist on the CBS/ABC quiz show *Celebrity Time*, which led to the job offer of a lifetime—hosting *What's My Line?*.

In July 1959, Daly and Associated Press writer John Scali reported from Moscow on the famed Kitchen Debate between USSR General Secretary Nikita Khrushchev and then-U.S. Vice President Richard Nixon.

Indeed, *WML?* oozed with class as the new medium of television entered into the homes of everyday people.

"I would pick up Dorothy and I was there at least every other week and we'd spend time there (at the studio) and then we'd go to Clarke's or somewhere or Copa. It was fun. It was an exciting period," Marlin Swing recalled of the show.

He described a game he used to play with Dorothy when she was on stage.

"Most times when the show was on the air, I was in the control room. And that's where they kept the mystery guests, so I got to meet all the mystery guests," he recalled. "Because I would know the answers I would try to mentally send messages to Dorothy and quite a few of them—it must have worked—because out of nowhere, she'd say 'do you have anything to do with animals?' or whatever."

Swing would socialize with the *WML?* panelists in the makeup room before the show.

"I'd take Dorothy over and then I'd sit up there and it was fun listening to them all talk," he said. "Quite often I gave [Bennett Cerf] a couple of puns that I had and he used them."

Almost from day one, DK would face insults about how seriously she took the game, with some pundits claiming the show was rigged.

"I don't feel that I'm a smarty pants, or that I'm aggressive," Dorothy reflected.

She credited Arlene Francis and Steve Allen for having "more professional experience" and being better at "clowning and making funny remarks."

The show's co-producer, Mark Goodson, said, "Dorothy is a girl of tremendous integrity. If we ever tried to give her the answer she'd quit the show immediately. Actually, she's the key member of the panel. The show would be a flop if she didn't hold the panel together."

Dorothy Grateful to Hearst

Aside from her father, Jim Kilgallen, it turns out Dorothy had another important mentor, but one whom she never met!

When William Randolph Hearst Sr. died in Beverly Hills on Aug. 14, 1951, Dorothy paid tribute to the man who had served as her boss since she was 17 years old. In her column, she revealed she'd never met the newspaper mogul in person, but was indebted to him.

"He must have believed that women—even very young girls—deserved an equal chance with men in the field of journalism, for when I joined the *New York Journal* at the end of my freshman year in college there were four other women on the city room staff, and they were not writing about cooking or mothers' clubs or how to make ruffled tiebacks, they were covering the news...

"...Under the system that prevailed at the *Journal* I became a reporter the natural way, as if my name had been Joe. I went through the tough, tiring, wonderfully stimulating mill of the city side reporter, from night court to ship news, from Bellevue morgue to Vanderbilt mansion, from politics to crimes of passion.

"In the beginning I was quite unaware that the eye of William Randolph Hearst ever fell upon the work of a cub reporter struggling to fathom the twin mysteries of the New York subway system and the journalistic style. He was a legend to me—a tall man directing an empire from what I pictured as a baronial desk in California—and it did not occur to me that he knew I existed."

Then one day the city editor called Dorothy into his office and announced he was assigning her to cover a big murder trial. He added "The Chief thought you did a great job on the last one..."

"The Chief" was Mr. Hearst himself, and Kilgallen was in disbelief that the legendary newspaper baron followed her column. She recounted, "The city editor looked at me wryly. 'He reads everything,' he said. In the years to come I learned that was true."

DK wrote it was Hearst who personally had approved of her taking her famed trip around the world, and would ask that Dorothy cover certain assignments, such as the Coronation of King George VI. Had he not allowed her to stretch her wings as a journalist, she wrote she would have quit the field to work in teaching, advertising or "painting forget-me-nots on china cups.

"The man I had never seen, never spoken to, read everything I wrote just as he read what everybody wrote in all his papers, and he guided my career from 3,000 miles away. His terse little notes, usually hand-written in the margin of a newspaper, never said more than 'How about Dorothy Kilgallen for this?' or "Suggest Dorothy handle this,' but they sent me to faraway places and on exciting assignments."

Dorothy Falls Hard For Bisexual Rock 'n Roller

Despite initially being rather dismissive of Johnnie Ray's music, DK began finding enjoyment in his records. She had an about face in 1952, enthusing in a column, "I've come to just love Johnnie Ray's record of 'Please, Mr. Sun.'"

She'd soon also come to love the man himself, despite her being married and he being fourteen years her junior.

Had they not been celebrities, it's unlikely Johnnie Ray's and Dorothy Kilgallen's paths would have crossed.

Called the "father of rock and roll" by Tony Bennett, in the early 1950s, Ray's emotional singing and sexually provocative performances made him an instant hit with teenyboppers. Ray had a hearing impairment from childhood and was also a heavy drinker and chain smoker.

Before finding fame, in June 1951, Ray was arrested in Detroit, Michigan for accosting and soliciting an undercover male vice-squad police officer for sex in the restroom of the Stone Theatre. He pleaded guilty and paid a twenty-five dollar fine, later being released.

Dorothy extolled the singer's merits to Marlin Swing and her makeup man Carmen Gebbia. Head over heels in love with Johnnie, she flew anywhere to be with him—sometimes forgoing discretion in public places.

A native of Oregon, Ray dreamed of becoming a movie star, but instead landed gigs in small, predominantly Black nightclubs in Detroit, including at the Flame Show Bar where he was discovered. Songs *Cry* and *The Little White Cloud That Cried* cemented his stardom. In 1954, Ray made his first and only film *There's No Business Like Show Business* co-starring Ethel Merman, Donald O'Conner, Mitzi Gaynor, Dan Dailey and Marilyn Monroe.

"The basis is sincerity. My need for sincerity traces back to when I was a child and lost my hearing. I became withdrawn. I had an emotional need to develop a relationship to other people," he said of his foray into the music business.

Despite being billed as a "Broadway" reporter, seen at all the hot night clubs and plays (sometimes with Ray), DK often wrote items pertaining to national security and geopolitics. She was obviously a well-spoken and worldly woman. She confessed to being "bored" with the 1952 presidential election and its "bad monologues" at campaign stops, teamed with the "bad dialogue" at dinner parties.

But what crossed the line from dull to infuriating was the political analysis of the female electorate—likely conducted by out of touch men. In 1952, women made up more than half of the voting block in the United States and politicos wanted to know who these lady voters would throw their support behind, as it had the potential to sway the election.

In an October column, Dorothy expressed her indignation at these so-called "experts" who were making their predictions based on sexist assumptions that women would vote for the candidate that appealed most to their emotions.

"I have read sober, not-kidding estimates of the number of women who may vote for Ike because he is sweet and homey and because he has Mamie, while other careful crystal-gazers point out that Adlai is an eligible grass widower and there are single girls and young housewives who find this irresistibly romantic."

She goes on to point out that women do not merely rely on "intuition" when determining which candidate to cast a ballot for.

"Women know the issues just as well as you lads. They are hep to high prices at the supermarkets, low values for the dollar in the clothing stores, housing problems, tax bites, and the mess in Washington. They have quite a lot to do with bearing and raising the young men who are shipped off to Korea, and equally share with the males in burying the ones who come back in coffins.

"So don't count too much on the number of girls who are going to vote for Adlai because he's lonesome or for Ike because Mamie is a grandma. Take it from me, the only thing you can be sure of is that women don't think the way you think they think."

A Visit To The Old South

On Feb. 6, 1953, Dorothy traveled to Augusta, Georgia to conduct research for an article on boom towns she was writing for *Good Housekeeping* magazine. Mayor Hugh Hamilton and *Augusta Chronicle* Woman's Editor Marguerite Stelling greeted her at Bush Field.

Louis Harris, the newspaper's editor, wined and dined her, eager to show off the city, which was experiencing a rise in commerce and construction.

"It is as if Scarlett O'Hara had come home from the ball, wiggled out of her satin gown, and put on a space suit," Dorothy remarked.

But when her article was published in April, Mayor Hamilton was aghast that DK wrote about the city's seedier side—its gambling dens. She pointed out Hamilton had run for office the prior year on a campaign promise to rid Augusta of this societal ill.

She wrote the town's "establishment" wasn't ready for modernity, noting, "The pretty ghosts of nineteenth century Augusta shudder under the dark pines."

To mark the sixty-fifth anniversary in 2018 of Kilgallen's visit, Bill Kirby of the *Chronicle* wrote, "After the article came out, Hamilton demanded an apology. He said he remained a strident foe of gamblers, and many of the places Kilgallen visited were outside his jurisdiction anyway. The Richmond County grand jury did have jurisdiction, how*ever,* and it vowed an investigation, dutifully announcing it on *The Chronicle's* front page. Well, you know what happened? Not much."

Some things never change.

Movin' On Up

The Kollmars relocated to a palatial, 13,000-plus-square-foot townhouse at 45 E. 68th Street in New York City, just a block away from Central Park. Their parties there were extravagant and even covered in the papers. They broadcast their radio show from the fourth floor studio. Its fifth floor was Dorothy's designated workspace she dubbed "the Cloop." She wrote and slept on this floor. It was her sanctuary, and she

Dorothy in her opulent, five-story townhouse, pens one of her syndicated columns. She and her husband Dick took care in decorating their home and hosted expensive parties there.

did not permit anyone else to be around her there. It had chartreuse carpeting, flowered wallpaper and embroidered organdy curtains tied back with taffeta bows.

Designed by architect C.P.H. Gilbert, the mastermind behind more than one hundred mansions in Brooklyn and Manhattan, the home features a rusticated stone base with Flemish bond brick with yellow headers at the upper floors; a heavy stone lintel on brackets over central entrance; a wrought-iron balcony across the second floor; and a modillion Renaissance-style roof cornice, according to real estate information obtained online. It was an elegant setting, with chandeliers, French doors, expensive artwork and original furniture from the film *Gone With the Wind*. The home sold for nearly seventeen million dollars in September 2021.

Dorothy enjoyed the attention and prestige that accompanied her fame. Stork Club owner Sherman Billingsley nicknamed her "Miss New York."

She told her dad she liked pretty things and Jim smiled when he recalled, "The room was an index to her character. Even when she was a cub reporter at $20 a week, she was a spender and inclined to extravagance. Her expense accounts were high and her personal taxi bills exceeded her weekly income!"

Dorothy Secures Pulitzer Prize Nomination

Dorothy often eclipsed the stars she wrote about. When she attended the Coronation of Queen Elizabeth II in June 1953, she wore a silver gown with 14,000 embroidered jewels and pearls that were encrusted at the scalloped neckline. She placed a tiara on her head, put on her white mink cape lined with silver lamé, grabbed her Western Union copy paper and headed off to Westminster Abbey, spending a week in England.

Her columns were labeled "Coronation Diary." She detailed the celebratory atmosphere of London, described the newly crowned monarch as much prettier in person than in photographs and called the occasion "colossal." She likened the veneration of the royal family to the hero worship of celebrities back home.

"She has a lush, beautiful mouth. In a Hollywood movie star it might be considered a note of sex appeal worthy of a fan magazine story, but I doubt if the British press will ever mention it. I have a feeling that on the tight little isle sex appeal in a sovereign is strictly coincidental," Dorothy wrote. She added, "In some doorways stood lifesize cutouts of Elizabeth and Phillip in elaborate finery, rather astonishingly like the cutouts of film stars we use for advertising current pictures in American movie house lobbies."

In her column published nationally June 4, Dorothy described turning down an invitation to attend a ball given by Mrs. Perle Mesta and

Mr. and Mrs. George Tyson because she was set to fly home to be present for her son Dickie's class day.

"This is not only an assemblage of some of the best crew cuts in the neighborhood, but it is the setting for Dickie's promotion to the 7th grade, and that drama involves more suspense than 'The House of Wax,'" she explained.

Perle's parties were legendary. She was a socialite, political hostess and served as United States ambassador to Luxembourg from 1949 to 1953. Dorothy noted she hoped to attend one of Perle's soirées in the future.

After concluding her coverage of the Coronation, Dorothy wrote (also in her June 4, 1953 column) that there were several details about it she wished she had shared in earlier installments.

"Doing the 'Running Story' on a big event as it happens is a good deal like having a verbal battle with someone you loathe—you always think of the most brilliant things to say afterwards," she noted.

The details included the orchestra playing *Greensleeves* during the ceremony, although it wasn't listed in the musical program, and observations about the royal jewels.

"And the diamonds in the royal gallery! Those could have been described more fully. When English royalty opens the safe and gets out the family jools [sic] it is quite a show. The diamonds around the Queen Mother's neck were at least four inches deep at the center, and the Duchess of Kent wore a high, closely fitted necklace of diamonds—almost a dog collar—that was blinding."

Dated June 7, 1953, Kilgallen discussed the grandeur—and logistics of reporting on the event:

"Add things I never thought would happen to this holder of a New York police card: My 'copy boy' in Westminster Abbey was a brigadier general. He was a wonderful old duffer, perfect casting, with a row of medals eight inches wide that showed he had fought in campaigns in India, Africa and Europe. Efficient, too—he lost no time napping with my envelopes from the place where I was sitting to the chute in the side of the triforium which was the transmission outlet for the working press.

"We became quite chummy, and after everything was over he conducted me out of the abbey, helping me to maneuver my dress up and down the steep narrow steps of the church. We must have made quite a picture wending our way through the almost deserted passageway, he with mustache bristling and sword clanking, me with tiara on head but Western Union copy paper under my arm. 'You want a train bearer with that gown,' he said, and forthwith did the honors."

Kilgallen earned a Pulitzer Prize nomination for her reporting on the coronation of Queen Elizabeth II. She also received an award from the Silurians Press Club—an all-male journalism society.

DK was frequently profiled in *TV Guide* magazine. The Oct. 9, 1953 issue featured a multi-page spread on her called "Career Girl, Plus." The color photo published on page one of the article showed her smiling alongside Dickie and Jill.

Dorothy Again Becomes a Mother

Dorothy and Dick's marriage was clearly lackluster, yet in her early 40s, DK became a mother for the third time.

Son Kerry Arden Kollmar was born on March 19, 1954, fair-skinned with freckles and red hair—looking nothing like DK's eldest children, which would later raise suspicions about his paternity.

Despite the rumors—and the declaration without evidence by Kilgallen author Mark Shaw that Kerry was fathered by Johnnie Ray—Marlin Swing did not believe Johnnie was Kerry's father. "No, no. Time-wise that wouldn't have worked," he said emphatically of Dorothy's later in life baby. "I remember she was very positive about the night that Kerry was conceived, because they (she and Richard) were an hour late to a dinner party, and she always said that was the night," he told *Midwest Today*.

It is worth noting Dorothy's mother Mae was a redhead and Richard had a touch of that hue in his hair as well. So the boy's reddish colorations could have come from both the Kilgallen and Kollmar sides of the family. Kerry today looks a lot like his mother.

Sitting in for Kilgallen on the *WML?* panel during her absence was popular writer Margaret Truman, only child of President Harry Truman. To honor the blessed occasion, DK's eldest two children served as mystery guests the evening of March 21. Reporter Robert Johnson wrote the next day, "What amused me most about last night's show was the appearance as mystery guests of Dorothy Kilgallen's other two children. The little girl, with every movement of her head and facial expression, is a remarkable miniature of her mother."

Now a mom of three, DK's home/work life balance must have required expert organizational skills. And despite that earlier concern of Hearst executive Richard Berlin that careers and motherhood don't mix, Dorothy's readers seemed satisfied with her work.

Because of how popular Dorothy's *Voice of Broadway* column was, it made sense for newspapers to subscribe to it to satisfy readers. On April 29, 1954, the *Muncie Evening Press* published this gushing item about DK:

"A Muncie police officer, the other day, said:

'If you want to make my wife and me unhappy just leave out Dorothy Kilgallen's column. We read it, without fail, every evening.'

"Of course, we do not want to make anyone unhappy and we know there are thousands of others who feel the same way about Miss Kilgallen's column. That's why it appears daily in the *Muncie Evening Press*.

"Unquestionably she ranks with the greatest of New York colum-

As in Deuteronomy 32:10, Dorothy was "the apple of her father's eye."

nists. In fact, she's regarded as America's greatest woman reporter just as her father, James Kilgallen, is regarded as the country's greatest reporter.

"Miss Kilgallen's column is another of those exclusive *Muncie Evening Press* columns. In Eastern Indiana her column appears only in this newspaper."

A late April 1954 *VOB* column kicked off with DK's love of springtime, which she said brought along with its gentle breezes a desire in her to travel. She told readers she wished she could be on the Rue St. Honore buying white kid gloves; at a seaside restaurant in Portofino dining on octopus soup; hailing a pedalo (boat) on a lake in Zurich; or on Waterloo Bridge that overlooks the River Thames in London, moon-gazing.

"Why does April stir the wanderlust in a soul, more than July or December?" she asked.

In her usual fashion, this column was a stunning mish mash of topics. She called Sid Caesar the greatest living comedian (with nobody a close second); predicted the publicity surrounding the H-bomb will cause a rise in the value of property that lies "beyond the danger zones," wherever those may be; was sorry to hear Frank Sinatra's mother was ill; relayed a story of a man who brought a bag of spareribs with him to the Apollo Theater and munched on them in the balcony, tossing the bones into the orchestra pit when he was through with them.

In June 1954, Jim Kilgallen penned a three-part series on Dorothy, syndicated in newspapers across the nation. Jim discussed DK's early love of journalism, the tough assignments that helped shape her as a journalist and factoids about her personal life.

Johnnie Ray came on *What's My Line?* as the mystery guest the night of August 22. On the panel was Dorothy, Bennett, Arlene and Steve Allen, all blindfolded for that spot on the program. Questioning began with DK, who asked Ray if he was "accustomed to appearing before audiences" (yes) and if he was an entertainer, an actor (yes) and if he was funny. He said he was not funny, which got Dorothy a "no," passing to Allen. (This was in the days before the show changed formatting, which restricted panelists to asking the celebrity guest just one question at a time, instead of going until receiving a "no" answer. This was likely because the more a panelist chatted with the guest—who was trying to disguise his or her voice and answer vaguely—the quicker the identity would be ascertained).

Arlene guessed who he was, after he agreed to briefly speak in his real voice. Ray said he vocalized his responses in a whispery tone because he thought Steve Allen would know who he was. Bennett then asked him to sing, to which Ray replied he could do an impression of himself, which film co-star Dan Dailey would do on the set, whereupon Ray sang a fragment of *Cry*, then smacked the side of his head, which received laughter and applause from the audience. Then Ray said he'd tell Dailey, who played his father in *There's No Business Like Show Business*, he didn't have to listen to him, and Ray would take out his hearing aid.

A Shocking Murder, A Shocking Verdict

Dorothy would follow up her eminent Coronation reports with coverage diametrically opposed in theme—reportage of one of the most notorious murder cases of the twentieth century—the Dr. Sam Sheppard trial.

On the morning of July 4, 1954, Sheppard's pregnant wife Marilyn was found bludgeoned to death, having sustained thirty-five stab wounds to the head, face and hands at the couple's lakeshore home in Bay Village, a suburb of Cleveland, while their young son slept in the next room and Sheppard was asleep (or drunk) on the couch downstairs.

The pair had entertained neighbors the night before, going to bed separately. Sheppard told authorities he heard Marilyn call for him, he then went to her and saw a "bushy-haired" man fighting with her. Sheppard was struck on the head and rendered unconscious. After the police failed to find signs of forced entry and learned of the doctor's extramarital activities, he became the prime suspect in the murder. In August 1954 he was indicted by a grand jury and a media circus ensued. A nine-week-long trial kicked off that October, which Dorothy covered for the *Journal-American*.

It wasn't unusual for Dorothy's arrival in the courtroom to draw admiration from members of both the prosecution and the defense. Sometimes judges would call out greetings to her from the bench, with autograph requests. Flattered, but unfazed, she was still able to carefully take notes of the proceedings to report them in her articles.

After the much-publicized trial—consisting of 214 exhibits, two million words of trial transcript and eighty-seven witnesses—the jury found Sheppard guilty of second-degree murder and he was sentenced to life in prison.

Dorothy couldn't understand how the jury had ruled with such confidence—yet went with the lesser charge—and called the verdict a "miscarriage of justice."

"The prosecutors for the State of Ohio did not prove he was guilty any more than they proved there are pin-headed men on Mars," DK wrote. "This is one the lawyers and the laymen alike are going to be arguing about for a long time, each in his own jargon and each for different reasons. It is a meaty judicial problem, just as it is a genuine puzzle for whodunit fans. The grandchildren of the Victorians who debated the Lizzie Borden issues will spend many an hour before the hearth worrying this bone."

Years later, Kilgallen would figure prominently in helping the doctor secure a new trial, which will be explored later on in this book.

The Nov. 13, 1954 issue of *TV Guide* magazine ran a story entitled "Dorothy Kilgallen: Girl Reporter" chronicling her coverage of the Dr. Sam Sheppard murder trial.

The very next evening, during a broadcast of *WML?*, brought DK some embarrassment. New York City firefighter Lt. Harold I. Gold was a challenger on the program. He had helped put out a fire at Dorothy's residence on Dec. 15, 1953. He signed in as "Hal" in case she had remembered his name, which she hadn't. DK quipped, "I didn't recognize him without his rubbers" noting he had done a "splendid job." Fred Allen then suggested with the remaining time, the panelists should try to guess how the fire had started, which drew a look of daggers from Dorothy, likely because she had worked to keep the incident out of the papers. But that wouldn't always be the case.

4
Communication Marvel of the Age

Dorothy was becoming a household name thanks to her syndicated column and by entering the homes of millions of radio listeners and those who tuned in weekly for *What's My Line?*. Her reach—and influence—was expanding.

Noted newspaper columnist and author Damon Runyon said of DK's talents, "She is one of the best of the women journalists in the history of the game. There isn't any kind of a story that the Kilgallen girl cannot do."

Time magazine wrote of her abilities, "Dorothy had the good journeyman's talent for catching accurate detail, as well as a sharp eye for the offbeat feature story on, say, an obscure trial witness."

Describing DK's adoration by the public, the *New York Post* daily magazine famously wrote, "Wherever Dorothy Kilgallen goes fame precedes her, envy follows her and a crowd looks on. She is one of the communication marvels of the age."

Journalism Comes First

Jim Kilgallen said of his daughter, "She had an unerring instinct for news. She had a brilliant style of writing. She was accurate and had a flair for the apt phrase. She had an uncanny ability to produce scoops and an inordinate speed in turning out copy."

Dorothy lived and breathed the newspaper business. She philosophized:

"There is nothing like sitting in an easy chair or on a subway seat or a railroad station bench or a porch rocker and unfolding a fat, crisp, wonderful-smelling, ink-damp, aggravating, satisfying, incomparable, indispensable daily newspaper. There is just no substitute for curling up with the evening editions or waking up to coffee and the morning paper. You can read on a train crossing the desert or on a plane 17,000 feet above the Atlantic—no static, no fading, no blips. You can read in the bathtub or while hanging onto a pole in a crowded bus. You can read as much or as little as you want, as fast or as slowly as you want. And if you read something you like you can tear it out and save it to read again some day. I enjoy radio and television, and I am gainfully employed by both, but I must admit they have their drawbacks. Did you ever try to clip a television program and paste it in your scrapbook? And if you got caught in a sudden rainstorm, would Lowell Thomas's newscast keep your hat dry?"

Kilgallen's contemporaries included Hearst reporter and radio news commentator Walter Winchell whom she dubbed "the daddy of us all," Louella Parsons, also with Hearst, and Hedda Hopper, who was with the *Los Angeles Times*. While most entertainment industry fans read them all, the celebrities themselves had their loyalties. But unlike the aforementioned gossip columnists, Kilgallen had a following as a hard news reporter, too, although it must be mentioned that Hopper was a Cold Warrior. She was a vocal supporter of the House Un-American Activities Committee hearings and championed the Hollywood blacklist.

When Dorothy went on vacation, her column still appeared—guest written by folks ranging from movie stars, producers, composers, critics, and more.

Johnnie Ray contributed a guest column when Dorothy went on vacation in June 1955. He discussed his journey to stardom and his starry-eyed view of celebrity when he first arrived in Hollywood.

"I worked as a bellhop, a car hop, soda dispenser. The crowds I always longed to mingle with didn't even know I was alive. But I still had the feeling deep in my heart that glamor, gaiety and crowds could spell happiness."

Kilgallen As Fashion Icon

What has never been explored in previous books on Dorothy is her status as a fashion icon. She was often included on "best dressed" lists and her wardrobe was highly discussed in rival columns.

Ceil Chapman created glamorous cocktail and party dresses for many celebrity clients. In September 1952, she guest wrote one of DK's columns. In it, she reflected of Kilgallen's style, "Dorothy is apt to stand with reluctant feet on the brink of a new fashion. But once she likes it, she is positively stubborn in her devotion to it. At the moment I have hopes of luring her into liking the new waltz length evening dresses. She adores white for evening, and also loves black velvet. She prefers her evening gowns strapless, but for television she covers her shoulders with a matching stole. To me, Dorothy represents the Scarlett O'Hara quality in women, and there are enough like her to insure that the bouffant dress with the tiny waist will never go out of fashion."

Dorothy was named one of the "Ten Best Tailored Women" in 1955 by the Custom Tailors Guild of America, Inc., in a poll conducted among the "topnotch career women across the nation." The list is as follows: Marguerite Piazza, night clubs; Mrs. Arthur Murray, business; Gloria Stokowski, society; Oveta Culp Hobby, public life; Kilgallen, journalism; Loretta Young, television; Roberta Peters, opera; Marlene Dietrich, recordings; Jane Pickens, radio; Grace Kelly, motion pictures.

Dorothy set off for Omaha, Nebraska for the Fall Festival of Fashion Style Show that September 9 and 10, sponsored by the Associated Retailers of Omaha. She presented the Ford Agency models, and also provided narration of the outfits being modeled. Tickets for the three performances sold for a dollar fifty and two dollars fifty cents, with proceeds benefiting the churches of Omaha.

On Jan. 20, 1956, Dorothy and Richard were interviewed live on Edward R. Murrow's *Person to Person* television program, which offered the public a rare look into the Kollmars' sumptuous home life.

Their twelve year old daughter Jill, and twenty two-month-old son, Kerry, made brief appearances on camera. They noted Dickie was away at school. The couple granted viewers a glimpse of their curios and furnishings, casting aside any doubt of Kilgallen's success as a television, radio and journalistic star.

The twenty-two-room townhouse was spotlighted, with special emphasis on their Black Room. There, the couple would have guests try to find the twenty-three eagles in the room (from furniture, furnishings to embroidery). The room also featured two life-size cigar store Indians, a television set and other items of Americana.

The Chinless Wonder

Dorothy Kilgallen had a very public and particularly nasty, ongoing feud with Frank Sinatra, despite the two having once been friends.

In early 1956, she penned a six-part series published daily on the crooner entitled "The Real Frank Sinatra Story." Far from a puff piece, it took several jabs at Frank's hedonistic lifestyle, debauchery and swollen ego. Dorothy may have been one of the few women in Frank's life not impressed by his bravado.

In Part I, dated February 26, the columnist noted ladies swoon over him despite Sinatra being the "little skinny sallow fellow that he is."

DK described the crooner in this first article, thusly: "When he was unappreciated and obscure, he was hot-tempered, egotistical, extravagant and moody. Now that he is rich and famous, with the world on a string and sapphires in his cufflinks, he is still hot-tempered, egotistical, extravagant and moody. His combination of dynamite talent and inflammable personality makes him the most fascinating character study in show business today—a 1956 version of Dr. Jekyll and Mr. Hyde dressed in sharpie clothes right out of a Broadway haberdasher's dream."

Part II included details about Sinatra's early years. She described his father as an "amiable fireman who had boxed professionally if not notably" and his mother as "a plump jolly little go-getter of a woman."

Part III detailed his relationship with his ex-wife Nancy Barbato Sinatra. DK praised Sinatra for being a hands-on father despite walking out on their mother.

Nancy tired of her role as second best when Sinatra was out cavorting with his latest conquest. Dorothy wrote, "She was faithful and patient. She was a good mother. All she wanted was Frankie and the children, and she got the children all right, and a mink coat and some pleasant luxuries, but she lost Frankie along the way."

In the fourth installment, DK highlighted the many women Sinatra had bedded such as Anita Ekberg, Lana Turner, Marlene Dietrich, Gloria Vanderbilt and Marilyn Maxwell, plus lesser known beauties. She wrote, "Many more, of course, have been the fluffy little struggling dolls of show business, pretty and small-waisted and similar under the standard layer of peach-colored pancake make-up—starlets who never got past first base in Hollywood, assorted models and vocalists, and chorus girls now lost in the ghosts of floor shows past. Others belonged to the classification most gently described as tawdry."

DK with "Frankie" Sinatra in happier times.

At the end, she concluded. "It took Ava Gardner, the volcano in female form, to really make him lose his head as thoroughly as a man has ever done without benefit of guillotine."

The fifth article in her series chronicled his turbulent relationship with Gardner. "The way Frank goes for women, Ava goes for men. He sings music, she plays it all day long. She is even-Stephen with him in earning capacity and one up on him in number of marriages. She is the kind of uninhibited girl who lights a cigarette when she sees a 'no smoking' sign and takes off her shoes when she feels like it."

Part VI, the last installment, kicked-off with this quip, "Frank Sinatra's climb up the stairway to the stars is proof that in this time and place there is no penalty for naughtiness if you are sufficiently attractive to a large number of people."

Sinatra responded by sending Dorothy a tombstone carved with her name. He derided her in his Las Vegas act as that "chinless wonder" comparing her profile to that of a car key. At a performance at the Copa, he told the audience, "Dorothy Kilgallen isn't here tonight. I guess she's out shopping for a new chin."

On one occasion, their paths crossed at the Stork Club. DK had on sunglasses.

"Getting up from his table, Frank walked past her and dropped a dollar bill into her coffee cup, saying, 'I always figured she was blind,'" Kitty Kelley wrote of the incident in her book *My Way*.

Unfazed, Kilgallen used her column to remind readers of Frankie's womanizing, mob ties and Rat Pack shenanigans.

Sinatra had a lot of running feuds with people so it's remarkable he remained so obsessed in his hatred for Dorothy Kilgallen. Given his mobster friends, some have wondered if he found a way to silence her.

Dorothy Continues To Get Yelled At By Men

Kilgallen scored another prestigious assignment when her newspaper sent her to cover the wedding of Grace Kelly to Prince Rainier of Monaco.

She embarked on her trip April 11. In a column filled with a touch of braggadocios name dropping, she explained one item in her luggage was to be hand-delivered to the future princess: a dress by prominent Russian-American designer Fira Benenson, to be worn at a party preceding the wedding.

"While my own luggage—11 pieces—is skimpy compared to the bride's," DK wrote. "I must admit it's more than I've ever taken on any previous assignment and twice as much as I took on my own honeymoon.

"When I think that I once went all around the world with just one small suitcase, and covered the coronation of Queen Elizabeth with a mere seven pieces, I begin to believe journalism is growing more complicated every day. My father, a one-suitcase, one-typewriter man from 'way back, would disown me forthwith if he could see me weighing in at the airport.

"But there's just no way of covering a royal wedding without the proper equipment in the way of ballgowns, garden party frocks, reception dresses and furs suitable for keeping off the chill in an ancient cathedral."

Dorothy's coverage of Princess Grace's wedding included discussion of Prince Rainier's other love interests—which drew letters of admonishment from *VOB* readers.

DK wrote the prince initially wanted to wed Marilyn Monroe but she turned him down! Kilgallen revealed that while attending a wedding anniversary party for composer Richard Rodgers and his wife Dorothy at the Ambassador Hotel in NYC on March 5, 1955, a friend of Prince Rainier approached her about a potential love match with Marilyn Monroe. She wrote she introduced the friend to Monroe, who attended the party with Milton Greene and his wife. The friend had even offered to split the "dower commission" with Kilgallen if the match was successful.

In addition, Dorothy penned a column that revealed the prince's true love was a French actress named Giselle Pascal, going as far as to write that the wedding was "haunted by the ghost of a girl who was very much alive." And it was the prince's own American-born priest, Father Francis Tucker, that had let the cat out of the bag.

"In his zeal to impress everyone with Rainier's splendid character and willingness to give up his heart's desire, the Prince's chaplain made it embarrassingly clear that Grace was definitely the second choice (or third, behind Marilyn) of the young ruler who took her as wife."

She said she spoke with one of Grace's bridesmaids who told the columnist, "I do hope Grace does not hear of it, she'd feel perfectly terrible!"

Father Tucker mentioned the French actress on at least three occasions, Dorothy confided to readers: once in his own bylined dispatch to a London newspaper; during a sermon at St. Charles Church; in an interview.

The news that the prince pined away for a woman he couldn't have was clearly not a secret, but was likely news to Kilgallen's readers back in the States. In her column, DK speculated that Giselle and Rainier broke off their romance because of her status as a "French commoner" and that the "French are not permitted to become citizens of Monaco." For years the press speculated as to what led to the breakup, including rumors that Giselle was barren. She married actor Raymond Pellegrin in 1955 and had a daughter in 1962.

But not everyone regarded the story as harmless fun that added "color" to coverage of the royal wedding. Dorothy would endure a harsh reprimand from Rev. Edmond P. McCarthy, O.S.F.S., for the following comments in her column: "Father Tucker is indeed a most unusual clergyman. In manner he is very much like a breezy Broadway press agent who has somehow acquired permission to say mass in addition to promoting his client."

McCarthy's belittling and misogynistic open letter to Kilgallen ran in place of her usual column in the *Philadelphia Daily News*. It's worth noting Grace Kelly's prominent Catholic family resided in that city. *The Tablet*, a Catholic newspaper, also ran the priest's tirade.

He wrote, "In your column of April 19, you have, once again, in your own vitriolic way, set yourself up as judge and jury to annihilate the character of a fellow human being. Indicative of a small mind, the entire column is based on wild and scandalous rumor. This means nothing to you, as your sophomoric comments in the past have proved that you like to 'play God.' It might be refreshing to your lilliputian mind to give serious thought to the following statements based upon facts and the truth."

The priest went on to defend Father Tucker's character and leadership.

"Every task assigned to Father Tucker in his long, fruitful and brilliant career has come to him through obedience, which to him means God's will. Would that everyone (even mothers-turned-columnists) could say that they are doing God's will, so that one day we might say of them that which we proudly say of Father Tucker today, 'He has done all things well.'"

Father McCarthy had no qualms about "annihilating the character" of Dorothy Kilgallen, a fellow human being and a Catholic, to boot. DK's observations of Father Tucker were based on matters of public record. It makes one wonder if McCarthy, while writing his poison pen letter, also pondered the morality of a rich movie star marrying a prince in what was clearly an arranged marriage—and the prince's priest running his mouth about the women that got away…

In her personal life, Dorothy endured every parents' worst nightmare: a child going missing. Around 8:30 a.m. on the morning of June 7, her eldest child Richard "Dickie" Jr. was discovered to be missing. Newspapers across the country ran an item reporting that the fourteen-year-old boy had vanished from his home with "a 14-state missing person alarm" issued. He returned home late the next day under undisclosed circumstances.

On June 14, Dorothy served as emcee for a special live portion of the *Four Star Playhouse* episode "Second Chance." Much fuss was made in the papers about Dorothy appearing on television in a non-*WML?* role. The show was a U.S. television anthology series, with the initial premise being Charles Boyer, Ida Lupino, David Niven and Dick Powell would take turns starring in episodes, with that eventually evolving into other celebrities guest starring.

Tom O'Malley and Bob Cunniff devoted some ink to their obvious dislike of DK in a series of items in their "Channel One" column. In June, Dorothy was included in a piece that had been written in Q&A style:

Q: "You're always saying snide things about Dorothy Kilgallen. Do you think you could do better?"

A: "Aw, c'mon. Dorothy's a girl, but we know a librarian on Forty-Second st. and Fifth ave. who could handle the job—at the same $750 a week."

Then in October, they claimed DK and Bennett Cerf were "keeping their distance" from each other during election season because in 1952 Cerf nearly walked off the show over "Dorothy's violent pro-Ike theorizing."

The duo struck again on November 23, alleging Dorothy was able to see through the mask she wore during the blindfolded mystery guest spots on *WML?*.

They wrote a "famous Hollywood-TV actress" was so mad DK had guessed her identity, the woman, "took a peek through the mask Dorothy uses on the show. To her vast surprise, she found she could see right through it. That's what is known as womanly intuition."

The men also speculated that the show's producers, Goodson and Todman, would deny the allegation. Their assumption backfired.

In January 1957, they had to publish a retraction noting the claim about Dorothy's see-through mask was "erroneous" and, "We hope that statement caused no inconvenience or embarrassment to Dorothy Kilgallen, 'What's My Line,' or its producers."

Sure, that hadn't been their intention at all...

Dorothy Befriends Billy Graham

One headline-grabber who dominated the news in 1957 was evangelist Billy Graham, who brought his Bible preaching to New York City beginning on May 17. Astoundingly, he attracted massive crowds to his nightly "crusades," held in Madison Square Garden, Yankee Stadium, Central Park, Harlem, Wall Street and a grass tennis court at Forest Hills. What he said each night often made the front pages of the nation's newspapers as he addressed current moral issues. His impact did not go unnoticed by Dorothy.

Far from being a "flash in the pan," Graham proved his enduring appeal, remaining in NYC until September 1, at which time he attracted

Dorothy chats with Rev. Billy Graham at his Montreat, North Carolina home.

a crowd estimated at 200,000 to Times Square. It was his one hundredth sermon in his fifteen and a half weeks in the city. He drew a total of well over two million people in this city of eight million persons.

Dorothy Kilgallen was quoted in a syndicated article about the crusades, saying, "Thrill seekers expecting hysteria at his meetings would be better off at a rock and roll concert: he does not court hysteria. Neither does he hypnotize individuals or masses... He is profoundly earnest about his mission. He has journeyed to this rich turbulent city to preach the message of Christ crucified. He will proclaim the hard truths of sin, punishment and Hell, and the glorious truths of repentance, redemption and Heaven. He attributes his flawless serenity to the peace that comes of being wholehearted Christian...

"The total calm is particularly remarkable as he prepares for this evening's drama at Madison Square Garden. An actor facing the opening night of a $900,000 production in which he was the star and sole attraction would be swallowing tranquilizers as if they were peanuts. To Billy Graham, Heaven is just as real as Chicago."

The popular evangelist's message obviously appealed to Dorothy, because she accepted an invitation to visit Billy and his wife, Ruth, at their humble mountain home in Montreat, North Carolina. There, beside the stone fireplace in the rustic, log cabin vibe of the Graham residence, Billy and Ruth showed Dorothy home movies of some of his crusades. They also sauntered along stone steps leading to a stream with a wooden bridge and explored forested walking paths. One photo shows Dorothy and Billy chatting on a foggy day in the crisp air.

Though Kilgallen was a Catholic and remained a steadfast adherent to Catholicism throughout her life—while no doubt accumulating stories to tell her priest during confession—she was obviously concerned about the great moral issues of the day.

Aside from the spiritual uplift Billy Graham provided Dorothy, there was an unexpected financial benefit, too. At the time, her husband Richard had just opened up a supper club called the Left Bank at 309 W. 50th Street, within walking distance of Madison Square Garden. Graham's nightly "crusades" surely drew business Richard's way. Journalist Jane Allison described the establishment as having a dark green-walled bar, a posh dining room that could seat fifty and an impressive art collection.

"Often Vic Damone or Judy Holliday or some other guest with a famous singing voice can be pressed into song, singing right from his table. Meanwhile, they will, of course, be sating themselves on exquisite food from the hand of chef Marguerite Lewis."

Speaking of hands, Richard owned a collection of two-hundred pairs of replica hands, crafted from plaster, marble, glass, clay, wood and porcelain, on display at his restaurant behind glass in the bar and on pedestals and shelves. He even possessed a porcelain hand piece which

Queen Anne Boleyn once used to hold rings.

Although supportive of her husband's business ventures (often promoting them in her column), Kilgallen was still openly dating Johnnie Ray, even being photographed with him in public.

Ray again came on *WML?* June 9, 1957 with DK, Bennett, Ozzie Nelson and Janet Blair on the panel. This time he stumped them, saying he'd expected Dorothy to identify his voice and that he'd spent time working on how to disguise it. A subtle flirtation, clearly.

In his television appearances, he came off mild-mannered, soft spoken and often poked fun at his hearing impairment. Privately, he offered Dorothy the attention and tenderness she desired in a man.

Dorothy Dazzles, Queen Elizabeth Shines

In the autumn of 1957, Britain's Queen Elizabeth and her husband, Prince Phillip embarked on a ten-day visit to North America, arriving in Ottawa, Canada on October 12 and departing from New York in the wee hours of October 22. The schedule included sojourns to Jamestown, Williamsburg and Washington. A worldwide press contingent of one thousand reporters and photographers trailed Her Majesty by plane, train, car and shank's pony.

The Queen traveled with ninety-five suitcases and trunks, plus an entourage of personal maids and ladies-in-waiting to help her with quick changes of clothes. She needed all this. There were one hundred and fourteen ceremonial occasions scheduled during her visit. The press had no such helpers and struggled to keep up.

Two and a half hours after their arrival in Canada, the Queen and her husband held a reception for the press. Stuart Keate, publisher of the *Times Colonist*, wrote, "I found myself next to Dorothy Kilgallen, savant of *What's My Line?*, who had at her elbow Miss Lotta Dempsey of the *Toronto Globe and Mail.*

"Never one to pass up a good story, Miss Dempsey was interviewing Miss Kilgallen, notebook in hand, as the line moved ahead into the Chinese Room, where the Queen and the Duke were receiving.

"I must say that Dorothy looked stunning and took this frontal assault with charming good nature. She was wearing some rich-looking outfit in black—a sort of long coat business, with mink at the collar."

Elizabeth Forbes wrote that amidst the mass of journalists following the royal couple, "Another personality that even blase and assured newsmen and women fought to meet was Dorothy Kilgallen, the United States TV performer and columnist whom Victorians know well as a member of *What's My Line? TV* show.

"Looking just as she appears on television and with the same almost little-girl voice and demure air, she kept pace with other members of the press from early morning to late at night.

"She expected no special consideration; rode the buses provided with the rest of us and battered out her copy on the first typewriter she could grab in the newsroom when she got back.

"At the press reception in Rideau Hall, Miss Kilgallen was as nervous as any of us, although she looked very calm and beautiful.

"Going slowly forward in the receiving line she suddenly turned to the next person and said, 'Do you know I can't remember whether it is correct to say Your Majesty or Your Royal Highness.' And so help me, it took half a dozen of us to decide which was right. We were all so jittery.

"It was Dorothy Kilgallen, still starry-eyed, strange as that may sound, at the end of the four-day Royal visit to Ottawa, who summed it up for us in a few words.

"'In this day of so many false values, the Queen seems the very symbol of goodness and integrity,' is what she said.

"Then with other members of the American press and radio she rushed off to a plane that went off to Williamsburg at the crack of dawn in order that the group might be there when the Queen and Prince Phillip arrived."

When the Monarch and party arrived in Virginia, Dorothy did not join other members of the traveling press who were positioned on top of a flat bed truck that had been provided so they could get a view of Her Majesty. Instead, "Dorothy...stayed on the ground to get closer up to the Queen shaking hands with the dignitaries lined up adjacent to the red carpet spread across the runway," noted Jackie Hudgins of the *Richmond News-Leader*.

"She had to shed her full-length black beaver by the time the plane arrived and still the Virginia noon-day sun was too warm on her belted black and blue basket-weave suit of wool.

"It was also too warm for her chinchilla beret but no one particularly minded because it went so well with her rather red hair.

"'I believe the United States is receiving the Queen with a bit more lift than Canada did,' she said. 'Their welcome was sedate. They seemed to be terribly pleased that she visited them and I have the feeling they love her dearly as individuals even though they may be embarrassed as a country because they aren't a republic.'

"Beset with more than the usual problems of finding a viewing spot, Miss Kilgallen at the crowd's request had to get into position for them to photograph her before the Queen appeared at the festival park."

To help Dorothy cover the Queen's visit in New York, William Randolph Hearst Jr personally arranged for DK to be escorted around by a chauffeur in a $24,982 Silver Wrath Rolls-Royce (price equivalent to $271,253 today). The car featured a leather interior, Persian lamb floor coverings, solid gold fixtures and even a French walnut bar.

Amusingly—and astonishingly—when the Royals arrived in New

Incredibly, Dorothy rode in the Queen's parade in a Rolls-Royce.

York, Dorothy's car managed somehow to segue into the motorcade during the tickertape parade. The Queen was in the first car, the Prince in the second, the governor of New York—Averell Harriman—in the third, followed by Dorothy in her Rolls. (In a way, the choice of DK's conveyance was appropriate. Even today, each Rolls-Royce—the epitome of a luxury automobile—is built by hand in England).

Press agent Emmett Davis saw the spectacle of Kilgallen waving to the crowd in her white gloves, in what he described as "the old Queen Mary gesture," and shook his head in disbelief, saying "I just stood there thinking, 'Now I've seen everything.'"

Time magazine took note of the limousine spectacle, reporting, "Inside, cool and elegantly dressed, sat columnist Dorothy Kilgallen, covering the event in her regal fashion. Wiping the perspiration from her forehead, an exasperated woman reporter murmured: 'There goes the Queen covering the Queen.'"

Despite the royal treatment Dorothy was accorded, there was one embarrassing incident she wouldn't soon forget.

Ed Koterba, writing in *The Times* of Munster, Indiana described how, at a reception at the Statler Hotel, a security agent "pushed a reporter back from a vantage point four feet from the Queen. 'Move back,' he snarled. 'We've got to have dignity here...'

"Dorothy Kilgallen quietly slipped into the vacated spot. She was blissfully staring at the Queen when the cop stepped up to her. 'Move,' he said. 'I'm *Dorothy Kilgallen,*' protested Miss Kilgallen. The policeman nudged her gently back into the crowd..." Apparently, he wasn't a fan.

In her typical fashion, Kilgallen's reporting contained her colorful prose. But aside from concentrating on the pageantry, she provided her readers with a view of real life.

She noted: "Elizabeth's final appearance at a large Canadian reception...came close to putting the Queen's right arm in a sling. In less than an hour and a half, she shook hands with 1,400 bemedalled men and expensively dressed women who snaked through three flower-filled ballrooms lighted by crystal chandeliers to pay homage to their sovereign.

"Warned by an aide at the door, 'Go easy on the handshakes, Her Majesty's hand is sore,' most of the guests barely touched the Queen's gloved hand as they bowed and curtseyed, but even the strain of standing in one spot, flashing that same warm memorable smile over and over again began to tell on her.

"Her enthusiasm never flagged, she kept her back ramrod straight in her taupe-and-gold cocktail dress, but by the time the last guest had filed past, her cheeks were so utterly white as the flowers someone placed on her arm as she walked out through a path cut in the murmuring crowd.

"She is truly a fairy princess in chains.

"Her life is mapped out for her, from hour to hour, from day to day...so powerless that she can't travel a mile without the permission of underlings.

"The only fun she gets is deciding, at the last moment, what tiara she'll wear.

"She has a staggeringly beautiful wardrobe that any woman would envy, but she wears her elegant ensembles to such boring events as cornerstone-layings, city hall book-signings and highway inaugurations.

"During this royal visit, Queen Elizabeth has spent ten frenziedly regal days showing herself to as many people as possible, shaking hands with thousands, smiling to millions, accepting countless bouquets and acknowledging innumerable silly honors conferred upon her by earnest if bumbling officials of cities she has never seen before and—if she's lucky—may never see again.

"So she has limousines always, and a new mink coat given to her by the mink men, and police escorts and a maid to put the diamonds away when she falls into bed.

"Still, who would like to spend every day from nine in the morning until midnight walking among strangers, asking—in a regal, but nonetheless suppliant way—to be liked.

"Nobody would like it...But Queen Elizabeth manages to look as though she's enjoying it."

Champagne at Maxim's

On Feb. 23, 1958, DK appeared alongside Sir Cedric Hardwicke on the game show *The Last Word* which aired on CBS Sunday afternoons. The show centered on discussing and debunking uses and misuses of the

English language—a likely easy task for a woman who made a living as a writer.

That April, Dorothy traveled to London to be among the who's who in attendance of the West End debut of *My Fair Lady*, which opened on April 30. Writing her usual "word pictures," DK described the premiere in fine detail.

"Elegant first-nighters who had flown in from the United States and capitals of Europe just for the evening as well as English theater-goers who arrived in Rolls-Royces and Bentleys from the haughtiest streets of Mayfair gave the event such uniformity, starched shirt pomp and jeweled dazzle that the audience at the historic Drury Lane might have been composed of movie extras carefully chosen and beautifully dressed to be photographed for a film about high society."

She praised Julie Andrews for surpassing her New York performance that evening in London.

Dick and Dorothy bid bon voyage as they depart for London.

Following that engagement, Dorothy and Richard traveled to Paris. She styled one column, written from the City of Lights, as a letter home to her parents.

"Dear Mother and Dad: I haven't written home because frankly this is such a swinging town there's just no time and besides my hand is bruised from being kissed by the French nobility."

She spoke of drinking champagne at Maxim's—the most famous restaurant in the world—and attending a party above it given by Maggi Nolan. She bumped into several European aristocrats plus Gene Kelly thrown in for good measure. She was pleased to report few French women were wearing sack dresses, which she didn't find flattering to the figure.

Unless you were living under a rock, most Americans knew of the scandal in Hollywood: Eddie Fisher's affair with Elizabeth Taylor. What made the infidelity all the more shocking to followers of celebrity gossip was the fact Fisher had been best friends with Liz's husband, Mike Todd. He'd been their best man at their wedding in 1957, while his wife, Debbie Reynolds, was matron of honor. The couple had even named their son Todd after the man. Sadly, four weeks after the child was born, Mike Todd perished in a plane crash, on March 22, 1958. Fisher provided more than just emotional comfort to Liz.

Dorothy wrote in September 1958 that Fisher's involvement with Liz had the potential to boost his television ratings and increase record sales, calling it "a tragic comment on current morality."

Harold Weir, writing in his "Matter of Hokum" column shortly after, cast doubt that DK cared much about the state of public morals. Calling her a "professional gossipmonger," Weir said the "essence of the Debbie-Eddie-Liz affair is not morals at all, but hokum. And hokum cooked up by Dorothy Kilgallen and her kind."

Dorothy again found herself in the spotlight for her dazzling wardrobe. In late October, the Fashion Foundation of America announced its list of the best-dressed women in the country. For the category of "television," Dorothy tied with Arlene Francis. Other winners included Mamie Eisenhower (in the public life category), plus "ambassador of fashion" Clare Booth Luce. Ingrid Bergman was also cited.

From at least mid-October through early November 1958, DK was unable to fulfill all of her usual professional commitments. The press reported she suffered from a serious virus which left her homebound and only able to do her morning radio show with Richard. She was allowed to appear on the Oct. 26, 1958 broadcast of *WML?* but then told to go home afterwards and rest. She sat on the panel alongside Tom Poston, Francis and Cerf. Last out on the panel, she was introduced by Poston as the star of radio and television—and the LeRoy Hospital. When Dorothy came out, she thanked the public for her many well wishes.

5
A Growing List Of Enemies

Dorothy's reporting on political and social issues continued to seep into her columns and bylined news articles. In February 1959, she wrote this item: "The international revolutionary junta, which is dedicated to destroying dictatorships in Central and South America, has decided on its next targets. It's out to get, in the order named, Trujillo of the Dominican Republic and Somoza of Nicaragua...If you talk to a New York cab driver during the next couple of weeks, try to make your conversation colorful; he may be using you as 'copy.' One of the local gazettes has assigned a reporter to get a hack license and drive around town as a cabbie to get material for a series of articles."

Rafael Leónidas Trujillo Molina, AKA "El Jefe," led a violent and corrupt regime known for inflicting state terrorism. On May 30, 1961, he was assassinated by a group led by the Dominican general Antonio Imbert Barrera.

The Somoza family ruled Nicaragua from 1936 to 1979. Luis Anastasio Somoza Debayle, who took office in September 1956, would remain the de facto leader of the country until his death from a heart attack in 1967.

DK Vocal Opponent of Castro

In 1959 and throughout 1960, Kilgallen penned several anti-Castro articles using first-hand accounts from Cuban exiles living in Miami.

Intriguingly, Fidel Castro and some of his scruffy compatriots appeared on the popular Ed Sullivan program in early January of 1959, where Sullivan described them effusively as "a wonderful group of revolutionary youngsters," as if they were the latest pop music sensation. He claimed that despite their appearance, Castro's followers were a far cry from the godless Communists depicted by the Cuban military's propaganda machine. Ed also noted they were all wearing Catholic medals and some were carrying copies of the Bible. Sullivan even compared Castro to George Washington!

Most of the U.S. media at the time were portraying Fidel Castro as a sort of Robin Hood. When the Cuban revolutionary visited America he was mobbed by fans as he ate a hot dog in New York City, spoke at Princeton, visited Mount Vernon and saw the Lincoln Memorial.

But Dorothy Kilgallen, visionary that she was, flagged Fidel as a bad hombre before the American public turned against him.

Comrades Castro and Khrushchev

In an April 6, 1959 column she observed, "Our government's intelligence reports on Cuba's Fidel Castro go back to the 1940s and aren't very pretty. They list him as a Communist and a killer."

In a piece published on July 15, 1959, Kilgallen commented: "If our state department heads in Washington deny they're gravely worried over the explosive situation in Cuba and nearby Latin American countries, they're either giving out false information for reasons of their own or playing ostrich, which might prove to be a dangerous game.

"U.S. intelligence is virtually non-existent if the government isn't aware that Russia already has bases in Cuba, and Russian pilots in uniform are strutting openly in Havana. Fidel Castro is the target for so many assassins they're apt to fall over each other in their efforts to get him.

"The Mafia want to knock him off. So do the Batista sympathizers, of course, and then there are his own disillusioned rebels, just for starters. He has machine guns and other ammunition mounted on every key rooftop near his base of operations, but the smart money doubts if any amount of precaution can change his status as a clay pigeon."

Based on the various columns she wrote about Cuba, especially in 1959, Dorothy obviously had sources amongst anti-Castro groups. Although she had been an ally of theirs in warning the American public about Fidel's treachery, if they participated in the Kennedy assassination in any way, they would not want that known and would therefore be motivated to try to prevent her from publishing such revelations.

She wrote about *Tonight Show* host Jack Paar's pro-Castro sympathies, which led to a feud that rivaled the one she had with Sinatra. Paar traveled to Cuba in February 1959 to interview the dictator, a move that was critiqued far and wide in the entertainment industry. His short time as host (1957-1962) was marred by moodiness and outbursts.

Paar would often attack Dorothy and fellow columnist Walter Winchell on the air, including on his final broadcast. He once referred to DK as "A puppet. She never moves her lips when she talks. She must use Novocain lipstick."

Dorothy's conflict with Sinatra continued. Her March 6, 1959 column "Frankie Not Talking to Sammy" can't help but bring a chuckle to the reader:

"Friends are trying to get Frank Sinatra to reconcile with his one time great pal, Sammy Davis Jr., who got the 'kiss of death' from Frankie for a casual remark made on a Chicago disc jockey show. Sinatra chose to regard the comment as treasonable, and the strong boys who have vested interests in nightclub singers may show their displeasure over the incident by expelling their cabaret."

Kilgallen's columns could also have an air of whimsy with personal touches, such as when she'd pen pieces describing a new experience she'd had. In late April 1959 she traveled to San Francisco for a few days. Despite having been the "girl around the world" and frequent traveler, this trip marked her first time taking a jet airliner. Accompanied by her husband, a visibly impressed Kilgallen marveled at the smooth ride and how they crossed the United States in five and a half hours. Describing the Boeing 707 as "silver with Chinese red on its swept-back wings," DK wrote, "We didn't seem to be moving a bit fast, but as I looked down at what scenery you can see from 31,000 feet, we passed a DC-7 the way a Rolls-Royce passes a pushcart. One of the three beautiful stewardesses advised we were only making 550 miles an hour. (Terrible headwinds, you know)."

Kilgallen's Caustic Wit

In September 1959, she reported on Nikita Khrushchev's stateside visit. In the piece she criticized his wife Nina's appearance. The headline rang out: "Our Miss K says Mrs. K's clothes fit like a slip cover." The columnist wrote: "The grisliness of her attire amounts almost to a demonstration of piety...It would be difficult to find clothes comparable to hers in the waiting room of a New York employment agency for domestic help; in this decadent capitalistic republic, applicants for jobs as laundresses, chambermaids, and cooks usually are far more a la mode than Russia's first lady."

Dorothy had been under FBI surveillance since the 1930s, and its agents were trying to dig up more dirt on the reporter. An internal memo to director J. Edgar Hoover dated Sept. 15, 1959, cited a confidential informant who "stated that [Dorothy and her husband Richard] have their own private lives," that Richard "has been dating other women...is interested in both sexes...and has his own private apartment..."

Johnnie Ray found himself in trouble in November when he was arrested at a downtown Detroit nightclub on a morals charge. Plainclothes Officer Eugene Caviston of the vice squad said the singer had made an indecent proposal to him. Ray was booked on a misdemeanor charge of accosting and soliciting. Dorothy couldn't keep the scandal from hitting the papers.

Marlin Swing first met Ray that year and recalled how happy the couple seemed, despite any whispers about Ray's sexuality and Dorothy being a married woman.

A Worrisome Libel Case

Dorothy was sued for libel by glamour girl-turned-journalist Elaine Shepard over a blind item published Dec. 22, 1959. In the article, Kilgallen insinuated that a female member of the Washington press group that had accompanied President Dwight Eisenhower on a tour of Europe was carrying on sexually with White House staffers. Because Shepard was the only woman among the eighty or so reporters present, she felt targeted by Kilgallen.

Shepard sued for an exorbitant and unrealistic amount: $750,000—the equivalent of $7,264,500 today. To prove libel requires proof of malice and if Dorothy had wanted to damage this individual, she would have printed her name.

The case dragged out for years, but the court ruled in Dorothy's favor.

DK could be crafty with the way in which she phrased blind items in her column. Take this tidbit from February 1960: "A famous comedian who'd never be suspected of hanky-panky by his devoted fans just gave the biggest diamond sparkler of the season to his illicit girl friend, who followed him from California to New York."

Then the next paragraph begins: "Marilyn Maxwell, the curvy blonde, is dreadfully depressed because Denise Darcel was summoned to replace her in the West Coast night club revue, 'Paygirls of 1960.'"

Clearly, this was a jab at the very married Bob Hope, who had an ongoing affair with Maxwell (and other women) despite his squeaky clean image. Hope and wife Dolores were married from 1934 until his death in 2003.

"Sometimes you make an honest error, and in that case, I'll take their word for it, and I print a retraction the very next day. But if I'm absolutely sure...I don't write a retraction," Kilgallen explained of her process.

Paris In The Sky

In early 1960, Richard and Dorothy opened a supper club in East Orange, New Jersey called Paris in the Sky. It was situated on the newly added eleventh floor of the Hotel Suburban, and featured a sixty-eight-foot terrace facing the New York skyline, a replica of an old Montmartre street and reproductions of six Parisian shops.

The New York Times wrote, "It offers musical trios and singers that are not loud, French décor, a bottle of champagne for every four persons, untouched scenic splendors, and a seven-course pheasant or sirloin steak dinner for $15."

The couple celebrated the achievement with a cocktail party attended by celebrities including Celeste Holm, Gypsy Rose Lee and Candy Jones, who were bused from the couple's townhouse to the restaurant for the evening. Journalist Mel Heimer wrote in his *My New York* column that the sight of famous people riding a bus was quite humorous. He reported the establishment had cost $500,000 to open.

In February 1960, Kilgallen received a star on the Hollywood Walk of Fame, located at 6780 Hollywood Blvd in the category of "television." It seemed her own personal star was rising high in the sky and she was in love.

Mike Connolly wrote of DK and Ray: "Dorothy Kilgallen tells me to tell you: be careful if you catch one of Johnnie Ray's shows—don't say anything nasty. The deaf-in-one-ear-and-getting deafer Cry Boy can read lips. 'We were dancing at Ciro's,' says Dorothy, 'and he told me a lady in the farthest corner of the room had just ordered Cointreau [a French orange liqueur]!' I asked 'Is that the way you get scoops?' Dorothy giggled, 'I ain't talking!'"

Famed comedian Steve Rossi, who was discovered by Mae West, was a witness to Dorothy and Johnnie's affair.

Dorothy steps out with Johnnie Ray at the premier of *Ben-Hur* in late 1959.

"I met her at The Copacabana. She had written a negative remark about me in her column," Rossi told show business author Kliph Nesteroff. "About a week later I went to The Copa to see Paul Anka and she was sitting at the front table with Danny Stradella. She was sitting there and Paul Anka introduced me. I said, 'Ms. Kilgallen, Steve Rossi.' She was kind of stunned, knowing that she had written something negative. I said, 'I just wanted to thank you for mentioning me in your column. I learned when I was very young that as long as you spell my name right, it's okay with me.' She started to laugh and we became the dearest of friends. The next week, Johnnie Ray was opening at The Copa. She said, 'I like you. I'd like you to be my escort.' I said, 'I've met Johnnie a couple of times, we did some TV shows together.' She said, 'Oh, do you know him personally?' I said, 'Yes.' So we go to the show and it was one of those exciting nights in show business. This guy just tore the place apart."

Rossi continued, "After the show we go backstage and she was just enthralled with him. She was married to a guy who she found out later was gay. His name was Dick Kollmar. He was a half-assed producer on Broadway and he had a lover in New Jersey that he was living with toward the end of their relationship...She fell madly in love with Johnnie Ray. They had a wild, mad, love affair and Johnnie Ray never slept with anyone else in his life other than Dorothy Kilgallen. Ironic, because she found out Dick Kollmar was gay—and Johnnie Ray had been gay."

A Love Triangle Turns Deadly

The *Journal-American* sent DK out to Los Angeles in early 1960 to cover the trial of Dr. Raymond Bernard Finch, a middle-aged surgeon, and his lover *femme fatale* Carole Tregoff. The couple was accused of murdering Finch's wife Barbara Jean in 1959.

In an article from May 1960, DK reflected, "The dream became a nightmare anyway on the night of July 18 (1959), when a single bullet drilled Mrs. Finch, and Carole cowered under a clump of bougainvillea while her lover ran."

The first of three trials spanned January 4 through March 12, 1960. It ended in mistrial.

"For three months, Carole sat in court, listened to testimony, heard herself called 'a modern Lady Macbeth,' walked the long marble corridors under guard, trying not to see the curious, smirking, sometimes accusing, sometimes sympathetic, faces in the crowd. At the end the jury couldn't agree on a verdict, and tears glittered in her eyes when it hit her that she would have to go through the whole thing again," Kilgallen opined.

DK wrote Tregoff had gotten embroiled in the lethal love triangle because she "wanted what millions of other girls want...everything."

Time magazine called Dorothy's efforts in painting a vivid word picture of the trial "the best coverage" the case received, while *Newsweek* said she was the "star attraction" of the court proceedings, noting as a journalist Kilgallen had "unquestioned talent."

David J. Krajicek wrote in the *Daily News*, "Dorothy Kilgallen, the scalpel-sharp New York scribe who'd seen it all as the queen of press row at murder trials, called it 'an absurdity piled upon an absurdity.'"

A second trial started June 27, 1960, and also ended in mistrial that November. The third time was a charm, and on March 27, 1961, Finch was found guilty of first-degree murder and Tregoff was found guilty in the second degree. Both were sentenced to life imprisonment, but in 1969, she got paroled and started a new life under an assumed name. Finch was paroled in late 1971 and took work as a doctor in the rural Ozarks. He died in 1995.

The Pot Boils Over

On Feb. 11, 1960, Jack Paar famously walked off the set of *The Tonight Show*.

Columnist Paul Jones chastised him in a column called "Paar Error: Talking Instead of Listening." Jones wrote, in part: "Paar got into trouble when he started popping off about Dorothy Kilgallen's profile and the manner in which the State department has mistreated Fidel Castro. These tongue lashings were not in line with the type of thing that Paar had been doing. Neither was his tirade against 'yellow journalism' in which he spoke out at newspapers which he said criticize TV for featuring so much violence and sex, while the papers at the same time feature stories about sex and violence in order to enhance their circulation and profits. The wrangle with Broadway columnist Kilgallen was hardly worth the time he devoted to it."

Jones continued, "The poke at the State department was ill-timed in view of the manner in which Castro's government has embraced the delegate from the Soviet Union, and, while criticism of the press might have some substance, I submit that Paar's importance has been substantially exaggerated by the press' attention to his frequent on-the-air squabbles."

On February 17, DK called out Paar's actions as nothing but a stunt to boost ratings.

"Jack Paar's fans can relax; he'll be back March 7. He made his 'peace' with the network in Miami yesterday. He never meant to quit NBC, and the executives at the network knew it, or they wouldn't have broadcast his emotional—but carefully taped—'farewell' scene when they could have kept it off the air and held their new contract conferences in private.

"The whole routine was as elaborately choreographed as an Agnes De Mille ballet. Paar felt the need of a great surge of audience sympathy to distract from the criticism he'd been getting, and NBC realized the stunt would cause front page headlines from coast to coast, so why not play the game with straight faces? It didn't hurt anybody, and gave the show and its star publicity that couldn't be bought."

In his *The Onlooker* column, John Moore fired back at DK, writing, "Dorothy Kilgallen, the Hearst columnist whose pride in her guessing ability is so evident in her panel show appearances, made a correct guess last week that Jack would be BACK.

"Miss Kilgallen's column is appearing only sporadically these days because her editor, rather intelligently, assigned her to cover a second-rate murder trial story (Finch-Tregoff) on the West Coast."

The piece concluded with an accusation that an episode of *What's My Line?* had been rigged with Dorothy's assistance.

"The Onlooker department, incidentally, is still waiting for a reply from Miss Kilgallen to the inquiry which our predecessor sent her.

"He pointed out that Miss Kilgallen, back on July 19 on *What's My Line?* (Channel 12), had made another of her triumphant guesses when she identified a girl guest as a bartender (Delores Naples).

"What the Onlooker wanted to know was how it happened that the same girl had been named as 'the most beautiful bartender in New York' in a Kilgallen column published July 15."

Could her *VOB* column have been where the show's producers got the idea to put Ms. Naples on *WML?* Dorothy wrote about hundreds of people each year. It was unlikely that any nefarious foolery was afoot.

Covering one of Old Blue Eyes' shows in her April 4, 1960 column, the biting scribe reported, "Frank Sinatra's recent engagement in Miami Beach not only packed 'em in when he was singing, but provided unscheduled entertainment for the hotel's guests. There were, for instance, the thrilling moments when Frank and Peter Lawford shot off firecrackers in the lobby, and residents in all sorts of attire came dashing down fearing the great noise was an atomic bomb, an earthquake, or some kind of an artillery attack by Castro."

Another Royal Assignment

Dorothy traveled to London in May 1960 to attend the wedding of Princess Margaret and Antony Armstrong-Jones at Westminster Abbey on the sixth. It was the first British royal wedding to be televised. Her *Voice of Broadway* column was written by a series of guests, in her absence. The *Liverpool Daily Post* reported on DK's wardrobe, noting she had traveled with fourteen outfits made by Canadian fashion designer Arnold Scaasi, who would enjoy a long career dressing First Ladies and movie stars. Her clothing included: one ankle length dress of ostrich feathers, shaded from pale green to seagreen with a white Ottoman silk coat lined with more feathers; a short white chiffon dress with lavender satin coat (she will wear this in the Abbey); a pale grey mink jacket; a dark mink shawl, and two sumptuous raincoats—one in white silk patterned with brown roses, and the other a tiger print silk. She also brought diamonds and pearls to accessorize.

Continues To Be Critical of Khrushchev and Castro

Dorothy Kilgallen even upbraided the President of the United States when she felt he deserved it. In a May 24, 1960 column headlined "I Told You So," she wrote: "Memo from this desk to Dwight Eisenhower. Dear Mr. President..."

She commented on Eisenhower's frustration at a recent Paris meeting with the Soviet leader. She wrote, "I tried to sketch Premier Khrushchev's character in my dispatches after observing him closely in Washington and New York. Anyone watching him objectively (and I was) could see that his occasional excursions into the role of Santa Claus or Soviet kewpie-doll were well-timed theatrics for propaganda purposes; basically he was a shrewd, ruthless boor, with an excellent sense of how far he could go in insulting his hosts and still emerge the chubby smiling chum of the 'little people...'

"I'm not a political expert, or even a political columnist, so I don't expect you to read what I write, Mr. President. I'm just a realistic reporter with some rather good sources. (As an example, I would like to point out that when you denounced Fidel Castro for his anti-U.S. policies—and thereby made front page headlines—you were more than two years behind my column.)

"Maybe [press secretary] Jim Hagerty could—? No, Jim's far too busy. Maybe some fourth assistant secretary to Jim's secretary could now and then scan these humble lines when they refer to the international situation—just to save your valuable time and taxpayer money.

"Meanwhile, I respectfully repeat: if you believe anything the Soviet chaps tell you on any subject more vital than the weather, you are taking a large historical wooden nickel."

Her July 8 column included a letter written by John Benincasa who criticized a recent exchange DK had with reader Morton Bernstein pertaining to Japan. Benincasa told Kilgallen she should read the June issue of *Life* magazine to bone up on the topic. In her usual way, she replied: "I read the *Life* article. *Life* is a swell magazine, very interesting to pick up in the dentist's waiting room.

"If you're interested in research, you might compare *Life*'s attitude toward Fidel Castro, in the first few weeks of his reign, with mine, which was quite clearly stated in my column. I think you will find that mine, at the outset, was far closer to the current feeling in the U.S. State Department. It just took the government a couple of years to face reality."

In her column the next day, DK found a way to thrust the knife deeper into an already bleeding Jack Paar. She noted, "Fans didn't see all of his gymnastic exhibition with the judo experts the other night. During one of his flips, his wig slipped, and NBC scissored the embarrassing moment."

Ouch. That had to hurt.

In September 1960, Dorothy wrote a piece entitled "All The World's A Stage," where she blasted the visit of "two murderous boors"—Fidel Castro and Nikita Khrushchev—to New York City and the ensuing "police state" it caused.

"WHO CARES whether Castro and Khrushchev are secure? Most patriotic Americans would like to believe they lie uneasy in their beds, the sword always above them, suspended by a hair.

"They are bad men, they are troublemakers in the world, and it is our world too; why are we treating them as if we believed they were capable of an honest impulse?

"Today, in New York, policemen who are Jews are being deprived of their high holy days because they are needed to 'protect' the atheist Khrushchev and the anti-religious Castro."

Then in October, she responded to those who felt her columns were becoming too political. She noted she'd received letters about an item she wrote expressing her opinion that the "Negro" vote would go to JFK because of Sammy Davis Jr.'s support of the candidate.

But she also received favorable letters about "All The World's A Stage" from people who shared her anti-Communist sentiments. For instance, Frances M. Nelson of Millinocket, Maine, wrote when her Jewish neighbor learned that Khrushchev was visiting the U.S., "she had a heart spell and almost died. Memories such as they have can never be erased. I feel as you do about Castro and Mr. K. And may the hair holding the sword break soon."

Dorothy defended her reporting. "There are those readers who think a Broadway columnist should not write about national or international affairs ('stick to the theatre and movies and night clubs' is their advice) but I ignore them," she said, citing the people of Broadway are U.S. citizens and have the right to their opinions and to vote, and that writers have the ability to cultivate sources in political realms.

"Hence the Broadway or 'gossip' columnist, however he or she is to be deplored, just might be in closer touch with the masses, or the public pulses, or whatever you want to call it, than the most brilliant of the ivory tower dwellers, or deplorers."

Dorothy Attends JFK Inaugural, Falls Ill in D.C.

In January 1961 the *Journal-American* sent Dorothy to cover the Inauguration of John F. Kennedy as the thirty-fifth President of the United States. Before the first Catholic was to become leader of the free world, DK filed a story from the Capitol, describing to readers the palpable excitement she felt, even from the Mayflower Hotel where she stayed.

"I keep thinking about Abraham Lincoln. This story I am covering is not just a rat race and a traffic jam, it is history. If I had been born in the era of hoop skirts, I would have been writing about the circumstances surrounding Mr. Lincoln's inauguration. (Or, more probably, some chap would have been writing about it)."

She revealed her plan to cover two of the five inaugural balls, outfitted in a floor-length white dress with silver bugle beads and a sleeveless white mink jacket. And while women no longer wear hoop skirts, DK noted, she expected the ladies at the balls would be wearing long, figure-flattering gowns accessorized with gloves and pearl necklaces—things that never go out of style.

It was a wonder DK had arrived in D.C. in time for the big occasion, given a blizzard had threatened the area. She was driven to the nation's capital by Roosevelt Zanders, who owned a Rolls-Royce car service.

At the pre-inaugural gala on Jan.19, 1961, Dorothy ran into Bette Davis who had been separated from her luggage en route. DK offered Davis the usage of her brocade coat, to which the actress replied, "It's terribly cute of you, but there's no use pretending that I'm anything that I'm not." When Davis took to the stage, she did so in her street clothes.

Unfortunately, sometime that night Dorothy became "ragingly ill," as longtime friend Jean Bach, (wife of CBS producer Bob Bach)—would relay. Jean had seen Dorothy accept a shot of Jack Daniels (on an empty stomach) and soon after got sick, requiring her to return to her hotel room early. By late evening, eight inches of snow blanketed the city, stranding motorists, hundreds of which abandoned their vehicles in the snow drifts.

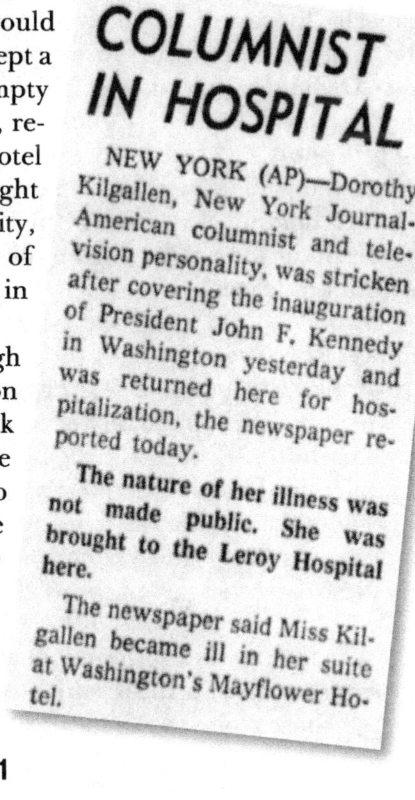

COLUMNIST IN HOSPITAL

NEW YORK (AP)—Dorothy Kilgallen, New York Journal-American columnist and television personality, was stricken after covering the inauguration of President John F. Kennedy in Washington yesterday and was returned here for hospitalization, the newspaper reported today.

The nature of her illness was not made public. She was brought to the Leroy Hospital here.

The newspaper said Miss Kilgallen became ill in her suite at Washington's Mayflower Hotel.

Dorothy recovered enough to attend the inauguration at noon the next day. She sat five rows back from the stage as JFK took the oath of office on the East Portico of the United States Capitol. She sat with columnist Bob Considine and Clifton Fadiman, a rep for *Life* magazine, shivering at the outdoor event that saw a wind-chill of seven degrees fahrenheit.

According to Zanders,

Kilgallen seemed to be under a great deal of stress, and again fell ill. Husband Richard's failing restaurant was causing financial turmoil and the two were having difficulties with their radio show. DK was visibly rundown, with the pressure of a busy schedule (in the middle of a snowstorm) likely compounding the situation.

Zanders made arrangements for Dorothy to receive help getting dressed and packed up to leave the hotel. He carried her to the back elevator and out to the waiting car. DK was driven directly to the LeRoy Hospital in New York City where she was treated for pneumonia.

Her column was not suspended during this time. In fact, following the inaugural, she thanked a reader in her column that expressed support of DK's right to print the news. She replied, "Thank you for your interest and support. I feel very lucky to be working for a newspaper that lets me write what I believe." How true that statement would continue to be during her probing of JFK's death less than three years later.

In late January, Kilgallen wrote about her admiration of Jackie Kennedy's taste in fashion, saying consumers could expect to wait only a month before the lower cost "replica" dresses and coats worn by the First Lady would hit department store racks. How fortuitous of DK to already sense that Jackie was becoming a fashion icon and would remain one for generations to come.

On February 5, after a brief hiatus from *WML?*, Dorothy surprised the panel by appearing as that evening's mystery guest. She told the panel, consisting of Arlene Francis, her husband Martin Gabel, Tony Perkins and Debbie Reynolds, that she sang, although not professionally. Once Reynolds asked if the mystery guest was associated with newspapers, Gabel guessed Dorothy's identity.

A shaky Kilgallen told the panel: "I'm scared to death. I'm so nervous, John's holding my hand." But Dorothy seemed pleased with the warm reception she received from the audience. It was good to be back home with her television family.

A Tropical Reprieve

Castro was again on Dorothy's radar. In her *VOB* column, sandwiched between an item on Sir Alec Guinness and one on Tony Martin's career, she wrote, "Food and drugs are the only items permitted, by law, to be sent from the United States to Cuba, but who's kidding whom? In the past month, German, Russian and other foreign ships have docked in Southern ports (New Orleans, for one) to pick up supplies for Castro's use: bottles, paper, sugar machinery, oil, radio parts and autoparts, for example."

Also that month, she and Richard went to Jamaica, enjoying some respite from the cold northeast winter back home. Whenever she traveled, DK would share some of the local color with her readers. One evening out in a nightclub, Dorothy saw nine "Disneyish" little piglets run across the dance floor. She wrote, "And so I say this to the proprietor of my favorite night club: You have your balloon nights, and your golden chain at the door, and your boxes of perfume, and your magnums of champagne, and that's all very well. You run a nice night club. But for goodness sake where are the pigs?"

In another column, styled as a letter to her boss, she described basking in seventy-eight degree weather, typing under a turquoise-colored umbrella on the terrace of her penthouse cottage at the Marrakesh Hotel overlooking the Caribbean Sea. She had on the radio, lamenting what she heard from a Cuban station saying the country was "the only free nation in America."

DK wrote going on the trip helped her to "thaw out" from the frigid conditions in New York after battling pneumonia.

She mentioned Elizabeth Taylor and Eddie Fisher recently stayed in the same penthouse and that Richard is "shook up at the thought that he is sleeping in the bed once occupied by Liz."

Springtime Boosts Dorothy's Spirits

Dorothy, who was an expert on all things New York City, wrote a festive column in March describing all the places tourists should visit. She recommended La Fonda del Sol at 123 W. 50th Street, which was one large area consisting of seven small restaurants and bars. For a steak, she suggested heading to Danny's Hideaway on East 45th Street, also offering glowing words to the veal Parmigiana, spaghetti and the Mack Gordon salad, which she called unforgettable. The Entertainer—Johnny Johnston's club—had good food and atmosphere, while the Tiana Tu on Central Park south was a romantic stop for lovers of Polynesian food. Billy Reed's Plush Room on East 55th Street was also a top pick for date night.

Dorothy was one of ten celebrities asked to design a room in a faux house, assembled by the National Design Center in New York City, for an exhibition called "Ten Best Dressed Rooms for 1961." Dorothy put together a summer dining room using foliage greens, silver and white by Everett Brown, AID. White wicker furniture, upholstered in velvety green washable nylon fabric, popped against the green carpet. The dining table was inlaid with brass strips.

The house remained on display through the summer.

Taking to her typewriter to again blast Castro, she wrote in late August that Fidel wished to meet with JFK for a conference, as per "scuttle-butt from Havana." DK wrote, "Please, Mr. President, DON'T DO IT!"

On September 2, Dorothy allowed her home to be used for the wedding of Allen Rubinstein and Ruby Wilson. Later that month, Dorothy wrote in her column that actor Tony Perkins had mailed her a postcard from Greece.

"It was addressed to me at the paper instead of my home, and a postscript gave the explanation: 'My address book blew out of a helicopter this morning.' (How many friends do you have who lose their little black books while flying over Greece?")

In November, Dorothy appeared on *Password* with Allen Ludden, alongside fellow guest Darren McGavin, as she was often recruited to "play" on other game shows.

More Litigation

Dorothy again found herself at the center of a libel lawsuit, but this time, she was the plaintiff. It began after DK read an article Cindy Adams penned about *What's My Line?* which she did not like. She then proceeded to devote ink in her column to Cindy and her husband Joey Adams, who was a comedian/humorist. In November, an incredulous Dorothy questioned why Cindy would be asked to tag along as Joey supervised twenty-five performers as they traveled the globe—a junket that cost $10,000 a week under the auspices of the State Department. The trip kicked off in late August and was set to continue through year's end.

Citing Heath Bowman of the Department of Cultural Exchange as her source, Dorothy wrote, "What's more, Mr. Adams' wife, Cindy, is along on the junket for the sole purpose of introducing the various acts in the language of the country being entertained.

"She does not know the language of the countries being entertained, I ascertained from Dr. Bowman, but someone in the State Department at each stop along the line whips up a phonetic introduction for her and she memorizes it. Mr. Bowman says, 'She is very good at it.' I have a seven-year-old son who would be good at it, too; he's a marvelous parrot of anything he hears. But so far the State Department hasn't asked for his services."

On Dec. 28, 1961, *Town & Village* published Cindy's "open letter" to Dorothy. As expected, Ms. Adams defended her involvement with the tour, but took her ill feelings for Kilgallen to the next level. She wrote that DK had a drinking problem, had relationships with younger men and was trapped in a joyless marriage. She called Kilgallen a "vulgar old crone" and concluded, "I don't have to try to hurt other people to get my satisfaction out of life. But just as David had to stand up to Goliath and hit him between the eyes, I'm warning you not to stick your chin out any more. You can't spare it!"

One day later, Dorothy had to face the public at several parties she'd arranged in honor of her daughter Jill, then a freshman at Northwestern University, as the young woman made her "informal debut into society." Joan Fontaine, Mary Martin and other celebrities were in attendance. Linda Shepard, niece of DK adversary Elaine Shepard, even showed up, as the girl was friends with Jill.

Kilgallen approached her libel lawyer Edgar Hatfield, and, referring to her copy of the book *Say It Safely*, outlined how she felt Cindy was in the wrong. One wonders how Ms. Adams could possibly know DK's true feelings for her husband? Was she a mind reader? And what evidence was there that Dorothy was "trapped" in a marriage that was "joyless"? Even if Ms. Adams had proved outside affairs, that would not have established that there was no love remaining between Dorothy and Richard. The fact the couple continued to do things together—including out of the public eye—argued against the premise that their marriage, however unconventional it may have been, was "joyless."

In the summer of 1962, a suit was filed against Ms. Adams for one million dollars. Adams and her spouse countersued not only Dorothy, but also Hearst, Hearst Consolidated, King Features, the *Chicago American*, the *Journal-American* and the Chicago American Publishing Company for one million dollars—each. Kilgallen let the lawsuit go. Hatfield sent DK a bill for $20,000—actually related to the earlier Shepard case—whereupon she dropped him as her counsel.

The lawsuits had been financially and emotionally draining for a woman who was often plagued by health problems and no doubt carried the weight of other stressors in her life.

Johnnie and Richard Vie For Her Attention

In January 1962, she and Ray attended a party hosted by film producer Joe Levine. While Dorothy was friends with his wife Rosalie, it was Joe who would figure prominently in the later years of DK's life.

In a newspaper article penned by Renee Francine, the couple were pictured petting "a tame lion." Riding one was more like it, since their affair at any moment threatened to devour their respective careers.

Francine wrote Levine was presiding at a "Night With the Gods" themed party celebrating a film premiere. "Slave girls hustled about the restaurant serving strange Roman delicacies, and in a corner, a scantily clad muscleman toyed with a 250-pound lion cub. The room was filled with celebrities from all areas of show business, politics and the press, each of whom was estimating how much this unlikely display was costing."

Although Dorothy and Johnnie carried on a flagrant love affair, the Kollmars still maintained a level of chumminess, perhaps more of a friendship and partnership than a sizzling romance. When Dorothy took a vacation in June 1962, Richard served as a contributor for her *VOB* column. He humorously outlined DK's various foibles, including her lousy cooking, poor sense of direction, love of shoes (she owned nearly four hundred pair) and how people were always messing up their surnames.

"Just remember, some night while you're opening an envelope addressed to Dorothy Kollgallen, I'm being introduced as Mr. Killmer," he wrote.

Kollmar ended the item, saying, "Darling, I know you'll forgive my exposé of your eccentricities but I want one thing clearly understood—as an eccentric, compared to me, you're a rank amateur. How you've put up with me for 22 years I'll never know. Perhaps a clue to the answer is we both have in common something which the 'beat generation' considers an eccentricity—love."

Gets Caught Up In Space Race, Loses A Dear Friend

Like many Americans fascinated by the Space Race, Dorothy watched John Glenn's successful mission as the first American to orbit the Earth on Feb. 20, 1962. In her *Voice of Broadway* column she waxed poetic, saying, "For the first time in my life I sat glued to a television set for five hours straight, eating peanut better sandwiches and crying."

She wrote of his patriotism and likability, even professing her love for him, and praised the scientists and team that made it all possible.

"Yes, that was quite a little thriller that NASA put on, and I hope Mr. (Newton) Minow, the television czar, approved of it, and I hope Mr. Khrushchev, the Russian czar, got an ulcer."

July 1961 brought personal sadness to Dorothy and to the literary world, with the death of Ernest Hemingway. He was an American novelist, short-story writer, and journalist. He had a strong influence on 20th-century fiction, while maintaining an adventurous lifestyle. He won a Pulitzer Prize and later a Nobel Prize for Literature. Hemingway penned *The Sun Also Rises*, *A Farewell To Arms*, *For Whom the Bell Tolls*, and *The Old Man And the Sea*. A fellow Illinoisan, Ernest adored Dorothy, calling her the greatest female writer in the world.

They shared an affinity for Cuba, where Hemingway spent a lot of time before Castro. He observed, "Writing, at its best, is a lonely life." After Ernest died, President Kennedy arranged for Mary Hemingway to travel to Cuba where she met Fidel Castro and retrieved her husband's papers.

DK and Ernest Hemingway

Always on the hunt for sources and tidbits for her column, Dorothy frequented P.J. Clarke's. She liked that establishment, on Third Avenue at 55th Street, as did lots of celebs. Buddy Holly proposed marriage there. Aristotle Onassis took Lee Radziwill to Clarke's. Nat King Cole named the bacon cheeseburger "the Cadillac of burgers."

Bartender Joe Allen remembered the night in the late 1950s when three people entered and sat at separate tables: Sen. Hubert Humphrey, Marilyn Monroe and mobster Frank Costello. "I thought, 'hmmm, this isn't bad,'" laughed Allen.

Dorothy was part of the Weekly Science Club that met Mondays at P.J. Clarke's. Some guests she brought to the meetings included actor Tony Perkins, boxer Sugar Ray Robinson and mobster Costello.

"It had nothing to do with science," Marlin Swing said of these peculiar gatherings. They were designed to chase away the Monday blues.

Frank Costello certainly helped Dorothy be more cheerful when he gifted her a large diamond cross. Hairdresser Marc Sinclaire said that it was so heavy, DK later (boldly) refashioned it into earrings.

"Dorothy was not only a very bright reporter, she was a very curious reporter. And it is totally in character for her to [invite him] to meet with her and her friends at P.J. Clarke's. Totally in character," opined Ron Pataky, who romanced DK in the final eighteen months of her life.

Costello (1891-1973) was an Italian-American Mafia don of the Genovese crime family. He served as inspiration for the character Vito Corleone in the *Godfather* films.

DK had connections. Lots of them. But sometimes her sources came up short. With deadly consequences.

Dorothy hobknobs with actors John Hodiak and Cesar Romero.

6
A Fatal Column

Immediately before Marilyn Monroe's death on August 4, 1962, Dorothy seemed obsessed with her. She mentioned her three times in her column that last week. The first was on Tuesday, August 1, and Kilgallen lead with this news:

"Marilyn Monroe, in an August magazine [interview], tells Alan Levy, 'I am trying to prove to myself that I am a person. Then maybe I'll convince myself that I'm an actress.'"

This was followed by a barb Kilgallen clearly aimed at Dr. Ralph Greenson, MM's Svengali psychiatrist. She wrote: "Marilyn, you're a person—I don't care what your psychiatrist says."

On Aug. 3, 1962, Kilgallen wrote what was in hindsight one of her most explosive columns with far-reaching ramifications she surely never intended. She referred cryptically to Marilyn Monroe's relationship with Robert Kennedy, without actually naming him. This column, titled "New Monroe Photo Creating a Stir" ran in the *Journal-American* on Friday and would also appear in some papers outside New York as early as the following day:

"Marilyn Monroe's health must be improving. She's been attending select Hollywood parties and has become the talk of the town again. In California they're circulating a photograph of her that certainly isn't as bare as that famous calendar picture, but is very interesting; Marilyn's dress looks as if it were plastered to her skin, and the skirt is hitched higher above the knees than any Paris designer would dare to promote in the fall showings. And she's cooking in the sex-appeal department, too; she proved vastly alluring to a handsome

DOROTHY KILGALLEN

New Monroe Photo Creating a Stir

NEW YORK — Marilyn Monroe's health must be improving. She's been attending select Hollywood parties and has become the talk of the town again.

In California they're circulating a photograph of her that certainly isn't as bare as that famous calendar picture, but is very interesting; Marilyn's dress looks as if it were plastered to her skin, and the skirt is hitched higher above the knees than any Paris designer would dare to promote in the fall showings.

And she's cooking in the sex-appeal department, too; she proved vastly alluring to a handsome gentleman who is a bigger name than Joe DiMaggio was in his heyday. So don't write off Marilyn as "finished."

gentleman who is a bigger name than Joe DiMaggio was in his heyday. So don't write off Marilyn as 'finished.'"

Perhaps as a gesture of détente, in the following day's column, Aug. 4, 1962, Kilgallen published a sanguine item in support of what was to be Monroe's final film project.

Under a headline that unfortunately read: "'Got To Give' Buried—But Is It Dead?" Dorothy wrote, "Don't faint if 20th Century-Fox sends *Something's Got to Give* before the cameras again with exactly the same co-stars who excited the headlined project in the beginning: Marilyn Monroe and Dean Martin. Marilyn has made it clear that she wants to make the movie and Dean has notified the bosses at 20th that he'll be available (and willing) this Winter."

On the evening of Saturday, August 4, Marilyn Monroe died in her home, her body "officially" discovered in the wee hours of August 5 by housekeeper Eunice Murray, whose story regarding the demise of her employer changed countless times over the years. The two doctors who had been treating MM, including her Svengali psychiatrist, Ralph Greenson, and MD Hyman Engelberg, told implausible and conflicting stories as well. All three had long-time and active associations with the Communist Party in America—a fact which was probably unknown to Ms. Monroe and was not told to the public. But this is irrefutable, and surely relevant, though not widely known even today. Suspiciously, both doctors came on the scene around the time Marilyn's affair with President Kennedy was heating up. (She had had occasional dates with JFK for years, as persons close to him confirmed. When that relationship cooled she briefly dated his brother, the Attorney General, Robert Kennedy).

Her publicist, Pat Newcomb, immediately led reporters, who arrived at MM's home as dawn was breaking, to believe the actress had killed herself, and this misinformation was put on the wire services, circulating worldwide before any determination as to cause of death could be made. Monroe's passing was marred by numerous unanswered questions and troubling contradictions in the medical findings.

Pat Newcomb, incidentally, then partied with Jack Kennedy on his yacht along with Peter and Pat Lawford—the latter being one of the president's sisters—a few days after Marilyn's funeral. Pat kept company with JFK for much of August 1962 while Jacqueline Kennedy was out of the country for weeks. The First Lady was making headlines cavorting with a married Italian playboy who was heir to the Fiat auto fortune. Then Newcomb spent months in Europe—making her inaccessible to the press—and upon her return got a job through Bobby Kennedy. She has never told all she knows about Marilyn's suspicious death and as far as is known, was never questioned by police though she was one of the last to see the actress alive.

Los Angeles Chief Coroner Theodore Curphey claimed Marilyn

swallowed at least sixty-four sleeping pills "in one big gulp" and "in a matter of seconds," yet hidden from the public was the disturbing fact that no pill residue was ever found in her body, even under microscopic examination. Her blood was said to contain a high concentration of barbiturates (but no alcohol), yet modern computer models show that she would have died before even thirty-five percent of the drugs she supposedly took could have been absorbed, if she had swallowed them. The assertion she OD'ed came from just one man, toxicologist Raymond Abernathy, who inexplicably rushed to destroy all forensic evidence before routine tests ordered by medical examiner Thomas Noguchi could be done. If that doesn't bespeak coverup, what does? Then Abernathy resigned soon thereafter and stonewalled, refusing to explain himself or cooperate further. Noguchi was also embroiled in subsequent controversies and fired.

Various eyewitnesses, including law enforcement officials and two former Los Angeles mayors, confirmed that Robert Kennedy was in L.A. on the day Marilyn Monroe died—taking leave of a family vacation on a ranch south of San Francisco. Credible reports establish he showed up unannounced at MM's home to confront her, most likely over the gossip about them that Dorothy had reported the day before. Marilyn called at least one close friend, respected movie hairstylist Sydney Guilaroff late Saturday afternoon and reported to him how Bobby Kennedy had manhandled her and threatened her. She was literally afraid for her life. Sydney tried to convince her to come to his home if she was so frightened, but after he spoke with her a second time on the phone, she seemed less fearful. Yet her final conversation with Guilaroff alluded to "dangerous" secrets she knew about the Kennedys.

However, as Larry Jordan persuasively argues in his epic new 760-page book, *The Real Marilyn Monroe*, the actress had no intention of holding a press conference and exposing the Kennedys. That myth was promulgated by Bob Slatzer, a fantasist and shameless self-promoter, who claimed to have once been married to MM. (He wasn't). He only told that story years later after Norman Mailer wrote a book hinting at Monroe being murdered. Slatzer wanted to sell his own book.

A true hustler, he once guest-wrote a column for Dorothy Kilgallen in 1952 in which he claimed he and Marilyn (who was a voracious reader) exchanged books long-distance. At that time Slatzer disavowed any romance with her. Unfortunately, Slatzer later embellished his story and was foolishly given currency by author Anthony Summers.

Jordan points out that Marilyn had "no history of vengefulness. Even when she was alive, reporters commented admiringly on her lack of bitterness, and how she always spoke highly of past loves, including her ex-husbands.

"Besides, she knew that the Kennedys were American royalty and if she ever aired tawdry allegations against them, she would destroy her career. Her friend Frank Sinatra also debunked the allegation that she planned to reveal dark secrets, even though Monroe knew some. Throughout her career she was an exemplar of utmost discretion and very adept at dealing with the press, and kept her private life private."

Jordan makes a compelling case that Marilyn was murdered, and has assembled fresh and irrefutable new evidence to prove it.

Marilyn Monroe wasn't the only one who knew Kennedy secrets. Many people did, including Dorothy Kilgallen. Lee Israel reported that DK "galvanized [a group of friends] with stories about all the Kennedys' extramarital capering."

"My God, why don't you print that?" one incredulous man asked.

"I couldn't possibly," Dorothy replied. "Nobody would."

The weekend the actress passed away, Dorothy was a houseguest at her friend Howard Rothberg's summer home at Amagansett, Long Island. When her editor called her early Sunday morning to report that Marilyn Monroe was dead, Dorothy was apparently so upset that her newspaper had to send reporter Bob Considine to the west coast instead.

According to Lee Israel, on the way back to Manhattan, Dorothy fell ill during the two-hour trip and had to be removed from the train and hospitalized.

Researcher Kathryn Fauble commented, "I could never confirm that she stayed in a hospital instead. Marc Sinclaire told us that he did not see her that weekend, but Dorothy told him later that a doctor had given her a vitamin B12 injection. Marc told us that the situation was not at all a crisis."

As luck would have it, DK was not due to appear live on *WML?* that Sunday night, Aug. 5, 1962. Fauble notes, "That episode had been videotaped months earlier. The August 12 telecast also came from a stockpile of videotape. Beginning a year before Marilyn died—1961—Dorothy, Arlene, Bennett, John Daly and various crew members and producers enjoyed long summer vacations. The invention of videotape made that possible."

Dorothy's indisposition is curious. She apparently was not well enough to write her column until Wednesday, August 8.

Had she realized her Friday item about a clandestine romance between Marilyn Monroe and a man of great importance had in some way triggered the beloved star's death? She confirmed to friends the person to whom she was referring was Bobby Kennedy. She had been told of their affair by a photographer who was close to Marilyn. DK had also previously reported that Marilyn and RFK had danced several times at an "after party" following her having sung *Happy Birthday* to JFK at a Madison Square Garden political gala in May 1962.

Dorothy's August 9 column was rather morosely devoted to Monroe. She reflected, "Yes, I think she committed suicide, but not in the conventional movie star way, with the well-chosen chiffon nightie and the tear-stained note to someone, destined to make him feel guilty all the rest of his life. I think Marilyn's was the involuntary suicide of a tortured creature running from the black shapes of nightmare into the path of an on-rushing locomotive."

Kilgallen speculated about the actress' frame of mind leading up to her death. "Among the things the friends kept asking was 'I wonder why she didn't leave a note?' Her whole life was a suicide note, written for everybody to read, but nobody would believe the message," the columnist opined. "So perhaps it is important for them to have a note in her own handwriting that they wouldn't comprehend, either. Sleep well, sweet girl. You have left more of a legacy than most, if all you ever left was a handful of photographs of one of the loveliest women who ever walked the earth."

Soon after that initial article was published, Kilgallen began openly casting doubt that MM had taken her own life. Something or someone obviously changed her mind.

On August 14, Dorothy wrote a column with the header: "Mystery Deepens In Marilyn Death." She assailed actor Peter Lawford, who came forward and publicly claimed to have been the last one to speak with MM on the phone (even though he dodged being questioned by authorities for thirteen years). Some newspapers that ran DK's column appear to have censored her references to Lawford by omitting them, probably because he was part of the Kennedy clan.

Kilgallen asked how it was possible Marilyn could have been: "allowed to lock herself in a room with a lethal dose of Nembutal...[Murray] certainly didn't tell much to the reporters. For instance, she told them, 'Marilyn seemed disturbed after the last telephone call. When she went to her bedroom she really was depressed.' But Mrs. Murray never explained what Marilyn did or said to convey the impression that she was disturbed and depressed and if Marilyn was so disturbed and depressed at 8 p.m. why did Mrs. Murray wait until 3 a.m. before checking on her? If she was just a housekeeper, why would she be checking on her employer at all, prowling around at three o'clock in the morning looking for a light under the [door]? She should have kept to her own quarters, not gone snooping and speculating."

Dorothy Kilgallen brazenly quoted an unnamed source as saying, "That 'psychological inquest' they've been holding is a big joke—although a sad one—when any good cop could ask a few questions and get the picture. What this case needs is facts, not theories, and the facts could be ascertained by asking the right questions of Mrs. Murray, Marilyn's doctors, and the Coroner."

Then she zeroed in on this point: "Of course that 'last' person to talk to Marilyn on the phone would be a great help if he'd tell the truth, but I think we both know who it was and I think we both agree he won't tell the whole truth."

Less than a week later, in her August 16 column, Kilgallen revealed her suspicions that Marilyn had met with foul play, in a piece entitled "Touch of Mystery to Marilyn's Death."

"One chum of Marilyn's said: 'The reporters out in California missed a bet in accepting the identification of Eunice Murray as a 'housekeeper.' If she's just a plain ordinary housekeeper, I'm a circus acrobat. Why didn't the press ask her where she'd kept house before, and for whom? I think they'd find out she was a personal friend, an interior decorator, and that she had moved in at the request of one of Marilyn's doctors with instructions to stick close and not let Marilyn out of her sight... you can wager a small sum that Mrs. Murray, by now, has sold her 'exclusive' version of the tragedy to a national magazine.'"

Dorothy concluded, "So poor Marilyn's death is liable to remain a mystery, quite unnecessarily, because Hollywood pulled another of its hush-hush jobs...In the land of Perry Mason, Marilyn's death has become 'The Case of the Prowling Housekeeper.'"

Kilgallen still couldn't let go of the story. Her August 20 column headlined "Marilyn's Story Really All Told?" held nothing back in her suspicions of the nefarious people who engulfed Monroe the evening of her death.

"If the woman described as Marilyn's 'housekeeper' [Eunice Murray] really was a housekeeper, why was her bedroom such a mess? It was a small house and should have been easy to keep tidy." Kilgallen also wanted to know, "Why was Marilyn's door locked that night, when she didn't usually lock it? If she were just trying to get to sleep, and took the overdose of pills accidentally, why was the light on? Usually people sleep better in the dark."

Dorothy couldn't reason why Mrs. Murray thought to call a doctor in the middle of the night simply because her employer didn't answer her knock on the door, given the fact that MM had presumably taken sleeping medication.

The columnist begged the question, "Why did the first doctor [to arrive on the scene] have to call the second doctor before calling the police? Any doctor, even a psychiatrist, knows a dead person when he sees one, especially when rigor mortis has set in and there are marks of lividity on the surface of the face and body. Why the consultation? Why the big time gap in such a small town? Mrs. Murray gets worried at about 3 a.m., and it's almost 6 a.m. before the police get to the scene."

Kilgallen declared, "The real story hasn't been told—not by a long shot."

Such bold reporting was not common in American journalism at that time. She couldn't possibly have known her own life would end under circumstances eerily similar to Marilyn's roughly three years later.

The Lead Up To Monroe's Death

Dorothy persisted in raising public doubts, but in so doing fell victim to misinformation imparted to her by someone wanting to twist the facts of the case. On Aug. 27, 1962 she reported that on a recent trip to the Cal-Neva lodge, located on the California/Nevada border, "A maid found [Marilyn] unconscious on the floor of her room there—from pills, not from liquor...[and] she was revived....but that night drank too much and passed out cold, in full view of several hundred guests of the lodge." She continued that Marilyn, "was then carried out and flown to San Francisco in Frank Sinatra's private plane."

In this instance, Kilgallen's source was not reliable.

Even she seemed to doubt her own story about MM's time at the resort, ostensibly owned by Frank Sinatra but whose principal, silent partners were Chicago-based mobster Sam Giancana and Joseph Kennedy, the president's father.

Dorothy asked a series of questions in her column:

(1) "Who was the maid who found Marilyn unconscious, and why hasn't she stepped forward to tell her story?

(2) "Is there a register at the Cal-Neva Lodge? Was Marilyn registered there?

(3) "How was Marilyn revived on that occasion, and by whom? Was a doctor called? Shouldn't there be a medical report available on that incident, which took place such a short time before the star's suicide?

(4) "Wouldn't Marilyn's name appear on the log of the last flight she ever took on Sinatra's plane?

(5) "Why did she go to the lodge on that occasion, anyway, during the period when she was trying to persuade Twentieth Century-Fox and various members of the press that she was really and truly too ill to work?

(6) "Aren't hotels in California and Nevada supposed to report attempted suicides to the police?"

What was not generally known at the time is that Marilyn flew to Cal-Neva on Frank Sinatra's plane in the company of Peter Lawford. His wife Pat flew in from Hyannis Port for the occasion. MM confided to close friend Ralph Roberts she didn't even want to go, but was talked into it by Pat.

Various biographers over the decades have tried to unravel the mysteries surrounding Monroe's trip to the infamous resort. But as Larry Jordan details in *The Real Marilyn Monroe*, the trip was much more convoluted than previously known. He goes into extensive and previously unknown detail about how MM had been used as a pawn not only by the Lawfords (acting on behalf of the Kennedy family), but also by mobsters.

While staying at the Mafia-run gambling haven, MM encountered Sam Giancana. Monroe did not normally socialize with members of organized crime, and shortly before her death confided to acting coach Paula

Strasberg she was afraid of them.

Kilgallen's scenario posits that the actress overdosed on pills, then miraculously recovered such that she over-imbibed that night, after which she was flown to San Francisco instead of being treated at a nearby Reno hospital.

But Jordan sorts out this confusing maze and explains why this is inaccurate. Monroe did not even leave the resort until Sunday. It is true she and her companions did fly to San Francisco. However, that was late on Sunday, whereupon Pat Lawford caught a plane back to the east coast and Peter and Marilyn returned post-midnight to Los Angeles on Sinatra's private aircraft.

In more recent years, some sloppy biographers have latched onto what they believe to be a legitimate memo allegedly signed by CIA snoop James Angleton the day before Marilyn died. It is supposedly a summary of a phone wiretap of a conversation between Dorothy Kilgallen and her friend Howard Rothberg, in which he tells her secrets about MM. So the story goes, the actress was planning to hold a press conference to expose the Kennedys, including details of her affairs with John and Robert; her knowledge of plots against Castro; and the fact that the president had gone to an air base to secretly view the remains of space aliens from a UFO.

Another version of this preposterous story has Kilgallen calling Monroe on Wednesday, August 1, during which time Marilyn supposedly spilled her guts to Dorothy about all these sensitive topics.

As Truman Capote attested, Marilyn didn't even like Dorothy, whom she felt had written "bitchy" things about her.

The presumed legitimacy of this so-called CIA memo collapsed with the public admission that it was a fraud, by the man who helped put it together. Furthermore, it was first introduced by a shady detective named Milo Speriglio, whom *The New York Times* referred to as a publicity hound. Speriglio and Bob Slatzer were in cahoots. Oddly, another partner in this ruse was Ron Pataky, whose ominous role in Dorothy's life will be explored more fully in later chapters.

There is one more sad tale about Marilyn Monroe that can be laid at Dorothy's doorstep. In a column she wrote that was obviously based on lies told to her by a studio rep, Kilgallen claimed that: "An executive at 20th Century-Fox, whose name cannot be revealed for obvious reasons, contributes this information:

'There really was no time at which the top brass considered resuming *Something's Got To Give* with Marilyn and Dean Martin in the leads.

'The bitter truth was that they had looked at the scenes that they had in the can, and they were pretty lousy, even the nude swimming-tank sequence...

'The studio never actually talked to Marilyn [about resuming filming].'"

Dorothy missed the truth by a mile. The fact is that shortly before her death—shrewd businesswoman that she was—Marilyn had confronted studio executives in a meeting in which she cogently outlined her case. Contrary to the fake news that was portraying her as all washed up, a has-been, a drug addict, MM was in better shape mentally and physically than she'd been in years. (*Even the Coroner's doctors said Monroe "was not an addict," that her use of sleeping medication was "light to moderate" and that she was not mentally ill*).

Marilyn was still radiant.

MM succeeded in getting herself rehired by Fox with a sizable raise and various other concessions, and the studio honcho who had fired her, Peter Levathese, even made pilgrimages to her home to get her back under contract. He brought along a revised script a week before her death. Years later when nine hours of film clips were smuggled out of the studio, viewers could see how stunningly beautiful Monroe looked and how adept she still was at her craft. She was completely functional, patient with the tyrannical director George Cukor, in good humor, and conveyed the subtleties of an accomplished actress. Q&A interviews she gave the press just before she died also confirmed she was articulate, poised, and focused.

Fox was on the defensive for making MM the scapegoat for its own problems, including the fact the script was not finished when filming commenced, there were constant rewrites, they were in violation of their contractual obligations to Marilyn, they were shutting down productions on other pictures due to massive cost overruns associated with the filming of *Cleopatra* (which was plagued by Liz Taylor's multitudinous problems), and the studio embarked on a campaign to destroy Monroe's public image both before and after her death.

Something's Got to Give was never completed. It had been intended as a remake of the 1940 smash hit *My Favorite Wife* starring Cary Grant, Irene Dunne and Gail Patrick. In 1963, the film was reworked as *Move Over, Darling* featuring James Garner, Doris Day and Polly Bergen.

Health Concerns And A Newspaper Strike

Since Dorothy would later succumb to a drug and alcohol-related death, some have surmised she may have had a substance abuse problem. Certainly while millions of people could be described as "functional alcoholics" not enough evidence exists to categorize Kilgallen in this manner.

As for hospitalizations, some have inferred she checked in to dry out or detox—and she may have at times—but she suffered from anemia which plagued her for years. She also had bursitis, which is characterized by inflammation of the fluid-filled pads that cushion joints. It commonly affects the shoulders, elbows, knees and feet.

The detective who reviewed her prescriptions after her death determined she was not over-using drugs, plus her autopsy showed her to be in good health for her age and bore no evidence of liver damage.

One online blogger referred to what he described as: "her long bout with alcoholism and barbiturate addiction which was at its worst in the immediate years prior to her death and is graphically visible in the reruns of *What's My Line?* where her speech is slurry and thick on numerous occasions."

While Dorothy did occasionally exhibit cottonmouth on *WML?*, albeit few and far between instances, the exact cause could be attributed to any number of reasons: nerves, medication side effects, a problem with her jaw—which Lee Israel made brief mention of in her book but about which she did not know any details—and not necessarily drugs or booze.

TMJ, for example, refers to the Temporomandibular Joint. That is a hinge that connects the jaw to the temporal bones of the skull, which are in front of each ear. It allows you to move your jaw up and down and side to side, so you can talk, chew and yawn. The condition can be caused by movement of the soft fusion or disc between the ball and socket of the joint, arthritis, stress, or the clenching or grinding of the teeth.

It's also documented that people with severe cases of anemia, which DK battled, can develop mouth ulcers and a sore or inflamed tongue.

Note that Sinatra always made fun of Dorothy's appearance by calling her—among other insulting names—"a chinless wonder," and the shape of her lower jaw might well have caused physical pain that sometimes interfered with talking.

Kilgallen was most likely a social drinker. Recall all the film and theater premiers she attended as part of her line of work, plus high society soirées where alcohol would have freely flowed. She was able to cultivate sources and score major scoops that made the front pages of newspapers across the nation. She churned out copy with record speed for her daily newspaper column. Had Dorothy turned up intoxicated for her live appearances on *WML?* or the live radio show she co-anchored with her husband, she would have lost those gigs. By all accounts, she was a good mother who was deeply involved in her children's lives.

Charles Simpson not only denied DK was an alcoholic, but said he never witnessed her imbibe.

"I never have seen her take a drink. I've seen her drink things, but I don't think it was alcoholic. Truthfully, in the evenings, when I would have a drink, she'd say 'Do you want a drink Charles? Go out to the bar and make one' and I'd make myself a Scotch and water or something, while I was doing her makeup or hair. She usually had a glass of iced water—almost always."

In a conversation with *Midwest Today*, Marlin Swing spoke of a "sad" evening he spent with Kilgallen at the opening of Irving Berlin's final show.

"Richard had several nightclubs and restaurants, so he was always occupied, so I went to most of the openings with Dorothy. And we went to the biggest opening of the season, because everybody knew it was going to be Irving Berlin's last show, *Mr. President* (which opened on Oct. 20, 1962, at the St. James Theatre).

"When I got to Dorothy's house, before we got in the car, I saw the condition that she was in. She could hardly stand up, and I was helping her put on her earrings, and I said 'you don't want to go, do you? Let's stay here.' And she said no, she wanted to go! She HAD to go to that opening.

"And the traffic, our limousine could hardly get through the street, and when we got to the theater...I held her elbow so tightly trying to lead her, so that she wouldn't fall down in the theater. Then at intermission, I knew she shouldn't talk to anybody, so we went across the street. I thought having a drink in a bar was less evil than having her talk to people. So we went over there. Afterward, the next day, her arm was black and blue because I had had to hold her so strongly. That was during one of her drinking periods."

He added, "I liked Dorothy very much. She was two different people. She was this professional bitch to the world, but to her friends, she was a soft, wonderful friend. Totally different."

A newspaper strike hit the *Journal-American* from Dec. 10, 1962 through March 1963. Although it's important to point out with her column being syndicated, this would only have impacted Dorothy so much. Also, she worked exclusively from her home office and was said to only stop by the newspaper office a few times per year. She wrote that readers were hungry for any news they could get their hands on.

"The newspaper strike has given an old national flavor to New Yorkers crushed on the subways. Straphangers are reading anything and everything available, with the luckier ones absorbed in newspapers from Washington, Boston, Newark, Philadelphia, and even as far away as Chicago, Denver and Los Angeles."

A Crowded Marriage

Richard knew of DK and Ray's relationship but did not intervene initially. One evening in early 1963, DK, Ray, his friend Allen Stokes and others, went out clubbing. They stopped at the Left Bank, the establishment Richard owned, whereupon Dorothy and Johnnie began necking in front of her husband who coped with the embarrassment by drinking.

The lovers then snuck off to Dorothy's townhouse where Richard found them in a compromising position in the Black Room. He ordered Ray out of his home, threatening to kill him if he ever saw his wife again. Dorothy begged Ray to take her with him, but he reminded her a scandal like that could cost her dearly, in terms of her television work and newspaper column. Dorothy agreed to remain behind, but was inconsolable.

Lee Israel related an incident, which on the surface, could have appeared to be a cry for help. One afternoon in mid-March, DK's assistant Anne Hamilton found her employer "wandering aimlessly on the fifth floor of the house." Was she depressed over Ray? Had she been drinking? Not wanting to leave DK by herself, Anne reached out to butler James Clement and maid Lempy Osterman for guidance. Finally Richard was summoned (he had been sleeping). Dorothy ended up spending a month in the hospital due to anemia.

Dorothy's blood had been detected as pink in color, and her symptoms also included mental confusion. This forced Richard to carry their radio show without her for about a month before it was suspended in mid-April.

Swing recalled Dorothy battled anemia most of her life but was otherwise in good health.

"She was afraid to eat because she was afraid of getting fat and she'd drink a lot of vodka," he said. "She smoked occasionally—one or two cigarettes."

A Summer Bride

In July 1963, Dorothy's daughter Jill Ellen Kollmar wed Lawrence A. Grossman at the Roman Catholic Church of St. Vincent Ferrer. Jill became an interior designer, later getting interested in clothing. At age fifteen, while attending boarding school at Knox School on Long Island, she had befriended a classmate named Marianne Smith. Years passed and the two women teamed up in 1976 to form the clothing brand Smith Kollmar, landing their products in department stores including Bergdorf Goodman, Lord & Taylor, Bloomingdale's and Macy's.

As Lee Israel explained of DK's relationship to her children, "Jill was not the first of Dorothy's children to marry. But this was the first marriage she deigned to talk about. When Dickie took a wife at least a year before, Dorothy apparently disapproved. Announcements were sent out by the bride's people. Bennett Cerf received his in the mail, and took it with him to *What's My Line?*. While the panelists were being made up, he shouted to Dorothy, 'Am I supposed to do something about this?' He was less concerned with gift etiquette than with teasing Dorothy, whom he knew to have an abundance of off-limit areas. She said nothing and looked sheepish."

The Profumo Affair And Putting Out A Fire

She felt reporting on court proceedings fulfilled her journalistic yearning to cover breaking news and the fast pace that work required. In the summer of 1963, she traveled to England for the much sensationalized trial of Stephen Ward which brimmed with a "bizarre cast" of characters she noted.

She described the first time she laid eyes on him thusly, "There was nothing at all dramatic in his appearance. He looked neat, and intelligent, and a trifle fidgety, like a man who badly wanted a cigarette...On the first day of studying him, he appeared to me to be a homosexual. There was a precision about him that seemed significant, a soft reluctance in the way he used his fine hands."

Ward was a British osteopath who figured into the Profumo Affair, a scandal that resulted in the resignation of John Profumo, the Secretary of State for War and led to the defeat of the Conservative government subsequently. Ward was convicted of living off the immoral earnings of prostitutes and died of a drug overdose on August 3 before he was sentenced.

"My paper gave (trials) a great play. They upped circulation for the paper which pleases you when you hear that," she later said.

Richard Kollmar was ambitious, but was also a troubled man with a drinking problem. Dorothy often had to care for him. For instance, in September, he fell asleep with a lit cigarette, setting his bed on fire. (The bed Dorothy would later be found dead in, in a room in which she did not usually sleep, as it was the "show bedroom" guests saw). DK, along with son Kerry and his governess Margaret Magee, dragged him from the room after discovering his condition. Carried out of their residence unconscious by firefighters, he was taken to Roosevelt Hospital for treatment of burns to his hands and "smoke poisoning," and discharged after one day.

He filled the void left from their radio show by sinking even deeper into a depressive state, while Dorothy furthered her career as a crime reporter and astute observer of geopolitics.

PART II

7
The Crime of the Century

According to Secret Service logs, President John F. Kennedy arrived in the Oval Office at 9:45 a.m. on Saturday, Jan. 26, 1963 and had a smattering of brief meetings. He spoke with the U.S. Ambassador to Senegal for fifteen minutes; David Ormsby-Gore (the Ambassador of Great Britain) for a half hour; and then chatted with family friend, painter Bill Walton and publisher of Gannett Newspapers, Paul Miller (the latter two off the record). By 12:35 p.m., the president was free to head for Glen Ora, the new home Jacqueline had designed and they had built at Middleburg, Virginia.

But JFK did not leave the Executive Mansion by helicopter until 1:53 p.m. He postponed having lunch and taking a nap—which he routinely did during mid-day—and instead played host to an old friend from New York: Dorothy Kilgallen.

She had taken her son Kerry to Washington, D.C. for the weekend and had called press secretary Pierre Salinger ahead of time to inquire about a tour of the White House. DK had a special affinity for Salinger, who once entertained her and other reporters by "playing the piano—everything from Bach, his favorite, to *Melancholy Baby*" for a half hour.

He told her to come at 1 p.m. and that someone in his office would be there to show them around. She and her son showed up a little early—which coincided with JFK's last meeting for the day.

Recounting the memorable visit, Dorothy wrote that the press secretary greeted her and Kerry and then, "The three of us were standing in the great long Cabinet room, examining the tall black leather swivel chairs that the Cabinet members take home with them when they leave office, looking at the silver name plaque on the back of each, when suddenly the door at one end of the room opened.

"A familiar silhouette stood in the doorway, waving and a familiar famous voice called out: 'Hi Dorothy. Come on into the office.'

"I was incredulous.

"'Is that the President?' I asked Mr. Salinger. He grinned. 'Yes. He asked you to go in.'

"I grabbed Kerry's hand and walked as fast as I could without running. President Kennedy waited smiling in the doorway. We shook hands, and I introduced my son. The President shook hands with him gravely and ushered us in.

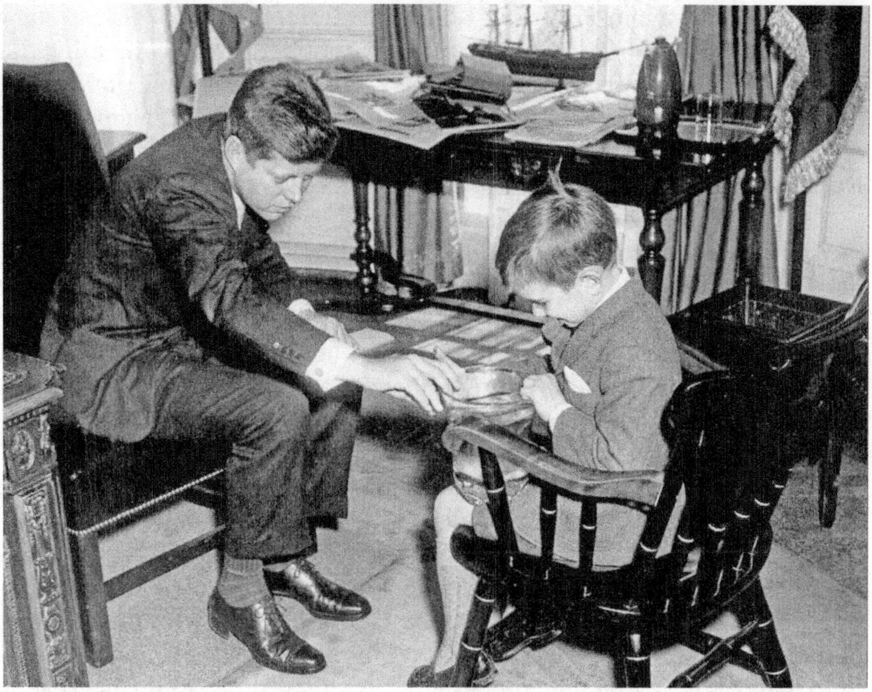

President Kennedy enjoyed welcoming young visitors to the Oval Office.

"'This is my office, Kerry,' he said. 'How do you like it?'

"He pointed out the presidential seal on the rug and showed us the whale's tooth which had been given to him by Mrs. Kennedy as a surprise, and which he liked so much she bought him another. He let Kerry hold it.

"The President took a gold tie clip modeled in the shape of the PT-109 and clipped it to Kerry's tie, which by an amusing coincidence was exactly like the 'old school' tie the President was wearing. As he did so he winked at me and said: 'I hope this is all right. I don't know whether Kerry is a Democrat or a Republican.'

"'I don't either, Mr. President,' I said. 'But I have a feeling that after today he may well be a Democrat.'

"Then, like a host who is concerned that he may not have done quite enough for an honored guest, the President called out again to Mr. Salinger and presented Kerry with a ballpoint pen engraved with 'John F. Kennedy' and 'The White House.'" Kerry explained to the president that every boy in his third grade class had written a letter, to be presented during the visit.

"I gave them to Mr. Salinger," Dorothy quoted her son as saying. "Our teacher told us that statistics show you can only read one out of every 50 letters you get, but she made us all write one, anyway."

"Well, I'll be sure to read yours, Kerry," he said. "Show me which one it is." Once again President Kennedy summoned his press secretary to bring him a thick packet held together by rubber bands, containing the handwritten letters from Kerry's class. "The President held them while Kerry sorted through them for his own," Dorothy recalled. The most powerful man in the world made sure he read the letter penned by young Kerry Kollmar.

After the visit to the Oval Office, JFK took the pair out on the terrace and pointed out the Rose Garden that the First Lady had worked so hard to restore, daughter Caroline's tree house out on the South Lawn, and where her pony, Macaroni also used to frolic.

It was the memory of this once-in-a-lifetime encounter that came to Dorothy's mind the afternoon of Nov. 22, 1963, when President John F. Kennedy was murdered in Dallas, Texas. Governor John Connally, who had also been riding in the motorcade, had been seriously wounded. About forty-five minutes later, Dallas police officer J.D. Tippit was shot dead in a residential neighborhood in the Oak Cliff section of the city. The crimes were soon blamed on a twenty-four year old ex-Marine, Lee Harvey Oswald despite his declaration of being "a patsy."

Even before the visit to the White House, DK had written glowingly of the president, which wasn't always a popular position to take. In a column dated Aug. 1, 1962, she published a letter she'd received from reader T.E. Sesbeau, in which he said the columnist had "a lot of nerve to state that JFK is 'America's Sweetheart'" because, "The thinking Democrats today know that JFK and his Harvard Socialists and 'pink' loving apologists have taken over their party." He went on to say how worldly he was and traveled even more than "a certain authority (?) named Dorothy Kilgallen."

She took him to task in her reply. "You are outnumbered, Mr. Sesbeau. And I really don't think that flying around in a plane makes you any more of a political or social expert than the average airline hostess. What do you learn in an airplane? I do agree with you that a newspaper writer has an obligation. As I look at it, that obligation is to tell the truth. I believe the truth is that if JFK ran for the presidency tomorrow—against anyone you can name—he would win. Sincerely, Dorothy Kilgallen, the authority."

Nightmare On Elm Street

Friday, Nov. 22, 1963 had started out damp and overcast in Dallas with 0.06 inches of rain as a cool front was making its way across northern Texas. The local weather forecast had called for more rain before the day was over, but it turned sunny and bright in the late morning hours. At 11:38 a.m. CST, President and Mrs. Kennedy arrived at Love Field airport in northwest Dallas aboard Air Force One after a thirteen minute flight from nearby Carswell Air Force Base, west of Fort Worth.

Barely a half hour before this, six key members of the president's Cabinet left Honolulu for Japan, after their plane refueled. It was highly unusual, if not unheard of, for so many high government officials to be away from Washington as a group at the same time. The fact that press secretary Pierre Salinger was sent to Japan instead of to Texas was also odd. If he had been on the visit to Dallas, he would have interceded when someone rearranged the sequencing of the vehicles in the motorcade and opened up lapses in security.

The two-day visit to Texas by the president was rather unusual in one important respect: the First Lady did not ordinarily accompany him on such political trips. Although all events except a Democratic fundraising dinner in Austin were organized on a nonpartisan basis, the tour was understood to be a prelude to JFK's impending campaign to win re-election. The itinerary included stops in San Antonio, Houston and Fort Worth the day before, with a luncheon scheduled for Dallas, followed by a stay at the ranch of Vice President Lyndon Johnson in Johnson City Friday night.

Local TV stations broadcast live coverage of the president's arrival in Dallas and had planned to carry the speech he was scheduled to give during a mid-day luncheon at the Trade Mart convention center.

But there had been concerns about the safety of President Kennedy as the city was a hotbed of reactionary conservatism and there was a feeling of hatred towards him. A few weeks prior, Ambassador Adlai Stevenson had been accosted and spat upon by protestors. So before the president arrived, Police Chief Jesse Curry had gone on local television to make an unusual plea to the citizens of Dallas. He said, "Because of the unfortunate incident that occurred here during the visit of Ambassador Stevenson, people everywhere in the world will be hyper critical of our behavior. Nothing must occur that is disrespectful or degrading to the President of the United States. He is entitled to the highest respect of all of our citizens. And the law enforcement agencies in this area are going to do everything within their power to ensure that no untoward accident or incident occurs. We will take immediate action if any suspicious conduct is observed. And we also urge all good citizens to be alert to such conduct."

Travel by the president was especially risky that November 1963, because authorities had learned of credible assassination threats against him in Chicago, Tampa and Miami, involving men with high powered rifles and telescopic sights planning to shoot JFK from a tall building and/or overpass. FBI head J. Edgar Hoover had alerted the Secret Service to the plots, and more information was gathered by the SS and Miami police.

A number of people close to Mr. Kennedy had fairly begged him to cancel his visit to Dallas—as he had aborted his Chicago trip—but he replied that the Secret Service had told him they were taking every precaution to assure his safety. He could not stop worrying aloud, however, sharing his concerns with his wife Jackie when they arrived in Texas.

On just the Fort Worth leg of the trip, at least 508 persons had participated in protective efforts. The police department there had assigned three hundred officers, the Carswell Air Force Base Police: eighty, the Tarrant County Sheriff's Department: sixty and the Texas State Police: five. The Secret Service provided thirty-two. The Fort Worth Fire Department and the River Oaks Police Department also contributed personnel to guard the exits and stairwells at the hotel where the Kennedys were staying that night. Every floor and window facing an area where the president might be was also checked.

By contrast, security in Dallas was shockingly lax. No orders were given to monitor open windows, the sheriff instructed his men to *not* participate in security, there were far fewer police officers in evidence than would be expected and at the last minute a motorcade route was approved which entailed a zig-zag between buildings that represented a unique opportunity for cross-fire.

In fact, David Belin, lead counsel for the investigative body that became known as the Warren Commission, later conceded to *Midwest Today* that the route chosen took JFK through what was probably "the only place in Dallas where someone could have looked out of a high window and aimed a rifle at the motorcade with a direct line shot."

A crowd estimated at more than eight thousand persons enthusiastically greeted the Kennedys upon their arrival at the airport, and the smiling First Couple reciprocated the warm feelings by shaking as many hands along a fence line as they could. Jack and Jackie had never looked more attractive and alive as a couple.

JFK was a marked man.

They, along with Gov. and Mrs. John Connally rode that day in the dark blue Lincoln Continental presidential limousine, code named SS-100-X, with the top removed, which turned it into a convertible. This left them exposed to the quarter of a million people who lined both sides of the streets, sometimes thirty deep, to catch a glimpse of and cheer the Kennedys. This sort of turnout for a president is unheard of today.

Nobody was more surprised by the warm reception

than the traveling press, who had been taking bets on how long it would be before the shooting commenced. Little did they know that their dark humor would become a dark reality.

The sun was so bright that Jackie kept putting on her sunglasses and the president had to gently remind her three times to take them off, because the crowd wanted to see how beautiful she was. Mrs. Kennedy was attired that day in a wool bouclé, double-breasted, raspberry pink, navy trim collared suit that was matched with a trademark pink pillbox hat and white gloves.

The president had told her, "There are going to be all these rich, Republican women at that lunch...wearing mink coats and diamond bracelets. And you've got to look as marvelous as any of them. Be simple—show these Texans what good taste really is." So she traipsed in and out of their room, holding dresses in front of her, so he could help her decide what to wear. She chose an outfit that was one of his favorites, one the trend-setting Mrs. Kennedy had worn on several occasions.

They were only five minutes from their luncheon destination when their motorcade made a right turn onto Houston Street on the outskirts of downtown. A short block later, as it got to Elm Street, it then swung sharply to the left—so much so the custom-built limousine (more than twenty feet long) had trouble avoiding the far curb. The driver, Will Greer, had to slow almost to a stop to make the tight, hairpin turn.

This was the area known as Dealey Plaza, and with the unusually sharp turn, the President of the United States was being taken into an ambush situation that would permit gunfire from multiple directions.

Local law enforcement officials knew that, and the Secret Service did too, because there had been several meetings to discuss security and the advance men had even driven the route. But no additional protection was accorded the motorcade in this area. In fact, SS agent Clint Hill, who had been riding on the left rear bumper in a crouched down position during much of the parade, incomprehensibly hopped off the back of the limo and returned to the left front running board of the follow-up car less than ninety seconds before the assassination.

Spectators were allowed to stand behind fences, trees and other visual impediments but police were told to keep the park-like triangle on the south side of Elm Street free of all onlookers and it was this area toward which bullets fired at the president were aimed.

As the car proceeded at 11.2 miles per hour down a slight incline and soft "S" curve on Elm Street, gunshots rang out. In a few seconds, a wife lost her husband, children lost their father, the United States lost its leader and the nation was forever changed. This unimaginable horror—the public execution of a president, boldly carried out under a brilliant blue autumnal sky and noonday sun by sinister forces for all the world to see—has forever left a dark stain on American history. The democratic choice of our top leader by millions of voters was nullified with the squeeze of a trigger, and the people responsible for this coup have never been brought to justice. And that's exactly what it was; a *coup* is defined as being "a sudden, violent, and unlawful seizure of power from a government." A cynical cover-up remains in place—weakened by informed challenges—but it's still the operative narrative that gets mindlessly embraced.

A Mad Dash To The Hospital

When the mortally wounded president arrived at Parkland Hospital in Dallas, Texas at 12:36 p.m. on Nov. 22, 1963, and Secret Service agents tried to remove him from the limousine, the First Lady resisted. She was still cradling her husband in her arms.

Jacqueline Kennedy's Secret Service agent, Clint Hill, remembered, "That's the one thing that I can't get out of my mind—the picture of him lying in her lap, with his head exposed to me, just looking into the back of his head, into his brain, his eyes fixed, blood and brains and bone fragments all over the car.

"The right rear portion of the President's head was missing...I saw a piece of his skull with hair on it lying in the seat.

"Mrs. Kennedy was completely covered with blood—there was so much blood you could not tell if there had been any other wound or not, and the problem was, she didn't want anyone to see him, because it was a very gory situation. So I removed my coat and covered the President's head and upper chest, and then she let go." Agent Sam Kinney helped.

Meanwhile, Vice President and Mrs. Lyndon Johnson had been hurriedly escorted into the hospital and isolated. Phyllis Hall, a Parkland nurse, described seeing "a very frightened" LBJ, who was observed holding his chest. Witnesses speculated to reporters that Johnson might be having a heart attack, given his health history.

The doctors and nurses at Parkland made a valiant effort to save the life of the thirty-fifth president of the United States, perhaps not immediately realizing that he had sustained fatal wounds. He had been brought in on a gurney, laying on his back, and there was no time to completely examine him before treatment commenced. He was making agonal attempts to breathe, so restoring airflow was a first priority.

Mrs. Kennedy had presumed her husband was dead, and was bewildered by all the rushing around the medical team was doing. She was largely ignored, left to wait in the hallway, her clothing drenched in blood, clots and brain tissue that was literally falling off her skirt. One of her white gloves was now stiff and red-brown; she had lost the other one. Finally, someone got her a chair. The Secret Service ignored her. Periodically she would go into Trauma Room One, where JFK had been taken.

Dr. Charles Carrico, a resident in surgery, was the first man in the room. The operating table had been shoved out the door. They did not want to jar the president by lifting him off the gurney. Then Dr. Malcolm Perry, an assistant professor of surgery, arrived.

He was soon joined by Dr. Charles Baxter, another assistant professor of surgery. More doctors rushed in. It is officially documented they were Robert McClelland, assistant professor of surgery; M.T. Jenkins, chairman of anesthesiology; Fouad Basheur, associate professor of internal medicine; Adolph Gisecke, clinical associate in anesthesiology; Paul Peters, assistant professor of urology; Ronald Jones, senior resident in surgery; Charles Crenshaw, surgery resident; Gene Akin, anesthesiology resident; Jackie Hunt, anesthesiology fellow; Don Curtis, oral surgery resident; and Kenneth Salyer, surgery resident. Kemp Clark, chairman of neurosurgery, had run all the way from the medical school. He was one of the last of the team to arrive, but he got there within five minutes.

The president's doctor, Rear Admiral George Burkley—who had been repositioned to the back of the motorcade under protest, was trapped on the bus that took White House staffers to the Trade Mart, blissfully unaware of what had happened farther ahead in the motorcade. So he had to hitch a ride to the hospital. Dr. Carrico recalled reading that Kennedy suffered adrenal deficiency and so he administered hydro-cortisone. (Burkley carried that with him but arrived too late at the hospital).

Dr. Jones began a "cut-down" on Kennedy's left arm to insert a catheter—a device to force more blood into a vein and keep the passage open. Curtis completed the same procedure on the left leg.

Lactated ringer's solution (sometimes called white blood and used until whole blood can be obtained) was pumped in. Soon a technician from the blood bank arrived with "O" negative blood (universal donor) and it was started. To feed the blood faster, hand pumps were used. The cart was elevated at the foot to help the blood get back to the heart.

John Kennedy had a small bullet hole in the front of his throat that looked like an entry wound, and was about three-eighths of an inch in diameter. One of the doctors noticed a frothing of the blood in the neck wound. "He's bubbling air," the doctor said. This means a possible hole in the lung. Peters and Baxter immediately inserted a tube into the right upper part of the chest, just below the shoulder, to re-expand the lungs to keep them from collapsing. A similar tube was inserted on the left.

Dr. Malcomb Perry asked his colleague, Dr. Robert McClelland, to stand at the head of the exam table and assist him with a small retractor as he slightly enlarged the anterior throat wound so as to be able to insert a breathing tube.

Seconds later, Joe Goldstrich, MD—who, at just twemty-five, was the youngest member of the Kennedy treatment team—stepped forward. Earlier that morning he had been "boning up" on having to do a tracheotomy on another patient under his care. In an interview done in 2020, Goldstrich said of JFK, "I saw the wound in the lower part of his neck. I looked in the neck wound and saw the cartilage of the trachea on the back side through the hole. I do not remember whether instruments had [yet] been used to expand the wound. I am clear, however, that I saw the posterior aspect of the trachea." This is significant, because it implies that a bullet entered the front of Kennedy's throat, and not the back side of the neck as the government later tried to claim.

Goldstrich, who went into the Army for two years in 1965, reflected that, "After a crash course in entrance and exit wounds by the field hospital commander (in the Dominican Republic)...based on what I had learned...I realized that JFK's throat wound was probably an entrance wound because the margins were so clean and the wound was so small." The doctor said that for years, he did not speak out publicly, "because I was afraid. There were so many people who were associated with the assassination who had died, sometimes by questionable means."

As treatment of the president was proceeding, Dr. McClelland—who was looking down at the leader of the free world from a vantage point of about eighteen inches above him—was shocked when he saw a massive wound in the back of Kennedy's skull.

He remarked to Dr. Perry, "'My God, have you seen the back of his head?' They said 'no, we just walked in here before you did, and we haven't seen anything but this hole in his neck.'

"I said, 'Well, there's a wound here in the back of his head on the right side that's at least five inches in diameter.' I could actually look down within the skull cavity and see that the whole right back half of the right southern hemisphere was gone. In fact, Mrs. Kennedy had come in carrying a portion of brain in her hand, and handed it to [a doctor] as soon as she came in.

"So the back half of the right side of his skull cavity was empty. And as I stood there, the right half of his cerebellum slowly fell out of that hole, onto the gurney."

Dr. Don Curtis said in 2013 that, "As soon as the doctor lifted the president's head, he said, 'Stop resuscitation. This is not compatible with life.'" Curtis reported that each physician in the room then looked at Kennedy's head. Curtis also looked, and he said, "the posterior part of his head was blown out."

However, the Parkland doctors apparently felt compelled to at least go through the motions of trying to save the president's life.

McClelland recalled, "Dr. Clark came in and stood over to the right side of the gurney, toward the EKG monitor and was looking at what Dr. Perry and Dr. [Charles] Baxter (the acting chief of surgery) were doing, and watching that monitor."

Kemp Clark wrote a letter labelled "TOP SECRET" to George Burkley dated Nov. 23, 1963 and later testified, "I then examined the wound in the back of the president's head. This was a large, gaping wound in the right posterior part...in the right occipito-parietal region...with cerebral and cerebellar tissue being damaged and exposed. There was considerable loss of scalp and bone tissue. There was considerable blood loss evident on the carriage, the floor, and the clothing of some of the people present. I would estimate 1,500 cc. of blood... As I was examining the president's wound, I felt for a carotid pulse and felt none. Therefore, I began external cardiac massage...Because of my position it was difficult to administer cardiac massage [so] cardiac massage was taken over by Dr. Malcomb Perry, who was more advantageously situated."

In his treatment summary memo to hospital administrator C.J. Price dated Nov. 22, 1963, M. T. Jenkins, M.D., Professor and Chairman of the Department of Anesthesiology was even more specific about Kennedy's injuries. He explained, "These described resuscitative activities were indicated as of first importance, and after they were carried out attention was turned to all other evidences of injury. There was a great laceration on the right side of the head (temporal and occipital), causing a great defect in the skull plate so that there was herniation and laceration of great areas of the brain, even to the extent that the cerebellum had protruded from the wound." **(Note: The occipital lobe is located at the *back* of the skull, just inside the hollow at the back of the head where the little bump is. The cerebellum is below that, at the base of the skull).**

Look at the diagram of the brain shown here. You can see how low on the back of Kennedy's head the major wound was, for it to involve the occipital lobe and cerebellum. This is indicative of an exit wound, not an entrance wound. (A bullet upon entry typically creates a hole about the same diameter as the missile; upon exit, after having tumbled, it creates a much larger hole, especially if a frangible, or "explosive" bullet is used, which appears to be the case in the head wound President Kennedy sustained).

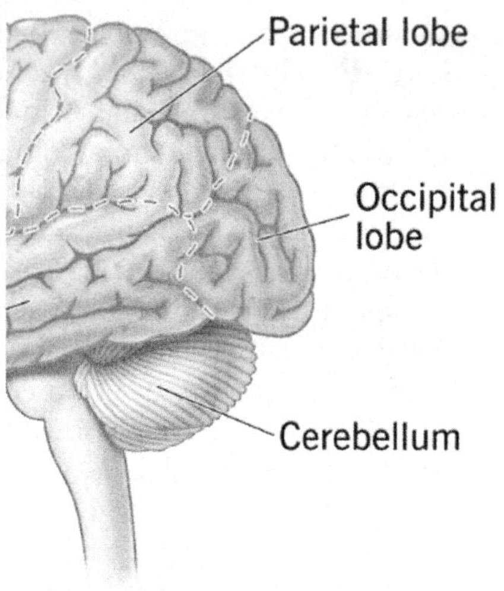

After being first struck by gunfire, with what appeared to be simultaneously inflicted wounds in the front of his throat and lower on his back, eyewitness photos and amateur movies show the president leaned over to the left, where Mrs. Kennedy was sitting, and turned his head more in her direction.

Some accounts say that JFK also had a small bullet wound in his right temple, (hidden by his thick hair), accounting for the massive blowout in the rear of his head. But a shot fired from above and behind could not have struck his right temple. It had to have come from the front.

Dr. Charles Crenshaw, who only spoke out years later, said, "In the occipito-parietal region at the right rear of the head, there was an avulsive wound nearly as large as a fist...I considered the throat wound to be an entrance wound and the large head wound to be an exit wound. Along with many of my Parkland colleagues, I believed at the time that President Kennedy had been hit twice from the front."

Later, to support the government fiction about all the injuries to Kennedy having been inflicted solely by a lone gunman firing from behind, the head wound was moved in a desperate and despicable ploy to make a "single bullet" theory seem more plausible. Audaciously, so-called autopsy pictures of the back of Kennedy's head entered into government evidence files show it to be intact, contrary to what multiple witnesses saw. They also depict an enormous wound *on the top* of the president's skull, which not a single doctor or nurse at Parkland ever observed.

Don Curtis, M.D., was just one of the doctors who later said that the photos he had seen, showing major trauma to the top of Kennedy's head, was not what he saw in Trauma Room One on Nov. 22, 1963.

So besides some photos being faked, it also became shockingly clear there had been alterations to JFK's corpse by the time the formal autopsy began at Bethesda Naval Hospital that night. Who had the power to do this? The mafia? Cuban factions? Obviously not.

Defenders of the lone assassin theory dismissively claim that the Parkland doctors were so busy treating President Kennedy they didn't have time to examine him closely. But that speculation is destroyed by the contemporaneous statements doctors made to the press, the previously secret and more detailed memos for the file and letters the Parkland medical team wrote on November 22 and 23, and vivid testimony they gave under oath within weeks. *All of the doctors present in Trauma Room One did examine Mr. Kennedy*. The only thing they didn't spot was a shallow back wound (that was not life threatening), because they did not turn him over.

Professor Joseph Valvano argues that, "Logic, reason, medical/forensic science, mathematics and biology dictate that the most important witnesses dealing with the assassination of JFK were the medical doctors and hospital staff at Parkland Memorial Hospital who...tried to save his life just after he was shot...Parkland Hospital had a reputation for medically treating patients from an economically disadvantaged neighborhood... The doctors and nurses who worked the emergency rooms were extremely experienced in severe medical trauma including gunshot wounds to the human body. It was these highly experienced medical doctors and nurses who were the first medically trained professionals to have access to the body of JFK within one hour of his being shot and who had the skill, the experience and the expertise to understand and be fully able to determine from what direction JFK had been shot based upon the gunshot wounds to his head and throat, wounds that they witnessed and tried to medically treat in Trauma Room One."

The Assassination Records Review Board (ARRB), which will be focused on later in this book, was the only independent agency to turn up additional major new evidence in the case. It found that at least forty-two credible witnesses saw the large wound in the rear of JFK's skull. This included highly trained medical staff at Parkland as well as at Bethesda, Dallas motorcycle escort officers, plus FBI and Secret Service agents who restated it to the ARRB years later. In addition, morticians who worked on Kennedy verified this and there were eyewitnesses close to the motorcade in Dealey Plaza who also described seeing the back of his head blasted away, confirming the statement that SS agent Clint Hill made during sworn testimony. He was the only agent who had run toward the car seconds after the last gunshot and climbed aboard, courageously sprawling over the back seat in an attempt to shield the First Couple.

Furthermore, Army experiments on skulls performed in 1964 showed that if a bullet *entered* that low on the skull, it would have exited from Kennedy's face. Yet no bullet exited his face.

SS man Roy Kellerman testified, "I walked around the president and wanted to look at his face—but I did not see any wounds on his face."

Parkland nurse Phyllis Hall said, "From the front, it didn't look bad at all. The damage was all back here" (patting the back of her head).

These contemporaneous observations are unimpeachable. Yet they have subsequently been altered and history rewritten to embrace the government's official storyline of shots only fired from the rear.

Dr. McClelland said that after "about seven or eight minutes, Dr. Clark looked at the [heart] monitor and saw that it had straight-lined. And he said, 'Mac you can stop now; he's gone.'"

Nurse Hall recalled that, "After doctor Clark had pronounced him [dead], he just walked right by Mrs. Kennedy without stopping and said 'Madam, your husband's dead.'" The time was 1 p.m. CST.

Meanwhile, shortly after 12:30 p.m., at Taylor Elementary in Cedar Rapids, Iowa, students returning from lunch were informed that the president had been wounded. Sixth grade social studies teacher Clara Johnson turned on a radio in her second floor classroom to listen to news bulletins over station WMT. Everyone sat in rapt attention as the drama unfolded. Allan Jackson, head anchor at CBS radio news headquarters in New York had interrupted regular programming, initially reading wire service copy off the teletype machines.

Dan Rather, a low-level CBS correspondent who was not even based in Dallas but who said he was in that city "by happenstance," called New York and was put on the air. This was his "big break" and he helped shape the public's perceptions—and misperceptions—of what transpired.

Rather told the network that there were unconfirmed reports that JFK had died. Jackson was handed a slip of paper reading "JFK DEAD" and immediately made the announcement at 1:22 p.m., reporting Kennedy's death as a fact (even though it had not been officially confirmed). Then the network played *The Star-Spangled Banner*.

Hearing this, Miss Johnson pointed her index finger at her students and said softly but firmly, "Class, always remember this moment. Because right now, the United States doesn't have a president."

Before school was dismissed at 3:30 p.m., principal Don Stonebreaker brought an early edition of *The Cedar Rapids Gazette* to Miss Johnson's sixth grade classroom to show pupils. A big black banner on the front page said: THE PRESIDENT IS DEAD.

At 1:33 p.m., Malcolm Kilduff, the assistant White House press secretary, made the official announcement in Dallas that President John Fitzgerald Kennedy had "died of a gunshot wound to the brain." He pointed to his right temple and cited Dr. Burkley as his source.

Dallas Reporters Encounter Censorship

Two of Dorothy Kilgallen's female counterparts who were reporters for Dallas newspapers tried to get out the truth about what happened, but were censored.

Mary Woodward was a junior reporter for the *Dallas Morning News*, who had walked over to Dealey Plaza during her lunch hour to watch the Kennedy motorcade. She was the journalist closest to the president and after witnessing the shocking spectacle of his murder right after he smiled and waved at her, rushed back to her office to file the story. She finished writing even before the formal announcement was made that the president had died. It ran under the headline: "Witness From The News Describes Assassination."

Ms. Woodward heard, "Three shots. And the second two shots were immediate; they came so quickly. The sound of one did not cease until the second shot. With the second and third shot, I did see the President being hit. I literally saw his head explode. So I felt that the shots had come—as I wrote in my article—from behind [where I was standing] and to the right, which would have been in the direction of the grassy knoll and the railroad overpass."

Her story appeared on the front page of an early edition of the newspaper. But because it contradicted the lone assassin theory—*which was already being promoted within minutes of Kennedy's murder*—Mary's eyewitness account was quickly pulled, and her version discounted.

"Civic leaders, responsible people—that would be the mayor, the managing editor of the paper—almost felt a responsibility to kind of not rock the boat perhaps," Ms. Woodward charitably lamented.

Dallas Mayor Earle Cabell was the brother of Charles Cabell, who

Dorothy's paper, the *Journal-American*, put out an "Extra" edition.

was deputy director of the Central Intelligence Agency until President Kennedy fired him in late 1962 along with Allen Dulles.

Another reporter who encountered censorship was Connie Kritzberg, who worked for the rival *Dallas Times Herald*. A couple of hours after the assassination, she did a phone interview with two of the doctors who had treated Kennedy at Parkland.

She explained, "I talked to Dr. Kemp Clark, who was neurosurgery, at Parkland Hospital and [also] Malcomb Perry. So I asked, 'how many wounds were there in the President?' And Dr. Kemp Clark said, 'there was a gaping wound in the back of the head.' And Dr. Perry said, 'of the wound I was working on was an entrance wound in the neck.' And I asked him where it was located; I asked him was it below the Adam's Apple. And he said 'yes, it was in the midline, in the front of the neck, below the Adam's Apple.' And he said three times it was an entrance wound from the front.

"And so I wrote a very simple story, only about twelve inches long and turned it in." The next morning, when she saw her article in print, Ms. Kritzberg was shocked to find that what she submitted was changed. "I found in the story, about the third paragraph, there had been a very unprofessional sentence inserted that said: 'a doctor admitted it was possible one wound.' Well I was very upset. I called the city desk and talked to one of the assistant city editors whom I respected quite a bit and I said, 'Who changed my story? Who put in that sentence?' And he immediately knew what I was talking about. And he said 'the FBI.' A story couldn't be printed because there was more than one shot and that one came from the front. It had to be altered no matter how crudely, to conform to the official story that there were three shots from one place from one man and there was only one man who committed the murder."

Obviously, these women didn't have the clout that Dorothy Kilgallen did, and hence they were at the mercy of their heavy-handed and cowardly editors who interfered with them telling their readers the truth.

It is clear that a sinister cover-up was already unfolding and the script had been written before any shots were fired. The media were fed a pack of lies and so misinformed the public.

There is absolutely no way that authorities could possibly be sure the attack was not part of a conspiracy—either foreign or domestic—before an investigation had even gotten underway. Yet the American people were told that the man guilty of murdering the president as well as a Dallas police officer had been arrested within an hour and a half of the shootings, that he fired three shots at the Kennedy motorcade, had acted alone, and that the case was closed even before formal charges had been filed!

This was absurd and not everyone was gullible enough to believe it. Dorothy Kilgallen knew a conspiracy was afoot and worked to prove it.

More Melodrama At Parkland

There are several major peculiarities that occurred that afternoon which suggest something diabolical was transpiring even more so than what was commonly known.

As Clint Hill had seen the massive head wound and knew that JFK was fatally injured, upon arrival at Parkland Hospital, he made a call to the local Dallas switchboard that had been set up to accommodate SS communications. He advised the White House Situation Room of what had happened. Then he phoned the O'Neal funeral home, the closest one to Parkland. He recalled, "I identified myself and told them that there had been a shooting and that we needed a casket IMMEDIATELY. The best one that they had. And that it was for the president."

Assuming O'Neal's—which was only two and a half miles away from the hospital—received the call by at least 1 p.m. and took fifteen minutes to load a casket, then another ten minutes to drive to the hospital, SS agents were in a position to quickly unload a heavy bronze casket upon its arrival at Parkland at least by about 1:25 p.m.

Meanwhile, Dr. Robert McClelland, who lingered momentarily in the trauma room, observed Mrs. Kennedy enter shortly after 1 p.m.—as soon as the president was officially declared dead. She first bent over and kissed JFK's bare foot, which was sticking out from under the sheet as he lay on a gurney. Then she walked along the cart and stood by the president's right shoulder. At that moment, a priest—The Very Rev. Oscar Huber—entered the room and walked over to the president's head on the left side and turned down the sheet.

Mrs. Kennedy bent over and kissed her husband's right cheek. Then she picked up his right hand, held it in both of hers, and pressed it on her left cheek, resting it on her husband's chest, then laid her head on it. According to McClelland, the priest leaned over and whispered in Jack Kennedy's ear, "If thou liveth..." as he administered the Last Rites of the Catholic Church. The First Lady then wondered what she could leave with Jack. They had already put his Saint Christopher's medal in the coffin with their prematurely born infant son, Patrick, who had died only three days after birth in August. (The medal is a popular symbol of protection and guidance for those who embark on journeys, both physical and spiritual). Lacking that, Jacqueline slipped off her wedding ring and placed it on her beloved spouse's little finger. Then she and the priest left the room, as did any remaining doctors. The time was 1:10 p.m.

Orderly David Sanders hurriedly began cleaning up Trauma Room One—which looked like a blood bath. There was so much blood, sheets had been laid on the floor to try to prevent the staff from slipping.

Twenty-two year old nurse Diana Bowron, who had rushed out to the emergency loading dock with a stretcher and tried to assist in removing the president from the limousine, was with him for the duration of his treatment. She was from England and had only been in this country three months. Ms. Bowron washed the president's hair after his death, and before he was placed in a casket. So she knew well the condition of Kennedy's head wound and confirmed it was in the back. She saw no other wounds on his head. Bowron and nurse Margaret Hinchcliffe spent roughly twenty minutes wrapping the president's bloodied body in sheets.

By happenstance, ambulance driver Aubrey Rike and his assistant, Dennis "Peanuts" McGuire, were on a call at Parkland Memorial Hospital. Rike said the Secret Service "told us we would have to remove the remains into a casket" that was soon to be delivered by their employer, Vernon O'Neal. Mr. McGuire said, "Mr. O'Neal come up in our '64 Cadillac hearse and we unloaded it and took the casket...into where the president was... [Then] we took him out and put him into the hearse. About two or three of the Secret Service men got into the hearse and just drove off and left Mr. O'Neal and the rest of us just standing there."

McGuire made it sound like after placing the president's body in a bronze casket, which occured around 1:30 p.m., the hearse left immediately. But it did not. First the Secret Service ordered everyone out of the room and told the men to wait outside in the parking lot. The hearse didn't depart the hospital for at least a half hour. Meanwhile, the casket into which JFK had been placed was in the sole custody of the SS. The importance of this will become apparent as this story unfolds.

First a dramatic scene played out at Parkland. Dr. Earl Rose, a forensic pathologist, professor of medicine and lecturer of law confronted

Secret Service agents who were preparing to take JFK's body from the hospital and put it aboard Air Force One. Dr. Rose informed them that state law required that he do a post-mortem examination before the body could be released. The federal government at that time had no jurisdiction over the president's remains. Informed of this impasse, Lyndon Johnson—before he left for Love Field at 1:26 p.m.—told the agents to shoot Rose if necessary. LBJ portrayed himself as chivalrous and wanting to consider Mrs. Kennedy's feelings. But he displayed no such chivalry by commandeering Air Force One instead of taking Air Force Two—an identical plane—back to Washington. He even took over the private bedroom on the aircraft and deprived Mrs. Kennedy of using it to lay down.

An impasse ensued whereby Rose phoned a justice of the peace to come to the hospital to mediate. The impasse lasted about forty-five minutes and drew everyone's attention. As the showdown reached a climax, a shouting match ensued in the main hallway, with the SS yelling profanities at Dr. Rose and Dallas police, while a grief-stricken and literally shell-shocked Mrs. Kennedy stood quietly by, observing all this.

Finally, Secret Service agents brandished guns and threatened the Dallas medical examiner. Roy Kellerman physically manhandled Dr. Rose by lifting him off the floor and setting him aside as they wheeled the casket out the door, over the objections of Dallas police.

Dr. Robert Crenshaw, who observed all this, later commented sardonically, "Strange, I thought, this president is getting more protection dead than he did when he was alive. How brave of these men, wearing their Brooks Brothers suits with icons of distinction (color-coded Secret Service buttons) pinned to their lapels, willing to shoot an unarmed doctor to secure a corpse...Dr. Kemp Clark wanted to physically detain the coffin [too], but the men with guns acted like tough guys with specific orders. A period of [many] years has neither erased the fear that I felt nor diminished the impression that that incident made upon me."

In a 1992 interview published in the *Journal of the American Medical Association*, Earl Rose said, "The law was broken" and that a "Texas autopsy would have assured a tight chain of custody of all the evidence." This was a curious statement on the part of Dr. Rose, hinting at the possibility Kennedy's body was at some point diverted before it was autopsied.

Was the Secret Service afraid that upon opening the bronze casket it would be discovered that Kennedy's remains had already been surreptitiously transferred to a body bag and a cheap military shipping casket so that it could be loaded unobserved aboard a military plane at Naval Air Station in Dallas and flown to Washington?

You read that right. There is evidence that *two* caskets left Dallas for Washington on Nov. 22, 1963 and that the one that everybody—including Mrs. Kennedy—assumed contained her husband's body was empty, while his remains were actually transported covertly. The possible reasons for this Machiavellian plan will be explored herein.

This is not some wild-eyed conspiracy theory. Contemporaneous official documents and testimony from multiple government witnesses suggest a military shipping casket said to be carrying the remains of President Kennedy arrived at Bethesda and was logged in at 6:35 p.m. EST, twenty minutes before the hearse carrying Mrs. Kennedy and the bronze casket (which was empty) arrived at 6:55 p.m. How to explain this?

It appears that an elaborate subterfuge took place so that Kennedy's corpse could be examined and altered after it left Dallas and before the autopsy formally commenced at Bethesda Naval Hospital in Maryland that night.

There is general agreement amongst most JFK assassination researchers that the two casket scenario took place and that Kennedy's body was probed for bullets (which were presumably removed) and surgical procedures done to conceal that he was fired upon by more than one shooter. That is based largely on the drastic differences between the wounds seen in Dallas and the corpse as it appeared when it arrived for autopsy. The chain of custody was definitely broken. But as to how and when the body ended up in a cheaper metal casket is open to speculation.

Some otherwise serious-minded researchers have come up with a scenario which this author finds truly preposterous, but it's worth mentioning, if for no other reason than to challenge it. The contention is that JFK's corpse was removed from Air Force One shortly after the bronze casket was taken aboard, and that this transfer took place right after the arrival of First Lady Jackie Kennedy at 2:18 p.m. and before Lyndon Johnson took the oath of office as the new president at 2:38 p.m. But that means barely ten minutes to accomplish a Houdini-like feat, unobserved by any of the more than forty passengers on the plane (nearly twice the usual number), who were crammed in there like sardines in a can, amidst sweltering heat.

The first problem with that hypothesis is that Mrs. Kennedy retired to the bedroom for a few minutes upon boarding the aircraft, where she was shocked to find Lyndon stretched out on the bed. Although he made a hasty retreat, she at least spent a brief while by herself. So that left little time for the switcheroo.

Esteemed Kennedy assassination researcher Douglas Horne, who served on the ARRB, seems to imply the body was simply removed from the bronze casket and carried out the aft galley door, and down the steps in broad daylight without anyone noticing! He assures, "There was plenty of space for a human body lying in a horizontal position in the aft luggage compartment." It is incomprehensible that this scenario played out because JFK's bloodied corpse would have made a mess in the plane, not to mention been observable by onlookers outside, if not inside, the aircraft.

According to Horne's hypothesis, after Mr. Kennedy is stuffed unceremoniously in the baggage compartment and the plane arrives at Andrews Air Force base hours later, along with the rest of the presidential party, JFK's corpse was supposedly removed in the dark to a waiting helicopter that took off at 6:23 p.m. (a mere three minutes after LBJ departed for the White House), and traveled to Bethesda Naval Hospital, where it landed in a nearby parking lot seven to nine minutes later. Someone there then inexplicably unwrapped Kennedy's sheet-clad body, rendering him naked, stuffed him in a zippered body bag, put him in a cheap military shipping casket—all of this in the dark, of course—and then drove him up to the loading dock by 6:35 p.m. *Seriously?*

While it is fairly certain Kennedy's body was indeed flown by helicopter to Bethesda and arrived at 6:35 p.m., such an arrival time offered little advantage in facilitating inspection of and alteration to his body at Bethesda—where Horne and some others have alleged it occurred—over the arrival of the bronze casket twenty minutes later at 6:55 p.m.

The alleged reason for this Keystone Kops scenario was because the Secret Service was supposedly so rattled and so scared that before Air Force One could take off from Dallas, a posse of local law enforcement officers might race out to Love Field, sirens wailing, and block the runway with their cars, thus preventing the plane from taking off! So they hid JFK's body in the luggage compartment.

This is laughable.

They had the new President of the United States on board, who was Commander-in-Chief of the Armed Forces. Dallas had a local military base and he could easily have ordered troops to assemble at Love Field and assure that Air Force One took off. No local law enforcement agency could ever dare to try to thwart a military operation like that. So the showdown at Parkland was a red herring.

Yet we still have the problem of there being two caskets.

How and why this could have taken place is an important but little known footnote to history, and one that Dorothy Kilgallen surely would have discovered had she had access to the documentation that only recently has been declassified. Based on a far more rational interpretation of events, this author believes the riddle can be solved.

But First...A Cover Story

An important clue has been overlooked. Curiously timed was the news bulletin broadcast on CBS television by Walter Cronkite at 1:23 p.m. on November 22 that stated: "A Secret Service man was also killed in the fusillade of shots." ABC News in Washington reported, "A Secret Service agent apparently was shot by one of the assassin's bullets." ABC repeated the story: "One of the Secret Service agents traveling with the president was killed today." ABC's Bill Lord then reported he "did confirm the death of the Secret Service agent...One of the Secret Service agents was killed...Secret Service agents usually walk right beside the car." Eddie Barker, KRLD-TV, a CBS affiliate in Dallas close to the scene, told viewers, "The word is that...one of [Kennedy's] agents is dead." He later updated the story saying, "Apparently this is correct, one of the Secret Service agents whose job it was to guard the life of the president was killed in his line of duty ...killed instantly...on the spot. We have it on good authority." Dallas TV station WFAA said, "A Secret Service agent [was] shot and killed." This fake news —which was officially confrmed—continued to be repeated and appeared in afternoon and evening newspapers nationwide.

The *St. Louis Post-Dispatch*, for example, carried a front page article from the Associated Press—dateline Dallas—indicating that, "A Secret Service agent and a Dallas policeman were shot and killed today..." Scores of other papers ran the same false AP story.

United Press International (UPI) issued a bulletin that was picked up and printed in newspapers across the country. It was bylined by veteran White House reporter Merriman Smith, who had traveled with the president. He reported, "One Secret Service agent was reported killed by the hail of bullets." Smith even won a Pulitzer Prize for his coverage.

Walter Cronkite said a SS man was killed.

Someone officially released this disinformation in Dallas. Thus a cover story was immediately in place in case anyone noticed another hearse leaving Parkland around the same time or spotted a second casket being loaded on a government plane at Dallas Love Field airport.

Secret Service agent Roy Kellerman had ordered the men who had been stationed at the Trade Mart, in anticipation of the president's speech there, to join the other agents at Parkland, which was located nearby. So this tripled the number of SS personnel at the hospital.

They had imposed security so tight they effectively blocked off part of the facility, making it inaccessible even to medical staff.

Parkland patient areas were racially segregated until 1964. There were separate restrooms, water fountains, elevators and dining facilities for African-Americans and whites. This arrangement could also have been advantageous for surreptitious movements by the Secret Service.

If a second casket transport had been planned, it would have been easy to put that aboard one of the planes at Carswell Air Force Base in

Fort Worth that was part of the presidential entourage that landed at Love Field. Alternatively, the Naval Air Station in Dallas would have been able to quickly supply a metal military casket.

Due to the physical restrictions at Parkland, in addition to the layout of the hospital, it is therefore entirely plausible that another casket was brought in unobserved and John Kennedy's body transferred to that container. Especially since the press had been redirected to a different part of the hospital for a news conference and then got busy filing stories.

The floorplan for Parkland Hospital in 1963 shows that a casket could have been wheeled in discreetly through the major medicine department on the north side of the building and potentially taken through an operating room that had doors on each end. Trauma One was next to this O.R. so the second casket could have been slipped around a corner. This route would avoid going by exam booths, the nurses' station, obstetrics and the triage desk, plus avoided the long hallway through which the president had originally been brought in from the south entrance.

SS agent Thomas "Lem" Johns said he was instructed by LBJ's agent Rufus Youngblood to ask Parkland Administrator C.J. Price if there was another entrance/exit to the hospital. An unnamed agent also inquired if there was "another way that the President and Mrs. Kennedy could be taken out of the building." There was indeed a "tunnel exit" that led to Harry Hines Boulevard. the press didn't know about. There is nothing particularly suspicious about agents looking for alternate routes for security concerns. But the existence of such a "back door" that presumably linked up with the room in which JFK's body was held, might have been used to bring in another casket, transfer his remains from the bronze casket that had arrived from the funeral home, then hurriedly exit Parkland via a different area of the large complex and put the second casket on a military transport plane before Mrs. Kennedy left the hospital.

It's not as far-fetched as it sounds, for reasons that will be outlined.

When questioned about this scenario, nurse Debra Bowron said that after she left Trauma Room One, "I went across to the nurses' station...[to] get me a cup of coffee...There's no way that they could have [brought in another casket] because I faced [the hallway]." She admitted, "I couldn't see the actual door, but the angle was such that anybody coming out of there I would have been able to see." That's debatable because the nurse's station was a bit offset from the end of the hallway leading to Trauma One and partially obscured by one of the tall partitions that divided exam booths.

At first Bowron said, "To get out of the building, it would have to come past where I was, with a lot of the other staff." But then she had second thoughts and remembered, "There *are* other doors. There was a connection between, there was an alleyway between, sort of toward the back of the emergency [area], not the trauma room where [Kennedy] was. He'd have to come out of there, go down, there was an alleyway...Any other way would have to come out past the nurses' station."

So despite her ambiguity, Bowron did not rule out the possibility and all it would take would be a few seconds to slip the metal shipping casket around the door from the operating room that had doors on both ends, and into Trauma Room One, and vice versa when it departed.

Presidential aide Ken O'Donnell had already gotten the First Lady to accompany him to a different area of the hospital so she wouldn't see them bring in the bronze casket. Plus she made phone calls to family members, including Robert Kennedy. Hence she was no longer sitting on the folding chair in the hallway outside Trauma One.

Interestingly, neither the Johnsons nor Mrs. Kennedy and the bronze casket exited the hospital via any doors other than the emergency entrance by which they had entered. A large throng of spectators had congregated outside, and still posed a security risk, so why was the "tunnel exit" or alleyway not used by the SS?

The military shipping casket could have departed from a different side of the hospital and nobody would have paid any attention to it.

While almost everyone was preoccupied with the kerfuffle unfolding between Dr. Rose and the Kennedy entourage, two men were known to have returned to Trauma Room One where the bronze casket was still sitting: Secret Service man Will Greer and White House doctor George Burkley. Neither of these guys had a good explanation for their return, and neither behaved in an exemplary fashion during or after the trip to Dallas. So assassination researchers have long viewed them skeptically.

Nurse Bowron never mentioned them so she obviously didn't see Greer or Burkley enter or exit the room. Were these the two persons who oversaw the transfer of the late president's body into a military casket?

By definition a military casket would have been brought in by members of the armed forces who would be under strict orders and subject to court-martial if they disclosed any details. They could have been wearing operating room smocks to protect their clothing when transferring Kennedy's sheet-wrapped corpse into a different vessel, and nobody in the hospital would look twice at them in such apparel. Significantly, two men attired exactly like this were observed delivering the shipping casket said to contain President Kennedy's remains to Bethesda that evening.

According to nurse Audrey Bell, "At the time the president and governor were brought to the ER, there were about twenty-three other patients receiving treatment in the area and seven emergencies were admitted within that two-hour period. Operations were also in progress."

There were typically 272 patients treated at Parkland every day in 1963, so ambulances and hearses routinely came and went.

With the airport officially closed, the public would not be able to see a second casket loaded onto a plane, and even if anyone did, it could be explained as being that of the Secret Service agent who was supposedly killed in the line of duty. The press at that point were congregated at the hospital and not in any position to observe what was happening.

Evidence For Two Caskets Shipped From Dallas

There apparently WAS another casket being shipped from Dallas to Washington that day. Secret Service man James Fox, who was working in the Executive Office Building next door to the White House Friday afternoon, later revealed that he was ordered to put together a group of *senior* agents to meet a plane in Washington in order to receive the body of a SS agent supposedly killed in Dallas. Of course, no agent had been killed; but the account by Mr. Fox dovetails with the suspicion that Kennedy's body may have been flown separately to Washington and was not aboard Air Force One as everyone thought.

This is not to imply that there was some vast conspiracy involving all Secret Service agents on the Dallas trip. It's likely some of them were either entirely unaware of the two caskets—because they were so dispersed around Parkland—or were given a different rationale, and thus were innocent pawns in the grand scheme of things without realizing it.

Rufus Youngblood—who took command, superseding agent Roy Kellerman when Johnson effectively became president—could have merely said they needed a "decoy" strategy to subvert efforts by Dr. Rose to prevent them from taking Kennedy's body back to Washington. He also could have capitalized on fears that the assassination was part of a broader conspiracy and that someone might attempt to even steal Kennedy's remains, as happened with Abraham Lincoln.

That would be one way of getting agents to eagerly participate in the ruse without their realizing the diabolical nature of it. This could have been made to appear that it was just a spur of the moment idea.

Any plotters smart enough to put together an elaborate conspiracy to kill the President of the United States in broad daylight in front of hundreds of witnesses would have realized that in the aftermath of his death, state law would prohibit his remains from being removed without a Texas autopsy. It was also predictable that Kennedy interests would surely not accede to that. So a showdown with the county medical examiner was inevitable because Dr. Rose was known to follow the letter of the law. Thus the drama could in effect have been staged.

Also, it's true that even to this day, decoy vehicles are commonly used during presidential travel. Thus any plan to put JFK on a different plane homebound would not have aroused suspicion even among Secret Service agents and there was no need to tell Mrs. Kennedy about this.

Probably few members of the security contingent in 1963 would have known the real reason for transporting JFK's body separately was so that it could be examined during the flight back to D.C. and attempts made to retrieve any bullets or alter wounds that might prove the existence of more than one gunman.

Was This Man An Accomplice?

Enter John Liggett. In 1963 he was a highly skilled embalmer and reconstructionist at a Dallas funeral home. The day of Kennedy's murder, he was attending the funeral service of his wife Lois' aunt when he was summoned to the phone. He then informed his spouse that he had to go to Parkland. She explained in a TV interview in 2003 that after she returned home, "John called me from Parkland. I could hear confusion in the background and I asked him what was going on...He said the president has died. And I said 'well did [your company] get the job?' And he said 'no—some other funeral home got the job' but he said 'I've got a lot of work to do. Don't try to call me. I'll call you as soon as I can.' And it was about twenty-four hours before I heard from him."

As a licensed mortician, Liggett had the tools of his trade to work on corpses—usually to improve their appearance for viewing. But he also could have helped extract bullets or made other surgical alterations. Some suspect he did that in the Kennedy case.

The fact that he did not return home until the next day suggests he may have flown with the body aboard whatever military aircraft it was that transported the cheap shipping casket to Washington. Since some staffers still had to ride on Air Force Two, it's most likely the second casket would have been placed on a different cargo plane than the C-130 which carried the presidential limousine and Secret Service sedan home to D.C. (as it didn't arrive at Andrews until 8 p.m. that night).

It would have only had a skeleton crew upfront in the aircraft. Liggett, under this scenario, would have been free to work on the corpse in the back of the plane without being disturbed. And he would have had ample time to do it. All of this could have occurred under the strictest military secrecy.

When John Liggett got home the next day, he was in a panic. He told Lois they needed to pack up and leave town right away. Lois said the family (including her three children) made a "high speed journey" to Austin and then San Antonio, ending up in a motel near Corpus Christi Sunday morning. Along the way Liggett was said to be in touch by telephone with relatives and persons unknown, engaging in private conversations to which Lois was not made privy. She was frightened and mystified by what was going on.

Finally, on Sunday, they saw Jack Ruby shoot accused assassin Lee Oswald on television. Lois reflected, "The minute he saw that he looked at me and said 'everything's okay now.' And you could just see his face. It was like all the pressure had been taken off of him."

Soon after the family returned to Dallas, Liggett came into a lot of money, and was now able to afford a new lifestyle and even move the family into a luxury home.

Lois' daughter, Debra, spoke of a visit from one of her stepfather John's eccentric friends from New Orleans.

"He was a rather freakish character and my sister claims we made merciless fun of him—my brother, my sister—because he was rather odd with the painted on eyebrows and the wig; this rather freakish man. John said to us that this was a friend of his from the Civil Air Patrol. That they had been in Civil Air Patrol together. And we believe that this was David Ferrie."

In 1966, Lois divorced John Liggett and moved out of state. It turns out he wasn't the loving, tender-hearted man she thought he was. According to reports in the Dallas newspapers, in 1974 he was charged with the attempted murder of a woman named Dorothy Peck. He beat, stabbed and set fire to her, and was also connected to another mutilation/burning killing in Dallas.

Mrs. Peck, incidentally—according to Johnson pal and swindler Billie Sol Estes—was the widow of Jay Bert Peck, who was said to be LBJ's second cousin and "official double" (whom Estes alleged Liggett also murdered. Mr. Peck was killed by an unknown assailant).

Ultimately Liggett was said to have been shot and killed by a sheriff's deputy when he tried to escape. At least that was the story. But Lois Liggett swore that sometime later, when visiting Las Vegas with friends, they saw a man who looked identical to her ex-husband. He also stared at her. She was convinced it was him and he was still alive.

JFK Returns Home

Before the plane took off from Dallas, Lyndon Johnson was hastily sworn in as the new president, with his wife Lady Bird on one side of him and the former First Lady on the other. Mrs. Kennedy later said the only thing she regretted was washing her husband's blood from her face before standing next to Johnson during his swearing in. That was a very revealing remark.

After LBJ took the oath of office, he turned to look at Congressman Albert Thomas, who winked at him. What did that mean?

JFK had just spoken at a testimonial fundraising dinner for Thomas the night before. Yet Thomas seemed gleeful that JFK was dead.

Mrs. Johnson could barely conceal her elation at her husband's elevation to the presidency. It also took the pressure off her for the various financial scandals in which she was also intertwined.

The plane took off for home at 2:47 p.m.—roughly an hour and forty-seven minutes after John Kennedy was pronounced dead. Plenty of time for someone to play a shell game with caskets.

When Air Force One lifted off from the runway, it made almost a vertical ascent. Pilot James Swindal seemed to want to leave not only Dallas but also the earth behind.

Late that afternoon, with the eyes of the nation focused on TV screens, the arrival at Andrews Air Force Base of Mrs. Kennedy and presumably the remains of the assassinated president were televised live. Floodlights were briefly turned on to pierce the darkness at the airport. Lyndon Johnson strode to a microphone and spoke briefly.

The nation was stunned to see Jacqueline Kennedy get off the plane and walk to a waiting gray hearse, her dress, legs and shoes still caked in her late husband's dried blood. She had refused to change clothes, telling others "let them see what they have done."

FBI Agents Francis O'Neill, Jr. and James Sibert were dispatched to Andrews "to assume jurisdiction over any violations that might fall within our purview." Sibert later explained this was "so there would be two of us to be a witness to whatever might happen." J. Edgar Hoover personally ordered the two agents to remain with Kennedy's body—obviously suspecting that something nefarious might occur.

Mrs. Kennedy rode in the hearse as the long procession made its way to Bethesda, Maryland, and the U.S. Naval Hospital there, a forty-five minute drive. As soon as the motorcade departed Andrews, the air base was again plunged into darkness as the TV lights were turned off. This meant any other activity there was unobservable.

Paperwork Raises Suspicions

It was the Assassination Records Review Board (ARRB) that discovered paperwork that buttressed the belief that two caskets—one empty, one with Kennedy's body inside—arrived at Bethesda Naval Hospital.

The first document was from the funeral home that handled the embalming of the president's body at Bethesda. A mortician made the notation: "Body removed from metal shipping casket at NSNH at Bethesda."

The second document was an official military report filed by Marine Corp Commanding Officer Sgt. Roger Boyajian which claimed, "At approximately [6:35 p.m.] the casket was received at the morgue entrance and taken inside." (Note that military time is usually rigidly precise). That was at least twenty minutes before Mrs. Kennedy even arrived in the hearse supposedly carrying her husband's body.

Paul O'Connor, one of the autopsy technicians, heard two helicopters land at Bethesda just before a black hearse showed up at the rear entrance to unload the metal military coffin.

Enlisted men who attested to the early delivery included E-Navy corpsman Dennis David, who went on to become a Navy officer and served in the Medical Services Corps. It was under his supervision that a team of sailors offloaded the cheap shipping casket containing the body of the late President Kennedy.

According to the ARRB, when David was interviewed by them, "He said the driver and the 'person riding shotgun' (i.e., front seat passenger) were wearing [operating room] smocks. Four or five men in blue suits, whom he assumed were federal agents, exited the back of the hearse, and supervised and observed while the Navy sailors (approximately seven or eight people) working for him, offloaded the casket which was in the hearse. He said it was a simple, gray shipping casket such as he frequently saw used later during the Vietnam War. His group of sailors took the casket into the anteroom directly adjacent to the morgue. He then dismissed them and went back upstairs to an administrative office on the second floor of the tower building, 'out front' toward the lobby."

The ARRB said David later saw an ambulance pull up outside of the front of the Bethesda Tower. "He went out on the curved, open second story balcony above the Bethesda Tower lobby and observed Jacqueline Kennedy, Robert [Kennedy], and several others immediately enter the Bethesda lobby from the motorcade, and go directly up to the seventeenth floor suite on the elevator (without stopping or pausing for anything). Mr. David said he knew what their destination was by watching the number indicators on the elevator. He was firm in his recollection that the motorcade out front with the gray ambulance arrived well after the gray shipping casket at the rear loading dock." David said that when he saw Mrs. Kennedy walking into the front of Bethesda, he knew what she did not know: the expensive bronze casket from Dallas did not contain her deceased husband. It was not offloaded until 7:17 p.m.

JFK's remains arrived in a shipping casket.

The ARRB reported "About 2:30-3:00 a.m. the next morning (November 23), [David] saw several corpsmen in the snack bar at Bethesda, and said that there was much discussion of two caskets coming into the complex that night...

"The next day (during daylight hours on November 23), Mr. David asked Dr. Boswell (one of the autopsy doctors) which casket the president had been in, and Dr. Boswell said, 'You ought to know; you were there.' He emphasized that he had no direct knowledge, by observation, that President Kennedy was in the gray shipping casket, but the implied sense of Boswell's remarks seemed to him to mean that President Kennedy was in the gray shipping casket which arrived in the black hearse..."

Multiple Witnesses To Two Caskets

There was apparent confusion at Bethesda the night of the JFK autopsy that even affected the military honor guard. According to a written report filed by Sgt. Boyajian, and dated Nov. 22, 1963, "The word was changed several times as to which entrance the ambulance was going to utilize and as a result a cordon detail of seven men was seen several times double-timing through the hospital on the heels of the Security officer."

Also attesting to the early delivery of JFK's body were E-4 Navy corpsman Paul O'Connor, E-5 Navy corpsman Floyd Riebe, E-4 Navy corpsman Jerrol Custer, E-4 Navy corpsman Ed Reed and E-4 Navy corpsman James Jenkins.

The latter expounded in a more recent TV interview. "All I saw was the body being brought in, in what I considered to be a shipping casket. That was striking in the fact that it's the president's body in such an ordinary thing," Jenkins reflected. Asked again if he saw the shipping casket, he affirmed emphatically, "Yes, I did. The casket came in, it was brought in by people, they were in business suits, and there may have been a couple of military officers with them. But it was brought in and it was brought into the morgue proper, sat down on the floor. Paul [O'Connor] helped them take the body out, and they put the body on the table in front of me. When the body was put on the table, everybody was asked to leave. The body was on the table, still wrapped in sheets. The head and the body was [wrapped] separate. And then Dr. Boswell left the morgue for fifteen or twenty minutes maybe. And I just assumed he was going back up to the laboratory to talk to Dr. Humes..."

Confirmation that there were two hearses and two caskets also came from First Lt. Richard Lipsey, who in 1963 was the 24-year-old aide to Maj. Gen. Philip Wehle (pronounced Weal), commanding general of the military district of Washington, based at Fort McNair.

Wehle was in charge of coordinating military ceremonial events at the White House and elsewhere, involving various branches of the armed services.

Two days after Lipsey and his boss had arrived in Washington in 1961, explained Lipsey, "General Wehle took me to the Oval Office. We shook hands with President Kennedy. He was affable; he could not have been nicer. He invited General Wehle to sit down. I was standing at attention. The president gestured at his rocking chair and said, 'Sit in my chair.'

"I often met with Kennedy in the Oval Office. I'd give him a briefing book, and he would scan it, sometimes ask a question. He was a real speed-reader with a photographic memory. He could skim through those things.

"As time went by, and I saw him more often, he'd call me Richard when we were alone...I found him sociable, charming. But he always had control of the situation. There was no doubt when you were in his presence who was in charge."

Both Lipsey and Maj. Gen. Wehle were at Andrews Air Force Base when the body of John Kennedy arrived around 6 p.m. EST. They then went to Bethesda and Wehle conferred with Mrs. Kennedy about what funeral arrangements she wanted made, while Lipsey was ordered to go to the morgue and observe the autopsy—something he had never done before. Lipsey recalled, "Gen. Wehle told me, 'Don't leave this body! You don't leave it.'" So again there was evidence that suspicions ran rampant.

In a 1978 formal interview with the House Select Committee on Assassinations (HSCA) that was tape recorded, Lipsey explosively revealed: "We had a decoy hearse because we knew there was a mob waiting at Bethesda Naval Hospital. So we got in a couple of these helicopters with our honor guard [at Andrews] when [the motorcade in which Mrs. Kennedy was riding] left and [we] flew over to the hospital to get there before they did. And when they came in, one of the hearses went right up to the front door. All of the crowd, of course, rushed over there. The one with the body in it went around to the back where the morgue was and we unloaded it. We met them in the back and unloaded it right there to avoid the news media and the crowd and everything else." But his account is somewhat flawed.

When Lipsey was asked to confirm what he'd just said, he replied, "The body was brought in the back door, backed right up to the loading ramp right immediately next to the morgue. And we unloaded it there and then Jackie Kennedy and her family and everybody that was, you know, flown to Washington and come back with the body, they came in the hospital the front way and went upstairs to the Presidential Suite at the hospital."

To further sort out the import of Lipsey's testimony: Since Jackie Kennedy was with the bronze casket that had been placed in the ambulance at Parkland, then photographed by a White House photographer being carried up the steps and loaded aboard Air Force One at Love Field, flown to Washington, and offloaded the night millions of Americans watched television and saw Mrs. Kennedy walk to the gray hearse into which the casket presumably containing the martyred president had been placed, and then driven to the front entrance of Bethesda. It can be said with certainty that JFK's body was NOT in the bronze casket as everyone assumed it was.

Lipsey clearly differentiated between the hearse that offloaded the Commander-in-Chief's body and the hearse in which Mrs. Kennedy was riding.

Lipsey confirmed he and General Wehle flew in a helicopter from Andrews AFB to Bethesda.

Lipsey claimed, "The body was in the procession and going through Washington but there were two hearses and one pulled right up to the front door and one went around with the body, went around to the back of the hospital."

But Lipsey was a bit confused. It's highly improbable that two hearses could have been in the motorcade that left Andrews and drove to Bethesda. The press was following closely and thousands of mourners lined the streets and would have seen a second hearse.

During live TV coverage of the arrival of Air Force One at Andrews, NBC's Robert Abernathy informed viewers, "A helicopter is standing by near the presidential jet, to take the coffin away." He was joined by co-anchor Nancy Dickerson, a close friend of Lyndon Johnson's. The next night, Dickerson and her husband were invited to dine with the Johnsons at their home.

Remember that autopsy aide Paul O'Connor talked about there being two helicopters that landed at Bethesda and even Lipsey himself referred obliquely to two. So it's likely the second one carried the military shipping casket that contained President Kennedy's body. After it landed on the grounds of Bethesda, it was then transported to the back loading dock area in the black hearse.

A Deliberately Flawed Autopsy?

Navy Surgeon General Edward Kenny ordered two Naval medical doctors, Commander James Humes and Commander Thornton Boswell, to conduct the autopsy. Humes served as the lead surgeon. Interestingly, Dr. Boswell called the decision to conduct the autopsy at Bethesda "stupid," and said that it should have been done at the specialized Armed Forces Institute of Pathology (AFIP) located just five miles away. Although both Navy men had done a limited number of autopsies, neither were trained or certified in forensic pathology (a subspecialty in pathology whose area of expertise is the examination of persons who die suddenly or violently and determining how, and by what means death occurred).

Milton Helpern, Chief Medical Examiner for New York City, observed that selecting Humes to lead the autopsy was "like sending a seven-year-old boy who has taken three lessons on the violin over to the New York Philharmonic and expecting him to perform a Tchaikovsky symphony."

Famed forensic pathologist Cyril Wecht pointed out Humes and Boswell, "had never done a single gunshot wound autopsy in their entire careers. This is something that really needs to be emphasized to every American...Democrat, Republican, liberal, conservative...this is your president. And you have multiple gunshot wounds to determine angle, trajectory, range, sequence, and then you have to correlate that with the multiple gunshot wounds of Connally. This is a formidable task that would have required two or three major forensic pathologists to undertake."

Wecht noted that several renowned pathologists were within one hour's driving distance or flying time from Bethesda and even had their bags packed waiting to go. But they were never called.

Admiral Burkley urged the doctors to expedite the autopsy. "All we need is the bullet," he idiotically insisted. But the commanding officer of the Bethesda medical center—Admiral Calvin Galloway—overruled Burkley and ordered a complete autopsy.

Unfortunately, as it turned out, there were about twenty routine procedures the JFK autopsy team failed to do, either because they were inept and/or inexperienced, or they were ordered not to do them; probably all of those things factored into what resulted.

Who Did Surgery To JFK's Head?

An FD302 report written at Bethesda, Maryland dated Nov. 26, 1963, by the two FBI agents, O'Neill and Sibert, reported: "The President's body was removed from the casket in which it had been transported and was placed on the autopsy table, at which time the complete body was wrapped in a sheet and the head area contained an additional wrapping which was saturated with blood. Following the removal of the wrapping, it was ascertained that the President's clothing had been removed and it was also apparent that a tracheotomy had been performed, AS WELL AS SURGERY OF THE HEAD AREA, NAMELY, IN THE TOP OF THE SKULL."

Who did this "surgery"? Certainly not the Parkland doctors!

In an unpublished manuscript, FBI agent Frank O'Neill said that it was Dr. Humes who pointed out that, "Some type of surgical procedure had been performed in the head region...to view the massive wound in the right rear of the president's head. The information relative to the surgical procedure was made by the physicians, not by the FBI agents. We merely reported what we heard."

Yet by the time the House Select Committee on Assassinations (HSCA) met in 1978 to supposedly re-investigate John Kennedy's murder, FBI agent James Sibert claimed the pathologists revised their initial suspicions of "surgery of the head area" and did so the same night the autopsy was performed. Sibert appears to have altered his testimony.

He said: "When the body was first observed on the autopsy table, it was thought by the doctors that surgery had possibly been performed in the head area and such was reflected in my notes made at the time. However, this was determined not to be correct following detailed inspection and when the piece of bone found in the limousine was brought to the autopsy room during the latter stages of the autopsy."

But if that were the case, why did Sibert and O'Neill even mention the suspected surgery of the head area when they dictated their report

FOUR DAYS AFTER the autopsy?

Still unanswered is why Kennedy's wounds looked so different.

Parkland nurse Audrey Bell, who stopped in Trauma Room One while the president was being treated, recalled asking Dr. Perry where Kennedy had been shot, because she couldn't see any evidence of it. So the doctor silently took ahold of JFK's jaw and turned his head to the side, thus exposing the huge wound in the back of his skull.

Dr. Malcomb Perry testified there was "a large avulsive wound on the right posterior cranium," in addition to the throat wound, but that in looking at JFK "*I did not see any other wounds.*"

Mrs. Kennedy told William Manchester that when she had re-entered Trauma Room One at Parkland after her husband was pronounced dead, and approached the gurney on which he was laying, she couldn't see that anything had happened to him. His face looked entirely normal. The head wound was hidden, (because it was on the back side).

Yet when John Kennedy arrived at Bethesda, the wounds to his head were five to six times larger than what anybody at Parkland saw.

Seeking to clarify this, in 1996, the ARRB took testimony from Dr. Thornton Boswell, and asked him to draw on an anatomically correct model of a human skull the area of Kennedy's head that was completely devoid of bone, prior to any autopsy incisions. What he drew depicted most of the back of the skull missing, with the wound extending forward to include most of the right side of the head above the ear, as well as the top of the head up to a point just behind the hairline above JFK's forehead.

The shocking damage to the president's head that Boswell depicted constituted compelling evidence that Kennedy's body had been altered by post-mortem surgery. At the very least, this was circumstantial evidence of obstruction of justice and a criminal conspiracy.

Autopsy doctors also noted a three-inch crescent-shaped flap on the right front side of Kennedy's head in the temple region that was hanging down. Michael Chesser, M.D. a neurologist with over thirty years of experience in private practice and academics, who has viewed and intensely studied the autopsy x-rays and photographs at the National Archives, comments: "All of this that you're seeing here was not seen at Parkland. This incision was not present at Parkland; we have witnesses who attested to that. [It is] my opinion...that this deep incision was done to somehow manipulate the evidence up in this area. There was no reason to do a V-incision like this as part of an autopsy. It's not done. You do an incision across from ear to ear to move the scalp back to access the brain. So it wasn't there at Parkland; it was there by the time the official autopsy began at Bethesda."

There is evidence of a very small wound in the temple region, however, that likely was obscured by how thick Kennedy's hair was. This would connote an entry wound of a bullet fired from the front.

Dr. Don Curtis said, "I did not see the right temporal wound, but my chief, Dr. Robert Walker, told me the following Monday morning that he did see what appeared to him to be a bullet hole in the right temple. He would know a bullet hole."

In addition, Dr. Chesser explained in a detailed analysis of Kennedy X-rays that the president also had what looked like a .22 caliber bullet hole above his forehead in the hairline.

Some claim there was evidence of a small bullet wound in the back of JFK's head but even i there was, it did not cause the big blow-out adjacent to it. President Kennedy was definitely struck by at least two bullets fired from the front.

It would have been easy for Parkland doctors, nurses and Secret Service agents to have missed seeing very small wounds on the president's head, that were likely concealed by his thick hair. But there is no way that they could have overlooked such a gigantic loss of bone mass as the autopsy doctors described.

Throat Wound Was Altered Too

The clearest proof of body alternation is that sometime between Dallas and Bethesda, the tracheotomy incision in the front of Kennedy's throat suddenly became a crude, three-and-a-half-inch gash. Dr. James Humes noted the size of the wound, and said it had "widely gaping, irregular edges."

Upon seeing the autopsy photos some years later, Dr. Malcolm Perry called the newly enlarged hole in the front of Kennedy's throat a "butcher job." It did not look like the incision that he made.

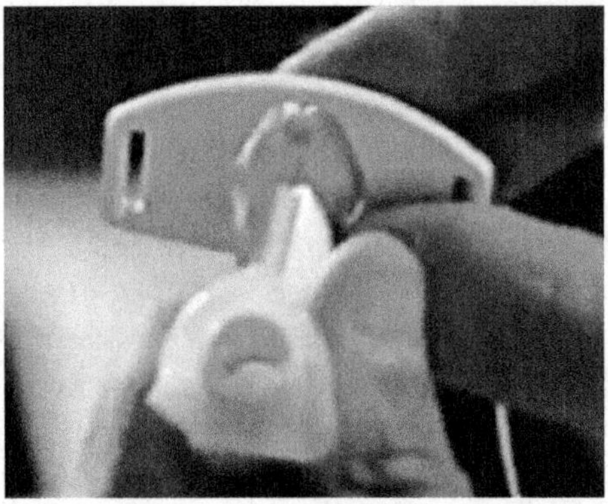

Parkland Dr. Charles Crenshaw held a tracheostomy tube showing how small it is. The bottom part goes in the hole in the windpipe. The flange at the top seals it. Kennedy had a 3/8-inch hole in the front of his throat at Parkland. It was only enlarged slightly to insert the tube. But a gaping 3-1/2-inch gash in his throat was seen at Bethesda that Dr. Perry at Dallas did NOT put there. Who altered it?

Charles Crenshaw, one of the doctors at Parkland who worked on Kennedy, told ABC-TV's *20/20* news magazine show in 1992 that after the tracheostomy tube and flange were removed from the president's neck following his death, that the very small incision made by Dr. Perry closed of its own volition, and that the bullet wound had NOT been obliterated and was still clearly visible!

Humes claimed that the autopsy team did not know that Parkland doctors performed a tracheostomy and that they didn't call Dr. Perry until 7:20 a.m. Saturday morning. But that's not true either. Bethesda called and harassed Perry yet Friday night, even threatening him with revocation of his medical license if he refused to go along with their story that the wound in the front of Kennedy's throat was an exit wound, and not a point of entry for a bullet as Perry and other medical staff at Parkland observed. Perry complained the next day to nurse Audrey Bell about not getting much sleep because of these calls. (Under pressure, Perry vacillated on this point when testifying in front of the Warren Commission, and said it could be an entrance or exit wound. But he continued to insist privately that what he saw in the front of JFK's throat was definitely an entrance wound. This will be detailed later in this book).

Robert Livingston, who was the Scientific Director of two divisions at the National Institute of Health (NIH) in Washington, phoned the Naval hospital early on the evening of Nov. 22, 1963 before the autopsy on John Kennedy had begun. Given Livingston's credentials, the duty officer put him through to Dr. Humes. Livingston recalled that Humes admitted he hadn't heard much of the news from Dallas. Livingston stressed he was calling to implore the autopsy team to closely examine Kennedy's neck wound. He had expertise in high-velocity wound ballistics plus considerable combat experience examining and repairing bullet and shrapnel wounds. Livingston later recalled, "I was confident that a small wound of that sort had to be a wound of entrance and that if it were a wound of exit, it would almost certainly be widely blown out, with cruciate or otherwise wide, tearing outward ruptures of the underlying tissues and skin.

"I stressed to Dr. Humes how important it was that the autopsy pathologists carefully examine the President's neck to characterize that particular wound and to distinguish it from the neighboring tracheotomy wound...

"I said, carefully, if that wound were confirmed as a wound of entry, it would prove beyond [reasonable] doubt that that shot had been fired from in front—hence that if there were shots from behind, there had to have been more than one gunman. Just at that moment, there was an interruption in our conversation. Dr. Humes returned after a pause of a few seconds to say that 'the FBI will not let me talk any further.' I wished him good luck, and the conversation was ended."

Livingston noted: "My wife can be good witness to that conversation because we shared our mutual distress over the terrible events, and she shared with me my considerations weighing the decision to call over to the Bethesda Navy Hospital. The call originated in the kitchen of our home on Burning Tree Road in Bethesda with her being present throughout. After the telephone call, I exclaimed to her my dismay over the abrupt termination of my conversation with Dr. Humes, through the intervention of the FBI. I wondered aloud why they would want to interfere with a discussion between physicians relative to the problem of how best to investigate and interpret the autopsy."

The Back Wound Location Keeps Changing

As the autopsy was underway on the president on the night of November 22 at Bethesda, Dr. Thornton Boswell marked the location of JFK's wounds on a pre-existing outline of a body, on a piece of paper called a face sheet. Notably, he placed the back wound much lower than the throat wound. The holes in Kennedy's shirt and suit coat confirm this was correct.

At some point following the autopsy, it was decided to claim that the hole in the front of Kennedy's throat was an exit wound.

But if Oswald fired at the president from a sniper's nest more than sixty feet above and behind JFK, the back wound would have to be at a HIGHER point on his body than the wound in the front of his throat.

If the entrance hole in Kennedy's back was at a lower point than the so-called exit wound in the front of his throat, how could an assassin have shot Kennedy from the sixth floor window of the Book Depository as was later alleged?

When subsequently quizzed about this contradiction—and eager to fall into lock step with the official storyline propounded by the government—James Humes disingenuously said, "Having seen the clothing I now know that I created a terrible problem with my own autopsy drawings. My drawings of the bullet holes on the night of the autopsy did not precisely match up with the actual holes in the clothing, because we were not aware that the president's suit jacket had humped up on his back while he waved at the spectators. These errors were later exploited by the conspiracy crowd to fit their premises and purposes."

But Humes did not diagram JFK's back wound based on the holes in his clothes. He based it on his and other witnesses' visual observation of the president's unclothed body in the morgue. They even measured the distance of the wound on his back in relation to his shoulder and placed a ruler next to it. Pierre Finck, of the Armed Forces Institute Of Pathology (AFIP) who was later called in during the autopsy, complained "I was denied the opportunity to examine the clothing of Kennedy."

Another Bullet Is Found

A preliminary summary of the observations by Sibert and O'Neill was contained in a teletype to FBI headquarters a few hours after the autopsy, on November 23. It stated that, "Total body X-ray and autopsy revealed one bullet entered back of head and thereafter emerged through top of skull. [Portion] of skull measuring ten by six point five centimeters later flown in from Dallas hospital and Xrays Bethesda revealed minute metal fragments from this piece where bullet emerged from skull."

These statements just add more confusion. No piece of skull was found at Parkland. However, according to Captain James Young—a thirty-four year-old Navy doctor assigned to the White House—during the autopsy, he sent two medical corpsmen (Thomas Mills and William Martinell) to the White House garage where the presidential limo was parked. There they found "varying sized pieces" of Kennedy's skull bones.

The corpsmen also found a fully intact bullet with a bent tip on the rear carpeting. Dr. Randolph Robertson, a diagnostic radiologist, described what happened next. "It went from Mills and Martinell to Young to Humes and it disappears. That evening, there may have been as little as four people who saw that bullet before it disappeared." So this shell was NOT in JFK's body and was therefore not shown on any X-rays. But it does raise major new questions about how many bullets were fired at the presidential limousine. Because there were also two shell fragments in a pool of blood that SS agent Paul Landis had briefly picked up and then redeposited in the limo after it arrived at Parkland. These were in addition to a bullet he retrieved from the car and placed on a stretcher upon entering Parkland. (A fuller explanation to come). And a bullet Connally confirmed fell from his thigh at the hospital (that also vanished).

Young subsequently wrote to former President Gerald Ford on Dec. 27, 2000, and explained that the day after the assassination, he "was staying in the White House to provide services to Mrs. Kennedy." He wrote that "I felt the need to write my feelings and my concerns..." This included "my twenty-three page handwritten description of our medical departments, the autopsy which I attended from beginning to the end and my preparations for President Kennedy's body and its disposition for the autopsy..." He said that upon recently re-reading his notes, in preparation for giving them to his children, "My particular problem is a description of what occurred at the autopsy...I have never seen anything written about the spent bullet in the Warren Report or elsewhere." Young was concerned because the bullet was never entered into evidence and he asked former President Ford if he knew what became of it.

Ford replied on January 9, 2001 and claimed, "I have no recollection of 'the spent bullet' you refer to." He then recommended Young read books by David Belin and Gerald Posner, a couple of "lone nutters."

Omitted Vital Evidence

FBI agent O'Neill described Kennedy's head wound as "massive": "[Dr.] Humes pointed out to Sibert and myself the gaping wound at the right rear of the president's head and the tremendous damage done to the brain therein." Yet in his final written notes, Dr. James Humes did not even mention the massive hole in the back of Kennedy's head, nor did he testify about that to the Warren Commission, which was soon to be impaneled to investigate the assassination! He later admitted he destroyed his original autopsy notes—under order—and burned them in his fireplace. Still later he also confessed to having destroyed a first draft of his autopsy report. Why?

The final report claimed JFK's brain weighed 1,500 grams, which is above average for an adult male brain. This notation is obviously a lie because as FBI agent Frank O'Neill told the ARRB, at least half of Kennedy's brain was missing due to the massive wound in the rear of his head.

Even Dr. Humes admitted "Two-thirds of the right cerebrum had been blown away." So how could the brain weigh that much?

There were also two brain exams days later.

Arlen Specter, assistant counsel to the Warren Commission, interviewed both Sibert and O'Neill on March 12, 1964. However, as a result of what they told Specter, they were never called to testify before the Warren Commission. Their FD302 report also became a classified document.

The background information the pathologists were given the night of the autopsy obviously tainted their conclusions. This is reflected in their written report. They stated: "Three shots were heard and the president fell forward bleeding from the head." That, of course, is FALSE. The impact of the fatal head shot had virtually lifted him out of his seat and propelled him violently backward and to the left, indicating a shot from the front.

The Bethesda autopsy report also noted that: "According to newspaper reports (including the *Washington Post* on November 23) Bob Jackson, a *Dallas Times Herald* photographer, said he looked around as he heard the shots and saw a rifle barrel disappearing into a window on an upper floor of the nearby Texas School Book Depository Building."

It is standard practice for pathologists to delve into the circumstances of a death in order to understand the context and hopefully enable them to reach the correct conclusions about the medical aspects of how death occurred.

However, in the Kennedy case, the information the autopsy team was given was grossly inaccurate and incomplete.

Although the official autopsy ended around midnight, Humes and Boswell claimed they remained behind several hours to assist in the embalming process, which was a curious assertion and certainly not one that pathologists would normally do. But then, nothing about this case was "normal."

The doctors lingering after the formal autopsy was completed would make sense if they participated in an elaborate deception, likely on the orders of their military superiors. Specifically: the partial reconstruction of the head by the morticians, at the direction of the pathologists, followed by photography that created the false impression that there was no exit defect in the back of the head. There is evidence that two sets of images were taken, with the misleading ones entered into the official record and the original, true evidence buried. The ARRB established through the testimony of ten witnesses that there are approximately eighteen images missing from the official record.

The point should not be lost that medical evidence was falsified, and provably so. FBI agent Frank O'Neill later stated under oath that the pictures of the back of JFK's head appeared "doctored," by which he meant the rear of the head had been put back together by the doctors. His FBI colleague, James Sibert, testified that the head looked "reconstructed" in these photos; he actually used the word "reconstructed" at his deposition. This author will further delve into this in a future chapter.

John F. Kennedy Comes Home

The body of the late President John Fitzgerald Kennedy was brought back to the White House at 4:40 a.m. Saturday, Nov. 23, 1963, entering at the northwest gate. The trees were bare of leaves but illuminated by bright lights and kerosene flares lined the curved driveway. The honor guard at the portico snapped to attention and began marching, their rifles with their brilliantly shining bayonets at "port arms" held diagonally in front of the body, with the muzzle pointing upward to the left. The men wore white gloves and dress uniforms as they accompanied the hearse to the north portico, with its tall columns. The doorway was draped with black mourning crepe as were rooms in the executive mansion.

One truly eerie matter that had to be addressed about the White House decor was that by some strange coincidence, Jacqueline Kennedy had arranged for the Oval Office to be redecorated while she and the president were in Texas. The dingy, blue-gray oval carpet in the room was most dreadful—a throwback to the Truman years—so she had one custom-made instead. The new rug was bright, blood red.

Workmen had moved furniture out of the Oval Office and unfurled the new red rug while Jackie and Jack were on their way from Fort Worth to Dallas. President Kennedy never lived to see it, but Jacqueline did. She make a point of hurriedly visiting the office which had otherwise already been stripped bare of her husband's things.

President Kennedy's body by this time had been placed in a new casket made out of African mahogany.

He lay in repose in the East Room for twenty-four hours. When Robert Kennedy viewed his brother's body, he fainted. Mrs. Kennedy had instructed chief usher J.B. West to follow the protocol and details of Abraham Lincoln's 1865 state funeral for her husband. Kennedy's coffin was taken to the center of the East Room and set upon the same catafalque used at Lincoln's funeral. Later that day, various officials and foreign heads of state were received and viewed the flag-draped coffin, surrounded by an honor guard in full dress uniform.

On Sunday, November 24, the body of President John F. Kennedy was taken to the U.S. Capitol rotunda. More than 250,000 people filed past his flag-draped casket to pay their final respects, some waiting for as long as ten hours in a line that stretched forty blocks.

The World Mourns

On November 25, the day of President Kennedy's State Funeral, Dorothy Kilgallen and her husband Dick were among the millions of people around the world who sorrowfully watched somberly as a horse-drawn caisson carried the casket down Pennsylvania Avenue to the White House. There the First Lady and mourners waited. They then walked with the procession—military escort, band, and the symbolic rider-less black horse with boots reversed in the stirrups—eight blocks to St. Matthew's Cathedral as drums played a solemn, muffled beat.

At least two hundred and twenty foreign dignitaries and heads of state from ninety-two countries, five international agencies, and the papacy, attended the funeral. Mourners included President Charles de Gaulle of France, Chancellor Ludwig Erhard of the Federal Republic of Germany, Emperor Haile Selassie of Ethiopia and Prince Philip of the United Kingdom. Many walked with Mrs. Kennedy. This was the largest gathering of foreign statesmen in the history of the United States and also posed the biggest security nightmare for American protective officials. The Requiem Mass was led by Cardinal Richard Cushing. After the service, more than a million people lined the streets to view the president's journey to his final resting place at Arlington National Cemetery. It was a place John Kennedy had visited with his young son exactly two weeks earlier, to lay a wreath at the Tomb of the Unknown Soldier on Veteran's Day. While there, JFK turned to Rep. Hale Boggs and said, "This is one of the really beautiful places on earth. I could stay here forever."

The horse-drawn caisson leaves the White House.

Fifty Air Force and Navy jets flew overhead, followed by Air Force One, which dipped its wing in a final tribute.

Jacqueline Kennedy lit the Eternal Flame at the head of the burial plot, the light intended to remain lit in perpetuity as a beacon of hope and remembrance for all who see it, a reminder of President Kennedy's legacy to our nation. In the next three years, sixteen million Americans visited the gravesite to pay tribute to JFK.

The most heart-breaking image was when "John John" saluted his father's casket. That day was the little boy's third birthday.

Many businesses and schools closed across the nation, as did government offices and the stock market. The *Dallas Times Herald* stopped printing comics in its editions until after JFK's funeral.

Concurrent with the services for the martyred president, bustling Times Square in New York City came to a standstill at noon, as pedestrians stood silently with heads bowed while two Boy Scouts played *Taps*. Railroads stopped trains, wherever they were, for a few minutes as passengers stood in silent tribute. At an old firehouse in Keokuk, Iowa and in the First Presbyterian Church in Springfield, Illinois, bells that tolled ninety-eight years earlier for another assassinated president, Abraham Lincoln, rang again. Navy warships in San Francisco Bay and the aircraft carrier *Franklin D. Roosevelt* in Bayonne, New Jersey boomed twenty-one gun salutes.

Meanwhile, Deputy Attorney General Nicholas Katzenbach was busy writing a memo to Bill Moyers, an assistant to the newly installed President Johnson. The memo suggested that a commission be formed, consisting of "unimpeachable personnel." He wrote: "We need something to head off public speculation or Congressional hearings *of the wrong sort.*" What did Katzenbach mean by "the wrong sort"?

Dorothy Pays Tribute To The President and Mrs. Kennedy

In the aftermath of the tragedy Dorothy Kilgallen penned two articles that eloquently honored the deceased president and his wife. The first piece detailed her January visit to the White House. She ended by saying, "The picture that stays in my mind is the one of this tall young man bending over a tall small boy carefully scrutinizing envelopes until he came to the name 'Kerry Ardan Kollmar—Grade 3B,' while the whole world waited."

In a bold typeface she concluded, **"This is the man who was assassinated in Dallas."**

What followed was a column called "Jacqueline, A Profile In Courage and More." In it, Dorothy wrote, in part, "She had so much more than beauty, as the months after the Inaugural revealed, and as the days after the assassination showed with heart-rendering impact. She had—she has—character and depth and courage and spirit and love and loyalty and a beautiful instinct for correctness...

"Her valor in the aftermath of catastrophe is the more remarkable because of her youth and her former gaiety. Those who remember her

water-skiing, laughing in the face of the ocean's spray, dancing at White House parties, smiling at the crowds that applauded her when she entered her box at the theater, sitting on the sand of a beige New England beach sipping vin rose, conversing earnestly in French with a foreign dignitary, always looking a little bit like a little girl, never dreamed of a day when they would see her as a figure of sorrow—in black, pale, shadowed by her widow's weeds, kneeling to kiss the flag on her husband's bier.

"When she was First Lady, she gave the nation much to enjoy and to emulate. She was a good example to the young people of the country because she showed that being beautiful and intelligent and graceful and modest was even better than just being beautiful.

"Many tributes have been paid by important men and women to the late president. Perhaps the greatest tribute ever paid to him in life was Jacqueline Lee Bouvier's promise to love him until death."

After Dorothy's poetic tributes to Mr. and Mrs. Kennedy, she was soon to turn her attention to the "murders most foul." She became a clarion voice for the truth and repeatedly assailed the lies being told to the world about the tragedy in Dallas.

Guilty Without Even A Trial

Beginning on Friday afternoon and evening of November 22, the depiction of 24-year-old Lee Harvey Oswald as the slayer of John Kennedy and DPD Officer J.D. Tippit was proceeding vigorously. Baseless conjecture by Dallas authorities and outright lies were leaked to the press.

The way in which the defendant was portrayed was an outrageous farce. There had not been any real investigation and yet he was said to be guilty. He was deprived of his right to counsel, and questioned for at least twelve hours without there being any documentation of what he said. A compliant press repeated these falsehoods. But the deception didn't stop there.

Oswald was described as a Marxist, a loner, a loser, a defector to the Soviet Union, a man who assassinated the president because he wanted to become famous, to "leave his mark on history." But if that was the case, he would have bragged that he killed JFK. Instead, he "emphatically" (his word) denied it. Repeatedly.

A big Texas wink at the concept of justice was seen in a sign hidden in Dallas District Attorney Henry Wade's office which said: "Any prosecutor can convict a guilty man. It takes a great prosecutor to convict an innocent man."

Yet on Saturday, Nov. 23, 1963, the *Dallas Morning News* ran a story quoting D.A. Henry Wade as saying preliminary investigation showed that more than one shooter was involved in the death of JFK. Cliff Carter, who was one of Lyndon Johnson's shyster lawyers, called Wade three times that day to say that LBJ "feels that any word of a conspiracy—some plot by foreign nations—to kill President Kennedy would shake our nation to its foundation." It was one of the first in a series of ploys to discourage a proper probe into the assassination by stoking fears of a threat to national security.

Also on Saturday morning, New Orleans attorney Dean Andrews called his secretary from his hospital bed to say that he would be representing Lee Harvey Oswald. Andrews said he was asked to take the case by a man named Clay Bertrand (a.k.a. Clay Shaw). But Oswald never received any legal counsel.

CIA Director John McCone told President Johnson and National Security Adviser McGeorge Bundy early Saturday that the CIA had confirmed that just weeks before Kennedy's assassination, Lee Harvey Oswald had traveled to Mexico City and visited the Soviet Embassy. Three hours later, McCone informed LBJ that Oswald had also visited the Cuban Embassy in Mexico City. McCone apparently did so during the time former President Dwight Eisenhower was meeting with Johnson at the White House for two and a half hours.

But after that meeting, at 10:01 a.m. on Saturday, FBI director J. Edgar Hoover told Johnson in a phone conversation that was recorded, that the CIA information was suspect. Hoover explained, "That's one angle that's very confusing, for this reason: We have up here the tape and photograph of the man who was at the Soviet Embassy using Oswald's name. That picture and the tape do not correspond to this man's voice, nor to his appearance. In other words, it appears that there is a second person who was at the Soviet Embassy down there."

This was not the first time someone was impersonating Lee Oswald. As far back as June 3, 1960—while Oswald was in Russia—Hoover personally sent a memo to the State Dept. in which he warned, "There is a possibility that an imposter is using Oswald's birth certificate." On Jan. 20, 1961, Hoover again noted in a memo that someone using Lee Oswald's I.D. was attempting to purchase trucks as part of an anti-Castro movement in New Orleans. All of this suggests that there was an effort to frame him well in advance of his arrest.

Hoover also debunked the CIA information in a memo to James Rowley, head of the Secret Service.

Dr. John Newman, who served as Executive Assistant to the Director, at the National Security Agency (NSA) said, "We can finally say with some authority that the CIA was spawning a web of deception about Oswald weeks before the president's murder, a fact that may have directly contributed to the outcome in Dallas."

In January 1964, when some of Hoover's subordinates told him that the CIA had promised to keep the FBI apprized of its operations within the U.S., the director replied in a memo, "OK, but I hope you are not being taken in. I can't forget CIA withholding the French espionage activities in USA nor the false story re Oswald's trip to Mexico City only to mention two of their instances of double dealing."

This author has reviewed a declassified FBI memo from Nov. 23, 1963 which reported, "Oswald stated that he had never been in Mexico except to Tijuana on one occasion."

In September 1977, David Atlee Philipps, CIA official station chief at Mexico City, admitted that "no evidence existed" that Oswald even made such a trip there, yet this remains part of the mythology surrounding the accused assassin.

John McCone was long suspected of withholding information from the Warren Commission. Now even the CIA says he did. A once-secret report written in 2013 by the CIA's top in-house historian, David Robarge, found that McCone and other agency officials were "complicit" in keeping "incendiary" information from the Commission. According to *Politico* in a 2015 article, the report "identifies tantalizing information that McCone did not reveal, including evidence that the CIA may have had communication with Oswald before 1963."

On the day after the murder of President Kennedy, a New York lawyer, Emile Berman—commenting on the case in Dorothy Kilgallen's flagship newspaper, the *Journal-American*—asserted "The District Attorney has a suspect, but not much more."

Nevertheless, on Saturday afternoon, barely twenty-four hours after Lee Harvey Oswald was picked up by Dallas police, the storyline was set. Capt. Will Fritz told the press: "Now I can tell you that this case is cinched. This man killed the president. There's no question in my mind about it. We are convinced, beyond any doubt, that he did the killing."

The dirty little secret is that shortly before Fritz made those comments—by his own admission later—he received a person-to-person telephone call from Lyndon Johnson Saturday afternoon, ordering him to cease his murder investigation. "You have your man," Fritz later quoted LBJ as telling him.

But FBI director J. Edgar Hoover specifically told Johnson in a recorded phone call that, "The case as it stands now isn't strong enough to be able to get a conviction." Hoover also wrote a memo saying that evidence pointed to Oswald's *innocence*. The knowledge that someone had impersonated Oswald for years was held very closely.

Once again Johnson demonstrated that he was the ringleader of the cover-up. His defenders claim that's because he was genuinely afraid that there had been Communist involvement in the assassination (which is extremely doubtful). It is a certitude he was merely trying to conceal his criminal participation in staging a "palace coup."

If he really feared the United States leadership was being targeted by foreign-sponsored assassins, Johnson would not have sat in Air Force One on the tarmac at Love Field in Dallas for one hour and forty-seven minutes after Kennedy died. He would never have left himself vulnerable to an on-the-ground attack. He would have taken off immediately, which is what the pilot, staff and security people urged him to do.

Johnson also made entreaties to Texas Attorney General Waggoner Carr. The A.G. testified that on the night of November 22, he received a call at home from the White House (though he claimed he couldn't remember who phoned). He was instructed that no mention of any conspiracy should be made in an indictment against Oswald. Johnson's influence over the A.G. wasn't completely successful. Carr took part in the prosecution of Johnson crony Billie Sol Estes. He also testified that Lee Harvey Oswald was working as an undercover agent for the FBI and was receiving $200 a month from September 1962 until his death. J. Edgar Hoover denied this.

D.A. Henry Wade was more cooperative. He claimed, "The wife (Marina) had said he had the gun the night before, and it was missing that morning after he left." But Mrs. Oswald never said anything even remotely similar to Wade's assertion. In fact, *The New York Times* reported on December 8 that Marina said she never knew her husband owned a rifle nor did she know he owned a pistol. The newspaper buried this item in the fourteenth paragraph of a story appearing on page sixty-three. The SS and FBI had her sequestered and would not permit interviews, thus enabling incriminating quotes to be attributed to her without her ability to refute them. When she was finally able to speak out years later, she disavowed a number of statements attributed to her in 1963 and 1964.

The American Civil Liberties Union (ACLU) later said, "If Oswald had lived to stand trial and were convicted, the courts would very likely have reversed the conviction because of the prejudicial pretrial publicity."

The group of lawyers also objected to "the treatment accorded Oswald," including depriving him of "his right to counsel," as well as "the nature of the interrogation, his physical security while under arrest, and the effect of pretrial publicity on Oswald's right to a fair trial."

An Oil Baron Is Briefed On Oswald's Security

Saturday afternoon, Haroldson Lafayette ("H.L.") Hunt—who seemed to take an unusual interest in the assassination—met with Jack Crichton, a former Military Intelligence officer then attached to Army Reserve Intelligence. Crichton was also director of Dorchester Gas Producing Co. with D.H. Byrd, who owned the Texas School Book Depository. Others serving on that board were Clint Murchison, H.L. Hunt and Sid Richardson. Big Oil during the 1950s and '60s was what the OPEC oil cartel was to the United States in the 1970s and thereafter. One of the main concerns of this group was the preservation of the oil depletion allowance which President Kennedy wanted to do away with.

Crichton was involved in the arrangements of the visit that JFK made to Dallas. His close friend, Deputy Police Chief George Lumpkin, and a fellow member of the 488th Military Intelligence Detachment, drove the pilot car of Kennedy's motorcade. One of Jack Crichton's closest friends was oil man and secret CIA operative George H.W. Bush.

Hunt's meeting on Saturday afternoon was to discuss, with Army Intelligence officers, the first interrogation of Marina Oswald. Strangely, a translator for Mrs. Oswald—who only spoke Russian—was provided to Dallas police by Mr. Crichton. According to Russ Baker, the author of *Family of Secrets*, there "were far from literal translations of her Russian words and had the effect of implicating her husband in Kennedy's death." When she later learned to speak English, she was aghast at some of the statements the government claimed she made but which she never uttered.

Marina and her young children had been taken to an undisclosed location by the Secret Service and basically held captive. The presumed reason was that it was to protect her from harm by persons upset about the assassination. But the SS also manipulated her. At one point, FBI agents were dispatched to the location where Marina was being detained, and a confrontation ensued between Hoover's men and the Secret Service, who refused to turn her over. *What was that all about?*

In any event, how did a private citizen have that much clout to be accorded a briefing and who authorized it? Why was Hunt so interested in knowing what the wife of the accused assassin had to say?

At that time, Mr. Hunt was described as the richest man in the world in 1963, worth billions of dollars. His assets included oil and natural gas, vast real estate holdings, and food production companies worldwide. He was certifiably a rightwing extremist and proponent of segregation. He financed a fifteen-minute daily radio program called *Life Line* that was distributed to about five hundred radio stations. It was personally costing him the equivalent of $50,000 in 2023 dollars each day. His program was designed to promote his radical views and business interests. Mr. Hunt believed that people with wealth should have a bigger voting right than average people or the poor. He and FBI director J. Edgar Hoover were friends, and spoke often on the phone.

John Curington was Hunt's right-hand man and attorney, from 1960-69. According to Gregory Doudna, who interviewed Curington, his range of duties included (as described by Curington): "running HLH Products (the 'food division'); covering up tax-evasion schemes; collecting gambling debts; handling matters involving Hunt's secret family—of which Hunt had two in addition to his public family in Dallas—and carrying out covert political operations."

Curington explained, "Hunt Oil company offices were in the Mercantile Bank Building there in Dallas. And [it] had windows that were about four by six foot in dimensions, and you could raise them up and be exposed without a screen or anything. And when the Kennedy caravan passed our offices on the day of the assassination, Mr. Hunt and I were in the window looking out, and John Connally was in...the limousine in which Kennedy was a passenger. He turned up and looked at our building and recognized Mr. Hunt, and he turned around and made a comment to Jack Kennedy. And Kennedy turned up and waved to Mr. Hunt."

It may have sent a cold chill down the president's spine to see the radical Mr. Hunt looking down at him from a Dallas building window, but if so, he didn't have long to ponder it. He was dead minutes later.

Curington revealed that Hunt began receiving threatening phone calls from people who wondered, "Could he have been involved in the assassination? And...did he feel any remorse by putting out programs that were detrimental to the Kennedy political agenda?"

Later on Saturday afternoon, Nov. 23, 1963, Curington said, "Mr. Hunt did call me and ask me to go down to the police station, and find out what security there was, if any, around Lee Harvey Oswald. Now at that period of time there was television on a twenty-four hour a day basis, showing the turmoil around the Dallas Police Department. And Mr. Hunt told me, that 'after you find out the information that I need on security, come back to Mount Vernon and give me a report' no matter how late it was. (Hunt had a home named after George Washington's—but it was five times bigger).

"I could depend on Lieutenant George Butler and Will Fritz—anything of importance I could depend on them to furnish me that information."

John Curington opined, "It was important that LHO not live to go on trial...not because Lee Oswald could directly implicate [Hunt] in the death of the president, but because a good defense attorney could poke holes in the story of Oswald's complicity. And this could arouse public demands for a more thorough investigation that could reveal Hunt's connections to a host of unsavory characters in the mafia and the government."

No Security, Free Press Badges...And Sandwiches

Curington said, "There was no security whatsoever around the jailhouse. A lot of news people, but nobody too concerned with se-security...Nobody asked for ID, nobody looked into my briefcase." Press badges were even laying on a table that anyone could pick up.

Incredibly—and supposedly serendipitously—Curington said, "I even got on an elevator, and Captain Will Fritz got on the elevator, and he had Lee Harvey Oswald with him. And Captain Fritz, of course we knew each other, and he just looked over and said, 'Meet the S.O.B. that shot the president.' Oswald didn't make a comment, I didn't make a comment."

Oswald was paraded in front of reporters on fifteen occasions, being taken up and down a corridor and getting jostled by the crowd, as if police were just hoping someone would shoot him. Jack Ruby certainly had the chance. He had been shadowing LHO since he was picked up by the police and had made several trips to the Dallas police headquarters.

Saturday night, Johnson lawyer Cliff Carter again called Dallas D.A. Henry Wade and demanded that he not pursue or even talk about the possibility of a conspiracy in the death of JFK. Wade then went to see Capt. Fritz to underscore that fact.

Unbelievably, Jack Ruby brought sandwiches to pass out to some of the policemen at the midnight press conference at which Lee Oswald was again put on display. Ruby was not a member of the news media, so why was he even allowed in the building?

Wade made a mistake when he told reporters that Oswald was a member of an anti-Castro faction called Free Cuban Commission (while in New Orleans). Astonishingly, Ruby spoke up to correct Wade, saying, "Henry, it's the Fair Play For Cuba Committee, a pro-Castro organization." LHO looked startled and one may fairly ask, how and why was Jack Ruby so interested in and familiar with the accused assassin's prior activities in Louisiana?

Dorothy Kilgallen questioned Oswald's mysterious life, and there is considerable evidence that he was working for the CIA, posing as a bonafide member of the "Fair Play For Cuba Committee" in New Orleans. It was actually illegal to represent the FPCC in Louisiana at the time, which was punishable with a ten thousand dollar fine. How did Oswald avoid being arrested for such pamphleteering? (He was taken into custody for a minor scuffle but not charged with illegally distributing these materials).

Significantly, the entire time Oswald was representing himself as a FPCC activist in New Orleans, District Attorney Jim Garrison was out of town. He had left to perform his National Guard duties the very day Oswald began his FPCC venture. Oswald ceased those activities the day the D.A. came back to work.

Something about the midnight press conference disturbed J. Edgar Hoover, because at 1:15 a.m., he contacted Dallas officials and urged them to make a secret transfer of Lee Harvey Oswald to the county jail. Parkland Hospital was warned to prepare for a possible emergency.

It is not clear whether or not H.L. Hunt's aide John Curington attended the late night press briefing, but while he said he arrived at the police department by around 6 p.m. Saturday night, he admitted he didn't get to Mr. Hunt's home until probably 2 a.m. Sunday morning, and Hunt was still up. "I gave him a report, that there was no security that I could see whatsoever around Lee Harvey Oswald, around the jail. And he said, 'If you would, I want you to go out and have The Man'—he called Joe Civello The Man—'come over to Mount Vernon.' That was the name of his home. And I did that and I went home."

Curington opined, "Civello, although he had a pretty bad reputation in the Mafia circles, look, all in all he was a pretty nice kind of a fellow. As far as I know I never saw him take a drink of whiskey, I never heard him use a word of profanity, he tipped his hat to the ladies. Outside of shooting one or two people he had a pretty fair background."

Don't laugh. That was John Curington's definition of a nice guy.

So consider what H.L. Hunt's reaction was to the news that there was no security around Oswald. He had his right-hand man wake up a mafioso in the middle of the night. Curington said Hunt "asked for that meeting right then." He said he believed the two men got together around dawn.

Without making overt accusations that Hunt plotted to assassinate President Kennedy, Curington wrote in his book, "During the period of time before the 1960 Democratic Convention and continuing after that, H. L. Hunt became more and more interested in what he called a 'Removal Group.' That sounded all nice, clean and sterile, but it was far from that. I nicknamed it the 'Kill Squad,' because that is what it was really going to be. Mr. Hunt always believed that his [radio] programs...would, over time, convince a certain type of listener to do things in accordance with the dogma that these programs were putting forward.

"In some of the more serious situations, however, it was clear that...might simply be too slow. If Mr. Hunt could develop a 'Removal Squad,' then in that event, results could take place almost overnight..."

A unique plan was developed and organized. Mr. Hunt wanted to establish four separate groups, each operating independently of each other, totally compartmentalized, and with no contact among the groups.

"What Mr. Hunt hoped to accomplish was to have as much insulation as possible surrounding the removal of a particular person—to have the 'Removal Squad' groups act independently of each other. This would give a high degree of insulation and protection between the group that said, 'This person should be removed,' and the group that said, 'Let's do it.'

"To my knowledge, this entire 'Removal Squad' plan—or 'Kill Squad' as I called it—never moved past the planning phase...I do have to say, however, that in looking back at history, when JFK was killed, his assassin Lee Harvey Oswald was shot in very short order...the 'killer was killed,' as Mr. Civello advised...

"Coincidence? Possibly. Still, it appears that—at least on the surface—there could have been other elements at work in these killings, and some of them could have been provided by my former employer, H. L. Hunt."

Vital Evidence Is Changed

At least thirty-two people in Dealey Plaza were known to have taken amateur movies or still photographs at or around the time of the assassination. Some of them had their film and even cameras confiscated on the spot by men claiming to be with the Secret Service or CIA, even though those agencies denied they had any personnel in that location at that time. Historic film—vital evidence—disappeared.

Tom Craven of CBS affiliate TV station KRLD in Dallas can be seen in photos standing on the grassy knoll filming in Dealey Plaza, with a family taking cover on the ground.

Yet the footage he took there that day was supposedly permanently destroyed during processing at KRLD due to water damage (whoops!), yet his Parkland footage was aired later that day.

One amateur video that survived was shot by Abraham Zapruder. Dallas-based Secret Service agent Forrest Sorrel and Zapruder took the film to the local Kodak lab for processing yet on Friday, Nov. 22. On Saturday morning, *Life* magazine consummated a deal under the auspices of publisher C.D. Jackson to buy photo rights to the film. According to Carl Bernstein, Jackson was "Henry Luce's personal emissary to the CIA." Zapruder later claimed in sworn testimony he received $25,000 and then gave this money to the Firemen's and Policemen's Benevolence. However, *Life* decided two days later to give him more money: He received $150,000 for the eighteen-second film (the equivalent of $1,430,000 in 2023 dollars) to buy all rights. Ultimately, in 1999, the government paid Zapruder heirs $16 million ($29,559,567 today) plus interest (they wanted nearly double what they got), yet allowed them to keep the copyright.

The government had to compensate the Zapruder family because the Assassination Records Review Board in 1997 declared the film the permanent possession of the people of the United States.

50 minutes after the Kennedys arrived in Dallas, Zapruder filmed JFK's murder.

The *Washington Post* reported that, "The Zapruder family had said the film should be valued like the works of Dutch painter Vincent van Gogh or pop artist Andy Warhol whose 'Orange Marilyn' silkscreen of Marilyn Monroe sold for $17.3 million last year." What a vulgar and insulting comparison—imagery of the cold-blooded murder of a president equated with beautiful artistic works.

"Government appraisers had said that without projection, the Zapruder film was a strip of celluloid wound around a plastic reel. They said that when Sotheby's auction house in New York sold 1,200 items from the estate of former first lady Jacqueline Kennedy in 1996, the highest amount paid for any one item was $1.4 million for an antique French desk where President Kennedy signed the Nuclear Test Ban Treaty.

"Some Kennedy assassination researchers...don't think the government should have paid a nickel to the Zapruder family. 'It's evidence in a criminal case,' Jim Lesar, president of the Assassination Archives and Research Center, said as arbitrators were deciding the compensation issue."

It is shocking that this purchase cost the taxpayers so much money. The Zapruder heirs then gave the copyright to the Sixth Floor Museum in Dallas, which demands licensing fees to use still photos from what should be public domain material since the taxpayers paid for it.

Some skeptics have suspected that the more than generous amount paid Abraham Zapruder for his film in 1963 was a form of "hush money" so he wouldn't reveal the alterations made in the original.

On Saturday, Nov. 23, 1963, the Z-film was supposedly flown to *Life*'s offices in Chicago. Then it apparently was handed over to the CIA and thereafter ended up in the nation's Capitol the same day.

That night, two Secret Service agents brought the original amateur movie filmed by Abraham Zapruder of the Kennedy assassination to the National Photographic Interpretation Center lab around 10 p.m.

This facility had recently relocated to Building 213 on the southeast corner of First and M Streets in Washington, D.C. It was top secret and Mike Wallace of *60 Minutes* fame once argued with a guard at the gate, attempting to get him to admit it was a CIA facility. No such luck. Security was tightened because at the NPIC's previous location, there had been a security breach. Dave Stinson relates, "On our hot D.C. summer days the large industrial-size windows were kept open." One day, a massive summer thunderstorm hit. Papers blew out through the windows and fluttered to the ground below. "The area was filled with government employees collecting the wind blown documents!"

Robert Kennedy then ordered the NPIC moved to a new facility to be located in a building with no windows.

In any case, the night after the assassination, the Zapruder film was closely examined. The chief photo interpreter, Dino Brugioni—wearing white gloves so as not to damage this crucial evidence—had quickly acquired a new projector from a local camera store after hours to show the film. He was asked to use the high-tech equipment the lab possessed to make a number of blow-up copies of frames the Secret Service selected. Brugioni recalled that the images were sharp. Curiously, the SS instructed him to focus on the Stemmons freeway sign, and the car frame by frame.

Brugioni and his team—including Bill Banfield and Ralph Purst—were instructed to make 20x22-inch color prints to be mounted on hinged briefing boards, to be sent to John McCone of the CIA. Brugioni prepared and typed accompanying notes himself. This work was completed around 4 a.m. Sunday morning, Nov. 24, 1963.

Dino—who had flown sixty-six combat missions and at least fifteen reconnaissance missions in WWII and been an Air Force photographer—routinely analyzed top security photographs such as were captured by U.S. spy planes in 1962 to document Soviet missile pads in Cuba that were presented to President Kennedy. He also made the briefing boards that were shown to the United Nations General Assembly proving the Soviets were installing nuclear missiles in Cuba. Even after retirement he was regarded as one of the world's preeminent photo analysts.

From viewing the original Z-film, Dino Brugioni concluded that Kennedy was struck at least six times from three different angles!

Z-Film Untrustworthy?

Brugioni was shocked to later learn that a second team of photo processors was summoned to the NPIC lab on the evening of Sunday, Nov. 24. This team made a second and different set of prints.

The briefing boards prepared Saturday night apparently convinced CIA director John McCone that JFK was not killed by a lone gunman, but rather by at least one other shooter. Hence there was a conspiracy. Those briefing boards cannot be located today.

So another copy of the Zapruder film was brought to the NPIC lab by a Secret Service agent named "Bill Smith," who said he had just come from Hawkeye Works, which was the world's premier research and development photo facility in Rochester, New York. It was Kodak's own R&D branch and also did highly classified work for the CIA. The agent told the work crew at NPIC that this was a camera original film and that it had been developed at Hawkeye Works. But that was not true; the camera original was developed Friday in Dallas; it's well documented.

Apparently, alterations of some type were performed at Hawkeye during the day on Sunday and a new film was created.

That night's crew at NPIC was different than the one that had made enlargements from the film the previous evening. This time, Homer McMahon, who was the head of the color lab, was in charge of the assignment. He was assisted by Ben Hunter. In a 1997 interview with the ARRB, McMahon said his salary was paid by the CIA. He confirmed that he and his small team were asked to make a set of up to forty prints from individual frames of the Zapruder film. NPIC had special, state-of-the-art equipment that could be used, as McMahon explained, to magnify each frame desired "forty times its original size for the manufacturer of internegatives." NPIC that night did not assemble briefing boards.

The Saturday night and Sunday night teams at NPIC didn't know about each other's work on the same project, and were told not to breathe a word of any of this to anyone—not even to their superiors—and that if they were challenged when they submitted requests for overtime pay, they were to advise their employer to contact "Colonel Sands."

When the Assassination Records Review Board (ARRB) interviewed Homer McMahon of the National Photographic Interpretation Center, he stated—according to an ARRB memo obtained by this author—that "his opinion, which was that President Kennedy was shot six to eight times from at least three directions, was ultimately ignored, and the opinion of SS agent Smith—that there were three shots from behind from the Book Depository—ultimately was employed in selecting frames in the movie for reproduction. At one point he said 'you can't fight city hall.' He said that it was clear that the Secret Service agent had previously viewed the film and already had opinions about which frames depicted woundings."

The use of silencers on some gun(s) used in Dealey Plaza could account for the varied statements as to the number of shots fired.

Upon viewing the second version of the Z-film, Dino Brugioni was flabbergasted. He couldn't believe his eyes.

In a 2011 video interview, Brugioni said he saw originally a different head explosion than what is now seen in the public version of the Zapruder home movie. He recalled the blood mist spray went up much higher and the debris in Frame 313 showed "way more than what you see" today. "We were shocked when we saw it."

The exit debris seen traveling to the left rear of JFK's head by numerous Dealey Plaza eyewitnesses nearby (the Willis family, Charles Brehm, Beverly Oliver and motorcycle escort officer Bobby Hargis, et al), was visible in the first version but not now.

One exception is a grainy and high contrast version of the Z-film posted on YouTube fifteen years ago, which surprisingly shows much more of the head explosion, including a larger cloud of blood spray that rises higher and can even be seen drifting backward. It's stunning. One can only infer that more recent versions of the video which are of sharper focus, have actually been sanitized. We are being deceived into thinking we are seeing a better view when actually, the full extent of the head shot has been erased. (*Search for "The Undamaged Zapruder Film" on YouTube*).

Dino Brugioni was further incredulous when told the head explosion comprises only one frame of the Zapruder movie. Since the film traveled through the camera at the rate of eighteen frames per second, that is totally implausible. It should have been captured in multiple frames.

Abraham Zapruder and his assistant, Marion Sitzman, who was standing with him on a four-foot high cement structure in front of a white pergola, (a shaded walkway comprised of vertical posts that support crossbeams and a sturdy open lattice—a unique architectural feature in Dealey Plaza built as a WPA project), both claimed that he started filming the motorcade before the car turned the corner from Houston to Elm Street. But this is missing from the current version of the film. Why was it removed?

Now all you see is motorcycle officers making the turn, and then the film jumps and the presidential limousine appears. But you never see it turn.

Brugioni realized that some frames had been edited out in the revised version of the home movie. An unintended consequence of alteration was the speeding up of the violent backward movement of President Kennedy's head and body as now seen in the official version of the film. JFK did indeed go backward and to his left, but it wasn't as fast as the Z-film seems to indicate. None of the Dealey witnesses described it that way. The rapidity with which he seems to go backward has been a subject of debate for decades. Now there is an explanation for what occurred. But the question arises: what was seen in the original, uncut version of the amateur footage that was so revealing it had to be excised?

Dino also believed that the back of Kennedy's head had been crudely blacked in to conceal his true head wound. The very dark patch is anomalous and does not look like natural shadow, and corresponds precisely with the location of the avulsed, baseball-sized exit wound in the right rear of JFK's head seen by Parkland medical staff, SS and FBI agents. After more recent, high-tech analysis by experts, there is agreement that the black area on the back of the president's head is blatantly fake. Anyone who has Photoshop can look at some of the images and adjust the contrast and see this for themselves.

The yellowish red blob on the side of his head people assumed was brain matter was likely also drawn in. The large head wound seen in the right-front and top of the head keeps moving around and appears to be nothing but artwork, for it is entirely inconsistent with the wound seen at Parkland.

When shown enlarged Zapruder film frames depicting a right-anterior wound, Parkland doctor Paul Peters responded, "I never saw and I don't think there was such a wound. I think that was simply an artifact of copying Zapruder's movie...The only wound I saw on President Kennedy's head was in the occipito-parietal (rear) area on the right side."

With a wry expression on his face, Dino commented, "I've never seen that film like the night that I looked at it." Meaning the film as it now exists has been altered and is different than the camera original.

Dr. Roderick T. Ryan, who served for many years as regional director of engineering services for the Eastman Kodak Company, has examined the Zapruder film. He has expertise in the field, having received an Oscar for his technical contributions to the motion picture industry during the 2000 Academy Awards.

When questioned about the mysterious "blob" that appears to shift around from frame to frame right after the fatal head shot at frame 313, Ryan said "it looked as if the blobs had been painted in." In some frames it even seems as though Jackie's face has been painted in.

This Proves It

The most dramatic and convincing evidence the Zapruder film has been tampered with is that when some of the individual frames are enlarged, they appear to show that the entire front half of President Kennedy's head is missing, following a horrific effusion of brain matter that is ejected from the right side of his head in the temple region.

The head wound clearly appears to represent such a catastrophic destruction of the top front of JFK's head and face that in Z-frame 337 we see Jackie's shoulder pad where JFK's face should be. But that is impossible. This fakery establishes the crudity of the 1963 alterations to the film.

The flathead appearance that is seen in enlargements of some of the frames cannot possibly be reconciled with the contention that the Zapruder film has not been altered.

From Dealey Plaza to Parkland to Bethesda to the White House, where family members privately viewed the body, not a single person noted any damage to the face.

Dino Brugioni was also dismayed to discover that sometime after the second set of enlargements were made, apparently dirty dupes were then created so that the Z-film is fuzzy and not crystal clear as he saw it.

The camera used by Abraham Zapruder was the best you could buy for the money (about $2,000 in today's dollars): the Bell and Howell 1440PD with a Perpetua Electric Eye "that adjusts lens even while shooting." It had great optics and was a brand-new camera. So the clarity of the original film was amazingly sharp. But even the best copies of the film available today, despite being stabilized, are comparatively poor.

As researcher Jeff Marzano writes: "The version of the famous Zapruder film which is in the public domain today was changed in many ways before they released it. Those photographic alterations were sophisticated for 1963 but not for today. Hollywood film experts who restore old movies can easily detect the many crude changes made to this movie footage. There's really only one group of people who had access to that type of critical evidence and the capabilities to change it and it wasn't the mafia or the anti-Castro nuts."

A media watchdog group called FAIR (for Fairness & Accuracy In Reporting) noted that Time/Life "paid $150,000 to buy all rights to the Zapruder film, and instead of making it available to experts or journalists, spent the next decade trying to prevent the footage from being seen or studied. *Life* publisher C.D. Jackson, who ordered the Zapruder film kept from public view, was a close CIA associate."

FAIR said, "While hoarding the Zapruder film, *Life* magazine repeatedly distorted what the footage showed. One *Life* article claimed that the fatal shot caused Kennedy's 'skull to explode forward.' Another argued that Oswald had shot JFK in the throat from the rear by claiming—falsely—that the film showed the president turning far around to wave to someone in the crowd.

"Meanwhile, *Time* magazine assailed Warren Commission critics as 'leftists,' 'Communists,' or, in the case of Bertrand Russell, 'that sometime philosopher.'"

While Nation Pays Tribute To JFK, Another Murder Occurs

Late on Sunday morning, just before Lee Oswald was taken down to the basement garage at Dallas police headquarters for transfer to the county jail, Inspector Thomas Kelley of the Secret Service spoke to the suspect quietly out of earshot of everyone else. He told Oswald that if he was not guilty, then Kelley would be "very anxious to talk with him to make sure the correct story was developing as it related to the assassination." Oswald said he would be glad to discuss this proposition "with his attorney" but, for the moment, had "nothing more to say." Oswald, still handcuffed, was then taken out of the small office by Dallas detectives.

As Oswald was being escorted through the department's basement for transfer to the county jail, he was supposed to be surrounded by what's called a "four star" configuration: one man directly behind him, one on each side, and one in front.

But DPD Capt. Will Fritz had not assigned a single man to walk directly in front of the prisoner and shield him from possible attack. Right before the shooting, Fritz—who was leading the way—suddenly speeded up and began to walk so far ahead, so fast that he became separated from Oswald. This opened up a large gap that left the prisoner exposed just as he was being led in front of a crowd.

A car horn honked twice, (a signal perhaps?), and low-level mobster and strip club owner Jack Ruby sprinted like the fastest football running back out in front of the crowd and pumped a bullet into LHO's left side. Oswald looked at Ruby fleetingly with what may have been a glimmer of recognition before crying out in agony and collapsing. As video from a different angle, captured live by a KRLD-TV camera shows, a car that was being driven down the ramp and into the basement garage—late—actually struck Jack Ruby from behind and knocked him off balance. Still, detectives had to struggle to subdue the assailant and prevent him from again shooting the dying man who was writhing on the floor.

An estimated eleven million people, many gathered in living rooms with their families, witnessed the murder of JFK's alleged killer on live television. J. Edgar Hoover privately called the shooting "inexcuse-

Fritz gives Ruby a chance to kill LHO and never even looks back at gun shot.

able." Oswald could have been given a bullet proof vest to protect him, and armed officers could have lined up to block him from view as he walked to the car. But despite the death threats, and the importunings of the FBI, the DPD failed to take those precautions.

Jack Ruby later said cryptically: "...and who else could have timed it so perfectly by seconds? If it were timed that way, then someone in the police department is guilty of giving the information as to when Lee Harvey Oswald was coming down."

Afterward, Oswald was dragged on the floor to a nearby room and an unknown officer started doing CPR on him. This severely reduced his chances of surviving the gunshot. For a person who has been wounded in the abdomen, like Oswald was, pressing on the chest intensifies the internal bleeding.

One of the two cops who was handcuffed to Oswald, Jim Leavelle (who was wearing the tan suit and hat), later complained in a TV interview, "The car was NOT in place. Consequently when I walked out, I was looking to my right, where the car was being backed into position. But it wasn't quite where it ought to be. I could see this crowd of people from my left which included police officers and news reporters, cameramen and so forth. I saw Ruby in this crowd to my left. He was standing in the front with a pistol in his hand down at his side. Had [the car] been in position where we were told it would be, that would have eliminated a lot of the area in which anyone would have access to [Oswald], because it would have been blocked by the car. In fact, if the car had been sitting where we were told it was going to be, see, it would have been sitting directly upon the spot where Ruby was standing when he fired the shot."

L.D. Montgomery complained, "Captain Fritz stepped out into this door leading out to the ramp...and told us [to] come on...We came out there. They crammed those mikes over there, and we had to slow up for just a second, because they was backing this car into position. It was supposed to have been in position when we got there, but it wasn't there, so, we had to pause, or slow down for the car to come on back."

Why did Fritz give the signal that everything was ready for the transfer when it was not?

The officers were shocked to find the press crammed into the basement, so much so one radio reporter stuck his microphone in the back of one of the officers. As the suspect was led out, the assembled news cameramen immediately snapped on their bright lights, momentarily blinding some of the police escort.

It was NBC-TV executive Robert Kintner who decided that his network should cover the transfer of LHO instead of the Kennedy ceremonies in Washington. As a result, the murder of Lee Harvey Oswald was televised live on national TV. Later on, Mr. Kintner oddly ended up joining LBJ's White House staff.

Richard Nixon immediately knew who Jack Ruby was the minute he saw him shoot Oswald on television. Nixon recognized Ruby as a "Lyndon Johnson man" from the 1940s whom LBJ had urged be placed on the House Un-American Activities Committee (HUAC) as a paid informant. Johnson and Ruby were seen together a few months before the assassination at the Adolphus Hotel in Dallas with H.L. Hunt, the oilman who was Johnson's biggest contributor.

Not long after Lee Oswald was taken to Parkland, President Johnson called the hospital. Dr. Charles Crenshaw, who had treated Kennedy two days before, was among those trying to save Oswald's life.

The doctor was shocked at being interrupted and summoned to take a phone call. As Dr. Crenshaw explained in an interview, "All of a sudden this voice like God comes across. 'This is Lyndon Johnson.' And he said 'How is the accused assassin doing?' I said, 'Well, he's holding his own. He's critical. He's lost a great amount of blood. We hope we can save him,'" Crenshaw said.

LBJ then demanded, "I want a deathbed statement from the assassin. There's a man in the operating room who will take the statement. I will expect full cooperation in this matter," and then he hung up.

Dr. Crenshaw also said he noticed in the surgery suite a man wearing scrubs and carrying a gun. He believed that was the man who would have been prepared to take a signed confession from Oswald had he regained consciousness. J. Edgar Hoover confirmed in a memo for his file that he had an FBI agent present in the Dallas O.R.

Dr. Paul Peters of Parkland also said, "There were Secret Service men intermingled with the operating room personnel; there were dozens of people in the operating suite at that time.

"Since it was known that [Oswald] was under little or no anesthesia, several people shouted in his ear 'DID YOU DO IT? DID YOU DO IT?'"

Dr. Crenshaw kept secret from the public for twenty-nine years what happened that day in regard to Lyndon Johnson, fearing recrimination. He rationalized that any entity powerful enough to kill a president wouldn't hesitate to kill a doctor.

When Crenshaw finally revealed it, his account was of course attacked by the national media and is still being assailed by anonymous bloggers. They point out that White House phone logs don't list a call to Parkland. But the custodians of records maintained at the various presidential libraries all stress the disclaimer that W.H. records are not necessarily complete or even accurate. They are known to be sanitized at times.

Corroboration for Dr. Crenshaw's account came from a Parkland Hospital telephone operator, Phyllis Bartlett, who initially answered the call from the White House and then heard President Johnson come on the line. Disgusted by Crenshaw being called a liar, she came forward.

As Leo Sauvage wrote, "Only two hours after Jack Ruby had disposed of Oswald in the basement of Dallas Police Headquarters, the case against him was declared 'closed' by Police Chief Jesse Curry and by District Attorney Henry Wade who boasted that he had 'sent men to the electric chair with less evidence.' That same evening, in a televised press conference whose transcript will stand forever in the international annals of justice as an example of fantastic irresponsibility, Wade spoke the final word for the Dallas authorities: 'I would say that without any doubt he [Oswald] is the killer. There is no question that he [Oswald] was the killer of President Kennedy.'"

That statement didn't satisfy everybody in the media, though the vast majority went along with the fairy tale. ABC's Howard K. Smith asserted on the air that "we don't know if Oswald really committed the crime and perhaps we will never know."

'A Forest Of Question Marks'

Foreign newspapers expressed the suspicions of millions of people around the world about what really happened in Dallas. *Die Welt* in Hamburg, West Germany said a "forest of question marks" was left by the assassination of President Kennedy and the slaying of his accused killer. The paper said, "There is a feeling of shame that the law, which should explore the facts, was prevented from doing so. Political mists which also gathered should have been cleared. Now they thicken to poisonous clouds."

UPI reported criticism of the Dallas police was general, particularly for the announcement that the investigation into the president's murder was closed with the death of Oswald. Newspapers voiced the suspicion that there remained much of importance still unknown in the case.

"The *London Daily Mail* reported 'whispers' that 'Oswald was a tool who was used and then liquidated.' The *Abdendpost* of Frankfurt, Germany, charged that Ruby, 'the dubious strip-tease boss, well-known to police, was not stopped when he approached Lee Oswald...Our photos show the guard did not even react when the murderer had already pulled his gun.'

"'Was Kennedy a victim of an isolated act or of a conspiracy?' asked *La Suise* of Geneva, Switzerland. East Germany's Communist newspapers said that extreme rightists assassinated Kennedy and then killed Oswald to cover up their tracks."

Dan Rather Misled the American Public

The same day as John Kennedy was laid to rest, TV newsman Dan Rather told the public untruths. After being one of the few to see the home movie of the assassination filmed by Dallas resident Abraham Zapruder, Rather gave the nation an inaccurate description of what transpired. In August 1963, after a shaky start at CBS in New York, Rather was transferred to New Orleans—the hometown of mafia kingpin Carlos Marcello and other members of organized crime. Instead of having reporters at the CBS TV affiliate in Dallas, KRLD, cover the amateur movie shot by Zapruder, Dan was assigned to it.

He later claimed he just happened to be in Dallas the day Kennedy was killed and just happened to be "on the other side of the railroad tracks, beyond the triple underpass," by his estimation a mere ninety feet from the grassy knoll. His job was to fetch a film drop from a camera truck at that location, and take it to the station for editing. He claimed he knew nothing of the assassination until he arrived at KRLD, despite having driven through Dealey Plaza. Yet he admitted, "The moment I cleared the railroad tracks I saw a scene I will never forget. Some people were lying on the grass, some screaming, some running, some pointing. Policemen swarmed everywhere and distinctly above the din, I heard one shout, 'DON'T ANYBODY PANIC.' And of course, there was nothing but panic wherever you looked."

Dan Rather claimed JFK's head "went FORWARD" after the fatal shot and demonstrated what he said he saw.

What did this supposedly astute reporter think had happened at the scene of the president's motorcade?

On Monday night, November 25, Walter Cronkite introduced Rather, who reported: "We have just returned from seeing a complete motion picture of the moments preceding and the moments of the assassination..."

He described the route of the motorcade as passing "right in front of the building from which the assassin's bullet was fired." But he could not know that ANY bullets came from that location, or that only one individual was involved. He claimed Kennedy put his hand up to the right side of his face and "at that moment...he lurched just a bit forward. It was obvious that the first shot had hit him."

That isn't the way it happened at all. Kennedy resumed smiling and waving after quickly touching his forehead to brush back his chestnut colored hair after his limo had turned onto Elm Street. There was a brisk easterly wind blowing that day, which he was heading into.

One thing about Rather's description that was inconveniently accurate—because it contradicted what the official government inquiry later claimed—was Connally turned around to look at the president after the first shot, something he could not have done if the governor had already been seriously wounded by the same bullet as the one that struck Kennedy, as the government later contended.

Rather said that while Kennedy "was still leaned over at that moment, another bullet obviously hit the head of the president." The president's head went "forward violently in this manner." Rather demonstrated this supposed reaction by bending his head forward, his clear intent being that he wanted to convince the public Kennedy was struck from behind. Why?

He even proclaimed there had been three shots, but since there was no sound recorded by the movie camera Zapruder used, and eyewitness testimony varied, this too was baseless conjecture.

(On Nov. 29, 1963, the FBI wrote a memo confirming that the Secret Service had concluded that Gov. Connally had been hit by a second bullet fired after the first shot struck the president. This was later changed to try to deceive the public into believing that there was no conspiracy).

It wasn't until March 6, 1975—almost ten years after Dorothy Kilgallen died—when Geraldo Rivera first aired a pirated copy of the Zapruder film on ABC television furnished to him by JFK author Robert Groden. Americans got to see for themselves what actually happened that day in Dallas. It showed that the fatal head shot literally lifted Kennedy out of his seat, propelling him violently backward and to his left, as his right arm flopped limply and his head exploded. This powerful imagery strongly suggested at least one shot came from in front of the motorcade, (though the angle was wrong for it to come from the "grassy knoll.")

Eyewitnesses reported a puff of smoke and the smell of gunpowder wafting from behind a wooden fence and underneath some trees, and hundreds of people spontaneously ran toward that location, as photos and film footage shows. Various people in the motorcade, including Mrs. Kennedy herself—who was mere inches away from being struck by gunfire as she saw her husband murdered beside her, as well as SS agents and JFK aides—thought shots had been fired from in front of the presidential limousine. Obviously, there had to be more than one shooter.

Even Dan Rather initially reported that the president came under fire from in front of the motorcade, telling TV viewers "the gunshot wound, the fatal wound inflicted on the president of the United States entered at the base of the throat and came out at the base of the neck *on the back side*." But then he fell in line with the cover up version of events and got a big promotion. Plucked from obscurity in New Orleans, he was selected to become the CBS network's White House correspondent beginning in 1964, covering Lyndon Johnson.

Fair & Accuracy in Reporting noted that after Rather's misleading account of the Zapruder film, "his rise up the CBS ladder was aided by major reporting assignments on documentaries (in 1964, 1967 and 1975) that did evidentiary somersaults in defense of the Warren Commission."

Dorothy Kilgallen Boldly Targets LBJ

Dorothy made a startling transformation from merely expressing sorrow for the death of JFK and admiration for him and his wife, to openly questioning the official account. The turning point seemed to be when Oswald was himself murdered.

Writing in the *Journal-American* on November 29, she cast suspicion on LBJ: "President Lyndon Johnson has been elevated so swiftly to his new high post that in one sense he has been snatched up into an ivory tower. As Chief Executive, he is no longer in a position to hear the voices of ordinary people talking candidly. If he could walk invisible along the streets of the nation and listen to citizens talking wherever people gather in normal human intercourse, he would realize that he must make sure that the mystery of Lee Harvey Oswald is solved and laid before the nation down to the smallest shred of evidence.

"If Lee Harvey Oswald was President Kennedy's assassin, he was the most important prisoner the police of this country had in custody in 100 years, and no blithe announcement in Dallas is going to satisfy the American public that 'the case is closed.'

"President Johnson, has, I realize, directed the FBI to look into every aspect of the case, and that was wise, but he must go a giant step further. He must satisfy the public's uneasy mind about this peculiar assassination of the assassin or he will start his term in office by making a dire political mistake that could cost him the 1964 election.

"As a token of esteem, I give to President Johnson the information that his countrymen are gravely concerned about this happening. The killing of President Kennedy shocked and grieved them, but the murder of Oswald made them bitter, ashamed and a little afraid. People who have never been to Texas, who were miles away from the place where it happened, feel queasy, as if they had just walked away from a lynching."

She then removed the gloves completely with this rejoinder: "The case is closed, is it? Well, Tex, write a footnote for me will you?

"I'd like to know how in a big smart town like Dallas, a man like Jack Ruby—operator of a strip-tease honky tonk—could stroll in and out of police headquarters as if it were a health club at a time when a small army of law-enforcers was keeping a 'tight security guard' on Oswald.

"SECURITY—What a word for it!

"Ruby had been hanging around the scene of the interrogation and the police knew him and knew who he was, and everyone knew he had at times carried a gun, but they didn't even frisk him before they let him in to watch the excitement. What's the answer to that one? The police check the credentials of the reporters and the guys pushing the television cameras around, but good ole Jack is such a buddy he just blends in with the scenery and they plumb forget to ask him to check his gun at the door...

"It certainly was humiliating to a lot of Americans...We are concerned, not just about what foreigners think is happening to our nation, but what we think is happening..."

She wrote the slaying of Oswald prevented due process. "When that right is taken away from any man by the incredible combination of a Jack Ruby and insufficient security, we feel chilled. Justice is a big rug. When you pull it out from under one man, a lot of others fall, too.

"That is why so many people are saying there is 'something queer' about the killing of Oswald, something strange about the way his case was handled, and a great deal 'missing' in the official account of his crime."

Despite the vile nature of the events of the previous few days, she felt the public was owed the truth. "The American people have just lost a beloved President. It is a dark chapter in our history, but we have the right to read every word of it. It cannot be kept locked in a file in Dallas."

What is striking about Dorothy Kilgallen's comments is she was boldly implying there was already a coverup in place and that the public was not being told the truth about what had transpired in Dallas. She was right. DK was virtually a lone voice in the wilderness because the rest of the press, with very few exceptions, was parroting the official line that Kennedy had been killed by a lone assassin firing three shots from the Texas School Book Depository Building and there was no conspiracy.

In fact, her own newspaper—the *Journal-American*—ran a banner headline on the front page: "OSWALD LONE KILLER. FBI REPORT TO PROVE IT." It quoted anonymous "government sources" but those sources turned out to be the FBI itself, ludicrously drawing conclusions before an investigation could barely get underway. The "fix" was in and obedient lapdogs eagerly devoured every tidbit fed to them by authorities.

Having covered major murder cases, Dorothy had good instincts about what was true and what was subterfuge. She smelled trouble.

The Parkland Press Conference Had Raised Suspicions

A few days prior, Kilgallen had seen on TV the president's assistant press secretary, Malcomb Kilduff, tell the press assembled in a nurses' classroom at Parkland Hospital, at 1:33 p.m. CST, that, "President John F. Kennedy died at approximately one o'clock Central Standard Time, today here in Dallas. He died of a gunshot wound in the brain..."

When asked for details, the perspiring and nervous White House spokesman, obviously struggling to keep his emotions under control, replied, "The president was shot once, in the head...Doctor Burkley (the president's personal physician) has told me that it was a simple matter of a bullet right through the head." Whereupon Kilduff pointed to his right temple, implying a shot from the front.

Shortly thereafter, NBC reported a shot both to the president's throat and right temple, citing Admiral George Burkley. At 1:45 p.m. another network carried a similar account. Then NBC's Chet Huntley reported a shot through the right temple as Robert MacNeil said on TV it was unclear to him how the president could have been shot through the throat and right temple if the assassin was firing from behind. Frank McGee called this "incongruous."

This sort of reporting, of course, undermined the cover-up that was already underway, so authorities brought pressure to bear on the NBC network (and others). It took awhile, but on December 11, a teletype from the FBI office in New York to J. Edgar Hoover stated that NBC had given the Bureau assurances that it will "televise only those items which are in consonance with Bureau report [on the assassination]."

However, at 3:16 p.m. on the afternoon of November 22, a press conference was broadcast live from Parkland, at which Dr. Malcolm Perry spoke about gunfire from in front of the president's motorcade.

In a calm manner he described in sequential order the steps that he and other doctors took in a doomed attempt to save the president's life. Most notably, he stated, "There was a neck wound anteriorly and a large wound to his head in the right posterior area."

Since Perry had performed a tracheotomy on the moribund Kennedy by slightly enlarging a wound found on the front of the president's throat, just below the Adam's Apple, there was this exchange:

Reporter: "Which way was the bullet coming on the neck wound? At him?"

Dr. Perry: "It appeared to be coming at him."

Reporter: "Doctor, describe the entrance wound. You think from the front in the throat?"

Dr. Perry: "The wound appeared to be an entrance wound in the front of the throat, yes, that is correct."

Immediately after the news conference, the doctor was accosted by a man in a suit and tie who grabbed his arm and warned him menacingly, "Don't you ever say that again!" The agent who did this was Elmer Moore of the Dallas Secret Service office. He also was assigned to badger other Parkland doctors into changing their accounts of what they saw. Subsequently, in testimony to a Senate Committee chaired by Frank Church, a witness testified that Moore went on a rant about Kennedy supposedly being a "pinko" who was selling us out to the Communists. It was said he became so agitated in talking about JFK that it was frightening.

Yet SS agent Elmer Moore got a promotion after harassing Parkland doctors to change their stories about the president's wounds. He became the *aide de camp* to Supreme Court Justice Earl Warren when the Warren Commission was formed.

Later, Moore claimed he acted on orders from Washington and Thomas Kelley, assistant director of protective services. Kelley was an interesting character, who had served as a consultant to several Far Eastern police agencies, as well as consultant to the Dominican Republic on protective matters.

On the day of Kennedy's murder, Kelley was said to be in Louisville, Kentucky and received word of the assassination from SS Chief James Rowley, who contacted him from Washington. Kelley did not even arrive in Dallas until Friday evening. While there, he sat in on at least four interviews with Lee Harvey Oswald. So it is unclear when instructions were conveyed to Mr. Moore or if it was even Kelley who told him what to do.

Agent Moore admitted that he coerced Dr. Perry to change his flat statement that there was an entry wound in the front of the president's throat, but added "I regret what I had to do with Dr. Perry [but I had been given] marching orders from Washington...I did everything I was told, we all did everything we were told, or we'd get our heads cut off."

This suggests that mere minutes after the president's slaying, there was already not only an active coverup in place, but that the script had been written in advance and shared with key people. It is abundantly clear that from the outset, the plan had been to promote the idea of a lone gunman firing from the rear. No other scenarios or suspects were even mentioned. Case closed.

Remember that Dr. Perry had been harassed by phone calls from Bethesda Friday night and pressured to change his story about the neck wound. This was also corroborated by Dr. John Ebersole, Acting Chief of Radiology at Bethesda Naval Hospital, during his formerly-secret testimony to the House Select Committee on Assassinations (HSCA) in 1978.

This blows the cover off of the idea that the autopsy doctors did not know about the anterior neck wound until the next day and hence they did not probe it. Obviously, not only did they know about it Friday night, they were trying to cover it up that night. This casts grave doubts on the honesty of the autopsy doctors, and makes it all the more suspicious that Kennedy's anterior neck wound was not dissected to track the bullet path.

Soon the story began to change. The anatomically precise expression "throat wound" turned into the less specific "neck wound" to give the impression that all shots had been fired from behind.

Reporter Martin Steadman of the *New York Herald Tribune* recalled that about a week after the assassination, he and two other newsmen were at Dr. Perry's home. The doctor explained that he thought it was an entrance wound because the small circular hole was clean. He pointed out that as a trauma room physician, over the years, he had treated hundreds of patients with similar wounds and certainly knew the difference between an exit and an entrance wound, plus he was an avid hunter and could readily tell the difference.

8
A Grand Design

On November 29, 1963, under intense public pressure and as a way to control the narrative, President Johnson created the President's Commission on the Assassination of President Kennedy, aka the Warren Commission, by Executive Order (E.O. 11130). The following men served on the Commission:

• Earl Warren, Chief Justice of the United States Supreme Court.

• Noted segregationist Richard B. Russell, Democratic senator from Georgia and chairperson of the Senate Armed Services Committee, former Governor of Georgia and attorney in that state.

• Allen W. Dulles, former Director of the Central Intelligence Agency. He oversaw the 1953 Iranian coup d'état, the 1954 Guatemalan coup d'état, the Lockheed U-2 aircraft program, the Project MKUltra mind control program and the Bay of Pigs invasion. A significant fact that must be mentioned here is JFK pressured Dulles to resign over the Bay of Pigs. On Nov. 28, 1961, Kennedy gave Dulles the National Security Medal at the CIA Headquarters in Langley, Virginia. The next day, the White House released his resignation letter. He had no "official" capacity within the CIA at the time of the investigation into Kennedy's death. He didn't belong on the Warren panel because *Dulles should have been one of the suspects.*

• Future President of the United States, Gerald R. Ford, Republican representative from Michigan and chairperson of the House Republican Conference. The duplicitous Mr. Ford had a close association with the CIA and also breached confidentiality by blabbing to J. Edgar Hoover about closed-door discussions as the Commission's work evolved.

• John Sherman Cooper, Republican senator from Kentucky, former county and circuit judge in Kentucky and United States Ambassador to India.

• Hale Boggs, Democratic representative from Louisiana and majority whip in the U.S. House of Representatives. (Daughter Cokie Roberts is regarded as one of the "Founding Mothers" of National Public Radio).

• John J. McCloy, lawyer, former president of the International Bank for Reconstruction and Development and former United States High Commissioner for Germany.

Notice Lyndon Johnson shrewdly constructed an entirely government-run investigative body. Thus it was always under his total control.

The point being that, because of their connections with the government, not one member would have been permitted under U.S. law to serve on a jury had Lee Oswald faced trial. So they were in "CYA" mode on behalf of the government. It is small wonder that the Chief Justice himself remarked that the release of some of the Commission's information "might not be in your lifetime."

Johnson literally blackmailed some of the members to agree to participate. After Warren refused several times to serve, Johnson called him to the Oval Office, which was a taped conversation, hinting that "Hoover told me about a little incident in Mexico City," after which a frightened Earl Warren began to cry.

In the case of Sen. Russell, a White House tape confirms LBJ alluding to scandalous behavior on the part of the senator and saying, "I can't arrest you and I'm not going to put the FBI on you but you're goddammed going to serve, I'll tell you that."

To assure that all the members of the W.C. and key law enforcement agencies were all under his influence, LBJ warned them it was imperative they convince the public Kennedy was killed by a lone assassin and there was no conspiracy, or it could precipitate a showdown with Cuba and/or the Soviet Union. According to the book, *The Johnson White House Tapes, 1963-1964* by widely respected historian Michael Beschloss, Johnson warned this could "check us into a [nuclear] war that can kill 40 million Americans in an hour." At least one key member of the Commission—Earl Warren—took that to heart. It was a way of Johnson instilling fear to make sure nobody probed too deeply.

White House tapes provide one of the most direct means of understanding how a cover-up was perpetrated by those, like Warren, who were not involved in the assassination and would not under normal circumstances be what Sylvia Meagher, an expert on the Warren Report, termed "Accessories After the Fact."

Johnson, of course, didn't really believe the Soviets or Cuba were involved in killing JFK. In fact, J. Edgar Hoover warned in a letter to a presidential assistant that the Soviet Union's intelligence agency, the KGB, had information tying LBJ to an assassination plot against Kennedy. The FBI had intercepted instructions from Moscow to the KGB residency in New York "to develop information" on Johnson.

Earl Warren Screws Up

From the onset, Earl Warren made a major mistake by deciding the Warren Commission didn't need investigators. Instead, he assembled a staff of fourteen lawyers and relied almost exclusively on the FBI for the legwork. He and his Commission did this despite being aware the FBI had already given them a hastily prepared report—written before they even began—that found no evidence of a conspiracy.

It was also unfair to impose the burden on the FBI whose agents were put in the awkward position of having to investigate and potentially report the shortcomings of colleagues they still had to work with in the future. So from the outset, there was a built-in predisposition not to reveal embarrassing information about fellow agents or the Bureau generally. In fact, pertinent records were in some cases destroyed, in violation of the law.

Chief Counsel of the Warren Commission, J. Lee Rankin, who was interviewed by Michael Ewing, staff member of the House Select Committee on Assassinations in 1978, was deeply troubled by what he learned after the fact about how Hoover and the FBI destroyed evidence that should have been given to the W.C. He said he found the FBI performance, "Quite disturbing in hindsight. We would have found their conduct nearly unbelievable if we had known about it at the time." Ewing related that in his talk with Rankin, "I commented that 'we have heard testimony to the effect that if the [Warren Commission] staff had known about it...that the decision to use the FBI for investigative work might have changed.' He agreed, saying, 'We couldn't have used the people involved in any further way, that's clear. The FBI would have to have been regarded as a suspect in that instance and that in turn would have affected everything.' He indicated that he would have gotten his own investigators at that point."

Michael Ewing said that Rankin "repeatedly expressed the view that both the FBI and CIA had concealed important material from the Commission, and that the CIA/Mafia plots would have had a 'very direct bearing on the areas of conspiracy which we tried to pursue.'"

One of DK's Fellow Journalists Shares Her Suspicions

Reporter Martin Steadman had been sent to Dallas, Texas to further look into the circumstances surrounding the JFK assassination. By happenstance, his paper had recently created a special investigative unit to probe important stories, headed by William Haddad, regarded as one of the best investigative reporters in New York. Haddad also had worked in the Kennedy presidential campaign in 1960 and became the first Inspector General of the Peace Corps before being lured back into the newspaper profession. Intriguingly, in 1962, JFK had dispatched Mr. Haddad to visit editorial offices of various publications on his behalf and dissuade them from running any stories about Kennedy's affair with Marilyn Monroe. Haddad complained about it later and said he was lied to by the president.

Steadman himself was uniquely qualified for the assignment of going to Texas because while previously working for Dorothy Kilgallen's newspaper, the *Journal-American*, he had spent three years tracking the Senate investigation of labor racketeering that was driven by Chief Counsel Robert Kennedy.

Steadman recalled, "On the plane from New York to Dallas, I thought I would come upon a beehive of law enforcement activity in Dallas. I knew immediately what Attorney General Robert Kennedy must have been thinking. He had to be looking at the connection between Jack Ruby and Paul Dorfman, (Jimmy Hoffa's partner in crime). He put in years of his life chasing down Hoffa. I imagined law enforcement was turning Jack Ruby upside down, inside out and every way but loose on his connections to Hoffa, Dorfman and the Chicago mob. I'm still stunned by how little interest J. Edgar Hoover had in following leads or suspicions President Kennedy had been killed by his most hate-driven enemies in organized crime."

Mr. Steadman spent eleven days in Dallas interviewing people and turning up new information that the FBI showed no interest in.

In a retrospective piece he penned in 2013, Martin Steadman opined that, "Of all the mysteries about the assassination that linger fifty years later, none is more baffling than the decision by Attorney General Robert Kennedy to distance himself and his Justice Department from the feeble inquiry that followed.

"When President Johnson and FBI Director Hoover agreed on the appointment of the Warren Commission and immediately provided the fledgling committee with an FBI report that said there was no conspiracy to kill President Kennedy, Attorney General Robert F. Kennedy and the Justice Department were cut out of the loop. The FBI works for the Attorney General, but in this case President Johnson decreed that Hoover would report FBI findings directly to the Warren Commission. The net effect was to muzzle all the talent and expertise of the Justice Department, including their power to convene grand juries. The nullification of Bob Kennedy's Justice Department was deliberate and to this day I can't get my mind around the enormity of that decision and Robert Kennedy's acceptance of it."

Steadman noted that, "Jimmy Hoffa's closest associates were in Jack Ruby's November telephone records, along with known associates of Trafficante and Marcello." Ordinarily, "Robert Kennedy and his Justice Department could not have remained silent.

"Which raises another question that is so difficult to comprehend. How could all of that talent and knowledge and experience at Attorney General Robert Kennedy's Justice Department have been silenced for the ten months the Warren Commission conducted its inquiry? Initially, Bob Kennedy removed himself from the events that followed the assassination of his brother, on the grounds that it would not seem proper for him to lead the investigation. But he and his powerful Organized Crime strike force accepted the role of unconcerned spectators totally. At no time from the murder in Dallas to the issuance of the Warren Commission Report ten months later was the Justice Department a factor in the process. What the hell happened then and thereafter?"

This would make sense if one viewed JFK's death as part of a conspiracy involving members of organized crime, perhaps disaffected CIA agents, and criminal elements associated with Lyndon Johnson such as some rich Texas oil men. (More about that later).

We now know Bobby Kennedy had led efforts to assassinate Cuba's renegade leader Fidel Castro. After the disastrous Bay of Pigs invasion, JFK wanted any efforts to get rid of Castro to be "invisible." He tasked his brother, the attorney general, with coming up with a covert plan that was known internally as Project Freedom. By September 1963 contingency plans were drawn up to take action against Cuba. Oversight of this was assigned to Lt. Col. Alexander Haig (who would go on to betray Richard Nixon, serve as Secretary of State in a Republican administration and make a spectacle of himself by claiming in rattled fashion to be in charge after Ronald Reagan was wounded).

The irony is that there were ongoing back channel discussions between the U.S. and Cuba over some form of a peace agreement even as Bobby Kennedy proceeded with plans to oust Fidel. This is all very strange because two widely divergent strategies for dealing with Cuba seemed to have been running concurrently within the Kennedy administration.

Jefferson Morley notes: "JFK kept alive the idea of making peace with Cuba. Kennedy was excoriated by Cuba hawks for refusing to order air support for the CIA brigade during the Bay of Pigs invasion in April 1961. In October 1962, he refused his general's unanimous recommendation that he order an invasion of Cuba during the Cuban missile crisis. In April 1963, he overruled CIA director John McCone and approved a crackdown on Cuban exiles launching freelance raids on the island, inciting bitterness and fury in Miami. In November 1963 Kennedy refused to rule out a diplomatic settlement, despite his own brother's opposition. JFK was serious about making peace with Cuba." Indeed, on Nov. 5, 1963, the president held a meeting on Cuban peace initiatives.

Fidel Castro himself stated, just before the president's death, "He (Kennedy) has the possibility of becoming the greatest President of the United States...He has come to understand many things over the last few months. I'm convinced that anyone else would be worse."

Yet RFK had approved a partnership with key members of organized crime to furnish the assassins. Those trying to protect him claimed he was surprised when briefed about it, but more recent revelations prove he was in the thick of things from the start. There is the suspicion that some of these assets were redirected against President Kennedy instead, which would be strong motivation for RFK to want to avoid revelations that would tarnish his family's legacy.

Hence Bobby Kennedy was forced to remain quiet.

Because truth is often stranger than fiction, *What's My Line?* host John Daly was married to Justice Earl Warren's socialite daughter, Virginia. The couple wed in 1960 and Virginia spent most of her time throwing lavish parties and traveling alongside the jet-set crowd including Conrad "Connie" Hilton, the founder of the Hilton Hotels chain. Daly had to have been privy to Dorothy's feelings regarding the Commission's findings.

Dorothy Zeroes In On Lax Security

DK's Dec. 3, 1963, column criticized the ineptitude of JFK's security: "Communique from Paris: 'People here and in Rome were appalled at the haphazard security measures taken during President Kennedy's visit to Texas.

"'How many Secret Service men were in the detail traveling with President Kennedy? A couple of hundred? In Paris, General De Gaulle always travels at a 60-mile-an-hour clip with 20,000 men of the security police lining his route. Traffic is suspended for two and a half hours before he rides through the city, and buildings are checked—every occupant is checked—through his concierges and by other means.

"'Do you know that DeGaulle seldom occupies the same office for more than a few days?' He keeps shifting his headquarters to foil assassination attempts—even in his own circle. One day he is in an office where you might expect to find him, a couple of days later he is in an office he's never used before.

"'Perhaps that is why he has lived to a ripe old age.'

"Perhaps, *mon ami*. But I think there has never been a President of the United States who would have wanted the job if he had to live like that. Including—in fact, especially—JFK."

Dorothy's guess that a couple of hundred Secret Service agents traveled with Kennedy to Texas is wildly off the mark. Only twenty-eight agents made the trip and just twelve were specifically assigned to guard the President and Mrs. Kennedy in the motorcade.

At least nine of them had been out the night before, until the wee hours of the morning, drinking at The Cellar, a dive in Fort Worth. It didn't even have a liquor license, was an unsavory hang-out, its waitresses wore only skimpy bikinis and the owner literally served moonshine to select patrons while they were seated (or laying) on old cushions on the floor. A sign on the wall said EVIL SPELLED BACKWARDS IS LIVE. Proprietor Pat Kirkwood was a licensed pilot who owned a twin-engine plane, and curiously flew to Mexico hours after JFK's assassination.

Kennedy's SS agents had recruited a couple of Dallas firemen to guard his hotel room door while they partied.

Comedian George Carlin was said to be performing that night and scared a few of the drunken SS men by doing an impersonation of

Kennedy that startled them into believing the president had entered the room.

All of them were sleep-deprived, if not hungover. Six of the agents stayed out until 3 a.m., and Paul Landis—who would ride on the right-side running board of the follow-up car behind the presidential limo—admitted he didn't go back to his hotel room until 5 a.m.

Even Clint Hill, Mrs. Kennedys' agent—and the only one who ran toward the car, albeit too late to save the president—stayed out until 2:45 a.m. and had a wake-up call for 6 a.m.

There were simply not enough men, agents were routinely overworked, even without their partying, and Secret Service man Gerald Blaine recalled that working double shifts since Kennedy became president was a common practice. He kept a few bags of peanuts in his flight bag and that would often be the only thing he would have time to eat all day.

It is unfathomable that despite the fact that plots against the president had been uncovered in Chicago, Tampa and Miami as recently as a few days earlier, no threat assessment information was conveyed to the advance team in Dallas, despite repeated requests.

The 112th Military Intelligence Group at 4th Army Headquarters at Fort Sam Houston was told to "stand down" over the protests of the unit commander, Col. Maximillian Reich, rather than report for duty to help guard the Commander-in-Chief, John Kennedy, in Dallas.

By comparison, in Tampa, Florida on November 18, one hundred and fifty military units from nearby MacDill Air Force base augmented local police for protective detail, as did seventy four from Orlando and McCoy AFB. All four hundred members of the Tampa Police Department—including those who were scheduled to have the day off—were assigned to provide security for President Kennedy and St. Petersburg and Clearwater officers helped out too. Forty-six Hillsborough County sheriff deputies participated, as did officers from Sarasota, Manatee, Polk and Pinellas counties. Twenty three troops from the Florida Highway Patrol were on hand as were reps from Sumter, Citrus, Hermande, Pasco, Polk, Pinelas and Millsborough counties. An Auxillary patrol assisted.

Military units secured all underpasses, rooftops, sewers, roadways—even a large stadium.

But in Dallas, John Kennedy was left vulnerable to attack.

The motorcycle policemen who typically rode alongside the presidential car were moved to the rear flank in Dallas and reduced in number, in contrast to the prior Texas motorcades in San Antonio, Houston, and Fort Worth on November 21-22. Dallas motorcycle officer B.J. Martin said that after the president's plane landed at Dallas Love Field, "While Kennedy was busy shaking hands with all the well-wishers at the airport, Johnson's Secret Service people came over to the motorcycle cops and gave us a bunch of instructions...They also ordered us into the damnedest escort formation I've ever seen. Ordinarily, you bracket the car with four motorcycles, one on each fender. But this time, they told the four of us [Martin, Hargis, Chaney and Jackson] assigned to the president's car there'd be no forward escorts. We were to stay well to the back and not let ourselves get ahead of the car's rear wheels under any circumstances. I'd never heard of a formation like that, much less ridden in one, but they said they wanted to let the crowds have an unrestricted view of the president. Well, I guess somebody got an 'unrestricted view' of him, all right."

During cross-examination by W.C. counsel David Belin, officer M.L. Baker confirmed the protection was changed. "When we got to the airport, our sergeant instructed me that there wouldn't be anybody riding beside the president's car."

Yet a memo dated Nov. 21, 1963 and sent to Dallas Police Chief Jesse Curry listed the names of the DPD motorcycle police officers assigned to help guard JFK, even specifying what positions they should assume in relation to the presidential limousine. There were to have been EIGHT motorcycles flanking both sides of the car and two behind him. But this plan was abandoned. Why?

Secret Service agents typically rode on special running boards that extended out on both sides of the custom-built Lincoln Continental presidential limousine, which was also equipped with handles they could hold onto. In addition, the limousine had special platforms built into the rear bumper—one on the left and the one on the right—for agents to stand on or crouch, holding onto special handles on the trunk lid. So six agents could be positioned around the perimeter of the vehicle.

But in Dallas they were told to stay off the car.

When one of the agents, Don Lawton, attempted to get on the back bumper of the president's automobile as the motorcade was about to leave Love Field, he was stopped by Emory Roberts, who rose in his seat in the follow-up sedan and ordered Lawton off the car. This was so unusual that—as you can see in the existing video captured by Dallas TV station WFAA—SS agent Lawton threw his hands up in the air three times in seeming disbelief, walking backwards as he addressed Roberts, appearing to question why he was not allowed to ride on the right rear of JFK's limo.

Asked about this, Clint Hill claimed, "Don Lawton's assignment that day was *not* to ride in the follow-up car. His assignment was to remain at Love Field and handle our return—secure the airport for us when we came back. We were going to fly onto Austin, Texas. And what he was doing was, when he came back off the car, he was saying 'okay you guys, I'm going to lunch. Have a good trip.' I talked to him during the last month and he reiterated to me the same thing again. That is exactly what he was doing. Making a gesture to us in the follow-up car—'See ya.'"

With all due respect to Mr. Hill, that makes no sense. If Lawton was going to go to lunch, how could he guard the airport? That's a contradiction. Besides, for any SS agent to take a lunch break during the president's visit to Dallas is just not believable.

Harder to explain is why the sequence of the vehicles in the Dallas motorcade was ominously changed. The president's physician, Dr. George Burkley, was assigned to ride on a bus with Kennedy's secretary, Evelyn Lincoln, and other WH staff, which was the twenty-fourth vehicle in the rear of the motorcade. JFK's military aides, Godfrey McHugh and Ted Clifton were in a car that was sixteenth. Burkley protested at the time, to no avail, and McHugh later said his positioning was "unusual."

The vital White House Signal Corps car that contained Chief Warrant Officer Arthur Bales and U.S. Army man Ira Gearhart—the "bag man" who carried the large briefcase that was handcuffed to his wrist and that contained the secret codes the president would need to launch nuclear missiles in the event of an attack on the United States—were relegated to the twenty-second car. This was an extreme departure from the norm as these two men are supposed to stay within very close proximity to the Commander-in-Chief at all times.

Thirty-four members of the White House press corps were crowded on two buses that occupied the seventeenth and nineteenth positions.

Crucially, cameramen were put in cars in the tenth, eleventh and twelfth spots in the parade. As lensman Tom Dillard pointed out, this effectively removed important potential eyewitnesses, as the press still and motion picture cameramen usually rode on a flatbed truck directly in front of JFK's limo—with cameras trained on the car in order to capture its movement along the parade route—not to mention the press bus which usually comes after the follow-up car.

What we have instead is film shot from the back of the motorcade which can't even see the president's car most of the time up ahead. In Warren Commission testimony Dillard said "we lost our position out at the airport. I understood we were supposed to be quite a bit closer..." Asked if they could see the president's car as it made its turn from Houston onto Elm Street, Dillard replied, "No; and the whole parade, the whole trip to town, I could only distinguish the president's car on very few occasions [when there was a rise in the pavement]. We had a very, very poor view of the president's car."

Had the sequencing of the vehicles in the motorcade been the way it normally was, film crews would have captured the assassination in vivid detail. Obviously someone wanted to prevent that. Dillard said the flatbed truck for photographers was canceled at the last minute and they were put in Chevrolet convertibles "which totally put us out of the picture."

So are we to believe "loner" Lee Harvey Oswald did this?

AP photographer Henry Burroughs said, "I was a member of the White House pool aboard Air Force One when we arrived with JFK in Dallas on that fateful day. We, the pool, were dismayed to find our pool car shoved back to about number eleven position in the motorcade. We protested, but it was too late."

Besides this, on November 21, Dallas Sheriff Bill Decker agreed to offer Secret Service Agent Forrest Sorrels his "full support" for motorcade security for November 22 (as verified in Sorrels' report), yet on the morning of the assassination, according to Deputy Roger Craig, this was nonexistent.

Craig explained in a TV interview, "A couple of hours before Kennedy was to arrive, the sheriff called us in, what I call the 'street people'—the plainclothesmen, the detectives—and he instructed us that we were to stand out in front [of the sheriff's office near Dealey Plaza] and in no way take part in the security of that motorcade. That we were merely spectators and nothing more."

Decker had his men standing idle on the corners of Houston and Elm Streets.

Asked if that seemed unusual, Craig replied, "It did to me at the time, because there were so many people around, and so few Dallas police officers. This was one of the first things I noticed, was the lack of the Dallas police officers, to keep the people back."

It was later claimed by Police Chief Curry these unusual "stand down" orders came to Decker via a call from Washington.

Later, the deputies almost unanimously agreed that they believed the shots originated from the railroad yard located just behind the grassy knoll. Of the twenty Dallas deputies who gave statements regarding the shooting, sixteen thought the assassin(s) had fired from that area while three had "no opinion" and only one "decided the shots came from" the Book Depository.

No orders to watch building windows were given, but there should have been. SS agent Winston Lawson couldn't remember if he told the Dallas police to watch the windows along the route. He testified: "I cannot say definitely that I told the police to watch windows. I usually do. On this particular case I cannot say whether I definitely said that. I believe I did, but I would not swear to the fact that I said watch all the windows."

The Motorcade Route And Protocols Not Followed

It has been claimed that the route of the motorcade was changed at the last minute. It would be more accurate to say the route was not finalized until a few days before the president arrived in Dallas.

It would have been possible for the Kennedy parade to follow a much more direct and hence shorter path from the airport to the Trade Mart, where he was to speak at a luncheon. But since this was a political trip, maximum exposure was desired. So forty-five minutes were allocated for a parade that would take JFK through neighborhoods and the downtown area, to enable people to see him and Mrs. Kennedy.

It has been argued that the only logical route was the one chosen. In order to be able to access the Stemmons Freeway after leaving downtown, the procession of vehicles had to turn off Main Street and head north one block, then west on Elm, because that's the only way to access the expressway on-ramp. A concrete curb prevented making a turn onto the highway directly off Main.

But a simple glance at Google maps shows that if the motorcade had turned west just one block earlier, from Harwood onto Elm—thus avoiding Main altogether—and headed west, it would have avoided the zig-zag that slowed down the procession. The better scenario would have enabled the presidential limo to pick up speed, making it less of a target—a strategy, incidentally, that the Secret Service had employed in Tampa. Instead, the route chosen meant the presidential procession had to backtrack and enter the one area of the city that would enable a crossfire.

That entailed going through a zig-zag between buildings. Dallas-based SS man Forrest Sorrels recommended the route and Winston Lawson, a member of the White House security detail, okayed it. But no defensive posture was planned or adopted to protect the president in this particular part of the parade. Simple logic should have raised the alarm that this traffic pattern offered a unique opportunity for crossfire from at least three directions. Strangely, while the details of the route were provided to various security agencies, the FBI was not informed. Was someone worried Hoover would foil another plot, given his prior warnings about a sniper team stalking Kennedy that November?

Indeed, the assassination occurred immediately after the motorcade was slowed by a turn of about one hundred twenty degrees to get onto Elm from Houston Street. It was the perfect spot for murder.

Secret Service protocols were incomprehensively not followed. Whenever the car carrying the president slowed, two agents on the running boards of the follow-up SS car were supposed to dismount and get on the special platforms on the rear of JFK's limo. Clint Hill, Mrs. Kennedy's assigned agent, had gotten on and off the left rear bumper at least four times, often riding in a crouched position during the forty-five minute procession. At no point during that day's parade did agents ever surround Kennedy, despite the threatening political climate of Dallas. And Mr. Hill jumped off the back of the car and returned to the follow-up vehicle less than ninety seconds before the tragedy occurred.

Why did he do this? Did Emory Roberts order him off the back of the limo like he had agent Lawton at the airport? This author posed the question to Hill via email but he did not reply, although his wife did say autographed copies of his latest book were available.

Previously questioned about this, Secret Service colleague Gerald Blaine claimed on CNN that by the time the motorcade reached Dealey Plaza, agents could no longer ride on the fenders.

"We were going into a freeway, and that's where you take the speeds up to 60 and 70 miles an hour. So we would not have had any agents there anyway," he said.

That is asinine. There were four Secret Service agents standing on the running boards of the follow-up car through Dealey Plaza. Yet Blaine claimed it was unsafe for two of them to be on the rear bumper platforms hanging onto special handles on the trunk of the presidential Lincoln? That makes no sense.

It's this sort of gaslighting that Mr. Blaine and others have done that is so egregious, and raises suspicions about their dedication to John Kennedy's safety and their willingness to be truthful.

JFK's limousine had slowed considerably to make the right turn onto Houston and then reduced speed to less than eight miles per hour making the hairpin left turn onto Elm. The SS knew in advance this was the most vulnerable point of the entire motorcade.

At a bare minimum, two agents should have been on the back of Kennedy's car through that area. Better yet, a total of six agents could have ridden on the running boards and both rear fender platforms of the presidential limo, as had been done in some prior motorcades.

There was plenty of time for the agents on the running boards of the SS follow-up car to get inside their big Cadillac convertible before they arrived at the freeway exit, considering Will Greer was only going 11.2 mph. And that's exactly what they did. But they waited until after the president was murdered, just before the motorcade raced to Parkland.

Even worse is that when the first shot rang out, Emory Roberts ordered agent John Ready, who was standing on the right front running board of the follow-up car a mere five feet away from the back of the presidential Lincoln, not to move. Had Ready done so, he likely could have leapt across the trunk of the Kennedys' car ahead and shoved JFK down in the seat, making him less of a target.

When SS man Sam Kinney was asked about this, he told Vincent Palamara, "Exactly right, and I'm involved in that, too!"

In his report, Emory Roberts lied and said the reason for the recall was because the president was twenty to twenty five feet in front of them. Video shows the two vehicles were five feet apart. Besides, he could not have known how much time would elapse between shots.

The only hero that day was Clint Hill, Jackie Kennedy's assigned agent, who disregarded Roberts and leapt into action. Yet if Hill had continued riding on the rear bumper through Dealey Plaza, it obviously would have been much easier for him to have acted fast enough by flinging himself across the trunk of the car and shoving Kennedy down onto the seat before the last shots were fired.

Similarly, if agent Ready had been positioned on the right rear of the presidential limousine, as he should have been, he also could have reacted to protect JFK given the time span of the shots. But these precautions were not taken and no one was held accountable.

Emory Roberts was never even interviewed by the FBI or the Warren Commission. One doesn't have to be a conspiracy fanatic to wonder why, after the murder of John Kennedy, Mr. Roberts was given a *promotion* to being Lyndon Johnson's appointments secretary, to replace Dave Powers. The news media were shocked when they observed Roberts greeting the Japanese ambassador in January 1965. The AP reported that the White House "has clamped a secrecy lid...on President Johnson's staff."

Besides the failings of the federal security personnel, Dallas Police Chief Jesse Curry did not explain why the Dallas Police Department decided to OFFICIALLY end its security supervision for the motorcade one block short of the full route through downtown. This unsupervised block includes Dealey Plaza.

Who gave those orders? Floyd Boring was responsible for the biggest part of it. He was the Assistant Special-Agent-In-Charge of the White House Detail, who handled the advance planning and on-the-ground implementation of security for the Texas trip. Mr. Boring chose Winston Lawson as the S.S. advance agent for the stop in Dallas.

Washington Post reporter Carol Leonnig—a three-time Pulitzer Prize-winning writer whose work has been described obsequiously and not entirely accurately by the *Wall Street Journal* as "a true and honest public service"—claims in her 2021 book on the Secret Service that Boring was blameless. She faults Kennedy for having supposedly told Boring on November 18 before leaving on the trip to Texas that protection of him was "excessive" and gave "the wrong impression to people."

But Leonnig's reporting is completely inconsistent with the statements President Kennedy made to his wife and close aides in which he expressed worries about his own safety, as recently as the morning of his death, as previously noted in this book. Although JFK would sometimes elude his SS detail by spontaneously taking a swim when at a beach, or make an impromptu stop somewhere, there was little risk in that because his actions were unannounced and therefore not known ahead of time to a would-be assassin. But Kennedy told Jackie: "We're heading into nut country today" and even warned somebody might "want to shoot me from a window with a rifle." He repeated that worry to aide Lawrence O'Brien in Forth Worth earlier that morning. O'Brien recalled, "I went in to visit the president and he was looking out the window [of the hotel] down at this open area, where they were putting the finishing touches on the platform (from which he was going to make brief remarks). And he made the comment to me, 'They talk about security, and protecting you, but look at this. If somebody wants to get you, they can always do it."

It's fair to ask Ms. Leonnig: Does that sound like a man who would tell Fred Boring to DECREASE security around him? It's this kind of whitewashing of history even by contemporary journalists that is so contemptible because it distorts the facts of this tragedy. For Leonnig to blame the victim is truly reprehensible.

By contrast, Vince Palamara—an expert on the Secret Service—writes, "Floyd Boring can be tied directly to at least ten instances of stripping security away from JFK." He said the advance team of Secret Service agents Winston Lawson and David Grant, "who worked hand-in-glove with Floyd Boring, were the in-the-field architects for the planning and implementation of security concerns (read stripping) in Dallas." They "had a hand in the motorcycle depletion and realignment, the overpass security, or lack of it, the press and photographers (dis)placement, and the planning of the motorcade route."

Eventually, Floyd Boring was interviewed by the Assassinations Records Review Board (ARRB) and the first thing he said was, "I didn't have anything to do with it, and I don't know anything!" What did he mean? That he didn't have anything to do with the assassination, or the Texas trip?

Incredibly, the man who was at the heart of the security lapses was never interviewed by the Warren Commission or the subsequent House Select Committee on Assassinations (HSCA). He managed to stay out of the spotlight and his name is not generally known to the public.

Boring said he had taken a day off and was at home November 22 when the tragedy occurred in Dallas. But he conceded to having gone directly from his home to Andrews AFB to meet the new president late that afternoon, and that he accompanied Lyndon Johnson on his helicopter from Andrews to the White House. He claimed he then went home.

But that's not true. Boring went to the White House garage where the presidential limousine and the follow-up car had been returned. He and another agent, Paul Paterni, inspected the vehicles from 10:10 p.m. the night of November 22 until 12:01 a.m. the next day—before the FBI had a chance to do so.

They reportedly recovered bullet fragments they turned over, but given Mr. Boring's suspicious conduct, is it likely he acted with complete honesty?

When asked who directed him and Paterni to search the automobiles, Mr. Boring said that no one had; he said he thought it might be a good idea and had suggested it himself to Paterni, and that they undertook this search as an independent action on their own initiative.

But Floyd Boring had just flown with Lyndon Johnson and after inspecting the presidential automobile it was soon shipped to the Ford

Motor Company in Dearborn, Michigan to be disassembled. (More about that to come).

Dorothy Reminisces

Dorothy's highly personal remembrance of the president in her earlier column struck a chord with readers. On Dec. 5, 1963, the *Philadelphia Daily News* carried a letter to the editor headlined "Kilgallen Tribute." The reader wrote: "I must be honest and say that up until now I have never been a fan of Dorothy Kilgallen's. Since this past terrible weekend I have read everything and anything about our beloved President Kennedy and his marvelous family. One of the most touching tributes, and in my estimation the most wonderful writing, was Dorothy Kilgallen's article in the *Daily News* on Nov. 26. I have read it over and over a million times and each time I read it I enjoy it more. From now on Dorothy Kilgallen has an ever-lasting fan." It was signed Sylvia Wasserman.

The Warren Commission met for the first time on December 5, 1963 and about a week later it became apparent that some revisionism was already going on with regard to the autopsy of the president.

Kilgallen Prepares For Ruby Trial

In anticipation of covering Jack Ruby's murder trial, Dorothy ingratiated herself with his co-counsel, Joe Tonahill and the infamous Melvin Belli, by contacting both men. Dubbed the "King of Torts" by *Life* magazine, Belli was a colorful figure known for getting his clients massive settlements in personal injury cases and for representing various mobsters such as Mickey Cohen. His celebrity clients included Errol Flynn, Mae West, Lenny Bruce, Mohammed Ali and years later, Jim and Tammy Faye Bakker. He was grossly unqualified to head the defense team of the "Trial of the Century" as a mere civil, not criminal attorney.

As Dan Abrams and David Fisher wrote in their 2021 book *Kennedy's Avenger*, Belli's, "San Francisco law office mostly resembled a 19th-century bordello; with mahogany paneling, Persian carpets, floor-to-ceiling bookshelves explored on a velvet-covered ladder, lavender tinted windows and four crystal chandeliers suspended from a gold-trimmed ceiling. It included a mahogany bar, a huge brick fireplace, red velvet drapes and upholstered chairs, an antique safe and rolltop desk and assorted Victorian pieces...

"He was known for wearing expensive European-cut suits with vests, both lined with bright scarlet silk, a gold chain draped loosely across the front, his handmade pastel shirts set off by Byronesque ties, and high-heeled, polished black boots. When appropriate he wore a Chesterfield overcoat with a fur collar and almost always carried his legal papers in a red velvet carpetbag. In court though, to emphasize his respect for the system, he wore a gray suit—an expensive gray suit—the finest fabric cut and sewn by the most-skilled tailors on the continent. But still a gray suit."

His courtroom antics were legendary.

Abrams and Fisher relate, "When the New York Giants baseball team moved to San Francisco he bought season tickets, then sued the team for fraud and breach of warranty because, he said, its Candlestick Stadium effectively became a frozen wind tunnel at night.

"After delivering his closing argument in a winter parka and boots, a jury ruled the team owed him over $1,500; when they were slow in paying, he convinced the sheriff to serve a writ of execution on Giants' property—specifically on centerfielder Willie Mays, whom he claimed to own a piece of until the judgment was paid."

An editorial in the Knight Newspapers chain warned: "Even Texas has never seen a performance that can match Belli at his best. The urbane Belli...is the greatest actor since Barrymore."

At a Dec. 10, 1963 press conference, Melvin Belli told reporters that Ruby's brother Earl had sought his legal representation, but he declined to comment as to who was financing the defense team. (His fee alone was $50,000, which the Ruby family hoped to raise by selling Jack's story).

Belli stated he and attorney Sam S. Brody of Los Angeles and J. H. Tonahill of Jasper, Texas, would join Tom Howard of Dallas in representing Ruby.

"Earl came to my home in Los Angeles and talked to me and spent a day there, and that was about four or five days ago," Melvin told the swarm of reporters.

He went on to say that Ruby "wasn't the man that I expected to see, and I was very impressed with his sincerity."

As will be elaborated on shortly, Melvin Belli was not the Ruby family's first choice to defend Jack. They sought a more experienced counsel but were lied to and manipulated into accepting the mob lawyer instead. In the end, Belli helped Lyndon Johnson and the CIA.

Dorothy Probably Knew Of CIA Plans In Re Castro

Meanwhile, Deputy Attorney General Nicholas Katzenbach sent Earl Warren and each member of the Warren Commission a letter urging they immediately issue a press release stating Lee Harvey Oswald was the lone assassin. He claimed the FBI "had made an exhaustive investigation into whether Oswald may have conspired with or been assisted by any organization, group or person, foreign or domestic, in carrying out this dastardly act...To date, this aspect of the investigation has been negative..."

The first witness the W.C. would hear was not even called for two more months. It is tempting to believe that Katzenbach was acting solely at the behest of Lyndon Johnson in trying to suppress facts. But remember, Bobby Kennedy was still (at least nominally) the Attorney General.

Surprisingly, on Dec. 9, 1963, RFK sent CIA director John McCone a memo about plans "for a coup in Cuba." As previously noted, this secret scheme had been personally run by Robert Kennedy for many months and even the death of his brother did not diminish his desire to proceed. It was to include a "palace coup" to eliminate Fidel Castro, allowing a new Cuban "Provisional Government" to step into the power vacuum, and would have been supported by a "full-scale invasion" of Cuba by the U.S. military, if necessary. The plan had been abandoned because of JFK's assassination. Officially declassified in 1999, "AMWORLD" is the cryptonym the CIA used for the plan in its classified internal documents.

As Joshua Zeitz, a *Politico* magazine contributing editor and author, who has taught American history and politics at Cambridge University and Princeton University, points out, "JFK had previously described his younger brother as 'kind of a nasty, brutal, humorless little fellow...moody, taciturn, brusque, and combative.'"

There were stories in the press prior to November 1963 about how Bobby was trying to abrogate to himself many powers that belonged to members of the Cabinet, and some of them were in open revolt. The point here is that Robert Kennedy may have pursued policies to which his older brother was not privy. Despite stories about how he felt in some ways responsible for his older sibling's death, Bobby apparently was not chastened enough to abandon his plans to assassinate Fidel Castro.

Dorothy Kilgallen had insider information regarding Castro and indeed the entirety of Latin America. Since her columns included periodic references to efforts to overthrow the Cuban leader, she was no doubt well-versed about this secret plan, if not its operational details.

Possessing knowledge like this could be very dangerous.

Finally, (on April 7, 1964) LBJ discontinued all sabotage and raids against Cuba. One CIA officer who was present at the Special Group meeting remembers LBJ saying, "Enough is enough." At least in this instance, Johnson was right.

In a syndicated column dated Dec. 11, 1963, Dorothy wrote President Kennedy's assassination seemed to be all people could talk about, be it those in her social circle, as well as her readers. She spoke of attending a party given by entertainers Nedda and Joshua Logan, wherein various celebrities including Truman Capote, Alfred Vanderbilt, Merle Oberon and the former president of Mexico, Miguel Aleman, were present.

"One might think this collection of sophisticates and celebrities might be tired of the topic by now; but they were not, obviously. And certainly the vast public is not, judging from the thousands of letters which have come to my desk since the tragedy."

She then quoted from these letters, which included compliments on the column about her and Kerry's visit to the White House. Some who wrote in expressed disgust at the hero worship of Jack Ruby. One person opined, "It has not been shown yet that he did not kill Oswald for far more sinister reasons than those given so far."

In the same December 11 column, DK also ran a letter from a reader who said: "Your article on 'The Public Needs the Truth' was right. Never has a person hit the nail on the head as you did. The many questions you asked have to be answered or I, myself, will never be satisfied as to what actually happened in Dallas." Interestingly, some newspapers edited out this passage from Dorothy's column.

The Warren Commission Begins 'Fact Finding' Mission

On Dec. 13, 1963, Congress passed Senate Joint Resolution 137 (Public Law 88-202) authorizing the Commission to subpoena witnesses and obtain evidence. The resolution gave the Commission the authority to compel testimony of witnesses by granting immunity from prosecution to witnesses testifying under compulsion. However, the Commission never used this powerful investigative tool to discover truths. Surprising?

Also on the same day, there was an urgent memo sent to J. Edgar Hoover in which it was reported that, "An article appearing in the evening Dallas, Texas, newspaper prepared by staff writer Bill Burrus, dateline Bethesda, Maryland, reflects a still unannounced autopsy report from the U.S. Naval Hospital reflecting President Kennedy was shot in the back and the bullet, which had a hard metal jacket, exited through his throat. THIS DOES NOT AGREE WITH THE AUTOPSY FINDINGS AT THE BETHESDA HOSPITAL, (*emphasis theirs*) as reported [in] the report of SA Robert Gemberling at Dallas of December ten, last, which reflects an opening was found in the back, that appeared to be a bullet hole, and probing of this hole determined the distance traveled by the missile was short as the end of the opening could be felt by the examining doctor's finger.

"The Bureau may want to have Baltimore obtain the unannounced autopsy report from Bethesda, Maryland, and disseminate to the Bureau and Dallas."

Dorothy Kilgallen

Slayer's 'In' With Police No Surprise

NEW YORK . . . Many New York variety acts who worked in nightclubs operated by Jack Ruby in Dallas say they weren't a bit-surprised at the revelation that Ruby and the local police were chummy—so chummy he was allowed to hang around headquarters while they were questioning Lee Harvey Oswald about the assassination of President John F. Kennedy.

Miss Kilgallen

The performers vividly recall jam sessions at which Dallas cops joined in the fun, some playing musical instruments, others doing turns as singers and comedians.

They also report that the town's gendarmes made Ruby's place their late late hangout, enjoying parties with the strippers and his men friends long after the official closing time.

Dorothy Exposes Dallas Police Ties To Ruby

Still obsessing about the appalling security lapse at Dallas police headquarters that allowed Jack Ruby to get close enough to Lee Oswald to kill him, in a December 17 article Dorothy reported that members of the force partied at Ruby's strip club. She wrote that "there were jam sessions at which Dallas cops joined in the fun, some playing musical instruments, others doing turns as singers and comedians...The gendarmes made Ruby's place their late late hangout, enjoying parties with the strippers and his men friends long after the official closing time." In future columns she further revealed secrets about the DPD.

President Truman Attacks CIA's 'Explosive' Acts

On Dec. 22, 1963—exactly one month after JFK's assassination—former President Harry S Truman took the highly unusual step of writing a lengthy opinion piece that appeared on the front pages of newspapers across the country. In it, he decried the abuse of power by the Central Intelligence Agency, an organization he helped start in 1947.

He bluntly told the American people: "For some time I have been disturbed by the way the CIA has been diverted from its original assignment. It has become an operational and at times a policy-making arm of the government. This has led to trouble and may have compounded our difficulties in several explosive areas.

"I never had any thought when I set up the CIA that it would be injected into peacetime cloak-and-dagger operations."

He said he wanted to see the agency better serve the president and move away from any extraneous operational duties. He noted, "At times the intelligence reports tended to be slanted to conform to established positions of a given department making it difficult for a president to reach the 'right decisions.'"

President Truman warned about the CIA.

He concluded: "There is something about the way the CIA has been functioning that is casting a shadow over our historic position and I feel we need to correct it."

Why had Truman felt the need to pen this column—at the height of the nation's mourning of President Kennedy's death—had he not believed rogue elements existed within the intelligence gathering arm of the government? Discerning people—reading between the lines—could reasonably infer the former president was hinting at involvement by the CIA with the assassination of JFK. Truman's use of the word "explosive" in describing what the agency had done could have been an oblique reference to Kennedy's horrific murder by gunshots.

His description of there being "cloak and dagger" activities clearly telegraphed his belief the CIA was involved in furtive operations that were independent from executive oversight or control.

While Truman never expressly linked President Kennedy's assassination to the CIA, his notes in the Truman Library indicate he started writing his opinion piece on Dec. 9, 1963, the day the FBI issued its initial report concluding Oswald acted alone. Truman's call for the abolition of the CIA was almost certainly motivated by the ambush in Dallas.

The former president may also have been aware of JFK's vow, after the Bay of Pigs failure, to "smash the CIA into a thousand pieces and scatter it to the winds."

Harry Truman had been in office for all or part of a number of important conflicts and events, including World War II, the atomic bombings of Hiroshima and Nagasaki, the Korean War, the Berlin Airlift, the Marshall Plan, and the beginning of the Cold War. Yet he was worried about the CIA. That should tell you something.

The 78-year-old former president had long settled into quiet retirement with his wife of forty-four years, Bess, in their modest 1867 Victorian-style home in Independence, Missouri. He had largely kept out of the public eye, except for the daily 7 a.m. strolls with his walking stick he was accustomed to taking even when he occupied the White House. Yet he was motivated to come forth and compose a strongly worded commentary that was perfectly timed for publication to mark the milestone of one month since President Kennedy's assassination.

Curiously, after Truman's article appeared, the Secret Service seized its criminal files from the Harry S Truman Presidential Library and Museum, saying that the agency wished to review them in light of the assassination. The SS never returned them.

Dorothy Writes A Bombshell Column Hinting At A Coup

In a DK column published the next day, on December 23, she wrote, "The producers of the forthcoming film *Seven Days In May* have every right to think that life imitates art in the most tragic way. Long before President Kennedy was assassinated in Dallas, they finished their picture about a military group hatching plans to overthrow the President of the United States. In the movie, the 'secret base' where the plot against the Chief Executive reaches its climax is a place in Texas."

This bombshell column no doubt detonated far and wide. She was clearly implying that John Kennedy had died as a result of a plot to stage a coup and that it had its origins in Texas (!)—the home state of Lyndon Johnson, who had fought so hard to capture the nomination for president at the 1960 Democratic Convention. Her clever invocation of a movie about a coup was obviously intended to make a very serious point. Who could pull that off except Dorothy?

President Kennedy had read the galleys for the novel *Seven Days In May* before its publication, and found its premise plausible. Its writers, Fletcher Knebel and Charles Bailey II, who were political journalists, had interviewed Air Force Chief of Staff General Curtis LeMay, who was incensed that Kennedy had refused to be coerced into providing air support for about 1,350 Cuban exiles, backed by the CIA, who launched a doomed invasion of their country in the Bay of Pigs in 1961 to overthrow Castro. It was a plan that had been concocted during the waning days of the Eisenhower Administration, and JFK was reluctant to go along with it only three months after he took office. As CIA Director Allen Dulles later admitted, Kennedy sought assurances from the CIA and the Pentagon that there was no chance the invading Cuban rebel force would fail, and that there would be no need for U.S. military involvement. But Dulles and the generals lied in giving the president those guarantees.

When the invasion faltered, Kennedy realized he had been drawn into a trap, and refused to order a U.S. strike on Cuba. Most of the generals were apoplectic, accusing him of being traitorous. Kennedy publicly accepted full responsibility even though the scheme was not his idea. Jacqueline Kennedy recalled her husband sitting on the edge of the bed crying about the disaster, one of the few times she ever saw him so upset. Knebel and Bailey realized that the military establishment and the intelligence community despised JFK.

In the fall of 1961, Gen. Lucius Clay, who had taken a civilian post in Berlin, launched a series of unauthorized provocations against the Soviets. He then threatened to knock down the Berlin Wall with U.S. tanks. This prompted the Soviets to respond by amassing their own tanks at a border crossing known as Checkpoint Charlie. A sixteen-hour standoff ensued. It was one of the most dangerous confrontations of the Cold War when, for the first and only time, U.S. and Soviet tanks squared off against each other.

With the Berlin crisis moving toward nuclear Armageddon, Khrushchev turned to KGB agent Georgi Bolshakov, a top Soviet spy in Washington, to communicate directly with JFK. Bolshakov somehow smuggled a letter, the first of twenty-one declassified in 1993, to Kennedy's press secretary, Pierre Salinger, in a folded newspaper. In it, Khrushchev expressed regret about Vienna and embraced JFK's proposal for a path to peace and disarmament.

In the autumn of 1962, when U.S. spy planes detected attempts by the Soviet Union to install nuclear missiles in Cuba—just ninety miles off U.S. shores—President Kennedy handled the crisis adeptly. Resisting pressure by the CIA, the Pentagon and the Joint Chiefs of Staff—the latter of whom unanimously urged him to launch a pre-emptive strike—Kennedy ordered a naval blockade instead. It ended up defusing a very dangerous situation and avoiding a nuclear war.

Gen. LeMay was then rude to the Commander-in-Chief at a White House meeting, accusing him of acting like Neville Chamberlain when JFK refused to attack Castro.

Kennedy asked LeMay what he thought the Russians would do if the U.S. bombed Cuba. "They'll do nothing," the general arrogantly replied. An incredulous President Kennedy responded, "Are you trying to tell me that they'll let us bomb their missiles, and kill a lot of Russians and then do nothing? If they don't do anything in Cuba, then they'll certainly do something in Berlin."

After the meeting, JFK commented to aide Kenny O'Donnell, "Can you imagine LeMay saying a thing like that? These brass hats have one great advantage in their favor. If we listen to them, and do what they want us to do, none of us will be alive later to tell them that they were wrong."

From the beginning of his term in office, Jack Kennedy was embroiled in an ongoing battle with top members of U.S. military and intelligence agencies, who hatched nefarious schemes to force him into escalating the Cold War into a hot one. Some of the generals with whom the president had to contend posed a threat to the survival of humanity.

Kennedy's hold on power was at times uncertain, as some of the generals and CIA officials engaged in flagrant insubordination in an effort to precipitate the need for a strike on Cuba. CIA spymaster William Harvey screamed at the president during a White House meeting: "We wouldn't be in such trouble now if you guys had some balls in the Bay of Pigs." Defense analyst Daniel Ellsberg, who later leaked the Pentagon Papers, observed, "There was virtually a coup atmosphere in Pentagon circles."

Gen. Curtis LeMay, the man who pioneered the use of napalm against civilians in Tokyo during World War II, urged his colleagues: "Why don't we go in there and make a strike on Monday anyway?"—even as the Cuban Missile Crisis was subsiding.

Tensions rose again when the Soviets shot down a U.S. reconnaissance plane. The Pentagon was ready to retaliate. In a secret meeting with Soviet Ambassador Anatoly Dobrynin, Robert Kennedy bluntly warned, "If the situation continues much longer, the president is not sure that the military will not overthrow him and seize power."

Soviet leader Nikita Khrushchev said afterward that Kennedy had won his "deep respect" during the crisis: "He didn't let himself become frightened, nor did he become reckless...He showed real wisdom and statesmanship when he turned his back on the right-wing forces in the United States who were trying to goad him into taking military action against Cuba."

John Kennedy was the only U.S. president to receive the Purple Heart medal. He knew how terrible war could be, having served in the South Pacific during WWII. On a moonless night in August 1943, the patrol boat he commanded was cut in half in a collision with a Japanese destroyer. Three of his men were killed. He towed one injured crew member to an uninhabited island with a rope clenched in his teeth as he and his mates swam almost six miles. JFK ultimately strategized their rescue six days later. Kennedy was a bonafide war hero. The injuries he sustained to his back resulted in four spinal surgeries between 1944 and 1957.

Khrushchev had participated in the Battle of Stalingrad, which took the lives of more than 2.6 million people. And, although Washington and Moscow generals were itching to test their armies in a battle against each other—as if it was all just a big game—the heads of the U.S. and the Soviet Union resisted the pressure.

Gen. LeMay's whereabouts on the day of the assassination had been a mystery for years. But a recently declassified recording of the radio communication between Air Force One and the White House Situation Room as the plane returned from Dallas to Washington on November 22 included an urgent attempt by some unnamed person to get a message to LeMay, who was supposedly flying back from Canada. An aide can be heard trying to contact LeMay and says the general is, "In a C140. Last three numbers are 497. His code name is Grandson. And I want to talk to him. If you can't work him now, it's gonna be too late, because he'll be on the ground in a half hour."

What was that all about?

Suspiciously, all references to Gen. LeMay were edited out of the tape when it was first released by the LBJ Library. Why? But a longer version—that included references to Kennedy's nemesis—was found in the possession of the late Army General Ted Clifton, one of JFK's military aides who accompanied him on the Dallas trip. Yet only one hundred forty-two minutes of the tape have surfaced, despite the fact the flight back to Washington took approximately two hundred forty minutes. Why has the remainder of the recording been kept secret?

Even more provocative is the question: Why was it that General LeMay turned up in the autopsy room at Bethesda Naval Hospital after the assassination, puffing on what seemed to be a celebratory cigar? When asked by one of the autopsy surgeons to extinguish the stogie, he rudely and defiantly blew a cloud of smoke in the man's face, despite the need to maintain a sterile environment during the delicate medical procedure which was of monumental historic and forensic importance.

Given all these behind-the-scenes difficulties John Kennedy endured from renegade generals and the CIA, it's no wonder he was so eager to see a film be made based on the book *Seven Days In May*, despite opposition from the State Department. According to director John Frankenheimer, the president even arranged a visit to the Kennedy Compound at Hyannis Port, MA. for a weekend so a movie crew could film inside the actual White House.

Press secretary Pierre Salinger said the novel and the movie based on it represented "a warning to the republic," and Arthur Schlesinger said Kennedy wanted the film made to "raise consciousness about the problems involved if the generals got out of control."

So Dorothy Kilgallen's great sagacity in drawing real-life parallels to *The Seven Days In May* revealed for her readers not only the possibility that JFK's death was literally the result of a coup d'état but that President Kennedy took the threat seriously, even suspecting his vice president was plotting against him.

Kennedy And Castro Both Worried About CIA

In a long-forgotten article that appeared on Oct. 3, 1963 in *The New York Times*, respected columnist Arthur Krock noted that Kennedy had publicly gone to war against the CIA over Vietnam. Krock quoted a dispatch from Saigon by Richard Starnes of Scripps-Howard, whom Krock referred to as a journalist with "an excellent reputation for reliability." Starnes reported that, according to a high-ranking White House source, "Twice the CIA flatly refused to carry out instructions from Ambassador Henry Cabot Lodge, and in one instance frustrated a plan of action Mr. Lodge brought from Washington, because the agency disagreed with it." Was that source John Kennedy himself?

The article continued, "The CIA growth was likened to a malignancy which the very high official was not sure even the White House could control any longer." Starnes said the agency "represents a tremendous power and total unaccountability to anyone." It concluded with this ominous warning: "If the U.S. ever experienced an attempt at a coup to overthrow the government, it will come from the CIA and not the Pentagon."

Krock observed, "Whatever else these passages disclose, they most certainly establish that representatives of other Executive branches have expanded their war against the CIA from the inner government councils to the American people, via the press."

Did President Kennedy or those close to him have some foreboding about his future?

A journalist for the French publication *L'Express*—Jean Daniel—had visited with John Kennedy at the White House late in the afternoon on Thursday, Oct. 24, 1963 for a half hour interview. The focus of the discussion centered on Cuba. JFK knew the writer was soon to also meet with the Communist leader. So this was an opportunity to exchange views in a back channel manner.

Mr. Daniel met with Fidel Castro on November 20, just two days before Kennedy was assassinated. Castro began by saying, "I am not forgetting the Machiavellian tactics, the deceits and the attempts at invasion, the pressuring and the blackmail, the organization of the counter-revolution, the blockage and above all the steps of retaliation taken...

"But I believe that Kennedy inherited a difficult situation, that a President of the United States is never truly free. Kennedy is now experiencing this lack of freedom; he realizes that he has been deceived, particularly with regard to the Cuban reactions at the time of the attempted invasion of the Bay of Pigs. I also believe that he is a realist. He understands the impossibility of making us disappear..."

Castro was eager to clarify what led up to the Cuban Missile Crisis that had unfolded about a year earlier. He explained, "Six months before the installation of these (Soviet) missiles in Cuba we had an accumulation of information telling us of new preparations for an invasion of the island, preparations undertaken by the CIA, whose directors were mortified by the failure of the Bay of Pigs and by the fact that they saw themselves as ridiculous in the eyes of the world and ill-treated by the American government (and Kennedy)."

"We knew also that the Pentagon would lend its authority to the CIA preparations, but we had our doubts as to the state of mind of the president.

"Some even believed that it was only necessary to alert him, to alarm him, to cause the project to fail."

However, following a visit to Washington by the son-in-law of Nikita Khrushchev, Alexei Adzhubel—who spoke with JFK—the Cubans and Russians concluded that Kennedy was taking a hard line against Cuba. So the missiles were regarded as a means of self-defense.

The point here is that even Fidel Castro understood the dynamics of the power the CIA wielded over American foreign policy, and the agency's ability to strong-arm a U.S. president. Such an entity, which was clearly out of control well before the autumn of 1963, was not only a danger to the Cuban leader but to John Kennedy as well.

Historian Arthur Schlesinger tellingly related that soon after the JFK assassination, Bobby Kennedy asked CIA Director John McCone whether the agency had killed his brother. McCone said he didn't think so, but continued to insist weeks later that he thought a second gunman was involved.

Lyndon Johnson, as vice president, was over the CIA. His interests and those of some members of the spy agency converged. There is no doubt. All he needed to do is give them a green light, and their problem—and his—with John Kennedy could be swiftly resolved. His rich oil friends and sponsors in the defense industry would applaud because he made them even richer with the Vietnam War.

Dorothy Harbors Suspicions About Lyndon Johnson

On Christmas Eve 1963, Dorothy led off her column with the startling claim that, "Attorney General Robert Kennedy will resign his Cabinet post and leave Washington early in 1964 unless he has President Johnson's assurance that he will be chosen as the next Vice Presidential candidate. Democratic brain trusters have been conferring daily about the possibility, but LBJ will make the final decision."

That was Dorothy—always coming up with something fresh nobody else had! It also may have been her way of needling Johnson.

A review of the columns and articles Dorothy Kilgallen wrote in the immediate aftermath of the assassination and the years that followed reveals that unlike so many other members of the press, she did not write laudatory articles about President Johnson to reassure the nation. Her refusal to do so may be because she suspected him of complicity in JFK's death.

As plugged into media circles as DK was, it is highly likely she knew that a team of top-notch investigative reporters for *Life* magazine had been engaged in a months-long probe into LBJ's corruption. This endeavor was undertaken at the behest of Attorney General Robert Kennedy. In fact, RFK had even called friendly reporters into his office to give them his blessing to look into Johnson's misconduct. Sterling Seagrove of the *Washington Post* said Bobby's effort to make public Johnson's litany of misdeeds was a poorly kept secret and that he was sure LBJ knew what was going on. Dorothy no doubt did as well.

In fact, in a column that appeared on Oct. 11, 1963, DK wrote "Sen. John L. Williams of Delaware is going to make a speech on the subject of Robert G. 'Bobby' Baker, former Democratic Majority Secretary of the Senate, that—if given—will curl the hair of some legislators and other politicians. It's not supposed to be good form for senators to criticize other members of the exclusive club, but Sen. Williams just might make an exception in the interests of patriotism."

Besides a sordid record of corruption in Texas politics, that included the deaths of some of Johnson's opponents—(LBJ henchman Mac Wallace committed cold-blooded murder, was convicted, but got a suspended sentence from a crooked judge in one case)—Lyndon was implicated in a long list of financial scandals. The most prominent were those tied to Billie Sol Estes and Bobby Baker, but included alleged kickbacks from corporations like defense contractors Ling-Tempo-Vought, as well as Brown and Root, plus many others. Bobby Baker made a career out of extorting suitcases full of cash on Johnson's behalf from agriculture, insurance, oil interests and anyone else that had business before the government. In November 1963, the U.S. Senate investigation into the Baker case was steamrolling ahead. Even the Democrats were cooperating, thanks to the Kennedys, and a lot of incriminating information was being unearthed—until Nov. 22, 1963.

That day a closed session of the Senate Rules Committee was hearing sworn testimony from a Bobby Baker associate, Don Reynolds, who told of a suitcase filled with $100,000 cash to pay off LBJ for his role in securing the Fort Worth TFX contract. Reynolds' testimony was interrupted by news of Kennedy's death. At the same time, interrelated congressional committees were investigating, along with Baker, lobbyists Robert Thompson, Irving Davidson and Thomas Webb who worked for multimillionaire Texas oilman and JFK hater Clint Murchison.

As LBJ biographer Robert Caro writes, "Johnson had been involved in pay-for-influence practices so pervasive that it had turned a lifelong government employee into a millionaire many times over."

Lady Bird Johnson was deeply mired in this scheme. The couple's holdings—including a string of radio and TV stations and massive real estate assets—were in her name, and Lyndon claimed he had no connection to these. That, of course, was a palpable lie since Texas is a community property state. When Mrs. Johnson wanted an expensive new color television set for a party she was holding, an insurance broker who had curried favor with LBJ was required to buy one and ship it to her overnight, and also purchase advertising on one of her Texas TV stations even though his firm was located in Maryland. The Johnson shakedowns were too numerous to count.

Johnson had strong-armed his way onto the 1960 presidential ticket by threatening to reveal JFK's womanizing as extensively documented by Hoover. Evelyn Lincoln, Kennedy's longtime secretary, witnessed a discussion between Jack and his brother Bobby regarding the matter, and their reluctant concession to Lyndon's demands. LBJ told friends he was happy to be selected as the vice presidential running mate because, he assured them, JFK would not live out his term.

By mid-1963 the Kennedys were determined to get rid of Johnson and one way to do that was to expose his scandalous conduct that in turn would force his resignation. In fact, President Kennedy confided to Evelyn Lincoln just before he left for Dallas that he planned to replace Johnson with another southerner, North Carolina Governor Terry Sanford. Sterling Seagrove of the *Washington Post* noted that, "JFK detested LBJ as one of the most corrupt men in D.C." He referred to Lyndon as "a riverboat gambler."

The belief that Kennedy needed Johnson on the ticket to win the South is widely held, but incorrect. He carried part of the South in spite of LBJ, who barely carried his own state of Texas in the 1960 election.

H.L. Hunt's right-hand man, John Curington, reflected, "Bobby Kennedy was going to indict a fellow named Bobby Baker. And that deal was already made. Bobby Baker would...turn against Lyndon Johnson, enter into a plea agreement on his deal...Johnson was going to be out in '64. No ifs, ands, buts, and maybes. And nobody realized this until about the...latter part of '62 or '63. Johnson was losing his skills every day, and Jack Kennedy was gaining more. So Mr. Hunt was almost at the stage where he didn't have much time to fulfill his obligation that Kennedy would not live—would not survive four years in the office there. That's really the essence of the Kennedy story. For Mr. Hunt to protect his empire, and to honor his commitment to Lyndon Johnson, Kennedy had to leave office."

James Wagenvoord, who in 1963 was 27 years old and the editorial business manager and assistant to *Life* magazine's executive editor, confirmed the explosive article on Johnson was nearing publication. He explained, "Beginning in late summer 1963, the magazine, based upon information fed from Bobby Kennedy and the Justice Department, had been developing a major piece concerning Johnson...On publication Johnson would have been finished and off the '64 ticket [which was the] reason the material was fed to us, and would probably have been facing prison time. At the time *Life* magazine was arguably the most important general news source in the U.S."

Wagenvoord said, "I had seen Department of Justice couriers coming in and out of the offices and knew that a lot of material was being fed directly to the magazine from the department."

Life magazine was scheduled to go to press with the major exposé on Lyndon Johnson within a week.

Drew Pearson, who wrote the *Washington Merry-Go-Round* column that was syndicated to 650 newspapers and had an estimated sixty million readers, was also set to publish a big story on Lyndon Johnson's massive corruption. Pearson was an aggressive investigative journalist who was notorious for uncovering scandals involving politicians of either party, including senators, cabinet members, generals and American presidents. He literally ruined careers, forced the resignations of unsavory characters, exposed hypocrisy, and was an unvarnished muckraker who was sued for libel one hundred twenty times but only lost one case. Though he was a friend of LBJ's, Pearson's obsession with uncovering scandals superseded his loyalty to any one person. The columnist could probably have single-handedly brought down Lyndon Baines Johnson.

Revealingly, one of the first things Johnson did after boarding Air Force One at Love Field in Dallas the day John Kennedy was assassinated, is place a call at 2:00 p.m. to Abe Fortas back in Washington. LBJ asked if Don Reynolds linked him to the Bobby Baker scandal during his testimony to the Senate Rules Committee. Instead of being preoccupied with the business of the nation as he was on the verge of assuming the mantle of the presidency, Lyndon was obsessed with his own political fate.

These official probes posed major and imminent criminal and political risks to the vice president unless John Kennedy was out of the way and LBJ was elevated to become the nation's chief executive.

Johnson told Sen. Mike Mansfield that he planned to use the FBI to investigate Republican campaign contributions to get back at them for

LBJ never looked happier than just before JFK was killed.

probing his family finances. He said in a taped conversation, "They've been down inspecting Miz Johnson's property in Texas and they've harassed and harangued her every day since we've been here. The FBI can look into their contributions and it won't look very good."

Kennedy Dies At A Convenient Time

Dorothy Kilgallen's suspicions about LBJ were no doubt fueled by the realization that if JFK had lived just a few more days, Lyndon Baines Johnson would have been toast. He would finally have been exposed in print as a corrupt and contemptible grifter, and forced to resign from office. Even his own grandmother predicted he'd wind up in prison.

Was it mere coincidence that Kennedy died at precisely the right time to save LBJ's skin?

Adherents to the lone assassin theory ludicrously ignore a monumental amount of countervailing evidence, including the historical context in which JFK's murder took place.

James Wagenvoord explained that, "On Kennedy's death, research files and all numbered copies of the nearly print-ready draft were gathered up by my boss—he had been the top editor on the team—and shredded. The issue that was to expose LBJ instead featured the Zapruder film. Based on our success in [exploiting] the Zapruder film I became chief of Time/Life editorial services and remained in that job until 1968."

An intriguing dynamic that should not go unexamined is that while the editorial department of *Life* was hot on the trail of Lyndon Johnson's reprehensible conduct, the publication's top brass (including Henry Luce and C.D. Jackson) were closely aligned with various U.S. intelligence agencies, hated President Kennedy's policies, and made various attempts to undermine him.

Drew Pearson also scuttled his planned exposé on Johnson, regarding it as too perilous to publish while the nation was traumatized by the loss of JFK. Johnson rewarded him by drawing the columnist closer such that Pearson was soon called "Lyndon's lackey." Unlike Dorothy Kilgallen—who clung steadfastly to her principles—Pearson sold his soul to LBJ, as did so many other members of the press.

There can be little doubt that Lyndon Johnson eagerly participated in a conspiracy that culminated in John Kennedy's assassination, in order to avoid his own political ruin. LBJ probably wasn't the mastermind, but as his actions clearly demonstrated, he was the most important enabler. He used his power over the military and other government entities like the FBI, CIA and Secret Service to suppress the truth. All it took was a few people in key positions to, in turn, wield enormous influence over how events turned out. "National security" was a ploy Johnson repeatedly invoked to secure cooperation from otherwise unwilling or unwitting participants in the cover-up. In order to secure the cooperation of the high ranking plotters he adopted policy changes favored by the assassination cabal within the national security establishment and private interests such as the oil barons and mafia.

The speculation that Lyndon Johnson knew a conspiracy against the president was afoot is given credence by a strange comment he made, as reported in the April 24, 1963 *Dallas Times-Herald*. While announcing that Kennedy's schedule would permit him to attend "a luncheon in Dallas" in November, he cryptically added, "At least wait until November before you shoot him down."

Investigative journalist Joachim Joesten says, "The Baker scandal then is truly the hidden key to the assassination, or more exact, the timing of the Baker affair crystallized the more or less vague plans to eliminate Kennedy which had already been in existence. The threat of complete exposure which faced Johnson in the Baker scandal provided that final impulse: he was forced to give the go-ahead signal to the plotters who had long been waiting for the right opportunity."

Doug Horne observes, "The proposed timing of the revelations (the week after JFK's Dallas trip) indicates to me how well the Kennedys were managing the news—arranging for the release of the exposé on Lyndon Johnson only AFTER the November 1963 trip was over" (and campaign cash raised in Texas). "Unfortunately, it seems that the Kennedy brothers' desire to delay publishing the LBJ exposé until after the Texas trip was unwise, for it allowed the timing of the assassination to precede the publication of the article, thus ensuring that it would never see the light of day."

Toppling Lyndon Johnson would also have had major repercussions for some of his cronies in the oil industry. They needed him to remain in office and would have been committed to perpetuating his power to do them favors.

On Oct. 10, 1963, Marquis Child, writing in his *Washington Calling* column, reported, "To a friend and long-time associate who called on him the other day President Kennedy expressed considerable bitterness on the subject of top-bracket taxpayers who use tax exemptions to spread propaganda of the extreme right..."

JFK singled out Texas oil man H.L. Hunt, who had an annual income of about thirty million dollars, but paid only small amounts of federal income tax. This was due to the 27.5 percent oil depletion allowance, which had been enacted by Congress in 1926 to provide an incentive for oil exploration, but had been inexplicably left in place and become a permanent means by which immense fortunes were amassed by those in the oil industry. Hunt was using part of his money to saturate radio, TV and print media with extreme rightwing propaganda, assailing the United Nations, foreign aid, Social Security and programs that help the poor.

President Kennedy proposed a sharp reduction in this benefit, that was expected to generate about one hundred eighty-five million dollars in additional revenues for the U.S. Treasury.

Matthew Smith, author of *JFK: The Second Plot,* wrote, "There was nothing in the world which would have inflamed the oil barons more than the president interfering with the oil depletion allowance."

Barr McClellan, a former law partner of LBJ lawyer Edward Clark, claimed Kennedy's assassination was paid for by oil billionaires H.L. Hunt and Clint Murchison, and that Mac Wallace was also involved. (A latent fingerprint found on one of the boxes in the TSBD was in recent years credibly identified as belonging to Wallace, and six photos taken in Dealey Plaza show a bespeckled man resembling him standing in a sixth floor window of the building at the time of the assassination).

The owner of the Texas School Book Depository building was D.H. Byrd, who founded the aircraft company Temco. He merged his firm with James Ling's electronics company and aircraft manufacturer Chance Vought Corporation to form Ling-Temco-Vought (LTV). Byrd became a director of LTV and bought, along with Ling, 132,000 shares of LTV in November 1963. Then he left on an African Safari for two months and when he returned his good friend Lyndon Johnson was president. A large defense contract was awarded to LTV to build fighter planes —to be paid for out of the 1965 budget which had not yet been approved by Congress—and was waiting for Mr. Byrd upon his return.

Mac Wallace, who received a five-year suspended sentence in the shooting death of a man in Austin, Texas went to work for D.H. Byrd's

Temco. Then Wallace got a job with LTV. The latter required security clearance to do defense department work. Despite being a convicted killer, Mac Wallace got his clearance. A Naval Intelligence officer handling the case said Lyndon Johnson used his influence. Four months after securing that new job Wallace was suspected of murdering Henry Marshall, who was hot on the trail of kickbacks Johnson was receiving. Also implicated in the financial scandal was Billie Sol Estes.

While still vice president, Johnson flew to Dallas aboard a military jet to privately meet with Estes and his lawyers on a plane parked away from the terminal. This trip would likely have remained secret except that LBJ's plane developed a problem when it landed. When reporters learned of this and tried to get the tower records for the flight mishap, the records were "sealed by government order."

Dorothy Realized Johnson Corruption Lead to Vietnam War

Dorothy Kilgallen was politically astute enough to grasp the complexities of realpolitik, and had covered enough trials to recognize corruption when she saw it. LBJ soon made clear he intended to maintain the 27.5 percent oil depletion allowance during his term, and it only dropped to fifteen percent after Richard Nixon assumed office.

Johnson took other steps that curried favor. Strong documentary evidence confirms that in October 1963, President John Kennedy had formally decided to withdraw from Vietnam, whether the U.S. was winning or not. A White House tape of a meeting on Oct. 5, 1963 contains a voice—either Robert McNamara or McGeorge Bundy—asking President Kennedy for "formal approval" of a recommendation to withdraw one thousand men from Vietnam by the end of 1963. McNamara was emphatic: "We need a way to get out of Vietnam, and this is a way of doing it," he declared. John Kennedy can be heard on the tape saying, "Let's go on ahead and do it." The Pentagon did not favor withdrawal.

Nevertheless, Kennedy issued directive NSAM 263, which called for the first stage of bringing U.S. troops home from Vietnam, and this had even been publicly announced yet in October of 1963.

James K. Galbraith writes that this decision by Kennedy, "Was also part of a larger strategy, of a sequence that included the Laos and Berlin settlements in 1961, the non-invasion of Cuba in 1962, the Test Ban Treaty in 1963. His larger goal after that was to settle the Cold War, without either victory or defeat—a strategic vision laid out in JFK's commencement speech at American University on June 10, 1963."

Kennedy believed in a strong military readiness posture and took the Cold War threats seriously. But he was highly skeptical of the advice he was getting from the so-called military experts and regarded force as a measure of last resort. It is now known that during the infamous Cuban missile crisis in October 1962, Russian forces in that island nation were authorized to launch a nuclear attack against any U.S. led-invading force without permission from Moscow. So Kennedy was wise to resist the pressure he was getting from the Joint Chiefs to authorize a military strike against Cuba, even after Soviet leader Nikita Khrushchev had agreed to remove the missiles.

President Kennedy was shocked by a July 1961 briefing he received from the Joint Chiefs saying the optimum time for a pre-emptive nuclear strike on the Communist world was late 1963. Their plan involved dropping 170 atomic and hydrogen bombs on Moscow alone, and destroying every major city in the Soviet Union, China, and Eastern Europe, killing hundreds of millions. Sickened by the radical idea, JFK walked out.

Mark White, a professor of history at Queen Mary, University of London opines, "In a crisis which brought America and the world closer to nuclear war than it had ever been, [Kennedy] had faced down the Russians. He had compelled Khrushchev to withdraw Soviet missiles from Cuba and had done so without making inordinately great concessions. No one could credibly claim, in the wake of the missile crisis, that Kennedy was incompetent in foreign policy and too weak to handle the Communists."

Yet following JFK's October directive, the CIA attempted to undermine the rationale of withdrawing from Vietnam, and thereby obstruct President Kennedy's orders.

U.S. intelligence even intercepted the final confidential communique from Krushchev so Kennedy wouldn't see it.

On Sunday, November 24—just two days after Kennedy's death—Lyndon Johnson reversed JFK's planned withdrawal of troops.

What was so urgent Johnson had to sign this paperwork on a Sunday? He acceded to proposals for a tough stance against North Vietnam, and he promised the military it could have what it wanted—short of a nuclear strike on the USSR. In so doing, he also gave his big benefactors in the oil and defense industries what they wanted: a war that would generate major profits for them.

On Nov. 26, 1963, Johnson signed NSAM 272—a significant departure from Kennedy's policy. It was a directive that approved intensified covert action against North Vietnam by the CIA. This was followed by NSAM 273, which led to seaboard raids and sabotage against North Vietnam that in turn lead to the Gulf of Tonkin incident and a wider war that ultimately killed 58,200 Americans. In addition, 75,000 were severely disabled, 23,214 were one hundred percent disabled, 5,283 lost limbs and 1,081 sustained multiple amputations. Of those killed, sixty one percent were younger than twenty-one years old.

Important to know is that in 1991, a draft copy of NSAM 273, prepared for LBJ by William Bundy, was discovered in the archives of the LBJ Library in Texas. It is dated Nov. 21, 1963—the day *before* JFK's assassination. This obviously was in anticipation that Kennedy would not survive the Texas trip. This is eerie and incriminating.

The unnecessary war in Vietnam resulted in massive social and economic upheaval. Journalists as diverse as Tom Wicker, Marvin Kalb and I.F. Stone perceived Johnson's November 1963 action as a "major decision," a "pledge" that determined "all that would follow."

Incidentally, in 1997, the ARRB deemed the tapes relating to Kennedy's Vietnam policies relevant to his assassination, and ultimately secured their release.

When Robert Kennedy criticized Lyndon Johnson's turnabout on Vietnam, White House tapes recorded LBJ as bellowing "I'll destroy you and every one of your dove friends in six months. You'll be dead politically in six months."

Lyndon Baines Johnson has been credited with having done good deeds with his Great Society initiatives but his venality must not be ignored. His behavior was beyond eccentric and qualified medical experts have termed it pathological. He had an unbridled lust for power and narcissistic impulses that drove his corruption and greed. His monumental hatred of the Kennedys was part of his pathology.

A most disturbing fact has emerged that on Nov. 18, 1963, John Kennedy told his friend Sen. George Smathers that LBJ was insistent that Jackie ride in the car with the president. In hindsight, given what now is apparent about Johnson's role in the death of JFK, it is shocking that the vice president would want to put the First Lady in physical danger too and expose her to the possibility of being killed!

It is indisputable that whomever concocted and carried out the assassination of President Kennedy showed a wanton disregard for the life of his wife, and was willing to risk her getting murdered. Remember, she was mere inches from being struck by bullets being fired at a moving target from some distance away. Imagine what an everlasting trauma it would have been for the nation had Jacqueline Kennedy been gunned down in Dallas that day too.

Dorothy Kilgallen's evident disdain for Lyndon Johnson was at least partially offset by her fear regarding the radicalism of Barry Goldwater, the likely Republican presidential nominee in 1964. On a TV show in Canada, when asked about her views on Sen. Goldwater, Kilgallen replied, "I haven't heard enough of his speeches, but every time I do hear one, he confuses me. I don't think I could support him. Some of the things he says strike me as being outrageous, really. [His beliefs] are so far behind what we've progressed to at this point. It's like turning back the pages of a calendar."

Goldwater was widely perceived as a warmonger but Lyndon Johnson promised he was not willing "to send American boys nine or ten thousand miles away from home to do what Asian boys ought to be doing for themselves." He lied. Over the course of the war, at least 2,709,918 uniformed U.S. military personnel were sent to Vietnam. Dorothy was apparently disgusted by both Johnson and Goldwater.

Meanwhile, Some People Were Being Petty

Despite the deeply distressing times the nation was going through, people were still willing to be petty and to snipe, and DK was not without her detractors. Writing in his Dec. 30, 1963, column, James Devane, TV-Radio Editor of the *Cincinnati Enquirer*, printed three letters he received from readers regarding Dorothy Kilgallen—and he also commented snidely on them.

Mrs. Erica Brandt wrote, "How can anyone criticize the looks of Dorothy Kilgallen? The letter writer who would do that must be sick, sick, sick. Dorothy has beautiful eyes and a lovely smile. She is such a sweet little thing." Devane responded, "Sweet, I must admit, is one of the last words I'd use to describe Miss Kilgallen."

An ad hominem attacker who was too cowardly to sign her last name wrote: "Dorothy Kilgallen overdresses something terrible if you ask me. She looks like a Christmas tree on *What's My Line?* All she needs is a few candles and a little angel on top of that thing she calls a hair-do." It was signed "Denise." Devane replied, "Come, come, Denise. Is that the Yuletide spirit?"

Next, an anonymous letter writer said, "I like Arlene Francis on *What's My Line?* but I sure could do without Dorothy Kilgallen. Can't they get rid of her? I'd like to see Betsy Palmer, Peggy Cass or Joan Fontaine get her job. Are they afraid of what Dorothy would say about them if they fired her?" Signed "P.L." Devane responded, "How would I know?"

It seemed Dorothy Kilgallen was growing more accustomed to criticism, be it of her physical appearance, writing or beliefs.

9
A Mixed Bag

The year of 1963 had ended so ghastly with the loss of the beloved young president and all the drama surrounding the murder case that a lot of people were morose and wanted respite from the sorrow. So they got away for a long weekend or—if they could afford it—even left the country.

That's what Dorothy Kilgallen did. She continued writing her columns, but did so from San Juan, Puerto Rico, spending the Christmas holiday and New Year's there.

There is a strong likelihood her vacation was facilitated by Joe Levine. Journalist Renee Francine described him as a "Midget Hercules" weighing two hundred ten pounds and standing a mere five feet and four inches.

Known for his business prowess, he was the founder of Embassy Pictures, and in 1963, Levine was offered a thirty million dollar deal with Paramount Pictures (making him a major shareholder) to produce films in the vein of his previous successes. His credits included *The Carpetbaggers, Two Women* (he was a mentor for Sophia Loren), *The Producers, The Graduate, Marriage Italian Style, A Bridge Too Far* and so many more.

Dorothy had been paying inordinate attention to Levine in her column, many items of trivial significance, while others were clearly an attempt at flattery. The only other people she may have written about with more frequency were Elizabeth Taylor and Richard Burton during their much publicized love affair. Levine even served as a guest columnist for DK in August 1960.

May 1961 saw DK lead off a column with news that Levine had secured Tony Randall for the film *Boys Night Out*. Writing in July 1962, DK enthused about the success of Levine's film *Divorce, Italian Style*.

"Joe Levine continues to make news daily. Now he's on the verge of announcing a headline-worthy deal with Brigitte Bardot," she wrote in January 1963. In November 1963, she reported that Sophia Loren had gifted Levine a Rolls-Royce. An item from a July 1964 column praised Levine's gala premier of *The Carpetbaggers* at the Festival Theater. She noted the occasion, "Brought out the celebrities, the fashions and the jewels, and Mrs. Levine's party afterwards at the Four Seasons was another triumph of lavish decor, luxurious cuisine and dancing belles and blades."

Then later that year, in December, Dorothy reported Levine's prowess as a producer of films, plays, and most recently, television. "And Levine is working on even more plays, while maintaining his position in the movie field and moving into the TV-film milieu full steam ahead."

February 1965 had DK reporting that Levine cast Red Buttons in his biopic *Harlow*, playing an agent "as a direct result of an offbeat item in this space, and he's delighted with the idea." Then that June, DK wrote that Levine took Bobby Vinton out to dinner for business talks.

Why all this attention paid by Dorothy Kilgallen to movie producer Joe Levine? Kilgallen had met with Levine about turning her long overdue *Murder One* book into a possible dramatic television series that she might even narrate.

Levine had reviewed a chapter she'd written on the Sam Sheppard case. He told an associate, "She's got some good stuff in there. It could be a helluva thing." Levine denied to author Lee Israel that Dorothy had shared anything with him about what she was writing regarding Jack Ruby and the Kennedy assassination, but what if she had? By confiding in a man she trusted, she may have put herself in jeopardy, as Levine had contacts with members of organized crime.

Several times during the course of research for this book, persons close to Dorothy named Joe Levine as someone whom they suspected may have had a peripheral involvement in her death. A man who befriended DK, Ron Pataky, also claimed to be chummy with the movie mogul.

Was it coincidental that Mr. Levine was in San Juan when DK was there? She was with him at the Ponce de Leon Casino, which she wrote "is the newest, and seems to jump the most."

Wanting to also give her readers some relief from the heavy-hearted news to which they had been subjected since Nov. 22, 1963, she rhapsodized about her vacation spot. As usual, her prose was colorful.

In a Jan. 6, 1964 dispatch from San Juan, she described the city as a: "Mixture of Latin-America and the Catskill Mountains of New York. You gamble with dice manufactured in Reno and playing cards from Cincinnati.

"In the hotels run by continentals for continentals (one does not say Americans because Puerto Ricans are American, too) it is easier to get lox, bagels, chopped chicken liver and cheesecake than frijoles or paella, and Rhinestone sweaters, chinchilla capes and sable stoles are de rigueur in the casinos.

"There are 11 gambling casinos in San Juan," she noted, then confessed it was, "All a complete mystery to me. I cannot figure out...why anyone should find it fun to put a stack of chips, representing money, on a table with numbers on it, whether he sees the chips swept away in the next moment or gets his stack doubled."

She confessed she had, "Even participated in those newspaper game pools where the reporters put in fifty cents or a dollar and take a guess at how long the jury will be out at a Page One trial, but there is no chance of blowing the grocery money in that kind of gambling, and you have the fun of putting your educated guess against the others.

"As far as I can see, any guess you make at a roulette or craps table has to be uneducated, so I don't see the lure for anyone belonging to the privileged classes.

"If a poor lady in a frayed shawl buys a 50 cent lottery ticket in hopes of winning $10,000 for her hungry family, I get the picture. But when I see a dame in a $4,000 chinchilla shoulder cover, wearing a $350 blonde wig and clutching a $275 beaded bag put three $5 chips on number 26 at the roulette table, I wonder.

"Suppose she wins $150 or $300 or $500, which I doubt? What is that to her? It would be important to the lady in the shawl who embroiders bedroom slippers for a living, but how can a few hundred dollars thrill a woman who already owns a mink coat, an alligator bag and a Cadillac—those staples of decent U.S. living and whose husband has taken her on a trip to Puerto Rico?"

In her column, Dorothy polished the apple a bit more when she said that, "At least Joe [Levine] smiled when he lost. Some of them—the gray-haired women who are playing alone, with no man in the background, the fellows who nurse their chips, looking desperate. And the ones who play almost every number on the table, a sure sign they have no hope in their luck—are downright depressing, like ghostly figures in a Fellini art movie, symbolizing futility against a vaguely moving background of cigarette smoke.

"And all the people you see in the Puerto Rico casinos are strictly gamblers. No boozers. You cannot buy a drink in any casino on the island—a direct contrast to the policy in Las Vegas, where they ply you with drinks and even snacks, as long as you keep putting your chips on the verdant baize."

Celebrates Fifteen Years on *WML?*

Dorothy and the other stars of *What's My Line?* celebrated the start of the fifteenth season on television Feb. 2, 1964.

AP critic Cynthia Lowry called it "a national habit and an institution."

In late January, the United Press International reported of the accomplishment, "The years marched by—and marched and marched —and so did the jelly bean polisher, the mosquito counter, the money burner, the ladybug salesman and the paper-pantry maker for lamb chops.

"The man who sells life insurance for chickens came and went, and so did the man who plays piano on an airplane, the man who makes false teeth for cows, the man who paints dots on dice, the man who drills

holes in bowling balls and the man who sells warships.

"There were the mattress tester, pillow stuffer, chicken plucker, egg breaker, salami knot-tier, mustache-wax wrapper, boxing-glove stuffer, whale counter, beehive inspector, false teeth modeler, pool table pocket crocheter, horse-hat maker, goose caller, spider raiser, tuba tester, chewing tobacco twister, nose-warmer knitter, false eyelash fitter, and the children eyeglass salesman. And did the occupations stump the panel? Over the span of 15 years, they did two-thirds of the time."

Show's director Frank Heller reflected, "Back in 1950, all of us were terribly fascinated with the mechanics of TV—the majority of the studio audience didn't have sets at home. What we really needed was the audience's attention to the stage. I took the cameras off the stage—put them way back with the longest lenses we could get; we have even longer now."

In February, John Daly was quoted in an article saying, "Early in the show's history, we had a bit of trouble with double entendres. That was the reason we evolved the business of my pulling at my left ear to warn the panel away from a dangerous area. But I haven't reached for my ear in years now."

A tribute piece written by Don Royal chronicled the show's history. He noted the producers worked to ensure the authenticity of each contestant's—or challenger's—profession. People were even required to sign an affidavit. Fun was poked at how contestants never left with more than fifty bucks in earnings, despite inflation.

"Over the years, all through the rise and fall of the big-money quizzes, we have felt proudly poor. Call it reverse snobbism, if you will,"

Mark Goodson said.

Gil Fates said a moment he relished on the show was when the panel was stumped by a contestant who worked as a candlestick maker—after a butcher and a baker had appeared on the show.

An estimated fourteen million people in the United States tuned in each week, and millions more watched it overseas or listened via radio.

Dicky Leeman, one-time producer of the UK's version of *What's My Line?* wrote: "When people complain to me that panel stars, like those on What's My Line...have found a wonderful short cut to easy money and easy fame, I find it simplest to change the conversation...The kind of person who is smug enough to suggest this idea could not, in his nature, have the imagination to conceive what it is like to 'be yourself' in front of the impartial lights and cameras of TV. They bring your every gesture, from an involuntary look of disapproval, to the nervous tapping of a cigarette, into several million living-rooms [sic]. If 'poise' is now the key to success and popularity in the new medium, let them remember that it is the hardest of all attributes to learn and the hardest to sustain under fire."

Friendly With, But Not Friends With, Arlene Francis

When asked about the dynamics of the *WML?* panelists, Dorothy said, "I think we're a good combination. We're all fairly amiable."

Journalist Margaret McManus wrote that although Arlene and Dorothy resided a few blocks from each other in NYC, they didn't socialize much outside of the show. "It is not likely that they run back and forth to borrow a cup of sugar, nor sit in one another's kitchen of a morning over a second cup of coffee."

Arlene Francis' son, the late Peter Gabel, echoed this view. Gabel was a law academic and Editor-at-Large of the progressive Jewish magazine *Tikkun*. He appeared several times on *WML?* as a mystery guest: July 5, 1964, as a guide at the New York World's Fair and again on March 12, 1967, alongside Jonathan Cerf, Bennett's son, for their role as co-editors of the *Harvard Lampoon*. Gabel was also a panelist for one week in the late 1960s. He later appeared as a mystery guest in 1973. Gabel stumped his mother each time he came on the show as a mystery guest, much to the audience's delight.

"My mother and Dorothy were—as far as I know—only really partners on WML. I never saw Dorothy outside of my occasional attendance back stage at the show, and mom rarely spoke of her at home," Gabel told this author. "They were very friendly, and were of course partners as the two women on the panel—each contributing to the magic of that ensemble in their own ways."

Dorothy And Marlin Swing Meet The Beatles

It was difficult for the participants in the Sunday night, Feb. 9,

1964 telecast of *What's My Line?* to reach the theater, because of the massive traffic jam and the crowd of hundreds of mostly teenage girls who converged on CBS-TV Studio 50. That's where *The Ed Sullivan Show* was broadcasting the first U.S. appearance of the British rock group, the Beatles. The panelists on *WML?* made references to it and John Daly told the audience the singing sensations were "next door."

George Harrison, Marlin Swing and DK.

On Monday, Dorothy attended a press reception at the Plaza Hotel and hobnobbed with the four young men. She brought along best friend Marlin Swing. In her column three days later she reported, "The Beatles are so funny and charming that everyone who worked with them on *The Ed Sullivan Show* loved them—including pretty, perky Georgia Brown of *Oliver*. The endearing thing about them is the fact that they don't take themselves one bit seriously, but they're enjoying every funny minute of the madness they've caused."

Ruby Case Mystery: Why FBI Helped Him

While Dorothy could sit back and bask in the adulation of her status as a female television pioneer who had incredibly diverse and fun experiences, her focus turned to the upcoming trial of Jack Ruby.

She arrived in Dallas, Texas on Wednesday, Feb. 19, 1964 as jury selection got underway. She said she would remain in the city until Friday, then return to New York City for the Sunday night broadcast of *WML?*. The *Fort Worth Star-Telegram* reported Dorothy, "May return to Dallas later to hear testimony in the case and may use some of the material in her column. She also said she probably will write magazine articles about the Ruby trial for some European publications."

That was a curious statement for her to make because one wonders why she wouldn't have anticipated writing for U.S. magazines. It might have had something to do with the fact that the American news media were embracing the official government line about the assassination and its aftermath, whereas foreign publishers were not intimidated by the pressure to conform to U.S. propaganda.

Ed Johnson of the *Star-Telegram* reported on the first day of jury selection, that Jack Ruby, "As usual, remained stony-faced during the hearing...Ruby, entering court after a recess, smiled broadly and bowed gallantly toward columnist Dorothy Kilgallen.

"Miss Kilgallen, who was in court for the first time Tuesday, replied with a broad grin."

This took place on Wednesday, which means that DK had already connected with Jack Ruby by Day Two of his court proceedings.

While fellow journalists were not probing too deeply into JFK's murder, they were openly incredulous about the DPD's security tactics.

George Dolan, writing in his front page column in the *Fort Worth Star-Telegram* on Feb. 20, 1964 observed that, "Dallas police are the butt of the latest elephant joke being circulated in correspondents' circles at the Ruby trial.

"One person asks: 'Did you know an elephant went through a window in the basement of the police department?'

"Another inquires: 'What did the police do about it?'

"The first replies: 'They did not notice it.'"

Dorothy's colleague Bob Considine made a shrewd observation when he attended the Ruby trial. In a column dated Feb. 21, 1964 he wrote, "The police guarding the courtroom know every bone in the bodies of the three hundred reporters, know those bones better than our doctors do. No matter how many times you enter the room, you get a thorough frisking from head to ankle. You can step outside, change your mind in

Dorothy arrives with Melvin Belli (Joe Tonahill in center) at the Ruby trial.

full view of the guard, start back in and they stop you for another frisk.

"Pity nobody thought of that the day they brought Lee Oswald downstairs."

Considine also reported: "Dorothy Kilgallen arrived in court and stopped the show. Judge Joe B. Brown, one of her fans gallantly granted her an audience in his chambers. Melvin Belli of San Francisco and his assistant, Joe Tonahill...took her to lunch at a nearby seafood house named Vincent's—whose oysters Belli declared are the best this side of his native city's Fisherman's Wharf.

"As Dorothy entered the courtroom and took her place, Tonahill was flailing away at a prospective juror on the matter of his reading habits. 'Do you read the *Dallas Morning News*?' Joe boomed, as if he was asking Bishop Sheen if he reads *Playboy*.

"The poor man whimpered some reply, and Dorothy whispered: 'This is where I left off in the Sam Sheppard trial, nine years ago, only then it was the *Cleveland Press* they couldn't read.'"

Jack Ruby: Defender of Virtue?

In her Feb. 22, 1964, column titled "Ruby Case Mystery: Why FBI Helped Him," Kilgallen wrote: "One of the best kept secrets of the Jack Ruby trial is the extent to which the Federal government is cooperating with the defense. The unprecedented alliance between Ruby's lawyers and the Department of Justice in Washington may provide the case with the one dramatic element it has lacked: MYSTERY.

"This was never a whodunit. It was only a why-did-he-do-it and what-will-he-get.

"But an arrangement that was made last month between the defense counsel and the FBI has a fascinating 'kicker.' It provides Ruby's side with reams of helpful information that they would never have been able to get without the G-Men—on the condition that they do not ask for anything at all about Ruby's alleged victim, Lee Harvey Oswald."

Kilgallen noted that back on Jan. 9, 1964, one of Ruby's lawyers, Joe Tonahill, had sent a letter to J. Edgar Hoover and to J. Lee Rankin, chief counsel for the Warren Commission.

She revealed, "Tonahill asked for the world." He asked to be given copies of all the evidence currently in possession of the W.C. Kilgallen reported that although he probably expected to be brushed off, to his shock "what he got was pure gold."

DK reported that on January 28, Assistant Attorney General Herbert Miller "informed Tonahill that (although it was unusual, to be sure), the FBI would be instructed to turn over to the defense...[information] which might be important to the case."

What could be the reason for this sort of extraordinary cooperation from Robert Kennedy's Justice Department?

The whole case had some very odd aspects. Notice that in all of the video of Jack Ruby supposedly shooting Lee Oswald, *you never see the assailant's face.* He is dressed in a dark suit and wearing a fedora hat. He has light-colored socks and is wearing cap-toe Oxford dress shoes. The back of his hair line is squared off, not as short and tapered as Ruby's. Slow motion video shows that within a second of the shooting, a bald man (either Louis Miller or Marvin Johnson) approaches the gunman and slips something over his head, as if to conceal his identity. The shooter keeps his head down, like a football player trying to sneak the ball forward over the line of scrimmage to get a first down. *None of the cameras present in the DPD basement garage ever got a picture of Jack Ruby's face.*

Jack Ruby

Shortly thereafter, when Ruby is photographed for booking, he is suddenly attired in apparel a Caribbean cabana towel boy would have worn at a resort in 1963. He has on white pants and a short-sleeved white casual shirt, black socks, and completely different shoes. Why was Ruby wearing a different outfit and where did the clothes come from? Suspects are typically photographed wearing the same attire they are arrested in, because that's forensic evidence.

Lee Oswald was upset—and justifiably so—because the brown shirt he had on when he was arrested was removed and not returned to him, so he had to appear in line-ups merely in his dirty and torn white T-shirt, looking unkempt. Capt. Will Fritz refused to give his brown shirt back and claimed they had nothing else for him to wear.

As Jake Ehrlich notes, "Ruby's white pants fit him perfectly in the waist and length. They are not too long or short. Same with his seemingly tailored short sleeve casual shirt. If this was some kind of prison uniform it would be baggier and not fit nearly as well."

Ehrlich points out, "Jack Ruby claimed until he died four years later he had zero memory of having shot Lee Harvey Oswald. He claimed during his trial that all he remembered was being woken up by men asking him why he shot Oswald. Ruby said, in his own words 'They told me I shot Oswald.'" What to make of any of this?

Even though DOJ was being helpful to Ruby's defense team, Dorothy Kilgallen said the "kicker" was that Assistant A.G. Herbert Miller wrote: "Information concerning Oswald's assassination of the President will not be available as it does not appear to be relevant."

This position was truly unthinkable to DK. "Say that again slowly," she taunted. "Oswald's assassination of the President will not be available? Perhaps it is dramatizing to say that there is an Orwellian note in that line. But it does make you think, doesn't it?

"I have covered many important murder trials. In most of them, as the character of the accused emerged through the days of testimony, so did the character of the victim," Dorothy wrote.

In her Feb. 22, 1964 column, DK went on to question, "Why is Oswald being kept in the shadows, as dim a figure as they can make him, while the defense tries to rescue his killer with the help of information from the FBI? Who was Oswald, anyway?"

Those were good questions that Dorothy Kilgallen posed, and we now have some answers.

The CIA, Oswald And LSD

Lee Oswald is often portrayed as an uneducated loser and malcontent. A good example is the highly deceitful or unforgivably stupid way Secret Service man Gerald Blaine described Oswald in a TV interview in 2010. (And Mr. Blaine is not ignorant. After the SS, he got a job with ARCO, a big International Oil and Gas company in Dallas, Texas as the Director of International Security, Government Relations and Foreign Affairs. Then he worked for Hill & Associates, an Asian-based consulting company).

Yet Blaine said disparagingly, "If you...follow Oswald's actions—taking a shot at General Walker—he had the type of personality he couldn't talk to anybody five minutes without totally alienating them, he had failed at everything he did, he couldn't even be a good defector."

Yet according to the *Washington Post* of Dec. 1, 1963, the associate pastor of First Unitarian Church, Dallas, Rev. Byrd Helligas, described Lee Oswald as "erudite." "He had a good vocabulary. No dangling participles or split infinitives. In the dictionary definition of the word 'intellectual' he was an intellectual." Helligas added that he sensed "no frustration through erudition. He was calm."

Samuel Ballen, described in the press as a "Republican petroleum economist in Dallas," said he found Lee Oswald to be: "an independent, thinking, inquiring young man. He was a rather frail person physically. At least to me, he was the kind of person I could like. I kind of took a liking to him, I wanted to help him a little bit...He had a kind of Gandhi, far-off look about him."

Roy Truly, the director of the depository where Oswald was employed, said of him, "He seemed just a normal, quiet young fellow."

Ruth Paine, with whom his wife and children lived and where he stayed on weekends, said, "Marina felt very favorably toward the president and his family. Most of what she learned of American news was provided by Lee, who translated from newspapers and news magazines. Marina said he never transferred any negative feelings toward President Kennedy."

In fact, Marina said that when President and Mrs. Kennedy lost their prematurely born infant son, Patrick Bouvier Kennedy on August 9, 1963, Lee actually wept at the news. The baby succumbed to respiratory distress syndrome three days after birth and his loss deeply affected the couple. The president even slept near a special incubator at Boston Children's Hospital which was located in the boiler room. Lee and Marina had a second daughter on October 20, 1963. By all accounts, Oswald was a doting father.

A handsome Marine, Lee Oswald.

Recently declassified government documents seem to establish with reasonable certainty that—despite previous denials by Allen Dulles and others over the years—a relationship existed between Lee Harvey Oswald and the Central Intelligence Agency. The extent and nature of that relationship remains somewhat murky but there are tantalizing clues.

The agency's interaction with LHO seems to have begun during his time as a young Marine at the Atsugi Naval Air Facility in Japan in 1957. Atsugi was the base for U-2 spy planes that were dispatched over the Soviet Union. It was also a hub for the CIA's research into psychedelic drugs, specifically LSD. Historians have noted that at the time, the CIA was one of the few suppliers of the psychoactive substance, which the agency used in human experimentation and mind control among the Marines at the Atsugi base where Oswald was stationed. One Marine from Lee's unit acknowledged being one of the human subjects.

A CIA memo entitled "Truth Drugs in Interrogation" revealed the agency practice of dosing agents who were sent on dangerous missions overseas. Did they do that to Lee Oswald too?

A 1978 CIA memo confirms that a finance clerk employed by the agency, James Wilcott, Jr., claimed, "The CIA hired Lee Harvey Oswald when Oswald served in Atsugi." This memo was declassified by the Trump administration in 2017. Critics claimed Wilcott didn't join the agency until 1960, but he was hired as a finance officer by the CIA in 1957.

Wilcott testified to the HSCA that he was working for the CIA in Tokyo when President Kennedy was assassinated, and began hearing the next day that Oswald had been with the CIA there. Wilcott gave the committee the names of seven other people who could confirm Oswald was still paid to do "CIA operational work." His testimony was kept secret for decades. In 1996, former Deputy Counsel for the HSCA, Robert Tanenbaum, testified to the ARRB "the Attorney General of Texas, Henry Wade, the District Attorney and Leon Jaworsky counsel to the Attorney General, on the transcript spoke to [Earl Warren] and said in substance, as I recall, that they had information from unimpeachable sources that Lee Harvey Oswald was a contract employee of the CIA and the FBI."

While serving at the U.S. military base in Japan, Lee Oswald had a "crypto" clearance (higher than "top secret") and regularly listened to the U-2 radio communications. Atsugi was the CIA's main operational base in the Far East; many U-2 spy planes departed from this base on their missions over the USSR and China. LHO was an adept radar operator. The Warren Commission absurdly claimed he taught himself Russian—a very difficult language to master. But W.C. Chief Counsel J. Lee Rankin later confirmed that Oswald's military records show he studied Russian while at the Army Language School in Monterey, California. He became so fluent in speaking the language that when he met his future wife, Marina, in Moscow she thought he was a native born Russian.

The fact LHO was taught Russian proves he was receiving "intelligence training," overseen by the Office of Naval Intelligence (ONI), which administers the language program through the Army.

Lee Oswald was discharged three months early due to a false claim of his mother being ill. Nine days later, he went by ship to England. Somehow, he flew on a U.S. military transport plane to Finland, staying at two of the nicest hotels in Helsinki, (the favored point of entry by the CIA), despite his officially having a mere two hundred and three dollars in his bank account. After this, he took an overnight train from Helsinki to Moscow. Once there, he went to the U.S. Embassy to formally announce he was defecting, though he never renounced his American citizenship. He spent two and a half years in the Soviet Union, living in Minsk, Belarus where he was given a government job, a nice apartment in the prestigious city-centre and also married Marina. The couple then had one child.

Just as curiously as he had defected, he was able to return home to the United States. His ability to do all this with such ease suggests he was playing some type of role in the inscrutable world of spycraft. The U.S. State Dept. even loaned him money. Such a loan, according to regulations, cannot be granted unless the recipient's "loyalty to the United States" has been established "beyond question," which it was in this case.

The U.S. passport office readily cleared Oswald and instructed the American Embassy to renew his passport so he could return home in August 1961. Meeting the Oswalds at the New York pier was the secretary-general of a private anti-Communist organization with close ties to the CIA. He was told by the State Dept. to give Lee, Marina and the one young daughter they had at that time any help they needed. Lee immediately went to work for a welding company in Fort Worth, Texas.

Biographers have pointed to the fact that by his seventeenth birthday, he had already "moved twenty times." The frequent moves weren't driven by his parents' employment opportunities. (Lee never knew his father, who was a distant relative of President Theodore Roosevelt and Confederate General Robert E. Lee). Instead, it was due to the unsettled nature of his mother, Marguerite's instability and the problems created by men who flitted in and out of her life.

But biographers make a mistake in assuming his upbringing meant that Oswald was a troubled adult. Many high achievers have come from difficult childhoods and surmounted early obstacles.

While in the Marines he finished seventh in his class of fifty at radar training school. An officer at the Marine Corps Air Station El Toro in California said that Oswald was a "very competent" crew chief and was "brighter than most people."

James Botelho, who later became a California judge, and was a roommate of Oswald's while he was in the Marines, said, "I knew he was not a Communist and was, in fact, anti-Soviet...I was sure that Oswald was on an intelligence assignment in Russia."

Ernst Titovets, a medical student who befriended Lee Harvey Oswald after the American defector's arrival in Minsk in 1959, told the BBC the pair went to dances and concerts together, they both enjoyed practical jokes, and both energetically chased young female students. David Stern reported, "Titovets, who spoke good English, was able to play Cupid's helper when Oswald met his future wife, Marina, whom he describes as 'attractive in a raw sexual sort of way.'

"'I just liked the guy,' says Ernst Titovets. What did he think when he heard Oswald named as the man who had killed Kennedy, and then was himself shot? 'I couldn't believe my ears,' says Titovets, now a spry 85-year-old bio researcher. 'I deeply believe he was innocent. He was incapable of killing anybody.'"

In 1959, Lee briefly considered studying philosophy at the Albert Schweitzer College in Switzerland and was accepted. Interviews prove he was articulate and knowledgeable. Besides English and Russian, he could speak Spanish passably well. Lee could discuss authors like Tolstoy and Dostoevsky—an impressive achievement for a high school drop-out who earned his GED while in the service.

He was a voracious reader and checked out at least twenty-seven books from the Napoleon Avenue branch of the public library in New Orleans, Louisiana during the summer of 1963. These included JFK's *Profiles In Courage* and William Manchester's idolatrous *Portrait Of A President*, neither of which suggest any anger toward Kennedy. A favorite of his was George Orwell's famous novel *1984*. Lee's literary tastes also ran from Ian Fleming's thrillers (*Goldfinger*, *Thunderball*, *Moonraker*, *From Russia With Love*) to numerous science fiction titles, many written or edited by Issac Asimov. As Matthew Stevenson of *Counterpunch* notes, "While his exaggerated public footprint that summer was that of a Marxist agitator, his background reading on Soviet Russia was anodyne, limited to *What We Know About Communism*, *Russia Under Khrushchev*, and *One Day In The Life of Ivan Denisovich*."

Oswald in 1959 when he "defected."

Bewilderingly, during his relatively short life, Lee Oswald came into contact with an incredible array of groups and individuals. Beginning with an uncle connected to organized crime, and an uncle by marriage who was in the Russian KGB, Oswald moved through the subterranean world of soldiers, CIA and Naval Intelligence agents, Russian Communists and anti-Communists, pro- and anti-Castro Cubans, FBI agents, oil men and right-wing extremists.

One of the most peculiar things was that a fellow Marine, Kerry Wendell Thornley, wrote a novel in 1962 based on Lee Oswald. It's hard to believe he did so simply because he found LHO such a fascinating human being pre-assassination. It's more likely he wrote the book because it was a way to establish a profile for an intelligence asset who would later be framed for one of the biggest crimes of the century. Thornley bragged that he was a friend of mobster Johnny Roselli, whom the CIA had recruited for covert operations against Castro.

In any case, Lee Oswald's well-publicized defection to and return from Russia made him a sort of *cause célèbre*.

This author turned up a lengthy letter in Dallas police files from *The Forth Worth Press* dated June 22, 1962 and addressed to Lee. The missive was signed by a man whose signature is unclear, except his first name was Johnny. He was requesting an interview with Oswald and said, "We are brothers under the skin...I believe you are a man of convictions...I could help you in any writing you might be working on." He advised, "With a 'teaser' for Scripps-Howard's 21 papers, the full meal could well turn out to be a story in a national magazine, even a book and possibly a movie." So Oswald was being treated like a hero.

In October 1962—the same month the world stood at the precipice of a potential nuclear war during the Cuban Missile Crisis—LHO moved his family to Dallas. There, despite having previously defected to the Soviet Union, within one week he had acquired a job with Jagger-Stovall-Chiles, which was under contract to the Pentagon to produce charts and maps for military use.

If Lee Harvey Oswald had no connections to U.S. Intelligence, and was a Communist, why was he given an extremely high security clearance and access to a variety of classified materials? The company he now worked for was also related to top-secret U-2 spy plane missions, including flights over Cuba.

The CIA's claim to have had no contact with Oswald is undercut by the fact George de Mohrenschildt, a CIA asset who was associated with the Dallas Petroleum Club, became close friends with Lee in the months before the assassination. Even Dallas Police Chief Jesse Curry expressed suspicions about this later. George had been born in Mazyr, Belarus in 1911 and was an anti-Communist political refugee with a background as a petroleum geologist. This was otherwise an unlikely friendship, given the great disparity in income levels between the two.

The day after Mr. and Mrs. de Mohrenschildt visited Lee and Marina at their Fort Worth apartment, the Oswalds packed up and moved to Dallas, where Lee got the job at Jagger-Stovall-Chiles.

An ambitious young man, he also sought freelance work. A letter discovered in Dallas police files by this author was addressed to Oswald by the Benjamin J. Davis Defense Company dated Dec. 13, 1962 thanking him for the "samples of photographic work you sent us."

He also had corresponded with another company who replied on stationery that had no company header. The writer, Bob Chester, said, "It is clear from your work that you are skilled at blow-ups, reversals and reproduction work generally." He asked questions about the scope of Oswald's abilities.

In the spring of 1963, de Mohrenschildt traveled to New York, Philadelphia and Washington. According to documents found in newly declassified government files, at the same time as his trip, the CIA's Domestic Operations Division—specifically case officer Gale Allen—was monitoring de Mohrenschildt.

The covert arm of this division was run at the time by E. Howard Hunt, a black ops specialist who later became a Watergate burglar. Hunt claimed not long before his death he had known in advance of a conspiracy to assassinate Kennedy that involved high-level figures in the CIA, among them Allen Dulles.

This author was able to find an interesting letter that had been locked up for years in a safe at the Dallas Police Department, and was addressed to LHO in the summer of 1963. It was from a man named Gene of the Jesuit House of Studies in Mobile, Alabama, inviting him to speak to a group of philosophy students on the subject of what life is like in the Soviet Union. The letter, signed only "Gene," indicates Gene's parents are the ones who suggested the invitation and offered to drive Lee from Dallas to Mobile for the speaking engagement.

Apparently LHO accepted the invitation to address the Jesuit group in Alabama on July 27, because another letter was located, this time from Paul Piazza, S.J., dated Aug. 1, 1963, thanking him for coming. Piazza said, "I feel that I came away from your talk with an understanding of the Russian people as a people, with ideals, goals, problems—normal, everyday human beings, something that is quite easy to forget with all the threats of war hanging in the air." So Oswald was a peacemaker?

Memos Imply CIA Gave Oswald An Assignment In 1963

Still-classified documents only partly unredacted refer to a covert operation approved by senior CIA officials three months before Kennedy's death, that suggest the agency used Lee Harvey Oswald for intelligence purposes in the weeks prior to the president's slaying.

George Joannides was a CIA agent who had close involvement with a group of Communist revolutionaries Oswald had infiltrated, and Joannides withheld information about his own role from Congressional investigators and also lied.

It is documented that LHO had interactions with an anti-Castro group known as the Directorio Revolucionario Estudiantil, or DRE that was founded, funded and operated by the CIA. Though he never revealed it, George Joannides was involved with that organization.

HSCA Chief Counsel Robert Blakey recently asserted that Joannides and his superiors were guilty of obstruction of justice. "I no longer believe that we were able to conduct an appropriate investigation of the [CIA] and its relationship to Oswald," he complained.

At one point, the *Washington Post* was offered a story about George Joannides, but editor Rick Atkinson wrote in an email, "Frankly it bored me." However, reporter Jefferson Morley pursued it and filed suit after the CIA failed to comply with a FOIA request. Ultimately about five hundred pages were released that established that Joannides had spent time in New Orleans and that he was in the loop of some sort of highly sensitive intelligence stream in June 1963. But when Morley's lawyer tried to collect attorney fees from the CIA for its failure to comply with a federal statute, judge Brett Kavanaugh sabotaged the effort and claimed the CIA deserved "deference piled on deference." Why? Later that day, Donald Trump nominated Kavanaugh to the Supreme Court.

Oswald In The Hub Of The Intelligence Community

It is a fact—not speculation or rumor—Lee Harvey Oswald had repeated contacts with Guy Bannister, who had formerly worked for the FBI for thirty years. The pro-Castro leaflets Oswald distributed on the streets of New Orleans (after he hired temp workers from a local employment agency to help him because his Fair Play For Cuba group basically had no members), briefly bore the address of 544 Camp Street. While Bannister's address was officially 531 Lafayette Street, they were in the same building, merely accessed by two different entrances around the corner from each other.

This location was a hub for U.S. intelligence agencies in New Orleans. Across Lafayette Square were the offices of the Secret Service in the post office building. Upstairs was the U.S. Naval Intelligence branch. Was it a coincidence Bannister's office was also across the street from the New Orleans offices of the CIA and FBI? Nearby was the Reily Coffee Co. where Lee Oswald officially worked during his pamphleteering. Local residents knew William Reily was active in anti-Castro activities, yet he had an employee who was supposedly pro-Castro. Next door was the Crescent City Garage, where Oswald often hung out when he should have been working. It was where the members of the FBI parked their cars.

Dorothy Kilgallen was soon to become fixated on what was going on in New Orleans and made a furtive trip there, and planned another not long before she died. (More about that later).

Bannister, whom witnesses claimed still spoke with J. Edgar Hoover on occasion by phone, was far-right politically. He headed the Anti-Communist League of the Caribbean and hired college students to monitor radical or even liberal groups on campus, and to infiltrate them. He believed racial integration of the schools was part of a plan formulated by Stalin and the Communist Party to create "dissension between the races." Banister was convinced the Soviets were contaminating American wheat but had no evidence this was the case.

In the summer of 1963, Oswald was to assume a much more public role. He was hired to establish his bonafides as being a Marxist, so he could gain the confidence of pro-Castro groups and keep an eye on them. In military parlance, LHO was an "agent provocateur." Another way of describing what was happening to him is he was being "sheep dipped"—a term the CIA uses to refer to giving someone a new identity.

When he got into a scuffle on the sidewalk on Canal Street in New Orleans with an anti-Castro person and was arrested and briefly jailed with others in August 1963, Oswald requested to see an FBI agent. He was then separated from the rest of the group and taken into a conference room where he met with Special Agent John Quigley. The FBI man later burned his notes from that meeting, a clear violation of Bureau policy and practice.

About a week after his arrest, someone arranged for Lee to participate in a radio program on local station WDSU. The subject to be discussed was Communism versus capitalism. Oswald articulately represented himself as a Marxist. Less than a week after his death, someone distributed copies of a tape of this broadcast to members of Congress and the media. The objective, obviously, was to portray Lee Oswald as a Communist (even though on the radio show he perceptively drew the distinction between Marxism and Communism). In short, Oswald was being set up as the "fall guy," though he didn't realize it until he was arrested on Nov. 22, 1963.

CIA Headquarters Lied To Its Mexico Branch

In October 1963, the CIA's Mexico City station sent a cable to headquarters in Langley reporting a suspicious phone call it had intercepted to the Russian embassy there. It stated: "AMERICAN MALE WHO SPOKE BROKEN RUSSIAN SAID HIS NAME LEE OSWALD." Headquarters responded that it had no information on LHO since May 1962—before he had returned to the U.S. from Russia. But that was a lie. Routing slips show that high-ranking CIA officials—including but not limited to Jane Roman, an aide to Counterintelligence Chief James Jesus Angleton—had deliberately misled their colleagues in Mexico. Why would they do this? It had to be because of compartmentalized operational secrecy.

A Senate Committee chaired by Frank Church in 1975 criticized the Warren Commission for ignoring "the significance of Oswald's contacts with pro-Castro and anti-Castro groups for the many months before the assassination." Oswald's behavior in the summer of 1963 looked to many critics like that of some sort of spy or agent provocateur. Senator Richard Schweiker, who chaired the Church subcommittee on the Kennedy assassination, said of Oswald, "Everywhere you look with him, there are the fingerprints of [U.S.] Intelligence."

Another New Revelation

It has also recently been learned that a CIA employee named Reuben Efron was reading Lee Oswald's mail for about eighteen months prior to the assassination. A memo has even surfaced that Efron sent to Betty Egerter at a CIA unit known as "the office that spied on spies." This clearly connotes the agency was checking to see if Oswald was a "double agent."

Tellingly, Mr. Efron was in the room when the Warren Commission interviewed Marina Oswald, in February 1964—the only one present whose title and role were not explained.

That Oswald was part of some undercover operation for the U.S. government seems beyond doubt.

That may be the reason why the Dallas Police Department supposedly never taped any of the more than twelve hours of questioning to which Lee Oswald was subjected by the DPD and FBI. They claimed they didn't have the "means" to record Oswald's interrogation, but that is absolutely false. The police employed five court stenographers and there were dozens of reporters in the building with recording equipment they could have borrowed if necessary. They also had the full power of the federal government at their disposal via the FBI which certainly had the capability to record Oswald interviews. Furthermore, on the schematics of the third floor of the DPD from 1963 it shows there was a "Recording Room" right across the hall from Homicide (Rm 317) where Oswald was being queried. This is just one more instance of gaslighting the public.

Dorothy Kilgallen perceptively deduced, "It appears that Washington knows or suspects something about Oswald that it does not want Dallas and the rest of the world to know or suspect.

"This is certain to emerge crystal-clear when the trial progresses to the stage where testimony is given. The least hip person, forensically speaking, is going to get the message that Lee Harvey Oswald has passed on not only to his shuddery reward, but to the mysterious realm of 'classified' persons whose whole story is known only to a few government agents."

Oswald May Have Saved JFK's Life In Chicago

Unbeknownst to the public at the time, a conspiracy was foiled to assassinate John Kennedy in November 1963 in Dorothy Kilgallen's hometown.

The president was scheduled to attend the Army/Air Force football game on Nov. 2, 1963, flying into Chicago's O'Hare Airport that Saturday, and arriving at Soldier Field at 1:17 p.m. Two bands would play *Hail To the Chief* and the national anthem. After that, the nation's top leader would toss the coin to determine the offensive and defensive roles of the two teams at the kickoff, set for 1:30 p.m. The entire program of four hours of military and athletic performance by the two football teams, the Army corps, and the Air Force wing, was to give Chicagoans their first opportunity in thirty-seven years to see an athletic contest between two of the nation's service academies. The game was expected to draw a crowd of 72,000 and football enthusiast Jack Kennedy was looking forward to it.

The Secret Service planned a motorcade route that would have unwisely taken JFK in an open-air vehicle from O'Hare Airport along the Northwest Expressway, exiting at Jackson Boulevard to pass through warehouses and crowds lined on sidewalks to Soldier Field. The motorcade would have to make at least one sharp ninety-degree turn that would slow it to almost a standstill, similar to what would occur in Dallas three weeks later.

But on Oct. 30, 1963, FBI director J. Edgar Hoover put the kabash on that by notifying the Secret Service in Chicago that at least one, four-man hit team with high-powered rifles, would attempt to shoot President Kennedy either from a warehouse or at one of the Northwest Expressway overpasses overlooking the president's motorcade route that coming Saturday. The men were described as paramilitary "fanatics" who owned rifles with telescopic sights, and at least one of the suspects had a "Spanish-sounding name" and might have been Cuban.

It was a tip from a reliable FBI informant named "Lee" that alerted Hoover to the Chicago plot. We know that Oswald was described as a paid informant for the FBI, so it may well have been Lee Harvey Oswald who saved John Kennedy's life that weekend.

Additional confirmation of the threat came the next day when a rooming house landlady phoned Chicago police to report that four men had arrived from outside the city and she observed high-powered rifles with telescopic sights and an outline of Kennedy's motorcade route in a room they rented from her near the Northwest Expressway.

A SS agent tailing two of the men blew his cover by failing to turn down his two-way radio when they passed his car and it spooked them. They were detained anyway and stonewalled, but the other two suspects got away.

Former Illinois state trooper Abraham Bolden, who was then with the Secret Service, said, "No one was sent to the room to fingerprint it or get an ID. The case was lost and that was the end of it."

The Secret Service is alleged to have deliberately destroyed documents related to the plot in January 1995 after they were requested by the Assassination Records Review Board.

Bolden ranked second in the nation in solving counterfeit and check forging cases. President Kennedy had personally invited him to join the White House protective detail, and thereafter introduced him to others as "the Jackie Robinson of the Secret Service," a comment Bolden found so touching he almost broke into tears.

But when he blew the whistle on the failure of the SS to thoroughly investigate the Chicago conspiracy against JFK, he was arrested on trumped-up charges of bribery. Following Bolden's conviction in a second trial, key witnesses admitted lying at the prosecutor's request. Bolden was denied a retrial and served several years in federal prison.

President Joe Biden's first pardon of his term was Mr. Bolden in 2022.

Yet another tip led to the Chicago arrest of former Marine and John Birch Society rightwing radical Thomas Vallee. He was found with an M1 rifle, a carbine, a handgun and 3,000 rounds of ammunition in his car trunk. Vallee shared similarities with accused JFK assassin LHO. Besides recently having landed work along a future Kennedy parade route, he had enlisted in the Marines when he was just sixteen in the mid-1950s like Lee did. He had also been stationed at a U-2 base in Japan like Oswald. He had apparently been recruited by the CIA to perform assignments. Vallee didn't defect to Russia, but he trained anti-Castro Cubans on Long Island. Both owned rifles and were loners, basically "perfect for a frame-up," wrote author Edwin Black.

At 10:15 a.m. November 2, with two potential snipers still at large on the streets of Chicago, JFK heeded the FBI's advice to abort his trip.

A news bulletin was issued mid-morning to state that President Kennedy canceled his plans to attend the game. It was said "the crisis in South Vietnam caused the cancellation, and Kennedy will remain in Washington to confer with top officials." But actually aides had readied a special communications station under Soldier Field stands to keep him on top of the news from Vietnam had he made the trip.

At about the same time as JFK was scheduled to visit Chicago, half a world away, South Vietnam President Diem and his brother Nhu were brutally murdered in a CIA sponsored coup. Kennedy had ordered the CIA multiple times not to proceed with their quest to kill Diem. Later, famed CIA agent E. Howard Hunt testified to a Senate committee that he was tasked "to create or fabricate cables [implicating Kennedy in Diem's murder] which were to substitute for the (legitimate) mission chronological cables." The plotters probably expected to get away with assassinating Kennedy in Chicago on the same day as the slaying in Vietnam and call it retribution.

That scenario had to imply involvement by U.S. intelligence in the planned murder of the President of the United States. No one was charged in the foiled Chicago plot.

On Nov. 4, 1963, President Kennedy recorded his thoughts on the Diem coup into a dictabelt machine in the Oval Office, in which he spoke analytically and even somewhat self-effacingly (complete with punctuation). He said, "I was shocked by the death of Chairman Nhu"...and "The way he was killed made it particularly abhorrent." Eighteen days later, Kennedy himself would be gunned down.

Strangely, on Feb. 11, 1968, Vallee wrote a letter to FBI Director J. Edgar Hoover, praising him and asking for a copy of a speech he had given four years before. Hoover personally replied on February 15, and sent Vallee a copy of the speech, but asked that he "not reprint this for [your] own use." Mr. Vallee was living in the same town as Ron Pataky: Columbus, Ohio.

There were other assassination plots swirling around Kennedy that autumn of 1963.

On Monday, Nov. 18, 1963, a Tampa assassination threat was thwarted by beefing up escort security for the presidential visit. Over six hundred law enforcement officers and military troops protected JFK.

Declassified documents show a credible threat against the president was investigated by the Miami-Dade Police Department during Kennedy's trip there later that same day. Bob Hoelscher was a countersniper and observer on the terrace deck of the airport hotel and confirmed the threat. Kennedy was transported primarily by helicopter to and from the airport to avoid a motorcade. When briefly in his limousine, he was driven at 50 mph.

As David Talbot writes in his book *Brothers: The Hidden History of the Kennedy Years* (2007), "Kennedy was, in fact, being methodically stalked in the final weeks of his life...In the final month of his life, John Kennedy seemed a marked man, encircled by a tightening knot of treachery." Because the Secret Service must have realized that JFK was in a dangerous situation, the rollback of protection furnished him on Nov. 22, 1963 in Dallas is very incriminating.

Knowing this makes it all the more improbable that a "lone nut" like Oswald killed JFK. Yet that lie just keeps rolling along...

Dorothy's Meeting With Jack Ruby

Soon after Dorothy had arrived in Dallas, attorney Joe Tonahill told her Jack Ruby had asked to speak with her. This exchange took place at the defense table, and was said to be brief. But she and the defendant would talk privately—and more extensively—soon.

On February 23, Dorothy penned a column called "Nervous Ruby Feels 'Breaking Point' Near." She revealed to readers she had met with Ruby in person. She wrote, "Jack Ruby's eyes were as shiny brown-and-white bright as the glass eyes of a doll. He tried to smile but his smile was a failure. When we shook hands, his hand trembled in mine ever so slightly, like the heartbeat of a bird."

Ruby discussed his desire "to be well enough someday to help people, to do something really worthwhile," perhaps seeking some sort of atonement. Dorothy said after their verbal exchange she left the courtroom "wondering what I really believed about the man."

Film footage shot at the courthouse during the nearly four weeks the Ruby trial unfolded confirms the mayhem that prevailed. With hundreds of members of the press from around the globe plus other persons crowding into the courtroom and the adjacent hallways like sardines in a can, it was a stressful scene. It was hot, grimy and noisy in the extreme. The sequestered jury probably suffered most.

Jury selection took fourteen days and one hundred and sixty-two people took the stand to be questioned. Max Causey, upon being selected as the first juror in the Jack Ruby trial, reflected, "In my thirty-five years on this planet I had never been exposed to a more devastating shock than at that moment. I suddenly felt as though the ceiling and all the upper seven floors of the Records Building had collapsed on my head. All of this publicity that we were getting was a little exciting but it was far more frightening. Everyone concerned with the security of the jury felt that no good could possibly come from this much exposure of the jury to the public." Their names, pictures and life stories appeared in the media throughout the world.

Despite the seemingly elaborate security of uniformed police officers present, seven prisoners escaped from the Dallas County Jail, fleeing past the door of the courtroom where Jack Ruby was on trial for murder! It was like a criminal version of the Keystone Kops.

Brandishing a "weapon," one prisoner frightened nineteen-year-old Karen Lynn Bennett, a dancer at one of Ruby's nightclubs, who was waiting in the hallway to testify as the first defense witness. "He's after me! He's after me!" she screamed, then slumped to the floor in a faint. She was revived in time to take the stand.

The artificial weapon had been carved in soap, painted with black shoe polish and held together with syrup. The barrel was made of rubber hosing. It is hilarious the jail escape could even occur with so many lawmen crowding the lobby outside the Ruby courtroom. Such was the inefficacy of law enforcement in Dallas.

Despite the serious nature of covering Jack Ruby's trial, Dorothy Kilgallen found a jocular way to describe the bureaucratic business of being frisked before entering the court room. Writing the next day—February 24—she noted the women in charge of frisking female trial attendees were "ladies with magnolia accents who wear bright-colored dresses, pearls and perfume." They chatted with Dorothy about *What's My Line?* and carefully examined items in her purse to ensure they were harmless.

"Mrs. Allen is the most dramatic of the friskers—sort of an Actor's Studio type. When she went through my purse she took out my ballpoint pen and examined it as if she believed it might be an infernal machine created by Dr. Wernher von Braun to blow up the courtroom," Dorothy joked.

At the end of this column, she mused that perhaps the time-consuming business of vetting the press each morning was a type of retribution by the Dallas Police Department for the criticism it received from the Fourth Estate after Ruby was able to access Oswald and kill him.

"...this is a trifling—if tickling revenge from a very courteous group of officers," she wrote.

In a column that ran on February 25 and headlined "D.A. To Link Ruby To Oswald?" Dorothy wrote this dispatch from Dallas:

"Among those who know the seamier side of Dallas show business, the betting is ten to one that District Attorney Hank Wade will produce witnesses who will testify that Jack Ruby and Lee Harvey Oswald were acquainted. Ruby has said repeatedly that he didn't know the alleged assassin of President Kennedy—but then Ruby's plea is temporary insanity and there are a great many things he doesn't remember, and isn't about to. To quote one observer:

"'The operation of Jack's Carousel Club had its unsavory aspects, but if Oswald checked in there a couple of nights a week, he could make some extra money. That could account for his ability to take trips—on a $50-a-week salary, and it also would account for his living in a room in the heart of Dallas five nights a week and joining his wife and children in the suburbs only on Fridays and Saturdays.'"

On March 7, 1964, Dorothy kicked off her column with a lone paragraph questioning whether or not Ruby was the actual cause of Oswald's demise.

"Spectators and press at the Jack Ruby trial in Dallas may expect forensic fireworks when the State offers medical testimony to prove the corpus delecti. Melvin Belli and Joe Tonahill, co-counsel for the defendant, will attempt to show that Lee Harvey Oswald did not die as a result of the single bullet pumped into him by Ruby, but because of 'bungled' surgery during which he allegedly suffered a fatal embolism."

Melvin Belli had told the court back on February 19, "We're not conceding any aspect of the charge against us is beyond controversy. That's why the surgeon who performed the post-mortem on Mr. Oswald is to be called as a witness."

A Private Chat

Also in March, DK approached Tonahill about the possibility of speaking to Ruby again, but this time without anyone else present in the room. She wanted to accomplish this before a verdict would be handed down. Kilgallen told the attorney she had a message to relay to Ruby from a mutual friend, a singer from San Francisco. Judge Joe Brown, likely a bit starstruck by the famed reporter, agreed to her request. The four sheriff's deputies who served as body guards for Ruby, traveling like a wolf pack everywhere the man went, were called off. Tonahill, Ruby and Kilgallen then walked to a small office off the courtroom behind the judge's bench, for this conversation held during the noon recess.

In an interview conducted by Kathryn Fauble and David Henschel in the 1990s, Joe Tonahill said he didn't pay close attention to their conversation, but felt it had been an impactful interaction from what he had observed.

"He wasn't uttering nonsense, because this interview with her was a very significant point in his class-less life," Tonahill said. "I think he enjoyed it very much and cooperated with her in however way that he could—told her the truth—as he understood it. It was just a very agreeable conversation between them. I can't understand people doubting the sincerity of that interview. I watched them. It was a very sincere discussion going back and forth."

DK and Ruby spoke one-on-one for at least ten minutes. Being as well prepared as Dorothy was, she could ask Jack Ruby a lot of pertinent questions within that span of time. But she never publically wrote about what she'd discussed with the "assassin of the assassin," likely saving these insights for her upcoming book on the circumstances of JFK's murder.

We Now Have A Clue What Ruby Told Kilgallen

Perhaps at the behest of Dorothy herself, Jack Ruby sat down and wrote out as best he could his thoughts on what happened. He compiled ten pages of comments on both sides of five pieces of paper. This confidential document was smuggled out of his jail cell and has been authenticated, though it is little known. Ruby implicated Lyndon Johnson as the brains behind the assassination, implying that he set the scene and put Oswald into position on that fateful day in November.

This author has examined the handwritten recollection and this is an excerpt:

Ruby wrote, "Who would ever dream that the m-----f----- was a Nazi, and found me as the perfect setup for a frame. It was perfect for them. Remember they had the president killed, and now with me in the picture, they'll make it look as though Castro or the Russians had it done. Anyone in their right mind would know that the Russians or Castro would never do something like that…it would only create worse hostilities...Remember the only one who had all to gain was Johnson himself. Figure that out. Remember all points. Also about Oswald who has been a drifter all of his life, suddenly decided to go to work in the book-binding building weeks before Kennedy himself knew he was coming to Dallas…Where did Oswald get the information that far in advance? It had to be someone pretty high in Washington who had made up Kennedy's mind about the trip. All that was planned by Johnson, no one would question the president about a conspiracy…Johnson could commit any crime he cared to because he knew he was going to be the president and have all the power he needed.

"The shooting at the ex-general's [Edwin Walker] home was to make believe…what a crackpot [Oswald] is. That to fool the people into thinking that there wasn't any motive in killing the president, and it was done by a crazy person…"

Given the possibility that anything he wrote would be intercepted and read, Jack Ruby was probably somewhat restrained in what he put on paper. But talking privately with Dorothy, he could let his hair down and speak more bluntly. He obviously pointed her in the direction of LBJ.

Ruby later commented, "I do not want to die. But I am not insane. I was framed to kill Oswald...They found some very clever means and ways to trick me and which will be used later as evidence to show the American people that I was part of the conspiracy in the assassination of

[the] president, and I was used to silence Oswald...They alone planned the killing, by they, I mean Johnson and others...Read the book *Texas Looks At Lyndon Johnson* and you may learn quite a bit about Johnson and how he has fooled everyone...In all the history of the U.S. never has a president been elected that has the background of Johnson. Believe me, compared to him I am a saint."

Jack had said that if Adlai Stevenson had been JFK's vice president, Kennedy would not have been assassinated. When asked by a reporter in a hallway to explain that, Ruby replied, "Well the answer is the man in office now."

Ruby Is Found Guilty

On March 14, Ruby was convicted of murder with malice and was sentenced to die in the electric chair. The jury hadn't bought Belli's claim that Ruby had suffered from "psychomotor epilepsy" and was of unsound mind when he killed Oswald. Belli was fired from the case and on March 19, it was announced prominent defense attorney Percy Foreman would replace him. Surprisingly, Ruby's sister Eileen Kaminsky said this was the man they'd wanted to retain as legal counsel in the first place.

"We preferred him to Belli. But Foreman was contacted by another man and there was some misunderstanding about what part Foreman would take in the case, so we went with Belli."

Ruby appealed his sentence.

In a column dated March 25, 1964, Dorothy cautioned her readers, "The point to be remembered in this historic case is that the whole truth has not been told. Neither the State of Texas nor the defense put all of its evidence before the jury. Perhaps it was not necessary, but it would have been desirable from the viewpoint of all the American people."

Somewhat later, Melvin Belli offered a harsh assessment of Lone Star justice. He said the trial had taken place in "a kangaroo court." He noted trial judge Joe Brown made frequent uses of the spittoon, jurymen smoked cigars and the judge and another courtroom official called each other "Joe" during the trial. He commented "you don't have to know much law to be a judge in Texas." He complained "not a single motion or move we made was sustained." Belli said he cited a long list of Texas cases which he believed would make Ruby eligible for bail, but when he confronted the judge with the citations, Belli said Judge Brown told him: "Don't cite those cases, Mr. Belli. They're all n----r cases."

Belli also bemoaned the lack of diversity on the jury, pointing out that 172 of the 178 people on the potential juror list were Southern Baptist, and all twelve of those picked to serve were of that faith.

Eventually, on Oct. 5, 1966—after Dorothy Kilgallen was gone—an appeals court ruled the motion for a change of venue before the original trial court should have been granted. Ruby's conviction and death sentence were overturned.

Plans were in place for a new trial to be held in February 1967 in Wichita Falls, Texas. Ruby became sick in prison, and died of a pulmonary embolism from lung cancer on Jan. 3, 1967. He had staked the claim he'd been injected with cancer cells—the hypothesis for his rapidly declining health. Paranoiac? Perhaps.

But the December 2022 National Archives release of thousands of previously classified documents collected as part of a U.S. government review into the assassination of President John Kennedy in 1963 has raised questions about a prominent psychiatrist who visited Jack Ruby in his jail cell. Louis Jolyon ("Jolly") West was funded by the CIA to conduct LSD experiments in the 1950s-70s. West was a prominent player in the now infamous MK-Ultra program in which CIA doctors gave powerful psychiatric drugs to Americans without their knowledge. The Citizens Commission on Human Rights International (CCHR), a mental health industry watchdog group, scrutinized West, largely because of his brainwashing and LSD experiments; a racist program called "the violence initiative"; his use of psychosurgery, and his links to well-known assassins, to evaluate their "mental states."

A document obtained under the Freedom of Information Act reveals the CIA set West up in a clandestine laboratory to perform "mind-control" experiments with hypnosis and LSD. A portion of the experiments were exposed in the mid-1970s by the U.S. Senate Select Committee on Intelligence.

Psychiatrist Colin A. Ross of the CCHR said West's work was of "direct relevance to mind control, non-lethal weapons development, creation of controlled dissociation and the building of Manchurian Candidates"—those who harm their own country because they are under the control or influence of another. West was also in contact with Sirhan Sirhan, the man convicted of killing Robert Kennedy.

What was Jolly West doing in Jack Ruby's isolated jail cell? In 1999, *The New York Times* flunked "Journalism 101" by failing to mention in West's obituary the salient fact he had worked for the CIA and had contact with an incarcerated Jack Ruby after which Ruby died.

Kilgallen Pillories LBJ And Boosts RFK

Besides covering the Ruby trial in Dallas, Dorothy of course continued her habit of multi-tasking. Her columns were filled with juicy tidbits about the famous, and she also took jabs at Lyndon Johnson and built up a man who posed a serious challenge to him.

In an article published March 26, 1964, Kilgallen reported, "Republicans all over the country are amazed at the rapidity with which the Texas millionaires lost their interest in [Barry] Goldwater as soon as President Kennedy was assassinated. They were willing to pour any amount into a Goldwater campaign to defeat Mr. Kennedy, but they faded away from campaign headquarters, taking their checkbooks with them, as soon as One of Their Own Boys, Lyndon Johnson, was installed in the White House."

What the politically astute DK was highlighting is the fact that the big money boys in Texas hated President Kennedy so much they were willing to fund an opponent, but Lyndon Johnson (despite being far more liberal than most of the tycoons) would play ball with them and protect their financial interests, and Kennedy wouldn't.

Four days later, Dorothy zeroed in on a political dynamic that historians have missed: How so soon after JFK's death, the Kennedy machine served notice to Johnson that they possessed the political clout to destroy him.

DK wrote, "Pierre Salinger's wealthy—very wealthy—backers don't really care whether he wins in California [in his race for U.S. Senate] or flops. His 'sudden' (really not so sudden) decision to quit as the White House press secretary was in fact a dramatic warning to the L.B. Johnson forces. The Democratic Party could be split wide open if Attorney General Kennedy is not chosen as the Vice Presidential candidate. Wise members of the party are aware of this political probability, and are frankly worried about carrying California, Michigan and New York—as well as the New England states—if Robert F. Kennedy doesn't run in the secondary slot. Salinger's ploy in California is just another way of telling the LBJ forces that the Kennedy team has not resigned from politics.

"Example: When President Johnson asked the Attorney General whether he was responsible for the write-in vote in New Hampshire, RFK denied it. A fellow named Corbin inspired the primary campaign. President Johnson ordered Bailey of Connecticut—chairman of the Democratic National committee—to remove Mr. Corbin from the committee, and it was done.

"But when the press was informed that Mr. Corbin had never been authorized to launch an RFK write-in, the disavowal was not made by the strong, frank, aggressive attorney general in person, but by one of his many assistants who kept referring to Mr. Kennedy in the third person. This was an oblique signal to Kennedy workers in the field that it was okay to proceed—and it should have been obvious to the Johnson team, no amateurs they."

Then on April 4, 1964, Dorothy wrote, "Politicians all over the country are having second thoughts about the possibilities for the vice presidency because of the tumultuous receptions that Robert and Edward 'Ted' Kennedy get wherever they go. In Milwaukee, the experts were astounded at the reception given [Teddy] and in Scranton squads of police were needed to hold back the crowds greeting the attorney general. It's obvious that the 'Kennedy magic' wasn't completely erased on the dark afternoon of November 22."

Dorothy Is Relentless In Pursuing The Truth

Kilgallen continued to pose thorny questions about the odd occurrences surrounding the tragedy in Dallas. She focused on the immediate aftermath of JFK's assassination and the official version of events. It was claimed that after leaving the TSBD, Lee Oswald followed some circuitous route by bus, cab and on foot, to get to his rooming house, where he stayed only briefly, before retrieving a jacket and walking to a bus stop on the corner, (which would have taken him in the opposite direction from where the W.C. claimed he ended up).

After that point, the Commission was unable to explain how the suspect traveled such distance on foot within the timeframe they claimed.

A patrolman named J.D. Tippit pulled his squad car over to the curb to talk to a man walking down the street, whereupon the officer was shot and killed after stepping out of his vehicle. Witnesses conflict on whether there was one assailant or two.

But could Tippit really have recognized Oswald on the basis of a very vague description which, moreover, would not have mentioned the tan zipper jacket he had put on since leaving Elm Street? It seems unlikely, and yet when Donald Janson summed up "The Dallas Mystery" in the *The New York Times* on Sunday, December 1, he wrote without hesitation, "He [Oswald] killed the policeman, another mass of evidence shows..."

What "mass of evidence" was that?

After supposedly having murdered Tippit, Oswald was later arrested at a movie theater.

Writing April 15, 1964, Dorothy commented: "A man who knows he is wanted by the authorities after a spectacular crime does not seek out a policeman, usually, unless he has decided to give himself up, and certainly Oswald was not doing that. By shooting officer Tippit, instead of trying to make himself inconspicuous, Oswald put himself in double jeopardy. His act almost guaranteed his arrest. Why?"

Dorothy made a very good point, as usual. If Oswald is the man whom officer Tippit stopped walking down the sidewalk, he could have played it cool. At that point no one could link him to the assassination. There were no eyewitnesses. Granted, he was an employee of the TSBD but he wasn't the only one who left the building early that day. It had obviously become a crime scene and so no work would be getting done. No one could have connected him to the rifle right away. That would take time. He would have had an opportunity to make his escape from Dallas and possibly flee the country.

Oswald would have had nothing whatsoever to fear as Tippit had absolutely no reason to arrest Lee. Besides, there were scores of men in

Dallas who fit the general description of the suspect.

Merely encountering a police officer on the street would be no more intimidating than when Officer Baker pointed a gun at him in the TSBD ninety seconds after Kennedy had been shot. Probably less so. Lee had remained unflappable then.

Those who saw Oswald right after JFK was slain said he was calm and not in a hurry. He seemed bewildered by what had just occurred outside the building. Similarly, police who interrogated him over the next two days, for twelve hours, also described his demeanor as calm, if not cooperative. Granted, he was incensed about being accused of murder, and raised his voice when being hustled physically by police through a crush of reporters and cameramen at DPD headquarters and protested his being deprived of legal representation. But LHO was not histrionic.

It does not make sense that Lee Oswald would panic and shoot the police officer.

'Car 10, Where Are You?'

There are many mysteries surrounding thirty-nine year old Dallas Police Officer J.D. Tippit—the man and his murder. (His legal first name was merely initials, a not uncommon practice in the South at that time).

He suffered from PTSD following his service during WWII and was a shy man. It was said he had trouble looking people in the eye. He was a big, strapping guy who could be gentle, but was also seen as someone who had a very rough side in the way he treated teenagers at Austin's—a barbecue joint where he worked from 10 p.m. to 2 a.m. on Friday and Saturday nights. The Tippits were struggling financially.

Former CIA Director Allen Dulles, at a Warren Commission hearing, asked Dallas Police Chief Jesse Curry if Tippit had any involvement with narcotics. What was the reason behind that question?

His best friend was a member of the John Birch Society but Tippit's family claimed he was a big admirer of

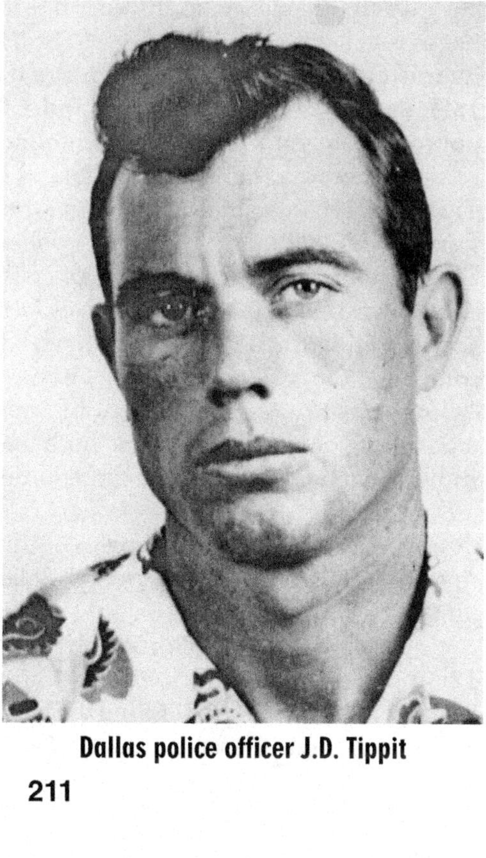

Dallas police officer J.D. Tippit

President Kennedy.

For some unknown reason, he had recently taken a sudden interest in studying Spanish. (His niece, Linda Christopher, said he "got pretty good at it.")

J.D. had gone home for a quick lunch his wife fixed him late Friday morning—something he did not ordinarily do. In talking about the president's visit to Dallas, he had remarked to her "you never can tell what's going to happen...One nut might try something."

The Tippits' oldest boy, Allen, who was thirteen, had faked being sick at school so he could avoid taking a test, and was home when his father arrived. Before leaving, Tippit hugged his son and said, "No matter what happens today, I want you to know that I love you." This was something uncharacteristic for J.D. to do, though he was a doting father.

After the assassination, all patrol cars were ordered to Dealey Plaza but Officer Tippit was cruising around the Oak Cliff section of Dallas. Why? Police later claimed he had been dispatched there. But that claim is suspect because Sgt. J.C. Bowels, the radio-room supervisor, revealed that federal agents "borrowed" the original police Dictabelts and took them to a recording studio in Oklahoma. These Dictabelts contained all recordings of police communications during the assassination on Channels One and Two. Did they edit or otherwise alter them?

That morning, there were a number of periods when Tippit was not in touch with headquarters. At 12:54 p.m. he reported his location as Lancaster and Eighth. But when the dispatcher tried to contact him at 1:03, there was no response. Around 1:08 p.m., Tippit twice radioed the police dispatcher but inexplicably got no reply.

Photographer Al Volkland and his wife Lou, both of whom knew Tippit, said that at about 12:45 p.m., they saw him as they drove past and waved to him. He was sitting in his police car at a Gloco gas station in Oak Cliff, watching the cars coming over the Houston Street viaduct from downtown Dallas. Three employees of the Gloco station—Tom Mullins, Emmett Hollinshead and J.B. "Shorty" Lewis—all of whom knew Tippit, confirmed the Volklands' story. They said Tippit stayed at the station for "about ten minutes, somewhere between 12:45 and 1:00, then he went tearing off down Lancaster at high speed" on a bee-line toward Jack Ruby's apartment and in the direction of where he was killed a few minutes later.

Who or what was Tippit expecting to see by watching the viaduct? And why did he leave so hurriedly? Police logs contain no instructions for him to go elsewhere.

Cab driver William Whaley said he picked up a young man at 12:30 p.m. at the Greyhound bus station and he—and authorities—believed it was Lee Oswald. Either he was wrong about it being Lee, or he was wrong about the time, because Oswald was still at the TSBD then.

Whaley told of driving across the Houston Street viaduct (past the Gloco station) at about the same time Tippit was reported there, and dropped the passenger off near his rooming house. Is it possible that Tippit spotted someone who looked like Oswald, and for some reason took off to intercept him? LHO was not yet considered a suspect and his name was not broadcast over police radio for about another hour.

Oswald's landlady, Earlene Roberts, said that Lee stopped by his room briefly at 1026 North Beckley, just before 1 p.m., and retrieved a light jacket. She said he then left via the front door at 1:04 p.m. and walked to the corner bus stop, on the same side of the street as the house. She observed him through the window standing at a point where he could catch a *northbound* bus. But officer Tippit was killed *south* of that location. What, then, was LHO doing awaiting transportation to take him in the opposite direction from that in which the W.C. claimed he went?

While he had been in his room, Earlene saw a police car pull up directly in front of the house with two cops inside and honk its horn twice—"tip tip", as she described it—then slowly pull away from the curb. It was car No. 207, assigned to Officer Jimmy Valentine, who was at the TSBD. The FBI was suspicious of this so a letter was prepared by Capt. W.R. Westbrook claiming the vehicle remained at the TSBD all afternoon. But Sgt. Gerald Hill said Westbrook had been in that car at some point.

Top Ten Record shop owner J.W. Stark and clerk Louis Cortinas claimed that at 1:11 p.m., Tippit rushed into the store on West Jefferson and made an attempt to reach somebody by phone, but was unsuccessful and then dashed out the door, heading north to Sunset, then east.

Who was he trying to reach by phone so urgently, rather than use the two-way radio in his squad car?

J.D. Tippit was gunned down at 1:15 p.m., about three minutes after leaving the record store. He was killed about a mile from Oswald's rooming house. How could LHO get there so fast? Then he was arrested eight blocks from the murder scene. Did Lee really cover all this distance on foot?

More importantly: why was Officer Tippit killed?

The simple fact is, the evidence against Oswald being the president's killer didn't surface fast enough for the police to be able to use it to arrest him. They needed another murder, if nothing else to muddy the water. Detective Jim Lavelle later said that Capt. Will Fritz admonished him that they'd better make the charges against Oswald stick when it came to the Tippit murder because they didn't have enough to convict him for Kennedy's death. That suggests LHO was viewed as a scapegoat.

The forensics of the Tippit shooting—more important even than any of the conflicting eyewitness accounts—fail to establish that he was killed by Lee Oswald

The ambulance that was summoned was based at a funeral home

just three blocks away and got there quickly, so Tippit's dead body was removed from the murder scene before the arrival of police.

Although history has been rewritten, a review of Dallas TV and radio broadcasts as the drama was unfolding that day tells a very different story. For example, WBAP-TV broadcast a news bulletin saying, "Dallas policeman J.D. Tippit was shot to death by an unknown man *in a car*." It then aired another bulletin awhile later stating the suspect "was picked up after Dallas police *put out a pick-up order on his car* following the shooting and the killing of a Dallas police officer."

This proves that the first reaction of police officers to arrive at the scene was that J.D. Tippit had been murdered by a man who drove off in a car, and they even had a good enough description of the vehicle they put out an all-points-bulletin (APB). The automobile containing the suspect was stopped by police about an hour later.

Their arrest of this individual occurred AFTER they had already surrounded the Texas Theater and a crowd estimated by one reporter as being between two and three thousand people had gathered there.

The police at the site of the Tippit shooting had radioed headquarters that they found spent shells and that the suspect was armed with an automatic weapon. They presumably based this on the type of spent cartridges found at the scene. However, when Oswald was arrested, it was claimed he had a .38 caliber revolver, not an automatic. The two guns do not use the same ammunition. Not only are the bullets not interchangeable, the .38 Super is a semi-auto round, whereas the .38 Special is designed specifically for revolvers like what Oswald had. The bullets are different enough visually that you cannot mix them up. The .38 Special cartridges are longer. Besides, they are clearly stamped on the bottom. One says ".38 Special," one says ".38 Automatic." So how could the assembly of police officers at the scene make a mistake?

Two very experienced witnesses (a police sergeant and former Marine) testified they were certain that the Tippit crime scene gun was an automatic pistol. Automatic shells would mean Oswald was not at Tenth St. and Patton Ave. when Tippit was murdered, and that the evidence was planted.

The story has been told that Oswald emptied the spent shells at the murder scene (to implicate himself? Get real!) and then ran.

Officer H. W. Summers in Dallas prowl car 221 (the designation for the squad car) reported that an "eyeball witness to the getaway man" had been located. The suspect was described as having black wavy hair, wearing an Eisenhower style jacket light colored, dark trousers and a white shirt. He was "apparently armed with a .32, dark finish, automatic pistol," which he held in his right hand. Moments later, Sgt Gerald Hill reported that "the shell at the scene indicates that the suspect is armed with an automatic .38 rather than a revolver."

Even more significant is the fact that the bullets in Oswald's revolver were never conclusively linked to the four bullets taken from Officer Tippit's body. Special Agent Courtlandt Cunningham, the FBI ballistics lab expert, testified before the Commission that he "was unable to conclude that *any* of the four bullets found in Tippit's body had been fired by the revolver taken from Lee Oswald." Also, there were two different manufacturers for the bullets at the scene, implying two guns, two shooters.

The autopsy report on Tippit was not included in the twenty-six volumes of the Warren Report. Why?

The killer supposedly discarded a light jacket as he left the murder scene and stashed it under a car parked in a lot behind a Texaco gas station. It bears a laundry tag with an item number on it. The FBI checked all 424 laundry and dry cleaning establishments in the Dallas/Ft. Worth area and 293 in the New Orleans area with no results. None of Oswald's clothing bore any laundry or dry-cleaning mark and noteworthy is that the jacket was a size medium; all of Lee's other clothing was size small.

Capt. W.R. Westbrook is the one who "found" the jacket.

At the end of November, a jacket purported to be Lee Oswald's was suddenly discovered on a windowsill of the sixth floor of the Texas School Book Depository building. Either the search was not thorough or evidence was planted in an attempt to place Oswald on the sixth floor.

LHO Went To A Movie Theater

The arrest of Oswald in the movie theater was equally bizarre.

Twenty-three-year-old Johnny Calvin Brewer, manager of the Hardy's Shoe Shop across the street, (a friend of Jack Ruby's), claimed he saw a man duck into the Texas Theater at 231 W. Jefferson without buying a ticket, but was not sure. Neither was the theater cashier, Julia Postal. But at Brewer's urging, she phoned the Dallas Police Department at 1:35.

The absurdity of it all is almost laughable. On a day when the President of the United States has been assassinated, the report of a man sneaking into a movie theater without buying a ticket is regarded as a crime so serious that twenty five police officers—the equivalent of a SWAT team—storm the building. Not to mention local broadcasts that cause a couple of thousand spectators to dash to the scene.

That man couldn't have been LHO because theater concession stand operator W.H. Burroughs said Oswald entered the movie house around 1:07 p.m., just as the theater began showing newsreels and cartoons prior to the main feature. He said Oswald bought popcorn from him at about 1:15 p.m. Witness Jack Davis, another theater patron, claimed LHO sat next to him during the opening credits of the first movie, several minutes before 1:20 p.m. But he was never questioned by the W.C. If Oswald was already at the theater at the time Tippit was shot, who was it that slipped in and attracted attention?

It's possible that Oswald merely stepped outside for a few moments to look for his contact, and then upon re-entering the movie house was spotted by Brewer, who mistakenly thought he hadn't paid.

It wasn't until Dec. 6, 1963—two weeks after Oswald's arrest and death—that Brewer claimed the man he saw was wearing a brown shirt. So he was malleable in what he told police.

Mr. Burroughs revealed to author Jim Marrs that Julia Postal knew that Lee Oswald had paid for a ticket earlier that day, but didn't want to admit it. She moved out of Dallas to avoid further questioning. But she was tracked down by researcher Jones Harris. When he asked Ms. Postal if she realized upon seeing Oswald's face that she really did sell him a ticket, she burst into tears.

Why did Oswald go to the Texas Theater? Witnesses noticed that he kept changing seats. He would sit down next to someone but stay only briefly, then get up and sit next to someone else.

He even sat beside a pregnant woman, who mysteriously vanished by the time the cops showed up.

The movie playing was called *War is Hell.* Oddly, the flick is now considered a "lost film," as no complete version is said to exist. The plot involves an unscrupulous American sergeant in the Korean War who fails to tell his platoon that a cease-fire has been declared. His plan is to attack unsuspecting enemy forces so he can win medals and adulation).

When Oswald got no reaction from the person he sat next to, he would get up and move to another seat next to someone else.

Would a guilty man bring this much attention to himself? His actions strongly suggest he was on a quest to meet a contact. In intelligence circles, an agent is told where to go if he runs into trouble. While in the theater, Oswald acted like he was waiting for his contact to show a form of identification, such as a torn dollar or a torn box top (Oswald having been given the other half of the dollar or box top. Rumor has it, LHO did have a torn top of a box on him when arrested).

The press was told that when officers approached Lee, he tried to shoot his way out of the theater, despite being surrounded by at least fifteen cops. How believable is this story? It was claimed he tried to kill one of the officers who approached him but that the weapon wouldn't fire because Detective Paul Bentley supposedly grabbed it and wedged his thumb between the hammer and the firing pin. Bentley was portrayed as a hero and had a big cigar in his mouth and smirk on his face when he escorted Oswald in handcuffs out the front door. What was funny?

Witnesses in the theater, however, claimed that Lee refused to resist, even when punched in the face. Oswald shouted several times "I'm not resisting arrest!" He didn't want to give the cops an excuse to kill him.

Sgt. Gerald Hill, who participated in the arrest of LHO at the theater, told David Belin of the W.C. that, "As to actually hitting anybody, or to actually seeing the suspect with a gun in his hand, I did not..."

Even the place he was seated in the theater is in dispute. Supposedly he was sitting three rows from the back, five seats from the aisle. However, an internal memo this author has discovered that was signed by Detective L.D. Stringfellow of the Criminal Intelligence Section and sent to Lt. Jack Revill of the Special Service Bureau of the DPD, dated Nov. 23, 1963, says that Oswald was "arrested in the balcony of the Texas Theater, 231 West Jefferson Blvd."

A quote attributed to LHO is also dubious. He supposedly said "Well, it's all over now."

The frenzied attempt to frame Oswald reached a fever pitch. DPD officer Nick McDonald lied to the press that LHO put up "a wild struggle," attempted to shoot him, and that the accused assassin boasted, "I killed me a president and a cop. Now all I need is two more!" That was a crazy lie. Oswald obviously made no such statement and in fact, repeatedly professed his innocence, telling newsmen "I didn't kill anybody."

Besides, Sgt. Hill said, "He didn't make boastful statements."

Capt. Westbrook showed up at the Texas Theater too, entering from the alley. Bernard Haire, owner of Bernie's Hobby House, located two doors east of the Texas Theater, saw police cars pull up in the alley behind his store. He watched as the cops brought out of the *back* door of the theater a young white man dressed in a pullover shirt and slacks. The guy appeared flushed, as if he had just been in an altercation with police. He was placed in a patrol car and driven away. Haire recognized one of the officers as being Capt. C.E. Tolbert.

For twenty five years Bernard Haire thought he had witnessed the apprehension of Lee Harvey Oswald. He was then shocked to learn that Oswald had been taken out the *front* door of the theater.

Detective Bentley claimed that as Oswald was being driven to police headquarters, he removed a wallet from the suspect's left hip pocket. But in 2013, ABC News ran a story about the claim by retired FBI analyst Farris Rookstool that the videotaped TV footage of a wallet supposedly found at the Tippit murder scene by Capt. W.H. Westbrook matched the one that was entered into evidence. That second wallet was likely fake and planted to incriminate LHO, along with the spent shell casings. This had to be premeditated, also implying Tippit was targeted to be killed, as part of a plan to claim Oswald shot a police officer after fleeing the TSBD.

It contained a drivers license for Lee Oswald and a Texas driver's license turned up at the Dept. of Public Safety the following week, even though he didn't even know how to drive.

The billfold "found" at the Tippit murder scene was later said to contain a forged Selective Service card for "Alek J. Hidell," that featured Oswald's picture on it and a different Selective Service number. Yet in his Warren Commission testimony, Sgt. Gerald Hill claimed the fake ID was found in the wallet removed from Oswald's pocket during the car ride downtown. Yet the arresting officers present in the car transporting LHO—Paul Bentley, K.E. Lyons, Bob Carroll, C.T. Walker and Gerald Hill himself—never mentioned to Chief Curry the second ID in the wallet they retrieved from Lee's pocket in route to the police station. In fact, the alias "Hidell" does not appear in any of the records or statements from the police, FBI, or Secret Service dated Nov. 22, 1963.

When officers W.M. Potts, E.L. Cuningham, Bill Senkel and Justice of the Peace David Johnson went to Lee's rooming house at 1026 North Beckley on the afternoon of November 22, they talked with property owner Mrs. A.C. Johnson and manager Earlene Roberts. But three witnesses at the scene said the officers never mentioned the name Hidell.

By the next day, authorities claimed the rifle found at the TSBD was purchased by mail on March 12, 1963 with a U.S. postal money order used by Hidell and listing Oswald's P.O. box as the place the gun was sent. Only then was it claimed LHO carried a bogus ID in that name.

Notably, Select Service cards did not contain a photo of the person—but the Hidell one had Oswald's.

There is no proof he ever made use of the Select Service card prior to the assassination; no testimony of anyone having seen this ID in his possession prior to Nov. 22, 1963; no indication his fingerprints were found on the card; no photos taken of the card on the 22nd; no listing of it on an inventory of LHO's personal effects at the time of his booking.

The postal money order supposedly used to purchase the rifle had no stamp indicating that it was ever used or deposited, and was bought at 10:30 a.m. when Lee's time card at Jaggers-Chiles-Stovall shows he was at work. USPS inspector Harry Holmes admitted that anyone who had access to Oswald's P.O. box could have picked up the rifle without even showing identification. Although post offices were required by law to retain "delivery receipts for firearms" for four years, no delivery receipt was found in this case. Yet Oswald supposedly bought the rifle using the Hidell alias.

Sgt. Hill said on the way downtown with the officers, Lee Oswald seemed bewildered and commented, "I don't know why you are treating me like this. The only crime I have committed is carrying a pistol in a movie..." Just before they got to the police headquarters, LHO was told that there were a lot of reporters waiting and if he wanted to duck down they would help him cover his face. His rejoinder was: "*Why should I hide my face? I haven't done anything I'm ashamed of!*"

Hill related that as he was filling out paperwork, Capt. Westbrook approached him and told him to change the heading on his police report to include Oswald as the suspect in the assassination of the president. It was Westbrook who quickly knew Oswald had been in the Marine Corp, had been to Russia, had passed out pro-Castro literature in New Orleans. How did he know all this so quickly?

Sgt. Hill also said Westbrook "added a paragraph to our report to include the fact that he was [at the theater] and the FBI agent was there. Now as to why this was done, your guess is as good as mine." Maybe it was to burnish his credentials. Capt. Westbrook resigned his police job and went to work for the CIA in South Vietnam and Operation Phoenix.

William Westbrook is one of the most suspicious persons involved in the Kennedy assassination story. He was forty-five years old and had a desk job. He was in charge of the Personnel Dept. for the Dallas police. He had nothing to do with Capt. Will Fritz's homicide and robbery division, yet following the shooting of President Kennedy Westbrook was everywhere. He showed up at the TSBD. He was likely one of the two police officers who drove past Oswald's rooming house at 1 p.m. as he was known to be in that specific vehicle at one point that afternoon. He was the first who turned up at the parking lot behind the Texaco Station in Oak Cliff where a jacket was "found." He was at 10th & Patton showing identification for Oswald and Hidell to fellow police officers and to FBI agent Bob Barrett. The FBI man said that Capt. Westbrook was the last person to have possession of the second wallet at the Tippit murder scene.

An Oswald Lookalike Nearby

Around 2 p.m. on Friday, Nov. 22, 1963, an Oswald lookalike was spotted sitting in a 1957 Plymouth with its engine running, near the Texas Theater. It was parked behind a billboard by the El Chico restaurant.

A mechanic who worked across the street, named T.F. White, saw the man and said it looked like he was hiding. With sirens blaring and police cars "all over the area," White became suspicious so went over to investigate. As he approached, the driver turned and looked at him, and then sped off. But White was able to get a good look at the man, who was wearing a white T-shirt. He also wrote down the license number of the car. That night when he saw Lee Harvey Oswald's picture on TV, he was convinced that was the man he had seen. The mechanic had been afraid to report the incident to authorities, although he did tell his employer.

However, by 2 p.m. when Mr. White observed the man in the Plymouth, LHO was already in custody. Had the driver of the automobile been impersonating him? Was he the guy who slipped into the Texas Theater, to deliberately attract attention and thereby lead police to Oswald?

In a plot twist worthy of a great whodunit, the license plates on the fleeing car were registered to Carl Mather, a longtime employee of Collins Radio (based in Cedar Rapids, Iowa). He was a close friend of Officer J.D. Tippit. Mather had a security clearance for electronics work. One of his assignments included working on Air Force Two, used by Vice President Lyndon Johnson. Collins Radio was deeply involved with NASA, and was also contracted by the CIA to play a role in plots against Castro and Cuba. On Nov. 1, 1963, *The New York Times* reported that Fidel Castro had captured a large boat being leased to Collins Radio, that had been used to ferry weapons into Cuba.

Wes Wise, a reporter for KRLD-TV and later mayor of Dallas, learned of the story regarding the suspicious man in the car, which had a license plate on November 22 associated with Carl Mather. He turned this information over to the FBI, and they went out to the Mather home, saw the car in the driveway, and spoke with Mrs. Mather. When asked where her husband was on the day of the assassination, she said he was at work at the Collins plant in Richardson, Texas and their car was in the parking lot there. But, claims Wise, by 2 p.m. that day it was at the Tippit home after J.D.'s wife, Marie, learned her husband had been killed and asked the Mathers to come over, which they did.

When the FBI interviewed T.F. White they tried to undermine his eyewitness account by intimidating and confusing him. In their report the FBI changed the car from a Plymouth to a 1961 red Ford Falcon.

The Mathers subsequently agreed to meet Wes Wise for a meal. and a person from the CBS network. Wise said Carl was "so upset and agitated" he was "too nervous to eat," but his wife was "cool, very cool." Carl had told them: "Put yourself in my shoes. I just can't explain it."

So now the FBI knew of a lookalike of the accused assassin of the president near the scene of the murder of a Dallas policeman who he is also accused of killing, sitting in a car belonging to a close friend of the victim, a friend who was employed by Collins Radio doing work on Lyndon Johnson's plane at the time. You can't make this stuff up.

Dorothy Appears On Canadian Television

Despite her determined quest to investigate the circumstances of John Kennedy's assassination, and keep up with her professional and personal responsibilities, Dorothy took time to travel to Canada.

She journeyed there to appear on the game show *Front Page Challenge* on June 16, 1964. In so doing, DK surprised her fellow *WML?* panelist, Bennett Cerf, who was also booked on the same program.

She was asked about various aspects of her life and career. Dorothy told the panel she very rarely endured editorial control of her columns, but Hearst attorneys did comb through her material.

"A lawyer reads my column at six o'clock every morning," she explained. "I usually get it in about four o'clock in the morning. He reads it when he gets down to the paper. If there's anything that looks dangerous, or possibly libelous, he has the right to cut it out," she revealed. "Then if I want to argue the next day and say, 'look I got this from a perfectly good source who will back it up in court,' then I can put it back in the next day after we discussed it. But they have an absolute right to do that to anything in the whole paper."

She said her staff was a lone secretary to answer the phone and

Dorothy on Canadian TV.

handle her mail and Dorothy always typed her own columns.

When asked if writing a regular column ever got to be a grind, she answered honestly, "I think anything you have to do six days a week and get it in by a certain time sometimes becomes a grind. But I love it most of the time. Because I am married and a mother, I couldn't be running around on assignments all the time, 52 weeks a year, but once or twice a year they manage to find some story to send me on like the Ward trial in England last year or the Coronation or Meg's wedding (Princess Margaret) or Princess Grace's wedding. That's definitely one week or two weeks. I love doing that best of all really—the news—if it's a good story, but there aren't that many good stories to make me want to give up everything else for it, to do it all year round."

DK Again Confronts LBJ

In early June of 1964, DK penned an open letter to President Johnson beseeching him to address the rampant crime New York City. She asked for the federal government to send additional law enforcement agents, especially in light of the city hosting the World's Fair and recent eruptions of violence in the subway. Kilgallen noted that with all eyes on NYC, negative news coverage could be embarrassing internationally.

She revealed, "I live just around the corner from the Russian Embassy where Khruschev spent a great deal of his time, and saw him make...[his] appearance on a balcony just a few feet above the sidewalk. It would not have taken the skill of an ex-Marine to polish him off as he stood there, bathed in light, not even a moving target. Yet our police were on the alert, and there was no 'incident,' not to mention an assassination."

She wrote, in part, "New York City has given generously of its police in the national interest whenever called upon...We have provided police protection for all manner of foreign visitors, friendly or hostile, because it was our duty to the United States as a whole.

"Now, how about some turnabout?"

Dorothy's Politics A Bit Of A Mystery

Like many journalists who try to maintain a level of objectivity in their reporting, DK did not publicly affiliate with any political party or candidate.

"I just say what I think from day to day, and I got a lot of people confused probably, including the publisher," she noted. "But I think they feel that a good paper should have room for all shades of opinion."

She criticized both Democrats and Republicans. Famously, in a July 1964 column she chastised former president Dwight D. Eisenhower for his attack on the press—and ensuing cheers from the crowd—during his speech at the Republican convention in San Francisco.

"The whistles blew, the horns tooted, the old men with the cigars in their mouths applauded, the sunflowers waggled, the Hawaiian leis bounced, the placards jostled each other and the arena really rocked—suggesting to the home viewer that the Republican delegates are much angrier at disrespectful 'commentators and columnists' than they are with those who deny equality under the law to Negroes.

"Well, now we know who the enemies are. Not the Communists. Not the church-burners, the child-killers, the lynchers. The ones you have to lick are the commentators and columnists.

"Hello Der, Thomas Paine!"

Dorothy Scores Important 'Exclusives'

A July 1964 column sought to further rattle the American people's confidence in the Johnson Administration. DK reported, "Washington is the setting for the nation's scariest legend. The insiders say the 'hot line'—supposed to be ready for emergency situations that might cause war between the United States and Russia—has, on three recent occasions, been severed by farmers in Finland ploughing their fields. And each time, according to the rumors, it was four days before either Moscow or Washington was aware that the catastrophe-deterrent phone was out of commission."

To be a fly on the wall of the Cabinet Room after officials reviewed that column!

One of the biggest scoops of Kilgallen's career came when she obtained the one hundred and two-page transcript of Ruby's testimony to the Warren Commission—before President Lyndon Johnson had even reviewed it. Its three-part publication, beginning on August 18, launched a federal investigation to determine how DK had come to possess the information. It also marked the beginning of those in her innermost circle being surveiled.

"And therein lies the tale," observed DK hairdresser Charles Simpson. "From then on, we were stalked. Our phones were tapped. They were trying to find out where she got her information from."

Earl Warren, Gerald Ford, Arlen Specter, SS agent Elmer Moore and some staff members—fourteen people in all—had made a surprise trip to Dallas on Sunday, June 7, and spent three hours and five minutes questioning Ruby in the interrogation room of the Dallas county jail.

Dorothy published excerpts from the documents and provided commentary. Readers were shocked at the hopelessly inept questioning of Ruby by Chief Justice Warren and by Warren's failure to follow up on the leads Ruby was feeding him.

They were further appalled to learn that Jack had pleaded eight times for the Commission to bring him to Washington, D.C. so he could speak freely, because he was fearful of remaining in Dallas. All he got was a bit of tea and sympathy from Earl Warren, and the panel failed to cooperate in pursuing the information he offered.

Newspapers across the country accompanied DK's exclusive columns with such editor's notes as published in *The Philadelphia Inquirer*: "Though the Warren Commission will not make public the findings of its investigation into the death of the President until sometime next month, Dorothy Kilgallen of the *New York Journal-American* obtained a copy of the original transcript of Ruby's highly important testimony through sources close to the Commission in Washington."

For example, on one column of the page, the testimony ran, accompanied by Kilgallen's bylined article on the other side, providing summations and questions in tandem.

Woman Columnist Gets Jack Ruby's Testimony

NEW YORK (AP)—Jack Ruby has been quoted from purported actual word-by-word testimony before the Warren Commission as insisting he killed Lee Harvey Oswald on the spur of the moment last Nov. 24.

In a copyrighted story yesterday by New York Journal-American columnist Dorothy Kilgallen, Ruby is quoted as having told Chief Justice Earl Warren during interrogation last June 7:

"I was never malicious toward this person. No one else requested me to do anything. I never spoke to anyone about attempting to do anything. No subversive organization gave me any idea. No underworld persons made any effort to contact me.

"It all happened that Sunday morning."

Stepped from Crowd

Ruby, now 53, stepped out of a crowd of newsmen and onlookers in the basement of Dallas police headquarters on Sunday, Nov. 24, and fired a single bullet into Oswald, who had been formally charged as the assassin of President John F. Kennedy two days hours after the assassination. Ruby mingled with a crowd of newspapermen that night during a confrontation with Oswald.

In the transcript which the Journal-American published with Miss Kilgallen's story, Ruby is quoted as telling Chief

DOROTHY KILGALLEN

The *Journal-American* agreed to publish this leaked information upon DK's assurance that she had obtained it through legal means.

In Part I of her reporting, DK wrote, "...Jack Ruby swears he didn't know Officer J.D. Tippit. And this is rather strange. Because according to the Dallas police, Ruby knew every cop on the force."

DK said she read the transcript three times in one sitting and observed, "It seemed to me that the Chief Justice and the Warren Commission's general counsel, J. Lee Rankin, were acutely aware of the talk both here and in Europe that President Kennedy was the victim of a conspiracy. They took the pains to prove to themselves and the world that no conspiracy existed."

Ruby asserted: "I never spoke to anyone about attempting to do anything. No subversive organization gave me any idea. No underworld person made any effort to contact me. It all happened that Sunday morning."

But, Dorothy pointed out: "The hint of conspiracy was very much in the air again when Rankin asked Ruby if he knew Officer J.D. Tippit."

She went on to reveal that J. Lee Rankin said it was known Ruby met with Bernard Weisman, Tippit and another person called "a rich oilman" at his club not long before JFK's assassination. She noted Weisman had published the famed anti-Kennedy ad the day the president visited Dallas.

"While Ruby never admitted that the reported meeting took place, he never directly denied it either," she added.

She described his statements throughout as rambling. "He opened the floodgates of his mind and unloosed a stream of consciousness that would have dazzled a James Joyce Buff and enraptured a psychiatrist."

Part II exploded in the papers the following day. The transcript revealed: Ruby's claim he was motivated to kill Oswald to spare Mrs. Kennedy the grief of a trial; his fear for his life and safety of his family; his desire to be transferred to Washington, D.C; feud with his lawyer Joe Tonahill, whom he accused of being a liar; how Ruby had not watched the presidential motorcade go by despite being present at a newspaper office along the route; his odd behavior leading up to and following murdering Oswald.

"And early Saturday morning, the balding striptease club owner did something else rather strange for a man as emotionally shattered by the President's death as Ruby claimed to be. He went to the *Times Herald* newspaper office and demonstrated a 'twist board' (an aid for dancing The Twist, named after the song) for one of the employees.

"I find it hard to reconcile the picture of Ruby performing on a twist board less than 24 hours after the president's assassination with the bereaved figure of a man who walked around in a state of emotional shock," Dorothy wrote at the end of the column.

In Part III, readers learned of Ruby's feeling that the John Birch Society was behind a smear campaign against him, as well as his supplications for truth serum or a lie detector test. He denied being part of a plot to kill JFK and said he acted alone in bumping off Oswald.

In this day's reporting, it was revealed the Commission subpoenaed attorney Mark Lane, who at that time was representing Oswald's mother Marguerite. Lane testified that a meeting among Ruby, Tippit, Weisman and the unnamed rich oilman took place approximately one to two weeks before the assassination, but he would not reveal the source of his claim. Ruby deflected the question.

During his questioning by Chief Warren and Rep. Gerald Ford, Ruby said if he could be taken to Washington he would be able to reveal more information relevant to the case.

"All I know is something can be saved. Because right now, I want to tell you this. I am used as a scapegoat and there is no greater weapon that you can use to create some falsehood about some of the Jewish faith, especially the terrible heinous crime such as the killing of President Kennedy. Now maybe something can be saved. It may not be too late, whatever happens, if our President, Lyndon Johnson, knew the truth about me. But if I am eliminated, there won't be any way of knowing," Ruby told the Warren Commission. "Right now, when I leave your presence now, I am the only one that can bring out the truth to our President, who believes in righteousness and justice. But he has been told, I am certain, that I was part of a plot to assassinate the President (Kennedy). I know your hands are tied; you are helpless."

DK wrote that Ruby feared being linked to the JFK's murder and kept referring to a nameless adversary, "they," as being after Ruby and his family.

Interestingly, many papers also ran an Associated Press story (on the same page in some cases) about the launch of a federal investigation into how Dorothy got the material and how outraged the Warren panel was about the "leaks." But as they did that, the AP also covered the revelations Kilgallen had reported—thus having their cake, and eating it too.

"No member of the commission or its staff has divulged or made available to any news media any portion of testimony before the commission," Rankin was quoted as saying.

Who had provided DK with this highly sensitive information?

Kathryn Fauble speculates, "I never have been able to guess who was Dorothy's longtime friend who gave her the Ruby transcripts with the condition of anonymity. When the FBI questioned her, she said the person was a man with whom she had been friends for a long time. That rules out Joe Tonahill [whom] she had known...for approximately six months."

The FBI sent agents to Dorothy's townhouse to interrogate her about the Warren Commission leak. She served them tea but did not give them any other information as to her source, except to say it was not her *WML?* colleague John Daly—the son-in-law of Earl Warren.

An FBI memo reported, "She stated that she was the only person who knew the identity of the source and that she 'would die' rather than reveal his identity."

Belli Calls DK's Reporting 'The Ruin Of The Warren Commission'

Despite the seemingly cordial relationship between Dorothy Kilgallen and Melvin Belli, in an article dated Aug. 22, 1964, and written by Robert Hassett, Mr. Belli was quoted as saying the publication of Ruby's testimony given before the Warren Commission (in advance of an appeal of the death sentence) "destroyed the integrity" of the body formed to investigate the Kennedy assassination.

"The leak to a columnist [Kilgallen] of Ruby's testimony before the Chief Justice has detracted horribly from the Commission and detracted from the efficacy of its report...[Warren] never should have gone [to Ruby's cell] and taken testimony from him before the appeal."

Warren Groshon of the *Redwood City Tribune* wrote that at a news conference, Belli implied the leak came via John Daly.

"[Belli] did not make a direct accusation, but in answer to a question, he said: 'Someone has pointed out that Daly, the interlocutor on the show, is the son-in-law of Earl Warren.' The *Tribune* attempted to reach both Daly and Miss Kilgallen in their New York offices but neither was available."

The *Tribune* further reported, "Belli said he has become increasingly concerned about 'the wild rumors' that have spread through Europe about the trial. He said he hopes the Warren Report will dispel rumors that Lyndon Johnson or the Central Intelligence Agency or some foreign country was behind the shooting of President Kennedy."

Dorothy Does Dallas...Again

At some point that summer of 1964, Kilgallen went back to Dallas, Texas. She wanted to investigate the context of President Kennedy's murder and try to understand what the setting was really like. Gary Cartwright of *Texas Monthly* described the era thusly:

"A lot of bizarre people were doing some very strange things in Dallas in...1963. Madame Nhu bought a dozen shower caps at Neiman-Marcus and tried to drum up support for the Diem regime in Saigon, even while her host in the U.S., the CIA, laid plans to assassinate Diem himself. Members of the American Nazi Party danced around a man in an ape suit in front of the *Times Herald* building. Congressman Bruce Alger, who had once carried a sign accusing Lyndon Johnson of being a traitor, went on television to denounce the Peace Corps as 'welfare socialism and godless materialism, all at the expense of capitalism and basic U.S. spiritual and moral values.' Zealots from the National Indignation Committee picketed a UN Day speech by Ambassador Adlai Stevenson; they called him Addle-Eye and booed and spat on him and hit him on the head with a picket sign. When a hundred civic leaders wired strong and sincere apologies to the ambassador, General Edwin Walker, who had been cashiered by the Pentagon for force-feeding his troops right-wing propaganda, flew the American flag upside down in front of his military-gray mansion on Turtle Creek. There were pro-Castro cabals and anti-Castro cabals that overlapped and enough clandestine commerce to fill a dozen Bogart movies. Drugs, arms, muscle, propaganda: the piety of the Dallas business climate was the perfect cover. A friend of mine in banking operated a fleet of trucks in Bogotá as a sideline. Airline stewardesses brought in sugar-coated cookies of black Turkish hash without having the slightest notion of what they were carrying."

It was into this milieu that Dorothy Kilgallen bravely trod. Her vigorous and repeated public challenges to the Warren Commission and the actions of Dallas officials did not exactly endear her to the local powers that be.

But just as courage is feared in some quarters, it is admired in others, and her trip to "The Big D" in the summer of 1964 yielded some important leads.

Exposes Dallas Police Chief's Lie

Dorothy followed up her reporting on the Ruby trial testimony about a week later with a powerful piece on Aug. 23, 1964 that once again contained exclusive information. In an article headlined "New Contradictions in JFK Murder Probe," that was copyrighted by the *New York Journal-American* but ran in newspapers coast to coast like the *San Francisco Examiner*, DK outlined troubling aspects.

She wrote:

"A previously unpublished and private report by the Dallas Police Department of events surrounding the assassination of President Kennedy conflicts sharply with some public statements of Dallas police officials.

"In the copy of that report which I have obtained, Police Chief Jesse E. Curry—who was riding in the presidential motorcade's 'pilot car' about a quarter mile ahead of President Kennedy's limousine—is quoted as transmitting by radio this order right after the shooting:

"'Get a man on top of the overpass and see what happened up there!'

"Twenty-four hours after the assassination, however, Chief Curry assured reporters that the sound of the shots told him at once they had come from the Texas School Book Depository and that 'right away' he had radioed an order to surround and search the building.

"But actually, as we see from the police department's official version of events, Chief Curry's immediate concern was not the depository, but the triple-tiered overpass toward which the presidential motorcade was moving.

"One of the two bullets that struck President Kennedy pierced his throat. This fact resulted in speculation that two snipers had fired on him—one from the overpass and the other, Lee Harvey Oswald, from the depository's sixth floor.

"Dallas police and federal agencies probing the assassination have dismissed this theory.

"Yet why did Chief Curry order a man to the overpass—which

the 'pilot car' had passed beneath perhaps a half minute earlier—rather than to the depository? How much time elapsed before a policeman reached the overpass? What—if anything—did he find?

"From Chief Curry's immediate response to the assassination crisis, we can also conclude that the overpass was unguarded. And this too is strange.

"I find the report—which was submitted to Chief Curry by three of his top assistants last Nov. 30—almost as fascinating as the transcript of Jack Ruby's Warren Commission testimony, which was published in full last week in the *New York Journal-American*.

"For the document—known officially as 'a chronological report of events prior to, during and after the assassination of President John F. Kennedy'—also bares this additional information:

"•Five hours before Oswald was slain by Ruby, Dallas police received a telephone warning that 'about one hundred men are going to take the prisoner Oswald and we don't want any policemen to be hurt.'

"•On the basis of this threat, Dallas police laid out an elaborate security system to safeguard Oswald. This even included bringing in two armored 'decoy' cars. Ruby, however, had no trouble piercing the security system.

"•The order to seal off the Depository building on the day of the assassination was given by Deputy Police Chief George L. Lumpkin, but only after a trip to and from Parkland Memorial Hospital. So perhaps twenty minutes passed between the shooting and the order. Quite a far cry from the statements by Dallas police officials that the building was buttoned up 'immediately.'

"•Two anti-Kennedy pickets and three men who came to their aid were arrested during a dispute with a crowd soon after the assassination. Later this was changed to trespassing. But it seems apparent that Dallas cops believed at first that President Kennedy was the victim of a plot."

This significant story by Dorothy Kilgallen did several things that would have contributed to a ferocious backlash against the journalist by powerful people.

They are as follows: (1) Once again DK had somehow managed to obtain highly sensitive internal paperwork—this time from the Dallas Police Department—proving her ability to cultivate sources and pierce the veil of secrecy surrounding the case. (2) Showed she was unafraid of publicly exposing the lies and other deceits by public officials. (3) Revealed the incompetence of Dallas police in failing to immediately seal off the supposed location of the assassin's lair, meaning crucial evidence could have been spirited away (or planted); (4) Fostered further public distrust of the official accounts of the president's assassination.

With this article—combined with her prior reporting—Dorothy

Kilgallen single-handedly laid the foundation for conspiracy theories to grow and flourish in the decades to come.

She covered a lot of ground in her exclusive and it's worth breaking it down. First, the significance of Kilgallen's revelation that Chief Curry had thought gunfire had come from in front of the motorcade. So too did key persons in the motorcade.

Roy Kellerman, White House U.S. Secret Service Agent-in-Charge of the Dallas trip—who was riding in the front passenger seat of the presidential limousine—testified the immediate reaction he had is that they were heading into an ambush situation.

Kellerman implied they were under fire from several directions as "a flurry of shells came into the car." He further challenged the Warren Commission by testifying, "President Kennedy had four wounds, two in the head and shoulder and the neck. Governor Connally, from our reports, had three. There have to be more than three shots, gentlemen."

Forrest Sorrels, Special Agent in Charge, Dallas District, U.S. Secret Service, was riding in the lead car, (in which Chief Curry was also a passenger), directly ahead of the presidential limo. He was sitting in the right rear and was looking out the right rear window keeping an eye on the president. He testified, "I looked towards the top of the terrace to my right as the sound of the shots seemed to come from that direction."

Special Agent Paul Landis was standing on the right side running board of the SS follow-up car. He testified: "My reaction at this time [of the fatal head shot] was that the shot came from somewhere towards the front, right-hand side of the road."

Thomas "Lem" Johns, Assistant to the Special Agent-in-Charge, Vice Presidential detail, testified: "The first two [shots] sounded like they were on the side of me towards the grassy knoll."

Close Kennedy White House aide, Dave Powers, riding only ten feet behind the president's car, concurred in the belief they were "riding into an ambush" and he claimed to have detected at least two shots from the grassy knoll in front of the motorcade. But he said he was pressured to change his story by the Warren Commission.

Kenny O'Donnell, another longtime friend and close aide to JFK, was also sure he had heard two shots that came from behind the picket fence on the grassy knoll. He confided to House Speaker Tip O'Neill, "I told the FBI what I heard but they said it couldn't have happened that way and that I must have been imagining things. So I testified the way they wanted me to. I just didn't want to stir up any more pain and trouble for the family...Everybody wanted this thing behind them."

Police Officer Bobby Hargas, who was riding a motorcycle to the left rear of the presidential car, said, "When President Kennedy straightened back up in the car the bullet hit him in the head, the one that killed him, and it seemed like his head exploded, and I was splattered with blood

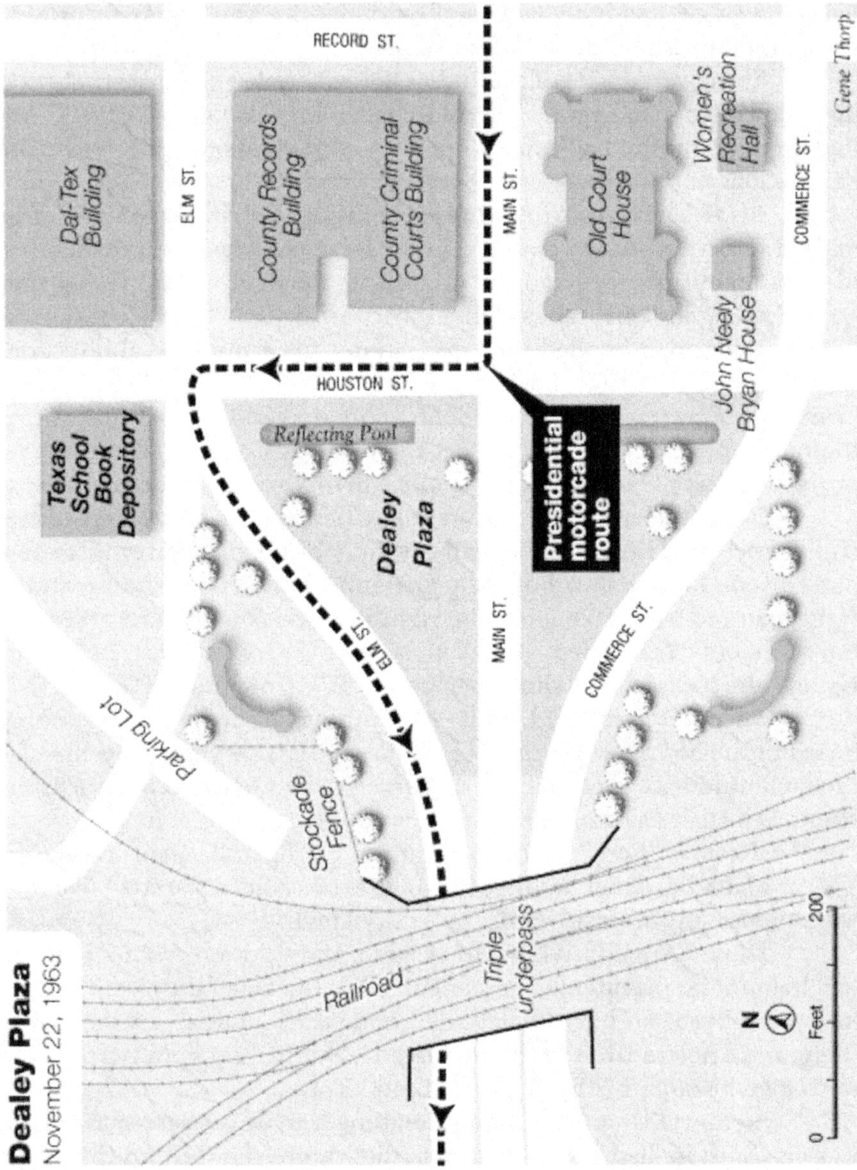

and brain, and kind of a bloody water...Well, at the time it sounded like the shots were right next to me."

Hargas was struck so forcefully by the blood and brain matter he first thought he had also been wounded. He then dismounted from his motorcycle and ran up the embankment of the grassy knoll, as did more than one hundred spectators. Films show this. They reacted instinctively, as if they were chasing down a suspect. The crowd ran into the parking lot beside the TSBD building.

A second police officer riding a motorcycle directly behind Hargas,

B.J. Martin, was also splattered with blood, bone and brain tissue from the head shot to the president, despite the fact he was even farther away but also to the left rear of the vehicle.

Gordon Arnold, who happened to be standing near the fence at the back end of the grassy knoll, had just completed basic training in the military, which included having to experience coming under fire with live ammunition. He was filming the motorcade passing by when he felt a bullet pass behind and near his left ear at the time of the fatal shot to Kennedy's head. Earlier, as he had tried to stand closer to the overpass to get a good view, some man claiming to be with the CIA told him to leave the area. So Arnold walked east, toward the grassy knoll. After the shooting, a supposed CIA agent immediately confronted him and demanded, then confiscated, his film, which likely would have provided potentially clearer images of the assassination than that of Abraham Zapruder.

Dallas Police Officer Joe Marshall Smith said in a sworn affidavit, "My instructions were...to hold all the traffic up when the motorcade was approaching...I was standing in the middle of Elm Street from the southeast curb of Elm and Houston Streets at the time of the shooting. I heard the shots and thought they were coming from bushes of the overpass." He said, "This woman came up to me and she was just in hysterics. She told me, 'They are shooting the president from the bushes.' So I immediately proceeded up there. Of course, I wasn't alone. There was some deputy sheriff with me, and I believe one Secret Service man when I got there. I pulled my pistol from my holster, and I thought, 'this is silly, I don't know who I am looking for,' and I put it back. Just as I did, he showed me that he was a Secret Service agent. He saw me coming with my pistol and right away he showed me who he was."

The Deputy Sheriff to whom he referred was Seymour Weitzman, who corroborated Smith's story.

DPD Sergeant David Harkness also reported encountering men in suits behind the TSBD following the assassination. He recalled, "There were some Secret Service agents there. I didn't get them identified. They told me they were Secret Service."

But the SS later said they had no agents on the ground there.

Larry Sabato, director of the University of Virginia Center for Politics, writing in *U.S. News & World Report* asks: "Who were the individuals representing themselves as Secret Service agents—with credentials good enough to fool Dallas policemen familiar with official identification—that appeared on the grassy knoll immediately after the shooting? The Secret Service has always insisted that the first agent to return to Dealey Plaza, Forrest Sorrels, did not do so until approximately 12:50 p.m.—a full twenty minutes after the presidential limousine came under fire."

The CIA routinely made Secret Service credentials, which were frequently changed for the agents.

To be clear, the curving white pergola sits about ten feet above street level on the so-called grassy knoll, and next to it is a wooden picket fence behind which is a parking lot, and further west is the railroad overpass. Any of those locations could have afforded a hiding place for any assassin(s) to deliver the fatal head shot(s). However, the anterior throat wound Kennedy sustained was not likely to have come from that area; the angle is wrong. The trajectory suggests that bullet came from southwest of Elm, probably from the tunnel-like area underneath the overpass.

There Was A Bullet Hole In the Windshield

To further expound on Dorothy Kilgallen's mention in her column that there had been gunfire from in front of President Kennedy, there is irrefutable evidence that there was a bullet hole in the windshield of the car, because there are photos that show this. It's visible in the Zapruder film, plus credible witnesses attest to it. The hole was slightly to the right and above the rear view mirror when the vehicle was viewed from the front. It can even be detected in an enlargement of one of the most famous pictures of the assassination.

In frame 306 of the Zapruder film, agent Kellerman can be seen touching his left cheek, possibly in reaction to the shot that came through the windshield. A second later he then dramatically ducks down, as if trying to get below the level of the dash, and driver Greer also ducks as much as he can behind the steering wheel. These actions have no explanation other than the two men appear to be reacting to gunfire coming at the car from the front.

Will Greer later told fellow agents, "I sure missed you guys today... You should have been there. Shots were coming from everywhere. One of the bullets came through the windshield, and almost got me."

Dallas motorcycle police officers Sgt. Stavis Ellis, James Chaney and Harry Freeman all confirmed the presence of a bullet hole in the windshield of the limousine when it was parked at the emergency room entrance of the hospital.

Ellis insisted, "Yes, I *did* see a hole in the limousine windshield, at Parkland Hospital. You could put a pencil through the hole."

Freeman said, "I could touch it. It was a hole."

Dallas Patrolman Nick Prencipe also noted the hole.

FBI Agent Charles Taylor wrote in his report "saw hole in the front window. Bullet fragments were removed."

Dr. Evalea Glanges, who was outside the hospital while Kennedy was dying, claimed she inspected a bullet hole, which she said clearly indicated the glass was shot from in front of the vehicle.

In a video interview, she explained, "We ran around the side of the building to the emergency room exit and the presidential limousine was there. I had been standing there for some time just watching the back of the emergency room, when I realized that there was a bullet hole in the windshield. At the time, I did not know any of the details of the shooting. I was quite shocked when I looked up and saw the bullet hole. But it was very clear it was a through-and-through bullet hole through the windshield of the car, from the front to the back. I don't believe that there are even any cracks associated with that bullet hole. It seemed like a high velocity bullet that had penetrated from front to the back in that glass pane. At which point a security officer of some type raced forward and jumped in the limousine and drove it off, even as I was leaning against it, to an area back of us somewhere. And that was the last time that I saw the limousine."

Minutes later, Glanges told Dr. Charles Crenshaw of seeing the hole in the windshield and he corroborated her story.

Other witnesses also remarked on seeing this damage. Richard Dudman of the *St. Louis Post-Dispatch* said in an article in the *New Republic*, "A few of us noticed the hole in the windshield. We were pushed away by Secret Service agents when we wanted to examine the hole." Frank Cormier, also of the St. Louis newspaper, concurred.

The Secret Service can be seen recklessly destroying evidence by cleaning the inside of the SX100 Lincoln Continental while it was still parked at the emergency entrance of Parkland Hospital. They had a bucket of water and some towels and were wiping the inside of the car and the back trunk, the latter of which had contained debris from the blow-out of the right rear portion of Kennedy's head. Afterwards, it was flown back to Washington on Friday where it was parked in the garage underneath the Executive Office building adjacent to the White House. Then it was sent to Michigan and quickly disassembled on orders from Lyndon Johnson.

George Whitaker Sr., a senior manager at the Ford Motor Company's Rouge Plant B in Detroit, Michigan, was surprised to see when he came to work one morning the unique, one-of-a-kind presidential limousine sitting there. One of the vice presidents of the division for which he worked directed him to report to the glass plant lab immediately. After knocking on the locked door (which he found most unusual), he was let in by two of his subordinates and discovered that they were in possession of the windshield that had been removed from the JFK limousine. They had been told to use it as a template, and to make a new windshield identical to it in shape, and to then get the new windshield back to the B building for installation in the limo that was quickly being rebuilt. Whitaker said in an August 1993 audiotaped interview, "The windshield had a bullet hole in it, coming from the outside through…it was a good, clean bullet hole, right straight through, from the front."

On Nov. 22, 1993—which was the 30th anniversary of the assassination—Whitaker documented everything he could remember. He wrote, "The hole was about four or six inches to the right of the rear view mirror [as viewed from the front]. The impact had come from the front of the windshield. If you have spent forty years in the glass [division] you know which way the impack [sic] was from."

Since it was his job to formulate a replacement windshield, he closely examined the condition of the existing windshield, and verified the hole penetrated through the glass, (which was not bulletproof), with fragmentation and beveling present on the inside. Shards of this fragmentation, called stippling, were known to have struck Kennedy in the face and neck. These were later removed by the mortician and were very minor.

Whitaker, who eventually became superintendent of his division and was put in charge of five Ford plant divisions, said the original windshield, with the bullet hole in it, had been broken up and scrapped—as ordered—after the new windshield had been crafted.

The Warren Report claimed the windshield was not penetrated by any bullet. A substitute windshield was shown to the Commission and subsequently given to the National Archives.

SS driver of the limo, William Greer, and agent Roy Kellerman—both of whom were front seat passengers—were emphatic in telling the Commission the car windshield did *not* have the big cracks in it like the one shown to the W.C. did.

During a Secret Service re-enactment of the assassination (using the follow-up car instead of the presidential Lincoln), you can see the position of the vehicle in a direct line of sight for a shot from the far left, underneath the railroad overpass (as indicated by the arrow). The grassy knoll is on the right and you can also see part of the white pergola where a shooter could have hidden.

A perfect place for sniper fire, under the overpass, accessible by a sidewalk.

United Press International (UPI) at the time reported, "A new windshield has been installed, lending credence to reports the old one was damaged in the shooting."

As for a hole in the chrome surrounding the windshield of the presidential car, the FBI claimed the damage had appeared prior to November 22. But photos taken the day before in San Antonio, when the vehicle was at Kelly Air Force Base, prove the chrome was intact.

JFK's Throat Wound Came From The Front

Just as Dallas Police Chief Curry had felt at the time, a least one shot had to have come from the area of the overpass.

As previously mentioned, when driver Will Greer turned left onto Elm Street from Houston Street—a hairpin turn so sharp it was said to be one hundred twenty degrees—he risked running the limousine up onto the opposite curb before straightening it out. He then maneuvered so as to be able to drive in the center lane on (three lane) Elm.

At that moment, the car was in perfect alignment for someone hidden in one of the "cubby holes" underneath the overpass, south of the east-bound lane of Commerce Street (which ran parallel to Elm), to shoot at the president. These "cut outs" were separated by vertical columns and had horizontal cement railings that offered a potential shooter a way to stabilize a weapon while aiming. They were also on the north side of Elm, and both were accessible by sidewalks. These were perfect places to hide in the shadows. The design created what one visitor to Dealey Plaza described as "walkway caves" or "tunnels" that were very dark and unlighted.

It is likely that some shooter(s) in Dealey Plaza made use of a suppressor or "silencer." This is a muzzle device that suppresses the blast created when a firearm (handgun or rifle) is discharged, therefore reducing the acoustic intensity of the muzzle report (sound of a gunshot) and jump, by modulating the speed and pressure of the propellant gas released from the muzzle. Silencers also reduce or even eliminate the muzzle flash.

President Teddy Roosevelt had a silencer attached to his Winchester 1894 carbine. "Father favored the silencer for early morning hunting expeditions to eliminate varmints around Sagamore Hill," his son Archie said. "He felt it best not to wake the neighbors."

During WWII, the U.S. Office of Strategic Services equipped guns with silencers. OSS Director William Joseph "Wild Bill" Donovan demonstrated the pistol for President Franklin D. Roosevelt at the White House. Donovan, an old friend of the president, was waved into the Oval Office, where Roosevelt was dictating a letter. When FDR finished, Donovan drew his weapon and fired a shot into a sandbag he had brought with him. He announced what he had done and handed the smoking gun to the astonished—and much relieved—president.

Greg Shaffer, former FBI and Security expert, commenting on the motorcade route, said "The threat of any one of those buildings would be great; it was putting the president in a very precarious situation. It's not just a left-hand turn. It's a sharp left-hand turn and then coming back at an angle. [The driver of the limousine] had to go at a very, very slow speed to make that hard turn."

After making the arc onto Elm and as JFK's limousine proceeded down Elm it was practically a stationary target for several seconds. The trajectory of a shot through the windshield from underneath the overpass lines up perfectly. A bullet nicked the left side of the knot in Kennedy's tie, connoting fire from that angle.

A silencer would increase the power of a bullet. But the fact the shot would have to penetrate the windshield during its trajectory could explain the compromised velocity that would result in a shallower wound path in the front of the president's neck. Officially, no bullet was retrieved from Kennedy's throat, but there is an explanation for that to come.

Prior to the assassination, Associated Press photographer James Altgens walked over to the triple overpass where Main, Elm, and Commerce streets travel under the railroad tracks. Two uniformed police officers, J. W. Foster and J. C. White, were stationed there and refused to let him take pictures from that vantage point. They claimed it was private property, a ridiculous excuse. Besides, they let at least sixteen other men stand on top of the overpass. So Altgens took up a position on the south side of Elm. When he heard the first shot, he snapped the shutter on his camera and captured the most famous photo. It shows JFK through the windshield, clutching at his throat, while agents riding on the running boards of the follow-up car look over their right shoulders.

As for Dorothy Kilgallen's groundbreaking reporting that the Texas School Book Depository building was not promptly sealed, she was once again pointing out something significant. Incredibly, three of the four doors on the north (back) side of the building remained unlocked even after the front entrance was sealed. Anyone could have gone in or out, planted evidence, or removed it.

Moments after the assassination, three men were seen running from the north side of the TSBD and getting into a station wagon parked across the street on Houston. Who were they?

It wasn't until 1:35 p.m. on Nov. 22, 1963 that Dallas Police Channel 2 said the TSBD is "being secured now." This is an hour and five minutes after the shots; about twenty minutes after the death of Officer Tippit; sixteen minutes before the arrest of LHO, and long after the departure of any or all who had anything to do with the assassination.

Dorothy Appears On The Big Screen

In the midst of aggressively pursuing leads into the assassination of President Kennedy and maintaining her otherwise hectic schedule, Dorothy somehow found time for a new challenge.

It's odd to think of Kilgallen as a movie actress (save for her 1936 minor role in *Sinner Take All*), but she filmed a cameo in the 1964 offbeat comedy *Pajama Party*, released that November. Son Kerry made several minor appearances throughout the film. He would say the word "mush" anytime he observed people getting romantic. Dorothy comes on camera at the 49:55 and 51:00 minute marks in the movie. She humorously lands on J.D.'s motorcycle and introduces herself as "Dorothy" before getting soon thrown off the back end (clearly the work of a stunt double).

In a whimsical August 1964 *VOB* column, she discussed how she'd been "discovered" for the role, having accompanied Kerry to the Columbia ranch in Burbank, California where the flick was being shot. Innocently accepting a ride on a motorcycle from one of the actors, she was then approached by James Nicholson, president of American-In-

Motorcycle mama Dorothy Kilgallen.

ternational Pictures, to ascertain if she'd care to appear in the movie doing just that.

"My son thinks it's all very thrilling, but there is a feeling among the more mature members of the cast that I am some kind of a nut. As I exited from the makeup room I ran into [co-star] Elsa Lanchester, who was having her hair done, and I said airily:

"'Wish me luck. I'm going to do my first scene.'

"'I heard all about it, my dear,' said Elsa in her most sepulchral tones. 'I hope you're heavily insured.'"

DK Focuses On 'Disappearing Witnesses'

Writing in late September 1964, DK relayed that Drew Associates' ten-minute documentary called *Faces of November* received the highest prize in the tele-documentary category at the Venice Documentary Film Festival. Her comments must have gotten under the bureaucratic skin of the men on the Warren Commission when she dryly wrote: "The same company—or another—could make an even more provocative program by collecting film clips of telecasts during those three days, showing interviews with people whose stories have since been 'erased' by the official version of the assassination. Some of the people can't be found now; others won't talk about what they said when the interviewers first reached them. It's amazing how many people who were pouring information into the radio and TV microphones in November are suddenly 'missing' or unavailable for comment."

Dorothy had been watching this phenomenon happen for months. As early as Dec. 5, 1963, *The New York Times* reported, "Most private citizens who had cooperated with newsmen reporting the crime have refused to give further help after being interviewed by agents of the Federal Bureau of Investigation."

What she had realized—before most others had—is there had been witness intimidation as well as a series of unlikely deaths of people who had been connected in some way to the Kennedy assassination. The list of individuals who died suddenly and under strange circumstances grew long quite quickly, and eventually included Dorothy Kilgallen.

Many witnesses were treated by Warren Commission staff lawyers with derision, disbelief, ridicule and scorn, sometimes threatened with charges of perjury if their testimony did not conform to the W.C.'s story.

There were countless complaints of how witnesses interviewed by Warren Commission staffers had their testimony changed when published, or how the important and highly relevant information they had supplied never made it into the Warren Report.

Eyewitness Jean Hill, who was on the south side of Elm Street and had a close-up view of the assassination, was belittled by Arlen Specter, an assistant counsel for the Commission.

Misogynist Specter snidely accused her of engaging in a "shabby extramarital affair" with DPD Officer J.B. Marshall, thirsting for publicity and notoriety, refusing to cooperate with federal authorities and proving herself "totally unreliable" as a witness. She was told that, once the official interrogation began, she was to give "proper answers" based on fact, not on her overactive imagination or "what some talkative cop told you while you were in bed together." This interrogation ended up as a nineteen-page testimony in Volume Six of the Warren Report. Jean described this testimony as a "total travesty"—heavily edited, completely distorted and shamefully fabricated. Specter's routine abuse of witnesses was deplorable.

Bonnie Ray Williams complained that he had been misquoted in written accounts attributed to him by the FBI. The FBI report says Williams stayed only about three minutes on the sixth floor in order to eat his lunch. But Williams said he told the FBI he stayed much longer than that, and he didn't finish eating until around 12:20 p.m.

Dr. Robert McClelland revealed that after being interviewed by Arlen Specter, the two men walked outside and Specter stunned him by commenting under his breath that the Warren staff had a lot of witnesses who were unwavering that shots had come from the grassy knoll, but Specter confided they were just going to "ignore them." Dr. Baxter of Parkland had a similar encounter with Specter.

One important person the Commission ignored was the president's own physician, Dr. George Burkley.Not only did the Warren Commission not call him, neither did the HSCA years later.

In early 1977, Burkley's attorney William Illig contacted HSCA counsel Richard Sprague, and indicated the doctor's eagerness to testify. Sprague wrote a memo about this, but it was inexplicably suppressed. So physician experts advising the HSCA were unaware of the crucial evidence being offered to them on a silver platter.

Sprague wrote, "Although he, Burkley, had signed the death certificate of President Kennedy in Dallas, he had never been interviewed and that he has information in the Kennedy assassination *indicating that others besides Oswald must have participated.*"

In January 1978 two committee lawyers—Andy Purdy and Mark Flanagan—contacted Burkley. But their sole objective was to get him to sign an affidavit saying that no one could have intercepted JFK's body before it got to the morgue, and that the president's wounds had not been altered between Dallas and the postmortem. Why would that have even been necessary unless there were, indeed, suspicions that alteration to Kennedy's corpse had been done by someone between the time his remains left Dallas and when the formal autopsy began at Bethesda? Burkley may have been put on the spot because the HSCA either suspected or even knew for certain he played a role in the casket switch.

It is bewildering that over the years Burkley vacillated between coming forward with evidence of a conspiracy and playing along with the coverup. He chose the latter. So he signed a statement that he remained "in the ambulance with the president's body in the casket and also on the plane; the casket was neither opened or disturbed in any way." And also that, "There was no difference in the nature of the wounds" seen in Dallas compared to those seen in the morgue. The latter was a bald-faced lie.

In 1996, Doug Horne of the ARRB contacted Nancy Denlea, a daughter of Dr. Burkley and the executor of his estate. She was asked if she would be willing to sign a release waiving attorney/client information from her father's attorney, William Illig, relating to the assassination. "She said that she would have no problem with that, and would be willing to sign such a form," Horne wrote for the file. But then "She changed her mind and decided NOT to sign the proposed waiver form drafted by ARRB general counsel. As a result, the ARRB never obtained access to Mr. Illig's files" pertaining to George Burkley's knowledge of any assassination conspiracy. Was Ms. Denlea afraid harm would come to her?

Many witnesses connected to aspects of the JFK assassination would do more than just lie, disappear or lay low to avoid publicity in the years to come. Some died in single car accidents; others "committed suicide" by shooting themselves several times in the back of the head, plus other equally bizarre circumstances. One man supposedly flung himself through a plate glass window to take his life. Mobster Sam Giancana was killed despite 24/7 police protection, when someone entered his Oak Park, Illinois home and shot him seven times in the head and neck in 1975, just before he was to testify to the Church Committee about the mob's collaboration with the CIA. Giancana's murder coincided with the discovery of the decomposing remains of Johnny Roselli in an oil drum floating off Miami; he had been shot and chopped up before being dumped.

One death that occurred in the fall of 1964 remains one of the most chilling unsolved murders connected to JFK.

Mary Pinchot Meyer was a former journalist and noted painter. She was also the ex-wife of high ranking CIA agent Cord Meyer and a serious romantic interest of John F. Kennedy up until his death. She regularly visited the White House (when Jackie was not in residence).

She was murdered on October 12—two days shy of her forty-fourth birthday—while walking along the C&O Canal Towpath in Georgetown, Washington, D.C. Mary was dragged twenty-five feet and heard calling out for help. She was shot execution style with a bullet to her temple and one that severed her aorta.

A twenty-five year old Black man, Raymond Crump Jr. had been fishing in the area and was soon arrested for the crime. The prosecution illegally deprived him of a preliminary hearing (that the courts ruled defendants are entitled to), and withheld exculpatory evidence: there was absolutely no forensic evidence linking him to Mary, despite the fact she had struggled with her attacker and had bled profusely from her wounds. Crump was a man of short and diminutive stature.

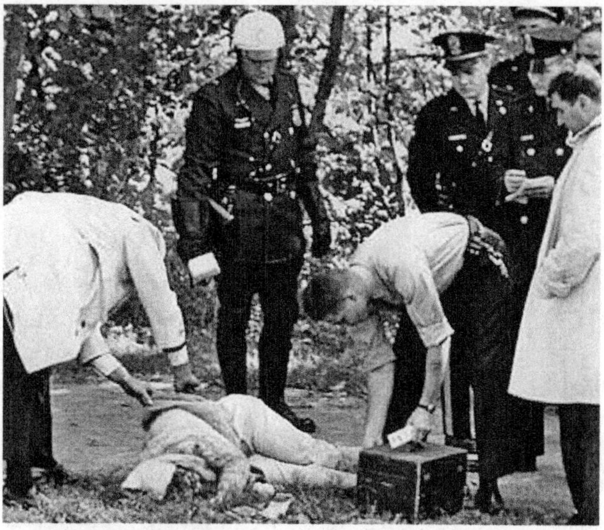

Mary Pinchot Meyer's murder was never solved.

Mr. Crump's public defender, Dovee Roundtree, was blocked from knowing any information about Ms. Meyer. "It was as if she existed only that one day on the towpath," the lawyer complained. This was probably because Mary was the ex-wife of a CIA bigwig.

Testimony from one man helped the prosecution's case. William Mitchell, a former Army lieutenant once stationed at the Pentagon, but by the start of the trial claimed to be teaching math at Georgetown University, came forward saying he saw a "Negro male" matching Crump's description following Mary on the towpath that day.

It was later revealed the address Mitchell provided as his residence turned out to be a CIA safe house; Georgetown had no records of him; the CIA was known to have its employees claim to be faculty at Georgetown to help provide cover; he soon disappeared.

The murder weapon was never recovered, even though Crump never left the scene and a large portion of the canal was searched by divers.

Mary died less than three weeks after the release of the Warren Commission Report. She had her doubts about the W.C.'s declarations, according to the book *Mary's Mosaic*, written by Peter Janney, a man who had been friends with the Meyers' son who had been killed as a child. Janney's father was also career CIA.

Realizing the immensity of the cover-up taking place, she may have confronted Cord and he in turn informed his colleagues at the CIA.

Mary's brother-in-law, Ben Bradlee of the *Washington Post*, covered up his having caught CIA Chief of Counterintelligence James Jesus Angleton breaking into Mary's home and art studio to retrieve her diary following her murder, and didn't write about it until his book came out thirty-five years later. Bradlee—who sanctimoniously demanded Nixon reveal the truth in Watergate—was willing to let an innocent Black man be convicted of murder. Fortunately, Raymond Crump was acquitted.

10
Love With The Proper Danger

While entrenched in her reporting of "the crime of the century," Dorothy began a relationship with a much younger reporter. She used him as a sounding board for her articles and had also confided in him about the book project she was working on for Random House. Kilgallen's biographer, Lee Israel, who published her tome in 1979, referred to this individual only as the "Out-of-Towner."

It wasn't until the 2007 *Midwest Today* magazine article "Who Killed Dorothy Kilgallen?" written by the author of this book, that the man was first publicly named in print: entertainment writer for the *Columbus Citizen-Journal* Ron Pataky. Magazine publisher Larry Jordan conducted multiple one-on-one phone interviews with Pataky over the span of several years, in which he confirmed having had a close bond with DK, but claimed it hadn't been sexual (despite evidence to the contrary).

Since Pataky's name has been publicly linked to Dorothy and suspicions aroused as to what role—if any—he played in her death, it is useful to delve into his background. There has been speculation about whether Ron had any association with criminal elements and/or U.S. intelligence agencies. This book seeks to shed new light on this subject by presenting startling new information no one else has ever reported.

This author has closely examined Mr. Pataky's academic record, including grade transcripts and confidential comments entered into his permanent student files by counselors and others, from his high school days to his attendance at Stanford University in Palo Alto, California and Ohio State University in Columbus, where he finished his undergraduate studies. His criminal record has also been scrutinized.

A probative look into this man's background is revelatory in terms of his character traits and how they affected his relationship with Dorothy Kilgallen and ultimately her fate.

Born Adam Ronald "Ron" Pataky on May 21, 1935, in Danville, Illinois, Pataky grew up a child of the war era. Never staying long enough in one place to put down roots, he ended up attending fourteen schools by the time he graduated high school. He chronicled his tumultuous childhood in his book *Over Here: A Young Boy's Journey Through World War II*. He wrote how he and his younger brother Gordon, who later committed suicide, lived "in near-constant fear of a young, emotionally-unprepared father with a blazing temper and precious little in the way of self-control."

In high school, Ron was an all-around athlete, participating in football, baseball, wrestling and swimming. He was a Boy Scout and enrolled in the Youth in Cadet program of the Civil Air Patrol. He was in a thespians group, was editor-in-chief of the school newspaper, and on the student council. He also engaged in church activities. He wrote that his special interests were "foreign languages and travel."

In 1953, during his senior year at Upper Arlington High School in Columbus, Ohio, Ron Pataky penned an essay for his freshman application to Stanford. The school, incidentally, was closely connected to the Central Intelligence Agency, as declassified government documents show.

He wrote to Stanford, "For years I have looked forward with great anticipation to the day when I might be successful in the art of living and getting along with others...I would like to enter your school of Hispanic Relations and to continue my Spanish in order to prepare for the Foreign Service." Just what kind of "foreign service" did Pataky have in mind?

The answer was soon to become clear.

D. Ellen Mann, a teacher of English and journalism at his high school, wrote on Pataky's application to Stanford: "Ronald has been in the middle section of his class scholastically. [But] one of his highest assets I think is his attitude that all things are possible. He secured a short interview and picture when Dwight Eisenhower was in Columbus last fall as a candidate. This fact proves his initiative; I believe few students could have succeeded with that assignment."

Ms. Mann admitted, "If you want the top bracket of pure scholarship, you probably wouldn't want Ronnie. If you want an all-around student, I believe I could [recommend him]."

This author has a copy of paperwork dated April 1, 1953 stating, "He passed the Navy College Aptitude Test, and is an applicant for enrollment in the Naval Reserve Officers' Training Corp, fall term 1953." In other words, he was trying to enroll in the Navy ROTC, which is a scholarship program that provides full tuition, stipends, summer training classes and more, so students can have a traditional college experience while preparing to serve as a Navy officer.

He succeeded in getting the scholarship, but was ultimately kicked out of the NROTC in April 1955 after which he dropped out of Stanford. So he never joined the Navy or became a commissioned officer.

Though Pataky was accepted by Stanford University and enrolled in the fall of 1953, he didn't do well. He earned "D's" in Navy Orientation, while earning "C's" in English, history and math. It had been previously noted his study habits "are not too good...doesn't spend enough time... doesn't fulfill his capacity, likes Western Civilization and Spanish best, English and math least."

In May 1954, while still completing his freshman year at Stanford, Ron ran into some trouble that made the front page of the *Stanford Daily* newspaper. He and two other male students were involved in a drunken altercation in which they tried to board a bus post-midnight. When the driver refused their boarding because they were so inebriated, they attacked the bus and he called the police.

Upon their arrest, they were also found to have bogus IDs. Possessing a fake California driver's license was punishable by a five hundred dollar fine (the equivalent of $5,517 today) and six months in jail.

Somehow Ron escaped the severest penalties, but not long after that, by his own account (told to *Midwest Today*), he apparently left the country. If he had ever written an essay on "what I did on my summer vacation," it would have been a doozy.

That chapter of his life will be revealed later in this book.

Pataky Attended Stanford As CIA Infiltrated Campus

At the time Pataky was enrolled at Stanford, the CIA had launched a clandestine project code-named MK-Ultra, which sought to control human behavior through such means as hypnosis, drugs (like LSD) and brainwashing. The covert operation commenced in 1953—the year Ron Pataky had enrolled—and lasted for ten years.

The New York Times reported in 1997 Stanford had "unwittingly lent its name to seven CIA (on-campus) research projects." This included "a survey of the ways in which criminals gave drugs to the unsuspecting."

Had Ron Pataky learned how to poison someone that way?

The Times reported, "The Stanford projects were financed either through foundations or through payments made directly to clinical faculty members, thus bypassing the university…Stanford has been making public every piece of information it can gather about its past involvement with the CIA's mind control research. It was the first institution with any major involvement in the program to do so…"

But the CIA refused to provide the university with the names of the faculty members or students involved. *The Times* noted, "The details of what human subjects might have been involved, if any, and what, if anything, happened to them, so far remains unknown."

The CIA was active on at least eighty-four college and university campuses, as declassified documents now prove. They cultivated students to keep tabs on others, and actively recruited those whom they felt would be useful for controversial and even dangerous assignments.

A Nov. 18, 1954 report on whether Ron should be allowed to continue to reside in housing operated by an on-campus fraternity stated, "He is not yet of the opinion that he is here to prepare for a life's work." The fraternity worked with Pataky to try to impress upon him the need for a "de-emphasis on [dating]." While his lack of academic rigor gave the impression he was not serious about anything, as will be seen, Ron was a split personality and there were some matters he took *very* seriously.

Pataky's 'Mental Conflicts'

A report in his file dated Jan. 15, 1955 stated, "Most of Ron's difficulties with his studies can be attributed to his age (and lack of maturity); his great interest in social activities. He has certain *deep-rooted social-mental conflicts* and as a consequence he puts out undue time on social activities." The counselor wrote, "As yet [we] know of no effective means to correct the situation. He is going to take a make-up examination and remove an incomplete (grade). This will take Ron off probation and there is a chance that it may bring him to minus C grade points."

But he was a malingerer who, on Feb. 11, 1955, attempted to get out of taking a hygiene class by claiming he'd recently had surgery on his eyes, the course required too much reading, and it wasn't worth it to him to expend the effort.

April 14, 1955, a counselor at Stanford wrote a memo to the professor of Naval Science at Stanford with the subject heading "Adam Ronald Pataky, Dismissal Of." It stated: "At the time of interviewing Ronald Pataky, I found his interest in the United States Navy to be of a very negative quality. It is my opinion that he not be given further consideration in being trained as a Naval officer."

Ron had been given a full NROTC scholarship before he flunked out. A summary dated June 15, 1955 as he was ending his enrollment at Stanford noted that while he was "very able to get along in any situation, liked by all (in social situations), his actions and opinions sometimes tend to alienate people." His study habits were described as "very very poor due to certain mental conflict." His social skills were said to be "well developed. It canceled out all other activity." Perhaps the most insightful comment was Ron Pataky had an "extremely amiable personality. Very able to understand people and why they tick." This was a skill he would exploit in the years ahead.

Ultimately, Pataky moved back home to where his divorced parents lived, and finished his undergrad studies at Ohio State in 1958, later earning a masters in journalism.

But strangely, he did not enter the journalism field at that time. Instead, he worked for an ambulance company. For much of his life, Pataky was very conflicted—straddling two worlds: one that was dark and treacherous and full of intrigue and betrayal—for which he at times seems to have felt guilt; and the other in which he projected sociability and lightheartedness, perhaps as a way of insulating himself from his conscience.

Before the 1960s, ambulance "attendants" were usually only required to complete a twenty-four-hour course in standard first aid through the American Red Cross or other training resource. According to William Atkinson, PhD., "Ambulance services provided little more than 'scoop and run' transport. Untrained personnel in hearse-type vehicles sped to an emergency scene, 'scooped' up the patient with no regard to injury, illness, or care and raced—sometimes with both the driver and an attendant (if present) riding in the cab—to an ill-equipped and poorly staffed emergency room. Such was the case in almost every community across this nation."

Since Pataky had fared poorly in biology, it is hard to see how he would have the aptitude or the interest in ambulance work.

Finally, his roommate—the notorious Bob Slatzer who later surfaced with bogus claims of having been married to Marilyn Monroe—learned of a job as an entertainment writer for an Ohio weekly paper and encouraged Ron to apply. He did, and this gig then led to his securing employment with a Scripps-Howard paper in 1961. He remained on the staff of the *Citizen-Journal* until it folded in 1985.

Pataky with Sandy Dennis; Miss America Laurie Lee Schafer; Alexis Smith.

Pataky's Suspicious Job

Despite being a young reporter for a newspaper in Columbus, Ohio—not a major city—Pataky was very well connected. He explained this by saying, "I worked for Scripps-Howard. They owned fifty-six newspaperss...and big ones: The *San Francisco Chronicle*, the *New York World-Telegram*, the *Pittsburgh Press*, *Rocky Mountain News*. I was headquartered, by choice, in Columbus because I'd gone to school here. My stories ran a lot of different places." Only part of his statement is true.

With very few exceptions, his articles only appeared locally. His columns were not carried by the United Features Syndicate owned by his employer.

Yet Pataky traveled extensively for his work, even to foreign countries, despite parent company Scripps-Howard News Service having reporters on the ground in most major cities that could provide the necessary coverage.

What was he really doing?

Pataky—charming though he was—managed to cross paths with an extraordinary number of celebrities and befriend them in a way most reporters don't actually get to know their interview subjects. Since his writing would only reach a limited market, why did celebs get so close to him? He even dated some of them.

Ron had all the appearances of someone who could, by dint of his ingratiating personality, manage to gain the confidence of people and then collect information that would be useful to his sponsors. The CIA was known to place writers in various media positions and even subsidize their salaries, to gather surveillance and also spin stories.

Pataky appeared numerous times on a local television show hosted by Nick Clooney, the father of actor George Clooney.

Ron was also an aspiring songwriter, who met with limited success. After his relationship with Dorothy Kilgallen heated up, she helped him form a song publishing company called Dawnlight Music. Besides Dorothy and Ron, its shareholders included singer Jerry Vale and Vale's manager Dee Anthony, who also managed Peter Frampton and Joe Cocker.

Pataky's songwriting credits include *While Stephanie Sleeps*, recorded by Johnny Mathis; *Give Me This Moment*, recorded by John Gary; and tunes for Jerry Vale and Al Martino.

In his conversations with Larry Jordan, Ron frequently mentioned his music compositions, one area of his life of which he was most proud.

"Tony Bennett took my review of his concert and took out a full page in *Variety* and ran just my review in the middle of it. And the headline—out of the column—was 'Tony Bennett Will Always Be A One-Man Show,'" Ron would later brag.

A Chance Encounter?

Dorothy Kilgallen first met the young man whom she dubbed "Beau Pataky" in June 1964 during a press junket.

With an unprecedented three major motion pictures in production, Twentieth Century-Fox flew one hundred and ten journalists on a chartered Lufthansa Airlines Boeing 707 to Europe to watch filming on locations in Britain, Austria and Italy.

At the reconstructed Booker Airport in England, reporters watched stunts for *Those Magnificent Men in Their Flying Machines* and interviewed stars like Sarah Miles, Terry-Thomas and Robert Morley. Each writer had their picture taken as a personal souvenir alongside a replica of a 1910 Antoinette airplane specially built for the film.

When the media arrived in Austria they were treated to a massive banquet at Schloss Klessheim in Salzburg where *The Sound of Music* was being filmed. Julie Andrews was interviewed and the reporters watched choreographer Marc Breaux rehearsing the *I Have Confidence* number as music pre-recorded in Hollywood was played back. Andrews and co-star Christopher Plummer were interviewed at Frohnburg Castle. Back in Ohio, Ron Pataky's newspaper ran a full page picture on the cover of a supplement section showing him interviewing Ms. Andrews.

Finally, the reporters arrived in Italy, where *The Agony and the Ecstasy* was being shot. They were conveyed up the perilous Carrera Mountains to the 4,700 foot Monte Altimissino to watch a scene being filmed in a quarry usually closed to visitors. Director Carol Reed, producer Darryl F. Zanuck and star Charlton Heston were on hand to welcome them. When Heston saw Dorothy, he called her "Dottie" and she called him by the nickname "Chuckles." *Journal-American* colleague Louis Sobel noted that DK attracted as much attention on the junket as the movie stars did.

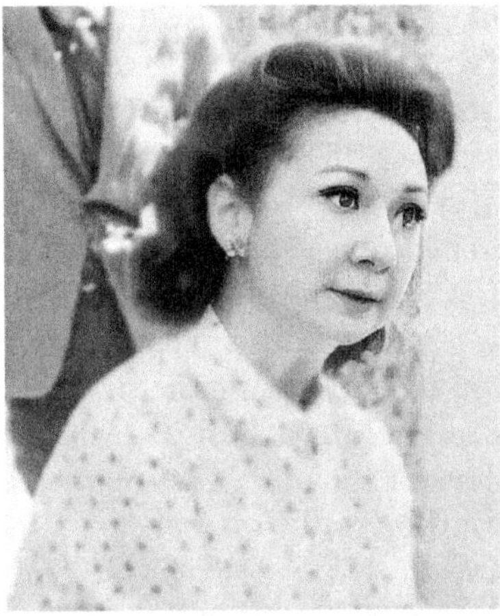

A candid pic of DK in Austria.

Actor Rex Harrison (playing the Pope) was interviewed outside a restaurant in Rome that bore the Pontiff's name.

As for how Ron Pataky and Dorothy Kilgallen met, he told *Midwest Today*, "[We were in] Salzburg, [Austria] on the set of *The Sound of Music*. And the bus had arrived at the set from the hotel. She walked up to the door of the bus and kind of tripped and I caught her by the elbow. She was on the outside of the bus. I looked at her and I said, 'Well, hello!' knowing instantly who it was. She said 'Thank you very much. And who are you?' flirtatiously. She giggled a lot. She was giggling the first thirty seconds we ever talked and kind of charming. And I said 'what are you doing after we get off the [bus]?' And she said 'Nothing.' And we went and had drinks."

But Pataky's account of chivalry is suspect. First, there's a good possibility he befriended her aboard the plane. Surely the press didn't remain buckled in their seats during the ten-hour flight from New York City. A sociable lot by nature, they would have been in a party mood during the long trans-oceanic trip.

Another reason for believing this scenario is that after they arrived in England they shared a cab from the airport. Pataky couldn't very well admit he targeted her by approaching her on the plane

In her June 19, 1964 syndicated column, she wrote of first encountering him while traveling in London: "At the airport, Ron Pataky, the Columbus, O., columnist invited me to ride into town with him. He said to the cab driver: 'I haven't any pounds with me. Will you take American money?' The hackie grinned. 'Hop in governor,' he said. 'It's the best money in the world.'"

Then on July 23, Pataky was once again included in her column (perhaps an item planted by Ron himself)?

"When Judith Hastings assumed the Sally Ann Howes role in '*What Makes Sammy Run*' on July 20, her No. 1 rooter was Ron Pataky, formerly betrothed to Anna Maria Alberghetti. And small wonder: Judith is not only a beauty but enormously talented. The movie companies would do well to have spies in the audience when she takes to the stage of the 54th St. Theatre."

Alberghetti appeared as a mystery guest on *What's My Line?* on Nov. 23, 1958 and then again on April 30, 1961. She and Pataky had dated briefly, having met in the summer of 1963 in Columbus when Anna starred in the play *Fanny*. In October 1963 it was reported in the press Ron was on vacation in Hollywood to visit her when she collapsed at a nightclub and had to be hospitalized. Pataky denied the pair was engaged to be married. The papers also revealed this little known tidbit, "[Pataky] has filed suit for divorce in Domestic Relations Court here (Columbus, Ohio) charging his wife, Sally, with neglect."

He and Sally Ann saw the divorce finalized Oct. 31, 1963. She by then resided in Phoenix. When interviewed by *Midwest Today*, Ron never brought up the fact he had been married. That December, Pataky and Anna Maria were involved in a bizarre incident at the home of Columbus-based bandleader Alvin E. Waslohn. According to Pataky, he slipped on a rug and cut his head on a glass door, whereupon medics were called. What then ensued was what Ron considered a beating by the police.

"Patrolman Charles West, one of two policemen who answered the call, said that the officers had to subdue Pataky and that he gave the critic a black eye," reported the press. After his injuries were treated at Riverside Hospital, Pataky was taken into custody by "two police officers, another patrolman and a sergeant, and was charged with intoxication and resisting arrest. He posted $45 bond."

Ron denied resisting arrest, saying he was "subdued by violence." He also failed to appear in court, forfeiting a bond of twenty dollars on the intoxication charge plus twenty five dollars for resistance.

On Sept. 12, 1964, Ms. Alberghetti wed Chilean-American director/producer Claudio Guzmán.

The Affair

"For all of her brashness in print she was very poetic," Pataky said of Dorothy. "She was a dyed-in-the-wool romantic, to be sure. A very soft person. I never saw her angry. I don't think, other than strictly business—something like discussing the Jack Ruby thing—[that] Dorothy and I ever really had a serious conversation. I knew Dorothy better than anybody. We talked daily. If we missed a day, we were aware we missed a day. Let's put it that way. And it was not a love affair...well it was a love affair, but not a physical love affair. She was a sweet lady, my best friend in the whole world."

Over the next fifteen months, Ron and Dorothy rendezvoused often. Sometimes she'd come to Ohio to see him, and he even took her to meet his mother. He'd frequently visit The Big Apple.

"[We'd] shuck the rest of these phonies and go off and do our thing," Pataky recalled. "We made trips together. We went to Florence together, we went to London together...We'd kiss hello on the cheek if I was coming into town. But there was no goodnight kiss when I dropped her off, and I dropped her off a lot of times. Because it wasn't that kind of relationship. Never. Not even close. I had my girlfriends. She knew about them."

Ron said he had nothing to hide. Although they did "openly meet at hotels...we never, ever spent any time in a hotel room."

Ron Pataky and Dorothy.

But that's not what Marc Sinclaire claimed. A well-known hairdresser to the stars, he was Dorothy's go-to-guy for hair styling and he became a close confidant. In 1966, *Vogue* magazine listed him as one of the world's top ten hair stylists. His celebrity clients included, among others, Liza Minnelli, former *Cosmopolitan* editor Helen Gurley Brown and Charlotte Ford.

Though he later discovered Dorothy Kilgallen's dead body, he was never questioned by the police and never spoke out publicly about his employer's death. His remarks were published for the first time in the *Midwest Today* article, the result of a videotaped interview conducted by researchers Kathryn Fauble and David Henschel.

Sinclaire noted Dorothy had several places she could go to have intimate time with Pataky, including Sinclaire's own apartment and interior designer Howard Rothberg's house.

"She had a key to mine, and she had a key to his. And I told her, 'why are you going to a hotel?' [And she said of Pataky] 'He wants to.'"

What could be the reason why Ron insisted on seeing DK in a hotel room? Did he have the room bugged? Or was he protecting himself against anyone who might entrap him by electronically eavedropping on his time with Dorothy at a private residence?

Ron admitted he would stay at the Regency during his frequent trips to NYC and Dorothy would even pick up his room keys for him.

Midwest Today obtained a copy of a note Kilgallen had sent Pataky in which she romantically referred to "our little spot on the 19th floor." Another time, she sent him a newspaper clipping showing a picture of her in a meeting with two men. On stationery marked "Dorothy Kollmar," Kilgallen wrote: "Notice that they were the wrong guys to be at the Regency with. Where were you when I wanted you?"

Asked about this evidence, Pataky told the magazine, "I had a lot of mail from her that was written in a kind of intimate fashion. We'd flirt."

He went on to say, "She would reach out if she respected you; she might well call you and say 'I want to read you something. Tell me what you think of it. And make any suggestions.' And she'd read it, and then go from there."

Marlin Swing said he knew Dorothy was romantically involved with the much younger reporter.

"[Pataky's] answers about their relationship were absolute lies because I spent one night in the Regency in that same bar with her, and when I first read about that contestant finding her there with a man (the last night she was alive), I thought maybe it was that night, because she had her head on my shoulder. She was feeling very—she wanted to talk about Ron and how wonderful he was and what a beautiful relationship and how he wrote her poems and he called her every night," Swing recalled. "According to her, it wasn't platonic, because she told me about their trysts in Italy and Florence, I believe, and various places. Switzerland."

Swing felt Johnnie Ray had been "one of" the loves of Dorothy's life, and her involvement with Pataky may have been a rebound relationship.

"The breakup with Johnnie had just happened, and then Ron appeared," he noted.

Swing never met Pataky and said he "wanted to keep it that way."

Pataky would state in later years, he rarely if ever watched *What's My Line?* despite his relationship with Kilgallen.

The handsome, twenty-nine year old Pataky was a ladies man. He squired Mia Farrow while staying at her mother Maureen O'Sullivan's New York apartment and bragged he "dated half of the females in Hollywood." He palled around with Peter and Pat Kennedy Lawford. So why the interest in Dorothy Kilgallen, who was old enough to be his mother?

11
The Dogged Reporter Remains Hounded

On Friday, Sept. 25, 1964, Dorothy scored yet another scoop, under the front-page headline in the New York *Journal-American* "Kilgallen Pre-Warren Exclusive." The subhead was "2 Witnesses Are Warned." The piece ran only in the *J-A* and not other newspapers in the Hearst chain, making it hard to find today. DK reported, "New and significant disclosures of events surrounding the assassination of President John F. Kennedy have been obtained exclusively by this newspaper.

"They are statements and affidavits.

"The important new points:

"1—A woman who witnessed the killing of Officer J.D. Tippit was warned by police that her life would be in danger if she talked about the case to anyone. She gave what seemed to be a vivid description of the slayer—a description which did not fit Lee Harvey Oswald—but she made her statement after being promised that her name would not be revealed. She said:

"'I'm not allowed to talk to anybody...Might get killed on the way to work...See, they'll kill people that know something about that.'

"2—Another eyewitness to the shooting of Officer Tippit—Mrs. Helen Markham, who identified Oswald in a police lineup—also said she had been told not to talk by 'several' persons whom she identified as FBI and Secret Service men, and four or five Dallas detectives...

"3—On Nov. 23, the day after the assassination, the Dallas police obviously were rounding up as many witnesses as possible and getting them to make statements and sign affidavits while the events were still clear in their minds.

"One of these was Seymour Weitzman, a Dallas policeman, who was one of two searchers to discover the alleged assassination rifle in the Texas Book Depository Building from which the shots were fired. He swore under oath:

"'This rifle was a 7.65 Mauser bolt action equipped with a 4/13 scope, a thick black leather sling on it.'"

Dorothy commented, "The Mauser seems to have been erased mysteriously from the case. The assassination weapon is now officially an Italian Carcano of another calibre. Lee Harvey Oswald owned a Carcano.

"4—On Nov. 23, a cab driver named William Wayne Whaley signed an affidavit saying he had picked up a fare 'who I now know to be

Lee Harvey Oswald' a few minutes after the assassination and drove him a short distance—95 cents on the meter.

"Yet on Nov. 24, District Attorney Henry Wade of Dallas County held a press conference in which he told reporters:

"'...he asked the bus driver to stop, got off at a stop, caught a taxicab driver, Darryl Click—I don't have the exact place—and went to his home in Oak Cliff, changed clothes hurriedly, and left.'"

Kilgallen commented sardonically, "William Wayne Whaley became Darryl Click almost as casually and rapidly as the Mauser became a Carcano."

There were two major problems. First, an inquiry at the City Transportation Company revealed no such taxi driver named Darryl Click had ever existed in Dallas. As for William Whaley, his log book showed a man matching Oswald's description had been picked up at 12:30 p.m. The president was shot at 12:31. This was never publicly corrected.

Most startling in Dorothy Kilgallen's exclusive was her statement that, "A reliable source close to the entire case has been informed that one of the Commission members, government advisor John J. McCoy, was given a photograph showing Oswald with a rifle in the sixth floor window of the Book Depository from which the assassination bullets were believed to have been fired.

"The photograph is said to have been taken by an amateur along the parade route, just as the bullets were being fired, or a second afterwards. It probably will be incorporated in the Warren Report as additional—and startling—evidence that Oswald was indeed the assassin."

On that last point, no such photograph has ever surfaced. Although it's worth noting that a picture by a Dealey Plaza witness does show a balding man with glasses visible through a window, who looks more like LBJ henchman Mac Wallace and does not resemble Oswald in the least.

The person who had seen Officer Tippit fatally shot, whose identity had been hidden at her request, was a Black woman named Acquilla Clemons. She lived on the north side of Tenth Street in Dallas and was sitting on her front porch when she saw the policeman gunned down.

She said she saw two men, not one, running from the scene of the crime, and neither fit Oswald's description. One was a "short guy and kind of heavy." The other was tall and thin in khaki colored trousers and a white shirt. Mrs. Clemons said after the shooting, the two men took off running in opposite directions.

Recall, Oswald had initially only been arrested for the murder of Tippit. The FBI interviewed Mrs. Clemons but did not take a formal statement from her because, the Bureau said, she was in poor health. (She merely had diabetes). Not only was she never called to give testimony to the Warren Commission, the Warren Report makes no mention of her and falsely claims "there was only one female witness" to the slaying of Officer Tippit. Had Mrs. Clemons failed to be taken seriously because of racial bias? Or was her story simply disregarded by the Warren Commission because it failed to point the (trigger) finger at Oswald?

Neighbor Frank Wright also saw two men, neither one of whom was Lee Oswald.

Adding credence to Acquilla's story of two assailants involved was the fact the bullets recovered from the policeman's body were from two manufacturers. There were four spent cartridges at the scene and the lead officer marked the shells with his initials before they were entered into evidence. However, the shells later produced by the FBI didn't have the symbols on them. Furthermore, when arrested, Oswald was carrying a revolver, not a semi-automatic weapon. Why would he have emptied the spent shells at the scene to implicate himself?

Helen Markham supposedly picked Oswald out of a police lineup, claiming she had reached her decision voluntarily.

Although considered the star witness, Markham's testimony was full of mistakes. She said J.D. Tippit was alive when the ambulance arrived, and when she talked to him, he replied, but the autopsy proved he died instantly. She also falsely claimed for the first twenty minutes she was the only person to attend the body, but a small crowd had formed around the fallen cop soon after he was shot.

It turns out Markham was so hysterical at the police station she was in no shape to go into the lineup room until after ammonia was administered to her. Lee Oswald was the only man in the lineup who was injured and in handcuffs, told his real name and where he worked. By then, his identity had already been on the news.

Even so, when Mrs. Markham appeared before the Warren Commission, she said six times she had been unable to recognize anyone at the lineup and changed her tune only after Assistant Counsel Joseph Ball asked her a leading question referring to "a number two man," who was Oswald.

The star witness in the Tippit shooting was best summed up by Joseph Ball himself. In 1964 he conceded in a public debate her testimony was "full of mistakes" and he described Mrs Markham as an "utter screwball." He further dismissed her as "utterly unreliable," the exact opposite of the Warren Report's assertion, "In testimony before the Commission, Mrs Markham confirmed her positive identification of Lee Harvey Oswald as the man she saw kill Officer Tippit."

Had Oswald ever gone to trial, any good defense attorney would have destroyed the "star witness" against him in the killing of Tippit.

Domingo Benavides was driving west on Tenth Street when he saw a patrol car parked a few feet away from the curb, heading east. He saw Tippit being shot, and then pulled his truck over to the curb. Benavides, who had perhaps the best view of Tippit's murder, said he could not identify LHO as the killer. His brother was shot and killed two months later. Domingo was not called to testify before the Warren Commission.

Warren Reynolds had heard shooting in the street and saw the murderer run off. The day after Reynolds was shown a picture of Lee Oswald by two FBI agents, but said he could not identify him, he was shot through the head by a man wielding a .22 caliber rifle who was hiding in his home. A suspect, Darrel Garner, was arrested for the crime but had an alibi supplied by his girlfriend, Betty Mooney McDonald—one of the strippers in Jack Ruby's nightclub. The Dallas police dropped the charges before Reynolds had regained consciousness, and might have been able to identify his attacker. Garner quickly disappeared, and shortly thereafter, the police arrested Betty McDonald on a minor charge. Then she supposedly hung herself in her jail cell. Warren Reynolds then changed his mind and said the man he saw at the Tippit murder scene was LHO.

Dorothy Notes The Change In Murder Weapon

A crucial component of Dorothy Kilgallen's exclusive had to do with the changing identity of the gun allegedly used to kill JFK. She cites Seymour Weitzman of the Dallas police as the individual who discovered the murder weapon in the northwest corner of the sixth floor of the TSBD.

"This rifle was a 7.65 Mauser bolt action equipped with a 4-13 scope, a thick leather brownish-black sling on it. The rifle was between some boxes near the stairway. The time the rifle was found was 1:22 p.m."

DK then noted in parentheses: "But the assassination weapon is now officially designated as an Italian 6.5 Carcano Carbine. Oswald owned a Carbine, which he had bought from a Chicago mail order house."

No doubt the original rifle was a 7.65 Mauser, because it was found by Deputy Sheriff Eugene Boone, Deputy Constable Seymour Weitzman and Deputy Sheriff Roger Craig. Moments later Capt. Will Fritz and Lt. Day of the DPD joined them and took possession of the firearm, and their immediate official declaration to the press was they had found a 7.65 Mauser.

Seymour Weitzman even wrote an affidavit before a notary public, and said it was a Mauser. This piece of information seemed so reliable that for three days TV commentators—including Walter Cronkite—repeated many times the model of rifle was a Mauser. A CIA report dated Nov. 25, 1963—after the assassination and after the rifle found in the TSBD was carefully examined—stated the weapon was a 7.65 Mauser.

On November 28, a second CIA memo, declassified under FOIA, notes, "As regards articles appearing recently in the Italian and foreign press concerning the presumed use of an Italian-made rifle in the slaying of President Kennedy, the following comments are made:

"The weapon which appears to have been employed in this criminal attack is a Model 31 rifle, 7.65 Caliber, 1938 modification...The description of a 'Mannlicher Carcao' (sic) rifle in the Italian and foreign press is in error."

So the cornerstone in the Warren Commission's case against Oswald—that Kennedy was killed by an Italian made weapon—was refuted by the CIA itself! But later, this was changed to being an Italian carbine Mannlicher-Carcano. Such a gun is clearly marked "made in Italy" on the shoulder stock, and cal. 6.5 is stamped on the side of the barrel. So how could trained law enforcement officers and the CIA, who examined the TSBD rifle, have ever been mistaken?

Dallas Deputy Sheriff Roger Craig—winner of the Man of the Year Award in 1960, for outstanding performance in the line of duty, (he helped capture an international jewel thief)—discussed in a video interview from April 1974 having participated in a search of the sixth floor of the TSBD on Nov. 22, 1963.

He related, "Deputy Sheriff Luke Mooney was with me when we found the shells. We found three hulls beside the window on the sixth floor, and they were laying three in a row not more than an inch apart, all pointing in the same direction." (This of course is not the way they would have appeared had they been randomly ejected from a bolt-action rifle in a rapid firing sequence. Instead, they looked like they had been planted there). "Of course, I didn't touch them. They hadn't been photographed or fingerprinted or anything..."

Roger Craig said that after finding the three spent cartridges and the one Fritz ejected from the rifle, "We began then to search for a weapon. Everybody took a different direction, and Deputy Sheriff Boone and myself just happened to head for the northwest corner of the building. And Boone was ahead of me by about eight feet. And there were a stack of boxes just at the head of the stairwell going downstairs. And Boone looked over into it and said 'here it is. Here's the rifle.' So I immediately...looked over and there was a rifle, but we didn't touch it until Capt. Fritz and Lt. Day from the...Dallas Police Department got there. Now Captain Fritz was chief of homicide; Lt. Day was from the identification bureau.

"Day pulled the rifle out and handed it to Cap. Fritz...He held it up by the strap and asked if anyone knew what kind of rifle it was. Well by this time, Deputy Constable Seymour Weitzman had joined us. And Weitzman was a gun buff. He had a sporting goods store at one time, and he was very good with weapons. And he said it looked like a Mauser and he walked over to Fritz, and Captain Fritz was holding the rifle up in the air, and I was standing next to Weitzman, who was standing next to Fritz, and we weren't any more than six or eight inches from the rifle, and stamped right on the barrel of the rifle were '7.65 Mauser.' And that's when Weitzman said, 'It is a Mauser,' and pointed to the 7.65 Mauser stamp on the barrel. The shells we found came from a 6.5 Italian rifle. The two don't relate. [The three cartridges that were] found at the [southeast corner] came from a 6.5 Italian carbine."

Even more telling is according to the Weitzman affidavit, Fritz had ejected one live cartridge from the rifle discovered at the TSBD. WFAA-TV cameraman Tom Alyea saw Capt. Fritz pick all the cartridges up off the floor with his bare hands. The caliber was printed on the end of the cartridges. The recovered shells were 6.5 mm and yet all of the five police officers present believed the rifle was a 7.65 mm Mauser.

Fritz then gave the shells to Det. Robert Studebaker. He "never saw the original placement of the casings, so he tossed them on the floor and photographed them. Therefore, any photograph of shell casings taken after this is staged and not correct," Alyea told the ARRB. "Lt. [Carl] Day and Det. Studebaker—these are the two crime lab men who dusted the evidence on the sixth floor. *Their testimony is false from beginning to end.*"

Also problematic is the gun Oswald allegedly ordered—and Kleins sent—was a 36 inch, 5-1/2 lb., slightly used rifle. Yet the Carcano said to be linked to Oswald and Army experts test fired was a 40.02 inch, 8 pound weapon. The FBI determined it did not have a unique serial number.

These experts concluded the Carcano (Vol. 3 Warren Commission Report pages 405-500) was unusable in its original state because of the scope, bolt and trigger defects. Here are some direct quotes from W.C. hearings:

"They [the U.S. Army marksmen] could not sight the weapon in using the scope." According to the FBI's firearms specialist, "Every time we changed the adjusting screws to move the crosshairs in the telescopic sight in one direction it also affected the movement of the impact or the point of impact in the other direction. We fired several shots and found that the shots were not all landing in the same place, but were gradually moving away from the point of impact.

"The pressure to open the bolt was so great that we tended to move the rifle off the target."

There was also a problem with the trigger mechanism. "In the first stage the trigger is relatively free, and it suddenly required a greater pull to actually fire the weapon."

This suggests the gun supposedly linked to Lee Oswald could not have caused any of the wounds to Kennedy or Connally, except by accident. And one major point that's been overlooked: the so-called murder weapon was a carbine (which had a shorter barrel), than a typical rifle. It had a muzzle velocity of around 2,000 fps, which means it is not a high-velocity weapon. Since the president's death certificates (1963), the Warren Report (1964), and even more recent articles in *The Journal of the American Medical Association* (1992) report JFK was killed by high velocity bullets, it stands to reason he was not killed by Oswald's weapon.

Incidentally, Lee Oswald has often been described as a marksman but there is zero proof of that. To the contrary, in the Marines, Oswald trained with an M1, a semi-automatic rifle. No bolt action, no telescopic sight, and no need to recapture the target after firing. Believed it or not, the first time Marines have trained by firing at a moving target of any kind was in 2011 at Marine Corps Base Quantico and a story in *Politico* in June 2022 told what happened to the first training group. (They didn't fare well).

When Oswald's gunnery sergeant, Sgt. Robert Block, was told that Oswald pulled off this feat of marksmanship from a sixth story window, he laughed. Block trained LHO at Air Control Squadron Nine at the Tustin air base. Lee arrived back in Orange County, California late in 1958 and stayed until the following September. He was no marksman.

Astonishingly, in an interview with the *Detroit News* in 1976, Dallas Police Chief Jesse Curry admitted "it's more than possible" the rifle originally found in the TSBD could have been switched, and said anyone wanting to substitute one suspected murder weapon for another "could have gotten away with it at the time," because no special precautions were taken by the authorities to isolate the gun as historic evidence.

Curry also admitted to news reporters years later, "We don't have any proof that Oswald fired the rifle and never did. Nobody's been able to put him in that building with a gun in his hand."

Remember that when someone makes an iron-clad assertion Lee Harvey Oswald murdered President Kennedy.

Assassination researcher Henry Hurt notes, "Another curious point is the failure by investigators to find a single Mannlicher-Carcano cartridge other than those, including a live round still in the rifle, discovered at the scene. No extra cartridge was ever found on Oswald or in his possessions. No evidence was found that he ever purchased ammunition at all. If he was the assassin, his only ammunition was at the scene—the cartridge shells lined up as evidence in the assassin's lair. There is no official explanation as to where Oswald supposedly got his four cartridges. Moreover, *there is no evidence that the Mannlicher-Carcano was even fired on the day of the assassination.*" In fact, the rifle was rusted.

Paraffin tests were negative for Lee Oswald's face. FBI agent Cortland Cunningham lied and said blowback wasn't expected from a rifle. Yet all of the FBI marksmen who tested the same Mannlicher-Carcano tested positive for gunpowder residue when given a paraffin test.

Oswald's hands were said to have contained small traces of nitrates, but that could have come from the fact that he worked in a book warehouse and came into contact with printer's ink there.

Other Guns Found At The Depository Building

A gun similar to the Mauser was owned by TSBD employee Warren Caster, who had recently brought his gun to work with him. Building manager Roy Truly admitted to the Warren Commission he had also brought a high-powered rifle into the TSBD a few days earlier and showed it to some of his co-workers. The late Jim Marrs, a newspaper journalist and best-selling author of books on the assassination, told *Midwest Today* in a 1992 interview that even "Wesley Frazier had a British 303 Infield (rifle) he'd brought up there a few days earlier that he was waving around. It's very odd." Frazier's weapon, with a fully loaded clip, was confiscated by authorities the night of the assassination.

This author has discovered a declassified FBI memo dated Nov. 23, 1963 which contains a typewritten description of part of the interview with LHO. It states: "Captain Fritz asked Oswald if he ever owned a rifle and Oswald stated that he had observed a Mr. Truly, a supervisor at the Texas Schoolbook Depository on November 20, 1963, display a rifle to some individuals in his office on the first floor of the Texas School Book Depository, but denied ever owning a rifle himself." His denial has weight because, as has been previously noted, it has been established he had been impersonated on several occasions, according to J. Edgar Hoover himself.

Scant Evidence

The public was shown photos of the so-called "sniper's nest" on the sixth floor of the TSBD, but Dallas police files declassified years later and examined by this author contained pictures showing various configurations of the boxes, as if they had experimented with different arrangements and staged the scene.

No prints of LHO were found on the floors, walls, window ledge, window frame or window. Only a movable cardboard carton, subsequently present at the police station while the defendant was also there, is now alleged to have his print.

DA Henry Wade told the press Oswald's palm print was found on the rifle but there is no photographic evidence of this and Lt. Day refused to sign a sworn affidavit that he found such a print. On that basis alone it would be inadmissible. FBI agent Vincent Drain said, "I just don't believe there was ever a print."

A Blown 'Cover'

Dallas Deputy Sheriff Roger Craig provided an important eyewitness account. After having talked to people on the grassy knoll immediately after the assassination, he crossed Elm Street to the south side. He noted, "Everybody was coming to the scene of the shooting, which is normal; people are just that way, you know. But as I was searching the south curb of Elm Street, I heard a shrill whistle, and I looked up. It just drew my attention. It was coming from across the street. And there was a light green Rambler station wagon driving real slow, west on Elm Street. And the driver was leaning over to his right, looking up at a man running down the grass. So I immediately tried to cross the street to take these two people into custody for questioning. Everybody else was coming to the scene. These were the only two people leaving. This was suspicious, in my mind, at the time. So I wanted to talk to them. But I couldn't get across the street because the city officer who was stationed at Houston and Elm had left his post and the traffic was so heavy, I just couldn't get across the street. But I did get a good look at the man coming down the grassy knoll. And he got in the station wagon and they drove west on Elm Street."

Craig recalled how a little later that afternoon, "I was thinking about this man getting away from me. And I called Captain Fritz in his office and gave him a description of the man I saw, and he told me, 'It sounds like the suspect we have in custody. Come on up and take a look at him.' So I went out and got in my unmarked car and drove to the city hall and went directly to Captain Fritz's office. The [suspect] was sitting in a chair behind the desk. And Fritz turned to me and said 'is this the man you saw?' And I said 'yes.' And it was. It *was*. So he turned to the suspect and said 'this man saw you leave.' At which time the suspect became a little excited, and he said 'I told you people I did.' And Fritz said, 'now take it easy, son...We're just trying to find out what happened here...What about the car?' [Fritz] didn't say station wagon, he said 'what about the car.' At which time the suspect leaned forward, and put both hands up on the desk, and said 'that station wagon belongs to Mrs. Paine. Don't try to drag her into this.

"Then he leaned back, and very disgustedly said, 'Everybody will know who I am now.' Now this was NOT a brag. I know it's been blown up to be a brag in the Warren Commission." Shaking his head no, Craig continued, "But this was not a brag. This was a man that...was disgusted that he had blown his cover or been caught or something, you know."

Capt. Fritz, in his testimony to the Warren Commission, denied all this, and critics attacked Craig, trying to debunk his story.

But Mrs. James Forrest was standing in a group of people who had gathered on the incline near the grassy knoll. She saw a man suddenly run from the rear of the Depository building, down the incline, and then enter a Rambler station wagon. She said the man strongly resembled Lee Harvey Oswald. "If it wasn't Oswald," Mrs. Forrest declared, "it was his identical twin." *Or it could have been one of the known imposters.*

Commission Document Five, which was not included in the Warren Report (but which is on file at the National Archives) states soon after the shooting, Marvin C. Robinson was driving west along Elm Street in heavy traffic. According to an FBI report dated the next day, just as Robinson crossed the Elm and Houston intersection, he saw a "light-colored

Nash [Rambler] station wagon" stop in front of the Book Depository. A white man walked down the grassy incline from the building, got into the Nash, and the car moved off in the direction of Oak Cliff. Robinson was unable to provide any additional information."

Bolstering Craig's story is the fact a photograph turned up a few years after the assassination showing the TSBD about ten minutes after the shooting. The Hertz clock on the roof reads 12:40. That picture shows a Rambler station wagon in the traffic on Elm.

Ruth Paine owned a station wagon but it is claimed hers was a Chevy, not a Rambler. But it was Lee Oswald who brought up her name and mentioned a station wagon in reacting to the statement he had been observed getting into a car outside the TSBD.

A person who *did* own a 1962 four-door Rambler station wagon was New Orleans businessman (and JFK conspiracy suspect) Clay Shaw of New Orleans, Louisiana. He insured the Dallas-based vehicle (buying only the required liability policy) through an out-of-town agency for his "son," (though he didn't have one), then canceled the policy after the assassination and presumably when he disposed of the vehicle. Correspondence from the insurance agent confirms all this.

Dorothy Targets Ruth Paine

In her Sept. 15, 1964 *Journal-American* exclusive, Dorothy also discussed what Ruth Paine, Marina Oswald's landlady, and her husband, Michael Ralph Paine—from whom she was separated—had to say of the events of that day. Michael said once he learned of the president's slaying, with the alleged shot coming from the TSBD, he immediately thought Oswald, who was employed there, may have been involved.

"I thought it unlikely that he shot the president, and that the FBI was fully aware of his presence there, and I did not want to contribute to his harassment which would be likely to occur due to his known Marxist views."

Mrs. Paine said she contacted the FBI after she got Oswald the job at the TSBD "but she believed he was working in the annex, not in the building along President Kennedy's parade route."

Why did Ruth Paine inform the FBI of Lee's employment soon after she got him the job? Was she working both sides of the street?

DK added, "But the FBI apparently gave no thought to Oswald's presence in the School Book building." She revealed a twenty-three-page police report submitted to Chief Curry outlined how law enforcement tried to protect JFK and how police came to the conclusion Oswald had shot both Kennedy and Tippit.

Almost everything that would convict Lee Harvey Oswald in the public mind—including the alleged murder weapon, the backyard photos of him supposedly holding a rifle, a page torn from the sporting goods store catalog from which he allegedly bought the gun—all came out of the Paines' garage.

One wonders why someone intending to commit a crime would allow such items to be stored in someone else's garage, instead of destroying the incriminating evidence. Michael Paine's testimony was used to confirm Lee had a rifle, even though Mr. Paine claimed he never realized it was a rifle. Yet he had been in combat artillery in Korea, and then in the Army Reserves for six years. Still, he supposedly could not recognize the feel of a rifle wrapped in a blanket. (No remnants of having been wrapped in a blanket were ever discovered on the alleged assassination weapon—nor hairs or fibers).

In a memorandum the Warren Commission suppressed from its report, J. Wesley Liebler, a commission counsel, stated, "The fact is that not one person alive today (including Marina) ever saw that rifle in the Paine garage in such a way it could be identified as being that rifle."

Michael Paine was an engineering designer who did highly classified work for Bell Helicopter, a major Defense Department contractor and held a security clearance. Ruth's father and brother-in-law had worked for the Agency for International Development in Washington, D.C., regarded by many as a cover for the CIA.

When Lee Oswald's widow, Marina, was asked why she cut off all contact after the assassination with Ruth Paine, the woman she had been living with, and in whose house much incriminating evidence against Oswald was found, Marina explained: "I was advised by the Secret Service not to be connected with her...She was sympathizing with the CIA. She wrote letters over there..." Is it not relevant that released documents show Ruth Paine's sister worked for the CIA, and her father was an informant for it?

Dallas Sheriff Deputy Buddy Walthers took part in the search of the Paine home. Walthers said investigators "found six or seven metal filing cabinets full of letters, maps, records and index cards with names of pro-Castro sympathizers." James DiEugenio has argued that this "cinches the case that the Paines were domestic surveillance agents in the Cold War against Communism."

As lawyer/assassination author Mark Lane commented, "Mrs. Paine and her friends had played a major role in the life of Lee Harvey Oswald. She brought Oswald's wife to Texas from New Orleans, and invited her to live in her home. Oswald came to Dallas from Louisiana because of Mrs. Paine. Mrs. Paine and her friends got Oswald a job in the book depository building on the president's motorcade route. And after Oswald was arrested, Mrs. Paine told him she would get a lawyer for him. He relied on Mrs. Paine to get him an attorney. She never did call a lawyer, and Oswald died, without being able to give his side of the story to [legal] counsel." As of this writing, Ruth Paine is stll alive and continues to be an assassination "celebrity" portrayed in the media as an innocent.

Dorothy Continues To Speak Out

DK was a guest on the October 6 episode of *Hot Line* and came on the show again October 20, 1964. She brought along a copy of the Warren Report, although was only given so much air time to voice her views.

A male caller asked Jackie Robinson, also on the show, what he thought of the Warren Commission's findings. The baseball great, who was likely not an expert on the topic, replied he was satisfied with what was concluded. Dorothy spoke up, summarizing the Click/Whaley story, and pointing out, "The names are not even alike. The whole report is riddled with these contradictions, and indeed, omissions."

A different male caller specifically asked what Dorothy knew of Mark Lane's personal background. She revealed she had met Lane on a couple of occasions and that she knew people who attended his lectures and found them interesting. Giving a middle of the road answer, only revealing so much, she said:

"I am convinced of his sincerity, whether he is right in what he believes anymore than what I am right and what I believe. I don't know. I don't think it has been proven one way or the other."

She went on to describe Lane as "very personable, very forthright, and has a very logical mind." Flattering, but DK was clearly holding back, perhaps wanting to keep her cards close to the vest.

Dorothy Takes Apart Howard Brennan's Testimony

In an article which appeared in newspapers nationwide on Oct. 10, 1964, Dorothy challenged the credibility of Howard Brennan, who supposedly gave police a description of the shooter immediately after the assassination.

She wrote: "Congressman Gerald R. Ford's explanation of the Warren Report in *Life* magazine is a study in contradictions that would make Sherlock Holmes swivel in his grave. In describing 'the most important witness to appear before the Warren Commission' in ten months, Congressman Ford immortalizes H.K. Brennan as 'a neat, Bible-reading steam fitter from Dallas.' One would assume that Mr. Brennan's powers of observation would be more vital to the case than his neatness or his reading habits, but to continue with the 'expert's' report:

"'In the shock and turmoil that followed, Brennan had headed for a policeman and given him a description of the man he had seen in the window. (The assassin). The police sent out a 'wanted' bulletin based on that description. Within the hour, police routinely learned that a Depository employee, Lee Oswald, was missing. By this time Oswald was already in custody for the murder of Officer J.D. Tippit. Tippit had heard the bulletin and spotted Oswald, who had shot him on the spot.'

"So far, swell. But get this:

"'Though Brennan later identified Oswald, his first description—gathered hastily from 120 feet—naturally varied from Oswald's appearance.'

"Naturally. So the hastily gathered description, not at all accurate, caused Officer Tippit to 'spot' Oswald, and thereupon die. If Dallas policemen were challenging suspects from Mr. Brennan's description—'hastily gathered' and 'naturally varied' from Oswald's actual appearance, it is a miracle that more officers in that fair city were not shot by indignant and innocent gun-bearing citizens who happened to fit the erroneous first 'bulletin.'

"Congressman Ford may be a splendid addition to the House of Representatives, but his powers of logic are ludicrous in evaluating a dreadful tragic event."

Howard Brennan's story was suspicious from the start. He was sitting on a retaining wall across the street from the TSBD, one hundred and twenty feet away from the alleged assassin's supposed position.

Brennan testified that after the assassination, he approached SS agent Forrest Sorrels and miraculously outlined that the shooter was white, slender, weighed about one hundred sixty-five pounds and was five feet and ten inches tall. This description was transmitted over Dallas police radio at 12:45 p.m. According to the Warren Commission, Brennan's description of the shooter led to the conclusion the shots came from the sixth floor, southeast corner window of TSBD. But Sorrels said he did not even arrive in Dealey Plaza until 12:55, ten minutes after the description was broadcast. And as Hoover noted a year later, the DPD claimed the description came from an "unidentified man" who saw a suspect "running."

Later, in his Warren Commission testimony, Brennan elaborated that following the assassination, "This man let the gun down to his side and stepped down out of sight...I could see this man from about his belt up...I believe that I could identify this man if I ever saw him again."

Except Mr. Brennan actually failed to pick Oswald out of a police line-up, not once but twice. This despite the fact he admitted "I saw his picture twice on television before I went down to the police station for a line-up." Even more absurd is that at four police line-ups, LHO appeared with two teenagers, a Latino, and men who were older, heavier and even blonde. He also gave his real name, which by this time was widely known. Lee complained bitterly—and justifiably—about the line-up.

Yet W.C. chief legal counsel David Belin continued to insist to *Midwest Today* that Brennan was "the most important witness of all...who not only saw the gunman fire the last shot, he described the gunman."

Intriguingly, declassified files show that no one ever convinced J. Edgar Hoover that the alleged witness Howard Brennan provided this tip. Hoover was not willing to go along with the Warren Commission's finding that credited Brennan as the source for this information.

Joseph Ball, a senior counsel to the W.C., found that in staging a reenactment of the assassination, Howard Brennan would have had difficulty seeing a figure in the window. And his testimony also contained a major error. He said he saw the gunman "standing up and resting against the left window sill." In actuality, with the window only partially open and the sill only a few inches off the floor, the shooter had to fire from a kneeling or sitting position. Considering the fact Brennan sought to estimate the height of the sitting man whom he thought was standing—as well as the man's weight (which he could not possibly provide from seeing only a portion of his body)—his description, motives and veracity are suspect. Notably, Brennan never offered any description of the man's clothes.

Is it not a wee bit suspicious that the tip largely matched FBI agent John Fain's May 12, 1960 memo on Oswald that CIA officer Bill Bright went to great lengths to include in the CIA's Records Integration Division files as being "five feet ten, 165"? The problem is, when LHO was arrested for the minor New Orleans street scuffle in August 1963, he had lost weight—he was 140 lbs.—and measured five feet nine in height. It appears that Oswald was swept into this case by someone with access to the FBI reports or the CIA description of him as "five feet ten, 165", and knew how to get it onto the police radio.

DK had been highly skeptical from the start about Brennan. So one evening, she had her husband, Richard, go to a window on the fifth floor of their Manhattan townhouse, holding a broom handle in his hand to represent a rifle. Then Dorothy walked down the opposite side of the street to a point that was the same distance as Brennan had been from the TSBD window. Despite it being dark, and the lights on in the room where Richard was standing, Kilgallen had trouble seeing him.

Critics have pilloried her for attempting to stage a recreation of Brennan's eyewitness account by pointing out it was dark outside when she did so and hence dissimilar. However, if anything, it should have been easier for her to see a man standing in a lighted upper story window, as opposed to the conditions that existed in Dealey Plaza the day Kennedy was gunned down, with the bright noon day sun overhead, the glare on the outside of the TSBD window glass likely obscuring a clear view inside, and Brennan having to squint upward to see what he claimed to have seen!

Dorothy would have been bemused to read Dallas Police Chief Jesse Curry's candid thoughts about Howard Brennan as expressed in Curry's 1970 book. He said that the "key witness" used by the Warren Commission in concluding that Oswald was a lone assassin had not told a consistent story to the police. He wrote: "Friday night, Nov. 22, 1963, Howard Brennan watched a police line-up...Brennan was unable to make a positive identification of Oswald in the line up. Brennan's later testimony to Federal Bureau of Investigation agents apparently varied from month to month after the assassination. Brennan was later to become the Warren Commission's key witness. At the time of the Warren Commission hearings, Howard Brennan was willing to positively identify Oswald as the man he saw in the windows."

Curry revealed that other eyewitnesses, who said they had seen *two* men standing at the window from which shots were allegedly fired, had been interviewed by the Dallas police and then turned over to FBI agents for questioning. But "no statement about the second man or mention of any accomplice appeared in the FBI report," Curry complained.

Why Was Oswald Even A Suspect?

It is still a mystery why Lee Oswald was a suspect so quickly after Kennedy was killed—even before he had left the TSBD. According to *The New York Times* on Nov. 26, 1963 Dallas D.A. Henry Wade said, "A police officer, immediately after the assassination, ran into the building and saw this man in a corner and tried to arrest him; but the manager of the building said he was an employee and it was all right."

(This account contradicted a Friday night report that Oswald was stopped outside the TSBD as he made an exit, but of course then authorities would have had to explain how he managed to get from the sixth floor to the street level within seconds of his encounter with a cop).

With regard to the scenario of Oswald being confronted inside the building, Wade failed to explain why the officer was going to arrest Oswald, because at that point, no description of the assassin had even been given to authorities by Brennan or anyone else. Of the seventy TSBD employees, why was he singled out?

Obviously Wade was trying to convey the impression LHO had virtually been caught red-handed. He neglected to mention the place in which Oswald was "cornered": the second-floor lunchroom, or describe Lee's demeanor at the time: calm.

The alleged assassin was sipping a soft drink and Jesse Curry let it slip there were "other persons" present. Who were they and why weren't they questioned? This admission was obviously a gaffe by Curry, never to be repeated.

Both building manager Roy Truly and Officer Baker admitted Lee Oswald did not appear to be out of breath. Surely he would have been had he just dashed from the supposed sniper's nest in the southeast corner of the building, wound his way through haphazardly stacked boxes of books en route to the northwest corner (where the staircase was), hidden his murder weapon, run down eight flights of stairs (eighty-eight steps) from the assassin's perch, bought a bottle of soda out of a vending machine in the lunchroom and had time to open it and sip it—and done all this in ninety seconds or less. (This was the estimated time the Warren Commission concluded it took for Officer Baker to encounter him).

If the cop had reason to single out Oswald for arrest for the assassination at that time, it seems unlikely the mere statement by Truly that this man worked in the building would have dissuaded the officer from taking Oswald into custody.

When the shots were fired, TSBD employee Victoria Adams and three co-workers were on the fourth floor looking out the windows, watching the motorcade. Victoria testified she and a colleague immediately ran down the same stairs from the fourth floor at the very time that Oswald is alleged to have been descending them from the sixth, but saw no one else.

Her story is credible and documented by others, but the Warren Commission ignored her and then said she was wrong about the timing.

But Barry Ernest, author of the 2013 book *The Girl On the Stairs*, explained, "In 1999, going through the files on (Victoria) Adams, as I did every time I went to the [National Archives], I found a document that hadn't been there before. It was a letter from Martha Jo Stroud, who was the assistant U.S. attorney in Dallas, forwarded to the Warren Commission: the transcript of (Victoria) Adams' testimony...The key line is the last paragraph where her supervisor...was quoted saying that she saw the building manager and policeman coming up the stairs after (Victoria) Adams and her coworker went down the stairs. The bottom line to that is that (Victoria) Adams went down in advance of seeing the policeman and building manager come up the stairs, proving that she did go down the stairs when she said she did."

Ernest says, "What that means is that Lee Oswald had to be down below the fourth floor before the girls went down, which is impossible based on the timeline the Warren Commission set up for his descent down the stairs."

The W.C. failed to interview the three other women who could corroborate Ms. Adams' account.

So why isn't her story a bigger deal today?

"It should be bigger," Ernest asserted. "This is a story that, in my opinion...is very crucial to the timeline of what the government had of what Oswald did immediately after the shots were fired."

Ernest, who is a former crime and court reporter, reflected, "I can't explain why the media doesn't show more of an interest in the legitimate controversy that's coming out, the contradictions that are coming out by legitimate researchers looking into this."

TSBD employees James "Junior" Jarman and Harold Norman had been standing outside the building, waiting to see the president, when they decided to go inside to get a better view from one of the windows overlooking Dealey Plaza. They said this occurred "between 12:20 and 12:25." Because of the crowd standing on the front steps, the pair used one of the building's rear entrances, where they had to walk past the "domino room"—so called because the floor had a domino pattern. It was one of two rooms where many of the warehouse employees usually ate their lunch. It was located in the northeast corner of the first floor of the TSBD.

A report written by FBI agent James Bookhout said that Oswald claimed to have been in that room and seen the two men, whom Lee described as "Junior" and "a short individual whose name he could not recall but whom he would be able to recognize."

Oswald's claim was very specific: that those two particular employees were in the vicinity of the domino room at a time when he was otherwise alone. He could not have known of their presence unless he too was in or near the domino room at the exact time when Jarman and Norman (the latter of whom was unusually short) entered the building. The two men's testimony buttressed Lee Oswald's contention he was on the first floor of the TSBD moments before the assassination. But the Warren Commission claimed he was lying.

Oswald was in the habit of reading the newspapers, so most likely saw an article in the *Dallas Morning News* on November 20, which stated that the motorcade was scheduled to arrive at the Trade Mart—about five minutes away from Elm Street—at 12:30. This would mean JFK would pass the TSBD around 12:25. Yet LHO was still dawdling downstairs. He told investigators he then went up to the second floor lunchroom briefly to get a soda from the Coca-Cola vending machine there.

Carolyn Arnold, a secretary to the vice president of the Texas School Book Depository, knew Oswald well by sight. She said she saw him in the second floor lunchroom as she was on her way out of the depository to watch the presidential motorcade. She left the building at 12:25 p.m. Her timing of this sighting has been corroborated convincingly by other employees, who noticed when she left her office.

As Ron Rosenbaum of *Texas Monthly* magazine asked: "If Oswald was planning to assassinate the president from the sixth floor, what was he doing calmly eating lunch...floors below, right before the president was supposed to come into view? Could he have been that hungry, that calm? And if that was Oswald in the lunchroom, who were the figures spotted moving around on the sixth floor by witnesses across the street from the building at just about that time?" Ms. Arnold was never questioned by the Warren Commission.

So how did Oswald get from the second floor lunchroom after 12:25 p.m., do all that he was alleged to have done, and gotten back to the lunchroom before Victoria Adams and her co-worker were themselves able to run down old, rickety wooden stairs to the second floor, where he was seen ninety seconds after the shooting calmly sipping a soda? None of the employees on the fourth or fifth floors reported seeing or hearing anyone dash up the stairs immediately before the shooting. And no one was encountered on the stairs afterward.

Jeraldean Reid, a clerical supervisor for the Texas School Book Depository company, recalled that within two minutes of the assassination, after she quickly ran from outside back into her office on the second floor, she also encountered Lee Oswald. She said he came to her door and asked "what is all the excitement about?" She said, "Oh, the president has been shot, but maybe they didn't hit him." She told the Warren Commission, "I had no thoughts of anything of him having any connection with it at all because he was very calm. He'd gotten a Coke and was holding it in his hands...*He was moving at a very slow pace. I never did see him moving fast at any time.*" That doesn't sound like a man who has just murdered the president, knows he has committed a capital crime of earth-shaking proportions, and is in a hurry to flee the scene, does it?

In a report Officer Baker filed with the FBI the next day, he confirmed Lee Oswald was drinking a Coke, as attested to by two competent witnesses. But the words "drinking a Coke" were deleted from the Warren Report, and any reference to the soft drink during Baker's testimony to the W.C. was stricken for obvious reasons: it undermined the Oswald-as-shooter scenario.

Workers had been laying a new floor on the sixth floor until shortly before noon. Because of this task on this date, the sixth floor had the most employees assigned to it of any of the upper three warehouse floors. Not exactly an ideal place for an assassin. Among the employees was Bonnie Ray Williams. After going downstairs to retrieve some food, he returned to the sixth floor and proceeded to eat his lunch until 12:15 or 12:20 p.m. He saw no one else on that floor. How could any assassin(s) be sure no other employees would be on that floor at the moment when the motorcade would pass by the building?

In fact, Williams told the W.C., "All of us were so anxious to see the president, we quit a little ahead of time, so that we could wash up and we wanted to be sure we would not miss anything. Well at the time everybody was talking like they was going to watch from the sixth floor. I think Billy Lovelady said he wanted to watch from up there. And also my friend; this Spanish boy, by the name of Danny Arce, we had agreed at first to come back up to the sixth floor. So I thought everybody was going to be on the sixth floor. [But] nobody came back up." Williams sat up there eating his lunch alone, near the third or fourth set of windows on the sixth floor facing Elm Street. Then he decided to go down to the fifth floor, where he found a couple of his friends.

Whoever the two men were who were observed on the sixth floor by several Dealey Plaza witnesses in the minutes before the assassination must have moved into position very quickly. It is very confounding how they could be sure Williams would finish his lunch and leave the sixth floor in the nick of time for them to go up there and shoot at JFK.

This author has discovered a rare and significant interview with TSBD building manager Roy Truly, conducted by a French journalist. When asked whether it had taken a long time for him and the motorcycle policeman to reach the lunchroom where they encountered Lee Oswald, Truly answered: "Oh, no! It was as soon as the last shot was fired when I saw the officer come running. As a matter of fact, it was so soon afterwards that I don't believe he was riding in the motorcade. He must have been off his motorcycle, standing nearby. Anyhow, it was right away after the shots. I knew they were shots, but had no idea they were fired from the building (even though Truly had been standing on the street directly underneath the sixth floor window)." He said, "I thought the shots came from the vicinity of the railroad or the WPA project." (He means the white pergola).

So too did TSBD Vice President Ochus Campbell, who told a fellow employee "it came from the grassy area down this way..." For the record he said, "I heard shots being fired from a point which I thought was near the railroad tracks located over the viaduct on Elm Street. In fact [I] had no occasion to look back at the Texas School Book Depository building as I thought the shots had come from the west."

In any event, Roy Truly encountered the cop running into his building. "I thought the officer wanted to get to the roof for a better look and I immediately offered to show him how...We took the stairs, the officer ahead of me. When I reached the second-floor landing, the officer was already at the open door of the lunchroom, some 20 or 25 feet away."

That's where the officer ran into Lee Oswald. Roy Truly described Lee as being "cool as a cucumber—although he seemed a little bothered by the gun."

Truly said he and the officer "searched the roof and a small room. Also checked the landing. We could look out over the tracks and the street below. We did not find anything."

Truly continued, "Some 15 minutes later I was checking our employees and I did not find Lee...I then...went up on the sixth floor where Capt. Fritz was and I told Capt. Fritz about Lee being missing and where he lived."

But Truly's timetable is off. Officers did *not* find the gun on the sixth floor that quickly and Fritz didn't arrive until after they did.

His statement is also illogical because Lee Oswald was not the only employee who was "missing" from the TSBD that afternoon. So too were: Jack Caso, president of the TSBD; Gloria Holt, Sharon Nelson, Bonnie Richey, Carolyn Arnold, Mrs. Donald Baker, Judy Johnson, Stella Jacob, Charles Givens, Virginia Barnum, Vida Whatley, Warren Caster, Spaulding Jones, Herbert Junker, Vicki Davis, Dottie Lovely, Mrs. Rudell Parsons, Joe Bergen, Scott Foresman, Maury Brown and John Langston. The list includes nine men besides the women. So why was Oswald singled out?

Who Was The Stranger On The Sixth Floor?

The author of this book discovered a little known affidavit that was part of the secret files of the Dallas Police Department and had been locked up in a safe for decades. It contains a statement by 18-year-old TSBD employee Danny Garcia Arce, which he wrote out longhand in front of a notary public on the afternoon of Nov. 22, 1963 at the Dallas police station.

He explained, "I was working on the sixth floor all morning...The only people I saw all morning was Bill Shelly, Bonnie Ray Williams, Charles Douglas Givens, Billy Lovelady and Jack E. Dougherty. The only [other] person I saw was a real old man, and he had on an old brown suit and a western type hat. I saw this man leave the building and drive off in an old black Buick. The man was not carrying anything in his hands when I saw him. This man was in the building after lunch. This man left in the car before the president was shot. I didn't see any other people in the building but this old man, other than the people that I named that worked there."

Since the topic of Danny Arce's affidavit was the people he encountered on the sixth floor, his mention of the old man implies that's where he saw the stranger.

Who was this man who did not belong in the building, just before Kennedy was killed, and attracted enough attention Mr. Arce apparently followed him and saw him drive off?

When Arce was interviewed by the FBI on Feb. 18, 1964, his story mysteriously changed and he claimed he encountered the old man outside the TSBD about forty five minutes before the assassination and directed him to a public restroom inside the building, after which he saw the man leave about five minutes later. (Note: there were no "public" restrooms in the TSBD). The FBI never challenged the witness over the discrepancy between his first and second accounts. The Warren Commission went with this version in its final report because by then the witness changed the timeframe when he saw this stranger in the building, which made it less problematic for the official story.

But this would mean Arce was outside the building at a time when he was known to be working with others on the sixth floor. He previously stated they did not take a lunch break until 11:55 a.m. and he stayed in the building.

Then when Arce was summoned to the U.S. Attorney's office and questioned on April 7, 1964 by counsel for the Warren Commission, his story changed again. Although he said he directed the elderly man to a restroom, he said this incident occurred ten to fifteen minutes before the assassination. The fact a stranger was in the building just before the president was murdered should have aroused their suspicion, but it did not. He could have smuggled in a gun, for example.

Several Dealey Plaza witnesses claimed to have seen a man in a brown sports coat in a sixth floor window, standing next to a man with a rifle. Could it be the same individual? Lee Bowers in the railroad tower next to the TSBD, saw a man driving around and out of the railroad car park in a black car ten minutes before the assassination with a "mike or telephone" up to his mouth. Bowers received death threats after speaking to the Warren Commission and Mark Lane. On Aug. 9, 1966 he died in a single car accident near Midlothian, Texas, having been run off the road by a black car.

If it had really been an innocuous encounter that had not aroused Danny Arce's suspicions at the time, why did he feel compelled to mention the stranger the day of the assassination in his original, handwritten statement about his time on the sixth floor?

Kilgallen Assails Lax Security At DPD

Dorothy Kilgallen was fixated on the lax security at Dallas police headquarters the morning Jack Ruby killed Lee Harvey Oswald on national television. So she brought up the subject again, months after her original reporting. The official account as propounded by the Warren Commission is Ruby's slaying of Oswald was an impulsive act because he happened to be downtown at the Western Union office that Sunday morning sending twenty-five dollars to a stripper who needed the money, when he noticed a crowd gathered at the police building and made his way over. Ruby claimed he merely walked down the ramp, saw Oswald and impulsively shot him. Defenders of the W.C. embrace this simplistic, nonsensical version of events with a stubborn resistance to suspicious circumstances which point to Ruby's actions as having been premeditated and assisted by key policemen and possibly even a Dallas lawyer.

As previously noted, there had been warnings phoned into authorities that Oswald would be killed. In the middle of the night, the local FBI office and the sheriff received anonymous calls from a person later recognized by Officer Billy Grammer as being Jack Ruby, warning that Oswald would be shot if he was led through the basement. The calls seem nothing less than a desperate, last-minute effort by Ruby to avoid having to kill Lee Oswald.

In a memo to the file dated Nov. 24, 1963, J. Edgar Hoover said, "We at once notified the chief of police and he assured us Oswald would be given sufficient protection." Hoover had also urged the suspect be transferred to the county jail in the middle of the night under the cover of darkness so as to avoid having him be exposed.

Chief Jesse Curry spoke to Capt. Will Fritz about using an armored truck to facilitate Oswald's transfer to the county jail, but Fritz disagreed with that suggestion and insisted a normal car should be used.

Still worried about Oswald's safety, Hoover noted that on Sunday morning, "We called the chief of police again warning of the possibility of some effort against Oswald and again he assured us adequate protection would be given."

Capt. Will Fritz rejected the suggestion of a couple of Dallas officers that Oswald could be secretly brought out from the DPD building by another exit, "leaving the press waiting in the basement, and on Commerce Street." Fritz also had delayed an earlier transfer of the accused assassin late Saturday, claiming he needed to finish interrogating him, even though he had conducted twelve hours of questioning.

On Sunday morning, Fritz kept further delaying Oswald's transfer. Detective Jim Leavelle, one of the men who would be handcuffed to Oswald, later said he never could understand the reason for the nearly one-hour delay in transferring LHO. Was Fritz merely waiting for Ruby to get into position?

Fritz even rejected a suggestion by Leavelle that the patrol car be parked closer to the elevator so as to reduce the distance Oswald would have to walk once he got off the elevator, thus limiting his exposure.

Recall that Fritz is also the one who handled the envelope containing a bullet retrieved from John Connally's thigh wound that went missing.

A well-regarded Dallas attorney, Travis Kirk, told the FBI he suspected Fritz as having "deliberately arranged to have Oswald shot, in order to close the case." According to Kirk, Fritz and Jack Ruby were close friends and Ruby was allowed by Fritz to have complete run at the police station, despite his reputation "of being a hood."

Nancy Rich, a Carousel Club employee observed, "I don't think there was a cop in Dallas that didn't know Jack Ruby. He practically lived at the station. They lived at his place." He employed off-duty officers as bouncers and they could come into his establishment and drink for free. Ruby also supplied women to some of the officers.

Another person suspected of complicity—both in 1964 during the Warren Commission investigation, and in 1978 by the HSCA—was Sgt. Patrick Dean. He was the senior Dallas cop specifically tasked with overseeing basement security for Oswald's transfer. As G. Robert Blakey noted, not only was Dean a good friend of Jack Ruby, he was on "very good terms with prominent organized crime figures" such as Dallas Mafia boss Joseph Civello, who was an operative of Carlos Marcello.

Dean was harshly criticized by W.C. member Burt Griffin for perjury, because of statements that were found to be inconsistent. He also failed a lie detector test.

The most surprising person to have possibly helped Ruby gain access to the basement and successfully finalize his murderous plan was his lawyer Tom Howard. Oddly, he arrived at Dallas police headquarters and walked up to the jail office window precisely when Oswald was brought down to meet his assassin, then turned around and left. Was this some sort of signal Ruby was in position? What was Howard doing there anyway?

Tom Howard was a lawyer for the underworld, who had a good record of defending persons charged with capital crimes, and none of his clients convicted of murder had ever been given the death penalty. Did he help convince Ruby to shoot Oswald with the reassurance he could get him a sentence of only five years at most, or maybe even a suspended sentence, by pleading him before a court as being guilty of "murder without malice" because his crime would not appear to have been premeditated? Incredibly, Texas law had been changed to allow for suspended sentences, as LBJ's henchman Mac Wallace received one after murdering a man, as has been previously noted.

It was Howard who first came up with the idea of Ruby as an "enraged patriot" who supposedly shot Oswald in order to spare Jacqueline Kennedy the grief of testifying at any trial.

Dallas-based FBI agent James Hosty, who had interacted with Lee Harvey Oswald in the months prior to the assassination—and who destroyed, on orders of a superior, a letter Oswald had written him—believed the police were lying about how Ruby gained access to Oswald.

Ruby claimed he simply walked down the ramp from the street level to the basement garage while an officer at the entrance had his back turned. Not likely. The HSCA believed Ruby entered the basement via a stairway accessible from an alley next to the Dallas Municipal Building. Unlocked doors along the stairway route and the removal of security guards from the area of the garage nearest the stairway shortly before the shooting suggested police collusion in the murder of LHO. There is also evidence that the DPD withheld relevant information from the Warren Commission concerning Ruby's entry to the scene of the Oswald transfer.

Jack Ruby, who almost certainly was gay, even though he ran a strip club featuring women, told a friend of his, Russell Moore, that he had no bitterness toward Lee Oswald and thought he was "a good looking guy." He compared him to the actor Paul Newman. Announcer Glen Duncan also said Ruby described Oswald as a "fairly nice looking kid" comparing him to Newman.

By this point in her inquiry, no doubt Dorothy Kilgallen was aware that the night before Kennedy was assassinated, Ruby had dinner at the Egyptian Lounge run by Joe and Sam Campisi. G. Robert Blakey, the chief counsel for the HSCA, later called Campisi "the Number Two man in the mob in Dallas," after Joseph Civello, who in turn was an underling of Carlos Marcello. After Ruby was jailed for killing Oswald, Joe Campisi "regularly visited" him.

Making this tangled situation even more convoluted, is the surprising twist that the third-highest official in the Kennedy Justice Dept., Howard Willens—who helped organize the Warren Commission—not only outlined the Commission's investigative priorities but *shut down an investigation of Jack Ruby's Cuban related activities*. An FBI report states that Willens' father had been a close acquaintance of mobster Tony Accardo, and his next-door neighbor. Accardo had allegedly recruited Ruby and other Mafia associates to make sure that a previous Dallas County Sheriff, Steve Guthrie, would not interfere with the mob's expansion into that city. Willens served as an assistant counsel to HSCA J. Lee Rankin—not a good scenario for getting at the truth.

As Blakey quipped, "It is difficult to dispute the underworld pedigree of Jack Ruby, though the Warren Commission did it in 1964."

In Explosive Memo, Hoover Alludes To Conspiracy

J. Edgar Hoover seethed about the killing of Lee Harvey Oswald while in police custody. He noted in a declassified memo he wrote for his file just forty-five minutes after Oswald was murdered, "It will allow, I am afraid, a lot of civil rights people to raise a lot of hell because he was handcuffed and had no weapon. There are bound to be some elements of our society who will holler their heads off that his civil rights were violated—which they were."

Hoover also wanted to control the narrative of the Kennedy case. Was that an attempt on his part to protect future prosecution(s), or because he wanted to bury the truth? He wrote:

"I dispatched to Dallas one of my top assistants in the hope that he might stop the Chief of Police and his staff from doing so damned much talking on television."

Hoover had a special antipathy toward Will Fritz. He observed: "Chief of Police Curry, I understand, cannot control Capt. Fritz of the homicide squad, who is giving much information to the press." Then **Hoover added a sentence that is of great gravity. He wrote: "Since we now think it involves the Criminal Code *on a conspiracy charge* under section 241, we want them to shut up."**

In the 1964 Warren Report on the Kennedy assassination, Hoover was firm in stating that he hadn't seen "any scintilla of evidence suggesting a conspiracy."

But in the Nov. 24, 1963 memo, Hoover was unequivocal in declaring he thought there had been a conspiracy. He clearly wanted the Dallas cops to keep their mouths shut. But was that just to protect the sanctity of the case until any conspirator(s) could be brought to justice, or did Hoover want to hide the truth from the American public?

His intent is ambiguous because in the same memo J. Edgar wrote

"The thing I am concerned about, and so is [Assistant Attorney General] Katzenbach, is having something issued so we can convince the public that Oswald is the real assassin."

Hoover elaborated, "Mr. Katzenbach thinks that the president might appoint a Presidential Commission of three outstanding citizens to make a determination. I countered with a suggestion that we make an investigative report to the attorney general with pictures, laboratory work, etc. Then the attorney general can make the report to the president and the president can decide whether to make it public."

If Hoover's suggestion had been followed, the FBI's report would have landed in the lap of Robert Kennedy, the attorney general. That would have put RFK in the awkward position of deciding how much information should be released publicly about the death of his brother when the A.G. submitted his recommendation to the new president. Complicating matters was that Bobby surely suspected LBJ as having been involved in JFK's death.

Possibly it was a way of Hoover showing deference to the attorney general due to the magnitude of the tragedy, instead of cutting him out of the loop like LBJ wanted to do. He may have thought Bobby would be upset enough about what had happened to his brother that he would let the chips fall where they may. One thing that Hoover and President Kennedy shared in common was an intense distrust of and deep disdain for the Central Intelligence Agency, which both men thought had gotten totally out of control. J. Edgar obviously suspected that rogue elements of the CIA were involved in JFK's death.

Hoover's actions in the Kennedy case are confusing and inconsistent. He was quick to publicly embrace the lone-assassin storyline, no doubt under pressure from President Johnson to do so. Yet at the same time, he personally stepped into the picture to bring forth very inconvenient and truthful information that his agents dug up. This included challenging the conclusions of the Bethesda autopsy doctors and specifically the nature and location of President Kennedy's wounds; the physical evidence whereby two FBI agents refused to vouch for a bullet supposedly found at Parkland that the Warren Commission considered crucial evidence; and even the shooting scenario the W.C. embraced.

It's true that the FBI director fraternized with people like Clint Murchison, guesting at the Texas oil tycoon's Del Charro Hotel in La Jolla, California for free, and visiting the local Del Mar race track to bet on the horses. Murchison was close to H.L. Hunt, long a suspect in helping finance the assassination of the president.

Yet Hoover's agents also assembled very incriminating evidence in the Kennedy case. It's strange, because the Warren Commission relied on FBI input to reach its conclusions, and yet internal memoranda circulated amongst the upper echelon of the Bureau show that Hoover never subscribed to the W.C.'s main theories.

A declassified Dec. 10, 1963 memo contains Hoover's curt, handwritten remarks about how the Bureau bungled the case. The FBI was receiving criticism for not having more closely monitored the accused assassin, Lee Oswald. Although J.Edgar publicly defended the FBI, privately he wrote "Certainly no one in full possession of all his faculties can claim Oswald didn't fall within this criteria" and should have received closer scrutiny. Hoover was angry because FBI agents in Washington, Dallas, New Orleans and New York all had been following investigative leads regarding various presidential security issues, yet were "flat on their feet" (his words) in the weeks before the assassination.

Dallas FBI agent James Hosty had been in touch with LHO, but failed to follow up. Hoover wrote Hosty's explanation for why he did not was "certainly an asinine excuse." (Later, Hosty claimed he discovered his written answers to the Director had been falsified by someone). In mid-December 1963, Hoover quietly censured and placed on probation at least seventeen agents, including Hosty, for shortcomings pertaining to the JFK assassination. When an internal review of the conduct of certain FBI agents acknowledged they made mistakes, Hoover wrote "They were worse than mistaken." He later expounded, "There is no question in my mind that we failed in carrying through some of the salient aspects of the Oswald investigation. It ought to be a lesson to all."

Incidentally, Section 18 of the U.S. Criminal Code, §241, involves "conspiracy against rights." This makes it unlawful for two or more persons to agree to injure, threaten, intimidate or kill a person in the United States in the free exercise or enjoyment of any right or privilege secured by the Constitution or laws of the United States or because of his or her having exercised such a right. Incredibly, there was no statute on the books in 1963 making it a federal crime to kill the president.

Also significant is that in his memo, Hoover admitted that the FBI had monitored Oswald phone calls and letters, the latter of which "we intercepted, read and resealed." But nothing incriminating was discovered in this surveillance. Hoover conceded the subject of LHO's correspondence with the Russian embassy only concerned obtaining an extension of his wife, Marina's, visa in order that she be able to remain in the U.S. But Hoover worried that "to use all that would reveal our failure to carry out international courtesy laws."

J. Edgar no doubt knew that when it came to how far he could go to really get at the truth of the assassination, he had to tread lightly. The savvy Director of the Bureau definitely knew of LBJ's immersion in corruption. A 1962 FBI report claimed Johnson consorted with "hoodlum interests." He dictated another long memo to the file dated Nov. 29, 1963 in which he recounted a lengthy phone conversation with the president. Lyndon told J. Edgar Hoover he thought of him "more than head of the

FBI" and that Hoover was his "brother and personal friend," that he knew Hoover "did not want anything to happen to his family" and that he had more confidence in Edgar "than anybody else in town." Clearly Hoover wasn't buying any of it and knew full well LBJ was trying to manipulate him. But he probably chuckled to himself, knowing that the only reason Johnson was buttering him up is because he was *afraid* of Director Hoover.

Pataky Claims He Helped Dorothy Write Some JFK Articles

Ron Pataky staked the claim he helped Dorothy write her article about the Warren Commission, adding, "I was interested in the story only because of Dorothy, because she was on it."

Marlin Swing knew of Kilgallen's FBI scrutiny due to her probing into the JFK assassination.

"All of our phones were tapped," he acknowledged. "Because the FBI was trying to figure out how she got the Warren Commission Report before it was published. She went through it and there were several hundred discrepancies—because she had a keen mind—and she picked out many discrepancies she was working on. So we discussed it quite often, that it definitely, in her opinion, was a conspiracy."

He added, "I do know that we had signals, certain signals, that a certain word meant that I should go to a certain phone booth and call her. In other words, it meant that she would go somewhere and call me. Because she knew the phones were tapped."

The Warren Report Is Released To The Public

Finally, the Warren Report was presented to President Lyndon Johnson in a White House ceremony on Sept. 24, 1964 and made public four days later.

The Commission concluded Lee Harvey Oswald was the lone gunman; there were three shots fired at President Kennedy from behind and they originated from the sixth floor of the Texas School Book Depository where he worked; the same bullet hit Kennedy and Texas Governor John Connally. The report also concluded Oswald was not involved in a conspiracy, he and Jack Ruby did not know each other, and Ruby's murder of the accused assassin was a spontaneous act out of compassion for the feelings of Mrs. Kennedy, and that occurred by happenstance.

Not surprisingly, *Life* magazine—which was practically the "house organ" of the CIA—called the Report the "most conscientious documentation of facts" ever assembled. *The New York Times* claimed the Commission's findings were "comprehensive and compelling" and declared that it "should destroy the basis for conspiracy theories that have grown like weeds in this country."

But Sylvia Meager, a research analyst at the United Nations World Health Organization, took a strong interest in the Kennedy assassination and read the twenty-three volumes of the hearings and exhibits, totaling 888 pages. She commented, "It was appalling to find how many of the Commission's statements were unsupportable or even completely contradicted by the testimony and/or the exhibits...I began to list what is now a long list of deliberate misrepresentation, omissions, distortions, and other defects demonstrating not only extreme bias, incompetence, and carelessness but irrefutable instances of dishonesty."

Meager published a vitally important subject index to the W.R. in 1965 to help researchers sort through the maze of disorganized information, and another book in 1967, *Accessories After the Fact: The Warren Commission, the Authorities and the Report*. She was unconvinced Oswald had been a lone gunman and concluded the W.C. had attempted to cover up details of the real people behind the assassination.

Dorothy's Reaction To The Warren Report

After the series of articles Dorothy Kilgallen had written that sent shock waves through the highest levels of the U.S. government, people were naturally eager to learn her feedback.

In a piece which appeared on Oct. 6, 1964, DK acknowledged, "Numerous readers have written to ask about this column's reaction to the Warren Commission report. My only possible answer:

"I have not read the entire Warren Commission volume—have seen only what appeared in the newspapers, and that seemed fragmentary—so I do not consider myself qualified to evaluate the tragic picture. However, from what I have read, I would be inclined to believe that the Federal Bureau of Investigation might have been more profitably employed in probing the facts of the case, rather than how I got them—which does seem a waste of time to me.

"At any rate the whole thing smells a bit fishy. It's a mite too simple that a chap kills the President of the United States, escapes from that bother, kills a policeman, eventually is apprehended in a movie theater under circumstances that defy every law of police procedure, and subsequently is murdered under extraordinary circumstances.

"The Warren Report made a great effort to note that the FBI and the Secret Service were delinquent in their duty, and that the press media—TV, radio and newspaper—also were responsible for the confusion that made Oswald's murder possible.

"Baloney.

"Oswald was not killed by a newspaperman. He was killed by a nightclub owner well-known to the police—Jack Ruby. How can the Warren Commission pretend to forget that?"

For those not alive in the 1960s, it is easy to underestimate the historic importance of Dorothy Kilgallen's challenge to the official findings.

There's one odd postscript to DK's column. She reported the late president's widow, "Jacqueline Kennedy was the rage of Shepheard's discotheque the other night when she appeared at a party given by Mr. and Mrs. E.T. Smith. She was wearing a simple black dress, but it could have been draped of neon judging from all the attention she caused."

It's interesting Dorothy chose to refer to the host couple the way she did, because Mrs. Smith was actually Florence Pritchett Smith, DK's friend and fellow *Journal-American* columnist, who'd had a years-long fling with JFK and owned a home in Palm Beach adjacent to the Kennedy family. Betty Spalding, whose husband Chuck was one of Jack's best friends since 1940, said that for Kennedy, "Over a long period of time, it was probably the closest relationship with a woman I know of."

Florence's husband, Earl, had been appointed Ambassador Extraordinary and Plenipotentiary to Cuba by President Eisenhower in 1957. FBI files reveal over the next two years, John Kennedy made more than a dozen trips to Cuba to rendezvous with Florence. He was often accompanied by a fellow playboy, Sen. George Smathers of Florida, and they weren't there to monitor the volatile situation in Havana. It was party time.

Thomas Paterson, author of *Contesting Castro: The United States & The Triumph of the Cuban Revolution*, writes, "In the 1950s the Batista government vigorously promoted tourism as a hedge against the always precarious sugar trade. Fancy hotels with gambling casinos went up and U.S mobsters shared profits with government officials...

"In search of rum, rhumba, and much, much more, some 300,000 tourists each year flocked to the island to partake in Cuba's bustling life of outdoor cafes, bars, nightclubs, brothels and casinos."

After Batista's ouster, Earl Smith became part of the anti-Castro community in the U.S. Did he and/or Florence offer some insider information to Dorothy about military/political goings-on in that small nation? Her *VOB* contained frequent mentions of Cuba.

Was it a coincidence the same column that contained Kilgallen's reaction to the Warren Report and the reference to Jackie and the Smiths also revealed, "Another anti-Castro invasion army is being organized in Central America, which explains the exodus of so many Cubans from Manhattan..." Had DK been given this insider info by Earl or Florence?

By her standards, Dorothy's reaction to the Warren Report seemed peculiarly anti-climatic, even tepid. Surely the voluminous report contained ample grist for DK's mill.

Instead, she all but stopped writing anything about it for Hearst, other than occasional very brief references that were not substantive. She did, however, take one parting shot at the Warren Commission almost a year later, just before her death.

Kilgallen never published any information she obtained from her private talks with Jack Ruby, but Ron Pataky said that's because she was "saving it for a book." She was under contract to Random House, Bennett Cerf's company, to produce a tome that was supposed to be a collection of stories about the famous murder trials she had covered.

But there would be a second book, claimed Pataky. "It would have been on JFK, the entire assassination. *That's what we were really working on.* Of course, who better to write it? When she got into the JFK thing, as we all know, the world went crazy. But given her background, given the people she spoke with, don't you think the obvious thing would be that that would be the book?" Marlin Swing agreed Dorothy was writing a second book, in addition to *Murder One*.

Ron's comments are important to note because he acknowledged he was collaborating with Dorothy on some of her JFK assassination research. But he did more than that. This author can now reveal by Pataky's own admission in a private conversation with *Midwest Today*, he also met on several occasions with at least two major figures investigating the assassination, and conversed with them at length. This stunning information further solidifies the belief Pataky's purpose for entering Kilgallen's life was not because he was beguiled by her charms, but that he had a mission to monitor her progress in probing the JFK matter. This will be explained more fully later in the book.

Lies, Lies, Lies

There were a large number of disturbing things contained in the Warren Report. It is rather surprising Dorothy did not write about them.

The first was the ludicrous and anatomically impossible "single bullet theory" conjured up by Commission counsel Arlen Specter in April 1964. It had been concluded (likely erroneously) that only three shots had been fired at the presidential motorcade. One bullet was said to have missed, because there was evidence the W.C. could not ignore. A shot hit a curb, a manhole cover and gouged the grass south of Elm. A piece of concrete also hit a bystander, James Tague, near the overpass.

That left only one shot to account for the seven wounds first sustained by Kennedy and Connally, and then one more bullet that struck the president in the head, which was fatal.

Coupled with that was Gov. Connally's insistence the single bullet theory was false: "There is my absolute knowledge that one bullet caused the president's first wound and that an entirely separate shot struck me."

Not one of the more than one hundred eyewitnesses in Dealey Plaza who testified said they thought the same bullet struck both men. Three of the seven commission members also expressed strong doubts about the single bullet theory. Sen. Richard Russell at one point even insisted he would not sign the Warren Report if it adopted that premise. (He did eventually relent).

Highly credentialed forensic pathologist Cyril Wecht, who was the first non-government expert to be given access at the National Archives to Kennedy forensic materials, pointed out, "The impossibility of the bullet flight path from the president's throat to the right side of the governor's back, and the large discrepancies between the wound angles and the postulated firing trajectories. To these could be added the visible difference in the times of reaction by the two men as seen in the Zapruder film and Governor Connally's own testimony that he believed he was hit by a separate shot...Another rifle is required to account for one of the shots."

Furthermore, a shot from the sixth floor of the TSBD would have passed through the left side of Connally's chest, not the right.

"The fact that both wounds were inflicted at substantial lateral angles is also supported by the horizontal elongation of the president's back wound and of the hole in the back of Governor Connally's coat...Moreover, the angles of the wounds in the vertical plane suggest that President Kennedy's wound was inflicted by a bullet fired from a low or intermediate floor, while Governor Connally's was inflicted by a bullet fired from a high floor or possibly the roof."

Though Wecht does not say it, this scenario suggests Kennedy's back wound was sustained from a shot fired from the second floor of the Dal-Tex building, diagonally across the street from the TSBD. It offered a clear view of the motorcade and was not obstructed by trees, unlike the alleged sniper's nest on the sixth floor of the Book Depository.

A 1999 trajectory test in Dealey Plaza, using lasers, determined shots could have been fired from the second-floor window of the Dal-Tex.

A window under a fire escape was open that day and led to a small utility closet—a perfect, hidden firing position for a gunman. There is speculation the bullet fired was undercharged, and that's why it didn't penetrate deeply into President Kennedy's back. Skeptics assert that no witness saw a rifle sticking out of that window. But skilled snipers don't allow a rifle barrel to protrude from a window, unless they are trying to create a diversion from other shooters.

View from Second floor, Dal-Tex with rifle scope.

Deceptively, when the *Saturday Evening Post* published an article about how easy it supposedly would have been for Lee Harvey Oswald to have shot the president, they ran a photo taken from the second floor of the Dal-Tex building, NOT the sixth floor of the Texas School Book Depository.

The angle of Connally's back wound which Cyril Wecht suggests originated at a much higher point could correspond with the Dallas County Records headquarters next door. A 30.06 mm shell casing was later found on the roof when the building was being re-roofed. What possible explanation could there be for a bullet to have ever been fired from any building in Dallas, much less one that overlooked Dealey Plaza?

Besides all this, among the files released in recent years by the Assassination Records Review Board was FBI evidence indicating a 7.65 mm rifle shell (the kind a Mauser uses) was also found in Dealey Plaza after the murder of President Kennedy. Nothing was known about the discovery of this bullet until an FBI evidence envelope, dated Dec. 2, 1963, was released along with other assassination materials. The shell had been removed from the envelope with a note left in its place that stated, "determined of no value and destroyed." Apparently that's because Oswald was alleged to have used 6.5 mm ammunition.

On Nov. 23, 1963, the *Fort Worth Star-Telegram* ran photos in its morning and evening editions of officers looking at what it claimed was a .45 caliber bullet that it attributed to the assassin. The Warren Commission was forced to admit that a shot missed. In case you've been counting, that means evidence of FOUR bullets, each of different caliber, connected to Dealey Plaza (including the one attributed to Oswald). There was also a bullet found in the limo, one on a Parkland stretcher and one in Connally in addition to bullet fragments retrieved from the two men and the car.

Two Suspects Arrested In Dal-Tex Building

With regard to the Dal-Tex location, immediately after the assassination, a man was apprehended in that building by deputy sheriffs and briefly detained. His real name was Eugene Hale Brading, 49, but in September 1963, he'd had his name legally changed to "Jim Braden" out in California. When he showed his new driver's license to authorities, they had no information on him under that name.

But the man had a long rap sheet of at least thirty-five arrests dating back to 1934 and convictions for burglary, illegal bookmaking and embezzlement. It was alleged he was a Mafia courier and had links to Carlos Marcello, Santos Trafficante and David Ferrie. In 1968 Brading was interviewed by the Los Angeles Police Department because of his presence in L.A. near where Robert Kennedy was murdered.

He was not known as an expert marksman or assassin but there is speculation he may have served as a radio coordinator for the shooters, whose role would be to give the signal for the assassins to fire in simultaneous volleys to conceal the true number of shooters and gunshots.

He was an interesting character who over the course of his life had twelve wives!

Though he was a two-bit hood, in February 1964 after the

Kennedy assassination, he suddenly came into considerable money, even helping found a well-known country club that still exists today near San Clemente, California.

But there was another suspect picked up in the Dal-Tex that day—a young man wearing a black leather jacket and black gloves. On a seventy degree afternoon? According to a police file, he "had been up in the building across the street from the Book Depository without a good excuse." However, no record appears to exist of the man or of any interrogation, and he slipped away from the sheriff's office and disappeared. Could he have been a shooter?

Ironically, when Brading/Braden had arrived in Dallas the day before, he had checked in with the U.S. Probation Office, which was required for interstate trips for four years after a convict leaves prison. He gave his real name. Records indicate Brading "advised that he planned to see Lamar Hunt and other oil speculators while here." Lamar was the son of Dallas oil billionaire H.L. Hunt. Mr. Brading remained in Dallas until November 26, when he once again checked in with the probation office prior to his departure from town. What he did during that interval is unknown. But it has been established the night before the assassination, Brading stayed at the swank Cabaña Motor Hotel (that had opened in January 1963 on the Stemmons Freeway). Jack Ruby visited the same hotel around midnight to see some Chicago friends.

Even FBI agents didn't pin down who Mr. Brading really was when they re-interviewed "Jim Braden" in January 1964, and only figured it out later. When New Orleans District Attorney Jim Garrison subpoenaed Brading during a probe into the JFK assassination in 1967, California Governor Ronald Reagan blocked his extradition to Louisiana. Why?

There are other odd stories associated with the Dal-Tex building. Besides owning the TSBD, Harold Byrd, a Texas oil man, also owned the Dal-Tex. It is alleged he allowed the CIA and an Israeli intelligence entity, Mossad, to run ops from and store weapons in those buildings.

Abraham Zapruder, who filmed the Kennedy assassination, also had an office in the Dal-Tex, for his women's clothing business, the same business Israel lied about and claimed a Dimona factory was making clothes for. (Dimona was later known to have been part of a covert Israeli operation to develop nuclear weapons capability. John Kennedy had been warned about this in briefings he was given by the Eisenhower Administration during the transition period before he took office. Kennedy applied pressure on Israeli Prime Minister David Ben-Gurion to allow U.S. inspections, which Israel resisted. JFK was steadfast in embracing nuclear nonproliferation, had signed the Limited Test Ban Treaty with the Soviet Union on Aug. 5, 1963 and made many enemies in both U.S. and foreign intelligence circles with his pursuit of peace.

Another historical coincidence(?): Zapruder had worked closely with Jeanne LeGon de Mohrenschildt, wife of CIA asset and Oswald best friend George de Mohrenschildt. All of them (except Oswald) were members of two alleged CIA fronts: The Dallas Council On World Affairs and The Crusade For A Free Europe, along with other members like George H.W. Bush, H.L. Hunt, Harold Byrd, Clint Murchison and other CIA/oil men, including the woman who swore LBJ in after Kennedy's death, Texas judge Sarah Hughes.

Was it just the hand of fate that Abraham Zapruder happened to be positioned in Dealey Plaza on a four foot high cement riser at precisely the optimum location to film the assassination of President Kennedy, who was killed directly in front of him and between yellow stripes that had been painted on the north side and top of the south curb the day before? Was it another coincidence that these twenty-four inch yellow stripes (for which there has never been any credible explanation) demarcated the "kill zone" and would have been helpful to shooters as "range markers" as well as an aid in target acquisition when one has to utilize a scope? Is it happenstance that after the third yellow mark, any subsequent shots would have been considerably more difficult to achieve?

Witness Jean Hill, who was standing on the south side of Elm even got some of the fresh yellow paint on her shoes (and still has the shoes). Was Zapruder chosen (unwittingly?) to take the unofficial film of the assassination so that it could be doctored by the CIA to portray a cover story of a lone assassin firing from the rear?

A Future President Helps Hide The Truth

Dorothy Kilgallen clearly thought Congressman Gerald Ford, a member of the W.C., was a dolt. She was right.

It was Ford who insisted the panel change its initial description of the bullet wound in Kennedy's back so as to make the single bullet theory more tenable. Ford's handwritten editing, revealed in newly disclosed papers in the possession of the late J. Lee Rankin, legal counsel for the W.C., were released by Mr. Rankin's son, James.

The initial draft of the W.C. findings followed what the autopsy report had concluded about JFK's back wound, and stated, "A bullet had entered his back at a point slightly BELOW THE SHOULDER to the right of the spine."

Ford wanted it to read, "A bullet had entered the BACK OF HIS NECK, slightly to the right of the spine."

The final report said, "A bullet had entered the base of the back of his neck slightly to the right of his spine."

This helped establish a fake trajectory that was part of Arlen Specter's "single bullet theory," which held that a bullet entered the back of the president's neck, passed through the front of his throat, exited and then made a sharp turn to the right in mid-flight to strike the far right side of Connally's back, etc. It is this crazy contention that is the *sine qua non* of the Warren Report. Without it, the whole house of cards collapses and you have evidence of a conspiracy.

Looking closely at the Zapruder film, you can clearly see when Kennedy has been wounded; his fists clench and he brings them up to his mouth and throat as if to cough and his elbows splay upwards. Meanwhile, Connally—who is sitting in front of him—still visibly has his white Stetson hat in his right hand, held by a wrist the W.C. claims had already been shattered. For a man whose body had just been pierced back to front by a bullet that collapsed a lung, took out a rib, struck his wrist and then became embedded in his left thigh, he sure looks unperturbed (Z-frame 230). W.C. defenders claim the governor merely had a "delayed reaction" to being shot. Such an assertion ignores the law of physics: contact with a

JFK's suit shows how far down the back wound was, NOT in back of his neck.

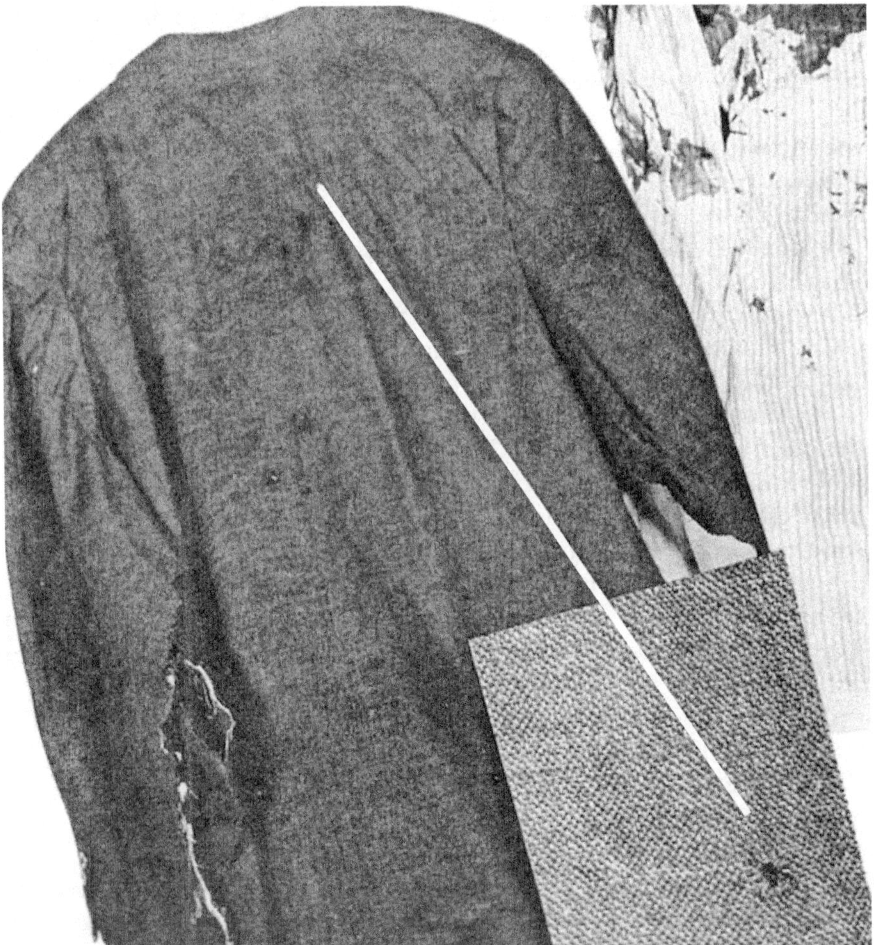

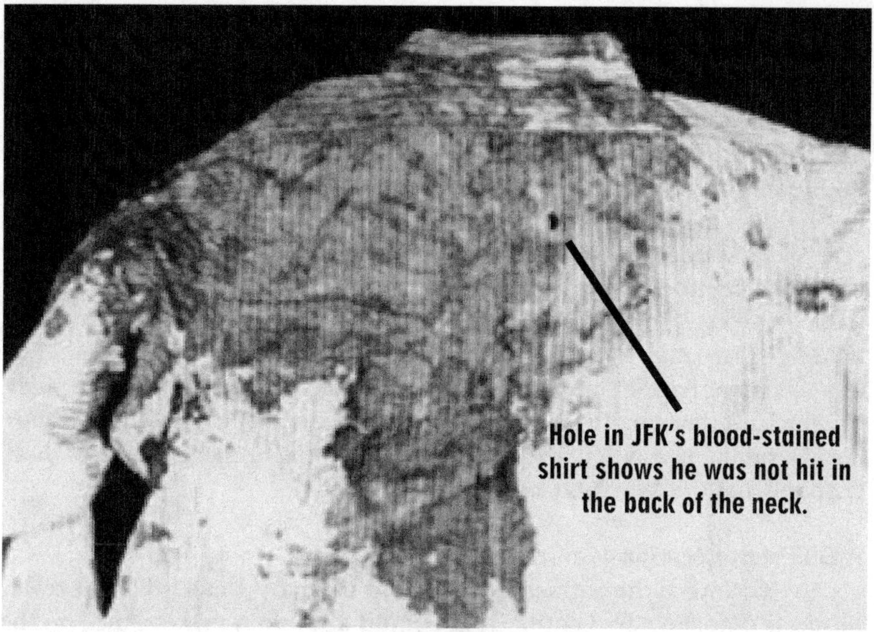

bullet powerful enough to have penetrated and exited his torso, then shattered one of the hardest bones in the body (in the wrist) would obviously have caused Connally's hand to move. But it does not.

Dr. Cyril Wecht pointed out that the radial nerve in the governor's wrist was partially severed, yet "the thumb which holds this large Texas white Stetson that is required for it to be in apposition with the index or index and middle fingers to hold that hat is innervated by the radial nerve. Note that the hat is still being held and Connally is not reacting."

The governor first shows signs of being wounded in Z-237; his right shoulder collapses, his cheeks puff out, his hair is askew. Yet he manages somehow to turn around 180 degrees in his seat and gaze right at the president, perhaps in a shock reaction. Mrs. Kennedy recalled looking at the governor and wondering why he was yelling. Then as Connally turns to face forward again, midway through his turn, he appears to collapse backward toward his wife, on the left, his face visible to Zapruder.

But something happens to the governor beyond that, which is truly puzzling and hard to explain.

Everyone who views the Z-film typically focuses on the fatal head shot to Kennedy. But look at Connally when this happens.

Simultaneously with the explosion of the president's head, as JFK goes backward and to the left, Connally is propelled violently forward, as if someone has tackled him from behind. He bounces off the back of the seat in front of him (where Kellerman is sitting) and then is pulled down by his wife, into her lap. People always focus so much on Kennedy they miss what's happening to Connally.

In his telling of what transpired, his perception was that he was wounded when he started to turn back around to face the front of the car. That could be true, because we see him fall back toward his wife and face the sidewalk. But then he is thrown forward. What accounts for this movement? Granted, Roy Kellerman also moves suddenly forward in his seat but he might have been reaching for the radio underneath the dash. Or was he ducking? Governor Connally may have been shot twice.

How does one interpret this sequence of events? It's not even clear how a bullet ended up in the governor's left thigh after supposedly having passed through his right wrist which, at the time of his wounding, was held up. The trajectory of this wound is unfathomable.

What happened in that limousine has defied clarity for decades, but the least that can be said is that more than one bullet caused the chaos, and Connally was NOT wounded by the first bullet to hit the president, despite what the Warren Commission claimed.

A Different Location For Sniper Fire

Granted, the immediate reaction of many Dealey Plaza eyewitnesses is that shots had come from behind a wooden picket fence on the so-called "grassy knoll" north of Elm and west of the TSBD. As previously noted, hundreds of spectators spontaneously ran toward that area, as if in hot pursuit of the shooter(s). Given the fake Secret Service credentials displayed to various people—including Dallas law enforcement officers right after the assassination—it would seem logical gunfire came from that area. But was it merely a diversion instead?

The problem is, given the documented location of Kennedy's exit wound in the right rear of his head, a shot fired from behind the *corner* of the picket fence closest to Zapruder—where some imagine they can see "badgeman" (dressed in a police uniform) firing a shot, complete with muzzle blast—would have been at the wrong angle.

The fence at that point was at a ninety degree angle to Kennedy's head, which was tilted thirty-four degrees left of center as well as somewhat downward. So it would have been virtually a broadside hit that would not have forced JFK's head rearward, but to the side, with the bullet potentially exiting near Kennedy's left ear and possibly even hitting Jackie.

If you ever visit Dealey Plaza, and go behind the fence (which is no longer the original picket fence but is now a new wooden one), you will realize there is no clear shot at the middle lane of Elm Street (where JFK's limousine was, now marked with an X on the pavement) until the instant of the head shot. The car would be obscured by road signs and a white retaining wall about ten feet in front of the fence, thus preventing tracking of a moving target and no earlier shots. A crowd of people who were lining Elm on Nov. 22, 1963 would also have interfered.

Some have argued that the fatal shot had to have come from a location farther down Elm Street, closer to the railroad overpass. A puff of smoke was seen wafting out from underneath some trees there.

But Kennedy sustained the fatal head wound just after the car passed directly in front of Zapruder, and before it had reached where a stairway comes down the grassy knoll toward the street. An aerial view makes clear that the limousine would have been aimed directly at the south end of the overpass at that point, (*take another look at the Secret Service re-enactment photo on page 234*), and had not yet gone around the last curve. So a shot fired from the extreme right anywhere along the picket fence would not have produced the head wounds that JFK sustained.

The only angle of fire that would have struck Kennedy in the front of the right temple (or the hair line of the right forehead as several witnesses reported) and blasted out the right rear of his head had to come from the south part of the overpass or south knoll area. This is a location that few have considered. Under this scenario, all the activity on the north side of the picket fence was designed to distract from the true location(s) of the sniper(s) toward the south and enable any assailant(s) to escape.

Special JFK assistant and historian Arthur Schlesinger Jr. even commented, "President Kennedy's assassination was the work of magicians. It was a stage trick, complete with accessories and false mirrors, and when the curtain fell, the actors, and even the scenery, disappeared."

Many witnesses (including at least six Secret Service men or sheriff deputies) described first hearing what they thought was a firecracker (which is a sound of very brief duration compared to a gunshot, which is more prolonged). It also sounded different than subsequent shots. This suggests the noise may actually have been a firecracker, intended to divert attention to the right front of the motorcade.

Sherry Fiester was the former head of the Forensic Investigative Unit for St. Charles Parish of the Louisiana Sheriff's Department. She testified as an expert in crime scene reconstruction and bloodstain pattern analysis in over thirty judicial districts in Louisiana, Mississippi and Florida. In her book, *Enemy Of The Truth*, she wrote: "There are standardized procedures for trajectory reconstruction that provide an accurate method to define where shooters are located. However, neither the Warren Commission, nor the House Select Committee on Assassinations used those uniform processes for trajectory analysis...Utilizing those recommended and recognized standards, **the results indicate the shooter was likely near the south end of the triple overpass or the parking lot adjacent to that portion of the overpass.** Addressing the location for the shooter, for that shot with proven scientific concepts, proves mathematically what areas are viable for locating a potential shooter, and *it does not include the grassy knoll.*"

It's crucial to realize that the Zapruder film creates the illusion that the presidental limousine is traveling in a straight line across the screen, but it was not. The lack of background reference points causes your mind's eye to imagine it but the reality is, there is a curve on Elm Street, especially in the area visible in the Z-film. As Zapruder pans his camera left to right, the road curves with him. This obscures the true orientation of the vehicle. In reality, the limo was pointed directly at the south knoll at the time the back, throat and fatal head shots were fired.

The New York Times reported on Nov. 27, 1963 that Dr. Kemp Clark, a surgeon who treated the president at Parkland Hospital and who signed Kennedy's death certificate, said that the fatal wound was "tangential" and it had been caused by a bullet which hit "the right side of his head." This is a view shared by others, including Dr. Robert McClelland who also used the word "tangential." Since at that point Kennedy's head was tilting downward and angled to the left, toward his wife, it was impossible for him to be shot in the right side of his head from the TSBD.

What does "tangential" mean in this case?

A tangential head wound is a specific type of injury caused by a missile grazing the head. It is unique in that forces generated at the point of impact cause more damage than the course of the missile per se.

Contrary to the instructions given to police, a number of spectators were allowed to stand on the overpass directly over Elm Street—the northernmost of the three adjacent roadways. It is possible a gunman equipped with a silencer could have been on the far south end of the overpass, the south knoll (where there was a parking lot), or even underneath the overpass south of Commerce Street (in the same area from which it is most likely the gunshot that inflicted the front throat wound originated).

The limo was on somewhat of an incline, so a shot from the front would likely have enabled a bullet to pass over the windshield and sun visors (which were in the up position) in the open car, and strike Kennedy's head in the right front region, and proceed in a downward trajectory to blow out the right occipital/parietal (rear) area of his skull, taking with it much of the right hemisphere. This is perfectly consistent with the expected effects of momentum, penetration and yaw on deflection.

There was radial and concentric fracturing at the site of entry, appearance and disappearance of backspatter within milliseconds, a trail of metal fragments on the lateral X-ray from the entry in the front of his head, 2.3-inch forward movement in the initial milliseconds followed by the dramatic back and to the left movement in billiard-shot response.

Proponents of the single bullet theory, which postulates a shot from behind, point out that between Zapruder frames 312 and 313, the president's head is propelled *forward* several inches (2.3 inches, according to one analysis), before strongly snapping backwards, beginning at frame 313. Gerald Ford and David Belin dismissed the snap of Kennedy's head and torso backward and to the left as merely a "neuromuscular reaction."

But neurologists say that given the injury to Kennedy's brain, the likelihood of any muscular reaction is very small. Any movement caused by a last-second excitation of nerve impulses would be general and random, and it would not throw the body in any particular direction.

Experts examining the Zapruder film with dissecting microscopes note that the change in direction of the president's body occurs in fifty-six milliseconds. The fastest reflex action known to science—the startle response—occurs in forty to two hundred milliseconds. An eyeblink takes forty milliseconds. Yet the movement of the president's head involves not the negligible mass of an eyelid but the larger mass of a human body previously moving forward under an acceleration of several g's. Of course, keep in mind the previously discussed suspicion that the removal of frames from the Zapruder film speeded up the appearance of JFK's recoil.

As for the initial movement of JFK's head forward, there is a physics concept called "movement into the force." As Ms. Fiester explained in her book, once the bullet enters the skull, if the design of the projectile limits penetration by distortion or fragmentation, the bullet immediately loses velocity. The loss of velocity results in the transfer of kinetic energy demonstrated by the instantaneous generation of temporary cavitation. The higher a projectile's velocity upon impact, the more kinetic energy is available to transfer to the target. The amount of kinetic energy transferred to a target increases with faster projectile deceleration. This initial transfer of energy causes the target to swell or move minutely into the force and against the line of fire. The greater the transferred energy, the more pronounced the forward movement.

More Evidence Of A Conspiracy

It is the testimony of Dealey Plaza witnesses recalling how close together the final two shots were that offers important evidence.

Roy Kellerman, sitting in the front passenger seat of the presidential limousine said, "Let me give you an illustration. You have heard the sound of a plane breaking the sound barrier, bang, bang? That is it. It was like a double bang—bang, bang." A sonic boom. Asked if this sounded different from the first shot, he replied "Yes. Definitely. Very much so."

Agent Sam Kinney agreed the final two shots "appeared to me completely different in sound than the first report and were in such rapid succession that there seemed to be practically no time element between them."

Clint Hill said it was "like the sound of shooting a revolver into something hard...almost a double sound."

SS agent George Hickey said of the final two shots "there seemed to be practically no time element between them."

This view was shared by SS agents Kellerman, Greer, Hickey, Hill, Kinney, McIntyre, Taylor, Sorrels, and Youngblood; sheriff deputies Seymour Weitzman, Luke Mooney and Roger Craig; railroad workers S.M. Holland and Lee Bowers; TSBD employee Joe Milina; Sen. Ralph Yarborough; Robert Jackson, Arnold Rowland, Mary Ann Mitchell, Jean Hill and even Ladybird Johnson—to name just a few who told the same story.

Yet their accounts were dismissed by the Warren Commission, despite the fact what they heard completely obliterates the W.C.'s contention there was only one assassin firing at the motorcade. The last two shots were too close together for that to be true.

Remember, the definition of a conspiracy is that two or more people were involved. Given all the information that has come out since 1963, how could the planning, coordinating and shooting have been pulled off by one person—Lee Harvey Oswald?

Obviously, Dorothy Kilgallen didn't find that plausible, and she continued probing the case until her death in 1965.

Did Ford Get Rewarded By Becoming Nixon's V.P.?

Contrary to Gerald Ford's manipulation of the evidence, it is a certainty that a bullet did not enter the back of JFK's neck. This is based on: (1) Dr. Boswell's diagram on the night of the autopsy; (2) President Kennedy's suit coat, which has a hole about six inches down.; (3) JFK's shirt, which has a hole in a similar location; (4) the death certificate signed by the president's physician, Dr. Burkley; (5) O'Neill's report on the autopsy for the FBI; plus (6) an ARRB release showing Congressman Ford had the final report changed to make it appear as if the bullet had entered the base of Kennedy's neck when it had not.

If JFK was wounded from above and behind, the angle of the shot would be such that—given the holes in his clothing—the bullet could NOT have exited his throat.

One can take the measure of the man by noting Gerald Ford voted against federal aid for education and housing, repeatedly resisted increases in the minimum wage, tried to block medical care for the elderly, consistently fought against measures to combat pollution and later opposed the Freedom of Information Act.

He had so little regard for truth, he unconscionably went around the country making money by giving lectures about Lee Harvey Oswald, a man whom Ford described as "that kill-crazy Communist." Ford contended Oswald killed Kennedy to prove his manhood in the eyes of his wife, Marina, because he was supposedly impotent. (This was just Ford's trash talk, and belied by the fact that Lee and Marina had two children, including a daughter who was thirty-three days old on Nov. 22, 1963).

When Spiro Agnew resigned, Richard Nixon was forced by Congressional leaders to accept Gerald Ford as his replacement, and when Nixon left office, Ford became president. Was this pay back for his having conspired to hide the truth of what happened to John Kennedy?

Ford also absconded with vital records—at least 4,000 pages, ninety-five percent of which were still secret—and all of which belonged to the American public. But they were kept in the sole custody of the Gerald Ford Presidential Library. What was he hiding?

Some have tried to explain away the holes in the JFK's clothing by claiming his jacket and shirt were riding up, making it appear he was struck lower than he was. But no amount of "riding up" could produce holes in his clothing from a supposed wound in the back of his neck. Besides, it is very clear in film footage that Kennedy's shirt can be seen above the suit collar in the proper position.

Collusion By Members Of The Secret Service?

Although the Warren Report was harshly critical of the Secret Service for its failure to protect the president, the Commission didn't go far enough. No one was disciplined for their failure to protect Kennedy.

The SS knew there were active plots in November 1963 against JFK—even including a four man hit squad not apprehended.

Bill Greer alone could have saved the life of John Kennedy. Instead, he wasted time turning around—twice—and looking over his right shoulder after the first shot was fired. He claimed he thought he heard the sound of a "motorcycle backfiring."

Just as any competent driver is capable of slamming on the brakes or stomping on the accelerator to avoid a collision, a Secret Service agent obviously could and should have immediately taken evasive action at the sound of the first shot. But Greer didn't.

Roy Kellerman, who had turned around to his left and saw the president reacting to the first bullet(s), told Greer they'd been hit and to get them out of there. But Greer turned around to look again. Kellerman sarcastically said later that he guessed Greer "didn't believe me."

Greer disingenuously claimed "I didn't really see the president at all" but the Z-film shows Greer saw the president's head explode.

Asked if he had ever slowed the car to an almost stop, Greer said "no, never." Even though the Z-film has been edited and doesn't show this, the Charles Bronson, Marie Muchmore and Orville Nix amateur films aimed at the motorcade from the south side of Elm show otherwise. Multiple eyewitnesses are emphatic that it did. (In fact, he slowed the car to less than five miles per hour).

Jean Hill, who was the closest witness to the car when Kennedy was shot, claimed, "The motorcade came to almost a halt at the time the shots rang out." The perception of James Chaney (one of the motorcycle escorts) was that, "After the shooting, from the time the first shot rang out, the car stopped completely, pulled to the left and stopped." Mary Woodward, a *Dallas Morning News* journalist and eyewitness wrote, "Instead of speeding up the car, the car came to a halt...after the first shot."

Senator Ralph Yarborough, who was riding with Lyndon Johnson, was highly critical of the actions of William Greer. "When the noise of the shot was heard, the motorcade slowed to what seemed to me a complete stop," he said. "After the third shot was fired, but only after the third shot was fired, the cavalcade speeded up, gained speed rapidly, and roared away to the Parkland Hospital...The cars all stopped...[The Secret Service] should be trained to take off when a shot is fired."

Roy Kellerman commented that the custom-build Lincoln Continental was an unusually responsive vehicle. He testified, "I have driven that car many times, and I never cease to be amazed even to this day with the weight of the automobile plus the power that is under the hood; we just literally jumped out of the goddamn road" (the acceleration was so good when Greer finally sped away). Jackie even commented on it.

Greer's own son questioned why his father was even driving the presidential limousine that day and made it clear the agent didn't like Kennedy. Greer was an Orange Irishman (Protestant). JFK was Catholic.

President Kennedy may have survived the assassination attempt if his usual driver had been behind the wheel. But on Oct. 14, 1963, SS man Tom Shipman died unexpectedly. He complained of feeling ill after eating dinner at Camp David. He went to bed and died in his sleep. No autopsy was performed and his wife was told by the president's doctor, Admiral George Burkley, to bury him quickly. Why did he say that? Also, Burkley had no jurisdiction in the disposal of the agent's body.

Shipman was preparing for the Texas trip and planned on having dinner in Dallas with his sister-in-law. He passed his routine medical examination and was pronounced in good health shortly before his death.

A Secret Service Agent Breaks Sixty-Year Silence

In September 2023, SS agent Paul Landis, who was riding on the right rear running board of the SS follow-up car on November 22, broke sixty years of silence with a bombshell revelation. He now admits after arriving at the hospital and helping remove the president from the car, he noticed an intact bullet in the seam of the tufted dark leather cushioning of the back seat where JFK had been sitting. He said he grabbed it to thwart souvenir hunters. He told *The New York Times,* "It was a piece of evidence, that I realized right away [was] very important. And I didn't want it to disappear or get lost. So it was, 'Paul, you've got to make a decision,' and I grabbed it.'"

He slipped it into his coat pocket and headed into the hospital, where he planned to give it to a supervisor, but in the confusion instinctively put it next to Kennedy on his stretcher instead. He assumed it could somehow help doctors figure out what happened.

It is regrettable Landis remained silent about this for six decades, because it allowed the Warren Commission to cover up the fact more than one shooter had to be involved in the assassination.

Landis said he feared he had done something wrong by handling

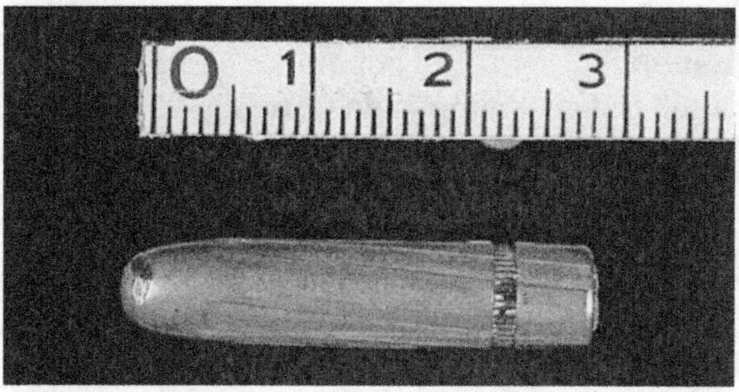

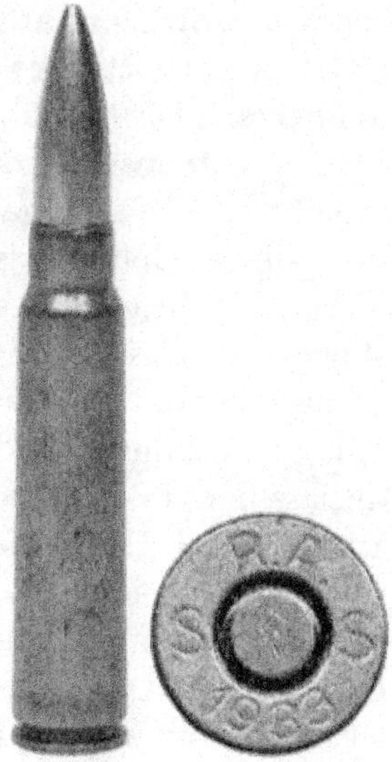

(Above) The pristine 6.5 mm "magic bullet" that supposedly caused seven wounds in JFK and Connally. At right is a 7.65 mm bullet like a Mauser fires.

this piece of evidence, and had been so traumatized by the assassination he couldn't even look at Kennedy's head because he knew he'd "pass out." After JFK's death, Paul was removed from the White House detail and assigned, along with a contingent of other agents, to continue protecting former First Lady Jacqueline Kennedy and her children. He found the experience so emotional that it took a toll on him. So at the age of only twenty-nine, he resigned from the SS in August 1964. He says he deliberately tuned out discussions of the assassination, not even reading any books on the subject until 2014. At that time he confided in Clint Hill about the bullet he'd retrieved from the back seat of the presidential limo, but Hill is alleged to have warned him to keep quiet, lest there be "ramifications."

The Warren Commission claimed the bullet came from Gov. Connally's stretcher, not JFK's. But that isn't true.

The so-called "magic bullet" (CE-399) was said to have been found by hospital maintenance man Darrell Tomlinson, at 1:45 p.m. Nov. 22, 1963, on a stretcher on the ground floor of the hospital. He testified he had brought one clean stretcher down in the elevator and placed it near one that was bloody, in the hallway just outside the emergency room.

Subsequently, when he attempted to reposition them so they wouldn't stick so far out in the hallway, they banged together, whereupon a bullet fell off one of them and onto the floor.

Since Tomlinson had not seen any bullet on the clean stretcher he'd brought down, it stood to reason that it was the bloodied gurney that had contained the projectile.

Furthermore, Kennedy had been pronounced dead forty-five minutes earlier and by this time had been transferred to a casket, so his gurney had been removed from Trauma Room One by an orderly.

But Commission counsel Arlen Specter went to work on the witness Tomlinson and turned what had been his tidy account into a mass of confusion. Specter harangued and browbeat Tomlinson with circular doubletalk and repetitious questioning, so that he got him to basically accede to Specter's fairytale about the bullet coming from Connally.

Tomlinson said that at 1:45 p.m., he contacted his supervisor. O.P. Wright, who in turn gave the bullet to SS agent Richard Johnsen, just before Johnsen left Parkland with JFK's remains. This bullet was given that night to SS head James Rowley in Washington. Later, both Johnsen and Rowley surprisingly refused to identify C-399 as the bullet they handled, because it looked different. Despite an FBI document which claimed that at least Tomlinson and Wright had confirmed the validity of CE-399, a declassified FBI memo dated 6/20/64 from Dallas FBI agent Gordon Shanklin to J. Edgar Hoover contradicts this and says that neither of those two men "can identify [the] bullet." Mr. Wright said in an interview that the Commission exhibit bullet did *not* resemble the one he and Tomlinson had handled. Describing the one they saw at Parkland, he said, "That bullet had a pointed tip." Parkland nurse Patricia Hall concurred. A Mauser bullet, of course, would match the type of rifle initially reported to be found in the TSBD, but which no one has linked to Lee Harvey Oswald.

Paul Landis now says he believes the bullet he retrieved from the limo may have been undercharged, and dislodged from the shallow wound in the president's back, falling onto the limousine seat when the fatal shot(s) struck his head. That's a reasonable hypothesis.

There is corroboration for his account in the form of a video interview from 2013 (that is still on YouTube). Nurse Phyllis Hall revealed that when Kennedy was brought into Parkland, she noticed, "On the cart, halfway between the earlobe and the shoulder, there was a bullet laying almost perpendicular there. But I have not seen a picture of that bullet *ever*, since that day." Obviously, nurse Hall saw the bullet Paul Landis had placed there. And she said that what she saw did not resemble the photos of C-399.

The "official" bullet, which had been fired but was nearly fully intact, was claimed to be positively matched through ballistics analysis to the Mannlicher-Carcano supposedly purchased by Oswald. But there is no proof he fired that weapon.

Importantly, Dr. Joseph Dolce, the U.S. Army's most senior expert in wound ballistics, challenged the pristine nature of the so-called magic bullet. He explained, "One bullet striking the President's neck, the Governor's chest and wrist, should be badly deformed, as our experiments at the Edgewood Arsenal proved." Dr. Dolce was not called to testify before the Warren Commission. The Edgewood Arsenal report, *Wound Ballistics of 6.5–mm Mannlicher–Carcano Ammunition*, was withheld from the public for ten years, and only made available as the result of a lawsuit under the Freedom of Information Act by the researcher Harold Weisberg.

Not surprisingly, neither the FBI nor the Warren Commission interviewed Secret Service agent Paul Landis, despite the fact he was a mere fifteen feet behind Kennedy when the president was murdered. He even had to duck to avoid being hit by blood and brain matter sprayed backward from JFK's massive head wounds.

A Second Bullet Is Found At Parkland

The Landis bullet isn't the only one that turned up at Parkland hospital that day. A bullet that actually struck Gov. Connally was found by a nurse on the second floor, while he was laying on a stretcher next to an operating room. Connally later wrote: "The most curious discovery of all took place when they rolled me off the stretcher, and onto the examining table. A metal object fell to the floor, with a click no louder than a wedding band. The nurse picked it up and slipped it into her pocket. It was the bullet from my body, the one that passed through my back, chest and wrist and worked itself loose from my thigh."

This discovery of a true Connally bullet took place at least forty-five minutes before the nearly pristine "magic bullet" (C-399) was said to be found by hospital employee, Darrell Tomlinson, at 1:45 p.m. on a stretcher on the ground floor of the hospital.

The Connally bullet was also seen by District Attorney Henry Wade, who rushed to Parkland. Wade told the *Dallas Morning News*, "Some nurse (either Mrs. Schrader or Miss Rutherford) had a bullet in her hand, and said this was on the gurney that Connally was on."

The nurse put it in a sealed brown envelope and gave this bullet to DPD patrolman Bobby Nolan. The FBI said that at 7:40 p.m., Nolan turned the envelope over to Capt. Will Fritz at Dallas police headquarters, and thereafter it disappeared.

FBI agents writing an utterly wrong report the day after, November 23, stated that nursing supervisor Audrey Bell handed a "metal fragment" that was removed from the "right arm" of Gov. Connally over to Texas State Trooper Bob Nolan, and no other metal fragment was removed from Connally's body. But there were actually FOUR fragments, and in any event, nurse Bell continued to insist years later to the ARRB that she did NOT handle these fragments. Furthermore, these had nothing to do with the bullet which Connally himself described as having come from his thigh before surgery even commenced.

Incidentally, when political aide Doug Thompson asked John Connally in 1982 if he was convinced that Lee Harvey Oswald fired the gun that killed John F. Kennedy, the governor replied: "Absolutely not. I do not, for one second, believe the conclusions of the Warren Commission." Thompson asked why he had not spoken out about this. Connally answered: "Because I love this country and we needed closure at the time. I will never speak out publicly about what I believe."

Dorothy wouldn't have seen the Zapruder film, because it wasn't shown publicly until 1975, but she took note of witnesses who came forth to contradict the official findings and commented on how they had been intimidated into silence. She obviously had confidential sources in Dallas and elsewhere. Debate about the single bullet theory and the medical evidence was also taking place during her lifetime. We know from insiders close to her DK was ratcheting up her private work probing the JFK matter even as she was publicly playing it cool.

There are other shocking aspects of the cover-up which were known to Dorothy and which no doubt engaged her investigative skills over the coming months. In the decades since, many revelations have been gleaned from declassified government files that confirm the importance and prescience of DK's hard-hitting columns. Later in this book, even more unsettling details will be revealed and it will become more apparent than ever why Kilgallen would have become a target.

Dorothy In Good Humor

As tumultuous as 1964 had been, with so much controversy aroused by the Jack Ruby trial and the Warren Report, Dorothy Kilgallen ended the year with some levity.

The American people voted to give Lyndon Baines Johnson a full four-year term in office as president.

On Nov. 10, 1964 Dorothy admitted in her column, "I am also painfully aware that before the San Francisco GOP convention I went out of my way to announce that if Barry Goldwater were nominated, I would eat my hat in Bergdorf-Goodman's (department store) window. This rash statement was based on nothing except my own 100 percent fallible womanly intuition; I simply did not believe the Republicans would be daffy enough to nominate someone who had absolutely no chance of winning.

"Several readers have written to remind me of my erroneous prognostication, and inquire about the hat-eating. I have taken this up with Mr. Andrew Goodman, and he has promised to have his millinery department whip up a chapeau of cookies, or candy, or something that won't kill me instantly.

"When the date is set, I will notify everyone, including Mr. Goldwater, who deserves a laugh."

12
Dorothy's Final Year Alive

Dorothy traveled to the nation's Capitol to attend Lyndon Johnson's presidential inauguration, which took place on Jan. 20, 1965. Her visit is marked by two key aspects: her enviable wardrobe and her reporting on what she felt were distasteful comedy routines by Johnny Carson and Woody Allen during the inaugural gala. Perhaps the latter being a visible representation of the public debate over censorship.

The outfit she wore to the arctic-temperature inaugural is one example of the voguish wardrobe she kept.

"Women reporters were craning their necks to see columnist Dorothy Kilgallen who showed up in a glittering white chinchilla coat, tight white trousers and white boots," wrote John Mort.

Critiques Johnny Carson, But Defends Lenny Bruce

Dorothy had a high regard for propriety, likely due to her Catholic faith. She was appalled by the off-color jokes she said the new president and his family were forced to endure.

"Johnny Carson bombed. The audience was appalled into almost total silence as Carson, host of a nightly television program, took to the stage directly opposite the President's box and announced he was more effective than birth control pills and made rude remarks about Senator Robert F. Kennedy's ninth child.

"He also poked fun at Texans for wearing spurs with their evening clothes. Very few people even snickered."

She wrote of Allen, "He elected in the guise of comedy, to make heavy points of prejudice deserving of a far more serious setting—and far more serious treatment. He might as well have been talking to himself so far as the fun-filled gala audience was concerned."

Carson was sanctimonious when talking about Kilgallen's criticism. He said on his broadcast his initial reaction was "outrage and hurt." After expansive comments about DK, he concluded by saying, "I have only pity and compassion for her. She is a symptom of a sick society." Scripps-Howard reporter Harriet Van Horne claimed Johnny kept "his dignity." Herb Lyons claimed Carson's "emotional answer to Dorothy on his TV show was sure in good taste."

But plaudits for the late night host were premature. At a White House photographer's dinner Johnny said, "Dorothy Kilgallen took issue with some of my material. That's like having your clothes criticized by Emmett Kelly" (who was a circus clown). "I don't know why Dorothy should take offense at a joke I made. I didn't when her parents made one."

Despite taking offense at what she deemed as profanity-laden shows that were growing in popularity, Dorothy was a defender of free speech stand-up comedian Lenny Bruce, whom she had first seen in Chicago at the suggestion of friends. She wrote of him in April 1964, "The interesting question: Who's after Lenny? True, he uses some impolite words in his act, but the same words have been used night after night on and off Broadway where controversial performances have received respectful reviews by dignified drama critics."

Dorothy testified on behalf of Bruce during his highly publicized six-month Cafe Au Go Go Trial, alongside fellow defenders Bob Dylan, James Baldwin, Norman Mailer and Allen Ginsberg.

In the summer of 1964 Kilgallen told the court Bruce was: "A brilliant satirist, perhaps the most brilliant that I have even seen and I think his social commentary—whether I agree with it or not—is extremely valid and important and I have enjoyed his acts on several occasions. I did not see the one that is in question here, but I read it. Of course, it is impossible to judge completely without having heard his voice and seeing his gestures, but I can say that on the occasion when I saw him I was very impressed with his intelligence, with his material, with his ability to comment on events of the day straight out of a newspaper, which was objectively adlibbed."

When asked about her views on Bruce's usage of swear words in his act, Kilgallen replied, "Well, I think that Lenny Bruce, as a nightclub performer, employs these words the way James Baldwin or Tennessee Williams or playwrights employ them on the Broadway stage for emphasis or because that is the way that people in a given situation would talk."

When Dorothy again appeared on the call in show *Hot Line* in 1965, she got into a debate about censorship. And clearly, as a woman of the press, it was something she vehemently opposed.

"You can't keep a child on a leash. If he has thirty five cents or fifty cents and wishes to walk up to a newsstand and buy a periodical, which you deplore, there is going to come a time when he does that—usually it's just a phase," she said. "If he's had the proper environment at home, and the proper training: religious, moral, whatever you wish to call it, he laughs at it a season later."

She even told listeners her eldest son Dickie had been interested in *Playboy* pin-ups when he was a teenage boy, lining the inside of his closet with them.

"Both his father and I thought it was kind of silly, but we didn't say 'take those down, you're defiling our home with these nude broads, or anything like that.' And now, he thinks it's funny."

Kilgallen would also wage a battle against suppression of information by the U.S. government until the day she died.

The Johnson Inaugural

While DK provided her newspaper with coverage of the inaugural, her mind and heart were with the Kennedys, and not the Johnsons. Charles Simpson would later recall DK telling him she swore she'd never vote in a presidential election again after JFK's murder. Writing on Jan. 21, 1965, DK reflected on Jackie's gentle elegance and maturity during her husband's big moment of just a few years prior.

"She was a new kind of First Lady to all of us. She looked like a princess doll that a good little girl might find under the tree on Christmas morning," Kilgallen enthused.

Dorothy praised the young widow for not attending Johnson's inaugural.

"It was tact. It was a decision of diplomacy and graciousness, it was Lyndon Baines Johnson's day of glory, and she would not have been true to her own high standards if she had arrived like a ghost at the past, distracting attention from Mr. Johnson and his family by her very presence, reminding him and them and the whole world that he is the 36th President of the United States today because the 35th President of the United States, her husband, was gunned down in the Johnsons' home territory, Texas."

Notice DK's subtle little dig—reminding her readers that Kennedy had been killed in the state where Johnson wielded such influence.

The former First Lady's decision not to attend LBJ's inaugural reflected her view of what happened to Jack. Unknown to the public at the time was that on Nov. 30, 1963—mere days after the assassination—Jacqueline and her brother-in-law, Robert Kennedy, used a family friend, painter Bill Walton, to relay a private message about what happened in Dallas to the leaders of the Soviet Union.

JFK had originally asked Walton to travel to Moscow to meet with Soviet artists and take their temperature about cultural exchanges. But in the aftermath of the assassination, Walton's assignment took on a new objective.

RFK arranged for him to meet with Georgi Bolshakov, the man who for more than a year and a half, including during the Cuban Missile Crisis, had been President Kennedy's back channel link between the White House and the Kremlin. The Attorney General instructed Bill to talk with Bolshakov before he checked into the U.S. embassy because neither he nor Jackie trusted the new U.S. ambassador, Foy Kohler. Kohler was a hardliner who thought Khrushchev was more dangerous than Stalin. Bobby later said of Kohler that he didn't regard him as someone "who could really get anything done with the Russians."

So Walton arranged to rendezvous with Georgi Bolshakov at the Sovietskaya restaurant. The message he delivered on behalf of Mrs. Kennedy and RFK was stark. He told the Russian that Dallas was the perfect spot for such a crime, and that they believed the president was the victim of "a large political conspiracy." Despite Oswald's portrayal as loyal to the Soviets, they were convinced JFK was killed by domestic "political opponents." Translated, that implies Lyndon Johnson and his backers.

Bolshakov was deeply moved by this revelation.

At the instruction of Jackie and Bobby, Bill Walton revealed to the Russian agent that national security adviser McGeorge Bundy had run the country because Johnson was out of his depth at the time. Walton also provided an assessment of LBJ that Khrushchev was deeply dismayed to hear when told of the conversation. The Kennedy message was that the selection of Johnson to be vice president was a dreadful mistake and that his close ties to corrupt businessmen would influence his policy agenda.

However, Walton confided that Bobby's plan was to remain as attorney general through 1964, then resign and run for governor of Massachusetts to gain political capital before launching a bid for president. The family wanted Khrushchev to know that only RFK could implement John Kennedy's vision for peace and the strain that might erupt in U.S.-Soviet relations due to President Johnson would not last forever.

On January 27, Dorothy wrote an introspective column reflecting on her and her father's long careers in journalism, in the context of just having returned from covering her fourth presidential inauguration.

"I went around the world in a plane, as the song goes. I visited Vietnam during a relatively quiet period. I learned the protocol of Westminster Abbey and the tinsel rituals of Hollywood.

"But a Presidential Inauguration is something else again. There is no training, no foxiness, no daring, no heroism that can lick the system—which is lack of system. You just get yourself to Washington, prepare to endure any kind of suffering this side of the Iron Maiden, and pray for the best."

She then complained of how the weather in Washington, D.C. is always bitterly cold in January with icy and snowy conditions the norm for the big event. She praised the British for how well-organized press credentials were handled for the queen's coronation and for Princess Margaret's wedding, compared to presidential inaugurations which leave it all to the last minute.

Trouble At Home

DK's friend Marc Sinclaire said one Sunday night in February 1965, as he was doing Kilgallen's hair at her townhouse just before she left to do *WML?*, her married young daughter, Jill, came by and confronted her mother. Jill "was very angry," Sinclaire alleged. She mentioned Ron Pataky by name and, "said that she was highly infuriated because her mother was going out with this man and sleeping with him all over town, and she said 'it's just too embarrassing to be seen in public with you.' And after she left, Dorothy cried. And she said, 'I don't know why Jill wants to behave this way. She knows about her father [and his indiscretions]. I've told her. And she knows a lot of other things.' Dorothy said 'I will never see [Jill] in public again.'"

Dorothy, Richard and daughter Jill.

And she never did.

Were her husband's extramarital activities less flagrant than Dorothy's more public ones?

Marlin Swing felt Kerry was the favorite of Dorothy's three offspring. "Richard, her one son, was kind of a lost cause. He went out to Montana or wherever to find himself, and Jill would have nothing to do with Dorothy because of (her extramarital affairs). She didn't even want to talk to her mother and wouldn't allow her mother to go into buildings that Jill lived in, because she didn't want Johnnie [Ray] to be seen in the elevator or whatever," Swing said. "She had trouble with those two [children] and Kerry caused her no trouble that way."

The Good With The Bad

In March, newspaper readers got a glimpse of another side of Dorothy: artist.

"I've always been interested in art but didn't have courage to paint until I timidly began work on this portrait of a clown, my first picture, for a charity art exhibit," she was quoted as saying. She confessed, "I don't know how I happened to select the subject matter, except that I have always been touched by clowns...especially sad ones...and the whole family seems to like clowns." She produced a 24" x 27" painting that was in a white-washed wood frame.

Artwork by Arlene Francis, Henry Fonda, Durward Kirby, Jack Paar, Jack Carter, Xavier Cugat and Cornel Wilde was also assembled for this two-page feature. She gifted her painting, entitled *The Blue Fireman*, to son Kerry who displayed it on his bedroom wall. The General Electric Company did an exclusive art reproduction of DK's artistic work.

Also that March, a Canadian newspaper, in British Columbia, published this letter to the editor, highly critical of DK's columns. Entitled "DRIVEL AND BILGE" it read:

"Some years ago the *Victoria Daily Times* ran Dorothy Kilgallen's column but then ceased its publication of her literary drivel and bilge. Now she has returned and we are being daily treated to increased dollops of the American scene.

"Now in both pain and anger I ask you, Sir, could we not concentrate more on things Canadian? Are there no Canadian writers who could give us mental refreshment instead of the nauseating outpourings of the Kilgallen pen? Are not people like Dorothy K. simply literary parasites who draw their livelihood from dealing in little snippers about 'show' people, many of whom pay her for keeping their names before the reading public?" Signed H. Cumberbirch

DK's wry humor was on display in a late March piece entitled "Jane's Got That Image Now."

"It's simply amazing the way the gazettes fall for cheap publicity—the most recent being Jane Fonda's nude picture on a billboard. Now her ballyhooers swear she 'doesn't want that image.' Baloney. Salami. A young woman of Jane's age—she isn't 12—doesn't pose for a naked picture unless she expects it to be used for her benefit. She got just what was intended—a lot of free space, so let's not kid the kidders."

In April (and again briefly in mid-June), Dorothy's column was suspended due to illness, with papers running Louis Sobol's column in place of *VOB*. DK having a broken arm was cited as the reason.

It's true she had fractured her left arm in a fall in March 1965. DK detractors love to claim every hospital stay was a result of her having to "dry out" from alcohol and drug abuse. What is the evidence for this?

Dorothy had some chronic health conditions, including serious anemia. That alone could account for several weeks of in-patient care as it is potentially life-threatening and can lead to multi-organ failure.

Earl Wilson wrote DK and Richard celebrated their twenty-fifth wedding anniversary (on April 6) in what had to have been less glamorous digs than the couple had been accustomed: the NYU Medical Center, dining on Chinese food. She "returned to the hospital, after trying to resume work too soon" he said of her condition.

That June, *The New York Times* reporter and critic Jack Gould found time to take a swipe at DK in a column lamenting the cancelation of what was apparently his favorite program.

"Sometimes there does not seem to be any justice in television," he groused. "Much the most delightful program of the past season, *The Rogues*, has been canceled, yet one of its Sunday evening competitors, *What's My Line?* has been signed for another season. Where else but in video could David Niven be dropped and Dorothy Kilgallen renewed?"

Some men just feel threatened by intelligent women.

On June 14, 1965, Dorothy wrote a tantalizing tidbit that proved her devil may care attitude when reporting on mobsters.

"Although gangster Sam Giancana was quoted as making angry remarks after Phyllis McGuire 'talked her head off' to the Chicago investigators into hoodlum activity, one of his close friends in the Mafia still predicts: 'There's going to be a marriage.' Of course, if Phyllis became Mrs. Giancana it might be not only the culmination of a great love but a smart legal move. As his wife, she would not be required to testify to anything detrimental to Sam in any future probe—or trial, if there should be one."

Then on June 22, she wrote an item about Castro, a man she'd been openly critical of since his rise to power. "Fidel Castro is now concentrating on Bolivia, sending arms as well as groups of well-trained mountain fighters who join rebel bands already fighting government troops in remote areas."

This notice, buried in her column alongside the high price of drinks in discotheques, Tony Bennett's movie career and the murder of circus clown Paul Jung, may have been skimmed over by the average reader.

Despite her career as a serious journalist, DK was a TV personality. She appeared regularly on other game shows, including *Call My Bluff*, which ran on rival network NBC. Appearing on the *Match Game*, she and Gene Rayburn served as team captains during the week of June 21-25.

Dorothy and Dick Host Elegant Parties

She was also known for her legendary posh parties. Les Wedman wrote of one over the top affair he attended in June 1965 where DK and Richard played host to one hundred and twelve Twentieth Century-Fox guests, who arrived via two chartered buses, courtesy of the studio.

He mused, "That visit was a mistake because now 112 newspaper publishers, magazine editors, and TV presidents can anticipate 112 demands for pay raises to allow the rest of us to afford even to pay the light bill on an elegant [five] story mansion such as that occupied by Miss Kilgallen, husband Dick Kollmar and their young son."

The writer noted the presence of a security detail at the party. He said there was a "private-eye type looking as conspicuous as a store detective at a convention of shoplifters" plus "two burly strangers" that prevented guests from traveling farther up than the third floor of the townhouse.

"Concern that Miss Kilgallen had slaved over a hot stove preparing for her guests was dispelled by the army of waiters shooting drinks and hors d'ouvres at the visitors. They were in the regalia of a luxurious New York restaurant and catering service, supplying everything from silverware to napkins."

Wedman quoted one party guest as joking, "I could retire if I just held the mortgage on this place."

Wedman continued, "In the midst of the luxurious furnishings is

Party guests were impressed by the opulence of Dorothy and Dick's home.

hi-fi equipment in a fireplace in the den. 'We decided we'd rather have a hi-fi in here than another fireplace,' confided Kollmar, Miss Kilgallen's showbusiness husband, a colorless but friendly individual with an obvious flare for self preservation.

"When he wasn't opening windows to let the smoke out (to reveal plastic greenery in their window boxes) he was removing soggy paper coasters from priceless antique sideboards.

"Every room into which access was permitted had a fireplace—not one of them used. Stairways were festooned with artificial flowers.

"There were bars set up in the dining room and one bedroom, and when it came time to move on, Miss Kilgallen told the white-gloved butler: 'Tell them they can take their glasses with them.'"

Then the guests got back on the party buses that would shuttle them from her townhouse to an off-Broadway Spanish restaurant, followed by a stop at Tavern-on-the-Green in Central Park for further merriment. (The buses were also furnished with bars).

"It was the first affair I'd ever attended where hostess and host left with the invited ones," Wedman quipped.

Guests also attended a swank *soirée* that included luminaries like Trevor Howard and Darryl Zanuck.

Wedman reported that at the end of the evening, "Miss Kilgallen and husband stopped dancing long enough to bid farewell to the thinning ranks of guests and to pish-tush Boston's Margery Adams' candid comment: 'You've made all of us jealous, you know.'

"'It's really nothing,' said Miss Kilgallen—inaccurate again."

Dorothy Embraces Her Irish Roots

Dorothy and her husband traveled to Ireland in the summer of 1965. She was in high spirits based on the content of her columns.

"The first thing to learn in Ireland, except how to get there, is to avoid playing darts in a pub unless you are a professor of higher mathematics with a deadly aim," she mused.

In another piece she waxed poetic about how much she loved the Emerald Isle: "There is something about Ireland, from the charm of the polite people with their lilting voices to the soft beauty of the long summer evening's silver gloaming that is above and beyond the call of most tourist attractions."

She and Richard spent time in Kildare with Tip and Liz Tippett who operated the Melitta stud farm, and also attended a horse race.

"I am a veritable jinx at any kind of gambling and the minute I refrained from placing a pound or two on Liz and Tip's horses the third entry, Gangster, won. I should rent myself out to horse owners for a large fee—not to bet on their entries. I could make a fortune and seal undying friendships."

In July, Kilgallen appeared as a guest star on the *Merv Griffin Show* alongside Anna Maria Alberghetti (ironically the former love interest of Ron Pataky), and Jose Feliciano. But she didn't discuss any of her work on the JFK assassination.

"When DK met Merv Griffin on that occasion, she confined her conversational topics to harmless entertainment stuff, including her recent conversation with Queen Elizabeth's husband Prince Philip, and in 1965, that was considered gossipy and harmless," Kathryn Fauble said. "Prince Philip and DK were among those who attended the London premiere screening of the movie *Those Magnificent Men In Their Flying Machines*. If Queen Elizabeth was there, Dorothy did not include her in the people she identified in her column that attended the screening."

Fauble added Dorothy also appeared on *Nightlife* with the telecast airing late Friday night, July 23, continuing past midnight. The hosts were Les Crane, Dave Garroway and Nipsey Russell. Bob Bach had helped DK secure the spot. As Lee Israel reported, this time Kilgallen had come prepared to discuss the JFK assassination, even bringing along with her a "thick folder full of material." But one of the show's producers, Nick Vanoff, asked her not to bring up the topic due to its controversial nature. At first Dorothy refused, but finally agreed to the demand. Vanoff then instructed Bach to send DK a dozen long-stemmed roses for her trouble.

It was apparent that Kilgallen was eager to publicly discuss the Kennedy assassination—at least during radio and television appearances—even as she refrained from writing about it in her syndicated newspaper work. That intriguing specter raises the question as to whether or not she had been told by her employer—the Hearst corporation—to refrain from stirring the pot for awhile. After all, she had been paid a visit by two agents from the FBI after she got ahold of an advance copy of Jack Ruby's Warren Commission testimony and published it the previous fall.

Frankie Still Pouting

Her long-standing feud with Frank Sinatra continued in his night club act and via her columns. Also that July, she wrote, "The world may be coming to an end. The annual *Downbeat* poll puts Frank Sinatra in 9th place among the vocalists, and everybody knows he's The Leader."

Secrets in Switzerland

In August 1965, a series of notables including Anita Bryant, Cy Coleman, Connie Francis and Robert Goulet filled in for DK, guest writing her column while she was in Zurich, Switzerland on vacation. She stayed at the Grand Dolder Hotel which was very, very opulent. Friends like Jean Bach thought she went overseas to rest and work on her book *Murder One*, which was four years overdue to her publisher. Lawyer Mort Farber was under the impression DK made the journey for cell therapy, a rejuvenation using animal embryo cells.

The Swiss resort where DK holed up, summer '65.

There is another possible reason why Kilgallen may have flown the 3,927 miles across the North Atlantic from New York to get to the Teutonic city of Zurich: because the Swiss have a long history of banking secrecy and client confidentiality reaching back to the early 1700s. Not that DK was stashing money there like a lot of tax dodgers do, but she had something more valuable she may have placed in a safe deposit box—a copy of her research materials for the Kennedy case. Granted, American banks also offer on-premises locked boxes that can be used to store valuables. But in this country, it would be much easier for U.S. authorities to gain access, especially if national security was invoked. In Switzerland, however, Kilgallen could secret away copies of her most important and sensitive JFK papers and tapes and do so anonymously, and thus be far more confident that no one would gain access.

This is a precaution that would have made sense for her to take because she could never be sure her townhouse wouldn't be burglarized, or the papers she carried around with her wouldn't be snatched. Even if she didn't actually acquire such a box in Switzerland, it's probable the thought at least crossed her mind. Because aside from the Alps and Swiss cheese, what is the country more famous for than its strict banking privacy?

Hopefully Kilgallen enjoyed more control over her personal belongings than Lyndon Johnson paramour Madeleine Brown. She was shocked to discover that a safe deposit box she rented had been drilled open from the opposite side and important papers that documented LBJ's connection to her and the son he fathered were missing.

Ms. Brown was the type of source that Dorothy would have loved to have met. She was a mistress of LBJ from 1948 to 1969 and she told *Midwest Today* that Johnson knew beforehand that Kennedy would die.

She spoke with the vice president on the morning of the assassination and "he was cussing the 'Irish Mafia SOBs' and said 'after today' they would never embarrass him again. I saw him next on New Years Eve (1963) after he had become president and at that time I told him 'I've got to put my mind at rest. People in Dallas are talking that you were responsible for the assassination.'" (She stated this conversation took place when she and Johnson rendezvoused at the Driskill Hotel in Austin, TX in room #254. Even today the hotel calls that the LBJ Room).

Brown said, "He told me at that time it was the oil people that I knew and the CIA. And the CIA connection was through the Dallas mayor (Earle Cabell)" whose brother (Charles Cabell) was the number two man under Allen Dulles. Kennedy had fired them both.

Brown recalled that Johnson "was over the CIA during the time that he was vice president. He called it 'the invisible government.'"

Madeleine was a well-connected businesswoman who knew all the movers and shakers and the dynamics of Texas politics. She worked at an advertising agency and her stories have since been investigated and confirmed by others. Her comments about the mayor of Dallas were validated only in 2017 when declassified documents revealed that Earle Cabell was a secretly paid CIA asset. Yet Brown told *Midwest Today* about this in 1991.

It "illuminated that the CIA's extraordinary penetration of domestic American institutions extended to the city where JFK was killed," says CIA researcher Jefferson Morley, who adds, "If anyone had said over the past [sixty] years that the mayor of Dallas in 1963 was a CIA asset, they would have been derided as a 'conspiracy theorist.' Now we know for a fact that he was."

Earle Cabell seemed unusually prepared for questions when he appeared on local Dallas TV immediately after the assassination. As if by rote, he said, "There is no question in my mind that every possible security precaution was taken. Every off-duty officer was called onto duty, we had several hundred reserves who were on duty, we had several hundred of the sheriff's department, and not only had they taken every precaution possible on their own, but worked in very close collaboration with and under the supervision of the Secret Service. It was just one of those things that couldn't happen, but it did." Of course, he lied.

Madeleine Brown spoke of the ongoing investigations into LBJ prior to JFK's death and commented, "Had Johnson not become president, some curious things could have happened to him." She called Mac Wallace Johnson's "henchman."

When asked if LBJ felt guilty about what he had done, Brown commented, "I don't think he felt guilty about anything. He was a great manipulator; he would always say, 'I've done what I've got to do.'"

Brown was hopelessly in love with Lyndon even though she also knew his dark side. He was manic depressive. She wrote a compelling book called *Texas In the Morning* that is now inexplicably out of print. Used copies sell for more than one thousand dollars. But it's worth searching for an affordable copy. Even skeptics will be impressed by Brown's details.

Dorothy was certainly familiar with the cold, hard realities of the book publishing world and how it could be difficult to convince a publisher to take a risk by printing a tome that contained highly charged material.

Maybe Dorothy was even shopping for a European publisher. Recall newspaper coverage that said DK would likely pen some magazine articles about the Ruby trial for European publications—feeling overseas readers would be less inclined to believe the lies and distortions of the U.S. government-based Warren Commission.

Curiously, during her last trip to Switzerland, Dorothy left behind nineteen items of jewelry in the Dolder Grand Hotel safe in Zurich. These items were appraised after her death at more than ten thousand dollars—the equivalent of $96,860 today. When Marlin Swing perused the posthumous inventory of her jewelry, he noticed flower-design diamond earrings set in platinum were missing, and Swing was surprised she would have left them behind as they were her favorite.

Surely DK envisioned returning to Switzerland at some point, and having them remain there also would have kept them out of the hands of any creditors who might seek to levy against her property. Recall there had been some prior costly libel suits.

Meets Up With An Old Flame

In September 1965, Johnnie Ray was booked to perform in New York for the first time in nearly five years, at the Latin Quarter.

Even after their romance cooled, DK remained Johnnie's biggest fan, continuing to give him coverage. Dorothy wrote that Ray was "such a smash in his current Broadway engagement, he's been signed for Las Vegas starting Oct. 5." She was said to have visited him discreetly backstage each night during his booking in NYC. Her ardor for Ron Pataky didn't dampen Kilgallen's enthusiasm for her one great love, "Mr. Cry."

Roughly a month before Dorothy would be found dead, rival newspaper columnist Mary Wood wrote an irreverent article exploring how television shows can influence the intensity, but not necessarily the content, of dreams. She mentioned a friend of hers who "hated" Dorothy Kilgallen and *WML?* but rarely missed an episode. This individual had a violent dream about the panelists being killed.

"Can't you imagine her joy in dreaming that the entire cast of 'What's My Line' is impaled on a giant shiskebab skewer, one by one, with the Lawerence Welk Orchestra playing 'The Ride of the Valkyries' in the background? Naturally, Dorothy Kilgallen would cry the loudest."

One wonders if a slow news day spurred Wood to write the degrading piece.

Her Last Column About JFK's Murder

The last reference DK made in print questioning the official findings of the Warren Commission appeared in syndication in early September 1965, when she challenged the authenticity of the famed image of Oswald supposedly posing with the rifle he used to kill President Kennedy. She also chastised Marina Oswald for vouching for it.

"Those close to the scene realize that if the widow of Lee Harvey

Oswald (now married to another chap) ever gave out 'the whole story' of her life with President Kennedy's alleged assassin, it would split open the front pages of newspapers all over the world. Even if Marina explained why her late husband looked so different in an official Dallas police photo and in the widely-printed full-length picture featured on the cover of *Life* magazine, it would cause a sensation. That story isn't going to die as long as there's a real reporter alive—and there are a lot of them alive."

Sadly, she wouldn't be one of them for much longer.

The controversial photo appears to show the accused assassin holding a rifle in his left hand and a left-wing newspaper in the other, with a pistol in a holster, posing in his back yard.

When initially shown the picture by police, LHO declared it was a fake—that his face had been superimposed on someone else's body. This seems plausible because at first glance, this picture and two others like it look strange.

David Belin, one of the most controversial Warren Commission lawyers, argued to *Midwest Today*, "If you have a negative to a print, and you have the camera, you can determine whether or not that negative came from that camera...It's just as individual as a fingerprint because there are minute differences in the manufacturing of every camera. After Oswald was apprehended and his belongings were searched, we found the camera, we found the negative, and indeed that negative came from Oswald's camera."

But photo lab experts say it would be relatively simple for someone to produce a montage photo using one background scene, a figure with a rifle, and a head shot of Oswald, all of which could be assembled and then photographed using the camera linked to him. Hence negatives from film advanced through the camera would appear genuine.

Suspicions as to the authenticity of the Oswald rifle photos were strengthened in 1992, after the Dallas City Council voted unanimously to open police files on the case. In January of that year, among the materials discovered in a safe were several versions of the photograph depicting Lee Harvey Oswald standing in his back yard with a rifle on his hip.

A negative "mask" of one of the infamous Oswald backyard photos had his image missing and only the background remaining. Since the material represented the intermediate step in making a composite photo, it seemed even more plausible that someone in 1963 had faked the pictures to make the case against him.

One of the newly discovered prints has Oswald's figure cut out as it would be in a darkroom procedure called matting. The technique can be used to impose an image on a photograph.

In response to this startling discovery, long buried in the Dallas Police Department's files, anti-conspiracy polemicists dismissed these materials with the speculation this was nothing more than an attempt by authorities to determine if the photo of Oswald holding a rifle could have been faked. That's a nice, simplistic explanation.

Photography analyst Steve Jaffe did a side by side comparison of two backyard photos supposedly showing LHO holding a rifle. He observed, "Whoever framed Oswald, evidently used only one picture of his face and planted it on someone else's body. Then to give the face on the right a different look, it seems they airbrushed some of the facial features, and tilted the head slightly. In doing so, they tilted the shadow under his nose." (Both photos show the same V-shaped shadow below the nose but on the image that has Oswald's head tilted, the shadow does not adjust for this tilt).

"The body on the right seems to be closer to the camera. If so, the head should be larger. However, you can see—when you slide it over to the face on the left, the faces are the same size. This means the body should be the same height. They are not."

LHO had a somewhat narrow and cleft chin but the chin of the man in the backyard photos is wider and rounder.

The shadows cast by the body are strange. Supposedly both pictures were taken moments apart. So why has the sun moved so much?

The Warren Commission said that the photos were taken by Marina Oswald on March 31, 1963 at the 214 West Neely address.

When the photographs are blown up to the actual height of Oswald (who was five feet, nine inches tall), the rifle in the photograph is too long. When the rifle is adjusted in the photograph to its proper length, Oswald's height is six inches too short.

Furthermore, the strap shown in the backyard photos is different and attaches to the weapon differently than the gun police held up to show the press the night of the assassination.

In these pictures Oswald is wearing a watch but all witnesses have stated that he did not wear one, no watch was found amongst his possessions and he was not wearing one when he was arrested.

The actual camera the alleged photographs were taken with was not found for several weeks but finally turned over by Robert Oswald, Lee's brother. He claimed he discovered the camera at the Paine residence even though the Dallas police had searched the home multiple times looking for it. Robert said the camera belonged to his brother Lee. But it was a reflex camera of very poor quality and Oswald was highly interested in photography. He owned several very expensive cameras worth more than $3,000 (the equivalent of $29,969 today). An inventory of his personal effects includes "one Minox camera." Later the word "camera" was changed to "light meter." The motive for this alteration may have been because the Minox was a "spy camera" not available to the public in 1963. The serial number is untraceable. This would have implied LHO's connections to intelligence activities. The W.C. never explained why Oswald would have his picture taken by a cheap camera for the backyard photos.

Oswald had also taken a series of pics while in Russia that show various subjects the CIA would be interested in but a tourist would not.

Dorothy Visits Las Vegas

Even though Dorothy Kilgallen had made no more references in print to the Kennedy assassination for almost a year, there is ample evidence that throughout 1965, she was still working hard on the case.

"We knew what she was doing. She said this would be the case of a lifetime—a story of a lifetime—that she would prove who assassinated the president," Marc Sinclaire confirmed.

Lee Israel wrote that in October, Dorothy confided in *What's My Line?* makeup man Carmen Gebbia that she was "all excited" about going to New Orleans to meet a source whom she did not know, but would recognize. Did that mean the person had a unique physical characteristic or would be carrying an item which would help to identify him to Dorothy? She said it was "very cloak and daggerish" and would yield details about the assassination. Gebbia told Israel Dorothy said to him many times, "If it's the last thing I do, I'm going to break this case."

Before going to New Orleans, she went to Las Vegas and was there on Thursday, Oct. 7, 1965 and left on an early flight the next morning. She wrote her October 8 column about her visit to Sin City.

DK had been flown there by Joe Levine, who was promoting singer Tony Bennett in his first motion picture role in *The Oscar*. Opening night was staged in the Versaille Room of the Riviera Hotel. Paramount Pictures had also flown in the entire cast of the film. The audience included stars like Jill St. John, Mike Douglas, Milton Berle...and notably, Dorothy and Johnnie Ray. Afterward they repaired to the Portrait Room for a black tie party where stars from the Strip included Vikki Carr, Allan Sherman, Jack Carter and others.

But DK wasn't especially fond of Bennett. Proving that you could always count on an honest opinion from Dorothy, she wrote that Levine, "Ought to do a favor for a friend and tell Tony not to wear a blue shirt with his evening clothes and to forget about the bit in his act where he takes off his jacket, then puts it on again and turns up his shirt collar. He could lose *Rags To Riches* too; that's a dog and always was. My feeling is that if a performer can't get through an hour on the stage without removing his costume (unless he's a stripteaser, of course), he ought to go into some other business. Tony is a fine singer; he hits the notes where they're written and his tempo is perfect, but he has become so rich and successful that no manager or agent or cafe owner will venture to tell him the truth about what's bad in his act. Maybe Joe can do it..."

Ouch!

The real reason Dorothy flew to Vegas—for only the second time in her life—was to see Johnnie Ray's show at the Tropicana Hotel's Blue Room. He opened the same night as the Bennett party and he and DK made their obligatory appearance. He got a good review from the *Los Angeles Times* and in an intriguing interview between shows commented, "I fulfilled an engagement at the Latin Quarter, but I want out of New York...I may locate somewhere...in Oregon, where I own a farm." He said his life was too hectic and he'd decided "never to run to anything again. The year in Spain changed my life. I came home to the United States a free man." Being in the spotlight was always challenging for him.

Trouble in New Orleans

It's likely Dorothy made a stop in New Orleans on her way home from Nevada. It would have been an investigative priority for her because it was the birthplace of Lee Harvey Oswald—who spent much of his last summer there. It was also the home base of mobster Carlos Marcello.

Dorothy had asked hairdresser Marc Sinclaire to meet her in New Orleans. Marc may have been invited to come along, not just to do her hair, but to act as an escort to accompany her out socially. And maybe also be a person who could be told, vaguely, where she was going and when she'd be back, in case she ran into trouble.

He explained, "She didn't tell me why we were going. She just asked me could I go with her, and I said 'yes.' She told me how I was to travel, where I was to go, what I was to do. And I'd never been to New Orleans before, so I didn't know anything about it. We didn't even travel on the same plane together. I went directly to my hotel, we talked [on the phone], and then I went over to her hotel and had dinner. And then I went back to mine. And the next morning, I was supposed to go do her hair and makeup, and she called me at my hotel and she said 'I want you to go to the airport, I've left a ticket for you, and I want you to go immediately back to New York, and never tell anyone you came to New Orleans with me...And don't ask me any more questions.' And I said 'okay' and I left. I did not do her hair."

Had someone or something spooked Kilgallen in the Big Easy?

Pataky opined, "Well I don't think it would have scared Dorothy, I just know her. She would have gotten belligerent before getting scared, but she didn't want Marc Sinclaire, her hairdresser, to be there: 'you go home.' She didn't come home. I think she did stay."

As has been established, Dorothy knew mobsters and counted New York crime boss Frank Costello among her friends. In fact, Marc spoke of the time he accompanied her to "a little tiny restaurant downtown. We went down there for dinner one night and [Costello] was there and he bought us drinks and he was very nice to us. She later told me who he was; I did not know who he was. We were probably safer with him that night than anyplace else we would be."

Asked if DK told him she was intending to pump Costello for information, Sinclaire scoffed and said, "She would never have told me that. NEVER. Yeah, I'm sure he did (give her help). But she would never tell me that she was trying to get something out of him. I'm not sure that we weren't there to see him that night, because it was really off the path for her, down in Little Italy." Meaning the encounter was not happenstance.

It was Frank Costello who—while planning the logistics of an expansion of his New York gambling operation into New Orleans—became aware of Carlos Marcello, then incarcerated in the Louisiana State Penitentiary—Angola—for "masterminding" the robbery of an A&P grocery store. After receiving a gubernatorial pardon, Marcello became available with his brother to help Frank install a few hundred pinball machines and jukeboxes in bars around New Orleans. With silent partner Meyer Lansky as an investor, Costello and Marcello then decided to open up some clubs of their own. The plum property was Beverly Country Club in Metairie.

Costello made his original money from bootlegging. Shortly before his death in 1973, he revealed for the first time that years earlier he had advised Joseph P. Kennedy—an Irish-American patrician from Boston—on how to improve his Scotch smuggling operation.

It's hard to imagine adventurous Dorothy making a trip to New Orleans without talking to Costello first. Stop and think: WHO would have set up the "cloak and daggerish" meeting with a Louisiana source? It's not inconceivable, given the high-profile people whom Kilgallen interviewed during her career, that she may have even convinced her friend Mr. Costello to facilitate a meeting with Carlos Marcello or at least one of his underlings for her sojourn to New Orleans. Not infrequently, an investigative journalist like Dorothy taps sources for "background"—not for public quotation. And Kilgallen no doubt was aware that organized crime knew a great deal about the government, and vice versa. Remember her printed comments hinting at a "coup"—implying LBJ involvement in JFK's death. She told friends "they" weren't willing to tell the truth about Kennedy's murder. She meant the government. So it's clear that she wasn't suspecting the mob per se as being behind the president's death.

Thinking hypothetically, it might even be the fact that Costello had providentially met Marc Sinclaire that, when he found out DK had asked her hairdresser to tag along to New Orleans, he raised the roof and that's why Kilgallen abruptly sent Marc packing.

Obviously, Dorothy had interviewed major criminals before, and Marcello certainly was one. On March 24, 1959, he appeared before the United States Senate Select Committee on Improper Activities in Labor and Management (also known as the McClellan Committee). Chief Counsel to the committee was Robert Kennedy. Marcello pled the Fifth.

The Committee was established on Jan. 30, 1957, and dissolved on March 31, 1960. In that time it conducted two hundred fifty-three active investigations, served 8,000 subpoenas for witnesses and documents, held two hundred seventy days of hearings, took testimony from 1,526 witnesses (three hundred forty-three of whom invoked the Fifth Amendment right to remain silent), and accrued nearly 150,000 pages of testimony.

Marcello liked to classify himself as a "$1,600-a-month tomato salesman who had done well with land investments." The New Orleans Crime Commission uncovered how under Marcello's leadership, the local Mafia made more than one billion dollars yearly from gambling, prostitution, burglaries and some above board businesses, according to the *Washington Post*.

On April 4, 1961, the U.S. Justice Department, on orders from Attorney General Robert Kennedy, arrested Marcello during a routine visit to the immigration authorities in New Orleans.

"Marcello was arrested, handcuffed, whisked away to the New Orleans airport, not allowed to call anyone, and flown to Guatemala City on a government plane," wrote RFK colleague, lawyer Ronald Goldfarb, in the *Washington Post* in 1993. "He had been shanghaied—denied notice or hearing. Within two months, Marcello worked and paid his way back to the United States through Central America; he said it cost him more in Guatemalan payoffs than he ever paid in the United States. In an act of high chutzpah, the INS (Immigration and Naturalization Service) brought an illegal entry case against him. That case was eventually dropped."

On Nov. 22, 1963—shortly after news broke of JFK's assassination—Marcello was acquitted in a New Orleans courtroom. He had been charged with "conspiracy to defraud the United States government by obtaining a false Guatemalan birth certificate" and "conspiracy to obstruct the United States government in the exercise of its right to deport Carlos Marcello." (He was actually a native of Tunis, Tunisia, born to Sicilian parents). He was later charged with "conspiring to obstruct justice by fixing a juror" and "seeking the murder of a government witness," but again was acquitted of those charges.

When asked by this author if he believes Kilgallen's death occurred under mysterious circumstances and whether or not it was linked to the JFK assassination, Goldfarb replied "I have no idea."

On her trip to New Orleans, being the good reporter that she was, Dorothy may well have met with more than one source. Ron Pataky continued to insist, "I know that she met with Jim Garrison." He was the District Attorney there, who would come to national prominence in 1967 when he launched his own investigation into the JFK assassination.

Those who doubt the two met—because Garrison did not become publicly known for pursuing the New Orleans connections to the Kennedy assassination until after DK was dead—overlook the fact that as the local D.A., he would know better than anyone what was going on in his city.

When Kennedy was hit in 1963, Garrison and his team surely did not delay in looking into the possibility that local mobsters were involved.

Next to Miami, New Orleans was the home for the largest influx of Cuban refugees from Cuba after Fidel Castro assumed power in '59. Acting on orders from its Langley, VA., headquarters, the New Orleans office of the CIA developed an extensive network of individuals assigned to engage in guerilla attacks against the Cuban government.

Three days after the assassination of John Kennedy in 1963, Garrison hauled in David Ferrie for questioning. He was a pilot who had been involved in gun-running on behalf of anti-Castro Cubans and burglarizing armoriess. The D.A. had been informed by Jack Martin, a part-time private investigator, that Ferrie had known Lee Harvey Oswald and might have been involved in the assassination. Ferrie told Garrison on the day of Kennedy's murder, he had driven 350 miles to Houston to go ice skating. Garrison handed him over to the FBI, which released Ferrie.

In 1965, Garrison was told by Sen. Russell Long and Hale Boggs—the latter being a former member of the Warren Commission from New Orleans—they believed Kennedy was killed by a conspiracy.

Boggs signed off on, but harbored doubts, about the Warren Report. DK could have paid him a visit during her trip to New Orleans. Boggs perished in a plane crash in Alaska in 1972. The wreckage was never found. Rumors were a bomb was planted aboard his plane. In 1971 he had made a speech on the floor of the House in which observed, "Over the postwar years, we have granted to the elite and secret police within our system vast new powers over the lives and liberties of the people. At the request of the trusted and respected heads of those forces, and their appeal to the necessities of national security, we have exempted those grants of power from due accounting and strict surveillance."

In response to this, Gerald Ford told President Richard Nixon he thought Boggs was either drinking too much or taking pills.

Boggs was the father of the late Cokie Roberts, a political analyst and journalist for PBS and ABC who was a "founding mother" of NPR, who died in 2019.

A Blockbuster Revelation

Ron Pataky said of Dorothy, "I knew she knew Jim Garrison because I remember when I told her 'I was with Jim Garrison' she [said] 'Oh, how was Jim?' So I knew that she knew him."

This author can also report the stunning revelation that Ron Pataky admitted to *Midwest Today* to having personally met at least twice with Jim Garrison—the first time less than two weeks after Ron had met with conspiracy author and lawyer Mark Lane. Pataky revealed he even "sat down a second time with Jim and talked and talked and talked."

This is significant because it establishes that Ron Pataky had more than a casual interest in the Kennedy case, and probably by virtue of his press credentials, had access to figures like Lane and Garrison. It further supports the theory Pataky's mission was to collect as much information as he could about probes being made into the JFK case—Dorothy's being the most prominent among them.

Apparently, Pataky even met Mark Lane before Dorothy did. "It was funny," Pataky mused, "because I mentioned Mark Lane and said 'he was here a couple of weeks ago' and she said 'well I don't know him. I've never met him.' She knew OF him."

However, in the weeks preceding her death, DK surprised Mr. Lane by phoning him at his New York office and inviting him to her townhouse. They met there several times, and Dick Kollmar sat in on a couple of the conversations. Lane recalled Dorothy described how she and Dick tried to re-enact the Howard Brennan scenario.

Garrison On The Trail

One of the most well known probes into JFK's assassination was conducted by controversial Orleans Parish District Attorney Jim Garrison.

Born in Denison, Iowa as Earling Carothers Garrison, he was a graduate of Tulane University Law School. He served in the U.S. National Guard, Army and Army Reserve and was stationed in Europe during World War II. In 1951 he briefly went on active duty. He worked as District Attorney of Orleans Parish from 1962-1973.

Garrison gained international prominence on March 1, 1967, when he arrested and charged New Orleans businessman Clay Shaw with being part of a conspiracy to assassinate President Kennedy. Shaw is the only person to have been prosecuted in connection with the assassination. Garrison believed anti-Communist and anti-Castro extremists in the CIA were behind Kennedy's murder. It is now proven that James Angleton sabotaged Garrison's investigation by illegal means, *in extemis*.

The enterprising DA secured a subpoena of the Zapruder footage from *Life* magazine, allowing the jury to view it (officially) for the first time. (It still was not aired on TV until 1975).

Garrison learned of a dispute between Guy Banister and an investigator, Jack Martin. Banister had worked for the FBI, been an assistant superintendent of the New Orleans Police Department and a private eye.

According to the *New Orleans States-Item* newspaper, Banister "participated in every anti-Communist South and Central American revolution that came along, acting as a key liaison man for the U.S. government-sponsored anti-Communist activities in Latin America."

Banister was implicated in a 1961 FBI raid on a munitions depot in Houma, Louisiana, in which "various weapons, grenades and ammunition were stolen...which were reportedly seen stacked in Banister's back room by several witnesses." The *States-Item* reported an allegation that Banister served as a munitions supplier for the 1961 Bay of Pigs invasion and continued to deal weapons from his office even in 1963.

Banister and anti-Castro activist David Ferrie began working for a lawyer named G. Wray Gill and his client, New Orleans Mafia boss, Carlos Marcello.

Guy Banister used Lee Oswald to try to find Castro's double agents who had infiltrated such groups as the Cuban Student Directorate (DRE), also located in New Orleans. The details remain classified.

On Nov. 22, 1963, Banister pistol-whipped investigator Jack Martin after an argument. Martin went to the police and the press about the incident saying Guy Banister was acquainted with a figure named David Ferrie, an associate of Carlos Marcello. Martin told New Orleans police Ferrie knew Lee Oswald, dating back to 1955 when the two had served together in the New Orleans Civil Air Patrol when Lee was sixteen. Martin said Ferrie may have been Oswald's accomplice in JFK's murder. An odd figure, Ferrie suffered from the skin condition alopecia areata, which led him to don a homemade wig and drawn-on eyebrows.

Less than a week after news of Garrison's investigation made the papers, Ferrie was found dead at his residence from a brain aneurysm, on Feb. 22, 1967. Garrison suspected foul play.

The star witness against Clay Shaw was Perry Russo, a twenty-five year-old insurance salesman from Baton Rouge, Louisiana. Russo testified he had attended a party at anti-Castro activist David Ferrie's home. Russo claimed Oswald, Ferrie, and a "Clem Bertrand," whom Russo identified in the courtroom as Clay Shaw, had talked about killing President Kennedy. The alleged conversation discussed a plan for a "triangulation of crossfire."

New Orleans D.A. Jim Garrison

In December 1966, Garrison interviewed Jack Martin who said in the summer of 1963, Ferrie, Banister and Oswald, plus a group of anti-Castro Cuban exiles, were involved in gun running and burglarizing armories.

Garrison wrote in his book, "The Banister apparatus...was part of a supply line that ran along the Dallas–New Orleans–Miami corridor. These supplies consisted of arms and explosives for use against Castro's Cuba." Note that in the weeks before her death, Dorothy Kilgallen followed that supply line in those three cities.

In 1969, after a thirty-four-day trial, the jury acquitted Shaw.

"The Clay Shaw trial involved strange characters," *The New York Times* wrote in Garrison's obituary in 1992. "One key witness died under mysterious circumstances (Ferrie). Others refused to repeat on the stand the statements that Mr. Garrison's investigators had attributed to them... Several students of the Kennedy assassination said that even though Mr. Garrison's investigation might have been seriously flawed, he served as a positive force in focusing attention on the inadequacies of the Warren Commission and in pressing for the release of many still-confidential documents."

Michael Kurtz, an American professor emeritus of history at Southeastern Louisiana University, wrote in *New Orleans* magazine, "Garrison's failure to prove his case in a court of law delighted defenders of the Warren Commission's lone assassin conclusion, but Garrison did raise certain questions that directly related to the New Orleans connection to the assassination."

One of them "was his accusations against the CIA for engaging in a willful cover-up of its New Orleans-based anti-Castro operations in the spring and summer of 1963. At the time, virtually all pundits and leaders of the national news media scoffed at Garrison's charges, but later developments proved him entirely accurate."

Kurtz elaborated, "A guerilla training camp was located near Bedico Creek, on the north shore of Lake Pontchartrain. There both Americans and Cuban exiles were instructed by CIA agents on guerilla tactics and even methods of assassination, since killing the Cuban leader remained the highest priority of the American intelligence agency.

"The activities carried out in and around New Orleans during the early 1960s became embedded in a morass of intrigue and intelligence operations that hasn't yet been totally untangled because of the continuing refusal of the CIA to release all materials in its possession relating to the assassination. Various anti-Castro Cuban organizations were established in New Orleans and served as fronts of undercover operations."

While Clay Shaw denied under oath having any CIA connection, for a period of eight years, commencing in 1948 and continuing until 1956, Shaw gave the CIA information on thirty-three occasions through its Domestic Contact Service (DCS). He was an observant businessman who traveled frequently, and his fluency in Spanish allowed him to pick up information on commercial and international matters that were useful to analysts for the U.S. government. He provided information about Czechoslovakia (which had been suddenly transformed into a Communist dictatorship). He also gave the CIA info on Central and South America—including Peru and Nicaragua—and interest on the part of Western bloc countries to trade with the Soviet Union. His reports were regarded as "of value" and "reliable."

It turns out that Clay Shaw's work for the CIA continued up to the time of the assassination, as he was on a "cut out" assignment.

This author has reviewed a 1967 memo obtained by the Assassination Records Review Board that also establishes Clay Shaw had been granted a special security approval in December 1962 for "Project QKENCHANT." In a memorandum to the ARRB, dated Sept. 18, 1998, the CIA states the following: "QKENCHANT was the name of a [Central Intelligence] Agency project used to provide security approvals on non-Agency personnel and facilities." In other words, the spy organization was hiring outsiders like Clay Shaw for a "covert" (their word) mission about a year before John Kennedy was killed. What was that all about?

It was revealed in 2017 that James Jesus Angleton, the notorious chief of the CIA's counterintelligence section from 1954 to 1975, was in charge of the CIA's massive—and ultimately successful—clandestine campaign to sabotage Jim Garrison's criminal prosecution of Clay Shaw.

Why was entertainment reporter Ron Pataky having long meetings with Garrison? Was he also helping the CIA gain insight into the prosecutor's work? He surely wasn't assigned to do this for his newspaper.

Why was the CIA so interested in assuring the acquittal of defendant Shaw, unless the assignment he had been given factored into the Kennedy assassination? Besides stage-managing the relentless, hostile media coverage of the New Orleans DA, the CIA's operation also obstructed justice by harassing prosecution witnesses, stealing documents and infiltrating Garrison's office with undercover agents.

Then the federal government brought false charges of corruption against Jim Garrison while he was in the midst of a re-election campaign for district attorney in 1973, and although he was found innocent, he narrowly lost the election. Five years later, however, Garrison won a seat on Louisiana's Court of Appeals.

In a 1976 television interview, Mr. Garrison reflected, "I said three things essentially: I said the Central Intelligence Agency was extensively engaged in domestic espionage; I said secondly, that it was apparent that the CIA was in the murder business; and I said, third, that it was also apparent that part of the CIA was involved in the murder of President Kennedy. New Orleans was an important city for the CIA. We found, as we dug into Lee Oswald's background...that nobody was associated with [him] who was not, one way or the other, connected with the intelligence structure. Whether it was a contract employee of the CIA like Dave Ferrie or Clay Shaw...all the way down to the part-time employees at the anti-Castro adventurers who were employed by the Central Intelligence Agency. So it was a case of our having bumped into so many, one after the other, that this very group of people, as we began to look at them after a year, and put them in perspective with regard to their function, we began to realize that we were dealing with the Central Intelligence Agency."

But Garrison clarified, "Let me put it in perspective where I think it belongs; first of all, when I speak of the Central Intelligence Agency, in connection with the murder of John Kennedy, the [CIA] was not involved as a structure, as an organization. That would be a mistake and I think it would be irresponsible to hold forth that theory. That's not my position at all. But it did become apparent that a part of the Central Intelligence Agency was employed...The CIA is a mansion that consists of many houses. But an important part of it from the Bay of Pigs thereafter were what you might call the alumni of the Bay of Pigs; these adventurists who felt so strongly about regaining Cuba. And many of them were Americans. Now from these people the assassination teams were formed. But the important thing to understand is—that is glossed over—is that these particular assassination teams, to the last man at the tactical level, had come to hate John Kennedy every bit as much as Castro, because they blamed him for the Bay of Pigs failure..."

From Dorothy Kilgallen's numerous references in her columns to information presumably gleaned from anti-Castro Cubans, it is apparent she had an inside track to them. The bottom line is that for DK to have targeted New Orleans by making a trip there in October 1965 as part of her efforts to investigate the JFK murder, made sense. It also made her a target for reprisal and she was dead mere weeks later.

Strange Bedfellows

After Dorothy Kilgallen's autumn 1965 trip to New Orleans, peculiarities were afoot.

Marlin Swing reflected, "I didn't know about that trip. I only heard about that afterward. She stirred up some trouble for herself."

Sinclaire added, "Up until then, I didn't think anyone could touch her."

On Oct. 24, 1965, only two weeks before her death, and just minutes before she was to do *What's My Line?*, an announcement came over the theater sound system that rattled Dorothy. A voice said, "The keys to Ron Pataky's room are waiting at the front desk of the Regency Hotel." No one knew who made the announcement or why somebody hadn't just brought her a note. Kilgallen was so shook up that as the show began and the panelists were introduced, Dorothy sat down too soon, and then quickly got up again—the only time that happened in fifteen years of her being on the show.

That "seems odd" Pataky conceded in one interview with *Midwest Today*. "I remember that story. They weren't my keys. I was not there then." Yet in a subsequent conversation, he admitted he was in the audience that night, adding that Dorothy liked to have him come to the show which he said he did "many times" when he was in town. His admission he was present when the incident happened raises suspicions he was behind it.

Had someone tried to frighten Dorothy with embarrassing personal disclosures? Ironically, she had sent Pataky a letter saying cryptically, "I will try to call you, hopefully before you get this, but it ain't easy." She suggested he visit New York "in late October or early November" so they could have "conferences and all that jazz."

Both of Dorothy's hair stylists, Marc Sinclaire and Charles Simpson, believed their telephone lines were being tapped and that they were being watched while both residing at 400 E. 58th Street in New York City.

They would frequently hear strange noises on the line when making or receiving calls. Plus they were being tailed.

"We used to come out the door and see them across the street and we'd wave at them. We knew they were following us. They'd follow us all over town," Simpson said. "First we joked and said they must be Mafia, but then I said they were CIA. We never figured out who they were actually, and then I moved out of there to the Pickwick Arms Hotel."

Charles Simpson

While residing at the Pickwick Arms, Simpson recalled an incident wherein he was approached by "four men in expensive suits" who "tried to entice me into a room." However, Simpson begged off. "I had a sixth sense and I didn't go in. When I got back to my room after getting something to eat, someone had gone in and gone through all my things. This was while Dorothy was alive, but at that time, I wasn't seeing her much."

Decades later, he said those four men were most likely the same individuals who were always tailing him and Sinclaire on 58th Street. When asked if he felt it was now safe to talk about what he experienced back in the 1960s, he paused for several beats before answering "no."

Simpson recalled how Dorothy would place a pearl Rosary on a little ledge of the second floor of her townhouse whenever he or Sinclaire were flying anywhere, leaving the Rosary there until they returned, for their protection. "She was always gracious," Simpson reflected.

Sinclaire and Simpson were sure the only reason they'd be under surveillance was due to their connection to the outspoken journalist.

"I figured, even though I didn't know anything about the assassination, these people didn't know that. They didn't know what Dorothy may have told us," Simpson speculated.

A Mysterious Trip To Miami

Former CNN television talk show host Larry King confirmed that Kilgallen guested on his Miami-based radio show in the fall of 1965, "a couple of weeks before her death," which would mean late October.

At that time, King was based in Florida and hosted a popular call-in radio show on station WMBM in Miami.

It is a certitude that DK discussed the Kennedy assassination, especially since King was interested in it too. In fact, King met Jim Garrison and helped raise money to fund his efforts. Since Larry King knew mobsters, it wouldn't seem likely he would have done anything to help the investigator of Kennedy's murder if the Mafia had really been involved.

Of course Miami was the nexus of the anti-Castro efforts. The first JFK conspiracy theory to surface after the assassination was promoted by CIA assets trying to blame Fidel Castro for the crime. A special edition of a Miami alternative tabloid published by the "Cuban Student Dirctorate" claimed links between Lee Harvey Oswald and Havana. The Directorate was receiving $56,000 per month from the CIA under a program code named AMSPELL. This was confirmed in 1967 by the CIA's top lawyer.

The Fort Lauderdale *Sun-Sentinel* reported, "Cuban underground sources here claim they have reason to believe Lee Harvey Oswald was in touch with Castro G-2 (intelligence) agents at least three times in the past year." This was proven to be false, but was promoted by "Frank Fiorini," a CIA operative whose real name was Frank Sturgis.

One of Jack Ruby's attorneys, Joe Tonahill, said his last telephone conversation with Dorothy Kilgallen happened "maybe a week before" she died. They planned to participate in a radio talk show about the JFK assassination, so this is another indication she was speaking out again. Author Mark Lane also talked with DK a few days before her passing.

A Deadly Confrontation?

Marlin Swing last saw Kilgallen about a week before she died. "I saw her quite often, but at that point, she was becoming so involved with Pataky, and so involved with working on the Kennedy thing, that she didn't have that much free time anymore," he noted.

Swing added Dorothy worried about her safety "not in a major way, but of course she did."

Marc Sinclaire recalled her telling him that she was going to buy a gun for protection. She was also freaked out when one of the New York newspapers (he couldn't recall which one), ran a photo of her son Kerry, running through Central Park. She wondered why he was chosen. Was that a message to her that somebody was targeting one of her children? On the Sunday night, Oct. 31, 1965 telecast of *What's My Line?*, guest panelist Steve Allen—in introducing DK—commented, "Her little boy is out tonight trick-or-treating in a limousine. How do you like that for class?" John Daly commented that it was a very cold night, so that might have been the reason. More likely is that DK was worried about the physical safety of her young son and that he might be kidnapped.

Sinclaire disclosed that Kilgallen called him on Saturday, Nov. 6, 1965—her final weekend alive. "We talked for about an hour," he said. "Her life had been threatened. I said, 'The only new person in your life is Beau Pataky. Why don't you ask him if all this information that is slipping out about you is coming from him?' Because she was concerned where the people were getting the information. I'm the one that suggested that she confront Beau Pataky with it. I call him 'Beau' (a name for a boyfriend or admirer) because that's what she called him. And she was dead two days later." Sinclaire never elaborated as to what "information" this was.

In response, Pataky claimed the confrontation "never happened." But he admitted the autumn of 1965: "was a funny period in retrospect because I was quick to realize after these things began to come out that there's a lot that Dorothy didn't tell me. Clearly she didn't want to worry me. She danced around problems. She did not want to tell me, for example, that she'd had death threats. She said she had some weird calls. Now these are my words. I'm not sure she said 'weird calls.' I probably said, 'Well what kind of weird calls?' and she said 'Oh you know, the kind we get' and I probably said 'Oh yeah...' That's the way it would have gone down."

DK knew her phone was tapped.

That final Sunday night, before *WML?* aired, Marc Sinclaire styled Dorothy's hair at her home. "She was subdued but no more than usual," he recalled. "She was tired. She was out the night before. But I would imagine that she was upset about Beau. I think he was the snitch, that she was telling him so much, and I think that's what she found out."

Sinclaire continued: "She'd

asked me if I wanted to meet her [later], because she did not have anybody she was going to meet with, and she was not dressing for a date-date. [But] I said 'No, I'm going to a movie.' [So she told me] she was going home after the show."

She had decided to wear a long, white silk filé evening gown and Sinclaire reminded her she had worn it the previous week. But she told him no one would notice. "So I said 'okay.' I helped her into it. She wanted to wear that dress. [It] was cumbersome, because that dress took up the back seat [of the limo]. We always discussed the clothes ahead of time, because...if it was an evening dress, I would do [her hairstyle] more elaborate, than I would do...for a shorter cocktail dress."

He had taken some silk flowers from a vase in Dorothy's home and incorporated them into her hair. But he was stunned to see, when Kilgallen appeared on the program a short time later, she was wearing a different outfit entirely: a low-cut, wing-sleeve short chiffon dress by designer Anne Fogarty (a woman who would go on to wed Richard Kollmar after DK's death). The hairdo Sinclaire had designed for the formal gown didn't look right with the short skirt, especially with the flowers.

"She couldn't take the flowers out because they were woven into the hairpiece," Sinclaire explained. "Obviously [there] was something to make her change that dress at the last minute. I don't know how she pressed the chiffon dress because there was no one left in the house to press a dress like that. After I left, I think she got a phone call [at home] from somebody, and she agreed to meet whoever it was at the Regency. That's my belief."

What man in Dorothy's life was so important, and knew her so well, that he could call her at home on a Sunday night just before she left to appear before millions on live television and make a late date with her for which she rushed to change her wardrobe at the last minute?

No one else comes to mind except Ron Pataky.

Swing said he was not with Dorothy the final night of her life.

"Usually I picked her up after *What's My Line?* and we went to Clarke's. But that particular night, I didn't go over. I don't know why," he reflected.

Her final appearance on *WML?* showcased her astuteness. She phrased questions with her typical shrewdness and correctly guessed the occupations of two of the contestants. However, she did at times speak a bit like she had cottonmouth. Was it mere nerves?

Bennett Cerf recalled before the broadcast, "She read me the preface of the book she was finishing for us at Random House, titled *Murder One*. I told her it was great."

Marc Sinclaire insisted—based on notes Dorothy carried around with her, and that she had opened one time in his presence—"I think *Murder One* wasn't the book that Dorothy had in mind."

Dorothy appeared to be in good health and good spirits on her last show.

Murder One was not intended to be Dorothy's swan song. Marlin Swing confirmed, "She was working on a second book—a different book—yes. And it would have been on Kennedy."

Pataky reiterated, "Her big deal—right up to the time of her death—was a book on the Warren Commission Report...It wasn't on Jack Kennedy per se, it was on ALL of the players. That was the thing."

Arlene Francis subsequently reflected, "That was the only night, in all the years we did the show, that Dorothy didn't kiss me on the cheek when she said good night."

It seemed she was preoccupied with something else.

After the show, Dorothy was observed getting into her Cadillac limousine alone. Kathryn Stone, one of the contestants on that night's broadcast, had traveled to New York City with a couple of friends. The male friend opened the door to the limo for DK, and she thanked him.

Kilgallen then went to P.J. Clarke's to meet Bob Bach, a *What's My Line?* producer, for a quick drink, as was her custom. She had told him in the past the Warren Commission Report was "laughable" and vowed she would "break the real story and have the biggest scoop of the century."

Clarke's confirmed Dorothy ordered her usual—vodka and tonic. She told Bach she had a "late date." Bach and Kilgallen were on a "don't ask, don't tell" basis regarding each other's personal affairs. He then walked his colleague to her car, "under the impression" she was headed to meet Ron Pataky.

In pondering the matter of Dorothy's "late date," one has to wonder: why couldn't the man have met her immediately after the show ended? Obviously, he couldn't, because she went first to P.J. Clarke's for a drink with Bob Bach. Then, at some point, she later excused herself and headed over to the Regency Hotel bar. DK wasn't dating anyone other than Ron Pataky. Her occasional encounters with Johnnie Ray were few and far between, even though Phyllis McGuire claimed to have seen Kilgallen dancing with Johnnie about three nights before her death, (a timeline which may not be precisely accurate).

In a statement that comes close to confirming at least part of the scenario theorized here, Ron Pataky told *Midwest Today*, "I think I talked to her that night early."

That is likely correct. But he didn't tell the rest of the story—that she confronted him with her suspicions (that Marc Sinclaire had planted in her mind). Ron probably assured her he would catch the first plane and fly to New York City yet that night to see her to clear the air.

Since it would have only taken about one hour and fifty minutes flight time to get from Columbus, Ohio to New York City, it's easily possible Ron Pataky could have boarded a plane that evening and flown to NYC while Dorothy was on TV. Then it would have taken him about fifty minutes to get from what was popularly still called Idlewild Airport (but had been re-named John F. Kennedy International following JFK's death) in Queens, to the Regency, located at 540 Park Avenue.

That would explain why Dorothy had to kill a little time before meeting Ron at the Regency post-midnight.

When Pataky admitted speaking with Kilgallen on the phone Sunday night, he was asked if she sounded suicidal. He replied: "No! No! The last time I talked to her, she was just normal. She always called herself my New York secretary and Suzie Creamcheese. 'This is your New York secretary reporting in.' That's how every call began from her."

Pataky added, "The last time I spoke with her, she was in great spirits. If you ever lose someone close to you, you will remember the last time you spoke with them."

He observed, "[The] Marina Oswald thing was two months before she died. Around the time she died, there were no big stories hanging around. I'd seen her through the Warren Commission thing."

This statement contradicts what others close to DK readily knew: her investigation of the JFK assassination had heated up, even though she was not writing about it publicly.

Katherine Stone from Madisonville, Kentucky, who had just appeared as a contestant on *What's My Line?* (she sold dynamite), was invited by the show's staff to join them for cocktails at the Regency. She rode over in a CBS limo. She remembered walking into the opulent piano bar, which was decorated in red, and located in the basement of the hotel.

"When we got there, there was this man sitting right next to [Dorothy]...and I mean close, because they were talking," Ms. Stone explained with a southern twang, in a videotaped interview conducted by researchers Kathryn Fauble and David Henschel. "Whether they didn't want anybody else to hear, I don't know. And I could see they both had a drink. There wasn't any laughter. The reason I know this is I kept an eye on her because I wanted to talk to her afterwards to tell her that I enjoyed being [on the show] and I was happy she guessed my line. I'd look over to see what's going on. That's the reason I was paying so much attention. Back in the corner where Dorothy was, was sort of a curved [banquette]. They wanted privacy. In other words, you wouldn't have felt like going up there. I knew they were talking serious business of some kind. I had that feeling."

Dorothy obviously knew the man in the hotel bar well or she wouldn't have sat so close to him. If this person's encounter with her was so innocent, and did not have sinister implications connected to her death, why has no one ever come forward to admit he was there with her (as Bob Bach did at P.J. Clarke's)?

When asked if she could gauge the age of the man accompanying Dorothy, Stone was uncertain. The police never followed up with her.

At 1 a.m., press agent Harvey Daniels ran into Dorothy in the Regency's bar. He described her as being in a good mood. Daniels left the bar at 1:30 a.m. Kurt Maier, the piano player, said Dorothy was still in the lounge and in high spirits when he got off work at 2 a.m. He added, "Of course, Dorothy was with a man. A true lady like her would not come by herself to hear me play."

Dorothy dialed the Western Union office at 10 E. 61st Street and sounded perfectly normal. Manager Dave Spiegel took the call and relayed the exchange:

"Miss Kilgallen called me at 2:20 in the morning. She sounded great as usual. She said, 'Good morning, Mr. Spiegel, this is Dorothy Kilgallen. Would you send a messenger over to the house to pick up my column and take it to the *Journal-American*? I'll leave it in the regular place, in the door.' I said, 'It's always a pleasure,' and sent the messenger. It was there as usual—the last column she ever wrote."

Though she had been drinking, Dorothy was apparently functional enough to have dialed the Western Union office. She probably called from the hotel, (there was a bank of phones in a hallway around the corner from where she was seated), having already left her column in the entryway at her residence, and remained in the bar for a while longer.

Since it was estimated that she died between 2 a.m. and 4 a.m., that leaves only an hour and a half for her to have become intoxicated. (She had a blood alcohol level of 0.15. Based on her weight, this represents four to six drinks. She was legally drunk at 0.10).

The barbiturates found in Dorothy's system would take a half hour to an hour to start working and then reach a dangerous peak level. This implies she consumed them between 2:30 a.m. and 3 a.m. The authorities should have pinned down her whereabouts at that time, but didn't.

Dorothy's favorite mixed drink, which she'd ordered that last night, included tonic water, which contains quinine. Quinine has long been used by murderers to disguise the bitter taste of barbiturates. If someone slipped her a Mickey Finn at the Regency Hotel bar, she might not have noticed, since she was already under the influence of alcohol. Her drink could have been spiked while she was on the phone to Western Union. Since it was dark in the lounge and she and her male companion had been sitting in a far corner, it would have been very easy for him to put something in her vodka tonic unobserved.

Timing was critical. A killer, especially an experienced one, wouldn't risk her overdosing by letting DK linger there in the bar. So her date likely hustled her out of there soon after she finished her drink.

The Regency was seven blocks from her townhouse but nobody knows how she got home in those wee hours. Marlin Swing speculated, "We were all fairly certain that [Pataky] was the one, the devil in the issue. She probably took the same [limo] service she used every Sunday night. She was with Bob Bach leaving the theater and then after that, nobody knows." For some unfathomable reason, this point was never pinned down.

Live-in butler James Clement stated that DK was accompanied by a man when she arrived home, and at some point he heard the back screen door close and assumed the man had exited that way. There is no word on whether he recognized this individual or how long he stayed.

It would make sense she would escort her companion to the third floor Americana Room (via the mirrored Otis elevator adjacent to the five-story staircase and skylight), since that's where she and Richard did most of their entertaining, and she had to go to that floor anyway to change clothes. Remember Dick had come home one night and found her there with Johnnie Ray, so it would not be unusual for her to do this. The bar was closed, she may have wanted to continue the conversation a bit and she was no doubt also feeling woozy—another reason for Pataky to offer to chivalrously escort her home.

Marlin Swing and Bob Bach were surely welcome guests in the Kollmar townhouse and were the two men who often joined Dorothy for drinks after *WML?* One of them would typically accompany her back to her residence so if Richard awoke on the fourth floor and heard muffled voices below—doubtful because he was normally "in his cups" by then—no suspicions would be aroused. So Dorothy would have felt safe in discreetly inviting the man in, who had dropped her off that last night.

She had covered major, mystery murder cases but tragically did not realize she was about to play a starring role in one.

PART III

13
'I Knew She Was Dead Right Away'

What happened in the bewitching hours post-midnight on Monday, November 8, 1965 at 45 East 58th Street on New York City's Upper East Side, as the full moon was scudding between clouds, will forever remain a secret that Dorothy Mae Kilgallen Kollmar took to her grave.

Would she have been likely to take a sleeping pill? She knew the hazards of combining alcohol with barbs and had even written about it. Yet powder residue from one barbiturate was found on one of the two glasses recovered at the scene. This suggests no pill was swallowed whole and that the drug was in powder form when she sipped from the glass—indicating a spiked drink. So the *coup de grace* was administered with a final drug after she was home.

If the account of James Clement can be believed, at some point, not long after Dorothy arrived home, she must have excused herself to go to the bathroom—located just off a bedroom which she never slept in—and that's where she collapsed. The butler supposedly found Dorothy in the bathroom (on the floor? In the shower? On the stool?) the next morning, although this is not the official version of what happened.

She was presumably attired in the clothing she wore when she arrived home since Mr. Clement commented to his wife (who was Dorothy's cook), that Dorothy was inexplicably dressed peculiarly a few hours later after she died.

A pink liquid found in her stomach was never analyzed so the medical examiner must not have thought it important; it may have been Pepto-Bismol. By the time she got home she was probably starting to feel unwell.

James Clement also claimed DK's dressing room was in disarray, which was unusual. Perry Mason would tell you that DK had to have been incapacitated—or even dead—when the man searched it, probably hoping to find her JFK papers. (Maybe he even did). She obviously would not have let him do that if she was awake. The back stairs from the third floor led to the screen door and that is another indication that he's the one who searched the room. He exited via the alley rather than the front door. If he had been above-board he would have left the same way he came in.

Later that morning, Marc Sinclaire went to Kilgallen's townhouse to do her hair, as she was supposed to be at son Kerry's school at noon. He arrived at the residence around 8:45 a.m. "I used my key," he explained, "let myself in, and went upstairs" (via the back staircase often used by servants).

He went to the small dressing room on the third floor where Dorothy had her hair styled. "The light was on and she wasn't there. So I turned on my curling irons and I walked into the (adjacent) bedroom, not thinking that she would be there," he said.

That's because, even though it was officially the master bedroom and was on the same floor as the "Americana Room" where she and Dick entertained, Dorothy hadn't slept in that room for years, and instead slept on the fifth floor. Dick slept on the fourth.

"She was sitting up in bed, and I walked over to the bed and touched her, and I knew she was dead right away," he recalled somberly. "The bed was spotless. She was dressed very peculiarly like I've never seen her before. She always dressed in pajamas and old socks and her makeup was off and her hair was off and everything." That morning, however, "she was completely dressed like she was going out, the hair was in place, the makeup was on, the false eyelashes were on." She was attired in a blue "matching peignoir and robe." Sinclaire insisted this was the kind of thing "she would never wear to go to bed."

Marc Sinclaire

He noted, "A book laid out on the bed. [But it] was turned upside down; it wasn't in the right position for if she'd been reading...and it was laid down so perfectly." The book was *The Honey Badger* by Robert Ruark. Sinclaire claimed she had finished reading it several weeks earlier, as she had discussed it with him. Dorothy needed glasses to read, but they weren't found in the room.

"[There was] a drink on the table, the light was on, the air conditioning was on, though you didn't need an air conditioner. You would have had the heat on. She was always cold and why she had the air conditioner on I don't know..."

Charles Simpson revealed Sinclaire, "Called me on the phone and told me that he had found her dead. And he said, 'when I tell you the bed she was found in, and how I found her, you're going to know she was murdered.' And I knew. The whole thing was just abnormal. The woman didn't sleep in that bed, much less the room. It wasn't her bed."

Strangely, she was in the middle of the bed—beyond the easy reach of the nightstand. "Rigor mortis had set in on the right hand and it had drawn up the covers a little bit," Sinclaire related. "And there was lipstick on the [left] sleeve of the Bolero jacket.

"I went back in the dressing room, picked up the intercom and rang for James [the butler]. I said 'James, I am unable to wake Miss Kilgallen. Could you please come up?' He ran up the stairs. I could hear him. He came up the front stairs and he ran like he was very excited and of course the door was locked. But I had come in through the back door. I don't think anyone knew I was coming. This was before 9:30 in the morning—this had to be nine, five after nine. So I opened the door to the bedroom and James came in, and at that time, I noticed a sheet of paper laying on the floor that had been pushed under the door. And James came in and he was very flustered. He wasn't himself at all."

Unfortunately, Sinclaire never picked up the piece of paper, so its contents are unknown.

Marlin Swing theorized, "Well that could have been an innocent note because James always slipped notes under the door." Then he paused and thought for a moment, before adding, "But he wouldn't have known she was in THAT room." That is indeed a mystery.

Marc never mentioned if he and

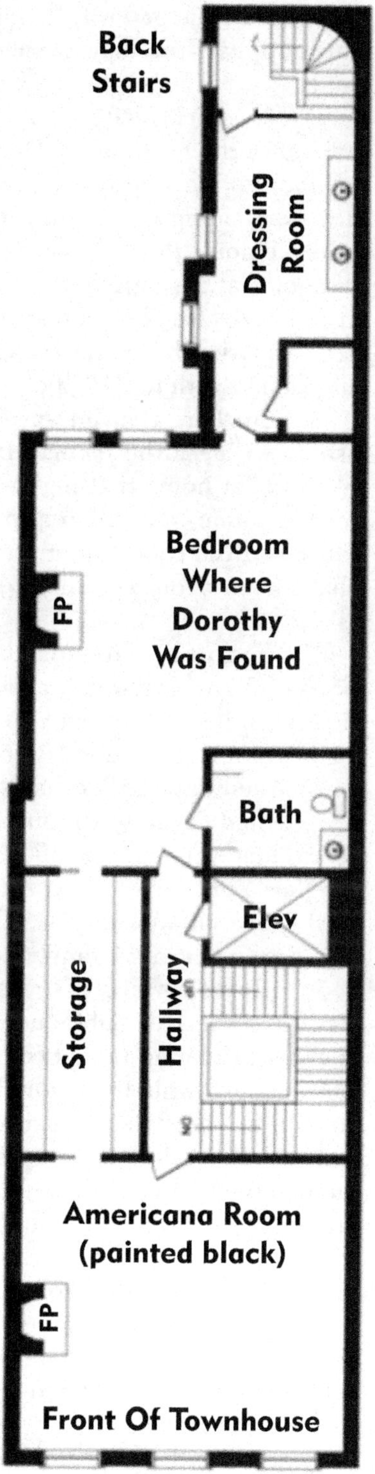

the butler exchanged words, and if so, what was said between the two men. But it appears the hairdresser wanted to beat a hasty retreat from the scene.

He quickly left the townhouse and discovered a police car parked in front of the residence. "There were two officers. They didn't pay any attention to me when I came out," he recalled. "I found it very strange they were sitting dead in front of the house and Dorothy was dead upstairs...I don't think I was the first one to discover Dorothy. I never thought that." A distraught Sinclaire left the residence without knowing any more details of what had transpired.

Curiously, he did not approach the patrol car out front and report Kilgallen's death to the officers. He must have been afraid to do so.

Sinclaire relayed an odd incident wherein Romola Metzner, a fashion writer at the *Journal-American*, wanted to speak with him. "They called me at home that night. My then-press agent Jan, I can't think of her last name, she called and asked me to come to Romola Metzner's house and the two of them interrogated me basically, trying to find out what I knew about Dorothy's death. I didn't have much to tell them."

Kerry's live-in tutor, Ibne Hassan, (who wished to remain anonymous when interviewed for the Lee Israel book), said that most weekday mornings, he took the boy to a bus stop where he caught a ride to St. David's parochial school. Mid-century New York Catholic schools typically started their days earlier than the public school system. Hassan said when he returned to the townhouse, presumably before nine in the morning, he was met with a police officer positioned at the front door, even though the New York Police Department wasn't officially notified of DK's death until later that afternoon. Evelyn Clement, the cook, told the officer he was "a member of the family" so he would be allowed inside.

Come to think of it, why would police guard the door unless foul play was suspected? Subsequently, Ibsen told a somewhat different version of events, claiming he noticed the household staff scurrying around the lobby of the townhouse before he left to go to college classes around 9 a.m. He said he asked them what was wrong and they told him DK was dead and probably drank too much alcohol. In another version of his story, he claimed the household staff told him Dorothy had committed suicide, but they later denied telling him that.

Obviously these stories are in conflict with the one about encountering the police after walking Kerry to the bus stop.

The tutor continued to live at the Kilgallen residence after Dorothy died, and completed a master's degree around 1966. He enrolled at Cambridge in England in 1974 and went on to have a career related to the United Nations.

Richard, Kerry and the tutor claimed to have heard nothing. But

Hassan said that was not surprising since it was such a sprawling residence.

This fact escaped Vincent Bugliosi, the former Los Angeles Deputy District Attorney who prosecuted the Charles Manson gang, and became a vociferous defender of the Warren Commission. He devoted two pages in his book, *Reclaiming History: The Assassination of President John F. Kennedy* to refuting points raised by Dorothy. But he did refer to her 1965 death as "perhaps the most prominent mysterious death" cited by assassination researchers. He contended that the presence of Kilgallen's husband and son in their five-story, 13,000-square-foot townhouse throughout the night when she died proves she could not have been murdered. Bugliosi said a burglar would have awakened her husband or her eleven-year-old son and then her husband would have called the police. *How absurd.*

That morning, a woman named Mary Branum received a bizarre call. "The phone on my desk rang, and when I answered, a voice said 'Dorothy Kilgallen has been murdered.' Before I could say anything, my caller had hung up. We put on a radio in the office and heard the news a little later. What made it odd was the anonymity of the call, and the fact that it had been made to me at all. I was hardly a reporter, just a managing editor of a couple of movie magazines."

James Clement's account remains murky. First, what time that morning had he allegedly discovered Dorothy's body? Whom did he notify? What happened between the time he found her and when Marc Sinclaire arrived? What exactly had she been wearing then that differed from when found by Marc Sinclaire? Had James moved her body in any way? What was written on that piece of paper shoved under the bedroom door? Who had the opportunity to move DK's remains, and why? Did he tidy up the messy dressing room and thereby disturb the crime scene? (Marc Sinclaire, who was very fastidious, never mentioned it was in disarray when he arrived that morning, and he surely would have noticed).

Usually in the case of a barbiturate overdose, the patient vomits as the body tries to expel the toxin. Had Dorothy thrown up?

What we know for sure is that the doctor who officially pronounced DK dead, Saul Heller, told Kerry Kollmar years later butler James Clement came to his house around 9:30 a.m. that morning as he was eating breakfast, and asked him to come immediately. This would have been right after Marc Sinclaire came upon her corpse.

Marlin Swing recalled a female friend of the Kollmar/Kilgallen family, Jean Stralem, being stopped by the police following Dorothy's death. The woman, who had been riding in a limousine from her Park Avenue apartment to her office around 10 a.m., was informed by an officer she needed to go to the townhouse as Richard wanted to see her right away. No mention was made of DK's death. Mrs. Stralem was perplexed by how the policeman located her in traffic, but complied with his request. She found Dick Kollmar drunk, very upset and crying.

Lee Israel theorized Dorothy's husband probably hoped to enlist the aide of family friends like Jean and her spouse, Donald Stralem—who were very wealthy—to arrange for his wife's body to be taken directly to the Abbey "before the official intervention of the police and the [medical examiner.]" Israel did not explain why she thought Kollmar would have wanted to do this. But it may have had something to do with the fact that he was concerned an autopsy would go against Dorothy's Catholic views.

Myrtle Verne, DK's secretary, told press agent Michael O'Shea by the time she arrived at the townhouse for work that morning around 10:30 a.m., Dorothy was already deceased.

Several hours elapsed before police and the medical examiner officially arrived at the townhouse. The butler claimed men in suits arrived that morning and carted off DK's files but it was unknown who these individuals were. Didn't they show any identification? Didn't he ask? Were they FBI? New York detectives? CIA? Who?

Ironically, that Monday, Kilgallen could be seen as a guest on a recently taped episode of rival game show *To Tell the Truth*. After it aired, CBS reporter Douglas Edwards announced at 3:25 p.m. Dorothy was deceased. It was only then a police commissioner claimed he officially heard the news and dispatched detectives.

Marlin Swing recalled an odd phone conversation that took place after he learned of Dorothy's passing. "I was at CBS. I called and I got who I thought was Anne [Hamilton] and I asked for Dorothy. She said, 'Well, she can't come to the phone right now, she'll have HIM call me back.' That was the message that I got at the home…I was so concerned, mainly to try to find out for CBS what was going on, that I didn't think murder or anything suspicious. I just thought maybe she got ill and had a heart attack or something, so I didn't suspect anything right away."

If all this isn't confusing enough, a supplementary report signed by homicide detective Peter McPartland states he was informed at 1 p.m. of Dorothy's death. Why was homicide notified? There is nothing in the records to indicate what, if any, investigation took place to deduce that DK was not the victim of murder. Yet a second detective in the homicide division, Richard Seiler, is officially listed as having witnessed the autopsy.

He proved to be uncooperative when Lee Israel tried to establish a dialogue with him. Seiler wrote her a nasty letter contending that "if the family had any doubs as to the cause of death of Dorothy Kilgallen they would have contacted me years ago...Your [letter] gave me the inference that your possible suspects will be Castro, CIA or FBI...Ridiculous!" What an odd response to a legitimate inquiry.

The medical examiner's office claims not to have been informed of Dorothy's death until 2:45 p.m., but the 19th Precinct insisted police were not aware of her passing until 3:20 p.m.

What does this convoluted storyline all mean?

Lee Israel told *Midwest Today*, ordinarily in the case of a woman's suspicious death, the police would "go out and at least ask *pro forma* questions of the people who were around her the night before." But the New York cops "did nothing. I mean *nothing*." The lead detective on the case, who had six children, abruptly resigned a short time later, forsook his pension, moved out of town, and opened a pricey restaurant. How?

After Ron Pataky claimed to magazine publisher Larry Jordan he was in Columbus when DK died, and Jordan pressed him with, "how do we know that?", Pataky replied, "because I was interviewed by police." When asked how they knew about him, he said, "I think they found my name written on a pad beside her bed or something." Was this true?

'Learning Not To Cry'

For the youngest member of the Kollmar household, Nov. 8, 1965 was even more traumatic. In an Oct. 7, 2009 post entitled "Learning Not To Cry" on his personal blog, Kerry described the day his mother died. He was informed of the news by his school's principal David Hume. He was driven home by a chauffeur, with his nanny Ellen O'Hara waiting to embrace him. Clearly a gifted writer like his mother, Kerry wrote:

"When I arrived at the house, Ellen met me with a wounded look and a heartfelt hug. She offered me anything she could do and together we went upstairs. In the elevator, on the way to the third floor, she said: 'Your father's in bad shape, Kerry. Just give him a little time.' This, as it turned out, was a sage warning, a wise predictor of what was to follow. This day would mark the beginning of the end of my respect for my father."

Upon arriving on the third floor, Kerry spotted his dad.

"He sat as he always did, perched on the right side of one of the pair of black, silk-covered loveseats, his shoulders stooped and rounded,

What really happened to this happy family?

elbows leaning on his knees, the fly of his pajama bottoms pinched open enough to make us all avert our gazes, hovering over a beer. He sipped one after the other; Ellen was sure to be working hard today, keeping plenty cold and at the ready during this mourning period, glasses of Heineken one after the next, two empty bottles on the table next to the coaster that held his half-full glass."

Kerry and Mom

Richard didn't utter a word to Kerry. "I wondered what my father was thinking about. I wondered why he wouldn't talk to me, particularly in this time of death and sadness. Didn't one comfort their child when times were hard? Did he not care about me? Or was it, perhaps, that he hurt so deeply, that he couldn't find the words or even some gratuitous gesture. Could he not come out of himself long enough to offer a hug to his eleven-year-old son who had, after all, just lost his mother?...I don't feel unforgiving toward my father for ignoring me or the opportunity that was missed when my mother died, just somewhat sad, even still. Sad that he missed so much love with his children. So much love, so many great experiences that he could have shared with us all. Perhaps. And for the rest of my childhood and well into my adult years, but for a couple of times that I was in excruciating physical pain, I never cried again."

Kerry, the only child still in the home, became estranged from his father following his mother's death. In a blog post dated April 6, 2009, Kerry wrote, "I was born into a life of privilege, the son of columnist and *What's My Line?* panelist Dorothy Kilgallen and producer Richard Kollmar. As a child of celebrities, I grew up in an environment surrounded by influences and events vastly different from many, probably most other people. Simply put, we were rich people, living a dream life on the Upper East Side of Manhattan. But boy, did that change."

One anecdote that Kerry shared but which he did not write about is that when his mother was alive, a wall in his fourth floor bedroom was covered with autographed photos of movie stars and papers signed by various performers. He had witnessed their signing many of them, and other signatures were acquired for him by Dorothy. These treasures remained on his wall for some time after she died, but one day when he arrived home he was surprised to find they were all gone. He never found out who took them down. If Dick Kollmar knew, he never mentioned it to Kerry, nor did any other member of the household.

Kerry reflected, "As the years unfolded, my life took many unexpected courses, some of them wonder filled, some harrowing, many of which I still look back at in awe. My mom died, I found myself thrown out of my house by age sixteen and, the rest, well, as they say—life happens."

He went on to write about his experiences meeting President John F. Kennedy as a child, as well as John Jr., John Lennon and John Belushi. He had his "first sexual stirrings" as a child enthralled by Jayne Mansfield, who had been a party guest at his parents' home.

One question that Kerry never addressed was: did he see his mother after he arrived home early from school and before her body was removed? It seems odd he did not mention it.

Tributes To Dorothy Abound

The *Journal-American* devoted seven pages to her life and death. Many newspapers across the country featured news of her passing above the fold. The *San Mateo Times* and *Daily News Leader* wrote above its banner: "DOROTHY KILLARNEY DIES." It reported that earlier in the day DI had died "in bed while reading," having suffered a heart attack.

Joan Crawford called her "one of the greatest women who ever lived." Producer David Merrick said, "Dorothy Kilgallen was one of the great reporters of our time. Her coverage of trials were journalistic mas-

WHY THE GIANTS LOST

New York Journal American

NEW YORK'S LARGEST EVENING NEWSPAPER

MONDAY, NOVEMBER 8, 1965

GALBRAITH: SAME TUNE

THE VOICE OF BROADWAY IS STILLED

COURTROOM COVERAGE . . . Dorothy was at her best covering courtroom dramas. Here, at the start of her scintillating career she tells fellow reporters of her insight during Bruno Hauptmann's trial for the kidnap-slaying of the Lindberg baby in the 1930s . . .

A BEAMING BRIDE . . . The happiest day in Dorothy's life was the day she married Richard Kollmar—April 6, 1940. It was a storybook romance. Meeting at a luncheon, they were engaged after six dates . . .

terpieces. She was a star and gave glamour and glitter to the world of journalism." Sammy Davis Jr. said, "Broadway won't be the same without her." Ginger Rogers applauded Dorothy's "journalistic talents and her television brilliance." Famed trial lawyer Louis Nizer said Dorothy had "keen insight, vivid and concise descriptive powers and an evaluating intelligence." Ed Sullivan said he was "heartsick."

Martin Hogan Jr, *Cincinnati Enquirer* TV columnist, wrote on Nov. 11, 1965, "I'm sure it rankled most newsguys, including myself, when Dorothy Kilgallen made a theatrical entrance into a courtroom during the trial of Jack Ruby. But Dorothy Kilgallen was Dorothy Kilgallen. Whether or not she wanted or deserved it, Dorothy Kilgallen was a celebrity, a big deal. She had an audience, a following for better or worse. And she never let them down."

Bette Kirchner Stevenson, co-publisher of the *Record-American*, recalled her first time encountering Dorothy at an American Newspaper Publishers Association meeting that was followed by a luncheon and hat show. Kilgallen asked Stevenson, then a girl in her teens, what she thought of several hats she'd tried on.

"I was in awe, for she really was a beautifully-dressed person and very charming, and besides my love for hats, I was really 'celebrity struck' to think she would want my opinion."

The two women met again on several occasions.

"Although I did not always agree with her views in her column, she was an excellent newspaper woman and a great writer and personality," Stevenson concluded.

Hy Gardner, who was an entertainment reporter with rival paper *New York Herald Tribune*, penned an intimate tribute to DK complimenting her brand of journalism, work ethic in a male-dominated industry and her likability:

"There were TWO Dorothy Kilgallens!

"One was the off-camera, off-typewriter, off-guard gal who was a gracious, witty and fascinating conversationalist with a satin lining of shyness peeking through her custom-tailored cloak of extroversion.

"The other Kilgallen was a rip-snortin', brass-knuckled competitor who relished a columnar brawl, who used every weapon at her command (and she had quite an arsenal) to talk or write a target into submission."

He went on to say, "Dorothy was an accurate, brilliant, sweet and sometimes sassy chronologist of the sham world of the celebrity. She etched findings with biting sarcasm rather than gooey syrup. Her style was readily recognizable because she was opinionated, for or against. She was tireless, fearless, dauntless, dedicated, determined but unforgiving. She never let a beaten enemy keep his sword.

"When they coined the phrase 'working reporter' they must have had her in mind. No journalist (even though she lived in a lush townhouse, traveled in a Rolls Royce, was draped with mink when she went to an opening and was treated like royalty) ever worked so hard, so long and so diligently on a man's assignment."

The AP noted DK "was known to colleagues and rivals as a hard-driving newspaperwoman. She had covered some of the biggest stories of her generation, including numerous dramatic courtroom trials."

Journalist Leo Aikman wrote a tribute column to DK. He said she would take notes on the *What's My Line?* panel while the others asked questions. She was always perfectly attired and made-up "with a keen mind, a good figure and a woman's vanity."

Murder Most Foul

Charles Simpson opined, "There was an unwritten rule. You only went so far. It wasn't like today...back in those days, people respected other people's space. The very people she wrote about in her 'gossip' column it was totally different than what goes on today. When it came to really big stuff, she pulled no punches when there was something that really needed to be exposed. Government people, things like that, she pulled no punches. But when it came to movie stars, she just put a tidbit in here or there."

Marlin Swing

Yet Dorothy's writing, national outreach, fearlessness and investigative skills got her killed. Her death was premeditated. The man suspected of doing the foul deed—Ron Pataky(?)—didn't just happen to have barbiturates with him and decide on impulse to drop them in her drink. He had to have come prepared to kill her, meaning he had time to reflect on the gravity of what he was about to do, and plan to avoid detection. So it was diabolical. But there is no known personal grudge that Pataky held against DK that would have compelled him to end her life. It had to be a case of him acting on behalf of someone else to silence her reporting.

Marlin Swing was convinced Dorothy had met with foul play, so much so he eagerly reached out to this author and her father after reading the story published in *Midwest Today* magazine, to say he was glad Ron Pataky's name finally got into public print, along with other explosive details contained in the article.

Asked to speculate on who was behind Kilgallen's death, Swing said, "I think it's a combination probably of the Jewish Mafia, the CIA and maybe the other Mafia, I don't know. The reason I mentioned the Jewish Mafia is because suddenly [film distributor and producer] Joseph Levine became very close to her in contacts and he sent her on these various junkets that she and Pataky would be on. So I'm sure that he had something to do with Pataky's suddenly becoming a friend of hers...because the breakup with Johnnie [Ray] had just happened, and then Ron appeared."

Pataky repeatedly bragged about his friendship with Joe Levine, even claiming he would sometimes sit around in Levine's office on Sunday afternoons and shoot the breeze. Why would a studio mogul befriend a lowly reporter from Columbus, Ohio? Ron said, "I was working on some music. Joseph E. Levine, Embassy Pictures, I sent him a song of mine called *La Notte è Dolce*, which is *The Night Is Sweet* in Italian. And he just flipped. He threw a party for me. I was the guest of honor, if you can believe that—I have no honor (laughs)—at the Four Seasons, and everybody was there." He even claimed Levine had promised to hire him to write the musical score for an upcoming motion picture, though he didn't say which one. Pataky said he went to New York fairly frequently, and "in the evenings I didn't have a lot to do. I was not seeing plays at that time. In New York at that time my purpose was not to see plays. I'll tell you what it was...I was a composer. I was working on some music."

While Dorothy faced times of melancholy, Marlin Swing did not think she could have committed suicide. He reflected, "There were very 'down' periods in her life. This particular period, mainly because of Ron, she was so happy and upbeat. She was excited about the Kennedys—things she was finding out—so it was a very upbeat time, so I really don't think she took her life," he said.

It was no secret the *Journal-American* was in financial trouble, ceasing publication in April 1966. But Sinclaire said even if Kilgallen had been troubled by the tumultuous nature of the newspaper business, "Dorothy was still being syndicated all over the country, plus she was working on television and had book offers." The family certainly lacked for nothing.

Sinclaire maintained his belief that Pataky had something to do with her death. "I think he had some problems with Dorothy. She was going to confront him...I think Pataky knows (who killed her). I don't think he did the actual work, but whoever his employers were did."

Marc went to the funeral home to do Dorothy's hair and makeup, at her sister Eleanor's request.

"I didn't like the funeral director because he was very rude about Dorothy's death. They brought her in and she had on a gold lamé Chanel-type dress and she was still wet from the embalming and she was very bloated. I cut the wig in half and started to put the hair on, because they had cut the head open, and so the back of the head was still there but nothing was in it. I said to Richard 'plug in my curling iron' and he went to plug in the curling iron and all the lights went out, and I said 'turn it off quickly, you're going to blow the lights out. Curling irons were fairly new then. So they would do stuff like that."

They discovered most of the city was blacked out—indeed a large portion of the northeast. At about 5:30 p.m. that evening, electricity went out from Ontario to New York City and Buffalo and to the eastern border of New Hampshire. It left more than thirty million people without power for about fourteen hours, impacting Manhattan, the Bronx, Queens and most of Brooklyn with some suburban areas not affected.

With DK's death, NYC went dark. Literally.

The blackout seemed emblematic of the tragedy that had befallen Dorothy.

Sinclaire said after leaving the funeral home he was so upset "of course I went to my doctor and I got a shot" (to calm his nerves).

Marc had to return the following evening to finish doing Dorothy's hair.

"I didn't like the way the family was behaving. I didn't like the way the press was behaving. I didn't like any of it. I knew more than they did, and I didn't want to be party to it."

Over ten thousand people filed past DK's coffin and 2,600 people paid their respects at Dorothy's November 11 funeral held at St. Vincent Ferrer Roman Catholic Church, Lexington Avenue and East 66th Street in the Upper East Side of Manhattan. Arlene Francis, Bennett Cerf and John Daly attended, as well as Ed Sullivan, Bob Considine, Joan Crawford and Joseph Levine. Notably absent were Ron Pataky and Marc Sinclaire.

Joan Hanauer of the *Journal-American* described Dorothy in her casket thusly, "Her auburn hair sweeping down to her shoulders, her throat encased in a pearl necklace, gowned in cream and gold satin brocade, with a pearl rosary draped in her hands. The hands held a pink bouquet of tiny flowers—from her children."

At the funeral, Dorothy's bereaved mother, Mae, angrily confronted Kollmar. The incident even made the *Journal-American*. Pointing a finger at him, she shockingly said, "You killed my daughter, and I will prove it." Jim Kilgallen led her away. But in Marc Sinclaire's view, "I don't think he could have done it. I think more than one person was involved in Dorothy's death."

Dorothy's casket is carried up the steps of the St. Vincent Ferrer Catholic Church.

Marlin Swing tended to agree Dick was probably innocent.

"I don't think he was ever sober enough to be suspected of being able to mastermind anything," Swing commented.

He speculated there was a police cover up. "I think they were paid off. There WAS a cover up in that respect," he said.

DK was buried at Gate of Heaven Cemetery in Hawthorne, New York, located twenty-five miles north of New York City. A Roman Catholic burial site, the cemetery is also the final resting place of Babe Ruth, Fred Allen, Sal Mineo, Condé Nast, Mary Higgins Clark and other notables.

After the funeral, Virginia Barry paid tribute to DK in her column for the *Asbury Park Press*, but also called her death an "eerie melodrama."

She asked, "How did it happen that a hairdresser, coming in from outside, should be the first to know about it? In a twenty-two room New York townhouse occupied at the time by her husband and son was there no one moving about who might have knocked on her door to inquire whether she would care for a cup of coffee or a late breakfast?"

Three days after Dorothy died, Bob and Jean Bach invited her widower Richard Kollmar over for dinner. Bob then asked him, "Dick, what was all that stuff in the folder Dorothy carried around with her about the assassination?" Richard replied, "Robert, I'm afraid that will have to go to the grave with me."

Dorothy's feud with Frank Sinatra continued even in the afterlife. Acclaimed journalist Gay Talese, writing in his groundbreaking article "Frank Sinatra Has a Cold" for *Esquire* magazine's April 1966 issue, observed the crooner's hatred of the late columnist:

"Later Jim Mahoney and another man walked in, and there was

talk of Dorothy Kilgallen's death in New York earlier that morning. She had been an ardent foe of Sinatra for years, and he became equally uncomplimentary about her in his nightclub act, and now, though she was dead, he did not compromise his feelings. 'Dorothy Kilgallen's dead,' he repeated, walking out of the room toward the studio. 'Well, guess I got to change my whole act.'"

Mr. And Mrs. Smith

Many conspiracy theorists list the death of *Journal-American* fashion editor Florence Pritchett Smith, 45, among the "convenient deaths" associated with the JFK assassination. Florence's death certificate indicates she died shortly after dawn, barely twenty-four hours after Marc Sinclaire's discovery of Dorothy's body.

There was speculation Kilgallen may have given Flo a copy of the research notes pertaining to her Kennedy probe. The rationale for that belief is if DK wanted to entrust a copy of her sensitive files to somebody, who better to confide in than Mr. and Mrs. Smith?

As previously mentioned, Earl was the former U.S. ambassador to Cuba who was active in anti-Castro circles, and Florence had had a romance with JFK.

Like Dorothy, Flo had also been a trailblazer among women. She was a journalist, model, radio commentator, author, conductor of her own television program *Leave It To The Girls* and publicist for the David O. Selznick Motion Picture Company.

Dorothy and Florence had been professional colleagues and friends for years. In fact, Florence filled in for Dorothy, writing her Aug. 30, 1946 column with this editor's note: "Dorothy Kilgallen is on vacation. Her guest columnist today is an expert on men, vivacious and glamorous Florence Pritchett."

Flo even was a substitute host on the *Breakfast With Dorothy and Dick* radio show on occasion, and also guested with them.

So those who try to argue the two women barely knew each other or were not friends, are dead wrong.

In Flo's obituary, it was noted she had been forced to stop writing her weekly column *The Mood and the Food* due to her battle with leukemia, in poor health since at least August 1965.

Her cause of death was listed by her family doctor, not a medical examiner, and was said to be a cerebral hemorrhage. Even that is viewed with skepticism by some. That's because it is statistically quite rare, occurring in only 0.5% of cases of acute myeloid leukemia (AML). If Smith had another type of leukemia, the chances of her dying from a cerebral event are even less than 0.5%.

Although there is absolutely zero evidence that Kilgallen ever gave a copy of her Kennedy notes to the couple, (or for that matter, to anyone),

Mrs. Smith's death on Nov. 9, 1965 understandably raised eyebrows, in the context of so many people dying suddenly, who had a Kennedy connection.

WML? Colleagues Pay Tribute

On the Sunday following Dorothy's death, *What's My Line?* began with words from John Daly, who looked visibly anguished as he spoke.

"These are sad days for us, as I'm sure they are for all those who learned about Dorothy Kilgallen's passing last Monday. Dorothy, Arlene, Bennett and I have been together on Sundays for the better part of sixteen years. Kitty Carlisle and Steve Allen, who've been kind enough to come and give us moral support tonight, are also, in a way, members of the family."

He said consideration was given in how to pay tribute to Dorothy. After consulting with her husband Richard, it was decided to conduct that night's show "just as it was when she was here."

Once the episode started, the panelists were already seated, with the usual conviviality gone.

As the panelists signed off for the night, Arlene Francis echoed Daly's sentiment about how members of *WML?* had become a family, and were not merely co-workers. Steve Allen noted the fact that the panel did not correctly guess the professions of the first three contestants—a visible representation of how Kilgallen was already missed.

Allen complimented her writing talents as a newspaper reporter, also saying she would be missed as a wife, mother and "a fine human being." Carlisle, who was sitting in Dorothy's seat, told viewers no one could ever take DK's place.

At the end, Cerf reflected, "A lot of people knew Dorothy as a very tough game player; others knew her as a tough newspaperwoman. When she went after a story, nothing could get in her way. But we got to know her as a human being, and a more lovable, softer, loyal person never lived, and we're going to miss her terribly."

Peter Gabel told this author, "My mother [Arlene Francis] and really everyone was shocked at Dorothy's passing. They were a team for a very long time. Although I do not believe my mother or Bennett, or Fred or Steve Allen—who were frequent guest panelists—were really friends with Dick and Dorothy, there was nonetheless a real bond among them from being challenged to play that challenging game together as the panelists for over a decade. Each would lateral to the others, would cover different areas and go in different illuminating directions based on their respective strengths...so I think it was really shocking to suffer the loss of one of them so abruptly."

14
'Circumstances Undetermined'

According to official paperwork, Dr. James Luke of the Manhattan Medical Examiner's office was notified of Dorothy's death at 2:45 p.m. on Monday, Nov. 8, 1965 and arrived at the scene at 3:10. He departed at 4:15. He made notes of his initial conversation with Richard Kollmar. Despite the fact that Dorothy's father, Jim Kilgallen, was present—as well as actress Joan Crawford—DK was listed as "Dorothy Kollmar (Killgallen)" with her name spelled incorrectly. Her age was originally written down as forty-two, then crossed out with fifty-eight written above the error. Her birthday was wrongly listed as July 13, 1913. At the bottom of the page Dr. Luke made a notation that Richard said Dorothy had returned home from *What's My Line?* around 11:30 p.m. (untrue) "feeling chipper" and went to write her column for the next day (also false). But Detective John Doyle—the first cop to officially arrive on the scene—said in a handwritten note that Kollmar admitted he had not seen his wife after she had gotten back home.

Richard is cited as having found her around noon unresponsive, yet maid Marie Eichler was also listed as having discovered her between noon and 1 p.m., dead in bed.

In Dr. James Luke's handwriting is the observation that Dorothy was attired in a "blue bathrobe and nothing else," and that the covers on the bed were pulled up to her chin—a description that conflicts with Marc Sinclaire's recollection of how he found her.

Dr. Luke stated in his initial notes that Dorothy had gotten a prescription filled for fifty, 100 mg capsules of Seconal exactly one month before her death. Detective John Doyle wrote in his notes that this empty bottle was found on the nightstand next to Dorothy. If true, this piece of evidence never made it to the Medical Examiner's office. But apparently the detective did visit the pharmacy Kilgallen used, and in reviewing her medication records, determined that over the previous three years, she had averaged two sleeping pills per night—establishing once and for all that despite the caricature of her as being addicted to drugs, she was *not*.

After Dorothy Kilgallen's body was removed from her residence, she became "Kollmar case number 9333" at the New York City Medical Examiner's Office, and an autopsy was performed by Dr. James Luke, junior medical examiner, in the presence of doctors William Sturner and Michael Baden. (The latter turned up as the senior medical adviser to the

HSCA investigating the Kennedy assassination. What are the odds?)

The report states her body was covered in extensive makeup about the face, neck and upper chest. This would appear to be stage makeup applied for her television appearance the night before.

Wouldn't Dorothy have normally removed this before going to bed at the end of the night? She was also still wearing false eyelashes. Any regular viewer of *WML?* knew she often struggled to re-adjust them after removing her blindfold following the mystery celebrity portion of the program. Smiling, she'd rub her eye(s) and try to wedge them back into place along the lash line, obviously with difficulty not having a mirror in front of her for accuracy.

"Rigidity absent save for jaws and fingers. Lividity posterior and involving the left neck and face," the autopsy report reads. There was a small abrasion on her right shoulder, described as measuring approximately six by three centimeters and was streaked and brown red in color, but considered superficial in nature. Notably missing is a temperature reading of the liver, which would have helped determine time of death.

Her hyoid bone was intact, as were the trachea and larynx, ruling out strangulation as cause of death. The heart was healthy with "minimal arteriosclerosis" and "no significant stenosis or occlusion," meaning there was no evidence of a heart attack, despite what various news outlets reported immediately following her death.

Looking at the pancreas, it was noted there was "considerable postmortem autolysis and congestion."

Fatty metamorphosis of the liver—moderate was detected, but there was "no evidence of cirrhosis." Other anatomical findings concluded she had slight pulmonary edema and visceral congestion, and at one point her uterus, Fallopian tubes and ovaries had been surgically removed (hysterectomy), maybe during one of her numerous hospital stays.

Eight days later, Luke concluded she died from "acute barbiturate and alcohol intoxication, **circumstances undetermined**." That was not a common phrase for his office to use.

Dr. Luke found the combination of alcohol and barbiturates had caused depression of Dorothy's central nervous system and resulted in her heart stopping. The estimated time of death was between 2 a.m. and 4 a.m. Luke would not speculate about the form in which Kilgallen had ingested the barbiturates. "We'd rather leave that up in the air," he said. "We don't want to give that out because—well, just because." Because *why?*

It would appear at least the medical examiner was leaving open the possibility that Dorothy had consumed the fatal barbiturate(s) in something other than pill form, such as being injected or dissolved in a liquid. That would connote suspicion of murder. Obviously, there was something unsettled in his mind. Unfortunately, no one followed up on that.

On Nov. 15, 1965, the UPI ran a story which reported, "Luke said the overdose of barbiturates may have been accidental. She left no notes, he said, and there were no other indications that she had planned to take her life. He said she apparently died peacefully, probably in a coma."

And that had been considered an acceptable response at the time?

"She was given [the drugs] somehow: injected, done in the back of the car, done in a drink," Marc Sinclaire said. "I don't know whether she walked out on her own power from the Regency Hotel."

One of the enduring mysteries is why the police never bothered to try to determine the "circumstances," which they admitted remained "unknown." They closed the case without talking to crucial witnesses. Suicide had never been seriously considered either, although the rumor mill floated the idea.

Since Dr. Luke had attended the scene the day of Dorothy's death and then did her autopsy, it would have been customary for him to sign her death certificate. But he did not. Instead, it was signed by Dr. Dominick DiMaio.

"I wasn't stationed in Manhattan [where Kilgallen died]," he asserted. "I was in Brooklyn. Are you sure I signed it? I don't see how the hell I could have signed it in the first place. You got me. I don't know why. I know nothing about the case. I never handled it," DiMaio insisted.

Medical Experts Harbor Suspicions

According to author Lee Israel, Dr. Charles Umberger, director of toxicology at the New York City Medical Examiner's office, privately suspected Dorothy had been murdered, and had inculpatory evidence to prove it. He remained silent, Israel theorized, because he understood the political implications of the matter and he wanted leverage over Dr. Luke, in an internecine feud.

In 1968, he asked a chemist who worked closely with him as his assistant to use some newly available technology to analyze blood and tissue samples he had retained from Kilgallen's autopsy, as well as the glass from her nightstand. Though Israel interviewed this chemist in 1978, she did not print his name. However, as the author of this book first revealed in *Midwest Today*, that man was John Broich. The new tests turned up traces of Nembutal on the glass but this was not the same as what she was prescribed (Seconal).

The more precise tests on the tissue samples were able, for the first time, to particularize a deadly mix of three powerful barbiturates in her brain: secobarbitol, amobarbital and pentobarbital (Nembutal). Broich reportedly told Israel that when he gave his findings to his employer, Dr. Umberger grinned and told him to "keep it under your hat. It was big."

Chemist At Medical Examiner's Office Reveals Distrust

In a much more recent interview by Larry Jordan, Broich elaborated: "There was some talk...whether the body had been moved and a whole bunch of stuff. But I don't know if it was ever resolved. I do remember that things were kinda screwed up. I think things were probably pretty unreliable. I wouldn't trust anything, you know what I mean? When I was [employed by the medical examiner's office], very few of the people knew what the hell they were doing. I was paranoid as hell when I was there. You never knew what was going to happen from one day to the next."

The educational and professional credentials of several of the people employed at the Manhattan Medical Examiner's office at the time were highly suspect due to their flagrant incompetence. Some were Sicillian and their records had supposedly been lost. No one wanted to challenge their legitimacy because of what was thought to be their strong ties to the Italian Mafia. Broich and a colleague, Steve Goldner—who was the supervising forensic toxicologist for the M.E. at the time—witnessed the ineptitude of some staff. They were also greatly disturbed by the influence of outside pressures on certain official findings of the office. The two men were expected to sign off on reports they felt were deeply flawed or even untrue. The situation became so acute that Goldner contemplated going public about the corruption by writing a book, but decided against it because, he said, he wanted to remain alive.

The chemist at the Department of Toxicology who originally did the tests on Dorothy noted he found quinine in her brain, bile and liver. But the lab findings of quinine were not reported to the Department of Pathology, although they should have been, as a matter of routine, because quinine is actually a drug used to treat malaria. It is also used as a flavoring agent in tonic water so as to give it a somewhat bitter taste.

Umberger said TWO glasses were found on her nightstand. But when tests were rerun, Lee Israel said the chemist found only Nembutal on a glass. What happened to the other glass? Whose glass was it? Were fingerprints ever found on the two glasses and if so, whose?

Disbelief At Dorothy's Demise

People who had come into contact with Dorothy were stunned by her death. The Western Union manager Dave Spiegel said, "I couldn't believe it the next day when I heard she was gone. I sat down and wrote a two-hundred word telegram to her dad, trying to tell him how much it had meant to us to help her move her copy and how much we'll miss her."

Bennett Cerf's wife, Phyllis Fraser, seemed unusually curious about Dorothy's death, and repeatedly questioned Marc Sinclaire about what he knew. He had never met the woman while Dorothy was alive and found it strange she suddenly sought out his services. "Afterwards, she came and had me do her hair. We didn't get along very well. I didn't like her very much, and she came to me for a year or two afterwards. She was always asking me questions about how Dorothy died." Sinclaire never revealed anything.

Phyllis, born Helen Brown Nichols, was an actress, journalist and children's book publisher. She co-founded Random House's imprint for young readers, Beginner Books, alongside Theodor Seuss "Ted" Geisel (aka Dr. Seuss) and his wife Helen Palmer Geisel. Her maternal first cousin was Ginger Rogers. Phyllis did appear on *WML?* in 1960, alongside the panelists' other spouses (Florence Randall, Dick Kollmar and Martin Gabel) as mystery guests.

WML? contestant Katherine Stone said when she learned of Dorothy's passing, "I was shocked to death. It made me mad that everybody thought that her medicine and her drinking caused her death. And I didn't think that at all. I thought that man probably did something to her."

Bob and Jean Bach were among those who suspected Ron Pataky knew something about Kilgallen's demise. But according to Pataky, "The next day [Monday] I had been in the office [in Columbus, Ohio] from 8 o'clock on. What did I do...hire my own jet, fly [to New York], kill her, and fly back in a hurry?" Some would say that was a possibility.

Pataky Tells Inconsistent Stories

Ron Pataky claimed he learned Dorothy had died when the news hit the wire. "Certainly, everyone knew it by 9 o'clock, 9:30."

But at that hour, Marc Sinclaire had just walked into the third floor bedroom and found Dorothy's body. The news could not have possibly been on the wire services that early. Police weren't officially dispatched to the scene until that afternoon, and a CBS broadcaster announced at 3:25 p.m. that DK had died. News of her death would not have been reported over the wire until much later in the day.

While Ron Pataky always denied being in New York at the time of Dorothy's death, a column he wrote which appeared in the Columbus paper on Nov. 10, 1965 suggests otherwise. He presented an extensive review of the new movie, *The Pawnbroker*, which (although it had been released in June) had been playing that week at the Playhouse Theater on 72nd Street in New York but didn't open until November 12 in Columbus. It was clear he had actually attended a showing of the film. It's possible, of course, he had seen it somewhere other than in NYC, but he wrote with such fresh piquancy and raw emotion, it would lead most readers to conclude he had just viewed it.

Since his was a morning newspaper, to get it into print on the tenth, he had to have submitted it no later than Tuesday, November 9, the day after Dorothy was found dead. Unless he scrambled to compose the review that evening, it seems most likely he viewed the film on the night of Monday, November 8—meaning he was in New York the same day her body was discovered.

Given the fact that the Medical Examiner's office at the time was known to be under the influence of organized crime, it is theoretically possible Pataky could have even been in contact with them regarding the handling of her autopsy. But let's not get too far into the realm of conjecture.

What Pataky wrote about the film is intriguing. The storyline is about a Jewish survivor of the Holocaust (portrayed by Rod Steiger) who relocates to New York after WWII.

The violence of the city causes flashbacks to his prior life in a Nazi concentration camp. But, Pataky writes, "What could be bitterness is instead complete apathy regarding his fellow man and the daily suffering he witnesses around him."

Pataky certainly supplied fodder for latter day armchair analysts when he penned, "We are told for the umpteenth time that hate, in any of its endless forms, breeds other kinds of hate, and that passing years do little to absolve the guilty or relieve the offender."

Then he adds, "The drama is one of seething discontent, which is to say it could only end in tragedy. Here, that tragedy leads to a cleansing or purification that no reviewer should attempt to describe. Suffice it to say that the torment builds until it can no longer contain itself, at which time it breaks out in violence."

What disturbing thoughts were going through Ron Pataky's mind within a couple of days of his "best friend" Dorothy's demise? Some of his writing seems to connote he actually loathed her.

Could it be DK's probing of the Kennedy assassination made her a target that Pataky in turn was required to destroy, and he felt both guilty and resentful about being placed in that position and blamed the victim instead? Did he view his actions as a sort of "cleansing" of his emotions?

We know by November 15—four days after DK's funeral—Ron Pataky was definitely in NYC because he was seen partying there.

Ten days after Dorothy's death, Ron penned a scathing attack on New Yorkers and said audiences there are "the stupidest collection of dull clods ever to set foot in a club or theater...If any of them ever had an original idea, the shock on the nervous system would send both the originator and his comrades to their great reward...They go where they hear they really should go." Seeming to take aim at Broadway columnists like his late friend Dorothy, Pataky wrote, "BIG people say go. The others follow suit and do just that. Then, through agony that no mortal—even these idiotic phonies—should have to endure, they pretend to like it."

In response to those who wonder why he was lavishing attention on a much older woman (when he said he wasn't interested in her romantically), Pataky noted he had other platonic friendships with famous older women including Myrna Loy, Alexis Smith, Arlene Dahl and Phyllis Diller.

Conspiracy buffs will no doubt seize on the fact Pataky told *Midwest*

Today, "I knew a lot of mobsters. I knew Sam Giancana through Phyllis McGuire. Drunk one night, I tried to put the make on her. That didn't work..."

The McGuire Sisters were a trio of real-life sisters who had popular hits like *Sugar Time* and appeared often on the *Ed Sullivan Show*.

Dorothy and Phyllis socialized together occasionally. A CIA memo on mobster Johnny Roselli states he and Robert Maheu went to the Copacabana nightclub on Sunday, April 8, 1962 and while there Roselli found himself facing a table at "ringside" at which Phyllis McGuire was sitting with Dorothy Kilgallen and famed pianist Liberace for the opening night of singer Rosemary Clooney. To avoid Ms. McGuire seeing him, Roselli got his companions to change their seating arrangement so that his back was turned to her.

Marlin Swing recalled dining with Dorothy late one evening when the pair crossed paths with Sam Giancana and Phyllis.

"A very funny thing happened. Dorothy and I were in Danny's Hideaway having a very late dinner one night and Phyllis McGuire was across the room, and anywhere that Dorothy would go, celebrities would come over and say hello to her, because they all wanted to get in the column. So Phyllis brought Giancana over to the table," Swing said with a laugh. "And Dorothy couldn't believe it, that Phyllis would introduce him to Dorothy. And that Dorothy would know that she was with him then. That was a very strange occurrence."

Phyllis McGuire told Dominick Dunne that at first, "Dorothy Kilgallen thought he was my attorney when she met him."

Ms. McGuire began dating the Chicago-based mob boss in 1960. But the FBI, which tracked Giancana's every move, decided not to expose the relationship, because such publicity would hurt McGuire's career. The agency still vainly hoped to recruit her as an informant.

In 1962, Phyllis was photographed with Giancana in Paris. She tearfully told Dorothy Kilgallen in an exclusive interview that she was going to stop dating the mobster.

In a September 15, 1965 column, Dorothy reported, "Phyllis McGuire, playing the Riviera in Las Vegas with her sisters, is quoted by chums as saying that her idyll with Sam Giancana didn't break up for any personal reason; it was simply because every movement she made was getting too much attention from the FBI."

But Phyllis lied about ending her relationship with Sam. She continued seeing him for another ten years—until his grisly execution-style slaying in 1975.

Years later, Ms. McGuire volunteered this tidbit: "Kilgallen was murdered. She didn't commit suicide. I saw her three days before, dancing at El Morocco (a Manhattan nightclub) with Johnnie Ray. She was murdered. I didn't believe the suicide story then. I don't believe it now.

Dorothy was the most beautiful corpse I ever saw."

Sam Giancana had famously been a target of Robert Kennedy. He began working for Al Capone in the 1920s. By the late 1960s, he had been arrested more than seventy times and served five years in prison for burglary and four years for operating an illegal still. He was also allegedly part of the plot along with other Mafiosos to help get John F. Kennedy elected president. Giancana was murdered on June 19, 1975, in Oak Park, Illinois before he was to appear before the Church Committee. He resided in a modest house, compared to mistress Phyllis who had a large complex.

When asked about Pat Kennedy and Peter Lawford's habit of socializing with mobsters at the Cal-Neva Lodge at the same time Robert Kennedy was prosecuting members of organized crime, Pataky told *Midwest Today*, "I know. I was very much involved in that whole thing at the time." He would not go into details.

Pataky certainly didn't staunch the speculation about himself when he published a poem called "Never Trust a Stiff At a Typewriter," soon after Dorothy's death. In it, he asserted there's a "way to quench a gossip's stench" "that never fails." He stated "one cannot write if zippered tight" and that someone who's dead can "sell no tales!" Some see in these lines a chilling reference to Dorothy and the way she died. But Pataky said he'd written 2,000 poems and asked *Midwest Today* magazine, "How in the hell did anyone come up with that one?" (It was posted on his website).

During one of his conversations with *Midwest Today*, Ron Pataky, in discussing the threat that Dorothy posed, observed that not only did she possess dangerous information, "she had the typewriter to make it public. Knowing is one thing, but knowing and TELLING can get you in TROUBLE." Then he chuckled.

Perhaps the most incriminating poem penned by Ron was a most curious one entitled *Vodka Roulette Seen as Relief Possibility*.

While I'm spilling my guts
She is driving me nuts
Please fetch us two drinks
On the run
Just skip all the noise'n
Make one of 'em poison
And don't even tell me
Which one!

Odd that he would pick vodka as the liquor mentioned in this poem—the very drink that Dorothy preferred.

Exclusive: Ron Pataky's Connection To The CIA

Pataky was evasive when asked what he did with his life during certain periods, such as in the year 1954 and then in 1955. Penn Jones, an early JFK researcher, alleged Ron attended a CIA assassinations school in Panama. When someone online attributed that to DK biographer Lee Israel, she erupted in anger (and possibly fear), and denied to *Midwest Today* that she had ever said that. (It is not contained in her book).

The school was actually run by the U.S. Army, which claimed it was a mere education facility. It said it should not be held responsible for those who may have attended the school briefly and then gone on to commit human rights abuses in their own countries. Students have included Manuel Noriega and Omar Torrijos of Panama, Leopoldo Galtieri of Argentina and Hugo Banzer Suarez of Bolivia.

When asked by Larry Jordan about the rumor he attended the Panamanian school, Ron said, "I'd tell you if there was any truth to it. Why not? Which by the way, there's no foundation for. I did go to Guatemala when in a small military thing. There was a Communist uprising in Guatemala. I did go, but nothing to do with assassins for God's sake. Or training."

It's interesting that, without being prompted, Pataky brought up Guatemala while answering a question about a CIA school in Panama. So there must have been a connection between the two.

Jordan then inquired as to why he had gone to Guatemala in the first place.

"Well, I don't get into that story, but I will tell you enough," Ron replied. "I was in the military then, and they sent a detachment of us down there because of this Communist uprising. They sent many, not just me. What am I gonna do? Tell the Commies to 'lay off you bastards' (laughs)."

Note: Pataky was never formally in the U.S. military, but as was previously mentioned in this book, he did attend Stanford for awhile on a Navy ROTC scholarship, but was kicked out.

When Jordan asked him how the story of the potential CIA training got started, Pataky replied he had once been asked if he'd been to Guatemala as part of the military. "I said 'Yes, it was military.' And that's the end of the story. Several hundred of us went. *We were highly trained.*"

Note that last sentence. He contradicted himself.

The U.S officially had no military troops in Guatemala during the timeframe in which Pataky admitted to being there.

Pataky Was Connected To U.S. Intelligence

In the summer of 1954, in trouble with Stanford over his fake ID and arrest, Pataky probably had something to prove to himself and the world. The CIA, which declassified documents show was present on the Stanford campus acting covertly at the time, swept up all sorts of people to be part of their nefarious operations. A healthy young man like Pataky—who excelled in Spanish and had an avowed interest in foreign service—would be a good candidate for their Guatemalan incursion.

Ron Pataky's time in Guatemala has never been explored but this author can now contribute a major revelation. Though he had denied ever attending a CIA run assassin's school in Panama, he later contradicted himself.

Larry Jordan recalls, "Pataky told me, in one of our last conversations, 'I always denied it, but I really *was* there.' I was shocked, but by that time he felt comfortable talking to me because he knew I was not out to 'get him.' He said it in a voice that suggested he was confiding in me. I don't know whether he was truly being confessional or what his intent was, but he definitely said that to me."

At the very least we know Ron Pataky was in Guatemala in 1954 when the CIA staged a coup d'état and got President Jacobo Árbenz removed from office. The covert operation to overthrow Árbenz was codenamed Operation PBSuccess.

Based on this author's review of original U.S. government source documents, including Department of State and Central Intelligence Agency telegrams, correspondence and National Intelligence Estimates, a clearer picture emerges of what happened.

The Guatemalan episode is relevant to the Dorothy Kilgallen story because Ron Pataky, by his own admission, was directly involved in what is now known to be a covert operation sponsored by the Central Intelligence Agency and sanctioned at the highest levels of the U.S. government, under the false pretext of combating Communism. It was really an effort to protect the profits of the United Fruit Company, to whom Secretary of State John Foster Dulles and his brother, CIA director Allen Dulles, had financial ties. The mission was overseen by E. Howard Hunt, with help from Frank Sturgis (both of whom were later prosecuted in the Watergate scandal). Also involved was David Atlee Phillips, another notorious CIA operative. Thus it could be fairly stated Pataky had an affiliation with the CIA at one point in his life. How long that lasted is debatable. But as someone has observed, "No one ever really leaves the CIA. They just die."

The CIA armed, funded and trained a force of at least 480 men who invaded Guatemala on June 18, 1954, backed by a heavy campaign of psychological warfare. The democratically elected Guatemalan President Jacobo Árbenz was deposed on June 27 in order to protect the profits of the United Fruit Company (UFC), which had vast land holdings there, and shipped a lot of bananas. What ensued was decades of brutal U.S.-backed regimes that committed widespread torture and genocide.

Árbenz and his family were the victims of a CIA-orchestrated and intense defamation campaign that lasted from 1954 to 1960—even after the family had fled the country and went into exile. The U.S. spy agency, with the imprimatur of the Eisenhower administration, justified their draconian action by falsely claiming Árbenz was a Communist. But this was not true. He was vehemently anti-Communist.

His administration was one of the most progressive in Latin America. He expanded the right to vote, the ability of workers to organize, fostered political activism and public debate, established minimum wage laws, increased educational funding and labor rights, and improved health care. The centerpiece of his policy was agrarian reform laws under which uncultivated, large land holdings were expropriated in return for compensation and redistributed to poverty-stricken agricultural workers. Approximately 500,000 people benefitted from this. A majority were indigenous people, whose forebears had been dispossessed after the Spanish invasion. Árbenz believed in capitalism but wanted to ensure its benefits went to the entire population.

In so doing, he ran afoul of the United Fruit Company (UFC), a U.S.-based corporation that owned a vast amount of land in Guatemala. The company also virtually owned Puerto Barrios, Guatemala's only port to the Atlantic Ocean. Under the Guatemalan dictator Jorge Ubico, the American company gained control of forty-two percent of Guatemala's land, and was exempted from paying taxes and import duties. UFC also owned the country's telephone and telegraph system, and much of its railroad track.

For the Guatemalan people, it appeared that their country was being shamelessly exploited by foreign interests that took massive profits without any regard to workers' rights.

Of the 1,719,740 acres the company owned, only fifteen percent were being cultivated; the rest of the land was idle. Árbenz bought back some of the unused UFC land at twice the price the company had paid for it. He reclaimed this land to benefit his country. Laudably, his actions resulted in a significant improvement in living standards.

As Mark Viskocil observes, "Árbenz's reform was far less confiscatory than previous ones in Europe and far more restrained than either the Mexican reform before it or the Cuban one after it. As further [evidence of] its modesty, the United States had already implemented similar agrarian programs in Formosa (Taiwan) and Japan, which led U.S. aid officials and the United Nations' Food and Agriculture Organizations' senior members to consider [Árbenz's] action as 'constructive and democratic in its aims.'"

The illiteracy rate in Guatemala was over ninety percent, so Árbenz instituted literacy programs, plus credit and agricultural tech programs that would help Guatemala's peasants utilize the newly learned methods of farming so they could benefit from their labors. His allotments of land averaged out to 10.5 acres per individual, giving 100,000 Indian families, or about 500,000 individuals, cultivatable land that was being unused. Almost overnight, President Jacobo Árbenz had brought some relief to one-sixth of the Guatemalan population and for the first time since the Spanish conquest, the government returned land to the Indians.

The Evil Influence Of The Dulles Brothers

But U.S. Secretary of State John Foster Dulles had close ties to the United Fruit Company, having served as the multi-national corporation's lawyer. His brother—then-CIA director Allen Dulles—was on the board of directors and owned stock in the company.

President Eisenhower's private secretary, Ann Whitman, was the wife of UFC's top public relations officer, Ed Witman, who had produced a propaganda film called *Why the Kremlin Hates Bananas*. It depicted the company fighting on the front line of the Cold War.

The Dulles brothers wanted to protect the fortunes of the American company so they duped Eisenhower into allowing them to misuse the power of the United States government to destroy the democratically-elected leadership of Guatemala. They created a fake coup, first by using absurd propaganda techniques.

Regrettably, President Árbenz was unaware that the CIA was orchestrating the covert paramilitary operation against him. So he turned to the U.S. government for help, placing his faith in a so-called ally that claimed to be committed to advancing and spreading democracy. But he got stabbed in the back.

Allen and John Foster Dulles

It's just astounding that Dwight Eisenhower, who had served as Supreme Commander of the Allied Expeditionary Force in Europe and achieved the five-star rank as General of the Army before becoming president, was so gullible. He allowed himself to be conned into believing a Communist takeover of Guatemala was underway.

Perhaps he later realized what had happened, and that's why in his farewell address to the nation, he warned of the dangers of the "military-industrial complex."

In a stroke of luck for the aggressors, the Guatemalan state radio station had gone off the air in mid-May 1954 for maintenance, so the CIA launched a pirate broadcast outlet called the Voice of Liberation on the same frequency. It aired reports of imaginary uprisings and defections and plots to poison the water and conscript children.

One fake broadcast reported, "A group of Soviet commissars, officers and political advisers, led by a member of the Moscow Politburo, have landed...In addition to military conscription, the Communists will introduce labor conscription. A decree is already being printed. All boys and girls sixteen years old will be called for one year of labor duty in special camps, mainly for political indoctrination and to break the influence of family and church on the young people...Árbenz has already left the country. His announcements from the National Palace are actually made by a double, provided by Soviet intelligence." The Guatemalan people were not fooled, and apathetically regarded these scare tactics as farce.

The State Department said publicly the day after the invasion began it assumed military equipment delivered under an aid program to Honduras and Nicaragua was not used to arm the so-called Guatemalan revolutionary forces. The Associated Press reported June 19, 1954 that military supplies were "rushed" to those countries. "The policy of the United States government has been to try to deal with the Guatemala situation by international action through the Organization of American States and not by backing or supporting some revolutionary movement." Of course, that was a lie. Meanwhile, Sec. of State John Foster Dulles conveniently fled to his Duck Island retreat on Lake Ontario which, UPI reported, "does not have telephone service."

The invasion force of which Ron Pataky was apparently a part, was called a "liberation army" and headquartered at Copan, Honduras, about four miles from the Guatemalan border.

But it fared poorly and most of its offensives failed.

Panicking, some of the on-the-ground CIA advisers kept imploring Allen Dulles to get airplanes to invade. In a Machiavellian scheme, Dulles called a major campaign donor of Dwight Eisenhower, William Pawley, and talked him into funding the purchase of three U.S. fighter planes. Pawley withdrew money from his bank, then personally drove the Nicaraguan ambassador to the Pentagon, where he gave the money to a general. Upon receipt of this money, the general transferred ownership of three Thunderbolts to Nicaragua. The planes arrived, fully armed, in Panama that night. President Eisenhower personally authorized their use by CIA pilots. This was all done to deceive the world into believing the U.S. had no role in this coup. Eisenhower didn't want to be seen as attacking a country in the Western Hemisphere.

At dawn, the planes flew over Guatemala, bombed troop trains, destroyed a radio station used by Christian missionaries and even sank a British freighter. Loudspeakers atop the American embassy blasted the tape recorded sounds of P-38 fighters soaring into the night to frighten the people.

"What we wanted to do is have a terror campaign to terrify Árbenz particularly, to terrify his troops, much as the German Stuka bombers terrified the population of Holland, Belgium and Poland at the onset of World War Two," explained CIA operative E. Howard Hunt years later.

The CIA succeeded. President Jacobo Árbenz and his family left the country. But before doing so, he ceded power to Col. Carlos Enrique

Diaz, who formed a junta and vowed to fight the CIA's hand-picked successor, Castillo Armas. The resistance lasted through August 1954—about the same amount of time as Ron Pataky was on summer break from Stanford.

According to the Central Intelligence Agency's own in-house historian, Gerald Haines, the agency compiled lists of individuals in Árbenz's government "to eliminate immediately in event of [a] successful anti-Communist coup." Planning for assassination included budgeting, training programs, creation of hit teams, drafting of target lists of persons and transfer of armaments. In declassifying this information and other related documents, the CIA deleted the names of the targeted individuals, making it impossible to verify that none of them were killed during or in the aftermath of the coup.

Vans of CIA-trained thugs would kidnap people on the hit list, and in some cases their mutilated bodies would be thrown out of a helicopter in front of a stadium during a sporting event to terrorize the local populace.

Since Ron Pataky finally confessed that he had, indeed, attended a Panamanian assassin school (after acknowledging he had denied it for years), one can only conclude the role he assumed in Guatemala fell within the scope of some of the CIA's most egregious terrorist activities.

The CIA's psychological warfare and fear of a U.S. invasion sufficiently scared the Guatemalan Army so much it eventually refused to fight. The coup was widely denounced internationally, dealt a death blow to democracy in Guatemala, and engendered long-lasting anti-U.S. sentiment across Latin America which continues to this day.

The CIA then sought evidence of Soviet influence in Guatemala among documents in Árbenz files, but didn't find any. (Sort of reminds you of those missing WMDs that were used as an excuse for the U.S. to launch a war against Iraq, doesn't it?)

Given Ron Pataky's experience in Guatemala as a paid participant in a paramilitary operation, it is not unreasonable to suspect that he further lent himself to other CIA-sponsored activities in the years ahead. Could one of those have been to befriend Dorothy Kilgallen, keep tabs on her progress in investigating the assassination of John Kennedy, and then eliminate her by methods he had learned from the CIA at Stanford (remember the course offering of how to poison people surreptitiously)?

In his columns, Pataky seemed to defend the CIA. In his review of the movie *John Goldfarb Please Come Home*, starring Shirley MacLaine, he noted officials of Notre Dame in Indiana had complained about the silly way their football team was depicted in the film. Pataky scolded that they were remiss for not also saying anything about the unflattering way U.S. intelligence agencies were portrayed in the movie. He wrote, "*Alma mater, si ? United States, no?*"

Frank Sturgis: Dorothy Kilgallen 'Got Whacked'

In 1993, *Vanity Fair* published a dizzying story on Marita Lorenz, a one-time mistress of Fidel Castro who was involved with the CIA. In the article, it was reported Lorenz confronted Frank Sturgis in 1977 about his role in various crimes. Sturgis "bragged about all his exploits" and said Dorothy Kilgallen "got whacked" because of her probing of the JFK assassination. Lorenz then asked if he'd killed JFK to which Sturgis replied, "So what if I fucking did it? Who's gonna prove it? I have a fucking alibi. I was home watching television."

Lorenz, who died in August 2019, gained notice after testifying before the House Select Committee on Assassinations, stating she was involved with a group of anti-Cuban militants, including CIA agents and Watergate burglars Frank Sturgis and E. Howard Hunt. The German-born Lorenz spent time incarcerated in the Bergen-Belsen Nazi concentration camp as a child, making her life story all the more complex.

In 2008, *Rolling Stone* published a piece on Hunt (after his death in 2007) which included his son Saint John's claim that his father confessed to having been involved in JFK's death, also implicating President Lyndon Johnson and CIA agents Cord Meyer (whose ex-wife, JFK mistress Mary Pinchot Meyer was murdered in 1964), David Sánchez Morales, David Atlee Phillips, William Harvey and Corsican assassin Lucien Sarti.

Saint John Hunt remarked of his father, "He thought of himself as a cool dude, suave, sophisticated, intellectual. He was Mr. Smooth. A man of danger. He was perfect for the CIA. He never felt guilt about anything."

E. Howard Hunt also played a key role in planning the 1954 coup in Guatemala. Hunt served thirty-three months in prison after pleading guilty to wiretapping and conspiracy in the 1972 break-in at the Democratic National Committee headquarters in the Watergate complex.

In 1985, E. Howard Hunt brought libel charges against the Liberty Lobby's tabloid, *The Spotlight*. Mark Lane served as counsel for the tabloid. In Lorenz's deposition, she claimed she met Lee Harvey Oswald in Miami in the early 1960s while working in the "Forty Group" which she said was a CIA-sponsored anti-Castro operation. She said in late November 1963, Sturgis told her to accompany him and Oswald to Dallas along with seven anti-Castro Cubans and run weapons. In its final report, the HSCA disregarded Lorenz's claims that Hunt or the CIA had any involvement in JFK's death.

E. Howard Hunt, called as a witness before the Senate Watergate Committee and testifying in closed session on Dec. 18, 1973, revealed that he had served as the first Chief of Covert Action for the Domestic Operations Division of the CIA. This division was set up in late 1961, shortly after the Bay of Pigs fiasco, and Hunt said many agency men connected with that failure were shunted into the new domestic unit. This sent a shockwave throughout the intelligence establishment when his confidential testimony was later leaked to and published by *The New York Times*, because the CIA's official and authorized mandate was only to do their work in foreign countries.

In a 1974 interview with the newspaper, Hunt confirmed he ran the covert domestic division of the CIA from 1962 to 1966. He explained that his division had subsidized and manipulated news and publishing organizations.

Thus immediately after the assassination of President John Kennedy, all the major news media in the U.S. dutifully reported that Lee Harvey Oswald was the lone assassin. Whatever the CIA wanted the storyline to be, that's exactly what the TV networks CBS, ABC and NBC and major media like newspapers and the weekly news magazines such as *Life* and *Look* told the public. The CIA financed and manipulated the media—including history books.

One of the few people who wouldn't go along with this deception was Dorothy Kilgallen. Either because she realized what the government was doing, or simply had the instinct to know the supposed facts of the case didn't add up. She resisted following along with the pack. She was a lone wolf on the trail of the truth.

Ann Louise Bardach, the author of the *Vanity Fair* article, described Lorenz as "a patron saint of conspiracy buffs" and wrote, "Over the years, at least 11 would-be biographers have been defeated by the messy sprawl of Lorenz's story. In interviews spanning more than a month, she agreed to tell it in its entirety, a saga that has the episodic, roller-coaster feel of a Spanish-language soap opera, but that also offers seemingly tidy resolutions to many of the questions voiced about the intelligence community throughout the '60s and '70s...while at least half of what she says is readily documented by the accounts of others and by FBI memorandums, the other half lacks any corroboration, and at times even flies in the face of existing evidence."

In a 1975 interview with the *New York Daily News*, Sturgis freely bared his braggadocio. "I was a spy. I was involved in assassination plots and conspiracies to overthrow several foreign governments including Cuba, Panama, Guatemala, the Dominican Republic, and Haiti. I smuggled arms and men into Cuba for Castro and against Castro. I broke into intelligence files. I stole and photographed secret documents. That's what spies do."

Even Pataky Admitted DK May Have Been Murdered

Despite Pataky's background in having been associated with the CIA, he continued to muse, "I would probably put it at seventy-five percent that [Dorothy] died naturally. My inclination, if I think about it at all, is that she accidentally O.D.'ed. Took a little too much pill and just a little too much whiskey. She was not a big person you know. She was a small gal. And it would not take a whole heck of a lot to just quiet her down to the point she stopped...[But] I'm not a fool. Of course she could have been murdered...It's not that she had a lot of enemies, but the ones she had were very, very powerful."

Pataky said he knew of her drinking and sleeping pill usage, "Because when we went to Europe three different times, I got up close and personal, not with her, but with the morning after. The long and short of it is that she could put it away. And I saw in her cupboard several times, not just overseas, but several times, medication and I knew the medication, and it was not stomach mints." What did he mean "in her cupboard"? This implies he had been in her townhouse, yet he earlier had denied it.

Pataky offered this observation: "She was advertising that she was going to blow the lid off the Warren Commission Report. And that might get the government involved. **You know, we've got some pretty nasty people the government hires, too [contract killers]**...It's entirely possible that she did die accidentally because she was on stuff that would kill you. And, the fact about the bedroom, I don't know. That's from a hairdresser, so I'm gonna discount ninety percent of that at the outset."

"I think the fishiest thing was there wasn't enough of any one thing to kill her," he said.

Jordan recalls of the conversation, "[Pataky] also kept deflecting speculation away from the mob and said 'If she was killed, it was the government who did it.' Now was he trying to give us an important lead, or was he just protecting his friends? He said if she was killed it was because of her threat to blow the lid off the Warren Report."

Pataky tried to steer suspicion to the U.S. government. Why? Given the fact he took part in covert CIA operations, plus his overlapping association with criminal elements, a strong *prima facie* case could be made that Ron Pataky had some involvement in Kilgallen's death, likely having worked on behalf of someone else. Had Pataky been paid to keep Dorothy under surveillance, "assist" her with research for her columns, and if necessary, also seduce her?

At points he seemed to possess insider knowledge. Besides saying that Dorothy sent him a copy of the Warren Report before it was publicly released, and agreeing that her scoop in revealing Ruby's testimony in advance would have aroused government interest, he cryptically added, "But that is not the, what I am trying to say—I'd love to have a phrase here—*it was not the straw that broke the camel's back*." How did he know what got her killed? He contradicted his earlier statement, but did not elaborate.

Pataky had a history of violence. In April 1971, he was involved in an argument with Jim Otis, a former Ohio State fullback. According to news reports, the fight had begun at Pataky's home and stemmed from a disagreement over religion. Pataky claimed Otis wrestled him to the ground until Pataky admitted he was a believer. Otis then got up and left, firing a shot at Pataky as he drove away. Pataky went back in his house and popped off four shots of his own with a revolver. Otis, however, told the police a different story. According to him, the two men had first met at a bar, having had mutual friends. Pataky then invited Otis and some other people over to his house where he pulled a blackjack from his pocket and held it over his head. Pataky was charged with discharging a firearm within the city limits, freed on a fifty dollar bond.

After Jordan stated there are many loose ends pertaining to the investigation into Dorothy's death, Pataky replied, "Well, the maddening point is they're gonna stay loose. I mean, they're still investigating the Lincoln assassination..."

A Close Friend's Theory About Her Death

Dorothy's inquiry into Jack Ruby's ties to the mob, and her relentless exploration of the Warren Commission's incompetence, threatened to uncover dark secrets that powerful people—both in and out of government—did not want exposed.

Steve Rossi, half of the popular comedy team Allen & Rossi, told Kliph Nesteroff that he always believed Dorothy had been poisoned over a period of time, and not merely drugged the night she died.

"To this day, the files are open in the New York police department on how she died. They never solved the case. They alleged that she died from an overdose of barbiturates, but I know for a fact that she wasn't taking anything at the time. She felt like she was being poisoned. And I think that's what happened. Once she started writing the book on the Kennedy assassination, I think somebody came in there and poisoned her," Rossi proclaimed. "She was turning yellow, you know. I saw her two weeks before she died. She looked really bad. And she thought she was being poisoned, but they couldn't detect it. You know, there's a lot of poisons out there that are undetectable. They're usually, you know, with the government (laughs). But...I'm not going to write too much about that. I've got a whole chapter on her, but who knows who's still lurking out there?"

Perhaps any yellowing of Dorothy's skin or eyes was the result of jaundice, which can be a complication of anemia, the condition DK struggled with throughout her life.

Rossi died on June 22, 2014, before any such book pertaining to Kilgallen was ever published. Steve was an immensely talented man: a singer, songwriter, actor, stand-up comedian. In 1963, Allen & Rossi were the first comedians to go to Washington, D.C. to lobby Congress on the House floor. They spoke on behalf of the Epilepsy Foundation.

Rossi and his comedy partner appeared on scores of television shows (including with the Beatles on Ed Sullivan's) and headlined Las Vegas. On Sept. 6, 1964 they were the mystery guests on *What's My Line?*

After Dorothy guessed who they were, Arlene asked them to do part of their comedy routine from the Sands. With Steve playing straight man to Marty, they tore up the show with their puns, and all the panelists and host John Daly could be seen laughing uproariously. It was a happy show that Dorothy was on. Both men hugged and kissed her on both cheeks as they said good night to the panel.

Dorothy with chum Steve Rossi

Arlene Francis's son, Peter Gabel, told this author, "To me, the Jack Ruby connection has always been so striking and makes her murder seem so likely. Points about her bed and the destruction of her papers increase this probability. I have always felt that my childhood friend Oliver Stone's *JFK* was a great movie...and I wrote an article myself about the social-psychological reasons for the rush toward the lone gunman theory, published in my first book, *The Bank Teller and Other Essays on the Politics of Meaning*."

There is no statute of limitations on murder, and there are people alive who could be questioned.

15
Dorothy's Legacy

Television producer Bill Todman noted finding talented panelists wasn't as easy as the public might think. While most of them were members of the entertainment business, some, like Dorothy Kilgallen and Bennett Cerf, gained their reputations from journalism and publishing. Todman had outlined this sentiment as a guest columnist for the *VOB* back in August 1964.

"We're constantly searching for new panelists because we cast more than one thousand celebrity 'spots' on nine shows each year, and there just aren't enough players in the dugout. That's why you occasionally see Dorothy and Bennett 'moonlighting' on other shows. But we expect them to be our regulars on their own show—along with Arlene and John—for a long time to come. I can't imagine *What's My Line?* without them, and I hope I never have to."

The Show Must Go On: The Fate Of *What's My Line?*

Television producer Gil Fates chronicled his many years in show business in the 1978 book *What's My Line? The Inside History* of *TV's Most Famous Panel Show*.

The book, long since out of print, offers a warm and witty look at the making of game shows during the 1950s-1970s. He said an article published in the July 23, 1966 issue of *TV Guide,* written by Muriel Davidson, amplified the fervor around finding a permanent replacement for Dorothy's seat on the panel.

Davidson wrote in her piece entitled "The Great Woman Hunt" how more than eight months after DK's death the show had only inched closer to being whole again, writing it was "one of the most determined woman hunts since David Selznick set out to find someone to play Scarlett O'Hara in *Gone With the Wind*."

Various celebrities were in the running, including Helen Gurley Brown, Joanna Barnes, Dr. Joyce Brothers, Jayne Meadows, Sheilah Graham, Dina Merrill, Joan Fontaine, Jeanne Paar, Pamela Mason, Betsy Von Furstenberg and Davidson herself.

Davidson revealed the network had three frontrunners in the search: Phyllis Newman, a cast member of the pioneering political satire show *That Was The Week That Was*; Dr. Suzanne Oakland Cott (later Director of Editorials for WCBS-TV in New York); and syndicated columnist

Aileen Mehle, better known under her pen name Suzy Knickerbocker. Who would inherit the one-thousand-dollar-a-week job, Davidson asked her readers.

"And so, nearly every day in the week, one hopeful or another is interviewed or tested for the vacant chair on the show. The hopeful is solemnly ushered into the executive conference room to face—usually—the gray-haired director Frank Heller, the dour Bob Bach and the tall and crew-cut Gil Fates. Two pages of mimeographed requisite questions which should be asked in both the 'product' and 'service' categories of *What's My Line?* are slipped under her nose. These she never gets to look at until she leaves. Now she plays the Game. And plays the Game. And plays the Game. And leaves—dizzy from firing questions, guessing right once or twice or not at all.

"She may be puzzled, too, as to who is minding the store on the 30th floor. Almost all day these grown men play the Game. Should she be asked to lunch with one of them, he will take her to a very nice restaurant, sit down and say, 'That girl sitting at the third table to your right is, uh,

THE GREAT WOMAN HUNT

The search for a 'What's My Line?' panelist
to replace Dorothy Kilgallen
has reached prodigious proportions

BY MURIEL DAVIDSON

salaried and deals in a product.' And before a menu is proffered, Hopeful is off and playing the Game again."

Davidson quoted Tony Randall's take on adding Kitty Carlisle to the panel on a permanent basis, "Arlene Francis is adorable. Kitty is adorable. And two 'adorables' on the same show was one adorable too many."

"We were inundated with mail," Fates wrote of the article. "But, as has always been policy, we answered every letter. Some writers suggested other people—sisters, wives, or friends. A college freshman suggesting his mother in place of Dorothy sent a knockout picture of her in a bathing suit. He described her as 'Bitchy (a little), Beautiful (very), and Bright (two degrees).' A helpful chap from Providence, Rhode Island suggested Bette Davis. But most writers suggested themselves."

Davidson ended her article by saying next fall's Nielsen ratings would determine if the network made the right hire.

Ultimately, Kilgallen was never replaced on the panel, with show regulars Arlene Francis and Bennett Cerf continuing on with two weekly guest stars to round out the four-person team.

Swing said despite Dorothy's popularity on the show, the producers did receive some complaints about her presumed competitive nature.

"I had dinner one night with [Mark] Goodson and [Bill] Todman and Dorothy at the Plaza and there was a discussion. They'd get so much hate mail about Dorothy. 'Get that woman off the show. We'll never watch it again.' It wasn't good. But she knew what people were saying about her," Swing noted. "[Dorothy] never wanted to get a 'no.'"

The Same But...Different

WML? left CBS in September 1967, sliding into syndication where it remained until 1975. When interviewed about the show leaving CBS, John Daly remarked that DK's death was not the reason for the change of format.

"We unquestionably miss Dorothy. We really could find no one to take her place, with her kind of incisiveness and competitiveness. Dorothy went for this like I would go for a Pulitzer Prize. You know, Dorothy came to success early in her life. Maintaining her place was important to her. Competitiveness was important. I remember finding her crying one night after the show. When I asked her what was wrong, she said, 'I didn't get (guess) anyone.' I said, 'Little one, this is a parlor game!' But that is how seriously she took this."

As Fates explained, "Taped for syndication means just that. The program is produced specifically for the syndicated market rather than for a network sale. These brand new, first-run programs are sold to television stations throughout the country—and indeed the world—on an individual basis, to be set into each station's broadcast schedule as that station's program manager sees fit."

By then the show was hosted by journalist Wally Bruner followed by actor Larry Blyden. Cerf continued to be seen on the show in syndication, years after he passed away in 1971. Ms. Francis also continued to appear on the panel. But the *WML?* of the late 1960s and early '70s did not possess the gloss and sophistication of the live show. Not by a longshot.

According to John Daly's 1991 obituary published in *The New York Times*, "When he agreed to take the job as host of *What's My Line?* in 1950, he was told it would last about six months. Its long life and his popularity on the show led to a vice-presidency at ABC in charge of news, special events, public affairs, religious programs and sports. When the show ended after 17 years on the air, Mr. Daly was named director of the *Voice of America*. He resigned after one year because of a dispute over personnel with the director of the United States Information Agency, which ran the *Voice of America*."

The Complete Directory to Prime Time Network TV Shows: 1946-Present offers a pithy assessment of why *WML?* enjoyed such longevity:

"That little game, by itself, hardly warranted an 18-year run, when other panel shows of the early 1950s came and went every month. But *What's My Line?* was something special, both for the witty and engaging panel, and for a certain élan which few other shows have ever captured. There were no flashy celebrities-of-the-moment or empty-headed pretty faces on this panel: they were obviously very intelligent people all out to have some genteel fun with an amusing parlour game."

The *Wall Street Journal* called the reruns, "A bracing antidote to today's dispiriting talk-a-thons, humiliating reality shows and hostile cable-news programs. What strikes you first is the civility."

Dorothy's Credibility As A Journalist

Dorothy Kilgallen was clearly a multi-faceted journalist. She reported on topics ranging from murder trials to entertainment news. She often used her *Voice of Broadway* column to provide commentary on various society ills and provide government watchdog reporting. In a July 1964 column, for instance, she even discussed New York City's drug problem, which would only continue to grow in the ensuring decades:

"The Treasury Dept. is puzzled. Its narcotics sleuths have scored with a record number of 'busts' during the past few months, yet New York addicts report there's more heroin—and even cocaine—available now than there has been in years."

In March of 1965 she correctly surmised the U.S. government would further escalate the situation in Vietnam, writing, "Officialdom isn't telling the public more than a whit about what's going on in Vietnam—and, more important, what is going to go on. The U.S. has a lot more over there (and near there) than the man in the street suspects, and the operation will get a lot bigger before we make our exit from that territory."

On Sept. 10, 1965 she warned, "There are now strong indications in Washington that the number of men needed for Vietnam will be raised dramatically. It will be closer to 200,000 than 125,000, the experts say—and it may go higher than that."

Dorothy scored the first exclusive interview with Bruno Hauptmann (the man convicted of the abduction and murder of the Lindbergh baby); followed FDR during his first presidential campaign; attended Queen Elizabeth's coronation as well as Princess Margaret's wedding; and was on hand for Khrushchev's famed U.S. visit. Her instincts led to a man wrongly convicted of murdering his wife to later be exonerated.

Time magazine wrote of Kilgallen in its Nov. 19, 1965 edition, "No one could fault Dorothy for her resourcefulness as a reporter. With the help of one of the most liberal expense accounts in the business and a smile that rarely came unstuck, she wangled stories that eluded others."

At the time of her death, she had a book deal with Random House. The work was published posthumously in 1967 as *Murder One*, with the aid of ghostwriter Allan Ullman. It did not contain any information about the JFK assassination. In Dorothy's inimitable style, the book relayed her experience covering six infamous cases: Finch-Tregoff; Greta Peltz; Eva Coo; The State vs. Robert Allen Edwards; the Creighton-Appelgate case; and in a chapter called "When Justice Took the Day Off," her coverage of the Dr. Sam Sheppard trial.

Dorothy divulged in her book: "To me and a number of my colleagues—who, coming from the 'outside,' had not been infected with the preconception of the doctor's guilt that hung like thick smog over the city of Cleveland before and during the trial—the decision of the jury was incomprehensible...When my story of the verdict appeared in the Hearst papers, the editors ordered Page 1 banners declaring 'Dorothy Kilgallen Shocked.' And shocked I was!"

In the book's introduction, she divulged her role in aiding the wrongfully convicted doctor. "Very few of today's readers know that among the documents that helped to persuade Federal District Judge Carl Weinman that Sheppard had not had a fair trial was a deposition of mine (given May 9, 1964). It concerned a matter that I could not reveal when I covered the trial, although daily it weighed on my mind."

Questioned by Sheppard's new counsel, F. Lee Bailey, Dorothy disclosed the judge in the first trial, Edward Blythin, had been prejudicial against the defendant during a meeting in the judge's chambers before the trial even began.

Bailey later served as legal counsel for several other well-known (and controversial) cases including Albert DeSalvo (a suspect in the Boston Strangler murders), heiress Patty Hearst's trial for bank robberies, U.S. Army Captain Ernest Medina for the My Lai Massacre, and as a member of the "dream team" in the trial of O. J. Simpson.

When asked why Dorothy would want to leave her post in New York City to cover an Ohio-based trial, she had replied, "Well, it has all the ingredients of what in the newspaper business we call a good murder. It has a very attractive victim, who was pregnant, and the accused is an important member of the community, a respectable, very attractive man. Then, added to that, you have the fact that it is a mystery as to who did it."

Blythin responded by calling it an "open and shut case" labeling Sheppard "guilty as hell."

Dorothy Kilgallen Shocked: Believes Reversal Likely

Journal-American

7TH SPORTS RACING SPORTS COMPLETE

Sheppard Case Jury In Doubt Till Last Day

Held at Gunpoint 24 Hours by Her Rejected Suitor

Facing It

20 Ballots Were Taken

Kidnap-Killing Case Dropped: Father Goes Free In Slaying of Girl

Girl Freed Unharmed

Wants Doom Prophet Held Mentally Ill

No Snow Slated For Christmas

Hiccoughs Again Upset Pope's Rest

School Fire In Stamford

8 way Gunmen Gets $4,000 Store Payroll

Dorothy Kilgallen's Opinion of Verdict

Liberace Takes Rest Due to Heart Strain

100 MPH Costs $100 Fine in N.J. Court

Kilgallen said court clerk Edward T. Murray backed up her claim, having also heard the judge proclaim Sheppard as guilty. Paul Holmes, who covered the trial for the *Chicago Tribune*, wrote in his 1961 book *The Sheppard Murder Case*, he felt the judge's behavior towards the defendant came off as biased.

In November of 1964, the doctor was released from prison. On June 6, 1966, the United States Supreme Court ruled Sheppard was entitled to a new trial, which was held in October and November of '66. Dr. Paul Leland Kirk provided testimony that turned the case on its side: a bloodstain from the bedroom definitely came from a third person; a left-handed person administered the blows Marilyn sustained to her skull. Sheppard was right-handed.

Sadly, Sheppard's life on the outside was short-lived. He self-medicated with alcohol, dying of liver failure on April 6, 1970. His saga loosely served as inspiration for the 1963 television show *The Fugitive* and the 1993 film of the same name, wherein a beleaguered doctor claims his wife was slain by a "one-armed man."

In 1989, Sheppard's son, Sam Reese Sheppard, launched an investigation of his own. He zeroed in on Richard Eberling, the Sheppards' window washer at the time of the murder. Eberling was serving time in prison for killing elderly widow Ethel May Durkin in 1984. Sheppard Jr.

successfully petitioned the courts to have his father's body exhumed.

A 1997 DNA test found that Eberling could not be ruled out as the source of blood and semen found at the crime scene because he shared a key genetic marker with those bodily fluids. However, the analysis could not definitively declare a match. Eberling maintained his innocence, but contradicted himself many times during interviews and in speaking with fellow inmates. He died in prison in 1998.

Launching An Investigation

Since the publication of the *Midwest Today* article "Who Killed Dorothy Kilgallen?" written by this author, interest in Kilgallen has increased exponentially. The piece has been much discussed on online blogs and referenced in several JFK books including *Hit List: An In-Depth Investigation into the Mysterious Deaths of Witnesses to the JFK Assassination* by Richard Belzer and David Wayne, published in 2013, plus *They Killed Our President: 63 Reasons to Believe There Was a Conspiracy to Assassinate JFK*, also released in 2013, authored by Wayne, Dick Russell and Jesse Ventura. The article also served as a springboard for author Mark Shaw's four books on Dorothy.

Before the *Midwest Today* exposé, the only other official resource for all things Kilgallen was a 1979 book written by Lee Israel, simply entitled *Kilgallen*. Israel was consulted for the magazine article and provided some valuable insights.

Sadly, Israel's reputation as a celebrated biographer of Kilgallen, Tallulah Bankhead and Estée Lauder was tarnished after it was revealed she'd spent years as a literary forger as a means of financially supporting herself. By the early 1990s, her career as a writer of books and magazine articles had fizzled. She turned to forging letters (estimated to exceed four hundred) posing as famed writers and actors. Her crimes evolved to stealing actual letters and autographed papers of celebrities from libraries and archives, then replacing them with fake copies she had created. Along with accomplice Jack Hock, they sold forged works and the stolen original items. Their criminal activity went on for more than a year until two undercover FBI agents were able to question Israel.

Her 2008 autobiography of this experience, called *Can You Ever Forgive Me?*, was adapted into the 2018 film of the same name starring Melissa McCarthy as Israel. Lee Israel died in 2014.

Ron Pataky referred to Israel as "a pain in the ass" saying, "She came to Columbus to interview me for the book. And I could tell right away that she had something, a chip on the shoulder. I finally said 'What is it about you that makes you sort of want to take the low road with me?' She said, 'Well I just don't believe that someone of Dorothy's beauty and talent could fall for an Ohio newspaper man.' I pulled out a handwritten note from London and it ended with 'Guess who stood on London Bridge last night and guess who she thought of?' And signed it always 'love.'" Elaborating on Israel he said, "I think she was a lesbian and in love with Dorothy. I was engaged to Anna Maria Alberghetti for God's sakes. She's a real beauty."

Pataky was caught in a lie when he told *Midwest Today* he was involved with the singer at the time he knew Kilgallen (and so couldn't have had a romantic interest in the columnist). Harrison Carroll noted in his *Behind the Scenes In Hollywood* column, which appeared on March 3, 1964, that her "romance with Ron Pataky has cooled."

Dominick Dunne's 2006 *Vanity Fair* piece "Spilling Secrets" revealed his decades-long fascination with Kilgallen and her mysterious death. "In later years, when I worked in live television, I became a friend of Dorothy's younger sister, Eleanor Kilgallen, who was the New York casting director for Universal Studios in Hollywood. A couple of times, after a couple of drinks, I asked Eleanor about Dorothy's death and the Ruby notes. She would never talk to me about it, and she made me feel like a skunk for asking, but I was dying to know the truth."

Dunne went on to recount a telephone call that he received while a guest on the *Larry King Live* show from a woman in Oklahoma who asked if he had any opinion of Kilgallen's death.

"What I recalled for the woman from Tulsa was a persistent rumor at the time that the sleeping pills in Kilgallen's stomach had not dissolved, which meant that they were undigested. Liz Smith, another famous gossip columnist, told me recently that the late Arlene Francis, who was also on the panel of *What's My Line?* [with Kilgallen], had been with Kilgallen the evening she had died, and she always maintained that Dorothy was not drunk that night. I forgot to tell the woman who called in that no notes or tapes from the Ruby interview [that Kilgallen had with Jack Ruby] have ever been found. Kilgallen told people that she was going to break the case, so Ruby must have told her something that someone important didn't want her to print. At least that's my interpretation."

Why hadn't law enforcement interviewed the residents of Dorothy's townhouse, her hairdressers or the bartender at P.J. Clarke's, for starters? What about Katherine Stone or the others from the television show who saw Dorothy that night with the "late date"? Surely, the police could have circulated a photo of Ron Pataky, asking those present at the bar that night if he had been the man seen with Dorothy. He could have rather quickly been ruled out, or confirmed, as a suspect. A sketch artist could also have been secured. It would have been simple to check flight logs to New York City from Columbus, Ohio to see if Pataky truly had an alibi for the night before Dorothy's body was discovered.

How had Kilgallen returned to her home the night of her death? If by taxi, drivers' logs could have been obtained if police had been so inclined to do the legwork.

Throughout his numerous conversations over a period of years with *Midwest Today*, Ron Pataky seemed strangely ambivalent about being accused of murdering Dorothy Kilgallen. Was that a sign of his innocence...or his sociopathy?

Decades later, Ron—then fifty-six—went on to earn a master's degree in Christian Counseling from Jerry Falwell's Liberty University in Lynchburg, Virginia, and a Ph.D. in Christian Counseling from Trinity Theological Seminary in Newburgh, Indiana via online courses. Had he turned to religion as a way to assuage his conscience?

Pataky died on May 16, 2022. His involvement in Dorothy's death may never be fully known.

The Mob And JFK

G. Robert Blakey is considered the nation's foremost authority on the Racketeer Influenced and Corrupt Organizations Act (RICO). He helped draft and secure passage of Title III on wiretapping of the federal 1968 Crime Control Act, as well as draft and implement wiretapping legislation in thirty nine of the forty-three states that have enacted those laws.

He served as chief counsel and staff director to the U.S. House Select Committee on Assassinations (HSCA) from 1977 to 1979, and helped to draft the President John F. Kennedy Assassination Records Collection Act of 1992. He was formerly a special prosecutor in the Justice Department under Robert F. Kennedy and was Chief Counsel of the McClellan Committee.

Blakey has stated he believes mobsters Marcello, Santo Trafficante Jr. and Sam Giancana orchestrated JFK's assassination. Recall the claim that Joseph P. Kennedy recruited the Chicago Mob, also known as the "Outfit" to help swing Cook County in favor of his son's 1960 bid for the White House. Blakey said FBI wiretaps confirm organized crime at the very least provided financial support of the candidate and helped stuff ballot boxes. "Can you say that mob money made a difference? My judgment is yes," Blakey said.

Blakey has theorized Trafficante recruited anti-Castro Cubans and that the assassination was not authorized by the Mob's national commission, but rather, based in Carlos Marcello's New Orleans—a scent DK's nose had also picked up on during her investigation.

But this author has reviewed a declassified CIA memo dated March 3, 1979 in which S.D. Breckinridge outlined details of his discussion with Blakey regarding what the final HSCA report would say about the Agency. It is clear that the CIA was successful in exerting major influence over the investigation to withhold from the public relevant information. Referring to Blakey's cooperation, Breckinridge wrote, "He said he thought we would find ourselves a minor part of it all, and that the headlines would address the role of organized crime..."

In 1978, Blakey reached out to the New York Medical Examiner's Office to request information about Dorothy Kilgallen's death. On April 13, Chief Medical Examiner Dominick J. DiMaio replied to Blakey, "Enclosed you will find the complete file on Ms. Kilgallen who died on November 8, 1965."

Blakey believed the famed journalist's death was "fishy." He told this author, "Look at how and who found her. How was she dressed? In short, why were the normal rules not followed? Why was a homicide investigation not undertaken?"

Blakey also revealed, "My deputy chief counsel recently ate dinner in the French Quarter. When (the) chef learned who Gary was he came out to the table and spent more than an hour telling Gary the inside story of LHO [Lee Harvey Oswald]. The French Q is a small place. Everybody knows everybody."

The Cover-Up Continues

Oliver Stone's 1991 epic movie *JFK*, which was inspired by New Orleans District Attorney Jim Garrison (who ironically played the part of Chief Justice Earl Warren in the film), aroused public awareness of the numerous flaws in the Warren Report. So Congress passed the President John F. Kennedy Assassination Records Collection Act of 1992. The Act mandated that all assassination-related material be housed in a single collection in the National Archives and Records Administration (NARA). Thus for the first time, a truly independent group—the Assassination Records Review Board (ARRB)—was created to collate all these materials from various agencies.

An important cornerstone of the JFK Act is that it required members of the ARRB board to be "impartial private citizens" who were not employed by the federal government and had not "had any previous involvement with any official investigation or inquiry conducted by a federal, state, or local government, relating to the assassination of President John F. Kennedy."

Significantly, the JFK Act had been passed over the strenuous objections of President George H.W. Bush, whose secret role with the CIA pre-dated the Kennedy assassination and was long before he was appointed as head of the CIA prior to his White House term. To try to stymie the work of the ARRB, Bush cravenly refused to appoint any members to the board, which had to await action by his successor, President Bill Clinton. This wasted eighteen months of the three-year mandate the ARRB had been granted. The joke was on Bush, however, because Congress went ahead and extended the mandate of the group to four years.

The ARRB was empowered to require federal agencies to disclose, forthwith, their records on the assassination and it gave the group the power to collect materials that the agencies themselves may not have identified as assassination-related.

The ARRB managed to assemble more than five million pages of assassination-related records, photographs, motion pictures, sound recordings and artifacts, many of which have been released.

The ARRB was never envisioned as an investigative entity as such, but it turned into one. Fortuitously, the group was given the authority to issue subpoenas and even grant immunity to witnesses. It hauled a whole bunch of important sources in for questioning. It did a masterful job of destroying the official account of Kennedy's assassination, which is probably why most Americans have never heard of it or been informed of its earthshaking revelations. The press in this country has largely ignored the ARRB's work, and although all of the records described are open for viewing and reproduction, *they are not available online*. Why?

According to the Assassination Records Review Board, "The [Warren] Commission failed to examine some of the most critical evidence in the case: the photographs and X-rays from President Kennedy's autopsy. The Commission relied instead on artistic renderings of the photographs prepared by an illustrator working from verbal descriptions provided by the chief autopsy prosector." This can be laid at the doorstep of Earl Warren who refused to allow the W.C. to examine actual images.

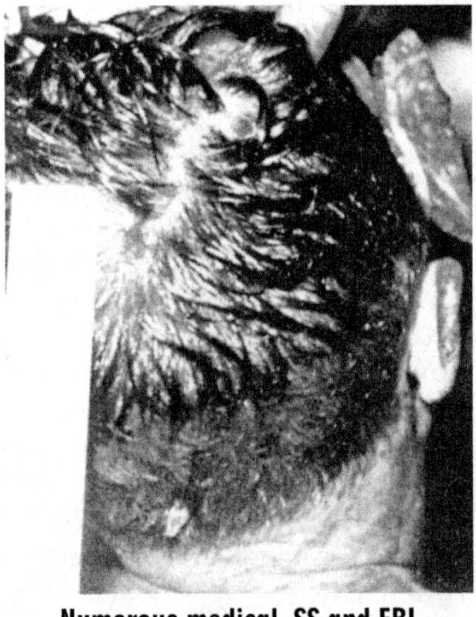

Numerous medical, SS and FBI witnesses claim this photo of the back of JFK's head is not accurate as it fails to show the big blow-out in back.

Probably fearing that eventually these incriminating materials would leak. Somewhere along the line, autopsy materials were altered to hide the truth.

The ARRB took depositions which established that some of the Kennedy autopsy photographs and X-rays have been altered, forged, or destroyed. John Stringer, the official autopsy photographer, testified that the official set of pictures of the brain now at the National Archives are not those that he took at the time. Robert Knudsen, White House photographer, had in his possession—at one and the same time—photos that displayed a major blowout in the rear of the president's head and others that did not (meaning the latter set were faked). Saundra Spencer, who processed the originals, contended that she knows they are not the same because they do not have the same physical features as other images she processed using the same

Dr. Charles Carrico

Dr. Charles Crenshaw

Dr. Paul Peters

Dr. Robert McClelland

Dr. Ronald Jones

Dr. Kenneth Salyer

PARKLAND DOCTORS POINTING TO THE LOCATION OF JFK'S HEAD WOUND

film, some of which she still possesses.

Experts who have studied the so-called X-rays of Kennedy's skull contend that they have been fabricated in at least two different ways: (a) the right lateral cranial X-ray has been altered by imposing a dense patch to conceal a massive blow-out to the back of the head; and (b) the anterior-posterior X-ray has been altered by adding a 6.5 mm metal-like object to implicate a 6.5 mm weapon. (Full body X-rays taken the night of the autopsy showed no such bullet).

The House Select Committee On Assassinations (1976-1979) interviewed the three autopsy pathologists—Drs. Humes, Boswell and Finck—and the radiologist, Dr. Ebersole, and asked each individually to point out on any one of several photographs and X-rays the location of the wound on the back of Kennedy's skull. Each doctor independently pointed out an area much farther down on the back of the head, almost to the base of the skull, and remained adamant about it. But the HSCA claimed the wound was a lot higher, nearly at the top back of the head, in the "collick" area.

SS Agent Clint Hill points to where Kennedy's head wound was.

To try to clarify these discrepancies, the ARRB summoned four Parkland doctors who treated Kennedy in 1963. They were interviewed by the ARRB in 1998 and for two and a half hours shared their recollections. ALL of them remembered a massive wound in the lower right rear of Kennedy's head. They expressed disbelief when seeing the photo purported to be the back of JFK's head, with the hair intact. But they also questioned skull X-rays which seemed to show the whole right hemisphere of Kennedy's head as missing. This, of course, is preposterous because they would have noticed such major damage if it had existed the day the president was brought into the emergency room. Plus his face was intact.

Furthermore, Thomas Robison, one of the morticians who worked on the late president at Bethesda, described JFK's wounds and the partial embalming process in notes as follows:

•Large gaping hole in back of head. Patched by placing piece of rubber over it. Thinks skull full of Plaster of Paris.

•Smaller wound in right temple. Crescent shaped, flapped down

•(Approx 2) Small shrapnel wounds in face. Packed with wax. HOW DO YOU GET SHRAPNEL WOUNDS—EVEN SMALL ONES—IN THE FACE IF SHOTS ARE COMING FROM BEHIND?

Notice that Mr. Robison made absolutely no mention of damage to the top or front of the skull. Yet the official story is that there was.

So the bottom line is, some of the X-rays and photographs on file at the National Archives today include materials that are likely not genuine and therefore cannot be trusted by researchers. Unfortunately, these materials have been relied upon by three separate investigative bodies—the Clark panel, the Rockefeller Commission and the House Select Committee On Assassinations. Former ARRB member Douglas Horne points out these groups supported "the Warren Commission's findings that President Kennedy was shot from above and behind, and [discounted] the expert observations from Parkland Hospital in Dallas that President Kennedy had an exit wound in the back of his head."

Life Without Dorothy

The *Journal-American* ceased publication in 1966, not long after Dorothy's death. The Hearst Corporation donated the photographic morgue to The University of Texas at Austin in 1968.

By the terms of the will Dorothy had drawn up in 1941 and never got around to changing, Richard stood to inherit almost everything. He got the jointly owned townhouse, sold it in 1966 for $290,000 (the equivalent of more than $2.8 million today) and then bought it back. DK had various insurance policies worth $90,000, and her husband was the sole beneficiary. There were also several pension funds. Only the Goodson-Todman profit sharing dividend of $82,000 was shared among the three children. There were $576 in government savings bonds for Kerry.

In 1967, Dick Kollmar married fashion designer Anne Fogarty, whose designs Dorothy often wore, including the night she died. Fogarty's ladylike clothes were aimed at women on a limited budget.

Syndicated columnist Jack O'Brian reported that Richard and his new wife were planning to do some remodeling of the townhouse, including knocking down two walls on the second and third floors. A "demolition party" was scheduled for May 6, 1968 at which sledgehammers and wrecking bars were supplied to party guests so they could participate in the deconstruction. Several days later, *Philadelpha Inquirer* fashion editor Rubye Graham (a friend of Anne Fogarty) reported the party had been a "smashing" success.

Marc Sinclaire said that some interior decorator (he never found out who) had done a lot to change what had been Dorothy's residence, but curiously did not change the lock on the front door of the brownstone. One day he decided to see if his key still worked, and it did. He boldly went roaming around and discovered the remains of DK's beloved doll collection in the basement. Strangely, the heads had been pulled off.

At age sixty, Richard died in his sleep at his home on Jan. 7, 1971. Some acquaintances speculated it was suicide. David Susskind's widow, Joyce, described Dick as "this guy who was always in his cups. He had the looks and the intelligence to do something with his life if he had not had this alcoholic cross to bear."

Marlin Swing had suspected Kollmar met with foul play.

"I can believe that he would have committed suicide because he was a very sad character and drunk a lot, but also it was suspect that something was done because he did have this material from her, from Dorothy, that he had control of, so there was some suspicion about him being murdered," Swing revealed.

James Kilgallen died on Dec. 21, 1982, at age ninety-four, having worked as a reporter for more than seventy-five years.

He once said: "I've covered railroad wrecks, airplane and ship disasters, sitdown strikes, beauty contests in Atlantic City, eucharistic congresses in New Orleans and Barcelona, Spain, the World Series, golf championships, major prize fights, courtroom dramas, executions and national political conventions—in fact every conceivable type of story in this country and abroad. In what other business would I have had such action?"

Dorothy's mother Mae died in 1985, also having reached an advanced age. She was 97 years old.

Johnnie Ray died Feb. 24, 1990 believing up to the end that Dorothy had been murdered. Well repected showbiz publicist Alan Eichler, who managed Ray, told this author, "Johnny said he knew who killed her, but he never said who it was. He said he couldn't prove it and that's why they didn't come after him. It had to do with her Kennedy investigations. Johnnie said she always slept in her office, but was found dead in the bedroom."

He continued, "I met her as a young press agent, but didn't really know her. I managed to plant a couple of items in her column and would hand-deliver things to her townhouse."

Ray received a highly coveted honor in 1982 when English pop band Dexy's Midnight Runners mentioned him in the intro of their now-iconic tune *Come on Eileen*. "Poor old Johnnie Ray/Sounded sad upon the radio/But he moved a million hearts in mono/Our mothers cried, sang along, who'd blame them."

Marc Sinclaire died May 19, 2006, at Palm Terrace of St. Petersburg under the care of hospice. He was seventy-two.

Arlene Francis passed away in 2001 at age ninety-three of Alzheimer's disease. Son Peter Gabel was a co-founder of the Arlene Francis Center for Spirit, Art, and Politics, located in Santa Rosa, California. He died suddenly on Oct. 25, 2022 from a heart attack.

Dorothy, her parents and Richard Kollmar are buried in the same plot at Gate of Heaven Cemetery. Sister Eleanor Kilgallen died Dec. 20, 2014. Her final resting place is George Washington Memorial Park, Paramus, New Jersey.

What Might Have Been

Had Dorothy been able to complete her research efforts and publish her account of what happened that day in Dallas, would the history books read differently? Would Oswald have been exonerated? Would she have been able to conclusively link Ruby and Oswald? Would Marcello and other mobsters have been indicted? Would agents from the CIA have been implicated, too? Would a Pulitzer Prize have rested on a shelf in her office, the "Cloop"?

What about her personal life? Had she lived, would she have rekindled her love affair with Johnnie Ray? Perhaps she would have found happiness with someone else. Would Dorothy have pursued additional work in television? Perhaps as a news anchor or documentary producer?

In all certitude, had Dorothy Kilgallen lived past November 1965, she would have closely followed the trial of Robert Kennedy's alleged assassin, Sirhan Sirhan. Her writings would have chronicled her thoughts on the escalation of military intervention in Vietnam, the election of Richard M. Nixon as president, and his fall from grace during the Watergate scandal. Her journalistic career would have continued into the 1970s and 1980s—even beyond. She would have scrutinized the Iran-Contra affair and been present when the Berlin Wall was demolished.

It's likely Dorothy would have received an invitation to attend and report on the wedding of Charles and Lady Diana Spencer (perhaps wearing the same tiara she donned at Queen Elizabeth's coronation)?

In time, her dishy columns and hard-nosed news articles would have appeared in fewer newspapers as publications merged or folded altogether. She would, however, have been a household name at the time of a natural death. She would have mentored the next crop of columnists, including "The Grand Dame of Dish" Liz Smith.

"Kilgallen was a friend I got to know when I was first starting out working as an assistant," Smith said in 2006.

Dorothy's writing would remain a little bit catty, very chatty and engrossingly inquisitive. She hadn't known any other way to be.

When Dorothy and her family appeared on Edward R. Murrow's *Person to Person* television program in 1956, Murrow asked Dorothy if she had to narrow her work down to just one profession, what would she choose. Despite her wholly unique career in a myriad of realms, one clear winner emerged.

She replied, "I love television. I have so much fun on *What's My Line?* playing the game, and I love our morning radio program too. But I think that I would have to settle for my first love, and my true love, the newspaper business. It still has me, and always will I think—I hope."

Epilogue

Writing a book on Dorothy Kilgallen seemed the inevitable progression of a project I began in 2006 at the age of sixteen, for my family business, *Midwest Today* magazine. I had discovered reruns of *What's My Line?* airing in the wee hours on the Game Show Network. Upon doing a Google search of Ms. Kilgallen, I found that although she was a long-time New Yorker, she'd actually been born in Chicago. Thus a Midwest connection was discovered, giving me the green light to do a story that was relevant to our reader focus.

I began writing the article, compiling the source materials available, while my father helped us score an interview with Lee Israel, whose 1979 book *Kilgallen* was the first in-depth look at Dorothy's life and death. We posted in an online chat room on the GSN's website, looking for leads. It was there we connected with some die-hard Dorothy fans and researchers including Kathryn Fauble, who at the time, wished to remain anonymous when being referenced or quoted. We learned the name of the mystery man who wooed Dorothy near the end of her life—a person Israel had only referred to as the "Out-of-Towner" in her book. My father—wanting to shield me from direct contact with a man who was (unofficially) suspected of being involved in DK's death—managed to befriend him.

Amazingly, they ended up having various lengthy conversations on the phone (all of which were taped), as the man continued to call us even after my article on Dorothy was published in 2007. In these chats, he became comfortable enough to reveal things about himself, which only strengthened suspicions about his possible role in Kilgallen's demise.

In 2008, I finished high school, then attended college at the University of Iowa, graduating with a bachelor's degree in American Studies and history. I then took employment at a daily newspaper as a reporter and began doing work as a freelance writer for magazines.

In 2014 Mark Shaw wrote to me requesting an interview. A San Francisco-based attorney and author, he wanted to learn more about the research that had gone into my article. He was in the process of writing *The Reporter Who Knew Too Much*, published in 2016. In an email to me, he commented, "When I discovered your article, I was most impressed with your investigative reporting skills. Dorothy Kilgallen would have been impressed as well since she admired those who dug deep to uncover the truth so that justice prevailed."

He wrote my father, (the publisher of *Midwest Today*), "Wow, and wow again. This is a great deal to digest...How blessed I am to have found you and Sara. Very much so."

We supplied him with rare source material and made important introductions, guided him in his research and stayed in touch with him through extensive email and phone contacts in the ensuing years.

Yet on his website, it states that "by pure serendipity, and Dorothy's guidance from the hereafter, [Shaw] was able to gain the trust of Kathryn Fauble, a Los Angeles-based researcher..." Actually, it was Larry Jordan who put those wheels in motion and made the introduction of Ms. Fauble to Mr. Shaw. Jordan comments, "I had to lobby hard for her to pay any attention to him."

While we have no reason to doubt the sincerity of his intentions, unfortunately we must respectfully disagree with many of his assertions.

In one video presentation Shaw stated, "I will tell you this right now. [Dorothy] was NOT interested in Lee Harvey Oswald." But DK was definitely interested in Oswald and probed that subject aggressively, as anyone can discern who has tracked her columns, as we have.

Shaw wrote that Dorothy's upcoming book, *Murder One*, would be "the dagger that would expose the conspirators." But as I have reported, and Mr. Shaw should know, a host of people close to Dorothy said she was writing a *separate* book about the Kennedy assassination.

He garnered headlines when the Manhattan District Attorney's Office agreed to reopen the probe into Kilgallen's death. The following month Shaw told me that the D.A. and even as assistant D.A. had been assigned to work with him to investigate the circumstances surrounding Dorothy's premature passing. He claimed he was continuing to receive tips and was passing them along to the prosecutor's office. He confirmed the focus was on Ron Pataky as being involved in her death.

In the summer of 2017, the probe into Dorothy's death came to a screeching halt. The D.A.'s office issued a statement saying, "Following a thorough, eight-month-long investigation into the death of Dorothy Kilgallen, the District Attorney's Office has found no evidence from which it could be concluded that Ms. Kilgallen's death was caused by another person...If new evidence comes to light, we will review it appropriately. We will decline further comment on this matter."

In August 2019, Shaw filed a 129-page petition to the Westchester County Clerk of Courts to have Kilgallen's body exhumed. In it, he claimed to be communicating with Kilgallen from beyond the grave. Speaking in the third person he wrote that after he decided to write a book on DK he "began to notice that he was somehow being 'guided,' so-to-speak, to certain evidence as he continued that research. In fact, petitioner felt like Kilgallen was somehow shouting, 'Investigate! Investigate!

Investigate!' regarding the circumstances surrounding her death which, of course, is subject to conjecture since there is no exact proof she was doing so."

The request for an exhumation was denied. DNA evidence was first used as a legal tool in 1986 with advancements being made daily. If DK's remains were ever exhumed, a forensic anthropologist could attempt to locate clues on her body that had not been detected back in 1965.

Shaw wrote to us in 2020 saying he was writing a book called *Collateral Damage* that would connect DK's death with Marilyn Monroe's. Ironically, my father was currently in the process of writing an extensive biography called *The Real Marilyn Monroe*. At the time, we'd even considered combining our efforts into one book that would chronicle both DK and MM. After informing Shaw of our project, he ceased communicating with us and we were not thanked in his next book.

He has stated, "I have great respect for women and their untold stories. I believe Dorothy chose me to write her story because we are both people of integrity."

I don't know if Dorothy "chose" me to write her story (I haven't tried contacting her via séance), but I'd like to think we might have been friends had I been alive back then. We have similar interests (celebrity culture, fashion and geopolitics), Irish-Catholic backgrounds, are journalists (and the daughters of journalists) and most importantly, share the bond of motherhood.

I have not given up hope that justice may someday be achieved for Dorothy. Although the main person of interest in the case, Ron Pataky, is now deceased as of 2022, as the old saying goes, "The wheels of justice turn slowly, but grind exceedingly fine." The investigation into DK's death can be reopened. It's happened before in other celebrity cases. Take the suspicious 1981 drowning of actress Natalie Wood.

In 2012, the Los Angeles County Coroner amended Natalie's cause of death from "accidental drowning" to "drowning and other undetermined factors." A supplemental coroner's report decided the bruises and scratches noted on Wood's body occurred before she ended up in the water, and were not the result of her body being tossed about in the ocean. In February 2018, her husband Robert Wagner was named a person of interest, but has refused to cooperate with law enforcement.

Unlike Wood, whose death was immediately labeled an accident, the cause of Dorothy's death always held a level of mystery to it with the circumstances of her drug and alcohol overdose listed as "undetermined."

Perhaps the person or persons involved in DK's death won't have their date in court. But her story isn't going to die, and to quote the lady herself, "as long as there's a real reporter alive—and there are a lot of them alive." ■

SELECTED BIBLIOGRAPHY

The works listed here include key books, newspaper and magazine articles, websites and interviews. It excludes films, television shows and musical works.

Note Dorothy Kilgallen's *Voice of Broadway* column was syndicated, appearing in newspapers across the United States (and Canada), often with a time delay from when first running in the *Journal-American*. The following citations are reflective of a variety of these publications, largely sourced from Newspapers.com.

Abrams, Dan and David Fisher. "The lawyer who defended Jack Ruby understood the new power of television in the courtroom." *The Dallas Morning News*. Aug. 8, 2021.

"Actor, Wed to Columnist." *The Washington Post*. Jan. 10, 1971.

"Adam 'Ron' Pataky." O. R. Woodyard Co. May 2022. https://www.orwoodyard.com/obituaries/Adam-Pataky/#!/Obituary

Aikman, Leo. "Dot Kilgallen Was Sharp." *The Atlanta Constitution*. Nov. 12, 1965.

Allen, Robert S. and Paul Scott. "Warren Report in October." *Orlando Evening Star*. Aug. 18, 1964.

Allison, Jane. "Dick Kollmar restaurant." *The Star Press*. Aug. 15, 1957.

"Anna Maria Albergheti—in hospital." *UPI* report. Oct. 6, 1963.

"Art by the famous." *Star Tribune*. March 7, 1965.

Bardach, Ann Louise. "The Story of Marita Lorenz: Mistress, Mother, C.I.A. Informant, and Center of Swirling Conspiracy Theories." *Vanity Fair*. November 1993. https://www.vanityfair.com/culture/2016/03/marita-lorenz-fidel-castro-conspiracy-theories

Barry, Virginia. "The Voice of Broadway Is Silent." *Asbury Park Press*. Nov. 14, 1965.

Basse, Craig. "Coiffeur had a style of his own." *Tampa Bay Times*. May 31, 2006. https://www.tampabay.com/archive/2006/05/31/coiffeur-had-a-style-of-his-own/

"Belli Successor Hired By Rubys." *Arizona Daily Star*. March 20, 1964.

Bennett, James. *Television Personalities: Stardom and the Small Screen*. New York: Routledge, 2011.

Besch, Bob. "Ex-Mansfielder Wins Recongition With His Songs." *The Mansfield News Journal*. March 13, 1965.

Blakey, G. Robert. Email correspondence. March 2020.

"Blame Alcohol, Barbiturates in Dorothy Kilgallen Death." *UPI* Report. Nov. 15, 1965.
"Bob Schieffer recalls driving with Lee Harvey Oswald's mother to police station after JFK assassination." *CBS*. Oct. 26, 2017. https://www.cbsnews.com/news/bob-schieffer-recalls-driving-lee-harvey-oswalds-mother-to-police-station-after-jfk-assassin tion/
Bradford, Rex E. "The Fourteen Minute Gap." *History Matters*. May 2000. https://historymatters.com/essays/frameup/FourteenMinute Gap/FourteenMinuteGap.htm
Brooks, Tim and Earle F. Marsh. *The Complete Directory to Prime Time Network and Cable TV Shows, 1946-Present*. New York: Ballantine Books. 2007.
Brown, Rita Mae. "What Did Dorothy Know?" *The Washington Post*. Nov. 18, 1979.
"Bullet holes in the limousine and extra bullets in Dealey Plaza." *YouTube*. HelmerReenberg. Oct. 12, 2008. https://www.youtube.com/watch?v=UtFoPCKVp-8&t=188s
Burnham, George. "Eyes Of The Press Are On Billy Graham." *The Gastonia Gazette*. May 23, 1957.
Carroll, Harrison. "Behind The Scenes in Hollywood." *St. Lucie News Tribune*. March 3, 1964.
Cartwright, Gary. "Who Was Jack Ruby?" *Texas Monthly*. November 1975. https://www.texasmonthly.com/news-politics/who-was-jack-ruby/
"Celebrity Captains Named For 2 Weeks of 'Call My Bluff.'" *The Times-Mail*. July 12, 1965.
Cheever, Susan. "Could the Secret Service Have Saved JFK?." *Vanity Fair*. October 17, 2014. https://www.vanityfair.com/news/politics/2014/10/secret-service-jfk-assassination
"CLASSICS: Two Men in Dallas." *Youtube*. Vince Palamara. Jan. 31, 2021. https://www.youtube.com/watch?v =0bUhHFqMWDE&t=2483s
"Columnist Dorothy Kilgallen on Air In New Program, 'Voice of Broadway.'" *The Tampa Times*. Aug. 19, 1941.
"Columnist, TV, Radio Personality; Dies N.Y." *Associated Press* report. Nov. 9, 1965.
Connally, John. *In History's Shadow*. An American Odyssey. New York:

Hyperion. 1993.
Connolly, Mike. "New Series for Marie." *Desert Sun*. Feb. 29, 1960.
Considine, Bob. "Lowdown on Dorothy Kilgallen." *Kingsport News*. March 22, 1960.
Considine, Bob. "The Last Person To Speak With Dorothy Kilgallen." *The Morning Call*. Nov. 17, 1965.
Considine, Bob. "Warren Commission Report." *The Morning Call*. Aug. 18, 1964.
Cranor, Milicent. "Navy Doctor: Bullet Found in JFK's Limousine, and Never Reported." *WhoWhatWhy*. Oct. 6, 2017. https://whowhatwhy.org/politics/government-integrity/navy-doctor-bullet-found-jfks-limousine-never-reported/
Crosby, John. "New Pseudo-Family is Behaving Royally." *The Macon Telegraph*. Nov. 21, 1963.
Davidson, Muriel. "The Great Woman Hunt." *TV Guide*. July 23, 1966, pages 15-18.
Devane, James. "You Said It." *Cincinnati Enquirer*. Dec. 30, 1963.
"Dorothy Kilgallen Hospital Patient." *AP* report. Jan. 23, 1961.
Dorothy Kilgallen interview excerpts from television show *Front Page Challenge*. Toronto, Canada. June 16, 1964.
"Dorothy Kilgallen, Noted Newspaper Writer, Weds Musical Comedy Star." *INS* wire story. April 7, 1940.
"Dorothy Kilallen, Pittston Native Wins $500 For Journalism Feat." *Sunday Dispatch*. Oct. 19, 1947.
"Dorothy Kilgallen's at Roosevelt Hospital with bursitis..." *Daily Press*. Oct. 6, 1952.
"Dorothy Kilgallen To Participate in Associated Retailers' Fashion Show." *The Omaha Guide*. Aug. 12, 1955.
"Dorothy Kilgallen Welcomes Viewers To Her 'Black Room.'" *Oklahoma City Advertiser*. Jan. 20, 1956.
"Dorothy's Our Gal." *The World-News*. May 15, 1957.
Dowd, Katie. "Mobsters, Marilyn and Sinatra: The legendary Cal Neva Lodge is preparing for guests again." *SFGate*. Oct. 19, 2019. https://www.sfgate.com/sfhistory/article/history-larry-ellison-Cal-Neva-Lodge-14496588.php
"Drivel and Bilge." Letter to the Editor. *Times Colonist*. March 9, 1965.
"Dulles, Allen W., June 1959-November 1962." *JFK Library*. https://www.jfklibrary.org/asset-viewer/archives/JFKPOF/029/JFKPOF-029-021
Dunne, Dominick. "High Roller: The Phyllis McGuire Story." *Vanity Fair*. June 1989. https://archive.vanityfair.com/article/1989/6/high-roller-the-

phyllis-mcguire-story
Dunne, Dominick. "Spilling Secrets." *Vanity Fair*. April 2006. https://archive.vanityfair.com/article/2006/4/spilling-secrets
Edelman, Susan. "Manhattan DA's Office probing death of reporter with possible JFK ties." *New York Post*. Jan. 29, 2017. https://nypost.com/2017/01/29/manhattan-das-office-probing-death-of-reporter-with-possible-jfk-ties/
Editors. "The Original Amazing Race." *Air & Space* magazine. Aug. 31, 2011. https://www.airspacemag.com/history-of-flight/the-original-amazing-race-52214251/
"Eleanor Kilgallen dies at 95; talent agent had legendary clients." *Los Angeles Times*. Dec. 23, 2014. https://www.latimes.com/local/obituaries/la-me-eleanor-kilgallen-20141224-story.html
"Ex-OSU Fullback, Newsman In Shootout." *The Akron Beacon Journal*. April 13, 1971.
Farquhar, Michael. "Nowhere to Hide." *The Washington Post*. Oct. 3, 1993.
Fates, Gil. *What's My Line? The Inside History of TV's Most Famous Panel Show*. Englewood Cliffs: Prentice-Hall, 1978.
Fauble, Kathryn. Email correspondence: 2006-2023.
Fauble, Kathryn. Videotaped interviews featuring Marc Sinclaire, Charles Simpson and Katherine Stone, Joe Tonahill and Ron Pataky. Conducted in 1999 and 2000.
Finn, Peter. "DNA Tests May Have Finally Resolved '54 Sheppard Case." *The Washington Post*. Feb. 5, 1997.
Fitz-Gibbon, Bernice. "Wad Ye Deny P-r-rint?" *San Bernardino Sun*. Nov. 29, 1961.
Flukinger, Roy. "New York Journal American Overview." *Harry Ransom Center The University of Texas at Austin*. https://norman.hrc.utexas.edu/NYJAdc/history.cfm
Forbes, Elizabeth. "Royal Vehicle Problem Solved In 'Simplest Way Pos sible.'" *Times Colonist*. Oct. 23, 1957.
"Former Castro mistress links Oswald, Hunt." *Lakeland Ledger*. Feb. 6, 1985.
Fox, James. "Johnnie Ray (1927-1990)." *The Oregon Encyclopedia*. March 17, 2018. https://oregonencyclopedia.org/articles/johnnie_ray/#.XkNbfoU_6Eq
Francine, Renee. "Midget Hercules: Joe Levine—overweight king of underdressed movie spectaculars?" *The San Francisco Examiner*. Jan. 14, 1962.

Frymer, Murry. "John Daly: What's His Line Now?" *Newsday* (Nas sau Edition). April 1, 1967.
Gabel, Peter. Email correspondence. March 2020.
Gardner, Hy. "'Second' Dorothy Kilgallen Gracious, Witty and Shy." *The Town Talk*. Nov. 13, 1965.
Garrison, Jim. *On the Trail of the Assassins*. New York: Sheridan Square Press, 1988.
Goldfarb, Ronald. Email correspondence. March 2020.
Goldfarb, Ronald. "What the Mob Knew About JFK's Murder." *The Washington Post*. March. 14, 1993.
Gould, Jack. "Stylish Series 'The Rogues' Deserved Another Season." *Corpus Christi Caller-Times*. June 13, 1965.
Grimshaw, M. "One woman's wardrobe." *Liverpool Daily Post*. May 6, 1960.
Hassett, Robert L. "Jack Ruby's Stories Seen Ruin of Warren Commission." *The Boston Sunday Herald*. Aug. 23, 1964.
Hedegaard, Erik. "The Last Confessions of E. Howard Hunt." *Rolling Stone*. April 2007. https://web.archive.org/web/20080618150441/http: //www.rolling stone.com/news/story/13893143/the_last_confes sions_of_e_howard_hunt/1
Hedrick, Sturgis. "Dorothy Kilgallen To Explore New TV Field Tonight." *The Buffalo News*. June 13, 1956.
Heimer, Mel. "My New York." *Simpon's Leader-Times*. March 1, 1960.
Hilty, James. *Robert Kennedy: Brother Protector*. Philadelphia: Temple University Press, 2000.
Hogan Jr, Martin. "Dorothy Was Top Reporter — But Not An Entertainer." *The Cincinnati Enquirer*. Nov. 11, 1965.
"Hoover Denies FBI Employed Oswald, Ruby." *The Montreal Gazette*. March 9, 1964.
Howard, Adam. "Acquilla Clemons: The black witness the Warren Commission ignored." *The Grio*. Nov. 21, 2013. https://thegrio.com/2013/11/21/acquilla-clemons-the-black-wit ness-the-warren-commission-ignored/
Howe, Marvine. "Earl Smith, 87, Ambassador to Cuba in the 1950's." *The New York Times*. Feb. 17, 1991.
Israel, Lee. *Can You Ever Forgive Me?: Memoirs of a Literary Forger*. New York: Simon & Schuster, 2008.
Israel, Lee. *Kilgallen*. New York: Delacorte Press, 1979.
Janney, Peter. *Mary's Mosaic: The CIA Conspiracy to Murder John F. Kennedy, Mary Pinchot Meyer, and Their Vision for World*

Peace. New York: Skyhorse Publishing, 2013.
"JFK Assassination Records." *National Archives*. https://www.archives.gov/research/jfk
"JFK Assassination 50th Anniversary: Interview with Robert McClelland, MD- Part 1." *YouTube*. PRSJournal. Nov. 21, 2013. https://www.youtube.com/watch?v=6Q1lYifmUXA
"JFK Assassination 50th Anniversary: Interview with Robert McClelland, MD- Part 2." *YouTube*. PRSJournal. Nov. 21, 2013. https://www.youtube.com/watch?v=VxC7YduICBY
"JFK Assassination 50th Anniversary: Interview with Robert McClelland, MD- Part 3." *YouTube*. PRSJournal. Nov. 21, 2013. https://www.youtube.com/watch?v=7HyoitsPlnk
"JFK shooting witness: nurse recalls day President Kennedy was shot in Dallas. *YouTube*. The Telegraph. Nov. 4, 2013. https://www.youtube.com/watch?v=36qUVsgCIpc
"JFK's Body Arrives at the White House on 11/23/63 (Sid Davis Reports for Westinghouse Broadcasting)." *YouTube*. David Von Pein's JFK Channel. Dec. 27, 2015. https://www.youtube.com/watch?v=qgZxpp8gfAA
"JFK's body brought to the White House." *CBS*. Nov. 21, 2013. https://www.cbsnews.com/video/jfks-body-brought-to-the-white-house/
Johnson, Ed. "Ruby Case Speeded." *Fort Worth Star-Telegram*. Feb. 20, 1964.
Johnson, Robert. "Margaret Sits In." *Press-Scimitar*. March 22, 1954.
Jones, Paul. "Paar Error: Talking Instead of Listening." *The Atlanta Constitution*. Feb 16, 1960.
Jordan, Larry. Phone conversations with Ron Pataky. 2006-2014.
Jordan, Larry. Phone conversations with Lee Israel. 2006-2007; email exchange 2013.
Jordan, Larry. Phone conversation with Marlin Swing. 2007.
Jordan, Larry. *The Real Marilyn Monroe*. PageTurner Books. 2023.
Jordan, Larry. "The Secret JFK Files, New Evidence and the Midwest Connection." *Midwest Today*. 1992.
Jordan, Sara. "Who Killed Dorothy Kilgallen? *Midwest Today*. 2007, pages 16-23.
Keate, Stuart. "Changing Role of Monarchy Demonstrated At Press Reception." *Times Colonist*. Oct. 15, 1957.
Kelley, Kitty. *His Way: The Unauthorized Biography of Frank Sinatra*. New York: Bantam Books, 1986.

"Kennedy May Testify in Hoffa's Trial." *UPI* report. Jan. 20, 1964.
Khiss, Peter. "Snarl at Rush Hour Spreads Into 9 States | 10,000 in the National Guard and 5,000 Off-Duty Policement Are Called to Service in New York." *The New York Times*. Nov. 10, 1965.
Kilgallen, Dorothy. "A Big Lawsuit." *Star-Gazette*. Sept. 19, 1964.
Kilgallen, Dorothy. "A Dorothy Kilgallen Pre-Warren Exclusive." *Journal-American*. Sept. 25, 1964.
Kilgallen, Dorothy. "After Inauguration reflections on career." *The Daily Journal*. Jan. 27, 1965.
Kilgallen, Dorothy. "All the World's A Stage." *The Mercury*. Sept. 23, 1960.
Kilgallen, Dorothy. "An Open Letter to Lyndon B. Johnson." *The Tribune*. June 8, 1964.
Kilgallen, Dorothy. "Asks Why Oswald Killed Policeman." *Ashbury Park Press*. April 15, 1964.
Kilgallen, Dorothy. "As long as there's a real reporter alive." *Edmonton Journal*. Sept. 8, 1965.
Kilgallen, Dorothy. "Astounding verdict." *The Bangor Daily News*. Dec. 29, 1954.
Kilgallen, Dorothy. "Attorney General Robert Kennedy." *The Springfield News-Leader*. Dec. 24, 1963.
Kilgallen, Dorothy. "Big LBJ Show—Carson Rapped For 'Rude' Gags.'" *Journal-American*. Jan. 19, 1965.
Kilgallen, Dorothy. "Broadway Fantasia." *Pittsburgh Post-Gazette*. April 21, 1949.
Kilgallen, Dorothy. "Can you believe this one?" *The Oneonta Star*. March 24, 1962.
Kilgallen, Dorothy. "Cary Grant Eludes Photographers." *The Cincinnati Enquirer*. July 5, 1964.
Kilgallen, Dorothy. "Castro Bolivia." *The Daily Journal*. June 22, 1965.
Kilgallen, Dorothy. "Celebrities Still Discuss Happenings of Nov. 22." *Fort Worth Star-Telegram*. Dec. 11, 1963.
Kilgallen, Dorothy. "Communique from Paris..." *The Springfield News-Leader*. Dec. 3, 1963.
Kilgallen, Dorothy. "Congratulations for Ruby Scoop." *The Daily Journal*. Sept. 18, 1964.
Kilgallen, Dorothy. "Criticizes Columnist on Kennedy Praise." *Asbury Park Press*. Aug. 1, 1962.
Kilgallen, Dorothy. "Cuba—'Explosive.'" *The Gazette* (Montreal, Quebec, Canada). July 18, 1959.
Kilgallen, Dorothy. "D.A. to Link Ruby to Oswald?" *Star-Gazette*. Feb. 25, 1964.

Kilgallen, Dorothy. "Dear John Benincasa." *The Record American.* July 8, 1960.
Kilgallen, Dorothy. "Dear mother and dad." *The Urbana Daily Citizen.* May 2, 1958.
Kilgallen, Dorothy. "Death Ends Fearful Dream for Marilyn." *Asbury Park Press.* Aug. 9, 1962.
Kilgallen, Dorothy. "Don't Be Foolish, Women Know Campaign Issues." *Muncie Evening Press.* Oct. 27, 1952.
Kilgallen, Dorothy. "Dorothy Not Sold On Warren Report." *The Oneonta Star.* Oct. 8, 1964.
Kilgallen, Dorothy. "Dorothy Relates Visit of Son with Kennedy." *The Times-Tribune.* Nov. 26, 1963.
Kilgallen, Dorothy. "Downbeat poll." *Republican and Herald.* July 28, 1965.
Kilgallen, Dorothy. "Drug busts." *The Times.* July 31, 1964.
Kilgallen, Dorothy. "Eat my hat." *The Daily Journal.* Nov. 10, 1964.
Kilgallen, Dorothy. "Echoes From the London Trial." *The Daily Jounal.* July 29, 1963.
Kilgallen, Dorothy. "Emergency Line." *The Bradenton Herald.* July 2, 1964.
Kilgallen, Dorothy. "Erased Witnesses." *The Daily Journal.* Sept. 24, 1964.
Kilgallen, Dorothy. "FBI Head To Answer Critics." *Tyler Morning Telegraph.* Jan. 12, 1942.
Kilgallen, Dorothy. "Foggy London town." *Newark Advocate.* June 4, 1953.
Kilgallen, Dorothy. "Frank Costello." *The Tennessean.* June 13, 1957.
Kilgallen, Dorothy. "Frank Jr. kidnapping." *Journal-American.* Dec. 18, 1963.
Kilgallen, Dorothy. "Frank Jr. kidnapping." (Updated mention). *The Springfield News-Leader.* March 18, 1964.
Kilgallen, Dorothy. "'Frisky' Side of Ruby Trial." *Star-Gazette.* Feb. 24, 1964.
Kilgallen, Dorothy. *Girl Around the World.* Philadelphia: David McKay Company, 1936.
Kilgallen, Dorothy. "Globe Racer Plans Three Meals in 3 Separate Countries." *INS* wire story." Oct. 6, 1936.
Kilgallen, Dorothy. "Guest column by Bill Todman." *The Bradenton Herald.* Aug. 15, 1964.
Kilgallen, Dorothy. "Guest column by Ceil Chapman." *Star-Gazette.* Sept. 18, 1952.
Kilgallen, Dorothy. "Guest column by Johnnie Ray." *The Journal*

Herald. June 7, 1955.
Kilgallen, Dorothy. "Guest column by Richard Kollmar." *The Bradenton Herald*. June 17, 1962.
Kilgallen, Dorothy. "Ike's Talk A Classic." *The Times-Tribune*. July 17, 1964.
Kilgallen, Dorothy. "'I Told You So,' Dorothy Writes Ike. *The Daily Journal*. May 24, 1960.
Kilgallen, Dorothy. "In London." *The Atlanta Journal*. May 8, 1958.
Kilgallen, Dorothy. "I Remembered Jackie." *The Record American*. Jan. 21, 1965.
Kilgallen, Dorothy. "Jack Paar's fans can relax." *Arizona Republic*. Feb. 17, 1960.
Kilgallen, Dorothy. "Jack Ruby Had Change Of Heart Toward Belli As His Attorney." *Lexington Herald-Leader*. March 25, 1964.
Kilgallen, Dorothy. "Jack Paar's wig slipped." *Republican and Herald*. July 9, 1960.
Kilgallen, Dorothy. "Jacqueline, a Profile in Courage and More." *Philadelphia Daily News*. Nov. 26, 1963.
Kilgallen, Dorothy. "Jamaica Bistro Offers Piglets in Floor Show." *The Times-Tribune*. Feb. 18. 1961.
Kilgallen, Dorothy. "Jane's Got That Image Now." *The Columbia Record*. March 22, 1965.
Kilgallen, Dorothy. "Joe Levine moving into the T-V film milieu." *Asbury Park Press*. Dec. 3, 1964.
Kilgallen, Dorothy. "Joe Levine Takes a Liking To Boy Singer Bobby Vinton." *The Times-Tribune*. June 4, 1965.
Kilgallen, Dorothy. "Johnnie Ray 'Smash.'" *The Salt Lake Tribune*. Sept. 19, 1965.
Kilgallen, Dorothy. "Kennedy Vs. Hoffa? Don't Bet on Bobby!" *Arizona Republic*. March 4, 1962.
Kilgallen, Dorothy. "Kilgallen Flies to Wedding." *Pittsburgh Sun-Telegraph*. April 11, 1956.
Kilgallen, Dorothy. "Kilgallen Says:" Ok, I'll Tell What It Was REALLY Like." *The Tennessean*. June 9, 1953.
Kilgallen, Dorothy. "Kim Novak Plans July Trip to Berlin." *Lancaster New Era*. April 15, 1964.
Kilgallen, Dorothy. "Las Vegas." *The Record American*. Oct. 11, 1965.
Kilgallen, Dorothy. "Leo Durocher Also Has Money Problems." *Journal-American*. April 4, 1960.
Kilgallen, Dorothy. "Let's Play Post Office." *Shamokin News-Dispatch*. Oct. 11, 1960.
Kilgallen, Dorothy. "Life imitates art in the most tragic way..."

Forth Worth Star-Telegram. Dec. 23, 1963.
Kilgallen, Dorothy. "London Jottings." *The Mercury*. June 4, 1953.
Kilgallen, Dorothy. "London Notebook." *The Record American*. Aug. 8, 1963.
Kilgallen, Dorothy. "London trip." *Morning Sentinel*. (Waterville, Maine). June 19, 1964.
Kilgallen, Dorothy. "London Turned Into Fairyland." F*ort Worth Star-Telegram*. May 12, 1937.
Kilgallen, Dorothy. "Loves Ireland's Charm." *The Ottawa Journal*. July 12, 1965.
Kilgallen, Dorothy. "Lyndon Johnson Elevated To Life in Ivory Tower." *The Daily Journa*l (Vineland, New Jersey). Nov. 29, 1963.
Kilgallen, Dorothy. "Marilyn Monroe." *Journal-American*. Aug. 5, 1962.
Kilgallen, Dorothy. "Marilyn's Story Really All Told?" *Arizona Republic*. Aug. 20, 1962.
Kilgallen, Dorothy. "Marina Oswald." *The Record American*. Sept. 9, 1965.
Kilgallen, Dorothy. "Mark Lane." *The Times-Tribune* (Scranton, Pennsylvania). Dec. 10, 1964.
Kilgallen, Dorothy. "Miss Kilgallen Is Applauded For Speaking Up On Politics." *Lexington Herald-Leader*. Oct. 7, 1960.
Kilgallen, Dorothy. "Marriage May Put Brakes on Singing." *Fort Worth Star-Telegram*. June 14, 1965.
Kilgallen, Dorothy. "Maybe You Didn't Know..." *Journal-American*. Sept. 30, 1964.
Kilgallen, Dorothy. "Midnight Memo." *Star Tribune*. Dec. 15, 1944.
Kilgallen, Dorothy. "Miss Kilgallen Basks In The Sun On Shores Of Caribbean Sea." *Lexington Herald-Leader*. Feb. 18, 1961.
Kilgallen, Dorothy. "Miss Kilgallen Is Applauded For Speaking Up On Politics." *Lexington Herald-Leader*. Oct. 7, 1960.
Kilgallen, Dorothy. "Miss Kilgallen Makes Report On The Preview in Washington." *Lexington Herald-Leader*. Jan. 21, 1961.
Kilgallen, Dorothy. *Murder One*. New York: Random House, 1967.
Kilgallen, Dorothy. "Nervous Ruby Feels 'Breaking Point' Near." *Journal-American*. Feb. 23, 1964.
Kilgallen, Dorothy. "New Contradictions In JFK Murder Probe." *The San Francisco Examiner*. Aug. 23, 1964.
Kilgallen, Dorothy. "New Levine Film to Star Randall, Novak, Garner." *Fort Worth Star-Telegram*. May 8, 1961.
Kilgallen, Dorothy. "New Monroe Photo Creating a Stir." *Asbury Park*

Press. Aug. 4, 1962.
Kilgallen, Dorothy. "Newspaper strike." *The Gazette*. Dec. 18, 1962.
Kilgallen, Dorothy. "Nothing Like Chummy Old General for a 'Copy Boy.'" *Fort Worth Star-Telegram*. June 7, 1953.
Kilgallen, Dorothy. "Now You Know All About Dorothy Kilgallen." *Muncie Evening Press*. Feb. 23, 1952.
Kilgallen, Dorothy. "Only in Ireland Can You Hit 4 and Score 7." *The Times-Tribune*. July 9, 1965.
Kilgallen, Dorothy. "Paris Film Work Curtailed By French Fuel Shortage." *Fort Worth Star-Telegram*. Oct. 27, 1948.
Kilgallen, Dorothy. "Portrait of a Mistress." *Pittsburgh Post-Gazette*. May 8, 1960.
Kilgallen, Dorothy. "Prediction: Ruby Won't Be Executed." *The Indianapolis News*. Feb. 24, 1964.
Kilgallen, Dorothy. "Prince's Chaplain Keeps Ghost Alive." *The Indianapolis News*. April 21, 1956.
Kilgallen, Dorothy. "Puerto Rico Gamblers' Paradise Minus Liquor." *Arizona Republic*. Jan. 6, 1964.
Kilgallen, Dorothy. "Q. and A. Text: Pity for Widow Led Ruby to Act." *The Philadelphia Inquirer*. Aug. 20, 1964.
Kilgallen, Dorothy. "Racing Reporter Arrives in Gaza." *INS* wire story. Oct. 7, 1936.
Kilgallen, Dorothy. "Riding a motorcycle." *Tyler Morning Telegraph*. Aug. 18, 1964.
Kilgallen, Dorothy. "Rolls-Royce." *The South Bend Tribune*. Nov. 17, 1963.
Kilgallen, Dorothy. "Ruby—a Man Full of Fears." *The San Francisco Examiner*. Aug. 19, 1964.
Kilgallen, Dorothy. "Ruby Case Mystery: Why FBI Helped Him." *Philadelphia Daily News*. Feb. 22, 1964.
Kilgallen, Dorothy. "Ruby Decision." *Fort Worth Star-Telegram*. March 24, 1964.
Kilgallen, Dorothy. "Ruby Fireworks." *The Ottawa Journal*. March 7, 1964.
Kilgallen, Dorothy. "Ruby's Testimony About 'The Plot.'" *The Philadelphia Inquirer*. Aug. 21, 1964.
Kilgallen, Dorothy. "Some producers do read Broadway columns." *Fort Worth Star-Telegram*. Feb. 11, 1965.
Kilgallen, Dorothy. "Son's Class Day More Important Than Party." *Muncie Evening Press*. June 9, 1953.
Kilgallen, Dorothy. "She does not know the language." *New Castle News*. Nov. 7, 1961.

Kilgallen, Dorothy. "Short Trip Across U.S. In Jet Age." *Fort Worth Star-Telegram*. May 1, 1959.

Kilgallen, Dorothy. "Suzy Parker And Hubby Reconciled." *The Bradenton Herald*. Feb. 26, 1960.

Kilgallen, Dorothy. "Sybil Is Ready To Relinquish Burton to Liz." *The Times-Tribune*. Jan. 16, 1963.

Kilgallen, Dorothy. "Tale of 'Oil Man' At Jack Ruby's Café Poses New Riddles." *The Philadelphia Inquirer*. Sept. 4, 1964.

Kilgallen, Dorothy. "The Celebrities." The Record American. Feb. 24, 1962.

Kilgallen, Dorothy. "The international revolutionary junta." *New Castle News*. Feb. 20, 1959.

Kilgallen, Dorothy. "The Latin Quarter." *Newsday* (Suffolk Edition). Sept. 7, 1965.

Kilgallen, Dorothy. "The Real Frank Sinatra Story." Part I. *Pittsburgh Sun-Telegraph*. Feb. 26, 1956.

Kilgallen, Dorothy. "The Real Frank Sinatra Story." Part II. *Pittsburgh Sun-Telegraph*. Feb. 27, 1956.

Kilgallen, Dorothy. "The Real Frank Sinatra Story." Part III. *Pittsburgh Sun-Telegraph*. Feb. 28, 1956.

Kilgallen, Dorothy. "The Real Frank Sinatra Story." Part IV. *Pittsburgh Sun-Telegraph*. Feb. 29, 1956.

Kilgallen, Dorothy. "The Real Frank Sinatra Story." Part V. *Pittsburgh Sun-Telegraph*. March 1, 1956.

Kilgallen, Dorothy. "The Real Frank Sinatra Story." Part VI. *Pittsburgh Sun-Telegraph*. March 2, 1956.

Kilgallen, Dorothy. "The Scuttle-Butt From Havana." *The Springfield News-Leader*. Aug. 22, 1961.

Kilgallen, Dorothy. "They Who Fight." *Star Tribune*. June 14, 1943.

Kilgallen, Dorothy. "This Is Morale, Mr. Jones; Some Fighting in Uniform, Others Busy in Greasepaint." *Fort Worth Star-Telegram*. Feb. 6, 1944.

Kilgallen, Dorothy. "Touch of Mystery To Marilyn's Death." *The Oneonta Star*. Aug. 16, 1962.

Kilgallen, Dorothy. "Tony Perkins postcard." *The Indianapolis News*. Sept. 21, 1961.

Kilgallen, Dorothy. "Tragic comment on current morality." *Arizona Republic*. Sept. 18, 1958.

Kilgallen, Dorothy. "Troubles Multiply For Earl Ruby." *Philadelphia Daily News*. Oct. 8, 1965.

Kilgallen, Dorothy. "Vietnam." *Republican and Herald*. March 11, 1965.

Kilgallen, Dorothy. "When It's Springtime in Manhattan." *The Journal Herald*. April 1, 1961.
Kilgallen, Dorothy. "Where Am I?" *The News-Herald*. April 26, 1954.
Kilgallen, Dorothy. "With the Celebrities." *The Bangor Daily News*. July 23, 1964.
Kilgallen, Dorothy. "W.R. Hearst…" *Republican and Herald*. Aug. 18, 1951.
Kilgallen, James L. "She's Just Good At Guessing, Is How Dorothy Kilgallen Puts It In Explaining Television Show." *Cincinnati Enquirer*. June 7, 1954.
Kilgallen, James L. "In News Offices Even As A Child, So She Grew Up Reporting, Dad Writes of Dorothy Kilgallen." *Cincinnati Enquirer*. June 8, 1954.
Kilgallen, James L. "Home Comes Ahead Of Career, As Dorothy Kilgallen Handles It; Columnist Has Three Children." *Cincinnati Enquirer*. June 9, 1954.
"Kilgallen Tribute." (Letter to the Editor). *The Philadelphia Daily News*. Dec. 5, 1963.
Kirby, Bill. "Journalist's trip to Augusta left mayor grumbling." *The Augusta Chronicle*. April 15, 2018.
Kollmar, Kerry. "Introduction." Testing the Waters. Blog. April 6, 2009. http://kerryslifeblog.blogspot.com/2009/04/introduction.html
Kollmar, Kerry. "Learning Not To Cry." Testing the Waters. Blog. Oct. 7, 2009. http://kerryslifeblog.blogspot.com/2009/10/
"Kollmar OK After Fire Hits Bedroom." *AP* report. Sept. 7, 1963.
Krajicek, David J. "A bumbling plot by philandering doc and his stunning flame gave tabloids a true crime bodice-ripper." *Daily News*. June 3, 2018. https://www.nydailynews.com/news/crime/ny-news-justice-philandering-doctor-true-crime-20180531-story.html
Krock, Arthur. "CIA Gets a Bad Press and Can't Fight Back." *Evening World-Herald*. Oct. 3, 1963.
Lambert, Bruce. "Jim Garrison, 70, Theorist on Kennedy Death, Dies." *The New York Times*. Oct. 22, 1992. https://www.nytimes.com/1992/10/22/obituaries/jim-garrison-70-theorist-on-kennedy-death-dies.html
Lardner Jr, George. "Ford's Editing Backed 'Single Bullet' Theory." *The Washington Post*. July 3, 1997. https://www.washingtonpost.com/archive/politics/1997/07/03/fords-editing-backed-single-bullet-theory/9054d41d-40e2-4e7f-8a52-fd8489aee9e5/

Larson, George. C. "Moments and Milestones: Once Around the Word." *Air & Space* magazine. September 2011. https://www.airspacemag.com/history-of-flight/moments-and-milestones-once-around-42265865/

"LBJ Gets Caught For Corruption—Almost." *DelanceyPlace*. June 13, 2019. https://delanceyplace.com/view-archives.php?p=3868

"LBJ Phone Calls - November 1963." *History Matters*. https://historymatters.com/archive/contents/lbjlib/contents_lbjlib_phonecalls_Nov1963.htm

Levin, Jay. "Eleanor Kilgallen of Paramus, agent to the stars." *The Herald News*. Dec. 23, 2014.

Lowry, Cynthia. "'What's My Line?' Starts 15th Year As National TV Habit and Institution." *AP* report. Feb. 3, 1964.

Lowry, Cynthia. "What's My Line? Television Miracle!" *AP* report. Feb. 23, 1964.

Lyman, Rick. "Phyllis Cerf Wagner, 90, Socialist and Collaborator With Dr. Seuss, Dies." *The New York Times*. Nov. 26, 2006.

Lynn, Frank. "James L. Kilgallen Dies At 94; A Reporter For Over 75 Years." *The New York Times*. Dec. 23, 1982.

"Mamie Tops in Fashion." *New York News Service*. Oct. 27, 1958.

"Marlin G. Swing." *Legacy*. October 2012. https://www.legacy.com/us/obituaries/nytimes/name/marlin-swing-obituary?id=25045997

Matthews, Dylan. "Manhattan DA Cyrus Vance's role in the Harvey Weinstein and Trump scandals, explained." *Vox*. Oct. 10, 2017. https://www.vox.com/policy-and-politics/2017/10/10/-16454182/cyrus-vance-harvey-weinstein-ivanka-donald-trump-junior-prosecute-donations-write-in

McManus, Margaret. "Francis, Kilgallen; Neighboring Careers." *The News and Observer*. March 24, 1957.

McKnight, Gerald D. *Breach of Trust: How the Warren Commission Failed the Nation and Why*. Lawrence: University of Kansas Press. 2005.

Meskil, Paul. "Frank Sturgis interview." *New York Daily News*. June 20, 1975.

"Morals Charge Brought Against Johnnie Ray." *AP* report. Nov. 21, 1959.

Morris, Bernadine. "Two fashion teams that started small." *The New York Times*. June 15, 1982.

Mort, John. "Events Follow Tight Schedule — Well, Almost." Fort *Worth Star-Telegram*. Jan. 21, 1965.

"Mrs. Earl Smith Dies in New York." *Palm Beach Daily News*. Nov. 10, 1965.

Nesteroff, Kliph. "An interview with Steve Rossi – Part One." *Classic Show Biz.* March 13, 2011. http://classicshowbiz.blogspot.com/2011/03/interview-with-steve-rossi-part-one.html

Nesteroff, Kliph. "An interview with Steve Rossi – Part Two." *Classic Show Biz.* March 16, 2011. http://classicshowbiz.blogspot.com/2011/03/interview-with-steve-rossi-part-two.html

"New windshield installed due to bullet hole." *Dayton Daily News*. Dec. 14, 1963.

"Obituary of Eleanor Esther Kilgallen." VanderPlaat Funeral Home. https://vanderplaatfuneralhome.com/tribute/details/1296/Eleanor-Kilgallen/obituary.html

O'Malley, Tom and Bob Cunniff. "Apology to Kilgallen." *The Courier*. Jan. 11, 1957.

O'Malley, Tom and Bob Cunniff. "Intuition Reveals Transparent Mask." *The Daily Times.* Nov. 28, 1956.

O'Malley, Tom and Bob Cunniff. "Readers Ask Several Timely TV Questions." *Wisconsin State Journal.* June 7, 1956.

O'Malley, Tom and Bob Cunniff. "Robert Stack Thanks TV For Choice Movie Role." *The Gazette*. Oct. 18, 1956.

"Only the press gives you this." *Muncie Evening Press*. April 29, 1954.

Oran, Nicole. "The doctors who tried to save the life of JFK discuss what really happened in new documentary." *MedCityNews*. July 24, 2015.

Pak, Eudie. "The True Stories Behind 'The Godfather.'" *Biography*. Dec. 15, 2020. https://www.biography.com/news/godfather-true-stories-books-movies

"Panelist's Son No Longer Lost." *The Spokesman-Review*. June 9, 1956.

"Post-JFK Assassination Air Force One Flight Deck Recording." *National Archives*. Aug. 15, 2016. https://www.archives.gov/research/jfk/air-force-one-tape.html

Potempa, Philip. "The gossip grapevine." *Northwest Indiana Times*. Jan. 15, 2006.

"Prince Eyed Marilyn Before Grace." wire story. Jan. 7, 1956.

Pritchett, Florence. "On Broadway With Florence Pritchett." *Journal-American*. Aug. 30, 1946.

"Racketeer's deportation ruled valid." Meriden Record. May 20, 1961.

"Raps Writer For Slurring Priest." *The Tablet*. May 12, 1956.
"Release of Sheppard is Ordered by Judge." *The World-News*. July 16, 1964.
"Reporters: The Triple Threat." *Time*. Nov. 19, 1965. https://content.time.com/time/subscriber/article/0,33009,834642-1,00.html
"Richard Kollmar, Actor on 'Dorothy and Dick' with Kilgallen, Dies." *The New York Times*. Jan. 9, 1971.
Rothman, Lily. "Queen Elizabeth 1957 North American tour." *Life*. https://www.life.com/people/young-queen-elizabeth-ii/
Royal, Don. "'What's My Line' in 15th Year." *Daily Press*. March 1, 1964.
"Sam Giancana." *Britannica*. https://www.britannica.com/biography/Sam-Giancana
Schwarz, Ted. *Marilyn Revealed*. Lanham: Taylor Trade Publishing. 2009.
Shane, Scott. "C.I.A. Is Still Cagey About Oswald Mystery." *The New York Times*. Oct. 16, 2009. https://www.nytimes.com/2009/10/17/us/17inquire.html?hp=&utm_source=substack&utm_medium=email
Secret Service logs January 1963.
Severo, Richard. "Melvin Belli Dies at 88; Flamboyant Lawyer Relished His Role as King of Torts." *The New York Times*. July 10, 1996.
Shafer, Jack. "The Posner Plagiarism Perplex." *Slate* magazine. Feb. 11, 2010. https://slate.com/news-and-politics/2010/02/making-sense-of-the-blog-statement-by-former-daily-beast-reporter-gerald-posner.html
Shaw, Mark. *Collateral Damage: The Mysterious Deaths of Marilyn Monroe and Dorothy Kilgallen, and the Ties that Bind Them to Robert Kennedy and the JFK Assassination*. New York: Post Hill Press. 2021.
Shaw, Mark. *Denial of Justice: Dorothy Kilgallen, Abuse of Power, and the Most Compelling JFK Assassination Investigation in History*. New York: Post Hill Press, 2018.
Shaw, Mark. "Mark Shaw's Letter to NYC DA Cyrus Vance, Jr. Demanding Re-Investigation of Dorothy Kilgallen's Death." *The Dorothy Kilgallen Story*. https://www.thedorothykilgallenstory.org/
Shaw, Mark. Phone/email correspondence. 2014-2019.
Shaw, Mark. *The Reporter Who Knew Too Much*. New York: Post Hill Press, 2016.

Shaw, Mark. "Verified Petition to Exhume Remains of Dorothy Kilgallen to Collect DNA Sample and Order One, Mr. Ron Pataky, to Submit DNA Sample to the Court." https://iapps.courts.state.ny.us/nyscef/ViewDocument?docIndex=M6FXN2oyMoCnCawoGmuhTQ==

Shogan, Robert. "Mafia Helped JFK to Win, Book Claims." *Los Angeles Times*. Nov. 9, 1997.

Shreve, Jr., Ivan G. "Happy Birthday, Richard Kollmar." *Radio Spirits*. Posted on Dec. 31, 2017. http://www.radiospirits.info/2017/12/31/happy-birthday-richard-kollmar/

"Sir Cedric 'Word' Guest. Dorothy Kilgallen Also to Appear As Panelist." *The South Bend Tribune*. Feb. 22, 1958.

Smith, Delos. "Alcohol and Barbiturates Mix Dangerously in Strange Action of Human Body Chemistry; Dorothy Kilgallen's Death Cited As Example." *The Vincennes Sun-Commerical*. Nov. 19, 1965.

Smith, Liz. "Kilgallen Case Is Still Open." *Detroit Free Press*. Dec. 22, 1976.

Smith, Liz. "Story Behind JFK." *Tucson Daily Citizen*. Dec. 20, 1976.

"Stafford County Museum - Stafford Stories - Dino Brugioni." *Youtube*. Kevin Henry. Dec. 15, 2013. https://www.youtube.com/watch?v=4ECiCH1pVXk

"Star's swain says police beat him. AP report. Dec. 6, 1963.

"S-T Column Writer at Ruby Trial." *Forth Worth Star-Telegram*. Feb. 19, 1964.

Steadman, Martin J. "50 Years from that Fateful Day in Dallas..." E*ve's Magazine*. 2013. http://evesmag.com/jfkassassination%20(1).htm

"Street's Corner: Doctor Recalls Kennedy's Last Moments (extended interview)." *YouTube*. KABB Fox San Antonio. Nov. 20, 2013. https://www.youtube.com/watch?v=s6_d2O47_qs

Sullivan, Patricia. "Virginia Warren Daly dies at 80; popular socialite in New York and Washington." *Los Angeles Times*. March 5, 2009. https://www.latimes.com/local/obituaries/la-me-virginia-warren-daly6-2009mar06-story.html

Talbot, David. "The Man Who Solved the Kennedy Assassination." *Salon*. Nov. 23, 2003. https://www.salon.com/2003/11/22/conspiracy_6/

Talese, Gay. "Frank Sinatra Has a Cold." *Esquire*. April 1966.

Taylor, Alan. "Looking Back on Queen Elizabeth's 90 Years."

The Atlantic. April 21, 2016.
"TELEVISION: The Return of St. Paarnard." *Time*. March 21, 1960. https://content.time.com/time/subscriber/article/0,33009,894807,00.htm 1
"Testimony of Perry Raymond Russo." State of Louisiana vs. Clay L. Shaw, Feb. 10, 1969.
"Tests on Cause of Death Of Dorothy Kilgallen." *UPI* report. Nov. 9, 1965.
"The Arlene Francis Center For Spirit, Art & Politics." https://arlenefrancis-center.squarespace.com/#home-section
"The Nation's Ten Best Tailored Women." *Madera Tribune*. April 23, 1955.
"The People vs. Lenny Bruce (Cafe Au Go Go Trial)."
Excerpts from the Trial Transcript. (June 16, 1964 to July 28, 1964 in New York City).
"The Warren Commission Report." Sept. 24, 1964. https://www.gutenberg.org/files/58031/58031-h/58031-h.htm
Thorpe, Jim. "Strictly Personal." *Times News*. June 4, 1964.
Tomasson, Robert E. "John Charles Daly Jr., the Host Of 'What's My Line?,' Dies at 77." *The New York Times*. Feb. 27, 1991.
Truman, Harry S. "CIA Needs Own 'Revolt.'" *The Miami News*. Dec. 22, 1963.
"Uncut Interview-JFK's Emergency Room Doctor: Dr. Robert McClelland." *YouTube*. City of Allen - ACTV. April 20, 2017. https://www.youtube.com/watch?v=lQ435lMaCng&t=649s
Van Horne, Harriet. "Trace of Blue Tinged Carson Gala Show." *The Albuquerque Tribune*. Jan. 20, 1965.
Wakin, Daniel J. "Arlene Francis, 93, Mainstay of 'What's My Line?' on TV." *The New York Times*. June 2, 2001. https://www.nytimes.com/2001/06/02/arts/arlene-francis-93-mainstay-of-what-s-my-line-on-tv.html
Waldron, Lamar. *The Hidden History of the JFK Assassination*. Berkely: Counterpoint. 2013.
Weir, Harold. "Matter of Hokum." *The Vancouver Sun*. Sept. 23, 1958.
Wenner, Cheryl. "Anna Maria: From A Sunny Beach In Italy To Carnegie Hall, Alberghetti Came Long Way (and Further Since)." *The Morning Call*. Oct. 10, 1985. https://www.mcall.com/1985/10/10/anna-maria-from-a-sunny-beach-in-italy-to-carnegie-hall-alberghetti-came-long-way-and-further-since/
West, Randy. *Johnny Olson: A Voice in Time*. Albany, Georgia:

BearManor Media, 2009.
"'What's My Line?' Boasts Beauty, Brains, Talent, All on One Sparkling Quiz Show." *Evansville Courier and Press*. Sept. 13, 1953.
"What's My Line? Stumps Old Age." *UPI* report. Jan. 26, 1964.
Whitman, Alden. "Bennett Cerf Dies; Publisher, Writer." *The New York Times*. Aug. 29, 1971.
Wilson, Earl. "What's Ugliest Four-Letter Word?" *The News and Observer*. April 12, 1965.
Winchell, Walter. "The Broadway Lights." *The Durham Sun*. Sept. 2, 1961.
Worth-Baker, Marcia. "East Orange's Golden Age." *New Jersey Monthly*. Dec. 23, 2013. https://njmonthly.com/articles/jersey-living/east-oranges-golden-age/
Wood, Mary. "TV Dream Brews Scalding Finale For Mrs. Olsen." *The Cincinnati Post*. Oct. 8, 1965.
"'10 Best Rooms' Are on Display." *The Knoxville News-Sentinel*. May 30, 1961.
"45 E 68th St, New York, NY 10065." *Zillow*.
https://www.zillow.com/homedetails/45-E-68th-St-New-York-NY-10065/2077848864_zpid//

ACKNOWLEDGEMENTS

Special thanks to long-time Kilgallen researcher Kathryn Fauble, who first provided *Midwest Today* magazine with video taped interviews of Charles Simpson, Marc Sinclaire and Katherine Stone, which she conducted with David Henschel. That material proved invaluable, first for my 2007 magazine article, and now this book. I appreciate her dedication to DK and her willingness to answer any questions I had while writing the book.

I'd also like to thank the late Peter Gabel who shared insights into his mother Arlene Francis' relationship with DK and further thoughts on the JFK assassination and conspiracy.

Thank you G. Robert Blakey who briefly answered a few questions related to Dorothy's death.

I also value the efforts of Miriam Gianni and Paul Friedman, staff at the General Research Division of the New York Public Library, who located Dorothy Kilgallen's ultra rare Sept. 25, 1964 column, which ran exclusively in the *Journal-American*.

My father Larry Jordan first introduced me to Dorothy Kilgallen and championed my completion of this book. He helped with research, fact-checking and encouraged me to keep probing into the complexities of DK's life and death. I am eternally grateful.

This project would have been impossible to complete without help from my mother Julie Campbell-Jordan who provided childcare for my young daughter Louisa so I could spend countless hours down the rabbit hole.

My love and appreciation goes to my husband Andy Heintz, a fellow writer, who was always available to play Devil's Advocate when I presented him with a variety of theories related to the JFK assassination. I hope you like the end result.

PAGE TURNER
BOOKS INTERNATIONAL

Printed in Dunstable, United Kingdom

73872752R00238